The History of the WWE
From 1985 to the Present
Volume XVIII: 2003

Jonathan Johnson

Imagine going back in time and reliving WWE history as it actually happened. Not as the WWE wants to present it, but as it actually aired. No longer would superstars disappear from the history books or angles be edited out because they're deemed too offensive to WWE's current corporate philosophy. Instead, you'd see the WWE as it aired, as you remembered it if you're old enough, or as it really happened for the first time if you're a younger fan. You'd see the WWE that turned a regional promotion into a global billion dollar powerhouse. You'd see the WWE that the fans who grew up on the product came to know and love.

Welcome to a year-by-year account of the WWE. This is the history of the WWE as presented on television. This series follows the weekly shows, PPVs, and major events that made the WWE the household name that it is. Love it or hate it, the WWE has become part of the world's culture and the events in this book helped define that culture.

In my previous series, *The Greatest Wrestlers of…* series, we reviewed the top wrestlers during three of the WWF/WWE's biggest periods. This time around, we'll be breaking things down even more, focusing on the WWE one year at a time. We'll be following along with the WWE's major wrestling programs, both on television and PPV. Other books focus only on the major PPVs, but those books miss out on one of the most pivotal parts of professional wrestling—weekly episodic television! Those weekly shows give meaning to the PPV feuds and really flesh out the WWE's legendary characters. Without the weekly shows fans are missing a huge part of the history of professional wrestling.

However, I'm not including house shows in this series other than to note any of the rare house show official title changes. For years wrestling companies have conditioned fans that "if it didn't happen on television, it didn't happen", so we're not going to buck that trend. For this year we'll focus on:

WWE Monday Night Raw*
SmackDown!*
All PPVs

The WWE had other shows running during the period, but most of those were recaps of other programs. As this book is already large enough, recap shows are not included. Contained within though, you'll find recaps of all of the major shows and the entertainers and angles that have entertained millions throughout the years. We'll look at all the champions, the contenders, and the ones who just missed out on their moment in the sun. After the recap, we'll crown the top wrestlers of the year as well.

Thank you for joining me on this trip back through the history of the WWE! Whether you're reading this to see for the first time what happened in the WWE's past or reliving your youth through the WWE's vast history, strap in and enjoy! This is the WWE…what the world was watching!

*Though some of these shows are taped and aired later, we'll be treating them as if occurring on their aired date.

2003

The Ruthless Aggression era kicked off in 2002, and 2003 would see the WWE continuing to move toward a blend of sexualized programming and top-notch in-ring work. While the Attitude Era largely focused on spectacle and brawling, the Ruthless Aggression era blended over the top storylines with the best in-ring work seen to that point in the WWE. Superstars were given longer matches on television to craft a story and some of the wrestlers really began to get over with just their in-ring work rather than having great promo skills or a bodybuilder physique.

For in ring storylines, 2003 begins with Triple H and Ric Flair ruling the *Raw* roost. Kane, Rob Van Dam, and Shawn Michaels are all chasing after the heels, but it is a heel dominant Monday night. The show features a few established feuds including Christopher Nowinski warring with Al Snow and Maven on the undercard, but for the most part, *Raw* is resetting into the Royal Rumble and the road to WrestleMania. On *SmackDown!*, Kurt Angle and Big Show's recent alliance with Paul Heyman to keep Brock Lesnar away from the WWE Title is the main event storyline. Like *Raw*, it's a heel led show, but unlike their Monday night counterpart, *SmackDown!* has a babyface waiting to burst through in Lesnar. *SmackDown!* also features the impending wedding of Dawn Marie and Al Wilson, frustrating Torrie Wilson, and the heel antics of Los Guerreros.

The champions to start the year were:

WWE Champion: Kurt Angle
World Champion: Triple H
World Tag Team Champions: Booker T/Goldust
WWE Tag Team Champions: Los Guerreros
Women's Champion: Victoria
Cruiserweight Champion: Billy Kidman

Alongside storyline resets, the title belts were also featuring restarts. The longest reigning champions—Los Guerreros, Victoria, and Billy Kidman—all won their titles at Survivor Series. The other champions all won their belts at the December PPV, Armageddon. The WWE eliminated several belts in 2001 and 2002 to try to streamline their shows. It wouldn't take long for more belts to emerge, especially in the mid-card area.

2002 was an exciting year for the WWE with the debut of young superstars like Brock Lesnar, John Cena, Batista, and Randy Orton. It also featured top established stars from multiple generations including Shawn Michaels, "Stone Cold" Steve Austin, and Hulk Hogan. 2003 would see the end of some careers and a changing of the guard as new top stars emerged and other established superstars took their next step toward immortality. With so many new faces and exciting new story options, the WWE had every opportunity to make 2003 one of the best years ever.

SmackDown!
January 2, 2003
Albuquerque, NM
Announcers: Michael Cole, Tazz, John Cena (briefly)

Rarely used voices introduce the episode promising the return of Brock Lesnar and the wedding of Al Wilson and Dawn Marie tonight ahead of the intro video.

John Cena (with B-2) def. Rikishi. Instead of fireworks, the heels come out, Cena rapping as he heads to the squared circle. He says Rikishi's butt looks like cottage cheese and chewed bubble gum. That brings the big babyface out to punch and chop his opponent. After tossing him out to the floor, Rikishi slams John's face into the ring steps and announce table. A leg drop back in the squared circle gets the big Samoan a two-count. When he sets Cena up for a Stinkface, B-2 drags his man out to the floor. That allows the heels to take control with a rapping heel back elbow and B-2 ram into the ring apron. John slows the pace afterwards with a reverse chin lock. It doesn't take the big babyface long to fight free and deck Cena. Unfortunately, he misses a corner charge. While he catches his breath, B-2 sets the steel chain on a turnbuckle. Mike Sparks catches him and takes it away. Unfortunately, while he argues with Cena's "dog", Rikishi slams John to the canvas with a modified spinebuster, but the referee doesn't see it. He's slow to make the count when he spots the cover and that lets John just kick out. Chaos reigns from there with the big Samoan dragging B-2 into the squared circle. Cena takes advantage and rolls up the big babyface for a three-count. Post-match, Rikishi chases the heels into the crowd.

Afterwards, Dawn Marie steps out onto the stage in her wedding dress. She says she looks beautiful in her dress, but the fans better not get used to it because tonight she's going to get married nude.

After a commercial break, Stephanie McMahon tells Dawn Marie that she's happy for her. However, so long as the wedding is on, the dress stays on. Stephanie warns that there will be "serious repercussions" if Dawn takes off her dress. Once the general manager leaves, Marie rhetorically asks Janet, the makeup lady, what those repercussions could be.

Bill DeMott def. Chuck Palumbo. After manhandling cruiserweights, DeMott steamrolls and clubs Palumbo. Chuck answers with some stiff shots of his own, but that just makes the bully mad. He responds with a corner splash and suplex. More hammering blows and a chin lock follow until Palumbo fights free. The two men then trade shots, Chuck getting the upper hand at last for a corner clothesline and overhead release belly-to-belly suplex. Fired up, Palumbo punches DeMott again, but when he attempts a discus shot, Bill surprises him with a clothesline. A reverse DDT afterwards gets him the win.

An Undertaker teaser package for his return at the Royal Rumble plays.

Backstage, Billy Kidman is surprised to see Torrie Wilson in attendance. Torrie says she doesn't support her father's marriage, but does support her father. However, she thinks Dawn Marie is the last person who should be wearing white. Billy then cracks her up impersonating both bride and groom.

Further backstage, Josh Mathews asks Kurt Angle, flanked by Team Angle, if he'll be prepared for Chris Benoit at the Royal Rumble. Kurt thinks he's just asking that because the Olympian is on crutches. That didn't stop him from choking out Benoit last week, which he shows with video footage. Angle then says he's not worried about who "the Crippler" picks to team with him tonight against Team Angle in their in-ring debut. Kurt says the only think he worries about is keeping his gold medals and WWE Title polished. When it comes to wrestling, the Olympian says he does it best. He's also joined by multi-time amateur champions, making them the "three best wrestlers in the history of the sport". Angle tells Benoit and whoever he picks as his partner tonight to worry.

Billy Kidman def. Eddie Guerrero (with Chavo Guerrero Jr.). Eddie has shaved his hair down short for the new year. It doesn't give him any luck to start the match as Billy starts fast until Guerrero dropkicks and punches the Cruiserweight Champion. A fallaway slam follows for a two-count before "Latino Heat" hooks a reverse chin lock. That brings out John Cena and B-2, the rookie rapping about Eddie's haircut and Los Guerreros working at Taco Bell. That sets off Chavo and he attacks B-2 while Cena runs away. Rikishi follows the heels out, brawling with B-2 until WWE officials separate them. While the referees are worried about B-2, Chavo, and Rikishi, "Latino Heat" and Kidman brawl at ringside into a commercial break.

Afterwards, Eddie and Billy are back in the ring while Cena joins the announce table to continue insulting Los Guerreros. While he does so, "Latino Heat" plants Kidman with a tilt-a-whirl backbreaker and spinning helicopter toss for a near fall. Once again, Guerrero slows the pace with a chin lock. Cole takes the opportunity to tell John that he doesn't have a lot of friends. When Billy escapes, Eddie stops his comeback with a back body drop out to the floor. Back in the squared circle, a slingshot somersault splash gets Guerrero another two-count. This time, he applies a sleeper hold while Cole compares Cena to Vanilla Ice. The rapping heel claims he's from the streets and listens to Biggie. Inside the squared circle, "Latino Heat" plants Kidman with a superplex, but misses his Frog Splash moments later. Billy answers with a powerbomb for his own near fall. A back body drop and dropkick follow before the champion flips free of a tilt-a-whirl backbreaker for a sit-out spinebuster and near fall. John continues rapping, calling Kidman "mild". He nearly scores the win with a face-first slam to the canvas and top rope flying cross body block. Cena blames Mike Chioda being out of position for the two-count. When Eddie slips free of a follow up attack, John blindsides "Latino Heat" with his steel chain, knocking him out while Chioda checks on Billy. Kidman capitalizes with a Shooting Star Press for the three-count.

Following a Brock Lesnar teaser, a video package plays for Al Wilson, Dawn Marie, and Torrie Wilson. Afterwards, Al heads out in an outfit that looks straight out of the seventies, complete with earring. He's followed by Dawn in her wedding dress. The preacher has a lot of flair as he asks if anyone has any objections. The fans do. So does Marie. She stops the wedding to say that she can't marry Al like this. She wants to keep her promise to remove her dress. While Stephanie McMahon says she can't get nude, she never said she couldn't get married in her underwear. She also didn't say Wilson couldn't get married nude. While Dawn Marie starts to disrobe him, the fans chant for him to keep it on. Although he's initially reluctant, he starts to dance around once in his white briefs. Marie finally stops leaving us with just an obvious imprint of something planted in Al's tights. He then bungles his lines and just tells her to trust him that he will take care of her for his vows. That's good enough for Dawn and she shares her vows before the couple seals the deal and kiss all the way down to the canvas. As they leave, Tazz says Wilson looks excited and the announcers talk about Marie being Torrie's mother-in-law.

Chris Benoit/Edge def. Team Angle (with Kurt Angle) by disqualification. The fans are excited to see Edge join Benoit tonight, but it's the "rabid wolverine" opening the match hammering Haas. Shelton tries to show his partner how it's done and tags in only to be trapped in the Crippler Crossface. Luckily, Charlie makes the save. Soon after, Edge tags in to chop and club Benjamin. A second rope missile dropkick nearly score shim the win before Haas grabs the babyface's hair while he runs the ropes. That swings the momentum with both heels attacking Edge ahead of a Shelton back suplex and two-count. Charlie returns afterwards, choking the babyface before Kurt gets in a cheap shot while Brian Hebner is distracted. Haas then scores a pair of two-counts with a belly-to-belly suplex. Team Angle follow right up by dropping Edge onto the top rope for Benjamin to leapfrog his partner and splash his opponent's back while Charlie holds him on the top rope. That gets Shelton a two-count, but the babyface is close enough to the ropes for the break. Haas returns afterward to club his opponents. When Edge starts to fight back, Benjamin hits him from behind for a Charlie slam and modified Texas Cloverleaf. Luckily, "the Crippler" makes the save. Moments later, Edge stuns Shelton with a face-first slam for both men to tag out. The fresh man, Benoit clubs and German suplexes both rookies. A snap suplex then puts Benjamin in position for a top rope diving headbutt and near fall before Haas makes the save. Edge returns soon after for a clothesline and stereo trio of German suplexes to Team Angle alongside the "rabid wolverine". Kurt grabs Edge and drags him out to the floor to help his team, but gets dropped with a Benoit baseball slide kick. When he traps Shelton in a Crippler Crossface, Edge returns to Spear Charlie. That brings in Angle to nail "the Crippler" with the WWE Title for the disqualification. Post-match, Team Angle attack Edge with the Olympian's crutch before Kurt chokes Tony Chimel and forces him to announce that Team Angle won. Cole calls the heels a "bunch of thugs".

After a commercial break, Paul Heyman is in the ring gushing over how proud he is of Team Angle and Kurt Angle. However, he knows that everyone is here to see his client, the "biggest professional athlete", Big Show. The giant then heads to the squared circle for Paul to issue a challenge to Brock Lesnar. That challenge is specifically to raise the stakes for the Royal Rumble match and to stop the "next big thing" from winning a WWE Title shot. Heyman wants to sign a Show/Lesnar "winner takes all" contest for the right to even compete in the Rumble match. Whichever man wins gets a spot in the Rumble while the loser has to sit backstage and watch. Unfortunately, Paul knows that Brock will never accept because he "can't beat the Big Show". Lesnar has had enough and slowly walks to the ring. Before he gets there, Matt Hardy and Shannon Moore bust open Brock with chair shots to the back of the head. Despite Matt's savage shot, the three heels can't keep Lesnar down and he recovers to chase them off.

After a commercial break, Funaki rushes over to catch Al Wilson and Dawn Marie, still in their underwear, before they leave in their limo. Dawn promises to film their honeymoon and show it to the fans next week. As the newlyweds speed off, Funaki "feels very dirty".

Nunzio (with Nidia/Jamie Noble) def. Crash Holly. Josh Mathews steps in as the ring announcer after Kurt Angle's earlier attack. Crash marches out to catch the rookie with a flying cross body block for a two-count. He also gets a two-count with a backslide before Nunzio starts to work on his arm with an armbar and slam onto the top rope. An armbar drop moments later scores the Italian heel a near fall. When he goes for a slam, Holly slips free for a roll-up and near fall. Unfortunately, Nunzio's kick out hurts Crash's shoulder and the rookie capitalizes with a tornado second rope armbar drop for the win.

After a commercial break, Matt Hardy brags about busting open Brock Lesnar to Shannon Moore. Matt says Shannon should have done that when he faced Brock a few weeks ago and that's why Hardy attacked him last week. Matt just wants Moore to be the best "Mattitude Follower" he can be.

Brock Lesnar def. Matt Hardy (with Shannon Moore). Brock is out first, having turned down medical attention to clean up his bloody head. Hardy follows with his Matt Fact saying that he always stays up until sunrise on New Year's. Although Shannon leads the charge, Lesnar decks him before hammering Matt and rocking him with a backbreaker. An overhead belly-to-belly suplex follows. Brock is in no hurry to put Hardy away, stomping him repeatedly. Lesnar doesn't even take this match seriously, wrestling in a t-shirt and his warmup pants as he slams Matt into a corner. A stiff clothesline and another slam into the corner follow before Moore distracts the "next big thing". Brock effortlessly tosses him aside and absorbs a Hardy side effect to belly-to-belly suplex Matt again. An F5 follows to Shannon, but Hardy capitalizes with a Twist of Fate for a near fall. When he attempts a second, Lesnar hoists Matt up for an F5 and the three-count. Post-match, Brock wipes his blood over his own face, Tazz saying he likes the taste of his own blood.

Post-match, Big Show and Paul Heyman step onto the stage. Lesnar dares them to get into the ring, but the giant only wants to motion for the WWE Title. Since they won't get in the ring, Brock picks up Hardy for another F5 to end the show.

Monday Night Raw
January 6, 2003
Phoenix, AZ
Announcers: Jim Ross, Jerry "the King" Lawler

Ahead of the intro video, a video package for Scott Steiner and Triple H plays.

Batista/Rico/Three-Minute Warning (with Ric Flair) def. The Dudley Boyz ("No Disqualification" match). The Dudleys' fireworks serve as the intro fireworks this week. As they step into the ring, Eric Bischoff and Chief Morley march out to promise a change in attitude on *Raw* for the new year. Eric then plays video footage of The Dudley Boyz helping JR and Lawler win their tag match two weeks ago. The general manager promises that he will get respect and signs the Dudleys' opponents tonight. On top of facing four men, the match will have no disqualifications so the heels can destroy the Dudleys. Batista is out last, announced as one of the fifteen *Raw* superstars to compete in the Royal Rumble match. Inside the ring, Bubba Ray and D-Von start strong, even giving Rico a 3D. Unfortunately, the "Animal" stops them from scoring the win with a two-handed chokeslam to D-Von and spear to Bubba. Not done, Batista whips Bubba Ray out to the floor for Morley to punch. Three-Minute Warning join him while the "Animal" gives D-Von a spinebuster. When Chad Patton refuses to count a cover, Eric threatens to punch and fire the referee. Reluctantly, the referee does drop down for the count, but Batista picks up D-Von's head to continue the assault. That brings Bubba back into the ring, but he's hammered down again before Flair joins the assault and hooks his Figure Four Leglock. Jamal capitalizes with a top rope Flying Splash. The heels then turn their attention back to D-Von, Jamal planting him with a pop-up Samoan Drop. Finally, Batista scores the reluctant three-count with a Sit-Out Powerbomb. Post-match, the heels continue their assault, culminating in a Bischoff slap to D-Von's face. The GM promises this will be "the year of Eric Bischoff". His music plays as the heels finally leave the ring.

After a commercial break, The Dudley Boyz are still down, but the announcers are more focused on Lance Storm and William Regal accosting them. The heels can't believe that they have a loss on their record to JR and "the King". Luckily for the announcers, the heels head to the ring to take care of the Dudleys. That includes a Regal brass knuckles shot to Bubba Ray, busting him open, while Storm locks D-Von in a sharpshooter.

Backstage, Ric Flair hypes Triple H up for his pose down with Scott Steiner. Hunter claims that he gets no respect and says his arm was injured two weeks ago when Steiner beat him in an arm wrestling match. The heels then show off Helmsley's *Flex* magazine cover until Scott bursts in to threaten them. He warns Ric that if he gets involved tonight, "Big Poppa Pump" will rip "the Game's" head off.

Molly Holly/Victoria (with Steven Richards) def. Jacqueline/Trish Stratus. While the babyfaces come out separately, the heels are unified. It helps them as they take early control of Jacqueline, each heel getting in some offense including a Molly handspring back elbow for a two-count. After she slaps Trish, the heels apply a combination Boston crab and camel clutch behind Charles Robinson's back. Unfortunately, Victoria misses a moonsault afterwards. When Holly tries to help her partner, climbing the ropes, Jacqueline shoves the Women's Champion back into her to crotch Molly. Trish gets the tag afterwards to fight both heels, flinging Holly off the ropes with her handstand head scissors. A Chick Kick to Victoria nearly gets Stratus the win, but Holly makes the save. She pays courtesy of a Jacqueline tackle. While the referee is distracted, Trish rolls up the "black widow" again, but Steven enters the ring and slams her down for Victoria to steal the win with a handful of tights.

Backstage, Terri interviews Booker T and Goldust. The five-time champion says if 2003 is the year of Eric Bischoff, everyone is in trouble. After reminding everyone of some of Eric's lowest moments in 2002, Booker promises that 2003 is going to be the World Tag Team Champions' year. Watching in his office, Bischoff says he won't put up with this and signs a title match for the champions.

Chris Jericho heads to the ring to say that he's had a recurring dream of late. That dream is him winning the Royal Rumble to reclaim "his" championship. Tonight, Y2J is happy to announce that Eric Bischoff has signed him to the Rumble match to make that dream come true. That brings out Shawn Michaels to a big pop. The "Heartbreak Kid" knows that they have gotten off to a rough start. However, Michaels says they are a lot alike, and Jericho needs acknowledgement as the best in the business. Shawn believes the only way to get that is to volunteer to be the number one entrant in the Rumble match and win the whole thing. Y2J believes he sees what the "Heartbreak Kid" is doing. He thinks Michaels just wants him to follow in Shawn's footsteps, but Jericho knows how to be the best, beating two men in the same night that the "Heartbreak Kid" never did. Regardless, Shawn continues to goad Y2J into entering the Rumble first. If Jericho doesn't, Michaels will himself. He also warns Y2J that he'll have to go through the "Heartbreak Kid" to win the Royal Rumble. Jericho doesn't want to wait until the PPV, but before they lock up, Randy Orton walks out for an RNN update. He's not wearing a sling this week as he steps into the squared circle. While he agrees that it's big news that Shawn is in the Royal Rumble match, Orton says the bigger news is that his shoulder is up to "ninety-three percent". He adds that he's the "new sexy boy" and his comeback story is more inspirational. Michaels has heard enough and decks Randy. Y2J capitalizes and tackles the "Heartbreak Kid", briefly turning him over into the Walls of Jericho until Rob Van Dam races out. He's followed by Christian to give the heels the numbers advantage again. It doesn't last long as Kane marches out to chase off the heels.

MUST SEE! Lance Storm/William Regal def. Booker T/Goldust (World Tag Title match). Storm and Booker open the match, the champion clotheslining and slamming his opponent to the mat for an exaggerated knee drop. Eric Bischoff isn't happy watching backstage. Goldust then tags in for his own knee drop and two-count. When Lance attacks the "bizarre one's" eyes, Regal tags in for more of the same treatment and a near fall before Booker T returns to chop and mount the Englishman. Luckily, Storm makes the save with a throat drop on the top rope. That swings the momentum and the challengers trap the five-time champion in their corner for a Lance back elbow and two-count. He then slows the pace with a reverse chin lock. When Booker starts to fight free, William returns for a series of strikes and his own near fall. The heels then trade chin locks until the champion surprises Storm with a side kick. Goldust gets the hot tag afterwards to hit both heels and powerslam Lance for a two-count. Luckily, Regal makes the save and kicks off a four-man brawl. After knocking the Englishman down, the champions score a two-count with a combination lift-up and side kick. At the last second, William breaks Charles Robinson's count with a kick to the throat ahead of a commercial break.

Afterwards, Booker scores a near fall with a spinebuster from the new referee, Chief Morley. He doesn't stay up for long, Booker T accidentally hitting him with a side kick when Lance ducks. The champion follows up with a Book End, but by the time Nick Patrick runs out, Storm has enough time to recover to just kick out. Goldust tags in afterwards to fight with the heels until Lance leads him on a chase around the ring for a William clothesline. That scores Storm a near fall back in the squared circle. Once again in control, the heels get another two-count with a Regal slam, but Booker makes the save. Back in, Lance applies another reverse chin lock. It doesn't take the "bizarre one" long to fight free, slamming Storm to the canvas before giving the five-time champion the hot tag. He proceeds to punch and back body drop both heels before planting Lance with a flapjack. Following a spinaroonie, Booker T connects with a Scissors Kick, but at the last second, Morley interrupts Patrick's count and drags him out to the floor. While the replacement referees argue, William hits both champions with his brass knuckles and drags Lance onto Booker for the Morley three-count.

After a commercial break, Lance Storm and William Regal tell Eric Bischoff and Chief Morley that it will be an honor to represent them as the champions.

A *Raw* Retro Moment shows Sable stripping off a potato sack in 1997 to reveal a tiny bikini. Afterwards, the announcers shill the special tenth anniversary show airing next Tuesday.

Test (with Stacy Keibler) def. Christopher Nowinski (with D'Lo Brown). Stacy gets a nice pop as she bends over to enter the ring. As the heels head to the squared circle, we see footage from earlier today of Nowinski asking D'Lo to be in his corner. He agrees that Keibler and the referees are prejudiced against Brown. Test is focused on him, dragging D'Lo into the ring only to be ambushed by the Harvard heel. In control, he focuses on the bodyguard's shoulder, whipping it into turnbuckles and the ring post ahead of an armbar. When Test escapes with a back suplex, he rushes out to keep Brown from getting to Keibler. A throat drop on the top rope and clotheslines follow from the bodyguard. After clotheslining D'Lo off the apron, Test nearly scores the win with a full nelson slam. Brown gets involved again, tripping the bodyguard to block a Big Boot, but Nowinski accidentally runs into his cornerman. Test capitalizes with a Rolling Cutter for the win. Post-match, D'Lo plants the bodyguard with Sky High.

After a commercial break, Christian tells Chris Jericho that he is also in the Royal Rumble. Y2J is ecstatic, telling his friend that he can help Jericho win the match. Christian wants to win too, kicking off an argument between the former champions. When they start making fun of each other, Christian calling Y2J's beard stupid and Jericho mocking his partner's tattoo, Randy Orton interrupts to tell them that he'll be in their corner tonight and they need to get on the same page.

From the announce table, the announcers talk about Scott Steiner previously appearing on the cover of *Iron Man* magazine before playing a video package of Scott and Triple H's confrontation two weeks ago. Afterwards, we see Hunter putting on baby oil and working out ahead of his pose down challenge.

After a commercial break, Triple H and Ric Flair head to the ring for the pose down. Jonathan Coachman is there to moderate the event, but he gives the microphone to Hunter to go over the rules almost immediately. After explaining that he'll go pose-for-pose with Scott Steiner, Helmsley says the fans are too jealous of him to serve as fair judges. Instead, he picks six people in the crowd to do the job. That's conveniently six men sitting front row. While they get in the squared circle, "the Game" gives Coach a set of poses to call out. Ric gives the men scorecards for them to pick between Scott and Triple H. Steiner then comes out to kick off the pose down. The first pose is a "front double bicep". Hunter takes his time flexing, but "Big Poppa Pump" gets right to it and receives a big pop. The second pose is a side bicep, Helmsley impressed and intimidated by Steiner's arm. The final pose is the "most muscular" and features "the Game" flexing everything. When Scott does the same, the rivals get in each other's faces until Coachman calls for a break. Instead of a fight, he wants the judges to make their decision. Not so shockingly, all six men select Triple H as the winner. Steiner can't believe he lost every vote. He smells a setup. Instead of the six men, "Big Poppa Pump" invites the fans to vote and the "freaks" pick Scott. Hunter doesn't want to let the fans make the decision. He calls the judging panel fair, but he understands that Steiner is upset. Since bodybuilding is subjective, Helmsley says some people might pick "Big Poppa Pump" as the winner. To be more objective, he challenges Scott to a pushup contest. Steiner accepts, the two men dropping down face-to-face for the contest before the six men attack "Big Poppa Pump". Unfortunately, they're just local talent and Steiner effortlessly fights them off while Flair and Triple H retreat up the ramp, ending this long fifteen-minute segment.

Kane/Rob Van Dam (with Shawn Michaels) def. Chris Jericho/Christian (with Randy Orton). After everyone heads to the ring and the final commercial break, the competitors trade fists to open the match. It doesn't take the babyfaces long to drive their opponents out to the floor, RVD with a clothesline to Christian and Kane a press slam to Jericho. Rob follows the heels out with a somersault plancha over the top rope. Afterwards, he fights with Y2J in the ring, but when he heads upstairs after a heel kick, Orton hops onto the apron to distract Hebner while Christian pushes Van Dam out to the floor. The heel then tags in to stomp and choke RVD. Jericho recovers quickly for his own shots and a back suplex. Afterwards, a trio of elbow drops nearly gets him the victory. The heels take turns wearing down Rob until he surprises Christian with a kick. The heel has the presence of mind to hold him back from the tag until Jericho can distract Hebner. That forces Van Dam to stay in the match. When Randy stomps him at ringside, Shawn comes over for the save with Sweet Chin Music. Unfortunately, Y2J nails the "Heartbreak Kid" from behind and whips him into the ring steps. Back in the squared circle, Van Dam finally makes a comeback, kicking down the heels before tagging in Kane to big boot Jericho and tilt-a-whirl powerslam Christian for a near fall. Luckily, Y2J makes the save. When the heels set up for a double suplex, the "Big Red Machine" suplexes both of his opponents instead. He follows up with a flying clothesline off the top rope to Christian, but Jericho saves his partner from a Chokeslam. Soon afterwards, the heels try to finish off the monster with a conchairto, but Kane dodges. Michaels then recovers to drag Y2J out into the crowd, the two men brawling while the "Big Red Machine" Chokeslams Christian ahead of a Five-Star Frog Splash for the victory.

Backstage, Eric Bischoff tells Lance Storm and William Regal that that's how he wanted to start 2003. However, he's interrupted by his phone ringing. Eric's mood quickly changes when he reveals that Vince McMahon will be on *Raw* next week.

SmackDown!
January 9, 2003
Tucson, AZ
Announcers: Michael Cole, Tazz, Matt Hardy (briefly)

Ahead of the intro video, a video package plays featuring the Big Show/Brock Lesnar rivalry.

Big Show (with Paul Heyman) def. Rikishi. As the heels come out, Tazz shows off Big Show's *Raw* magazine cover alongside Andre the Giant. Inside the ring, he knocks Rikishi down, but misses an elbow drop. That lets the big Samoan land a thrust kick, but he can't slam the giant. Show has no such problem, hoisting up the big babyface and slamming him to the mat. Stiff chops and a big boot follow for a near fall. Unable to get the three-count, Big Show applies a rare abdominal stretch. It takes quite a while, but Rikishi eventually escapes for a few more blows. One clothesline flips him completely around ahead of the Chokeslam for a giant victory. Post-match, Heyman promises that the heels will teach Brock Lesnar a lesson before the night is over.

John Cena (with B-2) def. Chavo Guerrero Jr. (with Eddie Guerrero). Pre-match, the "Doctor of Thuganomics" raps about "beating a Latino" and Chavo hating him because he's white being "reverse discrimination". B-2 adds, "booyah". The rap gets under Guerrero's skin and he clubs and back suplexes Cena to start the match. A head scissors and clothesline out to the floor gets Chavo a nice pop before he attacks John's leg ahead of another back suplex and near fall. Although he blocks a corner boot, Guerrero can't dodge Cena's clothesline. Following a one-count, the rapping heel plants Chavo on the top rope. Guerrero manages to elbow free, but B-2 gets involved and shoves him down to the canvas. That brings Eddie over to fight with B-2. When John joins his "dog", Chavo dives over the top rope onto them. "Latino Heat" then suplexes B-2 on the steel ramp before WWE officials escort both cornermen backstage. While they go, Cena suplexes Chavo over the top rope back into the squared circle. He takes too long climbing the ropes though and pays courtesy of a Guerrero superplex for a near fall. A DDT also scores Chavo a close two-count before he attempts a roll-up. Unfortunately, he's too close to the ropes and John grabs them to steal the win.

A video package plays for Al Wilson and Dawn Marie's wedding last week. Afterwards, we join Dawn in their honeymoon suite. She traipses around in red lingerie, inviting fans to join them in the couple's "most intimate" moments.

The *Raw* Retro Moment is "Stone Cold" Steve Austin giving Vince McMahon a beer bath.

Billy Kidman def. Matt Hardy (with Shannon Moore) (Cruiserweight Title match). This week's Matt Fact reveals that Hardy has a heated toilet seat and likes pulp in his orange juice. The Cruiserweight Champion starts fast in this non-title match with a head scissors and dropkick, but Moore makes his presence known with a trip and choke. Matt follows up with a modified side effect for a two-count before applying a sleeper hold. When Kidman reverses the hold, Hardy answers with a side slam. He can't keep Billy down and the highflyer answers with a bulldog and enziguri for his own near fall. When Shannon gets involved again, Kidman catches both heels with a Shooting Star Press off the top rope. Unfortunately, he hits his head on Moore's. Matt capitalizes with a side effect back in the ring for a two-count, but when he sets up for the Twist of Fate, Billy shoves him into his own MFer. That stuns Hardy long enough for the champion to roll him up for the three-count. Post-match, Matt tells Shannon to get in the ring and says that he understands what happened. Hardy is glad that Moore tried and failed rather than sit on the sidelines. Because of that, Matt forgives him and asks the fans to cheer for his MFer. He even hugs him, surprising the announcers.

Edge promoting WrestleMania XIX tickets in Seattle plays.

Backstage, Josh Mathews asks Torrie Wilson about last week's "disgusting" wedding. Torrie says Dawn Marie humiliated Al Wilson and she's going to get her revenge on her "evil stepmother" at the Royal Rumble.

Tajiri def. Jamie Noble (with Nidia). Jamie is focused, opening the match with strikes before fighting free of a Tarantula attempt to slam the "Japanese Buzzsaw" on the barricade. He follows up with attacks on the arm and a northern lights suplex for a two-count. When that doesn't work, Noble applies a hammerlock and knees Tajiri's arm. The "Japanese Buzzsaw" escapes with kicks and a roll-up for a near fall. Soon after, the wrestlers have the same idea and connect with simultaneous clotheslines. Although Jamie recovers first and attempts a charge, Tajiri dodges for a bridging German suplex and near fall. He also gets a two-count with a handspring back elbow. Noble won't stay down, rolling his opponent over into a reverse figure four leglock, called the Trailer Hitch by the announcers. Luckily, the "Japanese Buzzsaw" reaches the ropes. He holds onto them when Jamie attacks to apply the Tarantula. Afterwards, the two men trade counters, Tajiri escaping a Tiger Bomb and surprising Noble with a kick to the throat when he attempts a second rope dive. The Buzzsaw Kick follows for the victory.

Backstage, Kurt Angle gives Team Angle a pep talk and leads them to the ring.

A new superstar vignette shows a man bursting through a jail cell door while talking about serving ten years. Nathan Jones, his name displayed on the screen, says he's coming "in time".

Charlie Haas (with Kurt Angle/Shelton Benjamin) def. Edge (with Chris Benoit). Tony Chimel introduces the heels first and quickly bails out of the ring, wanting nothing to do with Angle. Edge then comes out alone, but before he locks up with Haas, Benoit hurries out to join his corner. That narrows the odds a little and allows the babyface to focus on his opponent. Although Charlie takes him down first, Edge recovers to attack his arm, the two men trading holds ahead of a heel northern lights suplex. The better technical wrestler, Haas stays a step ahead of his opponent until he runs into an arm drag and face slam for a near fall. Charlie answers with an overhead belly-to-belly suplex. A suplex moments later scores him a pair of two-counts before he applies a double arm rack. Eventually, Edge powers out and suplexes the rookie. Once again, Haas recovers quickly and scores another near fall with a German suplex. When he heads upstairs, the babyface counters his flying attack with a kick to the gut ahead of a belly-to-belly suplex to put both men down. Edge is up first to clothesline and back body drop Charlie ahead of an Edge-a-matic for a two-count. A flapjack follows and brings Kurt onto the apron. The "rabid wolverine" has had enough of him and pulls Angle back to the floor. Shelton is right over to help his mentor with a superkick. When he gets on the apron, Edge knocks him off with a Spear. A Spear follows to Haas, but Kurt pulls the babyface off his cover. Moments later, Angle catches Edge running the ropes and blasts him with a crutch for Charlie to steal the win with an Exploder Suplex. Post-match, the heels attack Edge until Benoit chases them away. "The Crippler" tells Angle that time is running out before Benoit makes him tap and takes the WWE Title. Before then, the "rabid wolverine" wants a match with Benjamin.

Chris Benoit def. Shelton Benjamin by disqualification. After a commercial break, the wrestlers circle each other while Cole reveals that everyone else has been sent backstage. Alone, Shelton makes his singles debut and, like his partner, tries to wear "the Crippler" down with amateur holds. Benoit answers with a forearm to chase the rookie out to the floor. There, Benjamin rams his more experienced opponent into the apron before scoring a two-count with a back suplex. A chin lock follows, Shelton using the "rabid wolverine's" own arms to do the damage. Afterwards, a butterfly suplex scores Benjamin a two-count before he changes tactics and applies a camel clutch. Eventually, Benoit powers out and picks up Shelton to slam him to the canvas. Despite that, the rookie surprises "the Crippler" with a twisting slam for a near fall. He also gets two-counts with a northern lights suplex, small package, and backslide. He makes a rookie mistake rolling up Benoit in the ropes though. Another rookie mistake follows when he misses a corner splash, opening the door for the "rabid wolverine" to deliver a trio of German suplexes. Following a top rope diving headbutt, Benoit locks on the Crippler Crossface. That brings Kurt Angle back out to argue with the referee so Mike Chioda misses Shelton tapping out. He does see Kurt hit "the Crippler" with his crutch and calls for the disqualification. Post-match, Benoit traps Angle in the Crippler Crossface until Charlie Haas runs out for the save. Edge follows, but the babyfaces are outnumbered. Once the heels knock Edge out to the floor, Kurt beats the "rabid wolverine" with his crutch ahead of a WWE Title shot to the head. Still not done, the Olympian traps Benoit in the Anklelock.

After a commercial break, Al Wilson is struggling to keep up with Dawn Marie, but she doesn't care. She wants him to get back in the shower with her. Reluctantly, he joins her.

Bill DeMott def. Shannon Moore. Matt Hardy joins the announce table to say that this match was Shannon's idea. He also says he forgave Moore for making a mistake earlier. While DeMott holds his opponent down with a front face lock, Hardy reveals a Matt Fact to say that Cole is biased. Eventually, Bill tires of his face lock and clubs Shannon. Matt says his MFer has to fight his own fights. He does so with a second rope springboard side kick, but when he attempts a second, DeMott meets him with a clothesline. A sit-out powerbomb follows for the three-count. Hardy says, "what doesn't kill you makes you stronger" before entering the ring to help Moore up. Shannon claims he tried his best and apologizes, but Matt hugs him again. This time though, he surprises Moore with a Twist of Fate. Tazz calls it "tough love".

An Undertaker teaser package plays for his Royal Rumble return.

Eddie Guerrero (with Chavo Guerrero Jr.) def. B-2 (with John Cena). Cena tries to rap again as he leads his "dog" to the ring, but Los Guerreros attack from behind immediately. That lets Eddie shove B-2 into the squared circle for a slingshot somersault splash. "Latino Heat" is fired up, repeatedly punching his bigger opponent. He can't keep B-2 down though, and the returning superstar recovers to punch and leg drop Guerrero for a two-count. Surprisingly, the fans chant for Eddie as B-2 continues his assault. After a flurry of fists, the heel scores a two-count with a back suplex and springboard clothesline. He also gets a near fall with a falcon arrow suplex ahead of a back body drop. Guerrero won't stay down, answering with a tilt-a-whirl backbreaker. That brings Cena onto the apron with his steel chain, but Chavo pulls him down to the floor and blasts the rapping heel with a title belt. Afterwards, "Latino Heat" scores the three-count with a back suplex and Frog Splash to B-2's lower back.

Back at their hotel, Dawn Marie crawls along the bed for another round with Al Wilson. He's too exhausted to move, laying face down on his pillow while she calls his name. Afterwards, the announcers laugh at Al before previewing the Royal Rumble PPV.

Backstage, Paul Heyman tells Big Show that they are going to teach Brock Lesnar a lesson tonight. A-Train enters to tell them that they can have whatever is left of Lesnar tonight after he's done with him, but first, the hairy heel wants to send a message.

Another Nathan Jones, an Australian man sitting in a jail cell, teaser vignette plays. Tazz calls him a "bad dude".

Brock Lesnar def. A-Train. Big Show and Paul Heyman are watching backstage as the wrestlers march out to try to establish their power advantage. They trade shots until A-Train surprises the former champion with an Albert Bomb for a near fall. Once in control, he clubs the back of Lesnar's head and taunts him. Showing off his power, he press slams Brock onto the top rope, but Lesnar doesn't stay down and answers with a powerslam. A clothesline and trio of belly-to-belly suplexes follow before the "next big thing" applies a bearhug. Despite the hairy heel headbutting free, Lesnar hoists him up and F5s A-Train for the victory.

Post-match, Brock calls out Big Show. The giant and Paul Heyman leave their locker room, but instead of confronting Lesnar, the heels head to the parking lot. Paul mocks the "next big thing", telling him that just when he thinks they are going right, they go left. Heyman is sure Big Show will stop Brock at the Royal Rumble from ever winning back the WWE Title.

The show ends back at Al Wilson and Dawn Marie's hotel room. Al wasn't just sleeping. He couldn't breathe. Paramedics rush in to help him, Dawn begging for him to wake up and breathe to end this action heavy show featuring nine matches. For fans of in-ring action, this is a great episode.

Monday Night Raw
January 13, 2003
Uncasville, CT
Announcers: Jim Ross, Jerry "the King" Lawler

The show opens with Eric Bischoff and Chief Morley anxiously waiting in the parking lot for Vince McMahon. They are interrupted by Earl Hebner and Charles Robinson who warn that the other officials are threatening to strike if they aren't treated better. Once Morley takes them away to try to resolve the situation, Scott Steiner marches down a ramp to demand a match with Triple H tonight. Instead, the general manager gives him a bench pressing competition with "the Game". Scott is tired of the games and storms off, refusing to promise that he won't put a hand on Helmsley ahead of their Royal Rumble match. Afterwards, the intro video plays and fireworks explode.

Victoria (with Steven Richards) def. Jacqueline and Trish Stratus ("Hardcore" Women's Title match). JR says this is the first ever divas triple threat "Hardcore" match in WWE history before Victoria comes out to find a Trish stand-up in a trashcan. She proceeds to tear it up before Stratus gets a kendo stick to hit the champion and her man. The "black widow" answers with a slam on a trashcan lid, but misses a moonsault for Jacqueline to kick off a trio of near falls. Although Trish breaks up the third count, the babyfaces team up against the champion until Steven trips Jacqueline and nails the vixen in the back of the head with a trashcan lid when she runs the ropes. That gives Victoria a very disappointing victory in a short "Hardcore" match. Post-match, the babyfaces briefly fight with the champion until Richards plants Stratus with a Hanging DDT. When the heels try to finish her off, The Hurricane runs out for the save.

Still in the parking lot, The Dudley Boyz confront Eric Bischoff and Chief Morley. The Dudleys have a problem with the way the general manager is running things. Morley tells them that if they have a problem with Bischoff, they have a problem with him. That's fine with the Dudleys and they attack the chief while Eric calls for security. Although he initially fires The Dudley Boyz, when Bubba Ray wonders if Stephanie McMahon is looking for a good tag team, Bischoff changes his mind and suspends them.

Maven/Test (with Stacy Keibler) def. Christopher Nowinski/D'Lo Brown. Despite D'Lo trying to distract him, Test starts strong hammering both heels. Following a boot to Nowinski's face and clothesline to Brown on the apron, the bodyguard tags in Maven for a double back elbow to the Harvard heel for a two-count. He also gets a two-count with a spinning kick before fighting with both heels. In the chaos, D'Lo stuns him with a throat drop on the top rope ahead of a Nowinski spinebuster. Brown also delivers a spinebuster for a two-count before the Harvard heel returns to stretch and slam the babyface for a two-count. Luckily, Test makes the save at the last second. Unfortunately, the heels follow up with a double-team attack and hard hammering blows. D'Lo then tries to sap the strength out of Maven with a shoulder lock. When the babyface fights free, Brown tries to follow up with a back suplex. Luckily, Maven flips free and tags in Test to clothesline D'Lo and slam both heels. Following a full nelson slam to the Harvard heel, the bodyguard tries to finish off Brown with a pumphandle slam. At the last second, Nowinski makes the save, but pays with a Test Drive, now the name for the bodyguard's Rolling Cutter. Unfortunately, Test misses D'Lo with a Big Boot and falls out to the floor while Maven returns only to walk into Sky High. Luckily for the babyfaces, Nick Patrick knows that the bodyguard is the legal man and refuses to count Brown's pin. Stacy then hops onto the apron to distract D'Lo until Test Big Boots the heel for the three-count.

During a commercial break, Eric Bischoff is excited to welcome Vince McMahon's limo. Unfortunately, it's "Mean" Gene Okerlund inside to advertise tomorrow's tenth anniversary show. When Bischoff calls him an "idiot", "Mean" Gene says that if Eric was a little smarter, they might be having a *Nitro* reunion show. Chris Jericho then approaches and asks for the number one spot in the Royal Rumble match. The GM tells him that he needs a *Raw* superstar to win the Royal Rumble and can't give Y2J the number one spot. However, if Jericho really wants to pick his number, Eric will give him a chance tonight to get number thirty in an "Over the Top Rope Winner Picks the Number Thirty Royal Rumble Spot" match.

Backstage, the F-View hidden camera catches William Regal making fun of "the King's" new book with Lance Storm. The Englishman promises to knock out Lawler tonight.

William Regal (with Lance Storm) def. Jerry "the King" Lawler by disqualification. Pre-match, Regal reads an excerpt from Jerry's book to make fun of him. When he wants to start the match, several officials swarm both heels looking for brass knuckles. They find weapons hidden by both men and escort Storm backstage while Jerry wraps a chain around his fist. After he levels William, Charles Robinson notices the chain on his fist and disqualifies Lawler. Despite that, "the King" takes the microphone to call himself the winner ahead of a Royal Rumble ad featuring Scott Steiner and Triple H.

Jeff Hardy def. Raven (Royal Rumble Qualifying match). The announcers say that this is for the last *Raw* spot in the Royal Rumble match. Raven returns here in simple black trunks and boots alongside much shorter hair. After both men trade shots, the hardcore superstar gets serious wrapping Jeff's leg around the ring post. He proceeds to kick and stretch the daredevil's knee until Hardy fights back only to miss a top rope moonsault. After Raven scores a two-count, he kicks Jeff's injured leg and applies a step over toe hold. Eventually, the daredevil kicks free. Following a series of kicks, a leg drop nearly gets Hardy the victory. Unfortunately, his leg is too injured and he slips on the top rope when going for a whisper in the wind for another Raven two-count. He follows up with a catapult into the top rope, but Jeff holds onto the ropes when the hardcore superstar attempts a Raven Effect. When Raven stuns himself, his head hitting the mat, Hardy races upstairs for a Swanton Bomb and the three-count. This ends Raven's WWE run. Despite some fun Hardcore Title matches, he never matched his ECW fame or even his brief time with WCW.

Backstage, Vince McMahon finally arrives. Eric Bischoff is happy to see him and says he looks better than ever. Vince tells him he's just here to make an announcement. As he heads to the squared circle, the WWE owner sees Randy Orton and asks how he's doing. Orton says he's up to ninety-four percent, but that number might be going down after Vince slaps his injured shoulder hard and says "good".

A Sean O'Haire teaser vignette features the heel telling fans to cheat on their wives.

After a commercial break, Vince McMahon heads to the squared circle. He's interrupted immediately by The Dudley Boyz. Bubba Ray speaks for his brother to say that the Dudleys have nowhere else to turn after getting suspended and Eric Bischoff is "a piece of crap". Vince interrupts to reinstate the Dudleys and give them a World Tag Title match this Sunday. All he wants from the babyfaces is for them to say, "get the tables", during their match. The fans love that and so do the Dudleys as they head backstage. Chris Jericho then heads to the ring. He's glad to see McMahon because "they" have a big problem since Eric won't give him the number one spot in the Royal Rumble match. Jericho proposes that Vince use his power to help him, but the WWE owner proposes that he shuts his mouth. McMahon does briefly make Y2J happy changing the main event's "Over the Top Rope Challenge" for the number thirty spot to a contest for any number in the Rumble match...except number one. Vince has already promised that number to Shawn Michaels. When Jericho reluctantly heads backstage, Bischoff interrupts. McMahon has had enough. When the GM complains that Vince is undermining him, the WWE owner tells him to shut up. He's tired of being interrupted and offers to give Bischoff a public evaluation. Despite the fans booing Eric, McMahon says he's been doing a good job. However, Vince hired him to do a "great job" and revolutionize *Raw*. The WWE owner is mad that he hasn't done that and gives him just thirty days to turn the show around before McMahon fires him.

After a commercial break, Eric Bischoff pleads with Vince McMahon in the parking lot for more time. When Eric says there's "not another man on the planet" that can replace him, Shane McMahon steps out of the limo to silently disagree. Vince warns Bischoff that he's got "thirty days".

Lance Storm (with William Regal) def. Booker T (with Goldust) by disqualification. As the heels head to the ring, Regal glares at "the King". Inside the squared circle, Earl Hebner checks them for weapons before Booker gets to work clotheslining and slamming Lance. An exaggerated knee drop scores him a two-count before Storm pokes his eyes. He follows up with knees in a corner, but when he attempts to lock on a sharpshooter, the five-time champion kicks free. Lance answers with chops, but runs into a flapjack to swing the momentum again. Booker T capitalizes with a side kick for a two-count before slowing the pace with an armbar. It doesn't take Storm long to drive the babyface into a corner for a string of shoulders to the gut and two-count. He also gets a near fall with a backbreaker. After nailing Booker's lower back with knees, the Canadian hooks a reverse chin lock. The five-time champion eventually fights free for a flying forearm and flurry of chops. When he goes for a side kick, Lance ducks and Booker T nearly hits Earl Hebner. Unfortunately, while he ducks out of the way, Regal hits Booker with a title belt. That brings out The Dudley Boyz to attack Storm and William for the disqualification. Although they set up to 3D Lance, the Englishman drags his partner from the ring for the save.

SmackDown superstars including Brock Lesnar and Team Angle are shown at The World.

The Hurricane (with Trish Stratus) def. Steven Richards (with Victoria). Trish holds her neck as she accompanies the superhero to the squared circle. When the heels come out, The Hurricane makes a mistake and turns his back. That lets Steven get in several shots until the superhero surprises him with a pair of clotheslines and a backward head slam. The masked man follows up with an overcast neckbreaker, but when he sets up for a shining wizard kick, Victoria grabs his leg. Luckily, Stratus rushes over for the save, fighting with the Women's Champion while the superhero scores the win with the Eye of the Hurricane. Post-match, the heels attack again until The Hurricane chases off Richards before the vixen sends Victoria flying with a Chick Kick.

A Nathan Jones teaser ad plays ahead of the announcers previewing the Royal Rumble.

Afterwards, Jonathan Coachman is on a stage beside the entrance ramp to introduce the bench press competition. He welcomes out Scott Steiner first. "Big Poppa Pump" is tired of playing games and says he's doing things his way. While the officials set the bar with 585 pounds, the JVC Tower of Power Extreme Blast of the Night is Steiner fighting with six men last week after Triple H set him up. Following a commercial break, Hunter steps through the curtain in a suit. He heads to the ring to say that he doesn't care about posing, arm wrestling, or bench pressing. Helmsley has only been messing with Scott because all that matters to "the Game" is the World Title. When it comes to wrestling, Triple H says he's the best. He lists all the men that he's beaten before saying that Steiner is no different than them. All "Big Poppa Pump" will do is talk a good game before going down this Sunday. Scott asks the champion if he's so confident, why don't they fight right now. Steiner then heads to the squared circle to toss around and strip Hunter, reminiscent of some beatings Helmsley's mentor, Ric Flair, has taken in his career. With "the Game" down to his socks and briefs, "Big Poppa Pump" tosses him out to the floor and does pushups over the World Title. As WWE officials hold him back, Triple H can only watch as Scott poses with the championship.

Chris Jericho def. Batista and Kane and Rob Van Dam ("Over the Top Rope Winner Picks Their Royal Rumble Spot" match).

Elimination Order	Wrestler	Eliminated By
1	Kane	Batista
2	Batista	Rob Van Dam
3	Rob Van Dam	Chris Jericho
4	Chris Jericho	Winner

As Batista comes out alone, JR reveals that Ric Flair had a family emergency tonight and had to miss the show. Once the bell rings, the "Animal" hammers RVD in a corner while Kane does the same to Y2J. The babyfaces soon switch opponents with Rob nearly knocking Jericho out of the ring. Once Y2J is down, the sometimes tag partners try to eliminate Batista, but Chris recovers and slams Van Dam. The heels then tease eliminations, the "Animal" picking the "Big Red Machine" up, but he can't slam him over the top rope. While he tries to, RVD accidentally hits the ring post shoulder-first. That lets the heels double-team Kane until Rob recovers only to run into a second rope missile dropkick. While Jericho tries to eliminate Van Dam, the "Animal" chokes the monster. It doesn't take Kane long to fight free and big boot Batista. Although the "Big Red Machine" teases fighting RVD, he shoves his partner aside to save him from a Y2J top rope attack. The monster follows up with a two-handed chokeslam before the babyfaces double-team the "Animal". Soon after, the wrestlers pair up for Jericho to nearly toss Rob out to the floor. Luckily, Van Dam lands on the apron and returns to drop Y2J for rolling thunder. Unfortunately, Batista flattens both babyfaces before hoisting up RVD. Although Kane saves his partner, Jericho low blows him for the "Animal" to clothesline the "Big Red Machine" out of the ring. Y2J tries to sneak attack Batista afterwards, but the big heel answers with a Sit-out Powerbomb. Before he can spot his other opponent, Van Dam kicks the "Animal" out of the match. Batista is a sore loser and quickly returns to shove RVD off the top rope as he sets up for a Five-Star Frog Splash. Jericho capitalizes, knocking Rob out to the floor for the win.

Post-match, Y2J says logic dictates that he take number thirty, but he doesn't care. If Shawn Michaels is number one, Jericho wants number two. That brings out the "Heartbreak Kid" to briefly fight with Y2J. Although Jericho gets the upper hand and tosses Shawn over the top rope, Michaels skins the cat and returns to fling Y2J out to the floor. The announcers wonder if the "Heartbreak Kid" will defy the odds again and win the Royal Rumble match this Sunday to headline WrestleMania.

Monday Night Raw
January 14, 2003
New York City, NY
Hosts: Jim Ross, Jerry "the King" Lawler, Jonathan Coachman, Stacy Keibler

This highlight special anniversary show opens with a montage of WWF logos and moments from the first ten years of *Monday Night Raw*. Interestingly, it's a Tuesday night episode. Instead of an arena show, the announcers are at The World where WWE superstars sit in the crowd waiting for the festivities.

Shawn Michaels heads to the stage to talk about being the number one entrant in this Sunday's Royal Rumble match. He then presents the "Diva of the Decade" award, saying that the division has come a long way since the days of "Bull Nakano and Bertha Faye". After claiming there's nothing wrong with full-figured women, he plays a video with the nominees: Sable, Sunny, Trish Stratus, Lita, and Chyna. Since only two are currently on the roster, it's obviously coming down to Lita and Stratus, Trish winning because she's healthier and has been on television lately. There's no doubt Stratus is an all-time female superstar, but in 2003 she had only competed for three years. Pathetically, someone chants for puppies while Trish thanks the fans and Fit Finlay for training her.

Jonathan Coachman and Stacy Keibler are excited to see what the fans voted as the top *Raw* moment. They'll introduce the countdown throughout the show beginning with number ten, the Mankind and Rock "This is Your Life" segment.

After a commercial break, Coach and Stacy talk about how the more things change, the more they stay the same with George Bush—albeit different generations—serving as the president both in 1993 and 2003. Shane McMahon then heads to the ring to present the nominees for the "Don't Try This at Home" award. They are: Big Show Chokeslamming The Undertaker through the ring, Jeff Hardy leg dropping Kane through a table from the top of a ladder, The Dudley Boyz powerbombing Mae Young from the stage through a table, and Kurt Angle doing a moonsault off the top of a cage onto Chris Benoit. The fans chant for Rob Van Dam despite him not being a nominee. Show assumes he won and heads to the stage first before Shane announces Kurt as the winner. He hugs Team Angle and shakes McMahon's hand before celebrating his victory, Charlie Haas and Shelton Benjamin holding an American flag behind him. Angle thanks the "Academy of Wrestling Arts and Sciences" for the "Ruckus Award" before reading a long prepared segment. The fans get under his skin chanting "what" before his music sounds, the producers playing him off the stage.

A video package of goofy gimmicks plays including IRS, Tatanka, and Gillberg.

The number nine fan voted moment in *Raw* history is "Stone Cold" Steve Austin driving a monster truck over The Rock's new car.

After a commercial break, Booker T heads to the stage. He says the last ten years have "been like a giant spinaroonie", leaving people dizzy but always entertaining. Booker says he's seen things he thought he'd never see like Chris Jericho's shiny outfit tonight. After telling him, "you go, girl", Booker T plays a video for the nominees for the "Tell Me I Didn't Just See That" award. They are the three faces of Foley, Eric Bischoff hugging Vince McMahon, Bart Gunn's "Brawl for All" performances, Kane setting a crew member on fire, and "Stone Cold" Steve Austin driving a Zamboni into the arena. Afterwards,

Goldust joins his tag team partner onstage in a golden smoking jacket. He talks about how excited his "golden globes" are. In a small surprise, Mick Foley wins the award despite not being here. He's on good terms with the company so he's a non-active competitor that can make fans think anyone can win an award. Booker accepts on Mick's behalf and tells everyone to "have a nice day". Afterwards, Coach asks Bischoff about losing. He doesn't care about this award. He's just focused on the next twenty-nine days and making *Raw* the best show around.

After a commercial break, the "sixteen-time World Champion", Ric Flair, takes the stage. He calls the WWE an extended family before noting the members of the family who have been lost in the last decade. A video package plays for deceased superstars and WWE employees like Andre the Giant, British Bulldog, Brian Pillman, Joey Marella, and Gorilla Monsoon. Also included are "Ravishing" Rick Rude, Yokozuna, and Owen Hart to "Tell Me a Lie", the song the WWF used for Shawn Michaels's knee injury years ago.

Afterwards, Chris Jericho interrupts JR and Lawler. He says his black leather suit was a tip from "Classy" Freddie Blassie. Y2J then introduces the nominees for the "Gimme the Mic" best talker award. The nominees are: "Stone Cold" Steve Austin, Shawn Michaels, Kurt Angle, Mick Foley, Vince McMahon, and The Rock. Jericho is stunned that the "Great One" wins. Since the "People's Champ" isn't here, Y2J accepts the award for himself. Suddenly, a big screen turns on. The "Brahma Bull" joins everyone via satellite from his latest film to say he's come back to New York City, getting booed. He tells Jericho to shine up the award and shove it up his butt. The Rock then rants about being a star before telling Y2J to get off his stage. Before he goes, the "Great One" tells him to leave the award and brush his teeth. He then addresses Angle, telling everyone that they made history in the ring once in Kurt's hometown, Pittsburgh. He calls Team Angle, "Team Suck Squad", before insulting Stephanie McMahon. She just laughs. Still not done, he calls Goldust a "sick freak". When he keeps talking, the fans chant "boring". Since it's prerecorded, The Rock ignores them while he thanks everyone for helping him get to where he is and warns that he'll be back in a month and a half.

The number eight fan voted top *Raw* moment is the *Raw/Nitro* Vince McMahon simulcast and Shane McMahon stealing away WCW.

Following another commercial break, Howard Finkel is outside to introduce the show. Tazz and Michael Cole then head to the stage to introduce the "Shut Up and Kiss Me" best couple award. The nominees are: Mark Henry and Mae Young, Chyna and Eddie Guerrero, Lita and Matt Hardy, William Regal kissing Vince McMahon's butt, and Stephanie McMahon and Triple H. Hunter and Stephanie win and are very uncomfortable together as McMahon calls Helmsley a loser while praising herself. "The Game" is feeling a little nostalgic and asks for a kiss for old times sake. She doesn't fight him about it, but instead of his lips, he pulls down his pants and moons her. Instead of kissing his butt, Stephanie spanks him and leaves with the trophy. Triple H can't help but smile as he heads backstage, barely pulling up his pants.

Also in his underwear, Vince McMahon is part of the seventh biggest moment in *Raw* history when Mankind introduces Socko and "Stone Cold" Steve Austin beats the owner in a hospital bed.

After a commercial break, Coach and Stacy introduce "Mean" Gene Okerlund and Pat Patterson. Okerlund gets several cheers before "Mean" Gene asks Patterson what he thinks about the WWE. Pat just wants to get to the point and the announcers introduce the "Network Difficulties" award. The nominees are: Mae Young delivering a hand, "Stone Cold" Steve Austin giving Santa Claus a Stone Cold Stunner, Three-Minute Warning interrupting "HLA", and Brian Pillman brandishing a gun. The fans want

Pillman to get the win, but Young's hand baby does. Mae heads to the stage, but argues with The Fabulous Moolah first. She then kisses the presenters before thanking the fans, the sound guys trying to play her off the stage quickly.

The sixth *Raw* Retro moment as voted on by the fans is D-Generation X impersonating The Nation of Domination.

Following a commercial break, Lilian Garcia introduces Brock Lesnar on the stage. Wearing a suit, the "next big thing" gets a nice pop before introducing the nominees for the *Raw* Superstar of the Decade. Brock says that he respects everyone in the room except Paul Heyman before playing video for the nominees: Mick Foley, The Rock, Bret Hart, Triple H, "Stone Cold" Steve Austin, and The Undertaker. Shockingly, Austin is the winner. Of course, he's not here. Instead, Vince McMahon steps on the stage and takes the award while the fans chant for Austin. Vince says he couldn't be here tonight, but he bets there's a good reason. McMahon knows that "Stone Cold" would be proud to accept a Ruckus Award and cause a stir. Vince says he knows the reason isn't here…because Austin wasn't invited. In the crowd, Coach asks Helmsley about losing the award. "The Game" says it's a popularity contest and leaves, Ric Flair following behind.

The number five *Raw* Retro moment is "Stone Cold" Steve Austin flipping off and fighting with Mike Tyson.

Following another commercial break, a video package plays for *Raw*'s greatest matches. The nominees are the 2002 Tag Title "TLC" match, Triple H versus Cactus Jack in 1997, Jeff Hardy and The Undertaker's 2002 "Ladder" match, and "Stone Cold" beating Kane for the WWF Title in 1998. JR and "the King" are proud to announce the winner is the "TLC" match. Christian and Chris Jericho are first onto the stage to argue about which of them deserves the Ruckus Award first. Kane takes the trophy away. Wearing a button down shirt and mask, the "Big Red Machine" says the award is for all of them. After over a thousand matches on *Raw*, Kane says it's an honor to be in the best of the best. D-Von Dudley then thanks the men who helped make the "TLC" match a big deal in the first place before Kane leaves with the award. Once everyone else leaves, Rob Van Dam stays on the stage to introduce himself as "everyone's favorite superstar".

The number four *Raw* Retro moment is D-Generation X invading *WCW Monday Nitro*.

After a commercial break, the number three *Raw* Retro moment is "Hollywood" Hulk Hogan and The Rock going nose-to-nose to set up their WrestleMania X8 match in front of a rabid crowd.

Following a shot of "Classy" Freddie Blassie in the crowd, the number two *Raw* Retro moment is footage from the Owen Hart tribute show.

After the final commercial break, Edge steps onto the stage to introduce the fan voted greatest *Raw* moment. He says he's just a fan like everyone in attendance before playing the moment, "Stone Cold" Steve Austin giving Vince McMahon a beer bath. Afterwards, Edge thanks the "true number one superstars in the history of *Raw*"…the fans. He then invites all of the WWE superstars to get onto the stage. JR is worried we might have a Royal Rumble tonight. Instead, the superstars keep the piece and thank the fans for watching for the last ten years. Really, this is a celebration of the last five years since nothing from 1993-1997 wins anything, but the WWE always has a short memory span.

SmackDown!

January 16, 2003
East Rutherford, NJ
Announcers: Michael Cole, Tazz

The show opens with a video package for Dawn Marie and Al Wilson's love, including Al passing away. Following a graphic of Al, Dawn is wearing black as she addresses the crowd in a prerecorded promo. She says a week ago she was so happy, but now her husband is gone. Dawn Marie claims that Al was a very public man who wanted their wedding and honeymoon to be public. To respect his wishes, she'll also have his viewing publicly tonight. Afterwards, the intro video plays and fireworks explode from the *SmackDown!* fist.

Los Guerreros def. B-2/John Cena (WWE Tag Title match). As they head to the ring, the champions talk about one of them winning the Royal Rumble in a prerecorded promo. They argue about who should win and who cheated the last time they fought before Eddie says so long as a Guerrero wins, the family will be happy. John then leads B-2 out, rapping about Los Guerreros selling fruit on the side of the road. Once again, B-2 adds, "booyah". When the bell rings, Cena and Eddie tie up. Neither can get an upper hand until Chavo grabs the rapping heel. "Latino Heat" takes advantage and slows the rookie before tagging in his nephew for a combination snap mare and dropkick. Another quick tag sees the champions deliver a back suplex followed by Eddie's slingshot somersault splash. When Chavo returns, he suplexes Cena back into the challengers' corner. That lets B-2 tag in for his own share of the punishment until John pulls the top rope down to low bridge "Latino Heat". The rapping heel follows up with a slam on the floor before B-2 welcomes the champion back in with a falcon arrow suplex for a two-count. When Cena tags in, he traps Eddie in a front face lock. Luckily, Chavo tags his uncle's foot only to run into a snap suplex and his own front face lock. Eddie doesn't even leave the ring, crouching in a corner for some reason while Chavo surprises John with a dropkick. "Latino Heat" then gets the tag, still in the ring, to DDT B-2. When Cena breaks up the cover, all four men fight. Los Guerreros capitalize with a pair of dives onto the challengers out on the floor. Chavo immediately takes over for his seemingly injured uncle, shoving B-2 back into the ring to dropkick and Frog Splash him for the win. Post-match, Chavo leaves to check on his uncle while John blames B-2 for the loss. When B-2 shoves him down, Cena retreats in a corner until a mystery man runs out to attack the heel. He follows up with a whip into the ring post and armbar, yanking on B-2's arm until the rapping heel tells him to stop.

A video package for Kurt Angle and Team Angle fighting with Chris Benoit and Edge plays. Afterwards, Benoit sits in front of a black screen to talk about his upcoming WWE Title shot at the Royal Rumble. He says all his sacrifices will mean something this Sunday. After complimenting Kurt as a competitor, the "rabid wolverine" promises that Angle won't be at a hundred percent after Benoit gets his hands on the Olympian tonight. He then jokes about showing his "toothless aggression".

Afterwards, Stephanie McMahon steps onto the stage to tease The Undertaker's return this Sunday. She then turns her attention to the Big Show/Brock Lesnar Royal Rumble match. Since both men want to get their hands on each other, Stephanie offers to sign them to a tag match tonight, giving the giant A-Train as his partner. She's going to let everyone wait to find out Lesnar's partner.

A Nathan Jones teaser plays.

Bill DeMott def. Rikishi. As he heads to the ring, Rikishi talks about living the dream this Sunday in the Royal Rumble match in a prerecorded promo. DeMott then steps onto the stage to say that everyone has been calling him a bully for picking on smaller guys. Tonight, he warns the big Samoan to get out of the ring right now. Instead, the big babyface nails the bully with a big fist. A hip toss and slam follow for a two-count before Rikishi works on his opponent's arm. It takes him a bit, but DeMott eventually fights free of the armbar to hammer the big Samoan's midsection. He follows up with a choke on the ropes and clubbing blow to the back. Afterwards, Bill applies his own armbar. Like his opponent, Rikishi fights free only to miss a corner charge. Following a two-count, the bully gets frustrated and wastes time before walking into a thrust kick for a near fall. Soon after, the two men bump heads. DeMott seems to get the worse of it, falling to the mat in a corner. When Rikishi tries to capitalize with a Rump Shaker, Bill hops up quickly for a powerbomb off the second rope. Alongside a handful of tights, that scores the bully the win.

Backstage, Billy Kidman makes fun of Shannon Moore to Funaki. Matt Hardy says Billy is just jealous that Matt is mentoring Shannon instead of Kidman. When Funaki asks Moore why he puts up with Hardy's "bs", Matt takes offense. He makes fun of the way he talks and offers to give him a shot of Mattitude before kicking off a brawl. It doesn't last long before the babyfaces chase away Hardy and Shannon.

Nunzio (with Nidia/Jamie Noble) def. Tajiri. In a prerecorded interview, Tajiri laughs and talks in Japanese about spraying mist and eliminating people this Sunday at the Royal Rumble. Inside the ring, he kicks and slaps the Italian heel until Nunzio snap mares him. The "Japanese Buzzsaw" answers with a heel kick for a two-count. When Tajiri attempts a swinging slam, the Italian heel holds onto his shoulder for a flying armbar. He continues working on the arm, stomping and stretching it in the center of the ring. When Nunzio tries to follow up with an enziguri, the "Japanese Buzzsaw" ducks, but a second rope flying leg drop to the standing babyface nearly gets the Italian heel the victory. Afterwards, he continues working Tajiri's arm until the "Japanese Buzzsaw" surprises him with a kick to the ribs and spinning attack. A German suplex follows for a near fall. With Noble cheering him on, the Italian superstar gets up only to receive more kicks and a handspring back elbow. Following another two-count, Tajiri walks into a corner kick and running armbar drop. He answers with a Tarantula, but when he sets up for the Buzzsaw Kick, Jamie hops onto the apron to distract him. The "Japanese Buzzsaw" instead kicks Noble and sprays green mist in Nidia's face before Nunzio finally capitalizes with a tornado armbar drop for the win.

Footage from *Raw*'s tenth anniversary plays.

Backstage, Josh Mathews asks John Cena and his mystery man what happened with B-2. Cena raps that it's time for a change and he's got a new man on his side, Redd Dogg. He barks and says that's what went down ahead of an Undertaker teaser for the Royal Rumble.

After a commercial break, Dawn Marie hesitantly walks around the funeral home. Tazz notes that she's not dressed like the "typical grieving widow", but she is wearing black. Dawn is clearly upset, crying on the funeral worker's shoulder before asking for a moment with her husband. Once the man leaves, Marie opens the casket and tells Al Wilson that he doesn't look so good. She thinks he looked better when he was on the gurney last week. Dawn cries as she promises to carry on the Wilson name before kissing him goodbye.

Backstage, Stephanie McMahon talks on the phone to her brother. She wants to know if Eric Bischoff is really going to get fired in thirty days. Before she gets her answer, Brock Lesnar interrupts. He doesn't want a partner tonight. Lesnar promises that he'll take down both A-Train and Big Show solo. Stephanie tells him that she wants him to win his match with Show this Sunday because he's her biggest star and she wants to protect her investment. Brock says that's fine, and he'll see his partner in the ring.

Ahead of the next match, A-Train and Big Show head to the squared circle where Paul Heyman talks about his "favorite client" facing Brock Lesnar in a match that neither man can afford to lose this Sunday. Paul assures everyone that the giant will stop Lesnar from competing in the Royal Rumble match because Brock cannot beat Show. And once Big Show wins their Royal Rumble Qualifying match, Heyman is sure that one of the giant, Team Angle, or A-Train will win the Rumble to face Kurt Angle at WrestleMania XIX. Lesnar has heard enough and steps through the curtain followed by the returning Rey Mysterio as his surprise partner.

Brock Lesnar/Rey Mysterio def. A-Train/Big Show (with Paul Heyman). The babyfaces race into the ring where Brock belly-to-belly suplexes Show ahead of an F5 to A-Train. The giant tries to answer with a Chokeslam, but Brock slips free and clotheslines Big Show out to the floor ahead of a 619 and slingshot splash from Rey to the hairy heel for the three-count. Post-match, Heyman leads his client backstage, trying desperately to hold back the giant.

Back at the wake, Dawn Marie hugs mourners. Everyone stops when Torrie Wilson enters. The women tensely stare at each other in front of the casket before we cut back to the ring.

Matt Hardy (with Shannon Moore) def. Funaki (with Billy Kidman). The Matt Fact this week says that Matt was in the academically gifted class in elementary school. Funaki then rushes out to pound on Hardy for insulting him. Matt answers with a side effect for a lackadaisical cover and two-count. He also gets a two-count with an elbow drop before choking the interviewer on the ropes. Shannon also chokes Funaki before Hardy applies a reverse chin lock. Instead of going for the submission, he slams the interviewer to the canvas for another near fall. When Funaki tries to fight back, Matt hot shots him ahead of another side effect for a two-count. He motions for the Twist of Fate to end things, but the interviewer fights free and bulldogs Hardy ahead of a dropkick for a near fall. Following an enziguri kick, Funaki nearly gets the win with a second rope tornado reverse DDT. Matt isn't even safe outside the ring as the interviewer dives onto him. When they return to the ring, Moore tries to get involved, but Kidman decks him. That distracts Mike Sparks and he misses Funaki's top rope flying cross body block and subsequent cover. When the interviewer gets back up, he accidentally runs into Shannon on the apron. That collision lets Hardy steal the win with a Twist of Fate. Post-match, Moore brags to Matt about getting things right, but Hardy shoves his MFer and says he did it on his own.

After a commercial break, Torrie Wilson cries at her father's casket. Dawn Marie angrily accuses her of killing her father with a broken heart. Dawn calls all this a performance and slaps Torrie hard. Wilson responds with her own slap and toss to the ground before yelling that she hates Marie. While she cries over her father's casket and apologizes, Dawn grabs a lamp and smashes the back of Torrie's head. It's such a big moment to the WWE that they replay the attack after another commercial break.

A Nathan Jones teaser plays. The announcers call him a "bad dude" before previewing the Royal Rumble card. Tazz wonders if Dawn Marie and Torrie Wilson will meet in a "Casket" match.

Kurt Angle/Team Angle def. Chris Benoit/Edge by disqualification. While the heels come out unified, Kurt is still on a crutch. Edge then comes out with a prerecorded promo playing of him listing his accomplishments. This Sunday, he promises to be the Royal Rumble winner. After everyone enters the ring, the show takes a commercial break. Afterwards, Benoit back suplexes Haas and dares the Olympian to get in the squared circle. Instead, he watches as the "rabid wolverine" chops Charlie and whips him into the ring post. The number one contender follows up with a back body drop and snap suplex before Benjamin distracts him and Mike Chioda for an Angle low blow. Once in control, Haas works on Benoit's arm with a reverse armbar. "The Crippler" escapes with a roll-up for a two-count and a snap suplex. That lets Edge get the hot tag to punch and back body drop Charlie. When he runs the ropes though, Shelton trips the babyface ahead of an overhead release belly-to-belly suplex. Kurt then tags in to pummel Edge and taunt Benoit. Unfortunately, the babyface quickly comes back to life with fists and a face slam, chasing the Olympian out to the floor. After running from the babyfaces, Angle lures the "rabid wolverine" into a Benjamin clothesline. Once he's down, Kurt resumes his attack, punching and German suplexing Benoit. He also cheap shots Edge on the apron before hooking an Anklelock. Although "the Crippler" kicks free, he knocks the Olympian into the heel corner and a Shelton tag. The babyfaces then take turns attacking him, Edge scoring a two-count with a top rope flying clothesline. Afterwards, he chokes and tackles the rookie in a corner. Unfortunately, the babyfaces are outnumbered and Team Angle distract the referee for everyone to cheap shot Edge. Back in the squared circle, Benjamin gets a two-count after a scoop slam and jumping leg drop. Team Angle then deliver their double-team leapfrog hotshot for another near fall. Moments later, Charlie gets his own near fall with a running bulldog. Kurt adds in a cheap shot before Shelton returns for a clothesline and two-count. He then slows the pace with a reverse chin lock. The babyface refuses to stay down, fighting free and dropping the rookie with an Edge-a-matic. Unfortunately, Haas gets the tag and elbow drops Edge before he can make the tag. That allows Team Angle to double-team the babyface some more before the Olympian tags back into the match. Cocky, he struts around and stomps Edge. The babyface answers with fists and a kick to the face before walking into an overhead belly-to-belly suplex for a two-count. Back in, Charlie wrenches Edge's neck. Although the babyface kicks free, Angle tags back in for more stomps until Edge surprises him with a clothesline. Before he can tag out, Kurt German suplexes him. He does so a second time before the babyface drops him. Shelton quickly tags in, but Benoit gets the hot tag to club him and Haas. He also German suplexes the rookies, giving Charlie a trio. When Benjamin saves his partner from a top rope diving headbutt, the "rabid wolverine" traps him in the Crippler Crossface. That brings in Kurt with the WWE Title, but Benoit sees him coming and locks the champion in the Crossface too. Chioda tries to get "the Crippler" to release his hold since Angle isn't the legal man while Edge takes care of Team Angle. Unsuccessful, the referee calls for the disqualification before the Olympian taps out. While Kurt taps, Edge dives off the top rope onto Team Angle. Post-match, Benoit attacks Angle with the champion's crutch, bending it over his back. The show ends with the "rabid wolverine" standing over the WWE Title and daring Kurt to come get it.

PPV: Royal Rumble
January 19, 2003
Boston, MA
Announcers: Jim Ross, Jerry "the King" Lawler, Michael Cole, Tazz

The show opens with a video package of superstars talking about winning tonight to kick off the Road to WrestleMania. This is the first time that there has been so much focus on the term "Road to WrestleMania", something the WWE will use from now on. Afterwards, the graphic plays featuring a rainstorm behind the event logo before fireworks explode to kick off the show.

Brock Lesnar def. Big Show (with Paul Heyman) (Royal Rumble Qualifying match). As Lesnar heads to the ring, Tazz says, "here comes the pain". The *SmackDown!* announcers get the honor of opening the show while the fans loudly chant for Brock. He answers them by driving Show into a corner and pummeling him. Although the giant headbutts free of a belly-to-belly suplex, he can't a second time. The babyface follows up with a second belly-to-belly suplex, impressing everyone. When he hooks a bearhug, Big Show breaks free and tosses Lesnar over the top rope to the floor. There, he knees Brock before shoving him back into the squared circle for a corner elbow. Stomps and hard chops follow, Cole wondering if the babyface can beat Show. It doesn't look like it as the giant tosses him around until he misses a corner splash. Lesnar answers with a German suplex for a two-count. Heyman has seen enough and grabs his former client's foot, giving Big Show the time he needs to recover and big boot Brock. The giant follows up with a sidewalk slam, but when he grabs the babyface for a Chokeslam, Lesnar rolls him up for a quick two-count. He follows up with a belly-to-belly suplex before dragging Paul into the ring. Luckily, Big Show saves his agent from an F5 and Chokeslams Brock for a near fall. Show can't believe he kicked out. Lowering his straps, the giant dares Lesnar to get back up. He ends up helping him up only to see the babyface shove Big Show into Heyman on the apron. Brock follows up with an F5 to the giant for the three-count. Cole wonders how much Lesnar has left for the Rumble.

Backstage, Terri interviews Chris Jericho. She asks Y2J why when he had the opportunity to pick any number he wants in the Royal Rumble match he picked number two. Jericho disagrees. He didn't have the opportunity to pick any number he wanted because Shawn Michaels stole number one. However, Shawn has never beaten The Rock and "Stone Cold" Steve Austin on the same night like Y2J, and tonight Jericho will start down the road to getting back a championship.

MUST SEE! The Dudley Boyz def. Lance Storm/William Regal (World Tag Title match). Pre-match, Nick Patrick searches the champions for brass knuckles, but doesn't find any. Inside the ring, Lance works on Bubba Ray's arm. The challenger returns the favor before barreling over Storm. The two men then trade fists, playing to Bubba's strengths. Following a modified powerbomb, Dudley locks on a single leg hold until Regal makes the save. D-Von tags in afterwards to punch and elbow both heels. Sporting bright green camouflage pants, D-Von scores a two-count with a slam and elbow drop to William. When he attempts a corner charge though, Lance pulls the Englishman out of the way to swing the momentum. Once in control, Regal gets a two-count with an exploder suplex. The champions then make quick tags, trapping Dudley in their corner and slowing him with wear down holds. Following a lengthy Storm reverse chin lock, D-Von finally escapes and tags in Bubba Ray who fights both heels. After tossing William out to the floor, he nearly gets the win with a side slam to the Canadian. He also scores a two-count with a German suplex to Lance before elbowing both heels. When he delivers a Bubba Bomb, the Englishman makes the save. He pays courtesy of a wassup drop. The Dudleys follow up with a double flapjack to Storm for a D-Von near fall. That brings out Chief Morley to argue with the referee while Regal dons his brass knuckles. Luckily, the Dudleys see William coming and drop him with a 3D. While Bubba decks Morley, D-Von dons the brass knuckles and drills Lance to crown new champions.

A Nathan Jones video package plays.

Torrie Wilson def. Dawn Marie Wilson. Following a video package for the match, Dawn comes out wearing a veil and announced with her new last name. Torrie follows, wearing white to contrast Marie's black. When Mike Sparks checks to see if Torrie wants to go through with the match, Dawn sneak attacks her. The babyface answers with hair pulls and a slingshot for the first ever stepdaughter versus stepmother match. Marie soon recovers to block a German suplex and apply an armbar. She adds in knees to the back for a two-count. A face-first slam from the heel follows before the women collide in a corner. The fans are not entertained. Despite that, Torrie nearly picks up the win with some roll-ups before Dawn surprises her with a springboard clothesline. The babyface answers with a swinging neckbreaker out of nowhere for the win. Cole wonders what the victory really means, noting that Torrie was grieving a lot more than Dawn Marie. Dawn says this isn't over.

Backstage, Eric Bischoff interrupts Stephanie McMahon shaking Randy Orton's hand. Stephanie is just here to say goodbye to Eric since he'll be fired in under thirty days. Bischoff teases an "atomic bombshell" that will save his job. McMahon has her own bombshell that she'll drop this Thursday night. She warns Eric that she's a McMahon and "blood is thicker than...urine". Bischoff calls her crass before telling her that "money is much thicker than blood".

A Sean O'Haire video package plays with him telling fans to taking control of their life. He ends with what will be his catchphrase, "I'm not telling you anything you don't already know".

Ahead of the next match, Lawler believes Triple H is scared of Scott Steiner before we see a video package for their World Title match. It's a great video package that makes the goofy segments the two have had leading up to the match look important.

Scott Steiner def. Triple H (with Ric Flair) (World Title match) by disqualification. Once the video package is done, Triple H is out first for once, sporting red trunks for this match. After Scott comes out for his first WWE match, Earl Hebner tells everyone that he's going to call this contest down the middle and he "won't put up with any crap". The two wrestlers then open the match trading fists. Steiner wins the exchange, clubbing Hunter down to the mat. A press slam follows, sending Helmsley rolling out to the floor. "Big Poppa Pump" follows, clubbing "the Game" some more before ramming his lower back into the apron and barricade. A suplex from the apron scores the challenger a two-count and some boos. The "Steiner sucks" crowd quickly quiet as Scott resumes chopping the champion. After hammering down Triple H again, Steiner locks on a sloppy Boston crab. It doesn't take Hunter long to reach the ropes before receiving another beating. Although he answers with a facebuster, it has no effect on "Big Poppa Pump" and the challenger answers with a bearhug. Helmsley has to go to the eyes to escape, but runs into a belly-to-belly suplex afterwards for a two-count. When he tries to apply the Steiner Recliner, a camel clutch, Flair pulls his man into the ropes. Scott backs "The Nature Boy" up before running into a corner boot to finally put the returning superstar down on the canvas. "The Game" follows up with a flurry of stomps and a whip into the ring steps. Back in the squared circle, a neckbreaker scores the champion a two-count before he stomps and chokes Steiner in a corner. Ric also chokes "Big Poppa Pump", getting the first good reaction in a while. Triple H follows up with another neckbreaker for a near fall. Back to the boots, Hunter wears down the challenger before distracting Hebner for another Flair choke. When Helmsley tries to Pedigree him, Scott fights free and suplexes "the Game". Steiner tries to follow up with a slam, but the champion flips over into a cutter for another two-count. Ric cheers on his man after a suplex, but instead of going for the cover, Triple H heads upstairs. "Big Poppa Pump" catches his leap for an overhead belly-to-belly suplex. Clotheslines and a back body drop follow ahead of a trio of belly-to-belly suplexes. The fans are really starting to boo the challenger now as he twists Hunter over with another belly-to-belly suplex for a near fall. When he delivers a double underhook powerbomb, Scott falls back and gets booed loudly ahead of a two-count. The fans really turn on him at this point and don't cheer any of his moves, including a second rope superplex for a near fall. That's enough for the heels and they try to leave, but Steiner nails them in the aisle. While the referee holds back "The Nature Boy", Helmsley tries to hit "Big Poppa Pump" with the World Title. Luckily, the challenger blocks the attack and slams the belt back into "the Game's" face, busting him open. Back in the squared circle, Scott gets booed again for an overhead release belly-to-belly suplex. That sends the champion scrambling into the crowd trying to get counted out. Instead, Steiner drags him back over the barricade and slams his face onto the announce table. Back in the squared circle, "Big Poppa Pump" does pushups in front of Triple H, the announcers ignoring the boos. Flair wants the match stopped for excessive blood loss. When he doesn't call for the bell, Hunter tosses Earl out to the floor. The referee teases calling for the disqualification, but changes his mind and orders Helmsley to wrestle. The challenger follows up with a twisting belly-to-belly suplex for a near fall. "The Game" can only answer with a low blow and roll-up for a near fall. When he grabs a sledgehammer, the champion gets a nice pop. Hebner tells him "no", but Triple H hits Scott for the disqualification and loud boos. Post-match, Earl saves Steiner from another shot. After Hunter shoves the referee down, "Big Poppa Pump" takes the weapon away and decks the heels for even more boos. The fans really hate every part of this match. Despite that, Scott locks Helmsley in a Steiner Recliner, forcing WWE officials and Eric Bischoff to come out and plead for Steiner to break his hold.

A video package plays for the upcoming WWE Title match.

MUST SEE! Kurt Angle def. Chris Benoit (WWE Title match). Following the video package, Kurt follows in Triple H's footsteps, walking out first as the champion. He's accompanied by Team Angle. They stop Benoit from getting his hands on the Olympian before the bell, but that sets off Mike Chioda. Alongside other *SmackDown!* referees, Chioda evicts Team Angle from ringside, making this a one-on-one match. That's good for "the Crippler" as he trips Angle and threatens to put him in a submission hold, chasing off the champion. When he returns to the squared circle, Benoit traps Kurt in a side headlock. The two men pick up the pace with the challenger dropkicking and punching the Olympian before Angle briefly applies a sleeper hold. Benoit responds by whipping the champion down to the canvas and applying a leg lock, but Kurt reaches the ropes quickly. Back up, the Olympian whips the "rabid wolverine" into the ring post shoulder-first. He follows up with clubbing blows and a suplex for a two-count. Back on their feet, the two men trade chops. Benoit wins that exchange ahead of a clubbing blow to the back of the head and knee to the gut for a near fall. More chops follow until Angle suplexes the challenger sternum-first onto the top rope. "The Crippler" answers with a throat drop on the top rope and DDT on the apron to knock out the champion. By the time he gets him back in the ring, Kurt just manages to kick out. Benoit heads upstairs quickly for a diving headbutt, but the Olympian rolls out of the way at the last second. He tries to follow up with an Angle Slam, but the "rabid wolverine" slips free and locks on a sharpshooter. Fortunately, Angle crawls to the ropes for the break. Still on the offensive, Benoit gets a two-count with a back suplex. The champion answers with a belly-to-belly toss before whipping "the Crippler" out to the floor. After catching his breath, Kurt follows him out for a slam on the barricade. Back in the squared circle, a clothesline scores the Olympian a near fall before he applies a rear chin lock and body hooks. Although Benoit escapes, he runs into another belly-to-belly suplex. A back suplex follows for an Angle two-count before he returns to his chin lock. After the challenger elbows free, the two men connect with simultaneous clotheslines. They work Chioda's count to nine before the "rabid wolverine" comes back to life with fists, clotheslines, and a back body drop. He follows up with two German suplexes before the champion answers with one of his own. Benoit ends the exchange with a final German suplex. He then slashes his throat and blows snot on Kurt before heading upstairs. The Olympian quickly hops up for a second rope belly-to-belly suplex and two-count. When he attempts an Angle Slam, the challenger slips free and locks on the Crippler Crossface. Although Angle reaches the ropes, "the Crippler" pulls him back to the center of the ring for an Anklelock. It doesn't take the champion long to reverse the hold before ending up back in the Crossface. Opposite of the last match, the fans love this. Kurt nearly steals the win with a roll-up, but Benoit just kicks out and reapplies his submission finisher. This time, the Olympian escapes with an Angle Slam for a two-count. Lowering his straps, Angle reapplies an Anklelock, but "the Crippler" escapes and rolls him up for another near fall. The men then trade German suplexes, Benoit flipping over the champion. The "rabid wolverine" follows up with a diving headbutt almost all the way across the ring for another close two-count. When he tries to follow up, Kurt reverse powerbombs him onto the top rope ahead of another Angle Slam and near fall. Benoit answers with another Crossface, but Angle counters with an Anklelock. The challenger fights to get free, but he can't escape. Eventually, he has no choice but to tap out to end this amazing match. Post-match, Team Angle puts Kurt on their shoulders. When they leave, the fans give "the Crippler" a big ovation. He even pounds his chest in response for the appreciation.

Backstage, Rob Van Dam stretches. Kane interrupts to tell his sometimes partner that he almost won the Royal Rumble two years ago. Tonight, if RVD is in his way, the "Big Red Machine" will not hesitate to eliminate him so that the monster wins the Rumble. Rob understands that and says it's "every man for themselves". He tells Kane to do whatever it takes to win because Van Dam will do the same.

Out at ringside, Howard Finkel explains the rules for the Royal Rumble match.

MUST SEE! Brock Lesnar wins the 2003 Royal Rumble match.

Entry	Wrestler	Elimination Order	Wrestler	Eliminated By
1	Shawn Michaels	1	Shawn Michaels	Chris Jericho
2	Chris Jericho	2	Christopher Nowinski	Rey Mysterio
3	Christopher Nowinski	3	Rey Mysterio	Chris Jericho
4	Rey Mysterio	4	Bill DeMott	Edge
5	Edge	5	Tommy Dreamer	Chris Jericho/Christian
6	Christian	6	Tajiri	Chris Jericho
7	Chavo Guerrero Jr.	7	B-2	Edge
8	Tajiri	8	Chavo Guerrero Jr.	Edge
9	Bill DeMott	9	Christian	Chris Jericho
10	Tommy Dreamer	10	Edge	Chris Jericho
11	B-2	11	Jeff Hardy	Rob Van Dam
12	Rob Van Dam	12	Rosey	Kane
13	Matt Hardy	13	Eddie Guerrero	Booker T
14	Eddie Guerrero	14	Chris Jericho	Test
15	Jeff Hardy	15	Goldust	Charlie Haas/Shelton Benjamin
16	Rosey	16	Booker T	Charlie Haas/Shelton Benjamin
17	Test	17	Test	Batista
18	John Cena	18	Rikishi	Batista
19	Charlie Haas	19	Charlie Haas	Brock Lesnar
20	Rikishi	20	Shelton Benjamin	Brock Lesnar
21	Jamal	21	Matt Hardy	Brock Lesnar
22	Kane	22	John Cena	The Undertaker
23	Shelton Benjamin	23	Jamal	The Undertaker
24	Booker T	24	Maven	The Undertaker
25	A-Train	25	A-Train	Kane/Rob Van Dam
26	Maven	26	Rob Van Dam	Kane
27	Goldust	27	Batista	The Undertaker
28	Batista	28	Kane	The Undertaker
29	Brock Lesnar	29	The Undertaker	Brock Lesnar
30	The Undertaker	-	Brock Lesnar	Winner

Since both men have been revealed on *Raw*, there should be no surprises with the first two entrants. Shawn Michaels dances out first to be followed by Chris Jericho. Instead of Y2J though, it's Christian dressed up like his friend. Jericho capitalizes, sneaking into the ring behind Shawn to give him a low blow. The heel follows up with a big chair shot, busting open the "Heartbreak Kid". Jack Doan admonishes Y2J before the countdown starts for the third entrant, Christopher Nowinski. He's in no hurry to get in the ring and stands at ringside to let Jericho continue to punish Michaels before eliminating him to boos. JR and Lawler, the only two announcers for the match, can't believe their eyes. The Harvard heel doesn't enter the ring until after Rey Mysterio runs out to dropkick and head scissors Y2J. He continues to watch as Rey plants Jericho face first to the canvas before Y2J recovers and press slams him. The heel tries to score another elimination, but Mysterio lands on the apron and springboard dropkicks his way back into the squared circle. He's followed by Edge who Spears both heels. Following a masked man flying head scissors off the top rope, the former WWE Tag Team Champions toss Jericho through the ropes to the floor. The two babyfaces then trade shots and counters before Rey head scissors his partner over the top rope. It certainly looks like both of Edge's feet hit the floor, but if they do he's back up so quickly that he's able to continue. He does so countering a springboard hurricanrana from Mysterio with a powerbomb. That sees both babyfaces down on the mat and the heels on the floor as Christian runs out at number six to hug Edge. Despite being brothers, Edge Spears Christian. The babyfaces tease a double-team move where Rey is on Edge's shoulders afterwards, but Nowinski returns to shove them over the top rope. Unfortunately, they both survive and deliver a double top rope missile dropkick, Edge landing on the Harvard heel's face and breaking his nose. Mysterio adds insult to injury with a bronco buster to Nowinski before the next man enters.

It's Chavo Guerrero Jr. at seven. He goes after Mysterio and slams him to the canvas, but the masked man counters a charge with a drop toe hold onto the middle rope. A 619 and West Coast Pop follow to Chavo. Christian also gets a 619, but when Rey goes for the West Coast Pop, the heel moves and Mysterio lands on Nowinski's shoulders. He proceeds to hurricanrana him out to the floor, back on his face. Rey follows right behind thanks to a Jericho clothesline to thin out the ring before Tajiri's entrance. He unloads with kicks to Y2J and Christian before Guerrero clubs and back suplexes him. The "Japanese Buzzsaw" answers with his modified airplane spin, but makes himself dizzy and gets trapped in a corner by Christian. Bill DeMott is in next at nine and he wastes no time running out to pound on everyone and toss Jericho over the top rope. Luckily, the heel lands on the apron and crawls back in while DeMott chokes Edge in a corner. Tommy Dreamer gets the number ten spot and brings a trashcan and kendo sticks with him. He uses a stick to wail on everyone until Edge gets a stick and joins him, the weapons wielding babyfaces knocking Bill out to the floor. Christian and Jericho then team up to smash Dreamer with trashcan lids before tossing him over the rope as well. While officials pull the weapons from the ring, Tajiri back elbows the heels. When he tries to give Y2J the Tarantula, Jericho shoves him out to the floor just before B-2 runs out, now wearing shorts after John Cena dropped him. B-2 doesn't last long at all, missing a corner splash for Edge to toss him out to the floor. The babyface follows up by tossing Chavo over the top rope and Spearing him off the apron for another elimination. Edge nearly eliminates Y2J too, but the heel skins the cat while the brothers wrestle on the other side of the ring. Jericho takes advantage, returning to push out both Edge and Christian. Alone in the ring, the camera focuses on the bloody knot on Y2J's head before RVD comes out at number twelve to unload with a flurry of kicks and a leg drop. He follows up with rolling thunder, but that puts Jericho down on the mat and makes him harder to eliminate. When the heel gets up, Van Dam catches his dropkick attempt to slingshot him over the top rope. Luckily, he holds onto the ropes ahead of the next entrant.

Number thirteen is Matt Hardy, joined by Shannon Moore. He gets in a Matt Fact tonight, stating that Matt "strongly dislikes mustard". RVD dislikes Hardy dropping him with a side effect. The heels then team up on Rob, Jericho catching him with a running face slam, but missing his Lionsault. Van Dam doesn't miss a Five-Star Frog Splash, but Hardy throws the babyface over the top rope. Luckily, RVD holds onto the ropes as Eddie Guerrero runs out to punch Matt. When he does the same to Van Dam, the popular superstar answers with a monkey flip before the two men nearly eliminate each other. Hardy makes the save and slams Rob to the canvas for a Frog Splash on the face. Matt quickly takes advantage and gives "Latino Heat" a Twist of Fate. Jeff Hardy is out next, but like Christian, Matt wants to work with his brother. Instead, the daredevil clotheslines him ahead of a jawbreaker. When Jeff tosses his brother over the top rope, Shannon props up his leader with his feet. Despite that, the daredevil gives his brother a Twist of Fate. Once again Moore comes to his man's aid, laying on him to try to prevent a Swanton Bomb. Unfortunately, Jeff doesn't care and jumps onto both heels before

Rosey marches out with Rico. The biggest man in the ring, Rosey throws his weight around and kicks RVD. Jeff teases eliminating Matt with a back body drop, but the heel holds onto the ropes while the daredevil joins Rob kicking Rosey in a corner. Test is out next, accompanied by Stacy Keibler. She watches as he slams Eddie and Matt. He also knocks Y2J over the top rope, but Jericho again holds onto the ropes to blindside the bodyguard. After ninety seconds of brawling, John Cena raps his way out, bragging about loving battle royals. He's got three reasons that he'll win including that he's going to slice people like a cucumber. Tazz, sitting at ringside but not providing commentary, loves it. Van Dam doesn't, tossing Cena into the ring while JR praises the rapping heel ahead of the next entrant.

Charlie Haas draws number nineteen and gets treated to a "you suck" chant as he runs out to slug Matt and Rosey. Moments later, Jeff attempts a whisper in the wind, but RVD shoves him off the ropes and to the floor for the elimination. Afterwards, Eddie stuns Jericho with a hurricanrana before Rikishi walks out, JR saying he's been in the most Royal Rumble matches in WWE history. For his eighth appearance he thrust kicks Cena and has a brief conversation with Rosey. The Samoans work together squashing Shannon Moore and Matt Hardy before Rosey surprises the big babyface with a clothesline. Jamal is out next at twenty to superkick Rikishi. The big Samoan is right back up and responds with thrust kicks to Three-Minute Warning before crushing Jamal in a corner. He then gives his fellow Samoan a Stinkface. That sets off the heel and he hammers Rikishi down to choke him. Rosey joins his partner while Jericho nearly eliminates Van Dam. Luckily, Kane is out next to help his sometimes partner. After punching and booting everyone, the "Big Red Machine" drags Rico into the ring for a Chokeslam. Rosey tries to help his manager, but gets back dropped out of the match. Kane follows up with a double Chokeslam to Hardy and Moore before nearly eliminating Jericho. Shelton Benjamin runs out to put a tag team back in the match, teaming up with Haas briefly. They are quickly separated when Matt nearly eliminates Benjamin. Things get worse for Shelton as the "Big Red Machine" hammers and chokes him while Hardy and Y2J trade fists. Booker T then comes out to a good pop to drop Kane with a Scissors Kick. He follows up with a flapjack to Matt and a spinaroonie for a bigger pop. Eddie tries to take advantage of the celebration, but Booker sees him coming and back body drops "Latino Heat" out to the floor. Everyone then trades attacks until the next man runs out.

It's A-Train who gives Cena and RVD Albert Bombs, sandwiching a Backbreaker to Benjamin. Rikishi slows his momentum with a thrust kick before again teasing eliminating Jericho. Luckily, the heel lands on the apron and returns to the ring. So does Shawn Michaels, sprinting out to punch Jericho before pummeling Cena and Hardy. Although Y2J knocks down Michaels, Test rocks the heel with a Big Boot to eliminate him. Shawn follows Jericho out with a slingshot dive over the top rope before WWE officials separate them. Maven is out afterwards, running out to punch the "Big Red Machine". Kane responds in kind before A-Train splashes Haas. With twelve men in the ring, everyone settles into brawls until Goldust runs out to fight with Team Angle. He also hammers Maven and drops him with Shattered Dreams. When he returns to fighting Team Angle, the heels work together to eliminate the "bizarre one", ending his short night. Booker T joins his oddball partner thanks to Team Angle pounding him out of the ring as well. Batista then emerges at twenty-eight with a great number. He clubs Cena and Jamal before Test stuns him with a full nelson slam. The bodyguard nearly tosses him out of the match, but the "Animal" holds onto the top rope and dodges Test's Big Boot to see the babyface fall out to the floor and out of the match. After spearing Benjamin, Batista clotheslines Rikishi out of the ring also. The men just get bigger as Brock Lesnar enters at twenty-nine. He clotheslines Shelton, Matt, and Maven before wailing on Cena. Team Angle quickly attack, working together to try to stop Brock from winning a WWE Title shot. Instead, Lesnar tosses them both out at the same time, Benjamin's feet just hitting the floor first. Brock follows up with an F5 over the top rope to Matt onto Team Angle for another elimination and a big pop. A-Train is Paul Heyman's last insurance policy and he crushes Lesnar in a corner before rocking Batista with a Scissors Kick. The final countdown starts and for those paying attention, it's the returning Undertaker.

Riding his motorcycle to ringside, the "Deadman" climbs into the ring to hit anyone stupid enough to get near him. Cena is the first to suffer the returning superstar's wrath and is clotheslined out to the floor. Jamal follows right behind, landing on John. Maven sneak attacks The Undertaker and celebrates after a dropkick, thinking he's eliminated the biker two years in a row. This year he doesn't even knock him over the top rope. The "Deadman" answers with a chokeslam before flinging Maven out as well. Unfortunately, he then turns into an Albert Bomb. Afterwards, Kane Chokeslams Lesnar. Down to six men, Van Dam is the smallest in the ring and kicks the hairy heel. The "Big Red Machine" then whips his partner into Batista for a spinning heel kick. A-Train is up quickly and teases powerbombing Kane. Instead, RVD makes the save before the babyfaces clothesline the hairy heel out to the floor. They continue to work together, the "Big Red Machine" offering to press slam Rob onto Batista. Van Dam leaps into his arms only to see Kane press slam him out of the ring and onto A-Train. That leaves four men, The Undertaker and Brock staring each other down. Before they can lock up, Batista and the "Big Red Machine" attack. Each show has two men in the ring, but it's *Raw* standing tall following an "Animal" spinebuster to the biker. Lesnar won't stay down, belly-to-belly suplexing Batista ahead of an F5 to Kane. That lets the *SmackDown!* superstars finally trade shots. The Undertaker gets the better of the exchange, big booting Brock. Lesnar tries to respond with an F5, but the "Deadman" slips free and answers with a Tombstone before clotheslining Batista out to the floor. Afterwards, The Undertaker helps Kane up only to toss his brother out of the match as well. The "Animal" returns with a chair, but the biker meets him with a big boot. He then smashes Batista with the chair before Brock grabs the "Deadman" from behind and shoves him out to the floor. The biker can only smile and curse as Lesnar celebrates his victory. Eventually, The Undertaker gets back in the ring to congratulate Brock.

The 2003 Royal Rumble is a show that starts slow and gets worse before picking up to end the show. The opening match isn't bad, but Big Show and Brock never go very long. Just over six minutes, the men hammer each other before Lesnar gets the needed victory to participate in the Royal Rumble match. The Dudleys then win the World Tag Titles in another quick match. It's fine, but nothing different than a weekly show contest. Torrie and Dawn continue to get screen time for their awful storyline that has gotten worse by the week. While *SmackDown!* is firing on all cylinders in the ring, this angle is dragging on and a mess, just like this match. The worst part is Dawn Marie threatening that they aren't done. The same could be said for Steiner and Triple H who have one of the worst matches of all-time. It is atrocious with several botches, two powerhouses barely moving, and little storytelling. Scott isn't a great babyface and the fans let the WWE know it. Earlier in his career, this could have been a great match. Now, Steiner has traded mobility for strength, and it comes at a price in long matches. At seventeen minutes, it's far too long. The tag match could have easily taken several of these minutes and spared the fans. Thankfully, Kurt and Benoit steal the show in a twenty-minute classic. It's **MUST SEE!** even without a title change and is a fantastic pure wrestling match. Everyone should watch it. The Rumble then rides that momentum to a good match. It's not the best Rumble ever, and the ending is pretty clear before the match even starts, but everyone entertains from Michaels and Jericho at the beginning to Lesnar and The Undertaker at the end. The only bad thing is due to each brand getting fifteen spots, there are no surprise entrants. Seeing some former teams cross paths and some big moves is enough to make the match a fun watch and cement Brock's spot in the WrestleMania XIX main event. Overall, skip the first hour or so of the show, but the last two matches are required viewing.

Monday Night Raw
January 20, 2003
Providence, RI
Announcers: Jim Ross, Jerry "the King" Lawler

The show opens with a video package of Vince McMahon giving Eric Bischoff thirty days to turn around *Raw*. Eric promises an atomic bombshell announcement tonight ahead of the intro video.

Afterwards, Triple H, sporting a black eye, and Ric Flair head to the squared circle. Hunter is so injured he can't even strike a pose as his music plays. JR isn't sure he'll give Scott Steiner a rematch, but if he does, Ross is picking Scott. Despite that, the announcer has to admit last night's match was ugly. Helmsley creates his own narrative, claiming that he beat Steiner for thirty minutes. No part of that is true. Nor is "the Game" saying that "Big Poppa Pump" was begging him to get the match over with. That was the fans. Scott has heard enough and storms out to demand a rematch tonight. Unfortunately, the champion has a note from his doctor that says he's not able to wrestle tonight. Triple H adds that he's not one to "buck authority", so he's going to have to listen to his doctor. However, if Steiner wants a match, Flair offers to give him a shot at Batista. The "Animal" then marches out while Hunter sneak attacks "Big Poppa Pump". Luckily, Scott fights him off and drives Hunter and Ric out of the ring where they hold Batista back ahead of a match later tonight.

Rob Van Dam def. Jeff Hardy. In this battle of babyfaces, the wrestlers open trading holds and counters. That includes Jeff dropkicking RVD out to the floor only to see Rob counter his barricade dive with a dropkick and leg drop on the guardrail. When he tries to take the fight back into the squared circle, Hardy counters his slingshot attack with a dropkick to the gut. The daredevil scores a two-count moments later with a leg drop onto Van Dam's legs. He also gets a near fall with a whisper in the wind. RVD answers with a rolling fireman's carry slam and second rope springboard moonsault. When he goes upstairs for the Five-Star Frog Splash though, Jeff rolls out of the way and responds with a pair of knees to the chin for a modified jawbreaker. Somehow, Rob manages to kick out moments later when Hardy hits a Swanton Bomb. The daredevil can't believe it. When he picks up Van Dam, RVD backslides him for the out of nowhere victory. Post-match, Jeff interrupts Rob's posing with a clothesline out to the floor. He teases hitting Van Dam with a chair, but thinks better of it and heads backstage.

Backstage, Christian tells Christopher Nowinski that he made the mistake of trusting Edge last night. Eric Bischoff interrupts to question what's wrong with the Harvard heel's face and tease his big announcement. Nowinski thinks he knows what it is, but won't tell Christian.

After a commercial break, Randy Orton stops Scott Steiner. He tells Scott that he was "dead wrong" when he said he'd be the new World Champion. Randy says he's just like the doctors who said Orton would be out a whole year. With his natural conditioning, the rookie says he'll be back in a third of that time. Scott doesn't care and slams him against a wall, threatening to send him back to his doctor.

In the general manager's office, Chief Morley shows Nick Patrick footage of D-Von Dudley hitting Lance Storm with brass knuckles last night. The referee admits he made a mistake. Morley tells him he better publicly apologize for it and leads him to the ring. After a commercial break, Patrick admits his mistake and apologizes. The chief wants him to reverse his decision now, but Nick says he can't do that. That leaves Morley no choice but to call out The Dudley Boyz. When they get in the ring, the chief asks them to forfeit their titles in the "interest of fairness". The Dudleys think he's crazy and blame William Regal for bringing the brass knuckles into the ring in the first place. Morley says he came out to stop that, but Bubba Ray calls that a "load of crap". The chief throws his weight around and tells the champions to give back the titles right now before they regret it. Bubba says he doesn't regret punching Morley last night and he knows D-Von doesn't regret hitting Storm with the knuckles. However, they do regret not taking Vince McMahon's advice and using tables. They try to fix that, hammering down the chief and setting up a table in the ring. Luckily for the chief of staff, William and Lance sneak attack the Dudleys and drive Bubba Ray through the table with a double flapjack. Afterwards, Morley signs a World Tag Title rematch right now.

MUST SEE! Lance Storm/William Regal (with Chief Morley) def. The Dudley Boyz (World Tag Title match). Nick Patrick is reluctant to ring the bell, but Morley tells him that he respected Nick's decision earlier to not reverse his decision. However, Morley makes the matches and he wants Nick to ring the bell. He eventually does so for Regal to receive an even more reluctant three-count and the belts back.

The Hurricane/Trish Stratus def. Steven Richards/Victoria. After The Hurricane gives a mask to a girl in the crowd, JR announces that this match will see the men wrestle the men and the women wrestle the women. Victoria doesn't get the message. After Steven slams the superhero to the mat, the "black widow" tags in to shove and slap him. He teases a chokeslam in response before clotheslining a charging Richards and tagging in Trish. She takes Victoria down with a head scissors ahead of a sloppy spot from the "Diva of the Decade" where she falls on the Women's Champion. When she mounts Victoria in a corner, Steven interferes, throat dropping the vixen on the top rope. Afterwards, the champion slams Stratus before missing a slingshot somersault splash. Richards rushes into the ring to grab Trish, but The Hurricane makes the save. When Charles Robinson forces the superhero back into his corner though, Steven attempts to give Stratus a Hanging DDT. Luckily, The Hurricane makes the save with a shining wizard kick. Afterwards, Trish drops Victoria with Stratusfaction for the win.

Backstage, Eric Bischoff tells Vince McMahon's assistant to let the WWE owner know that he's going to drop his bombshell next. Once he hangs up the phone, Eric throws darts at Shane McMahon's face.

In a prerecorded vignette, Sean O'Haire tells fans that God is everywhere and they don't need to go to church. He concludes with his catchphrase, "I'm not telling you anything you don't already know".

After a commercial break, Eric Bischoff heads to the squared circle. He brags about Vince McMahon watching at home right now before claiming that the *Raw* general manager had a "vision" during last week's tenth anniversary show. He plays footage of "Stone Cold" Steve Austin receiving the Wrestler of the Decade award before reminding everyone that the "rattlesnake" walked out on McMahon. Eric informs everyone that he stopped the presses on *Raw* magazine to give Austin a chance to tell his side of the story on why he walked out on the WWE last year. That's not his bombshell. Instead, Bischoff is inviting "Stone Cold" to make his return at No Way Out and come home to *Raw*. The fans boo that. They don't want to wait. The announcers are stunned, wondering if it's really going to happen.

Booker T/Goldust def. Three-Minute Warning (with Rico). JR compliments the babyfaces before calling the Samoans "Three-Count". Sporting green shirts with the number three on them, Three-Minute Warning aren't exactly memorable just a few months after their debut. Both Goldust and Booker take turns punishing Jamal until the five-time champion lowers his head too soon for a back body drop and gets kicked. The Samoan follows up with a big clothesline. When he attempts a corner charge, Booker T answers with a boot. A side kick follows before the "bizarre one" tags in to target Jamal's arm. Booker returns afterwards only to get decked ahead of Rosey tagging into the ring for the first time. He clubs and headbutts the five-time champion until Booker T stuns him with a spinning heel kick for a near fall. When Jamal tags back in, Booker catches him with a heel kick as well before tagging in Goldust to back drop the big Samoan. He tries to take advantage of Jack Doan arguing with Booker T to give Jamal Shattered Dreams, but Rosey makes the save with a superkick for a near fall. Three-Minute Warning then double-team and choke the "bizarre one" in their corner. Rico even gets in on the act with a cheap shot. When Rosey applies a neck wrench, Goldust fights free only to run into a knee to the gut for a Jamal two-count. He also wrenches the "bizarre one's" neck until the babyface elbows free. This time, he runs into a powerslam and near fall. The Samoan tries to follow up with a corner splash, but misses and Booker gets the hot tag to fight both heels. That includes a heel kick to Rosey before he crotches himself on the top rope trying to kick Rico. Despite that, he counters a double back body drop with a double DDT. A spinebuster to Jamal nearly gets him the win, but Rosey makes the save. Goldust joins his partner for a four-man brawl, but Three-Minute Warning get the better of the babyfaces, Jamal rocking Booker T with a superkick. Unfortunately, he misses a top rope Flying Splash. Afterwards, Rosey accidentally runs into Rico on the apron, stunning both men. Booker capitalizes, escaping a Jamal pop-up Samoan Drop to drive the heel to the mat with a Scissors Kick for the three-count.

Footage of Chris Jericho and Shawn Michaels from the Royal Rumble match plays, including Test eliminating Y2J.

Chris Jericho and Test (with Stacy Keibler) wrestle to a no contest. The announcers are mesmerized by Stacy's barely there outfit this week. Jericho then comes out to say that he had a dream, but it was stolen last night. He promises to take his frustrations out on Test, but early on it's all bodyguard. He punches, clotheslines, and slams Y2J until the heel attacks his eyes. A second rope missile dropkick follows before Jericho chokes and punches Test. Following a leg drop on the middle rope, Y2J back suplexes the bodyguard. In a foul mood, he yells at Keibler and hooks a reverse chin lock. With Stacy cheering him on, Test escapes and unloads with clotheslines and fists. A tilt-a-whirl slam gets him a two-count, as does a powerbomb. When he motions for a Big Boot, Jericho ducks only to be back dropped seconds later out to the floor. There, Y2J slips free of a pumphandle slam and rams the bodyguard into the ring post. He grabs a chair afterwards, but Test dodges his shot against the post. Unfortunately, Keibler is too close to the post and gets knocked out by the edge of the chair, the match stopping immediately. Even Jericho looks concerned as WWE officials run out to check on the diva and call for a stretcher. While Test ugly cries at ringside, referees lead Y2J backstage, the heel protesting that it wasn't his fault.

After a commercial break, Test continues crying while Stacy Keibler is loaded on a stretcher. The announcers say it's a dangerous business before kicking things over to Al Snow at The World to promote *Tough Enough*.

Backstage, Ric Flair hypes up Batista, telling him that if he beats Scott Steiner tonight, he'll be a "big time player".

D'Lo Brown (with Teddy Long) def. Tommy Dreamer ("Singapore Cane" match). The announcers are surprised to see Long accompanying D'Lo to the ring. Teddy says that Brown isn't a follower of Martin Luther King Jr. because King was a peaceful man. D'Lo isn't going to peacefully protest because he's being held down by white superstars like Dreamer who took his Royal Rumble spot. The heels promise to make everyone "down with the Brown" and "cane a white boy". Tommy answers with cane shots to chase D'Lo out of the ring. He's not safe there as Dreamer blasts him from the apron before missing a shot and snapping his cane against the ring post. Brown capitalizes, wailing on Tommy with the stick and choking him. A slam onto the cane scores D'Lo a two-count before the heel wails on the hardcore superstar over and over again with the weapon. Tommy loves the hardcore style and takes the cane away to chop Brown down for a leg drop and two-count. A DDT follows before Dreamer heads to the second rope with the cane. Unfortunately, he leaps into a cane shot to the gut and Sky High for the three-count.

MUST SEE! Scott Steiner def. Batista (with Ric Flair) by disqualification. His ribs taped, Steiner trades shoves with Batista. The rookie briefly adds in a side headlock before the wrestlers run into each other with shoulder blocks that don't move either man. Scott's clubbing blows in a corner do, but the "Animal" responds with his own hammering shots until "Big Poppa Pump" drops him with a twisting belly-to-belly suplex. That brings out Randy Orton to attack Steiner. Scott fights him and Flair off until Triple H sprints down to slug "Freakzilla". JR wonders about his note from the doctor and says this was a setup. It's a good one as the four heels pound Scott down, busting open his forehead. Although not named yet, this is the beginning of one of the most dominant teams in WWE history. The beatdown ends with a Helmsley Pedigree before the heels stand unified over the downed Steiner.

SmackDown!
January 23, 2003
Albany, NY
Announcers: Michael Cole, Tazz

The show opens with Stephanie McMahon promising the return of The Undertaker. She also has a bombshell to drop, leaning over a table as she promises a "big surprise" ahead of the intro video.

Chris Benoit def. Charlie Haas (with Shelton Benjamin). Benoit is out first to a big pop. When Haas gets in the ring, the two men show off their amateur skills with holds and counters. Eventually, "the Crippler" knocks Charlie out to the floor, but makes the mistake of following him out. There, Shelton distracts Benoit for Haas to slam the babyface's hand onto the ring steps. Back in the squared circle, the heel switches between a key lock and wristlock. When the "rabid wolverine" escapes, Charlie stops him with a dropkick and locks on an armbar. Once again, Benoit fights free, landing several chops before Haas takes him right back down and apples a hammerlock. The camera catches the name "Russ", Charlie's deceased brother, on his wrist tape. Eventually, "the Crippler" clubs his way free and DDTs Haas. After catching his breath, Benoit elbows and German suplexes the rookie. He follows up with a top rope diving headbutt. When he tries to apply the Crippler Crossface, his hand is too injured and Charlie escapes. He can't escape a roll-up out of nowhere as the "rabid wolverine" surprises him for the victory.

Rikishi def. Bill DeMott. The two big men go right after each other, Rikishi clubbing Bill in a corner. DeMott responds with shoulders to the gut, Cole noting the cast on the heel's left arm. He says he suffered an injury when eliminated at the Royal Rumble. The big Samoan targets it, slamming his arm on the top rope and crushing him in a corner. Stomps to the injured arm follow before the big babyface locks on an armbar. Despite a leg drop to the arm, Bill won't stay down. He answers Rikishi's attack with a spinebuster to put both men down for a Mike Sparks standing four-count. The big Samoan is up first, punching and squashing DeMott in a corner again. He also dodges the heel's charge moments later to thrust kick him and deliver a Rump Shaker, draping Bill's arm onto his chest for added punishment, to score the win.

A Nathan Jones vignette plays talking about Australian prisons and calling the newcomer "The Colossus of Boggo Road".

After a commercial break, Josh Mathews asks Big Show about The Undertaker's return considering the giant tossed him off a stage the last time they were on *SmackDown!* together. When Josh asks if Show is concerned, the big man wraps his hand around the interviewer's face and silently stares.

Further backstage, Matt Hardy tells Shannon Moore that he's impressed with how his MFer helped him during the Royal Rumble. However, he didn't save him from Brock Lesnar. Tonight, he wants Moore to teach Nunzio a lesson in Mattitude. When Shannon heads to his locker room, Hardy finds Nunzio and asks him to teach Moore a lesson. The Italian heel is happy to do so, relaying a story about doing the same to his nephew.

After a commercial break, The Undertaker heads to the ring to a big pop. He says he's here with bad intentions and to kick butt because there's too much talking. After showing footage of Big Show tossing him off the stage three months ago, the "Deadman" calls out the giant. Show doesn't make him wait long, stepping through the curtain in a suit. He says if he gets in the ring, one of them is going to get hurt. Like his agent taught him, Big Show has a contingency plan. Instead of the giant, the biker will face A-Train.

The Undertaker def. A-Train. While the hairy heel steps into the ring, the announcers rename his finisher the Derailer. He doesn't look like he needs it as he surprises The Undertaker with a flurry of shots for an early two-count. A-Train also traps him in a bearhug before the biker battles free. Afterwards, the two men trade fists and knees. The "Deadman" wins the exchange with a leaping clothesline and big boot for a near fall. The fight soon spills out to the floor for The Undertaker to slam his opponent's face onto the announce table and elbow him on the apron. A leg drop on the apron follows before the biker gets back in the squared circle for a pair of corner attacks. He even breaks out Old School before scoring a near fall with a chokeslam. The "Deadman" can't believe A-Train kicked out. When he sets up for the Last Ride, the hairy heel back drops free only to miss a big splash. Despite that, he quickly recovers and surprises The Undertaker with a Derailer for his own near fall. When he attempts to deliver a powerslam, the biker slips free and locks on his Taking Care of Business dragon sleeper for the tap-out victory.

A Sean O'Haire vignette tells fans not to pay their taxes.

Edge def. Shelton Benjamin (with Charlie Haas). As Edge heads to the ring, Cole talks about his theme song being nominated for a Grammy. Inside the ring, Benjamin has the superior technical skills, but a back elbow and spinning heel kick trump his amateur holds. A neckbreaker scores Edge a two-count before Shelton back suplexes him. The heel follows up with a bow and arrow against the ring post before scoring a near fall with a modified butterfly suplex. He then toys with the babyface, riding his back and taking him down until Edge responds with an Edge-a-matic. He tries to hit a quick Edgecution, but Benjamin fights free to clothesline the babyface for a two-count. Afterwards, he uses his own arms to choke him. It takes him a minute, but Edge fights free and answers with a belly-to-belly suplex. After catching his breath, the babyface nearly gets the win with a face-first slam. A flapjack follows, but when he goes for the Spear, Shelton leapfrogs him. Edge does throat drop Haas on the top rope when he hops onto the apron, but turns into a spinning heel kick and near fall. When he attempts a top rope attack, the babyface dodges and Spears him for the victory.

"Stone Cold" Steve Austin winning the *Raw* Superstar of the Decade plays.

After a commercial break, Kurt Angle berates Team Angle for losing. When he asks if they know what Team Angle stands for, Shelton Benjamin raises his hand. Kurt tells him to lower it before knocking their performances and asking them to "wake up and smell the coffee". The Olympian promises that the team won't lose three matches tonight and orders them to sit backstage and watch as he takes care of business. Angle is embarrassed of them and says it would be even more embarrassing if he lost to Rey Mysterio.

Nunzio def. Shannon Moore (with Matt Hardy). Cole is all over Matt's case as he watches Nunzio slam and hammer the cruiserweight. Focusing on the arm, the Italian heel slams it against the ring post ahead of an armbar. A second rope leg drop afterwards, called the Sicilian slicer by Tazz, gets Nunzio a two-count before he returns to the arm. Eventually, Moore answers with a springboard attack and flying forearm. A leg lariat and leaping neckbreaker nearly gets him the win and has Hardy worried. Shannon continues to look good, flying off the top rope onto the Italian heel before telling Matt that he's going to use his finisher. Unfortunately, Nunzio escapes a Twist of Fate to hit his Tornado Armbar Drop off the second rope, called Arrivederci by Tazz, for the victory. Post-match, Hardy chases Moore off before shaking the Italian heel's hand.

Still shots of Brock Lesnar winning the Royal Rumble are shown.

After a commercial break, Brock Lesnar sits in front of a black screen to talk about being goal oriented. He lists all the goals he's accomplished so far in his amateur and professional careers. After winning the Royal Rumble, Brock says his goal is to F5 Paul Heyman and beat Kurt Angle at WrestleMania XIX.

Backstage, Rey Mysterio heads to the ring. Shannon Moore nearly runs into him before he dives into a production crate and hides from Matt Hardy. Matt nearly finds him, sitting on the crate before searching some of the back rooms.

Kurt Angle (with Paul Heyman) def. Rey Mysterio. Heyman is back in Kurt's corner to get him ready for Brock Lesnar at WrestleMania XIX. He needs to get him ready for Mysterio because the masked man starts fast drop toe holding and dropkicking his opponent. That frustrates the Olympian until Angle catches him with a sit-out powerbomb for a two-count. A back suplex also gets the champion a near fall, Paul badmouthing Rey. Once in control, Kurt cockily punches and clotheslines the masked man ahead of a German suplex onto the head for a two-count. He then slows the pace with a front face lock. It takes him some time, but Mysterio escapes with a modified northern lights suplex. He then picks up the pace with a springboard attack and double front kick. When he attempts a hurricanrana, the Olympian tosses him onto the second rope. Rey bounces right back for a head scissors to chase Angle out to the floor. The masked man tries to follow him, but Brian Hebner stops Mysterio. When the referee checks on the champion, Rey leaps over his back out to the floor on Kurt. A springboard leg drop afterwards nearly gets the masked man the win, but the Olympian just kicks out. When he attempts a corner charge, Mysterio flips over the top turnbuckle and Angle hits the ring post. He still recovers in time to dodge a moonsault and trap Rey in an Anklelock. Although the masked man kicks free, he raises up into an overhead belly-to-belly suplex. The champion lowers his straps, but when he attempts an Angle Slam, Mysterio arm drags free. He tries to follow up with a 619, but Kurt catches him. Despite that, Rey slips free of his grasp for a bulldog and two-count. The Olympian also counters a West Coast Pop, catching and spinning around the masked man before slamming him face-first onto the top turnbuckle. Without letting go, Angle falls back with an electric chair drop and rolls through for the win. Post-match, he traps Mysterio in an Anklelock until Edge runs out to chase off the WWE Champion. He doesn't get far before Chris Benoit attacks him in the aisle and whips him back into the ring for a German suplex. Edge follows up with a Spear, Tazz saying that's not fair. Benoit doesn't care, German suplexing Kurt again before the babyfaces drape him on the middle rope for a 619. Tazz wants to know where Team Angle is, but Cole says the Olympian told them to stay backstage.

Also backstage, Funaki asks Stephanie McMahon what her surprise is. She says he'll have to wait until after a commercial break like everyone else. However, she drops a big hint staring at a Hulk Hogan poster on the wall.

After a commercial break, Hulk Hogan returns to *SmackDown!* to a big pop. When his music stops, the fans get even louder. The Hulkster is overcome with emotion as he waits through the cheers. Eventually, Hogan speaks over the fans to tell everyone that he's just signed a new contract and this time he's wearing red and yellow to "battle the forces of evil". He promises victory in what might be their final fight together. Just when it looks like the segment is over, Vince McMahon walks out with a bewildered look on his face. He says he showed up a few minutes ago just to see Stephanie McMahon's announcement and he's really disappointed. Since it's not 1985, Vince says Hulkamania and Al Wilson have something in common...they are both dead. Hulk tells McMahon that since this might be his last run, he wants to do things the right way. The right way is starting his run with a match against Vince. The WWE owner wants to know who Hogan thinks he is before telling everyone that he doesn't answer to anyone, including "the man upstairs". The Hulkster tries to help him make up his mind, decking McMahon and tearing off his good ripping shirt to leave it on the boss's stunned body. The fans love it as Hogan poses at the top of the ramp for another big pop to end the show.

Monday Night Raw
January 27, 2003
Chicago, IL
Announcers: Jim Ross, Jerry "the King" Lawler

The show opens with a video package featuring Triple H, Ric Flair, Randy Orton, and Batista teaming up to attack Scott Steiner last week. Afterwards, the intro video plays and fireworks explode.

Booker T def. Jeff Hardy. For the second week in a row, Jeff challenges a top babyface, Jerry wondering what's wrong with him. It doesn't look like anything is wrong with him in the ring as he trades amateur holds with Booker to open the match. The five-time champion briefly turns the tide with some clubbing blows and chops, but Hardy answers with a flying forearm and fists. A clothesline moments later gets the daredevil a two-count before he applies a reverse chin lock. It doesn't take Booker T long to escape with a side kick. A spinning heel kick afterwards gets him a two-count. Unfortunately, he runs into a corner boot and second rope flying dropkick for a near fall. Soon after, Jeff dodges a side kick to see Booker crotch himself on the ropes. Hardy tries to follow up with a whisper in the wind, but the five-time champion dodges and answers with a spinebuster for a two-count. When he goes for the Scissors Kick, the daredevil moves and responds with a jawbreaker. A leg drop and whisper in the wind nearly get Jeff the victory, but Booker T just kicks out to surprise the daredevil with a roll-up and three-count. Post-match, Booker entertains the fans with a spinaroonie before Hardy sneak attacks him. He tries to finish off the victor with a top rope dive out to the floor, but Booker T moves and Jeff hits the railing.

Backstage, Jonathan Coachman asks Scott Steiner's thoughts on what happened last week. He heads to the ring to address it while a Nathan Jones teaser vignette plays.

After a commercial break, Scott Steiner gets a big pop from the Chicago crowd. He accuses Triple H of masterminding last week's attack and calls him out. That brings out Hunter in a nice suit. He says he's proved over and over again that he's better in every way than Steiner. Helmsley teases heading to the ring before saying that when someone calls him out, they call out his friends too. That brings out Batista, Randy Orton, and Ric Flair to accompany "the Game" to the squared circle. Scott doesn't back down as the four heels surround the ring. "Big Poppa Pump" isn't worried because he's got a lead pipe taped to his leg and uses it to drive off the heels.

Following another commercial break, Terri interviews D'Lo Brown and Teddy Long about facing a superhero tonight. Teddy wonders why there are no black superheroes other than Black Lightning who can "shoot lightning out of his ass" and no one knows about him. If fans want a real black superhero, Long promises D'Lo will give them one tonight.

D'Lo Brown (with Teddy Long) def. The Hurricane. The superhero is out first to give a mask to a boy in the crowd. When Brown comes out, he wails on his opponent, the announcers trying to come up with a second black superhero. JR can only think of Shaft and Blacula, cracking up "the King". Following a D'Lo slam and two-count, The Hurricane briefly slows the heel with a head scissors. Unfortunately, the superhero lands on his neck and is right back on the defensive. After finally catching his breath, the babyface unloads with clotheslines and a head scissors out to the floor. The Hurricane follows him out with a flying dive over the top rope, JR noting blood in the superhero's mouth. Despite that, he nearly scores the win with an Oklahoma roll. That's as close as he'll get as D'Lo answers with a Sky High, now called the Fade to Black, for the victory.

After a commercial break, Chief Morley watches footage of Hulk Hogan decking Vince McMahon on *SmackDown!*. Eric Bischoff is in a bad mood and tells his chief of staff to turn it off. Morley says it's great for Eric because after what Stephanie McMahon did, Vince might give Bischoff more time. The general manager disagrees. He knows McMahon thrives on anger and Eric has just two weeks to save his job.

Backstage, Chris Jericho paces as Terri tells everyone that he has a number one contender's match next week with Scott Steiner and plays footage of Y2J hitting Stacy Keibler with a chair last week. After Terri reveals that Stacy received a grade two concussion, she says Jericho owes Keibler an apology. Y2J says he doesn't owe anyone anything, but he heads to the ring to "be a man". As he does so, JR wants him to apologize for his checkerboard pants too. Instead, Jericho says things happen that change the way people think out of nowhere. That's exactly what happened when Y2J found out that he has a number one contender's match next week. JR can't believe it. Jericho adds that he's not so shallow that he won't apologize to Stacy, and does so. That brings out Christian to say Keibler getting hurt was her fault. He says the ring isn't a dance floor and she was in the way. Y2J disagrees. He says the fault belongs to Test because if he was a real man, he wouldn't have ducked the chair shot. Jericho revises his apology to say he's sorry Stacy has a coward of a boyfriend. He reiterates that Keibler getting hurt is not his fault and Test got what he deserved for bringing her to ringside and eliminating Y2J from the Royal Rumble. Since the bodyguard isn't here tonight, Shawn Michaels steps through the curtain. He says it's ironic that Jericho is talking about what it takes to be a man wearing those pants. The "Heartbreak Kid" adds that a real man walks into a fight face-first rather than sneaking behind people. To prove it, Shawn says he's going to fight Y2J now and proceeds to do so, walking down the aisle to attack and chase off the heels.

Ahead of her "Chicago Street Fight", Victoria hits a picture of Trish Stratus taped to a trashcan with a cane.

Victoria (with Steven Richards) def. Trish Stratus ("Chicago Street Fight" Women's Title match). Trish is out first, Victoria immediately following behind to hit her with the stick and choke the challenger in the aisle. Stratus manages to reverse the choke, but the "black widow" is up quickly to toss the vixen into the ring steps. Trish answers with a Chick Kick from the crowd and clothesline off the barricade for a near fall. She can't keep the champion down and Victoria takes the fight back to the ring for a string of shoulders in a corner. Like the champion, Stratus is back up quickly, this time hitting the heel with a trashcan. After boxing her ears with lids, the challenger wedges a trashcan into a corner. Unfortunately, it's Victoria using it, catapulting Trish into it. Trashcan lid shots follow from both women before Stratus scores a near fall with her handstand head scissors from the corner. A kick afterwards sends the "black widow" out to the floor for a vixen diving attack. Back in the squared circle, a neckbreaker gets Trish a two-count. Richards tries to spray her with a fire extinguisher, but he can't figure out how to work it until Stratus moves and he sprays his own woman. That lets the challenger score a two-count before Steven breaks the cover. Trish responds with cane shots until Victoria levels her with a kick for a near fall. The vixen has one more comeback in her, but when she sets up for Stratusfaction, Richards grabs her legs. That lets the champion shove her off the apron and into the barricade for the three-count. Post-match, Victoria stomps Stratus until Steven stops her. When the heels head backstage, Jazz shoves her way past them to boot Trish's face. She follows up with a chicken wing slam, DDT, and fisherman's buster before applying an STF until Charles Robinson gets the break.

Lance Storm/William Regal def. The Dudley Boyz (World Tag Title "Tables" match). JR is really confused for this match, calling it a "Ladder" match. He corrects himself when the heels come out for the challengers to beat them with their own flags. Bubba Ray gets a nice pop when he breaks a Canadian flagpole over his knee before spearing Storm. D-Von and Regal then enter the ring for the challengers to crush the Englishman in a corner. A D-Von second rope clothesline and double-team neckbreaker follows. When Lance tries to help his partner, he runs into a 3D. The Dudleys follow up with a wassup drop to William before Bubba tells his brother to get a table. Unfortunately, there are no tables under the ring. The announcers can't believe it. JR smells a rat, and sure enough, Chief Morley steps onto the stage with a table. When the Dudleys go to confront him, Morley threatens to fire them. He doesn't need to worry as Three-Minute Warning attack the babyfaces, Rico directing traffic. The Samoans proceed to whip the challengers into the ring steps and crush them in a corner. When Bubba Ray tries to fight back, Jamal answers with a pop-up Samoan Drop. That brings out Spike Dudley to give Jamal a Dudley Dog. When he tries to do the same to Rosey, the big man dumps him crotch-first onto the top rope. Rico follows up with a Spinning Heel Kick. All five heels then set up a table for Rosey to powerbomb D-Von through it for the champions to retain their titles.

After a commercial break, Triple H and friends complain to Eric Bischoff about the upcoming number one contender's match. Hunter is worried about what will happen if Scott Steiner wins. However, looking at Batista he changes his mind and says they don't have a problem.

Further backstage, John Hennigan and Matt Cappotelli, *Tough Enough III* winners, are nervous about their upcoming match. Al Snow tells them they only have one shot to make a first impression. As he leads them to the ring, Christopher Nowinski glares in the background.

Even further backstage, Kane talks to Rob Van Dam about eliminating the popular superstar in the Royal Rumble. RVD says it's cool, but he wishes the "Big Red Machine" would have waited longer before turning on him. Regardless, the babyfaces are on the same team tonight. After Van Dam lists all their moves, he gets Kane to imitate his RVD pose and call himself the "Big Red Machine".

The *Tough Enough III* winners being announced Thursday night replays.

John Hennigan and Matt Cappotelli wrestle to a no contest. The rookies come out at the same time, accompanied by Al Snow for this "exhibition match". They wrestle in warmup attire and show off their amateur moves, Cappotelli hip tossing the future John Morrison for the first two-count. Hennigan responds with a dropkick for another two-count before Christopher Nowinski runs out and slams Snow's head into the ring post. The Harvard heel stops the match saying the last thing he needs is the two rookies rubbing it in his face that he didn't win *Tough Enough*. Tommy Dreamer follows, chasing off Nowinski with a cane before congratulating the winners. He tells them they are lucky to be standing in the ring on just their fourth day in the business. On behalf of all the men who paved the way, Tommy welcomes them to the WWE and blasts the rookies with his cane to a nice pop.

Sean O'Haire tells fans to enjoy their vices in another prerecorded vignette.

Afterwards, Eric Bischoff heads to the ring with a manilla envelope. He says "Stone Cold" Steve Austin isn't here tonight, but it's not his fault. He then plays footage from *WWE Confidential* of Vince McMahon and Jim Ross talking about Austin walking away from the company. That's one side of the story, but the other side is "Stone Cold's" and Eric says fans can read them in the new issue of *Raw* magazine. Hyping the magazine in his hand, Bischoff promises Austin's thoughts on the WWE and his divorce from Debra. The GM then teases "Stone Cold" possibly appearing at No Way Out. To remind the "rattlesnake" about how great his time in the WWE was, Bischoff plays a video of Austin's exploits.

Batista/Triple H (with Randy Orton/Ric Flair) def. Kane/Rob Van Dam. Batista opens the match hammering Kane in a corner. The "Big Red Machine" responds in kind until he runs into a back elbow and clothesline. The "Animal" follows up with a choke on the ropes and more stiff punches before Kane surprises him with a leaping clothesline. He adds a powerslam before tagging in RVD and slamming his partner onto Batista for a two-count. Kicks and a leg drop follow for another near fall before the "Animal" runs through Rob for his own two-count. Triple H then tags in to stomp and choke Van Dam. The popular superstar answer with a string of kicks for another near fall. Unfortunately, a high knee puts him down for a Hunter two-count. Batista tags back in afterwards to continue wailing on RVD, a clothesline getting him a near fall before the monster makes the save. The "Animal" doesn't overstay his welcome as Helmsley returns to work on Rob's leg. He doesn't get in much offense before Van Dam kicks him and tags in Kane to fight both heels. After he knocks "the Game" out to the floor, the "Big Red Machine" stuns Batista with a top rope flying clothesline. He tries to follow up with a rocket launcher, tagging in Van Dam, but "the Animal" moves. Flair, Orton, and Batista then assault the monster outside the ring, ripping off his mask and sending him running backstage while RVD gives Triple H rolling thunder inside the squared circle. He tries to follow up with a Five-Star Frog Splash, but the "Animal" returns to the squared circle to catch and slam him. A Sit-Out Powerbomb follows for the three-count. When the heels continue their assault, Scott Steiner runs out with his lead pipe to chase them away. Luckily, Chris Jericho follows close behind, knocking the pipe out of his hand. Although Y2J pays with a twisting belly-to-belly suplex, he distracts Steiner long enough for the other heels to return to the ring and bust open "Big Poppa Pump". Batista punctuates the attack, giving Scott such a powerful Sit-Out Powerbomb that he knocks down Steiner's pants. Ric follows up with a Figure Four Leglock before Triple H helps Scott pull up his pants only to finish him off with a Pedigree. When the four heels leave, Y2J pokes "Big Poppa Pump" with his boot, taunts him, and applies the Walls of Jericho to end the show.

SmackDown!
January 30, 2003
Green Bay, WI
Announcers: Michael Cole, Tazz, Kurt Angle (briefly)

Ahead of the intro video and fireworks, a video package for Hulk Hogan's return last week plays.

A-Train def. Rey Mysterio. Rey is looking for revenge after the hairy heel put him out of action for a month and attacks A-Train before the bell. Unfortunately, his hit and run tactics have less impact than one hairy heel slam and an onslaught of fists. Going back to what works, Mysterio runs away, luring A-Train out of the ring and back into it for a leg drop. A dropkick follows before the hairy heel surprises him with a Derailer for a near fall. As he continues his assault, locking on a full nelson at one point, Cole wishes Mike Sparks a happy birthday. Tazz doesn't care about the referee. He enjoys watching the masked man escape the full nelson with a jawbreaker. He then jumps onto A-Train's shoulders for fists and a tornado DDT, scoring a near fall. A dropkick to the back sets the hairy heel into position for a 619, but when Mysterio races into the ropes, A-Train stuns him with a bicycle kick. His over the shoulder Backbreaker follows, now called the Train Wreck, for the victory.

Backstage, Josh Mathews asks Paul Heyman if we'll see Big Show against The Undertaker tonight. Heyman wants no part of that. He says the biker is going to be very disappointed when he gets here tonight because the giant has the night off.

Eddie Guerrero (with Chavo Guerrero Jr.) def. John Cena (with Redd Dogg). Pre-match, Cena makes fun of Eddie's heritage and the Green Bay Packers. That fires up "Latino Heat" and he pummels the red basketball shorts wearing heel for an early two-count. All over the rapping heel, Guerrero back suplexes and stomps John. Cena answers with a press and drop before knocking Eddie out to the floor. While the rapping heel distracts the referee, Dogg slams "Latino Heat's" face into the ring steps. Back in the squared circle, John gets a two-count with a suplex. He shows off his strength with a delayed vertical suplex before clubbing Guerrero again. Another suplex follows for a near fall. He also gets a two-count with a sidewalk slam before hooking a reverse chin lock. It doesn't take "Latino Heat" long to fight free and rock the rapping heel with a dropkick. Redd Dogg pays off again, tripping Eddie for a Cena back suplex. Unfortunately, when John heads upstairs, Chavo shoves him down to the canvas for "Latino Heat" to steal the win with a Frog Splash.

After a commercial break, Paul Heyman tells Big Show on the phone that The Undertaker is here. The agent notices Brian Kendrick, a Shawn Michaels trained superstar in the background. Heyman gives the orange sweater with a flower on it wearing newcomer a sales pitch that he can make his career. Kendrick is willing to do anything to succeed.

Further backstage, Vince McMahon interrupts Stephanie McMahon on the phone. He wants to know why she brought back Hulk Hogan last week. Stephanie says she had no idea Hogan would hit him, but she's confused why he's upset that the Hulkster is back while Eric Bischoff is trying to bring back his nemesis, "Stone Cold" Steve Austin. She adds that she's just like her father doing everything to make *SmackDown!* the biggest show in the world. Vince says he has his own big surprise tonight.

Billy Kidman def. Shannon Moore (with Matt Hardy). Despite this being a Moore match, we get Matt Facts and Hardy's entrance music. The Matt Facts tonight are that Hardy believes Shannon has "an iota of Mattitude" and Matt lasted the longest in the Royal Rumble of all *SmackDown!* superstars. Once the match starts, Hardy distracts Billy for Moore to get in some cheap shots. One head scissors slows him and sends the MFer out to the floor. There, he surprises Kidman with rams into the barricade and apron. Back in the squared circle, Shannon shows off an aggressive streak, whipping Billy around for a two-count. He then tries to squeeze the life out of the Cruiserweight Champion with a reverse chin lock. When Kidman starts to fight back, Moore wails on him again and scores a two-count with a back suplex. He then locks on a crisscross arm choke, adding in knees to the lower back. Billy finally escapes and turns the tide with a dropkick. After catching his breath, he dropkicks and back drops the heel ahead of a reverse neckbreaker and two-count. Shannon answers with a springboard side kick for another near fall. Unfortunately, Billy Kidman slips free of his slam for a sit-out spinebuster and two-count. He can't finish off Moore who shoves him off the second rope for a flipping neckbreaker and another two-count. When he attempts to apply a leg lock, the champion surprises him with an enziguri. Shannon won't stay down, stopping him on the second rope, but he can't hit his superplex. Instead, Kidman shoves him down to the mat, kicks Hardy away, and scores the win with a Shooting Star Press. Post-match, Matt blindsides Billy and drops him with a Twist of Fate. After sending Moore backstage, Hardy delivers a second Twist of Fate. Tazz loves it.

After a commercial break, Vince McMahon heads to the squared circle where the fans get under his skin chanting for Hulk Hogan. Vince threatens to walk away right now before admitting that he made a mistake last week when he said Hulkamania is dead. While it might still be alive, it's "on life support" and he blames the fans. McMahon tells the crowd that they don't know the Hulkster like him and he's a "manipulative man-eating predator" of a businessman. As a person, he says he's even worse and "depraved". Despite that, the fans cheer Hogan again. That sets off Vince. He doesn't get Hulkamania, but he says he created it. Instead of accepting Hulk's challenge, McMahon signs the Hulkster to a match at No Way Out against The Rock. The fans don't like that. When Vince heads backstage, he introduces the "People's Champ" via satellite. Although they boo him, the fans do cheer when he says he's finally come back to Green Bay. Embracing the hate, the "Great One" says he's glad he's not physically in Green Bay. Regarding McMahon's match, the "Brahma Bull" says he doesn't answer to Vince. He answers to the people. The fans continue chanting alongside him as The Rock says he'll meet Hogan one more time at No Way Out in an "icon versus icon" match. He's looking forward to laying the smackdown on him, insulting the Hulkster before asking if the fans smell what he's cooking.

Bill DeMott def. Rikishi. The rubber match in the series, each man is looking for the definitive win here. Rikishi opens the match attacking DeMott's injured arm before Bill responds with stiff punches and a corner splash. The bully follows up with a heel abdominal stretch. When the big Samoan tries to answer with a belly-to-belly suplex, DeMott headbutts and slams him. He then heads upstairs, but is too slow and pays courtesy of an electric chair drop. After catching his breath, Rikishi punches and Samoan drops Bill. A thrust kick follows before the big babyface crushes the bully down in a corner. Instead of a Stinkface, he pulls DeMott up for a DDT, but the heel holds the ropes. As soon as the big babyface hits the mat, Bill covers him, still holding onto the ropes for the victory.

Post-match, The Undertaker nearly runs over DeMott as he rides his motorcycle to the squared circle. Once again, he calls out Big Show. After waiting through a commercial break, the biker says he's not here to entertain with his wit. He's got a new philosophy and that's to "shut up and fight". After he tells Show to be a man for once, the giant's music plays. Instead of Big Show, Paul Heyman steps onto the stage to deliver a "personal message". Brian Kendrick, dressed up like a bellhop, then rides a girls bike around the ring. The "Deadman" wants to know what the message is, but Kendrick is scared to death. Reluctantly, he delivers a singing telegram to tell The Undertaker that Show is "really, really sorry" and he'll never do it again. The biker wants to know if this is supposed to be funny, but Paul says it's a sincere apology. The "Deadman" warns Heyman that when he gets his hands on the giant, he'll truly be sorry. Once the agent heads backstage, Brian waits for a tip. The Undertaker says he has a lot of guts, but no brains. Luckily, the biker likes guts and gives him a hundred dollars before asking for a repeat performance. Kendrick barely gets a word in before the "Deadman" kicks him and delivers a Last Ride. Not done, The Undertaker takes back his tip and heads backstage to a big pop.

After a commercial break, Kurt Angle gives Team Angle a pep talk. He calls their upcoming number one contender's match the biggest of their careers. However, Chris Benoit and Edge are "as good as it gets". While Kurt has beaten them many times, it's "not as easy as it looks". He then talks about Vince Lombardi, the coach of the Packers "back when they were good". Quoting Lombardi, Angle says, "winning is the only thing" and Team Angle need to win for themselves. Charlie Haas disagrees. He says they are going to win for Kurt. That touches the WWE Champion and he hugs them.

The Brock Lesnar video package from last week replays.

Sean O'Haire's *Raw* vignette talking about vices replays.

Team Angle (with Kurt Angle) def. Chris Benoit/Edge (#1 Contender's match). While the heels come out together, the babyfaces enjoy separate introductions. Kurt joins the announce table afterwards to watch as Benoit slugs Haas in a neutral corner. Shelton helps his partner with a cheap shot to swing the momentum. Tagging in, Benjamin connects with a gutbuster, but only gets a one-count. A back elbow gets him a two-count while Los Guerreros watch backstage. Soon after, "the Crippler" answers with snake eyes on the top turnbuckle before tagging in Edge to flapjack Benjamin and give Charlie an Edge-a-matic. When Angle gets on the apron, the babyface Spears him. He then heads out to the floor while Benoit German suplexes Shelton. The "rabid wolverine" follows the fight out to the floor afterwards with a dive through the ropes onto Haas before Edge scores a two-count on Benjamin with a top rope missile dropkick ahead of a commercial break.

Afterwards, Edge traps Shelton in an armbar, but the rookie manages to kick free and tag in Charlie. The babyface also attacks his arm, softening him up for a Crippler Crossface. Benoit joins the assault, scoring a two-count with a northern lights suplex onto the arm. Back in, Edge continues stretching the arm. When "the Crippler" returns, he tries to lock on the Crossface, but Haas reaches the ropes. Edge is in afterwards to punch and kick the rookie until he runs into an overhead belly-to-belly suplex. That swings the momentum and Team Angle trap him in their corner for cheap shots and quick tags. Focusing on the leg, Benjamin stretches the babyface's knee, Kurt cheering him on. Charlie does the same, mixing in some leg drops before applying a side Indian deathlock. Shelton has his own variation of the hold, the Olympian yelling for him to break Edge's knee. Instead, the babyface reaches the ropes for the break. Back in, Haas continues the assault. When Mike Chioda gets distracted, Angle even attacks the babyface's knee, slamming it on the apron. Benjamin then applies a figure four leg lock, but the "rabid wolverine" has had enough and makes the save with a dropkick. Unfortunately, Charlie illegally switches places with his partner while the referee gets Benoit back to his corner. This time, Edge turns the hold over to force the break. He follows up with an enziguri before knocking Shelton back into a corner and tagging in "the Crippler". He goes to work fighting both heels and suplexing Haas onto his own partner for a two-count. When he runs the ropes, Kurt trips his rival for Team Angle to nearly finish him off with their combination leapfrog splash. Shelton tries to follow up with a superkick, but Benoit ducks and Benjamin knocks Charlie out to the floor. The "rabid wolverine" capitalizes with a trio of German suplexes and a diving headbutt to Shelton for a near fall. The Olympian tries to interfere, but Edge dropkicks him off the apron. Afterwards, Benoit traps Benjamin in a Crippler Crossface, but Haas makes the save. Edge soon Spears him, but while Chioda is distracted, Angle blasts "the Crippler" with the WWE Title for Shelton to steal the win and a match with Los Guerreros next week. Backstage, Eddie and Chavo don't look happy as the heels celebrate their tainted victory.

Monday Night Raw
February 3, 2003
Washington, D.C.
Announcers: Jim Ross, Jerry "the King" Lawler

The show opens with Eric Bischoff in Texas on the phone with Chief Morley at the arena. They can't hear each other so Bischoff complains about Texas before telling Morley that he's in charge this week. Even though the chief can't hear him, he tells Eric that the show is in good hands ahead of the intro video and fireworks. Hilariously, in the original broadcast of the opening segment, Bischoff is dubbed in Spanish, something that has been corrected on the network.

Afterwards, Stacy Keibler and Test head to the ring. She says she's getting better, but needs to be more careful in the future. However, she really wishes Chris Jericho would have apologized. Test demands that Jericho come out right now and apologize or get his butt kicked backstage. That brings Y2J out onto the entrance ramp to say he feels terrible. However, he has more important things to worry about tonight, namely his number one contender's match. Jericho then says he's gotten over hitting Stacy with a chair and suggests the bodyguard does the same. Test suggests that Y2J apologize again and gives him just a few seconds to do so. Unfortunately, Christian ambushes the bodyguard and knocks him into Keibler. When Christian looks at Stacy with ill intent, Test comes back to life to punch and whip the heel into the ring post. Afterwards, he helps Keibler up, some fans booing.

Backstage, Kane walks into Chief Morley's office where Rob Van Dam is already waiting. He wants a rematch with Batista and Triple H, but first wants to know why the "Big Red Machine" left him alone last week. Kane says he left because he lost his mask. RVD wonders if he gets his strength from his mask or if he's Spider-man. The monster thinks Rob makes a joke of everything. Before they come to blows, Morley interrupts only to tell them that they have a match later tonight…against each other.

After a commercial break, Test takes Stacy Keibler back to her hotel.

Three-Minute Warning def. The Dudley Boyz. Once the wrestlers are introduced, Chief Morley steps through the curtain to introduce the special guest referee, Rico. JR can't believe it and the Samoans capitalize with an early assault. Luckily, Bubba Ray dodges a Rosey split legged moonsault before putting Jamal on his shoulders for a Dudley Device. The stylist takes his sweet time even making the count. When he does count, it's super slow and only gets to two. The Dudleys don't let it bother them, setting up Rosey for a 3D. Before they can hit it, Jamal rolls up Bubba for a lightning fast three-count despite Dudley holding the ropes. Post-match, the losers deck Rico before Spike Dudley runs out to give Jamal a Dudley Dog. A clothesline follows to send Rosey out to the floor where Bubba Ray press slams Spike over the top rope onto the Samoans. Still not done, the Dudleys powerbomb Rico through a table from the second rope.

Still in Texas, Eric Bischoff is lost as he tells Chief Morley to handle *Raw* while he finds "Stone Cold" Steve Austin. Unfortunately, his limo driver is lost. Back in the arena, the announcers shill Austin speaking out in the *Raw* magazine.

Tommy Dreamer heads to the ring for his match, but he's interrupted by Batista, Randy Orton, Ric Flair, and Triple H. The WWE Champion is on a crutch, JR revealing that he's medically unable to compete right now due to a hematoma. Helmsley watches as his cohorts destroy Dreamer. Afterwards, "the Game" talks about the four men being an example of evolution. He praises each of his men, starting with Flair. Triple H says everything "The Nature Boy" did and embodies, Hunter has taken and put it alongside his brain to become the best in the business. Helmsley calls himself a diamond before calling "Dave Batista" the future and "unbridled destruction". Orton, he calls coal that will be squeezed into the next diamond. "The Game" warns that if you don't keep up, "Evolution will pass you by".

After a commercial break, Terri shows Scott Steiner footage of what Evolution has done to him lately. She wonders how he'll handle Chris Jericho tonight after all those attacks. Scott flexes his muscles and says with them he'll be just fine.

After seeing Evolution partying in a luxury box, we see Eric Bischoff in Texas. A countdown timer is shown in the corner telling fans that Eric has less than a week to save his job. Bischoff has finally found the house he's looking for, but "Stone Cold" Steve Austin isn't there. Buford says he's at the Longhorn Saloon. Jerry wants to know who Buford is.

Victoria (with Steven Richards) def. Molly Holly. Following footage of Jazz's return last week, Victoria heads to the ring for this non-title match. Molly doesn't wear typical wrestling attire, JR saying she looks like she's going to a Fleetwood Mac concert. Despite that, she takes the champion down by the arm and flips around impressively. After showing off with some nice moves, she runs into a back elbow and side slam for a near fall. The "black widow" then hammers her for another near fall before a delayed vertical suplex also gets her a two-count. When she sets up for the Widow's Peak, Holly briefly fights free only to be clubbed going for a handspring corner elbow. Victoria hits the Widow's Peak afterwards for the win. Post-match, Jazz hurries out to slam the loser with a double chicken wing. A DDT follows before the champion tries to get involved. Jazz shoves her down to the mat. That confuses the "black widow" and she leaves before Jazz gives Molly a second DDT.

Backstage Booker T tells Goldust that he's hyped up for tonight's World Tag Title match. The "bizarre one" tells his partner that the five-time champion has been so hot lately that he shouldn't be wasting his time chasing tag gold. Goldust makes him a deal. He loves Booker, but he doesn't want to hold him back. If they don't win the World Tag Titles tonight, the "bizarre one" says they go their separate ways.

Lance Storm/William Regal def. Booker T/Goldust (World Tag Title match). Following a shot of Evolution in their luxury box, the babyfaces head out to Booker's music. When the heels come out, Nick Patrick checks them for weapons before Storm and Goldust trade arm wringers. The "bizarre one" gets the upper hand and slows the Canadian with a punch to the jaw before the five-time champion tags in for a series of strikes. Lance answers with a forward leg sweep for a two-count. Booker T is right back up for his own cover after a clothesline before Regal tags into the ring. The babyface meets him with a side kick for another near fall before Goldust returns to hammer the champion's lower back for his own two-count. When Storm returns, the "bizarre one" arm drags him into an armbar. The heels finally swing the momentum when William kicks Goldust running the ropes. The champions then trap him in their corner to wear down the "bizarre one". That includes chin locks and strikes until Goldust dodges a dropkick for a roll-up and two-count. He then slams Lance to the mat before crawling to his corner for the tag. Unfortunately, Regal races around and pulls Booker off the apron to block the exchange. The Canadian follows up with a kick to the challenger. That wakes up the "bizarre one" and he fights both heels, nearly scoring the win with a powerslam to Storm, but William breaks his count. Afterwards, Lance shoves the challengers' heads together, stunning them for Storm to steal the win with a side kick to Goldust. Post-match, Booker T stops the music and tells the "bizarre one" to get back in the ring.

Booker says his partner has nothing to be embarrassed about and they had a great run. The five-time champion enjoyed each moment they had together and wants to end it with their heads lifted high, hugging Goldust before they go their separate ways.

After a commercial break, Eric Bischoff enters a Texas bar and gets mocked for ordering a martini. He finally accepts a cold beer before asking if anyone has seen "Stone Cold" Steve Austin. Unfortunately, the "rattlesnake" has already left for a different bar. The workers joke that Bischoff can get a martini there.

Rob Van Dam def. Kane by disqualification. When RVD does his customary taunt, Kane clotheslines him for a quick two-count. Rob answers with shots and a split legged moonsault for his own early near fall. Back up, the two men give each other respectful looks before the "Big Red Machine" slams Van Dam for another two-count. RVD answers with kicks, including one off the top rope to send the monster retreating to the floor. Rob meets him with a baseball slide kick and flying dive over the top rope. Kane is up first to clothesline Van Dam on the floor ahead of a sidewalk slam back in the squared circle for a near fall. RVD won't stay down, kicking free of a Chokeslam to connect with rolling thunder for a two-count. The "Big Red Machine" sits up and answers with a big boot and top rope flying clothesline. Unfortunately, Rob lands on his neck and doesn't look like he can continue. When the monster checks on him, Van Dam kicks his sometimes partner, playing possum. He tries to follow up with a Five-Star Frog Splash, but Jeff Hardy runs out to shove him down to the floor for the disqualification. He also slaps Kane and pays with a Chokeslam. RVD follows up with a Five-Star Frog Splash before shaking hands with the "Big Red Machine".

Backstage, Booker T looks for Goldust. Earl Hebner says he went back to his hotel room.

After a commercial break, Jeff Hardy is still laying on the canvas. Before he gets up, Shawn Michaels comes out to a big pop. He says he was planning on addressing Chris Jericho tonight, but Y2J has his hands full with Scott Steiner. Instead, Shawn is going to give Jeff some advice because he's been where Hardy is. When he looks at Jeff, he sees "wasted potential". After telling the story of kicking Marty Jannetty through a plate glass window, Michaels wants to know who Hardy is. Jeff says there's not enough time to explain who he is, but he's going to kick some butt starting with the "Heartbreak Kid". Shawn cuts off his attack with Sweet Chin Music to knock Hardy down again.

Sean O'Haire telling fans not to pay their taxes replays.

D'Lo Brown (with Theodore Long) def. Maven. When JR calls Long "Teddy", Jerry corrects him. He says it's Theodore now. Inside the ring, D'Lo and Maven trade headlocks and amateur holds. Brown changes tactics and clubs the young star ahead of a backbreaker for a two-count. Afterwards, he focuses on the lower back to Long's delight. Maven manages to slow him with a corner boot before unloading with a string of strikes and a spinning heel kick for a two-count. A roll-up and backslide also get him near falls, as does a flying leg drop off the second rope. When he heads to the top rope, D'Lo sidesteps his missile dropkick to hit the Fade to Black for the victory. Post-match, Theodore says his man is undefeated with him and tries to get the fans to chant "down with the Brown". No one does.

Back in the luxury box, Triple H tells Batista and Randy Orton that the number one contender's match is next and he wants to know if they know what to do. They do.

Back in Texas, Eric Bischoff enters another bar looking for "Stone Cold" Steve Austin. Unfortunately, the bartender hasn't seen him. When a young man laughs that Austin isn't here and Vince McMahon is going to fire Bischoff, the general manager smashes a mug of beer over his head. Eric is livid, yelling "screw Austin…and Texas". The announcers think that's poor negotiating.

Backstage, Batista and Randy Orton ask Goldust if he's seen Scott Steiner. When he doesn't answer to "hey loser", Orton slaps him. The heels then destroy the "bizarre one", tossing him into an electrical box. Crew are standing by to spray him with a fire extinguisher and call for EMTs to help the electrocuted superstar. JR speaks in his hushed serious tone to call it an "unfortunate accident".

Scott Steiner def. Chris Jericho (#1 Contender's match). Steiner is out second to point at Evolution in the luxury box before he shoves around Jericho. Y2J surprises him with a roll-up for a two-count and starts flexing. That just makes Scott mad and he clubs the heel. JR says "Big Poppa Pump" doesn't use technique "these days", but just beats people up. He proceeds to do that, hammering and stomping Jericho before doing some pushups after an elbow drop. When he attempts a belly-to-belly suplex, Y2J holds onto Hebner. That stops the move and allows Jericho to turn the tide with kidney shots and a knee out to the floor. There, Y2J whips Steiner into the ring steps before applying a rack back in the squared circle. It doesn't take Scott long to power out and catch Jericho attempting a leapfrog for a powerslam. A big back body drop and overhead belly-to-belly suplex follow. When he attempts a powerbomb, Y2J flips free and attempts to turn over "Big Poppa Pump" into the Walls of Jericho. Steiner is too strong and whips Jericho over before finally hitting his powerbomb. That gets him a near fall. When he attempts a corner charge, Y2J answers with a boot and cover, his feet on the ropes still only getting him a two-count. It does soften up Scott enough for the heel to lock on the Walls of Jericho, but "Big Poppa Pump" reaches the ropes. Soon after, Jericho stuns him with a throat drop on the top rope, but when he heads upstairs, Steiner crotches him. He follows up with a Samoan drop off the second rope for the three-count, concerning Triple H. Ric Flair assures Scott that he'll never beat "the Game".

Backstage, Chief Morley paces as he tries to tell Eric Bischoff that things have not gone to plan. It gets worse when Vince McMahon enters the office to say that things aren't going great for the heels. He reminds Morley that they are running out of time and if they don't impress him next week, Vince is going to fire both Bischoff and his chief of staff. The show ends with a shot of the countdown clock ticking down.

SmackDown!

February 6, 2003
Philadelphia, PA
Announcers: Michael Cole, Tazz

Following the intro video and fireworks, a crane removes a big box with a ribbon from the ring.

Rey Mysterio def. Jamie Noble (with Nidia). Fast-paced, both men race around and counter each other to start the match until Noble runs through Mysterio. He follows up with a gutbuster for a two-count. Jamie then slows the pace with an abdominal stretch. It doesn't take Rey long to fight free and bulldog the heel. A springboard cross body block and tornado DDT follow for a near fall. When he ends up on the apron and shoulder blocks Noble though, Jamie falls back into Jimmy Korderas. That lets Nidia trip the masked man and slam him on the apron. Despite that, Mysterio quickly recovers and sets the heel up for a 619. He has to avoid Nidia again letting Noble catch and powerbomb Rey for a two-count. Although Mysterio twists his knee moments later, he knocks Jamie back into position for a 619. This time, he knocks Nidia into position too to deliver a "1238" according to Tazz. Following the double 619, the masked man scores the win with a West Coast Pop.

Afterwards, The Rock is on the big screen to say he's finally come back to Philadelphia. Once again, he makes fun of the town, saying he's glad he's not really there and he doesn't like Philly cheesesteaks because he's "lactose intolerant". He'd rather have some "Tampa Bay tofu", getting boos. He tries to get the fans to chant his name, but they say "Hulk Hogan". The "Great One" is initially confused why the Philadelphia crowd boos him, but he realizes that they "boo greatness". One person they've never booed is Hogan. While the "People's Champ" loves the Hulkster too, he makes fun of him appearing in a ballet commercial before promising to beat him once again at No Way Out.

Rikishi def. Nunzio. The Italian heel attacks Rikishi before he can fully step through the ropes. That early onslaught lets him get a two-count before the big Samoan finally gets back up to his feet to slam Nunzio twice. A thrust kick follows ahead of a corner splash and the Rump Shaker for the win. Post-match, Rikishi starts to dance, but the Italian heel interrupts. He says the big Samoan just made a big mistake trying to embarrass him and the people he's with won't like that. Rikishi doesn't care, dancing after Nunzio runs backstage.

After a commercial break, Paul Heyman is in the ring with the ribbon-adorned crate. It's a present from Big Show, who isn't here this week, to The Undertaker. After Paul invites him out, the "Deadman" rides his motorcycle around the squared circle, chasing off Heyman. The biker then cautiously checks out the crate, slowly opening it to reveal Brother Love. He tells the man he brought into the WWF that he loves The Undertaker and it's good to see him again. From "one icon to another", Love wants to know if the biker remembers his lessons in love and forgiveness. The "Deadman" tells him to "remember this" before chokeslamming and Tombstoning him.

Backstage, Hulk Hogan shakes hands with some undercard wrestlers before staring down Brock Lesnar. The "next big thing" welcomes him back with a smile before both men walk away.

Billy Kidman def. Matt Hardy (with Shannon Moore). Hardy's Matt Facts reveal that he has a TV/DVD player in his car and "usually exceeds the speed limit". When Kidman marches out looking for a fight,

Matt hides behind his MFer and shoves him into the Cruiserweight Champion. That distracts Billy for a side effect and two-count. A leg drop moments later gets Hardy a two-count before he chokes the champion. It doesn't take Kidman long to recover and answer with a head scissors and dropkick. Clotheslines and a sit-out spinebuster get Billy a near fall before he runs into a face drop on the rope and ricochet elbow drop slam. He tries to finish off Kidman with a Twist of Fate, but the babyface spins free for a running bulldog. When he heads up the ropes though, Matt meets him and tries to counter with a superplex. The two men continue to trade counters as Billy tosses Hardy to the canvas only to leap into Matt's arms and another Twist of Fate attempt. One final counter follows as Kidman flips over him for a roll-up and three-count. Post-match, Hardy is shocked. He heads to the announce table to promise revenge, telling the announcers that he's going to lose ten pounds and take the Cruiserweight Title from Billy.

Backstage, Kurt Angle tells Team Angle that he can't be in their corner tonight because he's got his own match, but he wants them to win the biggest match of their careers and bring home the gold.

MUST SEE! Team Angle (with Paul Heyman) def. Los Guerreros (WWE Tag Title match). The champions are out first for Heyman to surprise everyone by joining Team Angle for this match. Inside the ring, Shelton and Chavo trade amateur holds before Eddie takes his shot at the amateur star. Neither man gets much of an advantage before Charlie tags in for his own amateur display. "Latino Heat" manages to get the better of him and holds the rookie for a Chavo dropkick. The younger champion follows up with a back suplex ahead of an Eddie slingshot somersault splash and two-count. When Chavo and Benjamin tag in afterwards, the champion clotheslines him ahead of a "Latino Heat" choke in the corner, Los Guerreros reminding everyone that they can cheat with the best of them. Eddie soon returns to pound Shelton down, Chavo adding a cheap shot. When Haas inadvertently distracts Mike Chioda, the champions drive Benjamin back crotch-first into the ring post. Eddie tries to slow the pace with a side headlock, but Shelton back suplexes free before the challengers work over the champion in their corner. That brings in Chavo for a four-man fight. In the chaos, "Latino Heat" dropkicks Benjamin into Chavo, knocking him off the apron and into the announce table ahead of a commercial break.

Afterwards, we see footage of Chioda stopping the match during the break to check on Chavo. The champion says he can continue so the match resumes with Team Angle double-teaming Chavo for a leapfrog splash. When they attempt a second, Eddie trips Shelton and attacks Haas. Soon after, Chavo counters a double back body drop with a double DDT. That finally lets "Latino Heat" get the hot tag and he works over both challengers. After knocking Benjamin out to the floor, Eddie catches Charlie with a trio of suplexes for a near fall. Los Guerreros follow up with a "Latino Heat" superplex and Chavo frog splash for Eddie to get a close two-count before Shelton makes the save. Afterwards, Chavo tornado DDTs Haas, but Benjamin shoves "Latino Heat" down to the floor to prevent his Frog Splash. Chavo answers with a flying dive onto Shelton leaving Charlie to press and drop Eddie ahead of a belly-to-belly suplex and two-count. When Chavo tries to help his uncle, Chioda cuts him off for Team Angle to give "Latino Heat" a double-team leapfrog splash. A Haas German suplex follows for a two-count before Chavo makes the save. Afterwards, the challengers attempt a second rope double-team maneuver, but Chavo electric chair drops Charlie ahead of an Eddie sunset flip powerbomb to Benjamin. When Heyman gets involved grabbing "Latino Heat's" boot, Eddie kicks him off the apron. Chavo follows up with a slingshot splash onto the agent while "Latino Heat" Frog Splashes Shelton. Unfortunately, he's not the legal man and the referee refuses to count until Charlie Oklahoma rolls Eddie for the victory.

Following a commercial break, Hulk Hogan heads to the squared circle for another huge pop. Eventually, The Rock interrupts on the big screen to tell the Hulkster he looks good. The "People's

Champ" is happy to listen to Hogan putting him over. Unfortunately, once Hulk starts to talk, The Rock yawns and says it's been a long day. He just wants the Hulkster to skip to the part where he rips off his shirt and flexes. When he starts to talk again, The Rock finds out his tofu is ready and leaves, but not before telling Hogan that he shouldn't bore the fans talking about vitamins and prayers. He does want Hulk to remind him to "whip that ass" at No Way Out though before going off to have some tofu and pies. The Hulkster isn't impressed. After hearing the fans boo the "Great One" out of the building at the *Raw* tenth anniversary special, Hogan doesn't think The Rock has any right calling anyone boring. He then rants about Vince McMahon, saying he's full of crap when he talks about creating Hulkamania. The Hulkster knows that Vince is really scared of Hogan and that's why he sent the "People's Champ" after him. That's okay with Hulk because he's looking forward to beating that "Rock-a-jabroni" and running wild on him at No Way Out. Backstage, several superstars watch the Hulkster flex. One of them is Brian Kendrick. Sean O'Haire sees him and tells the rookie that he's got guts. He was impressed with him last week. Brian says he'd do anything to make it in the WWE. O'Haire has a suggestion for him, giving him a scarf to streak through the arena.

A-Train def. Shannon Moore. When A-Train's music plays, Brian Kendrick races out in a scarf and boots, his crotch blurred out as he streaks into the ring, around the announcers, and through the crowd. Once he's gone, the hairy heel bicycle kicks and pummels Moore. He follows quickly with a Train Wreck for the win. Post-match, Kendrick returns, dancing on the apron and running under an A-Train clothesline before the officials corner him. Brian crawls under the ring and through a worker's legs to escape.

After a commercial break, Stephanie McMahon is on the phone trying to find out if Eric Bischoff signed "Stone Cold" Steve Austin when she's interrupted by the naked Brian Kendrick. He says he's "excited to meet her". She can tell. Afterwards, John Cena heads to the ring to rap a challenge to Brock Lesnar. After insulting his intelligence, Cena challenges Brock to a match next week, rewinding himself to repeat the challenge.

Kurt Angle (with Paul Heyman) def. Chris Benoit. A non-title match, the rivals know each other well and start fast trading fists and shoulder blocks. When Kurt attempts a corner charge, Benoit meets him with a boot and suplex for a two-count. The Olympian responds with an overhead belly-to-belly suplex. Once again, the two men club each other before Angle scores a two-count. That brings out Paul Heyman from the back to stand in his man's corner and double ax-handle "the Crippler". Back in the ring, the champion gets a two-count ahead of a suplex and another near fall. He then traps Benoit in a chin lock and body hook. When the "rabid wolverine" escapes, Kurt drops him with a knee to the gut for another two-count. More strikes follow ahead of a back suplex and near fall. Benoit answers with chops and a clothesline. When he tries to German suplex the Olympian, Angle counters with an Anklelock. "The Crippler" rolls through for a two-count before hooking the Crippler Crossface. Unable to break the hold, the champion picks him up for an Angle Slam, but Benoit rolls through for another near fall. Moments later, he arm drags free of another Angle Slam to return to his submission finisher. This time, Kurt breaks the hold with an Anklelock, but the "rabid wolverine" rolls back into the Crossface. Finally, the Olympian reaches the ropes for the break. After running through Angle, Benoit heads upstairs. The champion tries to block his attack with a belly-to-belly suplex, but "the Crippler" shoves him off the top rope. When he hops down, Kurt powerbombs him into a corner. Despite that, Benoit responds with a release German suplex. That scores a bloodied "rabid wolverine" a two-count. Afterwards, he German suplexes the Olympian again, but misses a diving headbutt. Angle capitalizes with a roll-up for a two-count. An Angle Slam follows for the victory. Post-match, Kurt offers Benoit a handshake. He takes it before Team Angle attacks, Edge attempting and failing to make the save. Brock Lesnar does, F5ing Charlie Haas and Shelton Benjamin while Angle runs away to end the show.

Monday Night Raw

February 10, 2003
Los Angeles, CA
Announcers: Jim Ross (briefly), Jerry "the King" Lawler, Jonathan Coachman

The show opens with a graphic for Mr. Perfect who passed away earlier in the day. He was just 44. Afterwards, a video package plays featuring Vince McMahon, Eric Bischoff, and "Stone Cold" Steve Austin. Tonight, the "thirty day" clock runs out after twenty-eight days. Following the intro video and fireworks, Eric steps onto the stage to say that he hasn't heard from Austin and has no idea if he'll be at No Way Out or not. He also says he may be fired when Vince gets here tonight, but Bischoff wants everyone to know that he's done everything he can to sign "Stone Cold". After being surrounded by "rednecks" last week, the general manager is happy to be back with his people and wants them to let McMahon know that they support him. The crowd booing sets off Eric and he demands that they support him. Bischoff says that so long as he's still in power, he's going to use it. That sees him turning his frustrations to JR and accusing him of not doing enough to get the "rattlesnake" back on *Raw*. Ross says it might be because Eric fired Austin back in WCW and Steve hates his guts. Bischoff remembers firing Austin and does the same to JR tonight until "Stone Cold" signs with *Raw*.

During a commercial break, Eric Bischoff sprints backstage to meet an entering limo. Instead of Vince McMahon, it's Evolution. Triple H mockingly asks if he's having a bad day.

Test (with Stacy Keibler) def. Christian. Lawler is on his own here as he tries to ignore Stacy's long legs to announce that Test will face Chris Jericho at No Way Out. Jerry also shills his autobiography before the bodyguard gets to work back dropping and choking the heel. Christian answers with a shot to the face and backward head slam on the top rope. A neckbreaker follows for a two-count before Coach joins the announce table. He says he's not prepared for the opportunity, but the GM told him to take it. While the announcers talk about JR, the wrestlers trade two-counts, Test with a tilt-a-whirl slam and Christian with a reverse neckbreaker after slipping free of a pumphandle slam. He follows up with a top rope flying cross body block, but the bodyguard catches him and rolls through for a military press slam. Although he misses a Big Boot, Test quickly recovers and picks up the win with a full nelson slam. Post-match, Christian hits the bodyguard from behind and drops him with an Unprettier. He then corners Keibler until Jeff Hardy runs out and pulls him from the ring for a barricade dive and a big pop.

Backstage, JR is on the phone trying to reach "Stone Cold" Steve Austin while Howard Finkel lurks in the background.

Following a shot of Rob Reiner in the crowd, a video package plays showing Booker T and Goldust going their separate ways. Despite them parting on good terms, the video takes a dark turn when Batista and Randy Orton toss the "bizarre one" into an electrical box.

Booker T def. D'Lo Brown (with Theodore Long). Pre-match, Booker dedicates the match to his friend "Goldy". The heels interrupt for Long to call Goldust a "white man" trying to keep the five-time champion down. He says Booker T should be teaming with D'Lo, but instead the babyface punches and kicks Brown for a near fall while Coach reveals that the "bizarre one" is dealing with a number of medical problems right now. D'Lo soon turns the tide with a string of fists until Booker rocks him with a side kick followed by the Scissors Kick for an easy win. Theodore doesn't like it as Booker T celebrates with a spinaroonie. This is D'Lo's last match with the company for five years.

Backstage, Chris Jericho interrupts Eric Bischoff and Chief Morley to complain about his match with Test at No Way Out. The GM says he has bigger problems. To make Y2J happy, Morley gives him a match with Jeff Hardy tonight.

The Starburst WWE Rewind is Jazz attacking Trish Stratus two weeks ago.

Jazz def. Molly Holly. Although Molly starts fast with takedowns, a dropkick puts her down for a Jazz two-count. The returning superstar follows up with a drop toe hold into a full body stretch, called Southern Comfort by Coach. When the fans chant "boring", Jazz turns it over into a backslide for a near fall. She follows up with a series of double underhook suplexes and another two-count. When she attempts a corner splash, Holly moves and comes back to life with kicks and clotheslines. Eventually, Jazz answers with a trip into a single leg crab. Molly tries to crawl to the ropes for the break, but the returning heel pulls her back to the center of the ring and locks on an STF for an unappreciated victory. Post-match, Jazz continues her assault with a double chicken win slam and STF before finally heading backstage.

Also backstage, JR finally gets a call from "Steve". Howard Finkel rushes up to find out what "Stone Cold" Steve Austin said, but Jim tells him it was a different Steve and wants the Fink to stop eavesdropping.

Kane/Rob Van Dam def. Three-Minute Warning (with Rico). Although Jamal starts with a slam, he misses his follow up attack and RVD splashes him. When the popular superstar heads to the top rope, the Samoan shoves him out to the floor. Rico rolls him right back into the ring for a Rosey splash and two-count. Back in, Jamal also gets a near fall with a superkick. When the Samoans attempt a double-team attack, Rob moves and Jamal hits his partner. Kane then gets the hot tag to punch and kick both heels. Following a side slam to Jamal, the "Big Red Machine" heads upstairs for a flying clothesline to Rosey. Although he recovers to save Jamal from a Chokeslam, Three-Minute Warning can't slow Kane's attack. Only him tagging in Van Dam does that, the popular superstar nearly getting the win with rolling thunder to Jamal. After Rosey makes the save, the monster tosses him out to the floor before planting Jamal with a Chokeslam. A Five-Star Frog Splash follows for the three-count.

After arriving and wondering why JR is backstage, Vince McMahon heads to the ring. He says on occasion he has to make heart-wrenching decisions, but not tonight. His decision is joyous as he invites Eric Bischoff and Chief Morley to enter the squared circle. They do so reluctantly. Vince deals with Morley first. While he planned to fire him, the WWE owner is going to give him a chance to save his job…in a handicap match with Spike Dudley and The Dudley Boyz. After sending him backstage to get ready, McMahon asks Eric if he's signed "Stone Cold" Steve Austin. The GM stammers before admitting that he hasn't yet. While Vince hates Austin, he would have let Bischoff keep his job had he signed him. Since he hasn't, McMahon prepares to fire him. Eric stops him to grovel and give Vince some action, specifically "HLA". That brings out two women and has "the King" going crazy. McMahon says there's a time and place for everything, but right now he's all about business. Vince tells him he's out of time and fires the GM. He's in such a good mood that he leads the crowd in singing goodbye to Bischoff.

After a commercial break, Lance Storm and William Regal tell Vince McMahon that he did a great job with the Eric Bischoff situation. Vince tells them to just and wait and see who the new GM is tonight.

Spike Dudley/The Dudley Boyz def. Chief Morley. While Morley paces the ring needing to win this match to keep his job, the announcers talk about the latest issue of *Raw* magazine. Afterwards, the babyfaces surround the chief of staff before Spike attacks from behind. Morley tries to answer with a back body drop, but the Dudleys catch their half-brother before giving the chief a double flapjack. The fans want tables, but instead the babyfaces squash Morley in a corner ahead of a Bubba Ray Samoan drop. Following an onslaught of stomps, the chief rolls out to the floor where Bubba press slams Spike onto him. D-Von follows up with a hard whip into the ring steps. Coach feels bad for Morley as the Dudleys continue slamming him on the steps before Bubba Ray rams them into his head. Back in the ring, the runt delivers a top rope double stomp. More strikes follow ahead of a Dudley Dog and 3D for the win. "The King" loves it and tells Morley that he's fired. Still not done, Bubba powerbombs the former chief from the second rope through a table.

Backstage, Eric Bischoff asks JR if he ever heard from "Stone Cold" Steve Austin. Jim says he hasn't. Accepting his fate, Eric offers Ross a handshake and says it was all business. He hopes they can be friends. JR tells him to clean out his desk.

Batista (with Ric Flair) def. Tommy Dreamer. The heels are out first for Dreamer to sneak attack Batista with a cane. Even his cheap shots can't keep the "Animal" down and he answers with a Sit-Out Powerbomb for the easy victory. Post-match, Booker T runs out to stop the heels from continuing their assault. Unfortunately, the other members of Evolution follow him, Randy Orton splitting his pants as he kicks the five-time champion. Once he's down, Triple H gets in a few shots before Scott Steiner runs out to chase him away and belly-to-belly suplex Batista.

Backstage, Jeff Hardy nods at a smiling Shawn Michaels.

Further backstage, Test wonders what Jeff Hardy was doing earlier. Stacy Keibler doesn't know, but she says she has a new marketing deal for the bodyguard from a group called "GGW". She promises it will be "great exposure". Test is happy about that.

In the former general manager's office, Eric Bischoff packs his stuff, but is interrupted by Spike Dudley and The Dudley Boyz. They sing "Na Na Hey Hey Kiss Him Goodbye" as he leaves.

Chris Jericho def. Jeff Hardy. Billy Gibbons from ZZ Top is in the crowd to watch this match. He sees Y2J slow Hardy with a headlock. When he slaps the daredevil, Jeff responds with several shots and a back body drop. A head scissors afterwards gets him a two-count before Jericho turns the tide with a clothesline. The heel proceeds to choke Hardy with his own shirt and chop him. Following a toss out to the floor, Y2J taunts the crowd before missing a second rope springboard attack. As he hits the floor, the daredevil follows up with an Asai moonsault and whip into the ring steps for a two-count. Soon after, he counters a second rope attack with a dropkick before heading upstairs. Jericho sees him coming and grabs Earl Hebner, shoving him back into the ropes to crotch Jeff. Y2J then climbs up next to his opponent for a butterfly suplex and near fall. A pair of backbreakers follow as the announcers speculate on who will be the new GM while the fans are distracted by something in the crowd. Jericho is too, turning around for a Hardy comeback and roll-up. When that nearly gets Jeff the win, Y2J springs up for a clothesline. He then chokes the daredevil on the middle rope and leg drops him. Afterwards, Jericho slows the pace with a reverse chin lock. When Jeff gets up, he dodges a corner charge to see the heel hit the ring post hard. Hardy follows up with knees to the chin and a neckbreaker for his own near fall. Unfortunately, Y2J answers with an enziguri kick for a two-count. The daredevil responds with a whisper in the wind for another near fall. Once again, the heel grabs Hebner and uses him to distract Jeff and lock on the Walls of Jericho. Luckily, Hardy is close enough to the ropes to crawl for the break. Afterwards, he counters a top rope attack with an arm drag to the canvas. After stripping off his other shirt, the daredevil nearly gets the win with a Swanton Bomb, but Jericho just drapes his foot on the rope to survive. Moments later, he counters a hurricanrana attempt with the Walls of Jericho for the tap-out victory.

Backstage, Evolution cross paths with Vince McMahon. They are leaving to party with Eric Bischoff's girls. Before they go, Vince tells Batista and Triple H that they will face Booker T and Scott Steiner next week.

After a commercial break, Vince McMahon is back in the ring and asks for the new general manager to come out. Instead, Jim Ross heads to the squared circle followed by Eric Bischoff. JR tells the WWE owner that "Stone Cold" Steve Austin has guaranteed he will be at No Way Out. Since Austin is reinstated, Vince gives JR his job back and tells him to head to the announce table. With "Stone Cold" back in the fold, McMahon also brings Bischoff back as the *Raw* general manager. Before he leaves, Vince recalls that Eric said he'd do anything to keep his job. The WWE owner wonders if he'd be willing to join a special club. McMahon calls it a "condition of employment" and pulls his pants and underwear down for Bischoff to kiss his butt. Eric can't do it. Vince promptly pulls up his pants and offers to kick Bischoff's butt instead. If that's what it takes to keep his job, the GM tells him to do it. Instead of McMahon doing it, the WWE owner signs Eric to a No Way Out match against Austin. JR and the fans love it while Bischoff pleads for his life. Vince doesn't care, leaving the ring to end the episode.

SmackDown!

February 13, 2003
Bakersfield, CA
Announcers: Michael Cole, Tazz

Charlie Haas (with Paul Heyman) def. Edge. Following the intro video and fireworks, Edge heads out and walks by a large wooden crate. It's from Big Show to The Undertaker again. Inside the ring, Haas takes the babyface down with a fireman's carry into an armbar. Edge responds with a drop toe hold and his own armbar until Charlie battles free, punching and choking his opponent. Heyman loves it. He doesn't like the babyface responding with a heel kick and shoulder tackle. When he attempts a second corner tackle, Haas moves, but Edge pulls up just in time not to hit Jimmy Korderas. The rookie capitalizes with an exploder suplex for a near fall. A belly-to-belly suplex also get him a near fall, as does a northern lights suplex. Backstage, Kurt Angle watches as Charlie applies a surfboard submission. Although Edge fights free, Haas pulls his hair to stop his comeback. When he attempts a back suplex, the babyface lands on his feet and answers with one of his own. Forearms, clotheslines, and a back body drop have Charlie seeing stars ahead of an Edge-a-matic and two-count. Haas nearly steals the win with a roll-up out of a DDT, but Edge just escapes for his own roll-up and near fall. He follows up with a flapjack, but when he sets up for the Spear, Paul hops onto the apron to distract him. Although the agent gets Speared, Charlie takes advantage and rolls up the babyface for the win.

Afterwards, the announcers reveal that Nathan Jones has signed a contract with *SmackDown!* and will appear next week.

After a commercial break, Kurt Angle is waiting in Stephanie McMahon's office. He compliments her hair and gives her a rose. When she says she wants to talk about a match, the Olympian says they are a "perfect match" and teases kissing her. Brock Lesnar interrupts to stare down the WWE Champion while Stephanie signs a No Way Out six-man tag match pitting the champion and Team Angle against Brock, Edge, and Chris Benoit. Lesnar likes that and invites Angle to watch his match ringside tonight when he destroys John Cena. After the number one contender leaves, Kurt takes his rose back.

The Nunzio and Rikishi match never officially starts. The Italian heel tries to sneak attack Rikishi before he gets in the ring, but the big Samoan catches and slams him to the floor. Afterwards, Johnny Stamboli and Chuck Palumbo, wearing black leather like Nunzio, run out to attack the big Samoan from behind. The Italian heel yells that they are family and they just taught Rikishi a valuable lesson. When the big babyface headbutts him, the heels hammer him down and Nunzio gives him the kiss of death.

Following a replay of The Rock's recent promos, the announcers tease his match with Hulk Hogan at No Way Out and the icons being on the show next week.

Rey Mysterio def. Matt Hardy Version 1.0 (with Shannon Moore). Tonight's Matt Facts are that Matt always gets more valentines than his brother and that he doesn't send flowers, only chocolates. Tonight, Hardy is announced as Version 1.0. Once the match starts, Hardy, wearing a rubber suit, shoves Rey down to the canvas and does jumping jacks. Since Matt has already lost eight of the ten pounds he needs to lose, Stephanie McMahon has given him a Cruiserweight Title match at No Way Out assuming he loses the rest of the weight. Here, Mysterio kicks him out to the floor only to miss a slingshot attack. Moore follows up with a string of kicks before Hardy drops the masked man sternum-first onto the top rope. A gut wrench suplex follows for a two-count. He also gets a near fall with a side effect before locking on a surfboard. When Rey starts to fight back, Matt clubs him ahead of a torture rack submission. Mysterio escapes with a bulldog to put both men down. Cole notes how tired Hardy looks as the masked man comes back to life first to hit a springboard butt splash. He then dodges a corner charge to nearly get the win with a split legged moonsault. Unfortunately, his follow up corkscrew attack is caught for a side effect and another near fall. Exhausted, Hardy sets up for a Twist of Fate, but Rey escapes and kicks off a series of counters. All the reversals wear out Matt and he collapses onto the middle rope for the 619 and West Coast Pop for the three-count. Post-match, Hardy says that doesn't count as a loss since he's lightheaded. However, Matt promises to drop two more pounds to make weight for No Way Out.

A Brian Kendrick video package plays before we see Sean O'Haire telling him that he made an impact last week. Kendrick says he got in a lot of trouble for entering Stephanie McMahon's office naked. Bill DeMott offers to help Brian make an impact, flinging him against a wall and stomping him. O'Haire intercedes, telling Bill that he's had enough, but he's not telling him anything he doesn't already know.

Chris Benoit def. A-Train. The hairy heel opens the match driving Benoit into a corner and trash talking him. "The Crippler" answers with chops, but they have no effect. A-Train's clothesline does, but Benoit won't stay down, teasing a Crippler Crossface. Luckily, the hairy heel reaches the ropes before delivering a backbreaker and elbow drops to the lower back. More shots to the lower back follow, including forearms before A-Train slaps and picks up the babyface in an inverted full nelson. Without letting go, he drops down to the canvas to crunch the "rabid wolverine". Moments later, the hairy heel gets a near fall with a scoop slam and corner bomb. Continuing to focus on the lower back, A-Train also applies a torture rack until Benoit fights free for a sunset flip and two-count. The hairy heel answers with a flurry of clubbing blows, but misses his corner charge. "The Crippler" answers with a trio of German suplexes. After blowing snot onto his opponent, Benoit goes upstairs but misses his diving headbutt. A-Train doesn't miss a bicycle kick, but the "rabid wolverine" kicks out. He also counters a Derailer with a Crippler Crossface for the tap-out victory.

Backstage, Joe Francis from *Girls Gone Wild* knocks on Torrie Wilson's locker room to invite her to a spring break party. She wonders if he really wants her since she gets pretty wild. That's exactly what he's looking for. This also removes Torrie from the atrocious Dawn Marie storyline.

Following footage of Big Show slamming The Undertaker off the stage last year, Paul Heyman is in the ring with another wooden crate from the giant to the biker. After Paul complains about the "Deadman" attacking Brother Love last week, The Undertaker rides his bike to the ring to a big pop. This week, Kanyon steps out looking like Boy George to ask who is better than him. When the "Deadman" turns his back, Kanyon nails him from behind with a microphone. The Undertaker responds with a flurry of fists and stomps before tossing the returning superstar out to the floor. Not done yet, he follows Kanyon out to continue his assault and grab a chair. With Heyman watching from the stage, the biker blasts the returning superstar's back twice ahead of a thunderous shot to the skull to end the assault.

Backstage, Shannon Moore cheers on Matt Hardy pedaling an exercise bike with all his might.

Further backstage, Funaki turns his cap sideways and asks John Cena, "what's up dog". Cena responds with a quick rap to say Brock Lesnar is getting smoked before slapping off Funaki's hat.

The Stacker2 Burn of the Week is Team Angle winning the WWE Tag Titles.

Shelton Benjamin def. Eddie Guerrero. The announcers reveal that Chavo Guerrero Jr. isn't here tonight due to having a stomach bug. Charlie Haas does accompany his partner to the ring, but leaves before the match starts so Shelton can prove what he can do solo. Inside the ring, the competitors tie-up and trade amateur holds until Benjamin gets a two-count with a powerslam. He then locks on an armbar, but Eddie escapes with a back suplex before applying a head scissors. Shelton shows off his power, picking up Guerrero for an electric chair drop and near fall. Afterwards, he hooks a reverse chin lock to keep "Latino Heat" on the canvas. It doesn't take Eddie long to fight free and score a two-count with a slingshot somersault splash. Benjamin answers with a big back body drop and backbreaker for a near fall. When he attempts a corner charge, Guerrero catches him and respond with an exploder suplex for another close two-count. He tries to follow up with a top rope attack, but the rookie follows him up and teases a second electric chair drop. This time, Eddie rolls through for a sunset flip powerbomb. When he heads back upstairs, Haas runs back out only to see "Latino Heat" dive onto him. He then slams Shelton's face into the top turnbuckle before attempting a Frog Splash. Unfortunately, he misses and Benjamin surprises him with a Dragon Whip kick for the three-count.

After a commercial break, Hugh Hefner teases a diva on the cover of *Playboy* soon.

Torrie Wilson def. Dawn Marie Wilson ("Valentine's Day Bra & Panties" match). While their feud over Al Wilson may be over, *SmackDown!* only has three divas who compete on the roster, so there aren't a lot of options. Dawn starts fast with a slam on the floor before stripping off Torrie's shirt. She follows up with kicks until Wilson teases a comeback. She can't get Marie's pants off, so she takes the fight out to the floor to kick and chop the heel. Afterwards, Torrie pulls off Dawn's shirt. A suplex follows before the two women tug at each other's pants. Dawn Marie tries to finish off the match with a fireman's carry slam, but Wilson rolls through for a series of pinning predicaments. Unfortunately, there are no pinfalls in this match. Instead, Dawn surprises Torrie with a second rope flying clothesline and scoop slam. When she heads up the ropes, Wilson capitalizes, ripping off Marie's pants for the win. Post-match, the final diva on the roster, Nidia, runs out to attack Torrie. Wilson fights off the heels with a double clothesline before stripping off Nidia's shorts and spanking her to a nice pop. Post-match, Torrie pulls down her pants while Tazz says the match wasn't a Kurt Angle/Chris Benoit classic. Cole believes it was as good as any Tazz match.

Brock Lesnar def. John Cena. After we see the tale of the tape, Brock heads to the ring to a nice pop. He sets up a chair at ringside for Kurt Angle. John follows to insult Lesnar's intelligence and say God forgot to give him a brain. That just makes the "next big thing" mad and he clubs the rapping heel before slamming him into a corner. Enraged, Brock delivers a backbreaker and stomps before flinging Cena out of the ring with a belly-to-belly suplex. Lesnar follows him out for a press slam onto the announce table. Although John attacks his eyes, the "next big thing" is right back up with hammering blows and another belly-to-belly suplex. While the rapping heel recovers, Brock removes a turnbuckle pad. That distracts Mike Chioda long enough for Cena to wrap his chain around his fist and blast Lesnar. He still can't score the three-count. After stomps and a back suplex get him another two-count, John applies a reverse chin lock with body hooks. Brock won't stay down, lifting the rapping heel up and slamming him into a corner, but Cena won't let go. Two more slams into the turnbuckles finally break the hold, but John follows up with a big clothesline and more clubbing blows. That wakes up Brock and he responds with shoulder blocks and belly-to-belly suplexes. He follows up with a face-first slam into the exposed steel bolt in a corner ahead of an F5 for the win.

Post-match, Lesnar yells at Angle to come out, but the Olympian isn't moving from backstage. Brock tries to get him to change his mind with an F5 against the ring post to Cena. Kurt says he's trying to punk him out, but Heyman tries to calm his client. It doesn't work and the WWE Champion steps onto the stage after a commercial break. Brock challenges him to a match right now. Angle is fine with that and steps into the ring to go nose-to-nose with the number one contender. Once he sees Lesnar, the Olympian backs down and says he has a sinus infection. Brock thinks he's chicken. Kurt argues otherwise, but proposes that the wrestlers give the fans the "greatest wrestling match" of all-time next week on *SmackDown!*. Lesnar accepts the challenge before decking and belly-to-belly suplexing the champion. He then takes the fight out to the floor to whip Angle into the ring steps and belly-to-belly suplex him at ringside. When he picks up the Olympian for an F5, Team Angle run out to attack the "next big thing". While he destroys them, whipping around Charlie Haas and Shelton Benjamin, Kurt retreats up the ramp. He doesn't get far before Brock F5s Benjamin and stalks after the champion. Instead of finishing him off, Lesnar looks at the WWE Title and continues backstage, the announcers reminding everyone about next week's stacked show.

Monday Night Raw
February 17, 2003
Columbus, OH
Announcers: Jim Ross, Jerry "the King" Lawler, Jonathan Coachman (briefly)

Rob Van Dam (with Kane) def. Lance Storm (with William Regal). Following the intro video, fireworks, and announcers previewing the episode, the babyfaces head to the squared circle for half of a preview of this Sunday's World Tag Title match. Once the bell rings, the wrestlers trade counters ahead of a RVD step over heel kick. After catching his breath, Lance unloads with shoulder blocks before running into a second rope moonsault for a near fall. Soon after, Rob attempts a suplex out to the floor, but Storm lands on the apron and drives Van Dam face-first into the barricade. Back in the squared circle, the Canadian scores a near fall with a springboard clothesline. A flurry of fists follow before RVD responds with a dropkick for his own two-count. Lance is right back on the attack, leg dropping the popular superstar for a two-count before applying a reverse chin lock. Eventually, Rob fights free and rocks Storm with a kick to swing the momentum. That lets him kick and clotheslines the Canadian ahead of a springboard kick for a near fall. Following another kick and two-count, Lance shoves Van Dam into the ropes and rolls him up for a single leg crab. It takes him a few seconds, but RVD reaches the ropes for the break. He follows up quickly with a kick and rolling thunder for another near fall. When he tries to head upstairs for a Five-Star Frog Splash, Regal hops up to distract him. Luckily, Rob fights him off until Kane comes over to take care of the Englishman. While he handles him, Van Dam finishes off Storm with a Five-Star Frog Splash for the three-count.

Backstage, Shawn Michaels talks with Jeff Hardy and wishes Eric Bischoff luck against "Stone Cold" Steve Austin this Sunday. When the babyfaces laugh at him, Eric warns them that they should pay attention to what he has to say next because they might be the ones needing luck tonight.

After a commercial break, Eric Bischoff heads to the ring to say that he's got some unfinished business with someone and he's going to take care of tonight. The fans think he's talking about "Stone Cold" Steve Austin, but he's talking about Chief Morley who comes out with a black eye to apathy. For his first official act as the *Raw* general manager again, Bischoff reinstates Morley. The chief of staff thanks his boss and asks the fans to give Eric a round of applause. They don't. The GM doesn't care. He remembers that they all turned on him, just like the wrestlers backstage. That includes Jeff Hardy and Shawn Michaels. To pay them back for laughing at him, Bischoff signs the babyfaces to a "No Disqualification" match against Chris Jericho and Christian tonight. He then plays footage of WWE security escorting The Dudley Boyz from the arena because they are now suspended. Spike Dudley isn't, and he'll pay tonight on the other side of a handicap match against Three-Minute Warning and Rico. Finally, to get ready for his match this Sunday, Eric signs himself a match. As an "eighth degree black belt" and world champion, Bischoff is ready to step into the squared circle with Austin's friend, JR.

Backstage, Steven Richards gets Victoria to talk to Jazz ahead of their match. The "black widow" respects what Jazz does in the ring, but she doesn't need her help. Jazz says she's in the WWE to take care of Trish Stratus and be the most dominant female in the business. When Victoria says she's the Women's Champion, Jazz tells her that's only for now.

Jazz/Victoria (with Steven Richards) def. Jacqueline/Molly Holly. As the wrestlers head to the ring, JR wonders why Eric Bischoff has signed him to a match tonight considering he was the one that got the boss his job back. Inside the ring, Jazz doesn't care about her partner, shoving Victoria to the side to attack Holly. After manhandling and leg dropping her, the heel tags in her partner only to see Molly roll her up for a two-count. The champion answers with a fireman's carry into a spinning side slam. The "black widow" proceeds to badmouth Holly and powerslam her for another near fall. When she goes for a slingshot attack, Jazz tags herself in to slam Molly before missing a body splash. Jacqueline then tags in to absorb a clothesline and punch both opponents. Unfortunately, Jazz recovers quickly to whip Jacqueline into Victoria. While the champion falls out to the floor, Jazz scores the win with a DDT. Post-match, Jazz gives Holly and Jacqueline chicken wing slams. JR says the crowd is stunned, but they're just silent as Jazz takes the microphone to say, "the bitch is back". Victoria has had enough and stops Jazz. When the returning superstar shoves her down, the "black widow" slaps her. Jazz just laughs.

Despite shots of the snow outside, the fans are still excited to be here. Goldust isn't here thanks to being thrown into an electrical box two weeks ago by Batista and Randy Orton. Following a replay of that attack, Booker T tells Terri that the "bizarre one" will be back in action in a few weeks, but there's something wrong with his head. Terri asks how Booker feels about Evolution joking about what they did to Goldust. The five-time champion warns them that they better enjoy laughing now because he's going to get payback tonight alongside Scott Steiner.

Further backstage, Evolution continues laughing, Triple H wondering why Booker T split up with Goldust especially now that they can be called "Booker and Cooker". After Randy Orton calls the "bizarre one" the "new most electrifying man" in sports entertainment, Hunter promises to put Booker T in a hospital bed next to him. Helmsley promises that they'll take care of Scott Steiner too.

With a little more prep time this week, a video package plays for Mr. Perfect's career after his passing.

Rodney Mack (with Theodore Long) def. Al Snow. Pre-match, Long introduces the former Redd Dogg and says that D'Lo Brown couldn't get the job done. For February, he's happy to lead a black man to the top of the WWE and wants everyone to "back the Mack". Al then marches out to punch the rookie until Rodney runs through him with a shoulder block. Following a belly-to-belly suplex, Mack powerslams and badmouths the home state star. He can't keep Snow down for long and the crazed superstar answers with a series of headbutts and clothesline. Following a back body drop, Al slams Rodney into position for a moonsault. Unfortunately, he leaps into a pair of knees followed by an underhook powerbomb where Snow lands on his head for the three-count.

Backstage, Chris Jericho is happy that he finally gets the chance to finish off Shawn Michaels tonight. Christian believes that Shawn and Jeff Hardy think they are so cool because women scream when they take their shirts off, but girls have been screaming at the heel when he does so for years. Tonight, Y2J promises a big surprise for the babyfaces.

Jeff Hardy/Shawn Michaels def. Chris Jericho/Christian ("No Disqualification" match). Since he arrived late and the airline lost his bags, Shawn wrestles in street clothes. That doesn't stop him from charging the ring and pulling Christian crotch-first into the ring post. Jeff then tosses Jericho out to the floor for a barricade dive. Unfortunately, the heel catches and powerslams him on the floor. Afterwards, he joins Christian in whipping Michaels into the ring steps. The heels follow up by handcuffing the "Heartbreak Kid" to the bottom rope. That leaves the daredevil all alone for a Jericho back suplex. For some reason, Christian stands on the apron and watches as Y2J taunts Shawn with the key. Despite there being no disqualifications, the heels take turns in the ring and tag each other in between assaults to Hardy. When the daredevil starts to fight back, Christian saves his partner with a reverse backbreaker. Once Jeff is down, the heels rip Michaels's shirt off and take his belt to whip him. Back in the ring, the former champions continue punishing Hardy before Jericho once again mocks the "Heartbreak Kid" with the key. He gets too close and pays courtesy of Sweet Chin Music while Jeff surprises Christian with a whisper in the wind. Once Y2J is down, Shawn uncuffs himself and tags in to punch and back body drop Christian. A springboard tackle and fists follow until Michaels walks into a back elbow. Despite that, he recovers fast enough to slam Christian off the ropes and tease Sweet Chin Music. Luckily, the heel dodges only to see the "Heartbreak Kid" toss him out to the floor ahead of poetry in motion. When Jericho tries to ambush him with a chair, Shawn drives it back into his face with Sweet Chin Music. Jeff follows up with a Swanton Bomb for the three-count. The announcers wonder if that will straighten out Hardy.

After a commercial break, Chris Jericho throws a tantrum and tosses around equipment about giving Jeff Hardy his first win in four months.

The Hurricane def. Christopher Nowinski. JR continues to talk about his upcoming match with Eric Bischoff as the wrestlers march out for the fans to chant "Harvard sucks". The Hurricane entertains the crowd with a clothesline and roll-up for a two-count. A hurricanrana out of the ring onto the floor follows, but when he attempts a flying attack back in the squared circle, Nowinski slams him to seize control. He capitalizes with hammering blows and a neck vise, keeping the superhero on the mat. A swinging neckbreaker afterwards gets the Harvard heel a two-count, but when he tries to apply a full nelson, The Hurricane rolls him up for a near fall. A tornado DDT and backward head slam follow for another two-count, but the superhero misses an overcast. Nowinski doesn't miss his spinebuster, but The Hurricane just kicks out. When the Harvard heel tries to finish off the superhero with an Honor Roll, the babyface reverses it into the Eye of the Hurricane for the victory.

Backstage, Chief Morley holds pads for Eric Bischoff to kick. Morley does a JR impression, wearing a black hat as Bischoff shows off his martial arts skill. The chief is sure Eric will handle Ross tonight and sits back to watch the upcoming handicap match.

The announcers thank Evanescence for No Way Out's theme song, "Bring Me to Life".

Rico/Three-Minute Warning def. Spike Dudley. JR calls this an "abuse of power" as the Samoans press slam and elbow drop Spike. Jamal follows up moments later with a running butt splash in a corner and pop-up Samoan Drop. Continuing the assault, the heels double-team headbutt the runt while Rico cheers them on from behind. Three-Minute Warning continue tossing around Dudley ahead of a Rosey spinning slam and Jamal top rope Flying Splash. JR wants Jack Doan to stop the match, but he waits for the stylist to cover Spike and pull his pants for the win.

Afterwards, the announcers shill the 2003 *WWE Preview* magazine available on the Shop Zone.

After the announcers preview No Way Out, Scott Steiner tells Terri that there will be no escape for Triple H this Sunday. Once Scott flexes and promises to win the World Title, Booker T tells him it's time for the babyfaces to kick "the Game" and Batista's butts.

Booker T/Scott Steiner def. Batista/Triple H (with Randy Orton/Ric Flair). Triple H and Booker open the match jockeying for position until the five-time champion connects with a spinning heel kick. A back body drop afterwards gets Booker T a two-count before he runs into a Batista knee. After Hunter rocks him with a high knee, the "Animal" tags in to crush the babyface with a corner clothesline for a near fall.

Another clothesline drops Booker and brings Helmsley back into the ring. Unfortunately for him, the five-time champion quickly rolls into his corner to tag in Scott for a pounding assault. Steiner follows up with a twisting belly-to-belly suplex and more fists until Flair trips him. "Big Poppa Pump" chases after him, but when he returns to the squared circle, "the Game" is waiting to stomp him. He also distracts Nick Patrick for Batista to throat drop Scott on the top rope. Randy also gets in on the attack, wailing on Steiner at ringside while JR yells that he has to be recovered by now. Back in the squared circle, the champion tries to put "Big Poppa Pump" out with a sleeper hold, but Scott escapes with a back suplex and tags in Booker T. He proceeds to punch both heels, slugging the "Animal" down in a corner before side kicking both men. With the fans cheering him on, Booker stops to deliver a spinaroonie. He pays courtesy of a Batista clothesline. When Triple H sets up the five-time champion for a Pedigree, Steiner makes the save with clotheslines. He then takes care of the "Animal" as Booker T comes back to life to stun Hunter with a Scissors Kick for the victory.

Eric Bischoff (with Chief Morley) def. Jim Ross ("No Disqualification" match). Coach steps in on commentary for JR once again before Bischoff heads to the squared circle. He asks Morley to hold boards for him so he can give a martial arts demonstration, punching and kicking through the wood. The chief of staff is impressed. To really show what he can do, Eric asks Morley to hold a watermelon. The GM pretends that it's "Stone Cold" Steve Austin's head and smashes it. Although he asks for a cinderblock, JR has had enough and marches down the aisle for a fight. Before they do so, Bischoff says he has all the power and makes this a "No Disqualification" match. He wants Austin to watch as he kicks his best friend's butt tonight despite the "rattlesnake" saving his job. Eric then strikes a crane pose to mock Ross. Jim responds with a slap, knocking the GM down. That's all Morley can take and he attacks JR from behind, hammering him down while the fans chant for Austin. The chief then holds the cinderblock over Ross's head for Bischoff to stomp it. Lawler has seen enough and races down the aisle to save his bloodied friend, but Morley attacks "the King" from behind and whips him into the ring post. That leaves JR alone for Eric to taunt with karate poses before doubling him over with a strike to the gut for the three-count. Post-match, Bischoff drinks a Miller Lite over Ross's bloodied face and says that's the bottom line because "Eric Bischoff says so".

SmackDown!
February 20, 2003
Indianapolis, IN
Announcers: Michael Cole, Tazz

The show opens with The Rock heading to the ring in black leather. He gets a great pop. The "People's Champ" takes his time telling the fans that he has finally come back, but before he finishes the word "Indianapolis" he stops himself and says, "who gives a crap". That draws a Hulk Hogan chant. The "Great One" was going to go through his usual routine, but he's afraid the fans don't want to hear what he has to say. He doesn't understand why they want to boo him. While he claims that he's committed to the WWE, the "Brahma Bull" stops to take a phone call from his personal assistant and asks the fans to "keep it down". On the phone, he makes fun of Indiana before asking the fans if they really want to boo him. He gives them one last opportunity to think about it, but when they boo him again, The Rock wonders why again. Since they've made their decision, the "Great One" promises a new "Brahma Bull" this Sunday and curses Hogan. When the Hulkster shows up later tonight, the "People's Champ" promises to tell him what he's going to do at the PPV to his face. He tries to finish his promo by asking the fans if they smell what he's cooking, but when the fans join him, he stops. "Sing along with The Rock is over". He then says it by himself before Tazz shills the "Great One" on the cover of *WWE Magazine*.

Ahead of a commercial break, Brock Lesnar and Kurt Angle's tale of the tape is shown for their upcoming match tonight.

Chris Benoit def. A-Train. Benoit is out first and has to walk between two giant crates for The Undertaker tonight. The hairy heel then marches out to club and clothesline "the Crippler". He shows off his power with a muscle buster, scoring an early two-count and impressing the announcers. When he wastes time badmouthing Benoit, the "rabid wolverine" surprises him with a Crippler Crossface. Although the hairy heel fights up to his feet, Benoit German suplexes him ahead of a roll-up and out of nowhere victory.

After a commercial break, Funaki tries to get a word with The Rock but is stopped by his personal security guards.

Rikishi def. Johnny Stamboli. Although Chuck Palumbo and Nunzio accompany Stamboli down the ramp, Mike Sparks sends them back to the locker room while Rikishi clubs their man. "The Bull" answers with an impressive press slam for a near fall. A top rope flying leg drop also gets the heel a two-count before he hammers the big Samoan in a corner. That wakes up the big babyface and he responds with fists and a Samoan drop. Afterwards, a thrust kick gets Rikishi the win. Post-match, Palumbo and Nunzio return for the heels to hammer down the big babyface.

Backstage, Team Angle help Kurt Angle warm up for his match with Brock Lesnar tonight. The Olympian says he's going to lead by example. He's not waiting for WrestleMania XIX to break Lesnar's ankle.

In a prerecorded vignette, Los Guerreros "lie, cheat, and steal" in California. There, they confuse a woman pushing a stroller with Pamela Anderson. While they distract her, "Latino Heat" steals her watch and wallet. Chavo steals the "ugly baby's" bottle too.

Matt Hardy Version 1.0/Shannon Moore def. Billy Kidman/Rey Mysterio. This week's Matt Facts are that Matt is miserable when dieting and that he finds Moore hard to teach. Despite that, Shannon is right at Hardy's side as he weighs in earlier today, stripping down naked to make weight for his championship match this Sunday. Inside the ring, Moore starts fast with a spinning heel kick to Rey before the babyfaces double hip toss him. Billy then tags in to toss his partner onto Shannon with a leg drop. Matt tags in afterwards to surprise the champion with a side effect and two-count. Fists and kicks follow ahead of a back suplex and another near fall. Afterwards, Hardy slows the pace with a front face lock. When he goes for a Twist of Fate moments later, Kidman escapes and answers with a dropkick. Mysterio tags in afterwards to fight both heels, surprising Matt with a springboard cross body block. After head scissoring Moore out to the floor, the masked man rocks Hardy with a 619. Luckily, Shannon saves his mentor from the West Coast Pop. Matt capitalizes with a slingshot sit-out powerbomb for a near fall. He tries a second powerbomb, but Billy blind tags into the ring for a missile dropkick. While the referee is distracted trying to get Rey out of the ring, Moore makes another save with a top rope guillotine leg drop. Somehow, Kidman kicks out at the last second. Moments later, he back drops his partner into a hurricanrana off the top rope. The champion tries to follow up with a Shooting Star Press, but Shannon distracts him. After knocking Moore down to the floor, Billy back body drops Mysterio over the top rope onto him. Unfortunately, he turns around into a kick to the gut and Twist of Fate for Hardy to steal the win.

Recorded earlier this week, Michael Cole sits down with monstrous Nathan Jones. The ex-con says he's done his time and he's looking forward to competing in the WWE. Nathan wants to win the WWE Title, but before then he wants to face the "biggest dog in the yard". Jones goes crazy, grabbing Cole's head and screaming about "tick" and "tock" and the "time in between" in a nonsensical introduction.

After a commercial break, the two crates are lowered into the ring. Tazz says the head games will end this Sunday when Big Show has to step into the ring with The Undertaker. The biker then rides his motorcycle around the squared circle. Paul Heyman doesn't set up the segment tonight. Instead, the "Deadman" just gets to work opening the crates. Inside the first is a puppy that he gives to a stagehand. He then bursts into the second crate, but it's empty. Show is waiting outside the ring to blindside him. The giant proceeds to ram The Undertaker into a crate before Chokeslamming him ahead of their No Way Out match. During a commercial break, Big Show speeds out of the arena.

Nidia (with Jamie Noble) def. Torrie Wilson ("Paddle on a Pole" match). After Torrie spanked her last week, Nidia is looking for revenge. The two women trade strikes to open the match before Nidia flattens Wilson with a clothesline. When the heel lowers her head for a back body drop, Torrie answers with a boot to the face and neckbreaker. She follows up with a clothesline to Noble when he gets on the apron and snap suplex to Nidia. That brings out Dawn Marie to distract the referee while Jamie powerslams Wilson. Nidia then climbs the pole and gets the paddle for the win. Post-match, she paddles Torrie until Funaki runs out to chase her away and catapult Noble to the floor.

Backstage, Hulk Hogan tries to get into The Rock's locker room, but his security force keeps the Hulkster out. Hogan promises to head to the ring to publicly say what he's feeling. After a commercial break, he does just that to a huge pop. Before he says anything, the "People's Champ" marches out to stare eye-to-eye with the legend. After clearing his throat and taking a drink of water, the "Great One" clears the air. He knows there have been some rude things said and done and the "Brahma Bull" wants Hulk to apologize for calling him a "Rock-a-jabroni". The Rock then takes credit for Hogan's career resurgence, saying he took pity on him. The Hulkster refuses to apologize, crediting the fans with the revival of Hulkamania. The "People's Champ", shuffling around the ring to stay away from Hogan, reminds Hulk that he beat him at WrestleMania X8. When he tries to get the fans to say "and millions" with him, they don't. That makes the "Great One" mad and he ridicules Hulk's promos. The Hulkster has had enough and starts to rip off his shirt, but the "Brahma Bull" calms him down. He's just joking around to make the match interesting. He offers Hulk a handshake, wanting to electrify the fans this Sunday. When Hogan goes to accept it, The Rock spits in his face and retreats up the aisle.

Following a commercial break, the announcers preview No Way Out.

A video package plays for Brock Lesnar and Kurt Angle's feud ahead of their upcoming match.

Backstage, John Cena is in a wheelchair. He raps as he declares war on Brock Lesnar, an Eminem poster in the background. John tells Brock that they are in jail and Lesnar "dropped the soap".

Ahead of the main event, Kurt Angle asks Brock Lesnar if he really wants to wrestle him tonight. Before they lock up, Kurt tells the number one contender that he must go through a Team Angle gauntlet to get to the champion.

Brock Lesnar def. Charlie Haas (with Paul Heyman) (Gauntlet match). Charlie is in the ring first for Brock to toss him over to the canvas. Haas answers with a takedown and front face lock. It doesn't take Lesnar long to power out, but he runs into a corner back elbow and German suplex. Right back up, the "next big thing" clotheslines and knees the rookie. Following an overhead belly-to-belly suplex, Brock effortlessly delivers a backbreaker and presses Charlie up into an F5 for the three-count.

Brock Lesnar def. Shelton Benjamin (with Paul Heyman) (Gauntlet match). Like Haas, Brock tosses around Benjamin. He adds in a delayed vertical suplex before Shelton comes back to life with a superkick. More boots follow to the arm ahead of an armbar drop for a two-count. Kane tells Benjamin that Lesnar can't F5 him with one arm. Shelton tries to take it out with an extended armbar. Brock proves him wrong, picking up the rookie with one arm and slamming him to the mat. Angle is nervous as Lesnar clotheslines and belly-to-belly suplexes Benjamin. When Kurt tries to distract him, Brock sees Shelton coming and catches his foot for an Angle Slam and another three-count.

Brock Lesnar def. Kurt Angle (with Paul Heyman) (Gauntlet match) by disqualification. Reluctantly, Kurt takes off his medals and gets into the ring. While Brock stares him down, Heyman grabs a chair and hits his former client from behind for the disqualification. The Olympian follows up with a choke, but Lesnar fights free and tosses Angle from the squared circle. He then hoists up Paul for an F5, but the champion returns to clip the number one contender. Alongside Team Angle, the heels pound Brock down for Kurt to hook an Anklelock. That brings Chris Benoit and Edge out for the save to a big pop. The show ends with the two teams glaring at each other ahead of their six-man tag match this Sunday.

PPV: No Way Out
February 23, 2003
Montreal, Quebec, Canada
Announcers: Jonathan Coachman, Jerry "the King" Lawler, Michael Cole, Tazz, Jim Ross (briefly)

Following the opening fireworks, Coach steps in for Jim Ross who is suffering from a concussion after his match Monday night.

Chris Jericho def. Jeff Hardy. Neither man wants to make a mistake early on, trading arm wringers. That quickly devolves into fists and a Hardy back body drop. He follows up with a head scissors and more fists, ignoring Chad Patton's instructions. Jericho takes matters into his own hands with a clothesline and back suplex while the announcers talk about the blizzard outside. The action is hot inside the arena as Y2J chops Jeff before missing a corner splash. The daredevil follows up with a modified Asai moonsault outside the ring. Inside the squared circle, a slingshot moonsault follows for a two-count. Back on the floor, Hardy connects with a baseball slide kick, but misses his barricade dive. Jericho capitalizes with a slam on the ring steps before taking the fight back to the squared circle. Once in control, Y2J stomps and suplexes Jeff until the daredevil surprises him with a small package for a near fall. Right back up, Jericho dropkicks Hardy ahead of a reverse chin lock. Although he fights free, Y2J continues his assault until he misses a corner charge and hits his shoulder against the ring post. That lets Jeff catch a second wind to punch and clothesline the heel. A jawbreaker onto his knees afterwards gets the daredevil a two-count before Jericho answers with an enziguri kick for his own near fall. The Canadian crowd chants for Y2J, cheering him on as he drives Hardy face-first to the canvas. Unfortunately, Jeff counters his Lionsault with a pair of knees and DDT for a two-count. He also gets a near fall with a whisper in the wind. When he attempts his own enziguri kick, the heel ducks and locks on the Walls of Jericho. The daredevil reaches down deep and crawls to the ropes for the break. When Jericho tries to follow up with a top rope attack, Hardy races up to hip toss him to the mat. He capitalizes with a Swanton Bomb, but Y2J drapes his boot on the ropes at the last second to stay in the match. Jeff tries to follow up with fists, but Patton steps in between the two men for some reason. Jericho tries to capitalize with his submission finisher, but the daredevil rolls him up for another near fall. He surprises Y2J again, countering a springboard attack with a dropkick. Following a neckbreaker, Hardy goes back upstairs for a Swanton Bomb, but Jericho moves and hits a Lionsault for his own close two-count. Afterwards, Jeff slips free of Y2J's slam for a roll-up and near fall. The heel answers with a flashback and two-count with his feet on the ropes. When he heads upstairs, the daredevil hits the ropes to crotch him. He tries to follow up with a top rope hurricanrana, but Jericho counters with a powerbomb. The Walls of Jericho follow for Y2J to finally score the tap-out victory. Post-match, Jericho refuses to break the hold until Shawn Michaels runs out to attack the heel. He's followed by Christian, the Canadians peppering Shawn with fists until he double DDTs them. Afterwards, a clothesline sends Y2J to the floor ahead of Sweet Chin Music to Christian. The Montreal crowd is very mixed in their reaction to Michaels.

Backstage, Kurt Angle tells Team Angle that Canadians have no Olympic heroes worth mentioning. He doesn't want his WWE Tag Team Champions to listen to the fans tonight when they say that they suck. Kurt refuses to lose in their first match together and has a plan.

Further backstage, Evolution arrives in a limo. The announcers are more interested by "Stone Cold" Steve Austin's truck in the background.

Lance Storm/William Regal def. Kane/Rob Van Dam (World Tag Title match). RVD and Storm cut a fast pace to open the match. It's the popular superstar getting the upper hand and driving Lance back into his corner. Regal then tags in to try to slow the pace, but Van Dam catches him with a kick and split legged moonsault for a near fall. Kane tags in to slam William for an awkward two-count. The Englishman looks to be in trouble and quickly tags out, the announcers noting that he's dazed. That leaves Storm to take the beating for the champions. The "Big Red Machine" punches and slams Lance while we get a replay of the monster slamming Regal on the back of his head. When Storm retreats to the floor, RVD tags in for a somersault plancha. A slingshot leg drop follows for a near fall before William tags back in to catch a kick to the chest. When Rob tries to follow up, Lance shoves him off the top rope and into the barricade. After Storm shoves Van Dam back into the ring, the Englishman back suplexes him onto his head for a near fall before Kane makes the save. The Canadian then tags in to pummel RVD, scoring another two-count with a leg lariat. Regal returns and scores a trio of near falls immediately. When Rob answers with a sunset flip, Lance tags in for a kick to the back of the head. A DDT follows for a two-count. Soon after, Storm slows the pace with a reverse chin lock. When he pulls Van Dam up for a suplex, the popular superstar flips free for a roll-up and near fall. William tags in afterwards to try to keep RVD from tagging out. While it initially works, the "Big Red Machine" eventually gets the tag to flying clothesline the Englishman. After fighting both men, he gets a near fall with a sidewalk slam to Regal. When he sets up William for a Chokeslam, Storm jumps on the monster's back and spins his mask around. That blinds him enough that he Chokeslams his own partner when Lance shoves Van Dam into him for the Englishman to steal the win.

Backstage, Josh Mathews asks Matt Hardy about making weight for his Cruiserweight Title match. Hardy says that he lost the weight because he has Mattitude and it's a state of mind that makes anything possible. In fact, it could even help his brother become a winner instead of losing every match he's in. Jeff Hardy responds with a slap to the face before Shannon Moore holds Matt back.

MUST SEE! Matt Hardy Version 1.0 (with Shannon Moore) def. Billy Kidman (Cruiserweight Title match). The champion is out first, followed by Hardy with his Matt Facts saying that he's annoyed by snow and ice. He also takes hot tea with milk and sweetener. Tazz and Cole take over on commentary for a run of *SmackDown!* matches. They watch as Matt dropkicks Billy and does jumping jacks. Hardy follows up with a scoop slam before flexing. Kidman answers with arm drags and a head scissors. The two men then reverse hip tosses until the challenger flings Billy onto the apron and rams him into the ring post. He follows up with elbows on the apron for a two-count. A leg drop also gets him a near fall. Controlling the match, a falling fist and neckbreaker score another pair of two-counts. Changing tactics, Matt applies a crisscross choke. When he goes for a side effect, the champion rolls him up for a two-count. Hardy slows him with an eye rake and scores his own near fall with a modified neckbreaker. He then stretches Billy and leg drops him on the middle rope for a two-count with his feet on the ropes. Following a front face lock, the challenger gets another near fall with a ricochet slam. Kidman answers with an enziguri kick. Catching a second wind, he clotheslines Hardy ahead of a sit-out spinebuster and two-count. Matt is quickly back up with a clothesline and second rope leg drop for a near fall. When he sets up for the Twist of Fate, the champion shoves him off into a dropkick out to the floor. Billy follows with a slingshot splash. The two men then trade counters until Moore hops onto the apron to distract Kidman. Hardy shoves the champion into his own cornerman for a side effect and near fall. When he attempts a back suplex, Billy flips free and runs into Shannon, running up him to bulldog the challenger. Unfortunately, he misses his Shooting Star Press. Matt capitalizes with a Twist of Fate, but somehow, Kidman kicks out at the last second. Hardy tries to follow up with an attack off the top rope, but the champion shoves him down to the canvas. Before he can follow up, Moore grabs Billy's foot. Matt takes advantage again, this time hitting a Twist of Fate off the middle rope for the victory.

Backstage, WWE officials, trainers, and Chris Benoit check on Edge laying on the ground. He's not moving. Stephanie McMahon wants to know what happened, but Benoit just walked by.

Ahead of the next match, a video package plays for the Big Show/Undertaker feud.

The Undertaker def. Big Show (with Paul Heyman). After he rides his bike around the squared circle, The Undertaker gets to work punching Show at ringside. The giant answers with a slam into the ring post and toss into the barricade. When he tries to enter the squared circle, the biker dropkicks Big Show. Apron elbows and a leg drop follow. Incensed, the "Deadman" grabs a chair and shoves Brian Hebner out of the way to try to use it. Instead, Show punches it back into his face before choking his rival. The biker quickly recovers to punch and kick the giant. He tries to scoop slam his opponent, but can't hold up Big Show's weight and falls back to the canvas for a giant two-count. Back in control, Show clubs and suplexes The Undertaker for a two-count. A string of elbow drops follow as Cole announces that Edge has been taken to a "local medical facility". With the fans booing, Big Show finally covers the biker for a two-count. When that doesn't score him the win, the giant applies a bearhug. It takes a few shots, but the "Deadman" eventually punches his way free only to run into a sidewalk slam and near fall. After tossing The Undertaker out to the floor for no reason, Show waits for him to return to bust open both men with headbutts. The biker tells him to bring it on, absorbing his fists and headbutts before fighting back with his own shots and corner splashes. He brings the crowd back to life when he motions for a chokeslam, but he can't lift the giant. He can knock him down though, scoring a two-count with a leaping clothesline. The "Deadman" follows up with Old School before the two men trade throat grabs. Hebner gets in the way and shoved aside for an Undertaker low blow and DDT. After that gets him a two-count, the biker tries to give Big Show a Last Ride, but the giant shoves him off for a spinebuster and near fall. Snake eyes and a clothesline follow from Show for another two-count. When he tries to follow up, the "Deadman" slips free of his grasp and locks on his Taking Care of Business dragon sleeper. Heyman has seen enough and hops onto the apron to distract The Undertaker. A-Train also runs out only to see the biker knock him down and fly over the top rope onto him. With the fans cheering loudly, the "Deadman" runs his thumb across his throat only to see Big Show Chokeslam him. He goes for the cover, but The Undertaker surprises the giant with a Triangle Choke to knock him out for the victory. Post-match, the "Deadman" grabs a chair, but A-Train stops him from using it with a Derailer. The hairy heel tells him that this is A-Train's yard before helping Show backstage.

Backstage, Stephanie McMahon accompanies Edge on a stretcher to an ambulance. She tells Brock Lesnar and Chris Benoit that they made their decision and need to worry about their match next.

Further backstage, Eric Bischoff and Chief Morley debate what kind of match the *Raw* general manager should have with "Stone Cold" Steve Austin. Bischoff says they have the power to make whatever match they want. Vince McMahon interrupts to tell Eric that he was so impressed by his martial arts display Monday night that he wants to see Austin face the GM one-on-one tonight. And if anyone interferes, McMahon promises to fire them immediately. The heels are stunned.

Brock Lesnar/Chris Benoit def. Kurt Angle/Team Angle (with Paul Heyman). Tony Chimel announces that this is now a handicap match as Team Angle comes out, the fans chanting that they suck. Cole reveals that the babyfaces had the option of picking a new partner, but they told Stephanie that they didn't want the help. Inside the ring, Benoit opens the match shoulder blocking and tossing around Shelton.

Haas soon tags in for a few shots before he runs into a back body drop and forearm to the chest. Brock then tags in to crush Charlie in a neutral corner and suplex him. He doesn't want Haas, tossing him into the heel corner. Lesnar dares Angle to tag in, but he won't. Instead, Brock press slams both members of Team Angle and resumes his assault on Charlie. When Haas reverses an Irish whip, Kurt knees and chokes the "next big thing". With Mike Chioda distracted holding back "the Crippler" from interfering, Benjamin superkicks Brock. The Olympian then tags in to trap his WrestleMania XIX opponent in a rear naked choke and body hooks. Lesnar tries to escape with a ram into the corner, but Angle won't let go. After a minute in the hold, Brock rams the champion into a neutral corner again, this time breaking the choke. Afterwards, both men tag out for Benoit to fight all three heels and German suplex Kurt. Shelton gets a trio of German suplexes before the "rabid wolverine" heads upstairs. Although it gets him kicked down to the floor, Haas holds Benoit's foot long enough for the Olympian to recover and belly-to-belly suplex "the Crippler" off the top rope. Afterwards, Lesnar grabs Angle from behind on the apron, but Benjamin makes the save with a flying forearm, knocking the "next big thing" out onto the ramp. Charlie then works over Benoit in the ring with a belly-to-belly suplex for a two-count. The champion is happy tag back in to stomp the downed "rabid wolverine". Team Angle also get in a few shots before the champion hooks a front face lock. Benoit won't stay down, rolling up Kurt three times for near falls until the Olympian plants him with a German suplex for his own two-count. Haas tags in afterwards to cheap shot Brock and draw him into the ring to distract the referee for a Team Angle leapfrog splash to the Canadian. That nearly gets Shelton the win, but "the Crippler" grabs the ropes to break the cover. Benjamin then hangs onto Benoit's leg, refusing to let him tag in a sweat-covered Brock. He can't stop the "rabid wolverine" for long and the "next big thing" explodes into the ring, clotheslining and suplexing Team Angle before setting up Angle for an F5. Although Shelton saves him with a dropkick, the champion falls out to the floor. Brock and Benjamin follow before Benoit German suplexes Charlie. He tries to German suplex Kurt when he returns, but the Olympian escapes to kick off an exchange of submission finishers between the rivals. Luckily, Team Angle makes the save. That sees Haas trapped in the Crippler Crossface too. When Shelton tries to break the hold, Lesnar knocks him from the ring. He then blocks an Angle attack with the WWE Title to F5 the champion. At the same time, Charlie taps out for the babyfaces to overcome the odds and score the victory.

A video package plays for the Scott Steiner/Triple H World Title match.

Triple H (with Ric Flair) def. Scott Steiner (World Title match). Triple H is sporting a bandage on his left leg, but Jerry says even at eighty percent he can beat most men. Scott isn't impressed, going nose-to-nose with Hunter. Lawler jokes that he'll lose that battle. "Big Poppa Pump" gets the early upper hand. Helmsley tries to fight back, but a knee to his injured thigh sends "the Game" retreating to a corner. Like the Royal Rumble crowd, the fans boo when Steiner is in control. They have a lot to boo as he clubs and elbow drops the champion. Instead of going for the cover, the challenger does pushups. He then pulls down Triple H's bandage to target his injured thigh with stomps and elbow drops. He also bends the leg back until Hunter punches free. He can't keep Scott down as the challenger kicks, back suplexes, and traps Helmsley in a figure four leg lock while the fans chant "Steiner sucks". Flair even gets a pop when he rakes Scott's eyes. That sends Steiner out to the floor to deck "The Nature Boy". "The Game" capitalizes with another punch, knocking the challenger face-first onto the ring steps. While the champion distracts the referee and the fans chant that Earl Hebner screwed Bret Hart, Ric chokes the challenger with his jacket. Following a whip into the ring steps, Triple H gets a near fall with a neckbreaker. Another neckbreaker moments later gets Hunter a two-count. He follows up with shoulder blocks in a corner and fists until he runs into an overhead belly-to-belly suplex. Unfortunately, "Big Poppa Pump" soon runs into a corner boot. When Hebner catches Helmsley's feet on the ropes during his cover, he thinks about disqualifying "the Game". Instead, he tells him that he's not going to let him out of this match. The champion gets a nice pop when he shoves Earl down. However, that gives Scott time to recover and deliver a twisting belly-to-belly suplex. With the fans chanting "boring", Steiner tosses Triple H out to the floor and continues hammering him. Following his own ram into the ring steps, the challenger takes the fight back into the squared circle for more fists and a belly-to-belly suplex. That gets him another near fall and boos. He follows up with a Samoan drop off the second rope, but Flair slides into the ring to pull his boot for the break when he goes for the cover. Moments later, Ric calls for help when Scott locks on the Steiner Recliner. Steiner greets Randy Orton with a fist and Batista with a clothesline and whip into the ring steps. He also decks Ric before escaping a Pedigree to drive Hunter from the ring. Still not done, he tosses Orton up and over the top rope onto the "Animal". Hebner has had enough and ejects all three members of Evolution. While he does so, Helmsley decks "Big Poppa Pump" with the World Title for an extremely close two-count. "The Game" immediately follows up with a Pedigree for the win. Post-match, Randy helps the champion backstage.

Backstage, *Raw* superstars, including Test prominently, mockingly wish Eric Bischoff luck in his match. A video package then plays for the events leading to Bischoff facing "Stone Cold" Steve Austin" tonight.

"Stone Cold" Steve Austin def. Eric Bischoff. Jim Ross joins the announce table to watch Bischoff get his butt kicked like Eric kicked JR's Monday night. The GM follows. He grabs a microphone and says there's still time for everyone to send Vince McMahon a message and call off this match. Eric is even willing to forfeit the match, but the glass breaks and Austin marches out to a massive pop. He paces the ring in his jean shorts while Bischoff pleads for him to let bygones be bygones. Instead, "Stone Cold" tackles the man that fired him from WCW and stomps a mudhole in him. The *Raw* wrestlers love it backstage. Eventually, Eric rakes his eyes and kicks the "rattlesnake". It has no effect and Austin chases him out to ringside to punch him and toss a drink in his face. Back in the squared circle, "Stone Cold" checks his imaginary watch ahead of a boot to the gut and Stone Cold Stunner. JR loves it. When the "rattlesnake" makes the cover, he picks up Bischoff's hand twice to break Jack Doan's count. He does so again after a second Stunner. Finally, he accepts the three-count after a third Stone Cold Stunner. JR goes wild as the fans cheer Austin's victory ahead of a post-match Stunner.

A video package plays for the main event.

The Rock def. Hulk Hogan. The Rock debuts new music and a new entrance video complete with a shot of a helicopter flying over a cityscape before he slowly walks to the ring to boos. Hulk comes out to a huge pop for this WrestleMania X8 rematch. After running from the Hulkster, the "People's Champ" tries to sneak attack him when his back is turned. Fortunately, Hogan sees him coming and chases off the "Great One". He takes his time returning to the ring, working Sylvan Grenier's count, making his debut in this series. This is a huge spot for a new official. He's got a front row seat as the "Brahma Bull" punches Hulk. The Hulkster quickly returns his blows, ramming The Rock's head into the top turnbuckle ten times before driving the "People's Champ" back out to the floor. This time, the "Great One" throat drops him on the top rope. He then delivers an early Rock Bottom for a near fall. The "Brahma Bull" mocks Hogan afterwards, putting on his bandana and whipping the icon with his weight belt. While the announcers talk about The Rock's new shoulder tattoo and short haircut, the "People's Champ" takes a water break. He pays when Hulk comes back to life and takes away the belt for his own shots. Fists follow until the Hulkster misses a clothesline. The "Great One" capitalizes with a DDT followed soon after by a sharpshooter. It doesn't take Hogan long to reach the ropes, but the "Brahma Bull" drags him back to the center of the ring to knock out the babyface. When Grenier checks his arm, Hulk powers back to life on the third drop, flinging The Rock out to the floor. The "People's Champ" remains in control, clotheslining the Hulkster at ringside before grabbing a chair. Luckily, Hogan ducks his shot and takes the chair away for his own blow to the back. When he tries to use the chair back in the squared circle, Sylvan grabs it and misses a "Great One" low blow. He follows up with a spinebuster and People's Elbow. A second one scores him a two-count before Hogan hulks up. Absorbing three fists, the Hulkster wags his finger and lands his own trio of fists ahead of a big boot. The Leg Drop follows, but when the referee counts two, the lights go out. When they come back on, Sylvan is out cold. Vince McMahon comes out wondering what happened to boos. He gets a loud, "you screwed Bret" chant while Hulk accuses him of turning out the lights. Vince confesses he did it while the referee slides The Rock the chair to blast Hogan. Grenier then lays back down until the "People's Champ" Rock Bottoms a bloodied Hulkster. Once he's down, Sylvan hops up to count three for the "Brahma Bull" to score the victory. Post-match, the three heels celebrate another "Montreal Screwjob". After he sends the "Great One" and referee backstage, McMahon returns to the ring to pie face Hulk. He also shows off his Hulkamania shirt that says it's "nothing" and "sucks". Vince poses over the Hulkster, ripping off his shirt and throwing it into his face to end the PPV standing tall.

No Way Out is a step back for the WWE while preparing the roster for WrestleMania XIX. On the plus side, it does build up several matches for the next PPV, but it's always tough to pay for a show that is focused on the next one. That trend starts in the opener when Jericho beats Jeff Hardy in a very good thirteen minute match. It doesn't feel important and ends up bringing Shawn Michaels out to set up his WrestleMania match with Y2J. A brief appearance from Shawn might be the best thing considering Montreal's unique history with the "Heartbreak Kid". The World Tag Title match follows, and the focus continues to be on Kane's mask as the heels use it to blind and defeat the babyfaces. This is nothing more than a *Raw* match with very little build. Matt Hardy winning the Cruiserweight Title feels like a bigger deal as *SmackDown!* has spotlighted him a lot of late. His attitude and Matt Facts are entertaining, as well as his quest to get his weight down for the match. He definitely brings some star power to the division. Big Show and The Undertaker go way too long at fourteen minutes, but this is the biker's revenge tour and he gets it before A-Train interferes and sets up another WrestleMania match. The six-man tag match is converted into a handicap match when Edge's injuries catch up to him and he requires neck surgery. Sadly, that will keep him out of action for over a year. It also takes away some of the fun of this match that again appears like nothing more than a weekly contest. It does serve as a good preview for WrestleMania when Kurt will face Lesnar. While the handicap match is entertaining, the fans continue to hate Scott Steiner's PPV efforts. He doesn't botch anything here, but it's a slow paced punch and belly-to-belly suplex match. Triple H being slowed doesn't help, but it's a terrible thirteen minutes. After two tainted finishes, it's worth wondering if the original plan was to have Scott challenge Hunter at WrestleMania XIX and possibly win the World Title. If so, that falls apart due to fan reaction. Austin's return is the shortest match of the night and it has the fans going crazy for five minutes as he destroys Bischoff. Not even a match, it's just "Stone Cold" destroying Eric to make the fans happy and set up some contentious weeks on *Raw*. With such a lackluster set of matches, it's no surprise that the Hogan/Rock rematch scores the main event. Sadly, it can't live up to the legacy of their WrestleMania X8 match. It also serves to set up Vince McMahon and Hulk's WrestleMania XIX match as well as solidify The Rock's heel turn. Overall, No Way Out isn't a great show. Other than Matt Hardy's title win and Vince screwing Hogan, there's nothing of note that happens. The show lives off of veterans this month rather than spotlighting future stars like recent PPVs. With Undertaker, Hogan, Rock, and Austin all getting big matches, the young stars are pushed down the card. After pushing so hard for young stars in 2002, it's odd to see the old guard elevated back out of nowhere, most of the big names making their return to PPV here after months away. No Way Out is a misstep for the WWE as the show is more focused on building up next month's show and living off legacy than pushing the next generation.

Monday Night Raw

February 24, 2003
Toronto, Ontario, Canada
Announcers: Jim Ross, Jerry "the King" Lawler, Steven Richards (briefly), Victoria (briefly)

Following the intro video and fireworks, Eric Bischoff limps out with his arm in a sling. JR doesn't feel bad for him. His face swollen and with a black eye, Eric says "Stone Cold" Steve Austin didn't get the job done last night and he's banned from the arena. Next week, Bischoff promises to have a welcoming committee for the "rattlesnake". Austin being banned is a big deal because he won't be a participant in tonight's number one contender's battle royal for a World Title shot at WrestleMania XIX. Not done with big announcements, the general manager welcomes out The Rock. The announcers are confused what a *SmackDown!* star is doing here. He takes his time entering the ring and addressing the crowd, telling him he's "finally come back to Toron...his mouth on all the candy asses". He then brags about beating Hulk Hogan last night for Vince McMahon. Since he did a favor for Vince, the WWE owner told the "People's Champ" that he could go and do whatever he wanted. That sent him to Toronto. When the fans cheer Toronto, the "Great One" hilariously mocks them for cheering the name of their city. The "Brahma Bull" then says this is where everything started when the fans turned on The Rock at WrestleMania X8. When the fans cheer for Hogan, the "People's Champ" reminds them that he's on *SmackDown!* and this is *Raw*. He stops to make fun of a "fatty" in the crowd before complaining about not winning the Superstar of the Decade award. The fans chant for that winner, "Stone Cold". The "Great One" calls Steve "nothing compared to him" and proceeds to say he's "bigger than a bear, stronger than a buck, and the biggest thing to hit Toronto because the Maple Leafs suck". That really sets off the hockey loving crowd and they tell him he sold out. He then enters tonight's battle royal before asking if the fans smell what he's cooking. When they try to chant alongside him, he tells them they were the first to boo him and first to lose "singalong with The Rock" privileges. Now, he tells them to know their role and "shove their boos up their maple syrup sucking asses". JR can't believe his new attitude.

Jazz def. Jacqueline. Steven Richards and Victoria join the announce table to watch this action. Jerry wishes they'd watch backstage. Jazz is out last to punch and slam Jacqueline. The babyface answers with a head scissors and dropkick to send the fight out to the floor. There, Jacqueline slams the heel on the apron and chops her. Back in the ring, Jazz explodes out of a corner with a clothesline ahead of a leg drop for a two-count. She tries to follow up with a powerbomb, but drops Jacqueline on her face. Luckily, the babyface is able to continue. Unfortunately, she gets trapped in a single leg crab and has to crawl all the way across the ring to reach the ropes. When she nearly grabs them, Jazz pulls Jacqueline back and locks on an STF for the tap-out victory. Post-match, Jazz brags until Trish Stratus comes out for a nice hometown pop. She goes right after the heel, punching her until Victoria races down the aisle to get kicked too. WWE officials then struggle to separate Jazz and Trish.

After a commercial break in prerecorded footage, Test finds out that GGW stands for "Girls Gone Wild". He joins Joe Francis on a bus with girls going wild. Joe has the bodyguard pick a finalist for Miss Girls Gone Wild. Afterwards, Test and Maven watch a monitor backstage, Maven telling the bodyguard that he's the luckiest guy in the world that Stacy Keibler set him up with the job. However, Test says Stacy isn't too happy now that she knows what GGW means before she enters to continue their argument. Chief Morley interrupts to tell the couple that they have bigger things to worry about after they laughed at Eric Bischoff last night. Tonight, they'll face the piper when they team up to meet Chris Jericho and

Christian. Keibler apologizes, but Morley says it's out of his hands. Test promises Stacy that nothing will happen to her.

Goldust getting electrocuted replays. In a prerecorded interview, JR then sits down with the "bizarre one". Goldust says he lived through the experience and Booker T has supported him through thick and thin. He has a twitch as he speaks and stutters, concerning Jim. The "bizarre one's" doctors believe that so long as he takes his medicine the problem will correct itself. He then gets serious to warn Batista and Randy Orton that they will never forget his name.

The *Cradle 2 the Grave* Slam of the Week is Kane Chokeslamming Rob Van Dam accidentally.

Kane (with Rob Van Dam) def. Lance Storm (with William Regal). Lance gets a nice pop from the Canadian fans before Kane clubs and slams him. Regal is in a suit tonight. He's suffering from a concussion and won't be in the number one contender's battle royal. Storm might not either after the "Big Red Machine" big boots and elbow drops him. Eventually, the heel turns the tide with a corner boot and top rope dropkick for a near fall. He follows up with a dropkick to the sitting monster's face and hammering blows before targeting Kane's mask. The "Big Red Machine" quickly fights him off with two Chokeslams for the victory. Post-match, RVD applauds his partner before they slap hands.

Backstage, Randy Orton and Batista don't think "Stone Cold" Steve Austin coming back next week is a big deal. Orton says the bigger deal is that he's ninety-nine percent and ready to step back into the ring tonight. Ric Flair tells them that Triple H won last night and they need to keep the streak alive.

The Lugz Boot of the Week is Booker T and Scott Steiner beating Batista and Triple H.

Booker T/Scott Steiner def. Batista/Randy Orton (with Ric Flair). Booker opens the match welcoming Orton back to the ring with chops and kicks for an early two-count. More strikes and a heel kick have the returning superstar seeing stars until Flair trips the five-time champion. That sends Scott after him, distracting Nick Patrick for Batista to give Booker T a spinebuster. He then tags in for hammering blows and a corner clothesline for a two-count. After ramming the babyface back into the heel corner, the "Animal" tags back in Randy for a powerslam and near fall. Booker answers with more chops and his own spinebuster. When Batista illegally enters the ring, the five-time champion rocks him with a spinning heel kick. That brings Ric up onto the apron to distract Patrick again while Evolution double-team Booker T. The "Animal" follows up with a bearhug. Soon after, Orton returns for a chin lock. It takes him a while to escape, but eventually the babyface does so and Scissors Kicks the big heel. Once again, "The Nature Boy" distracts the referee for his men to double-team Booker and stop him from making the tag. Scott has had enough and enters the ring to club, suplex, and press slam the heels to boos. JR says it's because he's got an American flag on his tights. When he traps Flair in a Steiner Recliner, Batista rushes to his mentor's aid, clubbing "Big Poppa Pump" while Randy goes upstairs for a Flying Cross Body Block to Booker T. When they hit the mat, the five-time champion rolls through for the three-count.

Clips of The Rock's earlier promo and a teaser for "Stone Cold" Steve Austin's return next week play.

Stacy Keibler/Test def. Chris Jericho/Christian by disqualification. JR reminds everyone about Y2J hitting Stacy with a chair a few weeks ago as the heels head to the squared circle. The babyfaces follow, Keibler getting a nice pop for her Maple Leafs outfit. Test doesn't wait for the bell, racing into the ring to chase off Jericho and tilt-a-whirl slam Christian. While he hammers Christian, Y2J pulls Stacy off the apron, having her fall face first to the canvas. The bodyguard is incensed and chases after Jericho. Unfortunately, he runs into Christian cheap shots. Test won't stay down, recovering to punch the heel again until Y2J grabs a chair and hits him for the disqualification. Post-match, Christian drops the bodyguard with an Unprettier before the heels handcuff him to the middle rope. That leaves Keibler alone for Y2J to trap her in the Walls of Jericho. While she cries, Jeff Hardy runs out only to be dropped by Christian with an Unprettier. The Canadian crowd chants for Shawn Michaels afterwards and he responds, running out to give Christian Sweet Chin Music and chase off Jericho.

Christopher Nowinski def. Jeff Hardy by disqualification. Following a shot of the Toronto Raptor's Vince Carter in the crowd, Nowinski comes out to mock Jeff. Unfortunately, his microphone isn't working. When he finally gets it to work, the Harvard heel calls Hardy a failure. Jeff responds with a twist of fate and Swanton Bomb for the three-count. Post-match, Hardy continues pummeling Nowinski so much that Jack Doan reverses his decision and gives the Harvard heel the victory by disqualification.

After a commercial break, Kane says he can't stand The Rock. He tells Rob Van Dam that the monster is going to eliminate the "People's Champ" from tonight's battle royal and go on to WrestleMania XIX. RVD is fine with eliminating the "Great One", but he says he's going to be the one facing Triple H for the World Title.

Further backstage, The Rock doesn't care if "Stone Cold" Steve Austin likes what he said earlier. He promises someone on the phone that he will take care of Austin if he has an issue with what he said before strumming a guitar. The heel is interrupted by The Hurricane telling him that he used to be a hero. The "People's Champ" wants to know who "in the green Hell he is". With the "H" on his chest, the "Brahma Bull" calls him the Hamburglar. Despite what he says, The Rock knows exactly who he is and says any superhero including Aquaman can beat him. The Hurricane knows one superhero he can beat…the Scorpion King. He then asks if the Scorpion King can fly because he's going to toss him over the ropes tonight in the battle royal. When the superhero flies off, the "Great One" hilariously looks up to watch him offscreen.

Jerry "the King" Lawler def. Chief Morley ("No Disqualification" match). JR calls the action solo, wondering what Morley and Eric Bischoff have in store for "the King" in this "No Disqualification" match. Early on, it's just the chief punching and kicking Jerry. Lawler likes that kind of match, answering with his own fists to take the fight out to the floor. There, Morley whips "the King" into the barricade before Jerry flings him into the ring steps. Soon after, the chief reverses a whip into the ring post. A slam into the steel follows before the action returns back into the ring for a string of heel suplexes and a near fall. Chops and fists wake up Lawler, but he runs into a spinebuster while the fans boo. Morley follows up with a Money Shot, but doesn't go for the cover. After arguing with Earl Hebner, the chief grabs a chair from ringside. When he slides it into the squared circle, Hebner kicks it back out to the floor. Morley can't believe it, yelling at the referee while The Dudley Boyz sneak into the ring to give the chief a 3D. "The King" follows up with a second rope flying fist drop for the three-count.

After a commercial break and "Stone Cold" Steve Austin teaser, Ric Flair tells Batista and Randy Orton that Triple H wants them to eliminate everyone in the upcoming number one contender's battle royal. After their earlier match, Orton wants Booker T.

Further backstage, The Rock walks the hall for the upcoming battle royal.

Booker T wins a twenty-man #1 Contender's battle royal.

Elimination Order	Wrestler	Eliminated By
1	Test	Chris Jericho
2	Chris Jericho	Chris Jericho
3	Jamal	Rob Van Dam
4	Tommy Dreamer	The Rock
5	Maven	The Rock
6	Steven Richards	Scott Steiner
7	Rob Van Dam	Batista/Randy Orton
8	Al Snow	Batista
9	Rodney Mack	The Hurricane
10	The Hurricane	The Rock
11	Jeff Hardy	Randy Orton
12	Randy Orton	Scott Steiner
13	Scott Steiner	Batista
14	Batista	Booker T
15	Rosey	Kane
16	Lance Storm	Kane
17	Christian	The Rock
18	Kane	The Rock
19	The Rock	Booker T
20	Booker T	Winner

Chris Jericho is out first, kicking off a string of individual introductions. Many of the competitors are introduced during a commercial break, The Rock's introduction being broadcast last. Test is the first man out, Jericho throwing him out in just seconds. When the bodyguard returns to the ring to chase him, Y2J eliminates himself and runs through the crowd to escape. Jamal follows soon after, The Rock tossing him out to the apron for RVD to knock him out to the floor with a top rope flying kick. Fists fly from everyone else, Jeff Hardy nearly being shoved over by Rosey while JR tells everyone that Owen Hart won the last *Raw* battle royal in 1995. Moments later, Lance Storm is nearly eliminated. Tommy Dreamer is eliminated thanks to fists from the "People's Champ". Seconds later, he clotheslines Maven out too. When Van Dam and Kane get close to each other, the "Big Red Machine" decks him. He continues attacking friends, punching The Hurricane in a corner. Not long afterwards, Scott Steiner flings Steven Richards over the top rope and out to the floor. Orton and Batista prove how dangerous a team can be, working together to eliminate RVD. Booker T rushes over immediately afterwards to sucker punch the "Animal". Batista doesn't stay down for long, knocking Al Snow out to the floor before The Hurricane flings Rodney Mack out of the ring. When The Rock attacks the superhero, he comes back to life with fists. The Hurricane teases a chokeslam, but the "Great One" answers with a low blow and toss out to the floor. The "Brahma Bull" also gets knocked out of the ring, but goes through the ropes courtesy of Booker. After slamming the five-time champion into the ring post, the "People's Champ" heads to the announce table to say he's too smart to stay in the squared circle. He promises to come back when the ring has cleared out. That happens in rapid succession with Orton tossing Hardy, Steiner eliminating Randy, Batista knocking out Scott, and Booker T tossing the "Animal" from the ring in one continuous flow of action. With just five men left in the ring, and The Rock talking at the announce table, Storm and Rosey team up on Kane. The Samoan squashes the monster in a corner while Lance goes to help try and eliminate Booker. While the Canadian's back is turned, the "Big Red Machine" clotheslines Rosey out. He tosses Storm out moments later before Chokeslamming Booker T. The "People's Champ" heads back to the squared circle while Kane big boots Christian. When he sets up for a Chokeslam, the Canadian heel counters with a sleeper hold. The "Great One" picks this spot to slide back into the ring and eliminate both men. That leaves the "Brahma Bull" alone with the downed five-time champion. Booker doesn't stay down for long, coming back to life with fists and chops, but a DDT puts him right back down for The Rock to taunt his five-time celebration. He tries to fling the babyface out to the floor afterwards, but Booker T reverses his whip and eliminates the "People's Champ" for a nice pop and spinaroonie. Sitting on the ramp, the "Great One" mockingly applauds Booker while JR hypes the five-time champion getting a shot at Triple H and the World Title at WrestleMania XIX.

SmackDown!
February 27, 2003
London, Ontario, Canada
Announcers: Michael Cole, Tazz

Following the intro video and fireworks, Vince McMahon heads to the ring with bad news. That's that The Rock will not be here tonight because he's earned the right to go wherever he wants, and he wants to be on *Raw*. Vince has good news too and that's that Hulk Hogan isn't here tonight with a "family emergency". McMahon says it has something to do with his son, but Vince says the real reason is that Hogan is a coward who is afraid of the WWE owner. McMahon brags about screwing over the Hulkster at No Way Out. He adds that Hulkamania is dead and he will show fans what he did to bury it at the PPV later tonight. Finally, Vince says it's time for "McMahonamania".

Funaki/Torrie Wilson def. Jamie Noble/Nidia. The men open the match, Funaki hip tossing and dropkicking Noble. Jamie answers with a spinning neckbreaker and stomps. Nidia tags in soon afterwards for a leg drop and double stomp before tagging back in her boyfriend. He slaps Funaki until the interviewer comes back to life pulling Nidia into the ring by the hair to catapult Noble into her. A bulldog follows for a two-count before both men connect with clotheslines. Jamie is closer to his corner and Nidia tags in for a top rope flying splash. Unfortunately, Funaki rolls out of the way and tags in Torrie to clothesline and toss the heel around by the hair. She also kicks and slaps Noble until he slams her down onto the back of her head. When he tries to follow up, Funaki answers with a baseball slide kick and flying slingshot splash out on the floor. Wilson then gets a two-count with a reverse leg sweep to Nidia. That brings out Dawn Marie for Torrie to whip Nidia into her ahead of a roll-up and three-count. Post-match, Stephanie McMahon steps onto the stage to tease a diva appearing in *Playboy*. After making seductive comments, Stephanie announces that Torrie will be in the magazine. Wilson is surprised and ecstatic, hugging Funaki while the fans cheer.

After a commercial break, Stephanie McMahon talks to Torrie Wilson about appearing in *Girls Gone Wild* and *Playboy*. Brian Kendrick interrupts Stephanie to tell her that he'd do anything to join the WWE. On top of streaking, he's willing to wrestle Kurt Angle for a contract. The general manager says if he can last five minutes with the WWE Champion, he'll be a *SmackDown!* superstar.

Eddie Guerrero (with Chavo Guerrero Jr.) def. Nunzio (with Chuck Palumbo/Johnny Stamboli). The heels are introduced as the Full Blooded Italians, or FBI. Once the match starts, Eddie starts fast with dropkicks and an arm drag off the top rope. Nunzio slows his attack with a whip into a corner buckle and stomps. "Latino Heat" can brawl too, coming back to life to wail on the Italian heel. Unfortunately, Los Guerreros are outnumbered and Palumbo trips Eddie for Nunzio to take back over. He capitalizes with more fists and a knee drop for a two-count after pulling down his knee pad. Guerrero answers with a tilt-a-whirl backbreaker. Catching a second wind, he punches and uppercuts the Italian heel. With the fans chanting his name, "Latino Heat" counters a victory roll with an electric chair drop. A waist lock suplex follows for a near fall. Although Nunzio moves out of the way of a Frog Splash, Eddie rolls to his feet to counter a roll-up for the victory. Post-match, the FBI attack until Rikishi runs out to even the odds and chase off the heels.

After a commercial break, Stephanie McMahon tells Paul Heyman that since Kurt Angle named his own stipulations last week in his Gauntlet match with Brock Lesnar, Stephanie is giving the "next big thing" the opportunity to do the same. If Brock beats Team Angle tonight in a handicap match, he'll get to face anyone he wants in a "Steel Cage" match next week. Paul doesn't think that's fair, noting that Lesnar will pick Kurt. Stephanie says life isn't fair.

Afterwards, the announcers talk about Edge's injury and him being out for a year.

Backstage, Chris Benoit tells Brock Lesnar that Kurt Angle will do anything to keep his WWE Title at WrestleMania XIX. He warns Brock that the heels took out Edge and they'll try to do the same to Lesnar. The "rabid wolverine" tells the "next big thing" that he needs to beat Team Angle tonight "by any means necessary" to eliminate a member of the team next week. Brock tells him to worry about himself. Benoit is counting on Team Angle targeting him, but "the Crippler" has friends.

A WrestleMania XIX teaser plays ahead of the announcers revealing that Limp Bizkit will be at the show.

Chris Benoit/Rhyno def. Matt Hardy Version 1.0/Shannon Moore. The heels are out first with the Matt Facts revealing that Hardy has a size 34 waist. He also thinks sweet potatoes are delicious. In a pre-match interview, Matt calls his Cruiserweight Title win a win for Mattitude before wishing Edge well. However, Hardy says if Edge was a MFer, he wouldn't have suffered such a "Twist of Fate". Back to real time, Rhyno races out to a nice pop after sixteen months on the sidelines. He goes right after Moore, spearing him in a corner before Benoit tags in to elbow the MFer. Fortunately, Matt saves his partner, tripping "the Crippler" from the floor. He then tags in to punch and side effect Benoit for a two-count. An elbow and leg drop follow before Shannon tags back in to club the "rabid wolverine". He also gets a two-count with a back suplex while the fans chant for Rhyno. Moore briefly quiets them with a chin lock before tagging in Hardy. When the heels attempt poetry in motion, Benoit dodges Shannon and German suplexes Matt. The man-beast tags in afterwards to back drop Moore and score a two-count with a spinebuster to Hardy. Shannon pays for breaking up the count courtesy of a Rhyno powerslam. "The Crippler" follows up with a top rope diving headbutt, but Matt knocks him from the ring. Unfortunately, he then turns into a Gore for the three-count.

Nathan Jones making strange comments about The Undertaker last week replay. After a commercial break, the "Deadman" rides his motorcycle to ringside. Instead of Jones, the biker calls out A-Train. He is joined by Paul Heyman to accuse The Undertaker of using an illegal choke hold to beat Big Show Sunday night. Paul also reveals that he's signed the hairy heel to a contract before Show marches out, still rubbing his neck. The heels surround the ring, but the biker manages to fight both men temporarily until the giant clotheslines and Chokeslams him. A-Train follows up with a corner bomb. Still not done, Big Show grabs a chair, but the "Colossus of Boggo Road" runs out for the save, chasing off the heels. The announcers wonder if he saved the "Deadman" or saved him for himself.

Backstage, John Cena raps about being a virus to Brock Lesnar as he looks at a computer. He promises to go on safari to hunt down the "next big thing".

Kurt Angle (with Paul Heyman) def. Brian Kendrick ("Five-Minute Challenge" match). Kendrick has to tell Tony Chimel where he's from and what he weighs for this challenge. If he lasts five minutes, he gets a contract. Kurt thinks this is a joke, laughing at the hopeful while the fans chant that the Olympian sucks. Angle gets down on all fours and offers to let Brian attack him. The champion ignores his blows and tackle, spinning around to slap Kendrick. Tazz says the hopeful should just survive. Considering Kurt is wasting time, that should be easy. A minute and a half in, the Olympian closes his eyes and dares Brian to attack him again. He does so with a kick to the jaw, but that sets off Angle. He answers with a belly-to-belly suplex and punch off the top rope out to the floor. The champion follows him out for a slam on the guardrail. Back in the ring, Kurt takes his time hooking an Anklelock, but he releases it immediately. A clothesline follows before he lowers his straps. Once again he plays with the hopeful, lifting him up for an Angle Slam, but dropping him to the canvas instead. With under a minute and a half left, Kendrick surprises the Olympian with a facebuster for a two-count and enziguri kick. He then dodges a corner charge to drop toe hold Angle. When he goes for a step up bulldog, the champion shoves him off and clotheslines the hopeful, just twenty seconds left on the clock. Brian responds with forearms until Kurt plants him with an Angle Slam for the win, two seconds left on the clock. Kendrick is nearly in tears as he realizes how close he came. Post-match, the Olympian tells Brian to stand up before realizing that the short superstar already is standing. He compliments Kendrick on a job well done and lifts his arm up as a show of respect before dedicating the upcoming beating to Brock Lesnar. That includes fists and a whip into the ring post. Still not done, he gives Brian an F5, stealing Lesnar's finisher.

After a commercial break, "Mr. McMahon's personally selected referee", Sylvan Grenier is introduced. He heads to the ring to boos before introducing the clip of Vince McMahon screwing over Hulk Hogan Sunday night. Following a lengthy replay of the finish of the match, Sylvan waves at the crowd. Afterwards, we see footage after No Way Out with the Hulkster warning Stephanie McMahon that he's going to beat up her father.

Backstage, Paul Heyman hypes up Team Angle. He says that together they are a strong unit and Brock Lesnar wants to rip them apart. Paul implores Shelton Benjamin and Charlie Haas not to let him and force their leader, Kurt Angle, into a "Steel Cage" match with the "next big thing" next week.

Brock Lesnar def. Team Angle (with Paul Heyman/Kurt Angle). Kurt smirks as he watches Brock walk down the aisle. Inside the ring, the babyface shoves Haas to the canvas. Charlie answers with fists and kicks. He can't overpower Lesnar though, and the "next big thing" fires back with knees and a toss to the canvas. A backbreaker and fallaway slam follow before Brock whips Haas into his corner to tag in Benjamin. Lesnar greets him with an overhead belly-to-belly suplex and more knees. When he tries to fight back, the "next big thing" rams him into a corner before running into a knee to the head. Charlie illegally enters the ring to clothesline the babyface out to the floor. While Mike Chioda admonishes him, Heyman stomps Brock. Back in the squared circle, Shelton punches the "next big thing" until Lesnar explodes out of a corner with a clothesline. Chops and a knee follow before Angle trips the number one contender. When Brock gives chase, Benjamin catches him with a baseball slide kick. Charlie then rams the babyface into the ring post ahead of a Heyman chair shot for a Shelton two-count. Soon after, Haas locks on a rear naked choke and hooks his legs around his opponent's waist. It doesn't take Lesnar long to power out and climb the ropes for a falling slam back to the canvas. That breaks the hold and has the Olympian worried. When Benjamin tags in, Brock clotheslines and shoulder blocks him. Belly-to-belly suplexes follow to both heels. When the "next big thing" knocks Kurt off the apron, Team Angle capitalize with a combination German suplex and superkick. They can't keep Lesnar down and he hoists up Charlie for an F5. Although Shelton saves him, he can't save himself and Brock scores the win with an F5. The announcers tell Angle that he's in trouble next week. Post-match, the "next big thing" slides Paul into the ring and sets him up for an F5. The champion makes the save with a chop block before yelling at his agent to get him out of the match next week. Lesnar interrupts them to say he's not mad. He's happy he just beat Team Angle and is set up for next week where he can pick any member of the squad for a "Steel Cage" match. Since he's got Angle at WrestleMania XIX, Brock picks Heyman as his opponent next week. Kurt can't help but smile while Paul is frozen in fear to end the show.

Monday Night Raw
March 3, 2003
Uniondale, NY
Announcers: Jim Ross, Jerry "the King" Lawler

The show opens in the parking lot with Eric Bischoff calling Three-Minute Warning and Rico his "first line of defense" for his "Stone Cold" Steve Austin welcoming committee. He wants them to "cave in his skull", but leave just a little bit for the general manager. Afterwards, the intro video plays and fireworks explode to kick off the episode.

Afterwards, Booker T comes out to talk about winning last week's battle royal and earning a "trip to WrestleMania". That brings out Triple H accompanied by Ric Flair. Hunter says the babyface is confused by his role because "someone like" Booker doesn't get to win at WrestleMania. "The Game" adds that the five-time champion isn't a wrestler—he's just an "entertainer". Helmsley wants him to dance for "the Game". The fans don't appreciate that, booing loudly as Triple H tells Booker to make him laugh with his "nappy hair and suckas". Hunter has been laughing all week thinking about facing Booker T. JR fails to see the humor. Helmsley then mocks Booker for being a WCW Champion, comparing him to other notable WCW Champions like David Arquette and Vince Russo. At WrestleMania XIX, "the Game" says that the five-time champion is going to do what "people like him always do" and lose. Booker T warns that he's going to "ragtag" Triple H and take his title. Hunter wishes him luck tonight in his match with Scott Steiner, wondering why Eric Bischoff would sign that match. With Steiner, Helmsley thinks the babyface will be lucky to even make it to WrestleMania.

Backstage, Three-Minute Warning hide for "Stone Cold" Steve Austin's arrival.

Christian def. Jeff Hardy. Jeff goes right after the heel, hammering him in a corner until Chad Patton steps in the way. That sees the daredevil take the fight out to the floor to kick Christian and catch him with a top rope flying tackle. After scoring a two-count back in the squared circle, Hardy strips off his shirt and heads upstairs. Unfortunately, the heel recovers and drops him on the ropes twice, the second earning him a near fall. A string of fists to the kidneys follow before Christian applies an abdominal stretch in the center of the ring. When Jeff tries to escape with a jawbreaker, the heel counters with a knee and reverse neckbreaker for another two-count. He can't keep the daredevil down for long though as Hardy fights back with fists and a mule kick. Just when he starts to build up momentum, Christian surprises him with a roll-up and handful of pants for a two-count. Jeff answers with a double leg drop and whisper in the wind for a near fall. He tries to deliver a reverse twist of fate, but Christian holds onto the ropes to block it. An Unprettier follows for the heel to earn the victory.

Backstage, Eric Bischoff tells Lance Storm that he and Chief Morley are going to be the second line of defense. The GM hands him a stick to give "Stone Cold" Steve Austin a warm welcome.

Chief Morley def. Spike Dudley. Pre-match, Morley says he can make his matches as interesting as he wants. To do so, he promises to reinstate The Dudley Boyz if Spike wins this match. However, if the Dudleys interfere, they will remain indefinitely suspended. That sends the runt running down the aisle to bite and kick the chief of staff. When he tries to score the quick victory with a Dudley Dog, Morley counters with a sit-out powerbomb. He gets too cocky with his cover though and nearly takes the loss when Dudley rolls him up. That wakes up the chief of staff and he hammers Spike ahead of a trio of suplexes, the third a slingshot off the top rope. The Money Shot follows for the victory.

Backstage, Christian tells Chris Jericho that he was on a roll earlier. Y2J promises the roll will continue tonight and he has a surprise for Test ahead of their match. Eric Bischoff interrupts to ask the heels to be his third line of defense tonight. Jericho says it would be a pleasure.

Jacqueline/Trish Stratus def. Jazz/Victoria (with Steven Richards). When the heels argue over who will start the match, Trish attacks from behind for the early advantage. Unfortunately, Victoria trips Jacqueline running the ropes for Jazz to dropkick her for a near fall. A big powerslam follows for a two-count before the "black widow" tags in only to accidentally kick her partner. She also kicks Jacqueline ahead of a spinning side slam and near fall. A snap suplex gets her a two-count before she runs shoulder-first into the middle turnbuckle. Stratus tags in afterwards for a Chick Kick and chops. A Thesz press and fists follow before the vixen knocks Jazz out of the ring onto Richards. While they argue, Jacqueline baseball slide kicks the heels. Trish tries to follow up with her handstand head scissors to the "black widow", but the champion shoves her off the ropes for a roll-up and two-count. Stratus answers with her own roll-up, stealing the win.

After a commercial break, Chief Morley says that he wants first crack at "Stone Cold" Steve Austin.

Further backstage, Jonathan Coachman knocks on The Rock's door. The "People's Champ" wants to know if he has an appointment. The "Great One" checks his "palm" pilot—his hand—to give Coach an appointment Wednesday. When Coachman doesn't like that time, The Rock tells him to take it and leave. As he goes, the "Brahma Bull" tells him to "wash your ass". He then looks for his guitar, but finds The Hurricane crouching in a locker like a gargoyle. The superhero wants to know "what's up with that" regarding the "People's Champ" having Eric Bischoff take care of "Stone Cold" Steve Austin. The "Great One" wants to know how long he's been in there looking at the "Brahma Bull" walking around naked. The Rock then reminds the "Hamburglar" about eliminating him last week. The Hurricane remembers Booker T throwing the "People's Champ" over the top rope. The "Great One" disagrees and argues with the fans. He calls the superhero "nothing" before taking a phone call from "Nothing". The Rock says they know each other and makes fun of The Hurricane for having braces. He wonders if he's "student body president" before reminding the superhero that he was chanting something from *The Scorpion King* while he eliminated The Hurricane last week. The superhero thinks it means he "has a tiny ding-a-ling". That sets off the "Great One" and he wants to know what The Hurricane wants. He says that the "People's Champ" is full of crap and afraid of "Stone Cold" before flying away. The Rock says he's not afraid of anyone and gives his crotch a pep talk.

Chris Jericho def. Test. Following a replay of Jericho attacking Test and Stacy Keibler last week, Y2J apologizes to Stacy that she was "stupid enough to hook up with a lying, cheating boyfriend". He then shows footage of the bodyguard signing chests at his *Girls Gone Wild* appearance. Backstage, Keibler can't believe him. Test argues that he did nothing wrong and demands that she stay backstage. The bodyguard then sprints out to punch and press slam the heel. Despite Test's instructions, Stacy limps out, Christian following right behind. The bodyguard spots them and attacks Christian, tossing him into the crowd. When he returns to the ring, Y2J surprises Test with elbows and fists. Despite a back suplex, the bodyguard is right back up for a tilt-a-whirl slam and corner clothesline. Although he misses another clothesline, Test blocks the Walls of Jericho to powerbomb the heel for a near fall. He tries to follow up, but Jericho hides behind Chad Patton. Christian capitalizes with a reverse DDT, but the bodyguard still manages to kick out of Jericho's cover. When Y2J grabs Stacy, Test rushes to his girlfriend's aid with a full nelson slam. Unfortunately, Christian distracts the referee long enough for Y2J to give the bodyguard a low blow and breakdown after Test Big Boots Christian. That scores Jericho the win, but he's not done. After chasing Keibler into hitting her injured back against the ring steps, the heels tease giving her a conchairto. Luckily, the bodyguard makes the save, but he gets a conchairto himself. Before Y2J can hit Stacy with the chair, Shawn Michaels runs out to fight the heels, dropping Christian with Sweet Chin Music. Unfortunately, he turns back into a chair shot to the skull, busting him open. Jericho threatens to end his career tonight, but changes his mind. He wants to finish off Michaels at WrestleMania XIX. Bloodied and crawling on the canvas, Shawn can't respond.

After a recap of the previous segment, a car pulls into the parking lot. Three-Minute Warning and Rico are still waiting for "Stone Cold" Steve Austin, but find Goldust stuttering and barking instead.

Inside the squared circle, Christopher Nowinski can't wait to see "Stone Cold" Steve Austin "get what's coming to him". The Harvard heel decries Austin's attitude. Surprisingly, the fans start to cheer. It's not for Nowinski, but rather The Dudley Boyz sneaking out of the crowd to 3D him.

After a commercial break, Christian tells Chris Jericho that they can call Shawn Michaels "the Head Break Kid" now. After dealing with him and Test, the heels are eagerly waiting to hit "Stone Cold" Steve Austin with their sticks.

Booker T def. Scott Steiner. JR tells everyone that the last time these two men faced off was on the final episode of *WCW Monday Nitro* when Booker beat Steiner for the WCW Title. After Scott gets in a few clubbing blows, the five-time champion answers with a leg lariat. He tries to score the early win with a Scissors Kick, but Steiner dodges and slams Booker T to the canvas. A belly-to-belly suplex and hard chops follow before "Big Poppa Pump" drops an elbow and does some pushups. When he returns to chopping Booker, the babyface fires back with his own shots and a flying forearm. A heel kick seconds later gets the five-time champion a two-count. Following another kick, Booker T drops down for a spinaroonie, but Scott blindsides him to boos. As he locks on the Steiner Recliner, Ric Flair and Triple H head to ringside. That sees "Big Poppa Pump" let go of his submission finisher. After yelling at the heels, Steiner turns back to the action at hand only to be rolled up for the three-count. While Scott chases after Ric and Hunter, Booker entertains the fans with a spinaroonie post-match.

Backstage, The Rock tells a member of the crew that he's not afraid of anyone and he wants Eric Bischoff to come see him. After a commercial break, the general manager does so, interrupting the "People's Champ" playing guitar. The "Great One" wants to know if Eric is trying to make him feel bad by having all the superstars waiting for the "rattlesnake". The "Brahma Bull" tells Bischoff that if someone gets to "Stone Cold" before he gets to Austin, The Rock won't be happy. The "People's Champ" promises to go back to *SmackDown!* if Bischoff doesn't make him happy. The GM quickly excuses himself to take care of business.

Further backstage, Rob Van Dam leaps up to kick a trashcan. Kane says that's hardcore ahead of their upcoming "Hardcore" match.

Kane/Rob Van Dam def. Al Snow/Tommy Dreamer ("Hardcore" match). Dreamer pushes a helmet wearing Snow down the aisle in a shopping cart to start the match, but the extreme wrestlers crash and burn. Soon after, RVD catches them with an Asai moonsault. When he tries to give Al rolling thunder in the ring, Tommy hits him with a kendo stick. Kane follows only to see the ECW pairing rock their opponents with trashcan lids. After knocking Rob out to the floor, Snow drop toe holds the "Big Red

Machine" onto a trashcan. Sign and lid shots follow before the monster responds with a double Chokeslam. Van Dam then has his partner stack up their opponents for a Five-Star Frog Splash and the three-count on both men.

Backstage, Eric Bischoff stops his welcoming committee from attacking "Stone Cold" Steve Austin just as the "rattlesnake" arrives in his truck. He nearly runs them over and threatens the heels with a tire iron before heading to the ring, the GM holding back his heel squad. Following the final commercial break, Austin gets a huge pop as he steps into the squared circle. He says he might be a little rusty, but first he wants to thank the fans here and at home. For the last seven months, he's been sitting at home. While he didn't bring his "ball" with him, referencing the WWE telling everyone that he "took his ball and went home", the "rattlesnake" did bring a "can of whoop ass". That brings out The Rock to boos. Standing on the stage, the "People's Champ" takes offense to the fans telling him that he sucks. The "Great One" tells "Stone Cold" not to thank the fans because they will turn on him. After insulting the fans for having no class, the "Brahma Bull" challenges Austin to "go one-on-one with the 'Great One'". Before he can respond, Bischoff bursts through the curtain with Chief Morley. He wants to make The Rock happy. To do that, he's giving the "People's Champ" a match next week with Booker T. If the "Brahma Bull" wins, he can choose to face either "Stone Cold" at WrestleMania XIX or challenge Triple H for the World Title. Unfortunately, the show is running long..."three minutes too long". That brings out Three-Minute Warning and Rico for the "rattlesnake" to give them Stone Cold Stunners. The Rock sneaks behind him as he finishes off the stylist, standing nose-to-nose with his long time rival, the fans chanting "Austin". The "People's Champ" just smiles before trying to cheap shot "Stone Cold". The "rattlesnake" is prepared and blocks his shot for several of his own. When he sets up for a fourth Stunner, The Rock bails out of the ring and retreats up the aisle to end the episode.

SmackDown!

March 6, 2003
Bridgeport, CT
Announcers: Michael Cole, Tazz

Rey Mysterio def. Jamie Noble (with Nidia) and Tajiri (Cruiserweight Title #1 Contender's match). Following the intro video and fireworks, Mysterio pops out of the stage for the opener. He's met by a Noble attack off the apron to kick off a fast-paced match. Tajiri capitalizes with a backslide to Jamie for a two-count. Rey then returns to hit Noble with a springboard butt splash for his own two-count. After Tajiri makes the save, he German suplexes the redneck for another near fall. The masked man is right back on top of him with a springboard attack before the "Japanese Buzzsaw" surprises Jamie with a handspring back elbow. Eventually, Noble comes back to life tossing Tajiri into the corner before slinging Mysterio out to the floor. Alone, Jamie traps the "Japanese Buzzsaw" in an armbar until he reaches the ropes. Soon after, Rey returns to punch both opponents. Tajiri tries to answer with a superplex, but Noble puts him on his shoulders first for an electric chair drop, the "Japanese Buzzsaw" superplexing the masked man at the same time. It takes him to the count of nine for Jamie to cover Tajiri for a two-count. He also gets a near fall on Mysterio before powerslamming the "Japanese Buzzsaw" for another two-count. Tajiri answers with a Tarantula and Buzzsaw Kick, but Rey breaks up his cover. The masked man follows up with a 619 to Noble, but the "Japanese Buzzsaw" makes the cover for a two-count before Mysterio returns with a slingshot leg drop from the apron. This time, Jamie makes the save, draping Tajiri's foot on the ropes. The masked man rewards Noble with a 619 on the apron, but he leaps into a Buzzsaw Kick to the jaw. When the "Japanese Buzzsaw" tries to suplex Rey back into the ring, Mysterio rolls through for the three-count and WrestleMania XIX title shot.

Los Guerreros def. The FBI (with Nunzio). Palumbo opens the match driving Chavo into a corner, but he makes the mistake of following the cruiserweight out to the floor and getting double-teamed by Los Guerreros. When Eddie tags in, Chuck briefly drops him with a back elbow before tagging in Stamboli. "Latino Heat" greets him with a dropkick, but Palumbo turns the tide with a cheap shot from the floor. Johnny then hammers down the former champion before Chuck returns for a press and drop. A Samoan drop follows, but Palumbo doesn't go for the cover. Instead, Stamboli returns for a choke and two-count. Afterwards, he shows off his strength with a bearhug. When Chavo tries to make the save, Jimmy Korderas cuts him off for the heels to switch places. The referee looks confused, but he lets the match continue. Eddie takes matters into his own hands with a hurricanrana before tagging in Chavo to dropkick both heels. A tornado DDT follows to Stamboli, but Palumbo makes the save. "Latino Heat" pays him back, hip tossing Chuck and himself out to the floor. There, he whips Palumbo into the ring post while Chavo slams Johnny. After he stops Nunzio from interfering, Chavo heads upstairs, but Stamboli catches his dive for a fallaway slam. When they hit the mat, Eddie surprises Johnny with a Frog Splash for Chavo to steal the win. Post-match, the heels attack and lay out the winners.

Backstage Paul Heyman complains to all of his clients about being locked in a steel cage with Brock Lesnar tonight. The agent yells that he can't be locked in a cage. Big Show assures him that the heels have his back. Kurt Angle promises to take advantage of his "personal relationship" with Stephanie McMahon to get Paul out of the match.

A WrestleMania XIX teaser plays. Afterwards, Kurt Angle and Paul Heyman enter Stephanie McMahon's office. Paul interrupts the Olympian to take over, saying that this is what he does for a living. He wants a "small little concession" from Stephanie, but it's just him groveling at McMahon's feet to get out of his match. Angle tells him to act like a man before reminding Stephanie about their shared history and how close they were on Valentine's Day. He slowly removes her jacket before telling her that they have a thing for each other. McMahon says they had something in the past, but he needs to think about his future. Him insulting her intelligence makes her so mad that she tells the champion that if Heyman loses tonight, Brock Lesnar will meet Kurt for the WWE Title next week.

Matt Hardy Version 1.0 (with Shannon Moore) def. Billy Kidman (Cruiserweight Title match). Hardy is out first with his Matt Facts telling fans that he likes looking at *Playboy* pictures and considers himself a sex symbol. The former champion tries to get his belt back with a head scissors and dropkick for a two-count. Matt answers with a catapult out to the floor where Shannon stomps him. Back in the squared circle, Hardy chokes and punches Kidman before scoring a two-count with a waist lock suplex. He then slows the pace with a surfboard until Billy escapes and unloads with an enziguri kick. Moments later, he dodges a corner charge to kick and crotch the champion on the top rope. A sit out spinebuster scores the challenger a two-count, as does a leg drop off the second rope, mocking Matt. Kidman quickly follows up with a bulldog off the middle rope, but when he sets up for a Shooting Star Press, Moore drags his leader out to the floor. Billy follows them out with a top rope flying cross body block. He then chases Shannon around the ring before running into a side effect back in the squared circle. When that doesn't get his man the win, Moore hops onto the apron to distract Kidman long enough for Matt to deliver a Twist of Fate for the victory.

A Brock Lesnar/Paul Heyman Moment sees the "next big thing" winning the WWE Title at SummerSlam.

A video package of Torrie Wilson's *Playboy* photo shoot plays.

Backstage, Josh Mathews interviews Nidia and shows footage of her visiting the Playboy mansion. Security intercepts her and forgets her name. Nidia wants Hugh Hefner to watch her on *Girls Gone Wild*'s PPV next week. She then challenges Torrie to a "Body Challenge" before flashing Josh. Matthews is speechless. The announcers step in to shill the PPV and remind everyone it's for mature audiences.

Further backstage, Hulk Hogan tells Jimmy Korderas to deliver a message to Vince McMahon. He promises to show the world who the real coward is before heading to the ring. Following a commercial break, the Hulkster makes his way down the aisle to a big pop. After calling the fans unbelievable, Hogan says he's tired of Vince. He's tempted to just walk away from the WWE, but he's had an issue with McMahon for over twenty years and there's only one way to settle it. He challenges the WWE owner to come out and face him right now. That brings Vince out onto the stage. He has no problem settling things with Hulk at any time, but he doesn't think Hogan is a man. McMahon can't believe he'd get called out after all he did for the Hulkster. Hulk tells him to shut up. He's heard enough from Vince and says Hulkamania was a success in spite of McMahon, not because of him. Hogan goes on to say that it makes Vince sick that the Hulkster was the one who built the WWE for him. Things break down from there as the two men curse each other, McMahon telling Hulk that he could have picked anyone to be the man like Hogan. The Hulkster disagrees, noting all the people who dropped the ball. He calls Vince delusional before challenging him to a match tonight. McMahon tells him there's "no chance in Hell" of that. He adds that he doesn't hate Hulkamania or the Hulkamaniacs, but he hates Hogan because he turned his back on him and joined WCW to try to put Vince out business. Even worse, in the trial of his life, Hulk testified against him. The Hulkster disagrees, saying he saved Vince and if he didn't, he'd be getting "screwed" in prison. McMahon can't believe he made Hogan "a fabric of Americana". Hogan might want a match, but he's not going to get it. Instead, he's going to get a fight at another one of

Vince's creations...WrestleMania. However, he wants it put in the contract that when the Hulkster loses, he'll retire forever. Hogan accepts, warning McMahon he better start saying his prayer ahead of their match.

Footage of The Undertaker helping Nathan Jones train earlier today plays. Nathan thanks him for living up to his word and helping him train after leaving prison. The biker is a man of his word and tells the "Colossus of Boggo Road" that he has to put in the work to be great. He then shows the rookie how to tie up and shoulder block an opponent. When Jones doesn't do it right, the "Deadman" yells at him. Jones snaps and kicks the enhancement talent before choking him out. The Undertaker steps in to say that's enough for tonight.

A-Train (with Big Show) def. The Undertaker (with Nathan Jones) by disqualification. The Undertaker is dominant early on, punching, slamming, and big booting the hairy heel. When he goes for the cover, Show pulls the biker out to the floor. That lets A-Train recover to powerslam the "Deadman" for a two-count. Unfortunately, he misses a corner charge and The Undertaker attacks his leg. When the giant gets involved again, the hairy heel clotheslines the distracted biker out to the floor. There, Big Show slams him against the ring post. While Jones backs up the giant, A-Train clubs the "Deadman". Show gets in his own shot to the face for a hairy heel two-count. Soon after, the two men trade shots before The Undertaker stuns A-Train with a leaping clothesline. Old School follows to the shoulder, but once again Big Show distracts the "Deadman". The hairy heel capitalizes with a Derailer, but when he goes for the cover, The Undertaker locks on a Triangle Choke. Show takes advantage of Nathan distracting the referee to stomp the biker and break the hold. Jones loses his temper and tosses aside Brian Hebner for the disqualification before the babyfaces take turns pummeling the giant.

Another Brock Lesnar/Paul Heyman Moment sees the agent screw his client at Survivor Series.

During the commercial break, Stephanie McMahon orders A-Train and Big Show to leave the arena for their own safety. They try to fight her over it, but she orders the monsters to leave.

Chris Benoit/Rhyno def. Team Angle. The champions are out first for this non-title match. Benoit opens the contest working on Shelton's arm before tagging in Rhyno. Together, the babyfaces connect with a double back elbow before Benjamin attacks the man-beast's eyes. Haas then tags in only to run into an overhead belly-to-belly suplex. Intense, Rhyno stomps the champion in a corner before "the Crippler" returns to score a near fall with a northern lights suplex. When Shelton tags back in, Benoit surprises him with a Crippler Crossface, but Charlie makes the save. Moments later, he scores a near fall with a powerslam out of a neutral corner. A "rabid wolverine" clothesline sends both men to their corners for tags. The man-beast attacks both heels, belly-to-belly suplexing Benjamin. When he sets up for a Gore, Charlie pulls his hair ahead of a Shelton superkick for a near fall into a commercial break.

Afterwards, Team Angle is in complete control, Haas propping Rhyno on the top rope for a Benjamin elbow drop to the neck. Charlie then wrenches on the man-beast's neck with a modified armbar stretch. Following a clothesline, Shelton tags back in to apply a neck vice. Even when he escapes, the champion slams the back of Rhyno's head on his knee. Tazz believes Mike Chioda should think about stopping this match. Instead, he lets the heels leg drop the man-beast on the top rope ahead of a Haas swinging neckbreaker and near fall. Eventually, Rhyno surprises Benjamin with a spinebuster to put both men down. A ball of fury, Benoit tags in to attack both champions ahead of a trio of German suplexes to Charlie. He follows up with a top rope diving headbutt, but at the last second, Shelton breaks the referee's count. The man-beast flings him out to the floor, but there, Benjamin whips Rhyno into the barricade. Inside the squared circle, Haas traps "the Crippler" in his reverse Indian Deathlock, called the Haas of Pain, but the man-beast makes the save. He then Gores Shelton only to see Charlie toss Rhyno out to the floor. Unfortunately, he turns back into a Crippler Crossface. With no other option, Haas taps out.

In another prerecorded vignette, John Cena warns Brock Lesnar that he's intense and he's going to fill the "next big thing" full of holes like a chain link fence.

Another Brock Lesnar/Paul Heyman Moment sees Kurt Angle signing Paul as his agent and getting his knee slammed against the ring post by the "next big thing" for his efforts. Afterwards, we see the "tale of the tape" for the upcoming "Steel Cage" match ahead of a WrestleMania XIX ad.

After a commercial break, Paul Heyman doesn't know what to do. He doesn't think he can beat Brock Lesnar, but Kurt Angle yells at him. He tells Paul that he will win so Angle doesn't have to defend the WWE Title next week in the Olympian's hometown. When Team Angle bursts in complaining, the champion quiets them and tells Heyman that he will win because they are a team.

Footage of *SmackDown!* on tour in South Africa plays.

Brock Lesnar def. Paul Heyman (with Kurt Angle/Team Angle) ("Steel Cage" match). Following footage of Brock earning the right to face Heyman tonight, the "next big thing" steps into the cage. He's followed by the heels, Paul wearing a suit and hat as he walks the aisle nervously. Before the match begins, Kurt scales the cage, but he's just distracting Lesnar for Team Angle to slip into the ring behind him. Together, the WWE Tag Team Champions wail on the number one contender ahead of a double flapjack. When Charlie Haas holds Brock for a Shelton Benjamin superkick though, the "next big thing" ducks. Afterwards, he whips both heels into the cage and knees them before tossing Team Angle out to the floor. Heyman apologizes profusely and lures Lesnar out to the floor where the Olympian attacks from behind. It doesn't take Brock long to drive him off, whipping Angle into the cage and busting him open. Finally, the "next big thing" shoves his former agent into the ring where he picks him up for an F5. At the last second, the champion climbs into the ring and makes the save with a chop block. He follows up with an Angle Slam for Paul to get a near fall. Not done yet, Kurt traps Lesnar in an Anklelock, but the number one contender holds onto Heyman's foot to prevent him from escaping. Eventually, he kicks free of the Anklelock, but Angle is all over him with a flurry of fists while Paul climbs up the cage. Before he can escape, Brock hammers the champion down and drags Heyman back into the squared circle. This time when he hoists up the agent for an F5, Lesnar sees Kurt coming and boots him. He quickly follows up with the F5 to Paul for the three-count. Post-match, a bloodied Angle stares at Brock, Cole reminding everyone that they won't have to wait until WrestleMania XIX to face each other for the WWE Title.

Monday Night Raw
March 10, 2003
Cleveland, OH
Announcers: Jim Ross, Jerry "the King" Lawler

The show opens with Eric Bischoff addressing the heels—except The Rock and Evolution—of the roster. He tells them that he made a mistake and wants to call off the attack on "Stone Cold" Steve Austin. The general manager doesn't want to spend his career feuding with the "rattlesnake". Once everyone else leaves, the "People's Champ" enters the dressing room to talk to Bischoff. Eric wonders if he's ready for his match with Booker T, but the "Great One" says that match isn't happening. While he's not afraid of Booker, he doesn't want to fight for the World Title right now. The only thing that's eating him alive is beating Austin at WrestleMania XIX. That's fine with Bischoff, but he's got advertisers who want to see the "Brahma Bull" in action tonight. The Rock understands, promising to find an opponent tonight.

Chris Jericho/Christian def. Kane/Rob Van Dam. RVD starts fast with a back kick and two-count. That chases Christian off and brings Jericho in to surprise the popular superstar with a flying forearm. He taunts Rob as he back suplexes and chops him. Moments later though, he attempts a springboard attack and leaps into a dropkick. Kane tags in afterwards to back body drop Y2J and knock Christian off the ropes. The "Big Red Machine" then heads upstairs for a flying clothesline and near fall. When he sets up for a double Chokeslam moments later, the heels fight free only to see Jericho back dropped out to the floor ahead of a big boot to Christian. Van Dam tags in afterwards to catch Christian with a flying kick off the top rope and rolling thunder. At ringside, Jericho whips Kane into the ring steps before RVD plants Christian for a Five-Star Frog Splash. Unfortunately, Y2J is the legal man and he races back in to Lionsault Van Dam when he hits the mat for the three-count. Post-match, Shawn Michaels sneaks behind Jericho on the ramp to give him Sweet Chin Music. He tells the downed heel that he'll see him at WrestleMania.

Since he doesn't have a match with The Rock tonight now, Booker T comes out to address what Triple H said last week. While he wanted to knock out "the Game" for his insults last week, Booker kept his temper in check. He proceeds to tell everyone that he is the youngest of eight kids who grew up without a father and spent time in jail. Since Hunter wanted to see him dance, the five-time champion invites Helmsley to walk down the aisle and he'll dance all over his face right now. Instead, Ric Flair comes out to tell Booker T that he's not Michael Jordan or Tiger Woods and he's not as good as Triple H. Flair says he's been dealt some good cards, but not one to be the World Champion. Since Hunter is a "class act", Ric says he isn't going to lower himself to Booker's level and fight with him tonight. However, next week, the five-time champion can put on a hat, carry their bags, and drive around Evolution. He can do that in St. Louis or get his butt kicked. Booker T has heard enough and decks "The Nature Boy" before heading backstage to find Helmsley. Following a replay of his punch, Booker finds "the Game" washing his face. When the five-time champion asks if he has something to say to the number one contender, Triple H throws a dollar at him and asks for a towel. Instead, Booker T punches him and slam a door in the World Champion's face.

After a commercial break, Ric Flair tells Triple H that him getting attacked was all "The Nature Boy's" fault. Hunter says he was jumped from behind and never saw Booker T. Flair proposes that the heels go find him.

Jeff Hardy def. Rico (with Three-Minute Warning). While Jeff arm drags the stylist, "Stone Cold" Steve Austin marches into the arena and knocks a tray of drinks onto a woman. Back to the action, Rico gets a two-count with a back stabber pair of knees to the back. The daredevil answers quickly with a whisper in the wind. When he runs the ropes afterwards, Rosey trips him. Hardy recovers quickly to back body drop the stylist over the top rope when he attempts a sneak attack. Jeff follows up with poetry in motion to Three-Minute Warning before rolling up Rico for the three-count. Post-match, he quickly runs away.

Backstage, Triple H talks to Maven and a member of the crew. When he slaps the crewmember, Maven takes offense and calls him "numb nuts". That sets off Hunter and he tells the *Tough Enough* winner to get his gear on for a match tonight.

After a commercial break, Goldust stops "Stone Cold" Steve Austin to bark and stutter as he explains that Eric Bischoff wants to apologize to the "rattlesnake" tonight.

Further backstage, The Rock asks The Hurricane if he's ready to go "one-on-one with 'the Great One'". The superhero is, wondering if the "People's Champ" is ready to "go toe-to-toe with the superhero". The "Brahma Bull" offers to let "all superpowers go" in their "No Disqualification" match. However, he wants to know what superpower The Hurricane is going to have and if he's going to throw a hamburger at The Rock. The superhero says he's bringing his "Hurri-powers, bitch". The "People's Champ" tells him that he's low class and wants The Hurricane to bring it tonight for the biggest match of his life. He even shakes the superhero's hand before jacking his jaw with a cheap shot.

Jazz and Trish (#1 Contender's match) wrestle to a no contest. Following technical difficulties that keep the show off the air for several minutes, Jazz marches down to kick Trish. Stratus answers with a handstand head scissors before Victoria rushes out to blast both women with the Women's Title for the no contest. Presumably, this match would have gone longer without the technical difficulties.

After a commercial break, Eric Bischoff heads to the ring. He says he has never been beaten as bad as he was at No Way Out and he let his personal feelings get in the way of business last week. He apologizes to "Stone Cold" Steve Austin for trying to have him attacked. He also apologizes for firing Austin from WCW by FedEx. He even apologizes to JR for smashing a cinderblock over his head. However, Eric takes credit for "Stone Cold's" career, saying if he didn't fire him the world would never have found the "rattlesnake". Bischoff adds that they are the "same animal" since they both wear jeans, like to hunt, and went toe-to-toe with Vince McMahon to reinvent the industry. That brings out Austin to a big pop. The GM offers his hand to "let bygones be bygones". "Stone Cold" flips him off instead. He doesn't like Eric and thinks he's boring. The "rattlesnake" promises that the only thing he wants to bury is his foot in Bischoff's butt. That brings The Rock out onto the stage to loud boos. The "People's Champ" doesn't want to shake his hand—he wants to slap his face. Austin invites him to try. Instead, the "Great One" says there's just one thing left that he wants to accomplish. The way "Stone Cold" remembers it is he's beaten the "Brahma Bull" twice at WrestleMania and The Rock is cruising for a third. The "People's Champ" just laughs and calls Austin "nothing". The "rattlesnake" invites him to enter the ring right now, even laying down on the canvas for him. The "Great One" postures and teases, but decides, "nah". He'll wait until WrestleMania XIX. Since the "Brahma Bull" won't fight him now, "Stone Cold" stomps a mudhole in Bischoff in a corner. The Rock teases a sneak attack, but when Austin turns around, the "People's Champ" retreats and heads backstage, the "rattlesnake" glaring at him.

Triple H (with Ric Flair) def. Maven. Triple H is wearing red trunks for this non-title match as he clubs Maven down and whips him out to the floor. There, he slams the babyface back into the ring steps. When Maven tries to fight back, Hunter answers with a stiff clothesline and face rake. Helmsley also grinds his elbow across his opponent's face while "the King" compares Maven to Booker T. The WWE is walking a very fine line right here with "the Game's" feud. While Jerry toes that line, the champion locks the babyface in a sleeper hold. He doesn't wait for Charles Robinson to check Maven, throwing him down to the canvas. When he pulls Maven up, the babyface surprises Triple H with a jawbreaker and fists until he runs into a spinebuster. Hunter follows up with a Pedigree for the three-count. Post-match, he tosses Maven over the top rope, but the babyface's head gets caught in the ropes. When Al Snow rushes out to help his student, "the Game" Pedigrees him too.

Backstage, Eric Bischoff complains to Chief Morley about "Stone Cold" Steve Austin spitting in the general manager's face. Morley says he went above and beyond because Vince McMahon never even tried to make amends with the "rattlesnake". That gives Eric an idea. Since Vince is distracted by Hulk Hogan on *SmackDown!*, he's going to make "Stone Cold" feel his wrath next week in a one-on-one match under "Bischoff's rules".

Backstage, Stacy Keibler is on the phone. She tells Test not to worry because Chris Jericho got laid out by Shawn Michaels. She then hears girls in the background, realizing that her boyfriend is at a *Girls Gone Wild* party.

Further backstage, Terri interrupts "Stone Cold" Steve Austin talking to Scott Steiner to tell the "rattlesnake" about his match with Eric Bischoff next week.

Afterwards, The Dudley Boyz head to the ring, JR revealing that they've been reinstated. Chief Morley then comes out with Lance Storm and security to tell the Dudleys that there's been a mistake. Only D-Von is going to be able to compete tonight. If he wins, The Dudley Boyz will be reinstated, but if he loses or Bubba Ray interferes in any way, the Dudleys will remain suspended. Security then leads Bubba out.

Chief Morley/Lance Storm def. D-Von Dudley. While D-Von tries to calm down his half-brother, the heels attack from behind. Dudley refuses to stay down, whipping Morley into his own partner for a roll-up and two-count. A corner clothesline and DDT also get him a near fall before Storm punches D-Von from the floor. The Canadian tags in immediately afterwards only to run into a clothesline for a two-count. With the fans chanting for tables, Dudley clotheslines and flapjacks Lance for another near fall. A powerslam also gets him a two-count before Storm attacks his eyes. Soon after, the chief of staff knees D-Von running the ropes ahead of a Lance leg lariat. Morley follows up with a Money Shot for the win.

Following a video package for the Chris Jericho/Shawn Michaels feud, Lawler is in the ring to host a wet t-shirt contest. He brings out four women in orange tops to spray them with a water gun. Before he starts, Stacy Keibler marches out to a nice pop. She says she's as wild as anyone and grabs the water gun. While "the King" introduces the girls, Stacy sprays them down in a segment that is another example of the WWE's priorities at the time, wasting valuable camera time. Before a winner can be announced, Keibler reveals that she'll be at the *Girls Gone Wild* PPV and wants to show her wild side by getting shot with the water gun tonight. Jerry is happy to spray her backside to end the segment.

The Hurricane def. The Rock ("No Disqualification" match). As the heel heads to the ring, JR lists all of his accomplishments, but points out that he's never beaten "Stone Cold" Steve Austin at WrestleMania. When the superhero comes out, The Rock slaps him. The Hurricane answers with fists before running into a Samoan drop. Once in control, the "People's Champ" dons the superhero's cape. That makes The Hurricane mad, but a "Great One" clothesline flattens him. The "Brahma Bull" pretends to fly before removing the cape and suplexing the superhero for a two-count. A choke on the ropes follows before The Rock slows the pace with a chin lock. When The Hurricane starts to fight free, the "People's Champ" rakes his eyes. The superhero answers with a neckbreaker to put both men down. He catches a second wind moments later to punch and clothesline the "Great One". A shining wizard kick has the "Brahma Bull" seeing stars before The Hurricane nearly scores the win with a top rope flying cross body block. He also gets a near fall with a second rope overcast before The Rock comes back to life with a DDT out of nowhere. When he tries to give the superhero a Rock Bottom, the babyface fights free and teases a chokeslam. The two men then trade counters until The Hurricane finally hits his chokeslam for a long two-count. He can't follow up as the "People's Champ" plants him with a spinebuster. When he runs the ropes for the People's Elbow though, "Stone Cold's" music plays and he marches down the aisle. That distracts the "Great One" long enough for the superhero to roll him up for the three-count. The Hurricane immediately races out of the ring and up the aisle as Austin flips off the "Brahma Bull" and taunts him to end the show.

SmackDown!
March 13, 2003
Pittsburgh, PA
Announcers: Michael Cole, Tazz

The show opens with shots of Brock Lesnar and Kurt Angle arriving at the building for their WWE Title match. While Brock looks confident and happy, Kurt is sporting a black eye and looks despondent. After the intro video plays and fireworks explode, Team Angle heads to the ring for the opener.

Team Angle def. Billy Kidman/Rey Mysterio. Kidman opens the match looking strong, head scissoring Haas down for a two-count before catching Shelton's arm and holding him for a Rey sunset flip and near fall. Mysterio follows up with a helicopter spin head scissors for another two-count before Billy returns to atomic drop his partner onto Benjamin with a modified leg drop. Kidman follows up with shots to both heels until he misses a corner charge and stuns himself hitting his shoulder against the ring post. Shelton capitalizes with an armbar drop for a near fall. When Charlie returns, he locks on an armbar. To add to the punishment, he wraps the arm around the ropes, drawing a warning from Mike Chioda. The champions remain in control, Benjamin tagging in to continue the assault on the injured limb. Following a cheap shot to the masked man, Shelton tags back in Haas for their leapfrog double-team splash. Luckily, Rey recovers to break up the cover. Moments later, Billy surprises Charlie with an enziguri kick and gives Mysterio the hot tag. He fights both heels, stunning Charlie with a springboard splash. When Benjamin tries to slam him, the masked man flies onto Haas for another two-count. Kidman returns moments later for a near fall after a face slam to Charlie. After knocking Shelton from the ring, Billy holds Haas for the 619. Rey then dives out of the ring onto Benjamin while Kidman gives Charlie a Shooting Star Press. Unfortunately for the babyfaces, Shelton makes the save. When Mysterio returns to the ring, he ends up distracting the referee long enough for Team Angle to score the win with a combination German Suplex and Superplex to Billy. Post-match, Kidman is in a bad mood.

Backstage, Brian Kendrick interrupts Stephanie McMahon's phone call and gives her flowers. He thanks her for the opportunity to wrestle Kurt Angle two weeks ago.

After a commercial break, Jamie Noble takes a taxicab to the Playboy Mansion. When he can't get inside, he rants at a worker that Nidia is more beautiful than Torrie Wilson. Noble wants Hugh Hefner to watch his girlfriend on tonight's *Girls Gone Wild* PPV. The worker has head enough and calls for security, two large men who chase off the redneck.

Rikishi def. Chuck Palumbo (with Johnny Stamboli/Nunzio). Outnumbered, Rikishi decks Nunzio and kicks Stamboli before turning into a Palumbo boot and one-count. Chuck follows up with a belly-to-belly suplex for a near fall. The heel continues his assault, unloading with haymakers and a clothesline in a corner. Johnny gets in a few cheap shots too until the big Samoan comes back to life and catches Palumbo for a series of fists and a Samoan drop. A thrust kick and corner splash follow, but before he can finish off the heel, the rest of The FBI sneak into the ring. That brings out Los Guerreros to drive Nunzio and Stamboli from the squared circle. Rikishi then gives Chuck a Rump Shaker for the win.

Ahead of a shot of The Undertaker backstage, the announcers tell everyone that the "Deadman" will team with Nathan Jones at WrestleMania XIX to face A-Train and Big Show. Afterwards, the biker finds his partner sitting quietly and rocking in a dark room. Jones says after ten years in jail he appreciates moments of peace. The Undertaker appreciates that, but wants Nathan to join him in watching their WrestleMania XIX opponents next.

A-Train/Big Show def. Funaki/Tajiri. After the announcers let everyone know that Paul Heyman isn't here tonight due to the F5 he took last week, a prerecorded segment from the babyfaces plays. In it, Funaki is worried about facing the giants, but Tajiri promises to chop them down. Instead, Big Show clubs and press slams the interviewer. He then joins the announce table to complain about The Undertaker using an illegal hold to beat him at No Way Out while A-Train crushes Funaki in a corner. When Tajiri tags in, the babyfaces unload on the hairy heel with a flurry of kicks. They can't put him down and he drops the "Japanese Buzzsaw" on the top rope. Heavy blows follow to his opponents. When Funaki returns, A-Train slingshots him into the middle rope. He tries to finish off the interviewer with a press slam, but Tajiri makes the save with a string of kicks. That brings Show back into the ring, but the "Japanese Buzzsaw" catches him with a Buzzsaw Kick. It doesn't slow him for long and he responds with a Chokeslam while A-Train nearly takes Funaki's head off with a bicycle kick. A Train Wreck follows to *SmackDown!*'s number one announcer for the three-count.

Following footage of Brock Lesnar beating Paul Heyman to earn a WWE Title match, fans predict who will win tonight.

After a commercial break, Sean O'Haire notices that Dawn Marie is down in the dumps. She's upset that Torrie Wilson was picked for *Playboy* over her. O'Haire says she's beautiful and can prove she's more deserving of the opportunity than Torrie. When Dawn asks if he's telling her to flash the crowd, Sean says he's not telling her anything she doesn't already know.

In a prerecorded promo, Torrie Wilson shows fans her *Playboy* cover.

Afterwards, Dawn Marie heads to the ring to say she has a "voluptuous body". While girls will go wild later tonight on the PPV, she's going wild tonight, opening up her shirt and flashing Tazz, the ring ropes conveniently in position to cover up anything unfit for air.

After a commercial break, John Cena is sitting in a doctor's office rapping and insulting Brock Lesnar. He vows revenge when he gets back.

Chris Benoit/Rhyno and Los Guerreros (#1 Contender's match) wrestle to a no contest. Benoit and Chavo trade arm holds to open the match. When neither gets the advantage, Eddie and Rhyno give it a go. "Latino Heat" is faster and a better mat wrestler, but one shove from the man-beast puts Guerrero on the canvas. Back up, he tags in Chavo to snap mare, punch, and dropkick Rhyno. Both men tag out soon afterwards for Benoit to lace Eddie with a string of chops. When "Latino Heat" fights back, he misses the man-beast tagging in to club Guerrero. Eddie doesn't stay on the defensive for long, tagging his nephew to back suplex Rhyno for a two-count. He can't keep the man-beast down and Rhyno drives him back to his corner for the "rabid wolverine" to return with a side backbreaker and two-count. A back suplex also gets him a near fall, but when he goes for a second, Chavo shifts his weight and lands on Benoit for his own two-count. "Latino Heat" is in right afterwards to punch and dropkick "the Crippler" for his own near fall. Once again, the two men trade shots before Benoit locks on the Crippler Crossface. Unfortunately, he's close enough to the ropes for Eddie to escape. When the "rabid wolverine" doesn't break the hold immediately, Chavo kicks and punches Benoit illegally. "Latino Heat" tells his nephew to think before tagging him in so he can legally attack "the Crippler". That includes a reverse chin lock in the center of the ring. After a minute, Benoit elbows free and nearly steals the win with a roll-up. Chavo answers with a cross chop and tag to his uncle for a somersault slingshot splash and another near fall. "Latino Heat" follows up with an armbar. When he tags back in Chavo, the "rabid wolverine" nearly surprises him with the Crippler Crossface, but the younger Guerrero rolls Benoit out to the floor. Unfortunately, he misses a slingshot plancha, but Eddie hits his. Rhyno then clotheslines "Latino Heat" at ringside ahead of a commercial break.

Afterwards, Chavo traps Benoit in his own Crossface. He can't get him to tap out before "the Crippler" reaches his boot out to Rhyno for the tag. The man-beast nearly gets the win with a belly-to-belly suplex before hooking a reverse chin lock. It doesn't take Guerrero long to fight free and stun Rhyno with a second rope missile dropkick. Soon after, both men tag out for Benoit to kick Eddie. "Latino Heat" responds with a back suplex and head scissors. When he heads upstairs though, the "rabid wolverine" catches him. The two men fight on the ropes until Eddie surprises Benoit with a sunset flip powerbomb for a near fall. At the last second, the man-beast makes the save and tosses Chavo over the top rope. Unfortunately, he misses a corner charge, but still has the presence of mind to break up "Latino Heat" rolling up "the Crippler". Benoit answers with a back suplex over the top rope to the floor. Chavo is back in the squared circle, dropkicking and uppercutting the "rabid wolverine" until Benoit traps him in a Crippler Crossface. Luckily, Eddie makes the save with a Frog Splash, but turns into a Gore. Afterwards, Chavo head scissors himself and Rhyno out to the floor while "the Crippler" covers "Latino Heat" for a near fall. When he reaches the ropes, Benoit responds with a pair of German suplexes. Before he can hit a third, Eddie counters with his own pair of suplexes. Like Guerrero, the "rabid wolverine" blocks the third and briefly applies the Crippler Crossface. "Latino Heat" has him well-scouted and slips free only to be German suplexed a third time. Before either man can score the victory, Team Angle runs out to hit both men with the WWE Tag Titles, ending this solid match in a no contest. The announcers wonder who will face the champions at WrestleMania XIX now.

A clip of Hulk Hogan and Vince McMahon agreeing to a match at WrestleMania XIX last week plays.

After a commercial break, Stephanie McMahon yells at Team Angle, ending their celebration. She tells them that since they ruined the number one contender's match, they'll face both Los Guerreros and Chris Benoit and Rhyno in a triple threat WWE Tag Title match at WrestleMania XIX.

A Hulkamania video package plays to "Real American". It also features Vince McMahon introducing the Hulkster and the friendship between the two. After Vince thanks Hogan for Hulkamania ahead of WrestleMania VIII, McMahon addresses the crowd on the Titantron. He plays a clip multiple times, highlighting Hogan thanking him. Vince says that was the only time the Hulkster ever thanked him. The WWE owner considers that sad since they were close friends for a long time. However, McMahon says Hulk changed and it hurt Vince. Now, McMahon realizes that Hogan wasn't saying "thank you", but rather "screw you". Vince rants that the Hulkster didn't appreciate the WWE owner bringing him back into the company last year. Worst of all, McMahon is mad that at WrestleMania XIX he will have to kill his creation, Hulkamania. Vince warns Hogan that he will never forgive him for that.

The Pittsburgh Penguin def. Matt Hardy Version 1.0 (with Shannon Moore) by count-out. This week's Matt Facts are that Hardy has never locked his keys in his car and that he hates cleaning his carpet. Backstage, Rey Mysterio scouts his WrestleMania XIX opponent. Inside the ring, Matt tells the fans that he will not defend his belt until WrestleMania, but he's willing to give a display of his talents against any cruiserweight other than Rey tonight. That brings out a man wearing a penguin mask. Tony Chimel introduces him as being from Pittsburgh. The fans are firmly behind him despite Hardy slamming him to the canvas to open the match. He follows up with a whip into a corner before walking into a head scissors. Matt takes offense, yelling that this is an exhibition before cheap shotting the Penguin. Moore then joins in the fun with a choke ahead of a middle rope leg drop. A ricochet slam nearly gets Hardy the win, but the masked man just kicks out. When he starts to fight back, Matt rakes his eyes and applies a surfboard submission. The Penguin escapes with kicks, but runs into a tilt-a-whirl slam. Hardy has had enough and unmasks the Penguin to reveal that it's Brian Kendrick. Surprised, Matt runs into a springboard dropkick and facebuster onto the knee for a near fall. A step up DDT also gets the rookie a two-count before he whips Hardy into his MFer. After escaping a side effect, Brian walks up Shannon to give Hardy a step up bulldog. Moore has seen enough, pulling his mentor from the ring for the count-out. During the commercial break, Mysterio congratulates Kendrick on a great match. Brian wishes him luck at WrestleMania XIX.

A three-minute video package plays for the Brock Lesnar/Kurt Angle feud ahead of the main event. We also get to see the tale of the tape for their WWE Title match.

A WrestleMania Moment sees Hulk Hogan facing Andre the Giant at WrestleMania III.

Kurt Angle def. Brock Lesnar (WWE Title match). The champion is out first, wearing a hoodie as he prays over the belt in a corner. Lesnar follows and blindsides Angle, hammering him in the corner before he can even lower his hood. A man possessed, Brock F5s the champion, but after the count of one he stands up and looks confused. The announcers don't understand. Team Angle then hurries down the ramp to distract the "next big thing" while Kurt switches places with his brother Eric. When Lesnar returns to the squared circle, Angle small packages him for the win. Post-match, Kurt runs off, leaving his brother to take a beating and F5 against the ring post. Tazz calls what Angle did tonight "pure genius".

Monday Night Raw
March 17, 2003
St. Louis, MO
Announcers: Jim Ross, Jerry "the King" Lawler

The show opens with a graphic dedicating the episode to the men and women of the US armed forces. Afterwards, Eric Bischoff is standing in the center of the ring to announce that his match tonight with "Stone Cold" Steve Austin tonight will be a "Lumberjack" match featuring all of the superstars on the *Raw* roster. If anyone doesn't want to do it, Eric promises to fire them. After he wishes Austin good luck, the intro video plays and fireworks explode.

Kane/Rob Van Dam def. Chief Morley/Lance Storm. While the babyfaces come out separately, the heels are unified for Morley to wish William Regal well in his recovery from injuries he suffered at No Way Out. He then warns The Dudley Boyz that if they interfere in the match in any way they will continue to be suspended indefinitely. Inside the ring, Kane opens the match hammering the chief of staff. Even when he runs into a corner boot, the "Big Red Machine" clotheslines Morley and slams him for a RVD top rope guillotine leg drop. That gets the babyfaces a two-count. A step over heel kick and moonsault follow for another near fall. When he attempts a monkey flip, the chief hotshots him on the top rope. Storm then tags in only to walk into a spinning heel kick. Morley tries to help his partner and grab Rob, but Lance ends up hitting the chief. The heels finally get their acts together, Morley tripping Van Dam for a Storm DDT and two-count. Back in, the chief gets a near fall with a clothesline. A spinebuster and armbar follow before RVD rocks the heel with an enziguri. That lets him tag Kane to fight both heels. After chasing the chief of staff from the ring, he stuns the Canadian with a top rope flying clothesline. Before he can give him a Chokeslam, Morley returns for the heels to double DDT the "Big Red Machine". Van Dam rushes to his partner's defense with a flying kick and rolling thunder to the chief. He follows up with a mule kick that knocks Lance into a Chokeslam for the three-count. Post-match, Van Dam teases giving Morley a Five-Star Frog Splash, but the heel rolls out of the ring. The Dudleys stop him from leaving, shoving him back into the squared circle and setting up a table while Lawler says the match is over, so they aren't risking any punishment. They don't have to worry as they blindside RVD before putting the monster through the table with a 3D. Morley is confused, but likes it.

After a commercial break, The Dudley Boyz tell Chief Morley that they aren't happy about it, but they've made a choice to join Eric Bischoff's team to feed their families. The chief of staff officially lifts their suspension and shakes their hands. He wants them to stick around and serve as lumberjacks later.

Afterwards, Triple H and Ric Flair head to the squared circle to say that Booker T doesn't deserve a World Title shot at WrestleMania XIX because he attacked the champion last week from behind. Hunter calls him a "common street thug" and challenges the five-time champion to walk down the aisle right now. Instead, Goldust heads to the ring. Jerry says Booker is "probably in jail". When the "bizarre one" stutters saying "cockles", the heels crack up. Helmsley stops him to say that Goldust is killing them. He can't keep a straight face as the "bizarre one" stutters once again. When "the Game" mocks him, Goldust attacks, hitting both heels until Flair holds his leg long enough for Triple H to hammer him down. He tries to finish off the "bizarre one" with a Pedigree, but Booker T runs out for the save, decking Ric in a corner ahead of a side kick to the champion. A thrust kick follows to "The Nature Boy" before Goldust knocks Hunter out to the floor. There, he pulls Flair out of the ring to escape a Scissors Kick and retreat backstage.

After a commercial break, Triple H throws a tantrum in his locker room and demands a match with Goldust tonight.

Maven def. Rico (with Three-Minute Warning). After the wrestlers open the match trading takedowns, Maven elbows and slams the stylist. While he locks on an armbar, cameras catch The Rock arriving backstage. Back to the action, Rico kicks and knees the babyface. He then distracts Chad Patton for Jamal to throat drop Maven on the top rope. A kick afterwards gets the stylist a two-count. Following more kicks and another near fall, Rico applies a neck wrench. It doesn't take the babyface long to fight free, but a neckbreaker puts him back down for a two-count. After he lands an elbow, the stylist heads up to the second rope for a flying elbow drop, but misses. Maven catches a second wind afterwards to clothesline and back body drop Rico. A second rope flying bulldog nearly ends the match, but the stylist just kicks out. When Maven tries to follow up with a dropkick, Rosey holds onto Rico's leg to save his man. He can't stop the babyface from backsliding the stylist for the win though. Post-match, Maven runs away.

Backstage, Shawn Michaels walks past Terri to enter "Stone Cold" Steve Austin's locker room. The "Heartbreak Kid" tells Austin that he's going to be a lumberjack tonight and if "Stone Cold" leaves the ring he'll throw him back in. However, if he sees Chris Jericho, he'll take care of him. Michaels reminds Austin that The Rock will be a lumberjack too. The "rattlesnake" thinks he's trying to stir up trouble. Steve isn't worried about the "People's Champ" because he beats him whenever they get into the ring. And if Eric Bischoff thinks he's going to beat Austin tonight, "Stone Cold" is going to take him down too.

Further backstage, Theodore Long hides a copy of the *WWE Magazine* with The Hurricane on the cover from The Rock. When he sees it, the "People's Champ" takes offense. Long promises that Rodney Mack will take care of the superhero tonight. Mack agrees, but that just makes the "Great One" madder.

A WrestleMania XIX teaser plays.

The Snickers Cruncher WrestleMania Moment is Andre the Giant slamming Big John Studd.

The Hurricane def. Rodney Mack (with Theodore Long) by disqualification. Lawler doesn't think the superhero actually beat The Rock last week. The Hurricane doesn't care, clotheslining Mack and getting an early advantage until Long distracts him. Rodney capitalizes with a powerslam for a near fall. Moments later, he barks following a second rope flying shoulderblock. When he misses a corner charge, the superhero comes back to life with a neckbreaker. He quickly follows up with a head scissors and shining wizard kick. A top rope flying cross body block then gets him a near fall ahead of an overcast. He motions for the chokeslam afterwards, but the "People's Champ" runs out to attack him for the disqualification. After The Hurricane gets in a few punches, the "Great One" DDTs and tosses him over the top rope. Not done yet, he atomic drops the superhero on the barricade and punches his crotch. Embarrassed, he then wails on The Hurricane with a steel chair repeatedly.

Steven Richards/Victoria def. Jazz/Trish Stratus. JR questions this match after announcing that Trish, Jazz, and Victoria will meet at WrestleMania XIX for the Women's Title. As the heels head to the ring, we see footage of the "black widow" talking to her Women's Title. Richards interrupts to say his history with Jazz is in the past and he knows Victoria will successfully defend her championship at WrestleMania XIX. Inside the ring, Jazz forces the "black widow" back into the ropes. The champion responds with a slap and kick. A powerslam afterwards gets her a two-count ahead of shoulder tackles in a corner. Jazz won't stay down, answering a dropkick and powerslam for a near fall. She follows up with a string of fists before yelling at her partner and tagging her hard. Stratus is met with an eye rake and chops. She answers with a string of clotheslines and a dropkick for a two-count. A Chick Kick also gets her a near fall before she attempts a victory roll. The champion counters by tossing her to the canvas for a moonsault and two-count. Richards tags in moments later, but takes too long posturing on the ropes and Trish whips Victoria into his crotch. The vixen follows up with a handstand head scissors before the "black widow" recovers to toss her around by the hair. A surfboard in the ropes follows, but Victoria misses a somersault leg drop. Steven also misses a bronco buster, crotching himself. That gives Stratus time to crawl to her corner for the tag, but Jazz short arms her and walks away. Richards capitalizes with a sit-out spinebuster ahead of the champion's Widow's Peak for the victory. Post-match, Steven teases a DDT on a chair, but Jeff Hardy runs out for the save. When Victoria grabs his hair, Jeff shoves her into a corner where Richards accidentally squashes her. Hardy tries to Swanton Bomb her, but Steven recovers to pull the "black widow" from the ring before Jeff checks on Trish and kisses her.

A video package of memorable Shawn Michaels moments at WrestleMania plays. Afterwards, Chris Jericho tells Jonathan Coachman that Shawn's legacy is impressive. Y2J used to dream about being Michaels, but now his dream is ending the "Heartbreak Kid's" career and he will in thirteen days. Christian interrupts to tell Jericho that their tag match is next. Y2J doesn't know who Test's partner will be, but it doesn't matter to him.

After a commercial break, Stacy Keibler tells Test that Chris Jericho is not going to be ready for their surprise next. The bodyguard agrees, but needs a minute alone before heading to the ring. When Stacy walks away, Test unveils his hidden issue of *Playboy* with Torrie Wilson in it.

Chris Jericho/Christian def. Scott Steiner/Test (with Stacy Keibler). The heels are surprised to see Scott joining Test. The bodyguard takes advantage of the shock, racing out to punch Y2J and press slam him over the top rope onto Christian. After Steiner decks the heels, Test resumes his attack in the squared circle until he lowers his head too soon for a back body drop. Jericho answers with a kick to the face and tag to Christian. "Big Poppa Pump" joins him to slam the heel into a corner and slug him. An elbow drop and pushups follow before the bodyguard returns for the babyfaces to hammer Christian. When Test turns his attention to Y2J, Christian takes advantage with a spinning heel kick. Jericho tags in afterwards for a leaping back elbow. Christian returns moments later only to run into a clothesline. When Scott tags back in, he clotheslines and slams the heel. He also chops Jericho before press slamming Christian. Y2J tries to help his partner, but runs into a belly-to-belly suplex. "Freakzilla" follows up with an exploder suplex to Christian for a two-count. When he tries to finish him off, the heel grabs Earl Hebner for Jericho to low blow Steiner. Once in control, Y2J chops "Big Poppa Pump" and mocks him with pushups. He tries to follow up with a second rope attack, but leaps into Scott's arms for an overhead belly-to-belly suplex. Test tags in afterwards to slam and clothesline the heels, nearly getting the three-count on Jericho. When he goes for a powerbomb, Y2J flips free ahead of a Christian chop block. Jericho and the bodyguard then trade counters, Test finally hitting a pumphandle slam, but Christian breaks the count. He also breaks a cover moments later when Steiner belly-to-belly suplexes Y2J ahead of a Test powerbomb. When Christian goes after Stacy, "Big Poppa Pump" chases him away. He also saves Keibler when Jericho hits the ropes ahead of a Test full nelson slam. After Scott catches Stacy to save her from falling to the floor, the bodyguard gets upset and loses his focus. Y2J capitalizes with a roll-up for the three-count, leaving Keibler to explain to a frustrated Test what just happened.

Triple H (with Ric Flair) def. Goldust (with Booker T). Lawler doesn't think it's fair that Booker is in Goldust's corner and wonders if the five-time champion's parole officer knows he's here. Inside the ring, the "bizarre one" punches the champion ahead of a butt bump. A shot to the injured arm slows him briefly, but Goldust recovers for a back body drop. Unfortunately, he feels a delayed pain in his arm and drops to the mat. Helmsley capitalizes, working on the arm ahead of a spinebuster. Instead of going for the cover, he taunts Booker T. That gives the "bizarre one" time to recover and punch the champion. He nearly picks up the win following a roll-up to counter a Pedigree, but Triple H just kicks out. Moments later, he runs into a pair of clotheslines and a fist to the jaw. An inverted atomic drop and clothesline gets him another two-count, but when he misses a clothesline, Hunter tosses Goldust out to the floor. There, Flair attacks the "bizarre one" until Booker rushes to his friend's defense. From the crowd, Randy Orton smashes the five-time champion with a crutch. Back in the ring, Goldust bulldogs and punches Helmsley. When he sets up for Shattered Dreams, pain in his arm drops the "bizarre one" again. "The Game" capitalizes with a high knee and Pedigree for the victory.

Fred Durst talks about Limp Bizkit performing at WrestleMania XIX in a prerecorded clip. He's looking forward to it.

Backstage, Eric Bischoff is in his karate gear talking to The Rock. When he tries to touch the "Great One's" guitar, the "People's Champ" stops him. He says the guitar is special and signed by Willie Nelson. He offers to give everyone a Rock concert. Eric thinks he's talking about tonight, but the "Brahma Bull" says St. Louis is disgusting and doesn't deserve it. Instead, he'll play next week. Bischoff wonders if he'll see the "Great One" at ringside in his "Lumberjack" match next. The Rock wants to talk to the GM about that. He thinks a "Lumberjack" match makes Eric look weak and talks him into changing the contest. Instead, Bischoff and "Stone Cold" Steve Austin will meet in a "No Disqualification" match with the "Brahma Bull" waiting to make his mark.

The announcers preview the WrestleMania XIX card.

"Stone Cold" Steve Austin def. Eric Bischoff (with Chief Morley) ("No Disqualification" match). Eric doesn't want to get into the ring with Austin and runs away from him. When he hides behind Morley, "Stone Cold" clotheslines and stomps the chief of staff. He then punches Bischoff at ringside before shoving him into the squared circle to stomp a mudhole in the GM. The "rattlesnake" follows up with a Boston crab, but lets go to threaten Morley. When he sets up for a low blow to Eric, the chief returns for his own low blow shot. That gives Bischoff control and he chokes and kicks Austin. He can't keep him down as the "rattlesnake" stomps another mudhole in him ahead of a Stone Cold Stunner. After he tosses Morley out of the ring, The Rock runs out to give Steve his own Stunner. Somehow, he recovers in time to kick out of Bischoff's cover. That brings the "Great One" back into the ring, but he misses a People's Elbow. After knocking the "People's Champ" from the squared circle, the "rattlesnake" gives Morley and Eric Stone Cold Stunners for the three-count. Post-match, the "Brahma Bull" flips off "Stone Cold" ahead of a Rock Bottom. With the fans booing, The Rock raids Austin's beers and has a drink on the ramp to end the show.

SmackDown!

March 20, 2003
Louisville, KY
Announcers: Michael Cole, Tazz

The show opens with clips of famous WrestleMania opening anthems and shots of WWE superstars with the US armed forces. A flag graphic says that the WWE is always thinking about the troops. Afterwards, a video package plays showing Kurt Angle outsmarting Brock Lesnar last week ahead of the intro video and fireworks.

Rhyno (with Chris Benoit) def. Charlie Haas (with Shelton Benjamin) by disqualification. The man-beast goes right after the heels, hammering both of them and chasing off Haas. After he swings around a title belt, Rhyno continues his assault on the rookie. Charlie turns the tide whipping the man-beast into a Benjamin low bridge and superkick. Although Benoit chases off Shelton, the damage is done and Haas capitalizes back in the ring with a belly-to-belly suplex. He then works on Rhyno's knee with kicks and submission holds. When the man-beast reaches the ropes after a knee bar, Benjamin cheap shots him. Charlie follows up with a knee breaker and stomps before applying another submission hold. Eventually, Rhyno kicks free and slows the rookie with a back suplex. Hard shots and a shoulderblock follow before the man-beast belly-to-belly suplexes his opponent. When he sets up for the Gore, Shelton trips him. The "rabid wolverine" tries to help his partner, but Benjamin slips free of his attack to hold Rhyno for a Charlie title belt shot to the head and disqualification. Post-match, Benoit chases the heels away.

Bob Costas talks about the "twenty years in the making" Hulk Hogan and Vince McMahon WrestleMania XIX match. He says big time feuds have to be settled in public.

The New Balance Slam of the Week is Brian Kendrick beating Matt Hardy last week. While Kendrick is proud of his effort, Stephanie McMahon isn't. She calls him a liability because he's not part of the SmackDown! roster. Brian apologizes, but Stephanie doesn't want his apologies. She offers him a chance to earn a contract tonight by beating Shannon Moore. If he does, McMahon tells him that he better start listening.

In another prerecorded vignette, John Cena issues an open challenge to any rapper for a WrestleMania XIX freestyle battle. He also warns Brock Lesnar that payback is coming and promises to be back in action next week.

In yet another prerecorded vignette, Los Guerreros interrupt a pair of golfers. The men say the joke is over and the kitchen is back at the clubhouse. Eddie and Chavo threaten them before telling the pairing that they are playing golf together today. The men back down and are suddenly okay with a "foursome". Los Guerreros don't like that term, but they do enjoy playing the men and cheating them out of all their money and watches despite being terrible golfers. The skit ends with Los Guerreros telling everyone that "if you're not cheating, you're not trying".

Los Guerreros/Rikishi def. Nunzio/The FBI. Eddie starts fast slamming Nunzio. Things get worse for the Italian heel as Chavo powerbombs him. He then whips Nunzio into Stamboli and out to the floor. While the fans chant for Eddie, his nephew head scissors Palumbo. Eventually, Chuck slows the former champion with a forearm to the back and single leg crab. When Chavo reaches his corner, Jimmy Korderas is distracted and misses the tag. "Latino Heat" then inadvertently distracts the referee as Johnny joins his partner with a pair of single leg crabs. Nunzio follows up with a Sicilian slicer. Moments later, Palumbo nearly gets the win with a Samoan drop, but Guerrero just kicks out. He does one better when Chuck attempts a powerslam, countering with a tornado DDT. Chavo finally gives Eddie the hot tag to punch and head scissors Palumbo. He also dropkicks Stamboli and punches Nunzio off the apron. A double takedown follows to The FBI before Rikishi tags in to kick Chuck. Johnny gets a boot too while the Italian heel stomps "Latino Heat" at ringside. When he enters the squared circle, the big Samoan crushes all three heels in a corner at the same time. Once the babyfaces get rid of everyone else, Rikishi squashes Palumbo ahead of a Frog Splash from Eddie for the three-count.

In another twenty years in the making clip, Bobby Heenan says anything can happen when Hulk Hogan and Vince McMahon bump heads.

Rey Mysterio def. Jamie Noble (with Nidia). A tune-up match for his Cruiserweight Title shot at WrestleMania XIX, Rey flies around the ring until Jamie powerbombs him into a corner. A back suplex follows for a two-count. Afterwards, Noble flings Mysterio out to the floor where Nidia hurts her arm clotheslining the masked man. That's a sacrifice she's willing to make as her man scores a near fall back in the ring. The redneck follows up with a hanging stretch until Rey escapes with a tornado DDT. Chops and a springboard cross body block follow for a two-count, but Mysterio can't keep Jamie down and runs into a powerslam and near fall. When Noble heads upstairs, the masked man dropkicks him ahead of a head scissors to the mat. Nidia gets involved again, grabbing Rey's mask. After chasing her off, Mysterio flies onto the diva with a slingshot splash. That sets off the redneck and he baseball slide kicks the masked man. When he sets up for a Tiger Bomb on the apron though, Rey fights free for a 619 and West Coast Pop to score the victory.

Backstage, Kurt Angle tells his brother, Eric, that he feels bad that he got hurt last week. As his brother limps around on crutches, Kurt tells him that they should go to the ring and speak their mind about Brock Lesnar. After a commercial break, they do just that. The Olympian brags about beating Lesnar last week and being the greatest athlete in WWE history. He adds that he's the smartest too before revealing that Eric distracted Brock long enough for the WWE Champion to get the win. Angle loves his brother and hugs him, but says his love is different than the Kentuckians have for their family members. Eric loves his brother too and says their mother is right, Kurt "doesn't suck". The Olympian promises his brother that Lesnar will never touch him again. Angle rants that the "next big thing" is a disgrace to wrestling, amateur and professional. He wants an apology from Brock for what he did to Eric last week, saying "what you do to one Angle, you do to all Angles". Instead, Stephanie McMahon comes out to apologize that not only will Kurt have to defend his belt at WrestleMania XIX, but if anyone interferes or Angle is disqualified or counted out, he'll forfeit the championship. She says he owes it to the fans to have the best WrestleMania match of all-time. The Olympian is fine with having the best match in history, but he's going to do it for himself. When the champion refuses to leave the ring, Lesnar finally comes out to a big pop. When he charges the ring, Kurt shoves his brother into the "next big thing" and runs away. Brock isn't concerned with Eric, clotheslining him before lunging for the champion, but he should be as the injured superstar slows him with a low blow. The Olympian follows up with a crutch shot to the face and Angle Slam onto a chair. Afterwards, he locks on a full body chin lock, his knee in the number one contender's back to injure his WrestleMania XIX opponent.

The Undertaker def. Bill DeMott. The Undertaker starts strong, trapping DeMott in a headlock and leg bar while Nathan Jones watches backstage. The announcers are excited to see his in-ring debut next week. This week, the biker gives Bill snake eyes before walking into a spinebuster and near fall. The "Deadman" is back on the attack moments later with peppering fists and a leaping clothesline. He follows up with Old School, the announcers noting that he looks better than ever. When he tries to chokeslam the bully, DeMott counters with a belly-to-belly suplex and a two-count. He can't avoid the chokeslam forever and The Undertaker catches him moments later ahead of a Tombstone for the win.

After a commercial break, a trainer checks on Brock Lesnar's ribs. The "next big thing" says it's the same one that he broke last year and he can feel the same pain.

Brian Kendrick def. Shannon Moore. Moore comes out to Hardy's music and Matt Facts stating that Matt "graciously" included Shannon in his book and that he's the rookie's idol. Speaking of his book, Hardy gives his and Jeff's book to Tazz. After Kendrick comes out to no music or fanfare, he shoulder blocks Shannon and rolls him up for a two-count. When he attempts a victory roll, Moore slams him to the mat, but the rookie won't stay down. It takes a clothesline and pair of suplexes to slow him enough for a Shannon two-count. The MFer then takes a page out of his mentor's playbook and applies a surfboard. Brian continues to fight back, chopping and punching Moore ahead of a facebuster and springboard missile dropkick for a near fall. When he attempts a dropkick, the MFer holds the ropes. He tries to follow up with a back suplex, but Kendrick lands on his feet for a leg lariat and another two-count. When he attempts a twist of fate, Shannon counters with a fireman's carry into a facebuster for his own near fall. After his man gets in a string of strikes, Matt slams Brian face-first on the ring steps. Somehow, Kendrick still kicks out of Moore's cover. Following another Hardy cheap shot, Rey Mysterio runs out to head scissors Matt. That distracts Shannon long enough for Brian to score the win with a Step Up Reverse Bulldog to land a WWE contract.

The WrestleMania Moment is "Rowdy" Roddy Piper and Mr. T's WrestleMania 2 boxing match. Afterwards, the announcers talk about the Miller Lite Catfight Girls being at WrestleMania XIX and preview the card.

Footage from this week's WrestleMania press conference play featuring WWE superstars hyping up the show.

Backstage, Vince McMahon and his attorney look over his WrestleMania XIX contract stipulating that if Hulk Hogan loses their match he'll never wrestle again.

Chris Benoit (with Rhyno) def. Shelton Benjamin (with Charlie Haas). A classic wrestling trope, this is the second singles match of the night pitting the feuding tag teams against each other. "The Crippler" is fired up as he chops and back suplexes Benjamin for an early two-count. A pair of clotheslines score him another near fall before he unloads on Shelton in a corner. Eventually, the rookie responds with a backward head slam onto his knee. Afterwards, a back suplex gets him a two-count. Showing off his own intensity, Benjamin chokes and knees Benoit ahead of a chin lock. Cole picks the "rabid wolverine" and Rhyno to win the WWE Tag Titles at WrestleMania XIX, but Tazz says that's a mistake since they both have suffered serious injuries. Benoit shows why he's a good pick locking on a Crippler Crossface. Although Shelton manages to escape that one, when he misses a spinning heel kick, "the Crippler" reapplies his hold. The man-beast stops Haas from breaking it, Goring him before Benjamin taps.

In another twenty years in the making clip, Jesse Ventura says there's never been a bad WrestleMania. He calls the show physically and mentally draining while complimenting Vince McMahon's tenacity.

After the final commercial break, "Mean" Gene Okerlund is in the ring to officiate the contract signing for Vince McMahon and Hulk Hogan's "twenty years in the making" WrestleMania XIX match. "Mean" Gene also reminds everyone that should the Hulkster lose the match, his career will be over. Afterwards, Hogan comes out to a huge pop. He knows what he's in for and promises that he won't let the Hulkamaniacs down. The fans don't even care what he says, loudly cheering Hulk as he makes fun of McMahonamania and says that the Hulkamaniacs made Vince. When he challenges McMahon to come out, the WWE owner walks the halls telling his employees to watch what's coming. It's a prerecorded trap as Vince sneaks out behind the Hulkster to smash him repeatedly with a chair. McMahon spits venom as he yells that he made Hogan. When Hulk gets up, the WWE owner blasts him with the chair one more time to the skull, busting him open. Vince then signs the contract before stabbing the Hulkster with the pen. He makes Hogan sign the contract in blood to boos.

Monday Night Raw
March 24, 2003
Sacramento, CA
Announcers: Jim Ross, Jerry "the King" Lawler

Continuing to support the US troops in Iraq, Lilian Garcia sings the "Star Spangled Banner" to start the show to a big pop. Afterwards, the intro video plays and fireworks explode before "Stone Cold" Steve Austin heads to the squared circle. Charles Robinson tries to get him to leave, telling the "rattlesnake" that it's time for a match. Austin doesn't care. He's in a foul mood after The Rock gave him a Stone Cold Stunner and Rock Bottom last week. "Stone Cold" refuses to leave until the "People's Champ" comes out. Instead, Test and Stacy Keibler head to the ring for their match. The bodyguard doesn't want to disrespect Austin, but Bischoff told him to head to the ring. The "rattlesnake" gives him a Stone Cold Stunner. Afterwards, he sits beside Lilian Garcia as Lance Storm hurries out to cover Test. Instead of Robinson making the count, "Stone Cold" slides in to count to two. He stops abruptly and gives Lance a Stunner too. That brings out Eric Bischoff. He's had enough and tells the "rattlesnake" that this is his show. To make sure Austin never touches him again, Eric has a restraining order. The general manager sends twelve armed officers to ringside to ask Steve to leave or get arrested. After thinking it over, "Stone Cold" leaves peacefully. At the top of the ramp, Bischoff taunts the "rattlesnake", but Austin doesn't take the bait. He calmly walks away for Eric to tease tonight's Rock concert.

Jeff Hardy/Trish Stratus def. Steven Richards/Victoria. A mixed tag match, the men can only wrestle the men. Jeff starts fast with Steven, leg dropping his midsection before the heel answers with a string of fists. A whip into the corner and double kick sends Richards crawling to his corner for the tag. After Victoria goads Hardy, Trish enters to rock her with a Chick Kick. Steven tries to break up the count, but Jeff meets him for the men to fight outside the ring while the "black widow" plants Stratus with a spinning side slam for a near fall. Unfortunately, she misses a standing moonsault. That stuns her long enough for the vixen to recover for a corner handstand head scissors. She sets up for Stratusfaction afterwards, waiting for Richards to return to knock him into the ropes where she climbs up him to bulldog Victoria for the win. Post-match, Trish nearly kisses the daredevil, but Jazz hit her from behind. While Steven fights with Hardy, Jazz lays out both Stratus and the champion.

After a commercial break, Jonathan Coachman interrupts Eric Bischoff on the phone. Coach says security has an emergency.

Further backstage, Booker T interrupts Goldust checking out Torrie Wilson in *Playboy*. Ahead of their tag match tonight, the "bizarre one" stutters as he tells Booker how proud he is of his friend facing Triple H for the World Title this Sunday. The five-time champion appreciates it, but wonders if Goldust is okay. He will be when he hears the fans cheering on his friend.

Afterwards, security shows Eric Bischoff footage of "Stone Cold" Steve Austin pacing the parking lot. A guard tells the GM that his restraining order is only good for inside the arena and they can't do anything to the "rattlesnake". Bischoff wants Jonathan Coachman to tell Austin to leave or Eric will make his life a living hell. Coach doesn't want to go. The GM understands and gives him a choice too. He can deliver the message or get fired. That doesn't leave Coachman much choice and he heads to the parking lot.

Scott Steiner def. Christian. Scott easily overpowers the heel to start the match, clubbing and press slamming him. JR wonders how anyone can wrestle "Big Poppa Pump". Christian answers, slipping free of a press slam for a reverse neckbreaker and two-count. He follows up with a choke and neckbreaker for another near fall. Following more chokes, the heel flexes to mock Steiner. Scott quickly answers with fists to boos. An overhead belly-to-belly suplex has fans divided, as does a powerslam to block a Christian leapfrog. When he runs into a corner boot, some of the fans cheer the heel as he nearly steals the win with his feet on the ropes. He follows up with a throat drop on the top rope, but takes too long climbing them afterwards and Steiner catches him for a second rope Samoan drop and three-count. Post-match, "Big Poppa Pump" dedicates his win to his freaks and gets a decent pop, the crowd clearly divided.

In the parking lot, Jonathan Coachman approaches "Stone Cold" Steve Austin's truck to deliver Eric Bischoff's message. Austin doesn't say a word before Coach rushes off to tell the GM that his message was received.

The Snickers Cruncher WrestleMania Moment is Shawn Michaels beat Bret Hart at WrestleMania XII.

MUST SEE! Backstage, Chief Morley tells Terri that due to William Regal's injury the World Tag Titles haven't been defended in thirty days and he and Lance Storm must be stripped of their championships. As the chief of staff, Morley names the new champions, himself and Storm. Kane and Rob Van Dam halfheartedly congratulate them before challenging the new champions to a match tonight. The chief says that they haven't had time to think about challengers. The babyfaces feel they are the top contenders since they beat the new champions last week, but Morley disagrees. He thinks The Dudley Boyz deserve a title shot. Kane proposes that they have a number one contender's match tonight with the winners getting a title shot this Sunday. The chief of staff likes that and agrees. As he walks away, the "Big Red Machine" says hello to Storm, slapping the back of his neck hard.

Booker T/Goldust def. Ric Flair/Triple H. Following separate entrances for everyone and Lawler making fun of Booker's criminal history, Goldust drives Flair into a corner to jack his jaw. He follows up with a back body drop before threatening Triple H. The "bizarre one" gets a piece of him moments later when he tags in before racing to his corner to tag the five-time champion. A WrestleMania XIX preview, the championship competitors lock up with the fans cheering for Booker T. He answers them with a hip toss and chops until Hunter runs through him and tags back in Ric. "The Nature Boy" unloads with chops, but that just fires up Booker and he laces the legend himself ahead of a side slam and two-count. Flair responds with a rake of the eyes before Helmsley tags back in to run into a kick to the face. Luckily, Ric chop blocks the five-time champion to give his partner control. He takes advantage with strikes and a whip out to the floor. There, Goldust stops Ric from attacking his partner ahead of a commercial break.

Afterwards, "The Nature Boy" has Booker T trapped in a Figure Four Leglock. It takes him a few seconds, but eventually the babyface turns over the hold, forcing Flair to break. Afterwards, the wrestlers trade chops again. Once again, Booker gets the better of Ric. The "bizarre one" then gets the hot tag to fight both heels, countering a double back body drop with a double uppercut. He follows up with inverted atomic drops and a double clothesline before missing "the Game" and flying out to the floor. The champion capitalizes with a whip into the ring steps before Ric takes advantage of Nick Patrick being distracted for a low blow and choke. Triple H tags in afterwards to stomp Goldust and taunt the five-time champion. The "bizarre one" tries to fight back, but a neckbreaker puts him down for a two-count. When he returns, "The Nature Boy" gets a two-count with a knee drop. Moments later, Goldust reaches his corner for the tag, but Patrick misses it. He also misses Hunter illegally entering the ring while trying to hold back Booker T. Despite missing that tag, he lets Helmsley stay in the ring punishing the "bizarre one" until he rolls to his corner and gives Booker the hot tag. He proceeds to fight both heels, kicking them until Flair attacks the back of his leg again. This time, the babyface quickly recovers to whip "the Game" out to the floor. When Ric attempts his corner flip, he falls face-first into the middle turnbuckle. That lets Booker T slam the champion's face into the ring steps, busting him open. Fists follow in and out of the ring. When "The Nature Boy" attacks the five-time champion again, Booker drops him with a Scissors Kick. Unfortunately, Flair isn't the legal man and Triple H attacks the babyface from behind. When he tries to finish him off with a Pedigree, Booker T counters with a catapult into the top turnbuckle ahead of a Scissors Kick for the three-count. JR says he has the momentum heading into WrestleMania XIX.

After a commercial break, a bloodied Triple H stares at the World Title while Ric Flair tells him that Booker T's win was a fluke. He adds that Booker can't beat him. "The Game" responds that no one told Booker T that.

Afterwards, Chris Jericho heads to the ring to boos. He's serious as he talks about his history with Shawn Michaels and invites him out to the ring for a face-to-face conversation. Y2J promises no tricks. When the "Heartbreak Kid" comes out, Jericho says that he was really impressed by Shawn's video package last week. It reminded him that Y2J modeled his career after Michaels and he shows video clips and pictures of him emulating the "Heartbreak Kid". Everyone thought Jericho was going to be the next Shawn Michaels, but Y2J says he's surpassed Shawn. While Michaels was at home, Jericho was in the WWE being the workhorse and first ever Undisputed Champion. With all the opponents he's faced so far, there's no one he's more excited to beat and embarrass than Michaels. Y2J promises their match will be special and the "Heartbreak Kid" will have to admit that Jericho is the better wrestler. When Shawn doesn't look at him, Y2J slaps the babyface. Michaels laughs ahead of his own slap. Now it's Jericho laughing, the two men going face-to-face and laughing ahead of a commercial break.

Backstage, Eric Bischoff tells someone on the phone to keep an eye out for "Stone Cold" Steve Austin until The Rock interrupts with an idea. Bischoff notes that every time the "People's Champ" has an idea, the GM gets his butt kicked. The "Great One" tells him that he took care of business and did just fine last week. He then says Austin is hanging around because he wants to hear the Rock concert. He wants Eric to get Chief Morley to put some speakers outside so "Stone Cold" can hear the concert later.

Kane/Rob Van Dam def. The Dudley Boyz (#1 Contender's match). Despite vying for a World Tag Title shot, the babyfaces come out separately again. Although the Dudleys come out together, Kane pounds them down. Bubba Ray doesn't stay there, surprising the "Big Red Machine" with a German suplex. D-Von then tags in for a clothesline and elbow drop. After that scores him a two-count, the monster slams Dudley and tags in RVD for a slingshot leg drop. The fans chant for tables as Rob hurricanranas D-Von and kicks him. Rolling thunder afterwards gets Van Dam a near fall. When he attempts a monkey flip in a corner, Dudley moves and answers with a neckbreaker. Bubba returns afterwards to drop a trio of elbow drops on the downed babyface for a two-count. He then slows the pace with a neck wrench while the fans chant for RVD. Rob quickly fights free and drops Dudley with a step over kick. Kane tags in afterwards to clothesline and back body drop D-Von. He also decks Bubba Ray on the apron ahead of a powerslam to his half-brother for a near fall. When he attempts a flying clothesline, D-Von moves and the Dudleys answer with a double flapjack. Van Dam rushes to his partner's defense, kicking both heels until Bubba catches him with a hip toss into a neckbreaker. Despite that, RVD quickly recovers and drops Bubba Ray with a springboard kick. That brings out Chief Morley to distract Chad Patton. While he does, Lance Storm tries to give Rob a leg lariat, but Van Dam ducks to see the Canadian hit D-Von.

RVD and Kane then interrupt Bubba arguing with Lance, knocking them both out of the ring before the babyfaces score the win with a combination Chokeslam and Five-Star Frog Splash to D-Von.

Backstage, WWE crew set up large speakers beside "Stone Cold" Steve Austin's truck. Before he can do anything about it, the "rattlesnake's" phone rings and he answers it.

After a commercial break, The Rock comes out for his concert. He says the best part about being here is that in half an hour he's going to leave Sacramento. He then sings a song about Sacramento and the big women that he wants to get away from. He promises to come back when the "Lakers beat the Kings in May". That gets him a huge booing. All his singing is cut from the WWE Network including him spoofing "Hound Dog" to sing that "Stone Cold" Steve Austin is nothing but a redneck. He then notes that Willie Nelson signed his guitar and he can't "wait to whip Austin's ass again". Finally, he sings about facing the final curtain at WrestleMania XIX and beating Austin to the tune of "My Way". As he jokes about a woman fainting in the crowd, an ambulance pulls up to the building. "Stone Cold" uses that opportunity to drive his truck into the arena. The "People's Champ" has seen enough and calls for security to surround the ring and protect him. When the truck drives down the aisle, it's The Hurricane driving. The "Great One" calls him the Hamburglar again and tells the cops to arrest him too. They do so, leaving the "Brahma Bull" alone in the ring. That's bad news for him as Austin crawls out from under a blanket in the back of the truck to attack The Rock and drive him from the squared circle. When the "People's Champ" runs away, "Stone Cold" holds his Willie Nelson signed guitar hostage. He teases giving it back before stomping it to pieces for a huge pop.

After a commercial break, Vince McMahon heads to the squared circle to brag about what he did on *SmackDown!*. He then plays footage of his contract signing with Hulk Hogan. After the complete replay, the WWE owner says he's proud that he created Hulkamania and this Sunday he'll be proud that he ended it.

Following another commercial break, Kurt Angle attacking Brock Lesnar on *SmackDown!* replays. Afterwards, JR thanks the network for giving the WWE extra time to hype up WrestleMania XIX and shills the upcoming PPV.

SmackDown!

March 27, 2003
San Jose, CA
Announcers: Michael Cole, Tazz

Matt Hardy Version 1.0/Shannon Moore def. Brian Kendrick/Rey Mysterio. Following the intro video and fireworks, Rey pops out of the stage to get the fans hyped up. The heels follow with Matt Facts stating that Mattitude will make WrestleMania a success. It also says that Hardy is "very humble". He is also on the apron to start the match as Shannon and Kendrick cut a fast pace. Mysterio gets involved illegally dropkicking Moore for the upper head. The babyfaces follow up with a Brian giant swing and masked man dropkick for a two-count. Afterwards, Shannon catches Rey with a pair of boots on corner charges before we get a preview of the WrestleMania XIX Cruiserweight Title match. Mysterio gets the upper hand, punching and dropkicking the champion for a two-count after a snap mare. Back in, Kendrick is hip tossed by his own partner into a sunset flip to Matt for a near fall. Moments later, the heels cut their own corner with a double-team powerbomb and clothesline for a two-count. When Moore returns, the heels stomp Brian in a corner. Shannon scores a near fall afterwards with a side suplex. Hardy returns soon after for a sit-out crucifix bomb and near fall. When Shannon tags back in, Kendrick absorbs a snap suplex to surprise the MFer with an innovative facebuster. Rey then gets the hot tag to dropkick and springboard butt splash the champion. Moore saves his mentor after a springboard leg drop, but is chased from the ring by Kendrick. Moments later, Brian gets a blind tag to block a Twist of Fate with a springboard tornado DDT and near fall. After Mysterio takes care of Shannon, he hurricanranas Matt out of the ring. Moore returns afterwards to trade kicks with his fellow rookie while the masked man runs into a barricade slam. Hardy quickly slides back into the ring after Kendrick drops Shannon with a Step Up Reverse Bulldog to give him a Twist of Fate and steal the win. Post-match, Rey returns and chase off Matt ahead of a 619 to Moore. Before he can finish him off, Hardy surprises the masked man with a Twist of Fate. He stares intensely at his downed WrestleMania XIX opponent as he heads backstage.

Also backstage, Hulk Hogan arrives with his son, Nick, and Jimmy Hart. He tells them to wait in his locker room.

In a twenty years in the making clip, "Rowdy" Roddy Piper talks about the history between Vince McMahon and Hulk Hogan. He says that after this Sunday "there will be a McMahon or a Mc-Nothing".

A video package of Vince McMahon attacking Hulk Hogan last week plays. Afterwards, the Hulkster head to the ring to a huge pop. While the fans cheer for him loudly, the announcers wonder if Hulkamania is running wild for the last time. Finally, Hogan says that Vince fears Hulkamania to quiet the crowd. Once upon a time, Hulk says he was friends with McMahon and over the years he's seen him do some "illegal things". While Vince might be a genius, the Hulkster says he's an "evil genius". He then talks about the WWE owner screwing him at No Way Out. After what McMahon did last week, Hogan wonders if he made a mistake putting his career on the line this Sunday. However, he's a man of his word and Hulk knows that this won't be his last time on *SmackDown!*. The Hulkster is sure he can beat McMahon in a fight. Hogan promises a fight like no one has seen before because he will do what it takes to beat the WWE owner and leave him laying in a pool of his own blood at WrestleMania XIX.

Eddie Guerrero (with Chavo Guerrero Jr.) def. Charlie Haas (with Shelton Benjamin). After Team Angle enjoyed a pair of matches with Chris Benoit and Rhyno last week, they step into the ring tonight against Los Guerreros in two more singles matches. Once the bell rings, the wrestlers trade takedowns until Eddie surprises Haas with a head scissors. A dropkick follows, but "Latino Heat" hurts his shoulder as he lands. It comes back to cost him when he shoulder blocks the rookie. Charlie spots the weakness and hammerlock slams Guerrero's arm onto the top rope. A whip into the ring post follows. Despite an arm drag, Haas remains in control stretching and slamming Eddie's injured joint. Eventually, "Latino Heat" escapes an armbar with a back suplex. He comes back to life afterwards with fists and clotheslines from his good arm. A unique jawbreaker and roll-up follow for a near fall before the rookie slams him on the top rope ahead of a hammerlock northern lights suplex and two-count. When he attempts an arm slam, Guerrero rolls Charlie up for the out of nowhere three-count.

Backstage, Josh Mathews tries to get a word with John Cena. The rapping heel says he's on the hunt for Brock Lesnar and he's going to call him out tonight.

In a prerecorded vignette, Nunzio and The FBI walk around New York City. When they meet a man who asks for more time, the heels take him down an alley off camera to deal with him. As they walk back into the shot, Nunzio says the guy took a "nasty fall".

After a commercial break, Josh Mathews tells Brock Lesnar that John Cena is going to call him out. Brock says Cena can do whatever he wants. Lesnar is just focused on his WrestleMania XIX WWE Title shot.

Further backstage, The Undertaker asks Nathan Jones if he's ready for his debut. Nathan opens a locker room door to say his match is already over. Inside is a downed Chuck Palumbo. The "Deadman" chuckles and says that Jones will have to wait until this Sunday for his debut. He then leads the rookie away to explain why what he did was wrong.

Even further backstage, Jamie Noble and Nidia pass a blown up picture of Torrie Wilson's *Playboy* cover. After smacking her boyfriend for not immediately saying that Nidia is the hotter of the divas, Nidia promises to rip Torrie's face off later.

The WrestleMania Moment is "Rowdy" Roddy Piper spraying Morton Downey Jr. with a fire extinguisher.

A video package of Stephanie McMahon and Torrie Wilson, alongside Hugh Hefner in Los Angeles, hyping Torrie's *Playboy* appearance plays.

Torrie Wilson def. Nidia (with Jamie Noble). Torrie is wearing yellow tonight. The announcers love the color. Noble doesn't, badmouthing the diva until Nidia sneak attacks her. After tossing Wilson out to the floor, the heel poses and grabs a chair. Torrie baseball slide kicks it into her face for a near fall. Chops to the back follow for another Wilson two-count. When she runs the ropes, Jamie gets involved and trips her for a Nidia dropkick and near fall. She gets in a few uppercuts before she runs into a corner boot and neckbreaker. Unfortunately, Jamie distracts Mike Sparks and the babyface for Nidia to recover and roll up Wilson for another two-count. Torrie won't stay down, surprising the heel with a tornado DDT for the three-count. Post-match, she runs away before Noble can grab her.

Backstage, A-Train and Big Show walk by Nathan Jones. They tell him not to worry. They'll deal with him this Sunday and question his sexuality after spending time in prison.

In a prerecorded vignette, Sean O'Haire tells fans to eat what they want.

A-Train/Big Show def. Chris Benoit/Rhyno by disqualification. As the giant heads to the ring first, the announcers talk about him appearing on *The Hollywood Squares* this week. Once everyone is out, the fans chant for A-Train to shave his back. Instead, he trades pummeling blows with Rhyno in a corner. When he attempts a charge, the man-beast meets him with an elbow and shoulders to the gut. Benoit then tags in to chop the hairy heel. Although A-Train answers with a big shoulderblock, he misses his splash. He doesn't miss a back elbow and tags in Show to corner "the Crippler". Benoit won't back down, chopping and attempting to trap Big Show in a Crippler Crossface. Instead, the giant chops and shoves around the "rabid wolverine". Afterwards, he tosses him halfway across the ring, showcasing his size and power advantage. A knee lift and headbutt follow before the hairy heel returns to stomp Benoit and yell at the fans. He also locks on a reverse full nelson, but rather than wait for the submission, A-Train drops to his knees for a two-count after the modified backbreaker. Unfortunately, he soon leaps into a pair of knees ahead of a drop toe hold into the middle turnbuckle. "The Crippler" impresses with a German suplex afterwards before crawling to his corner for the tag. The man-beast proceeds to hit both heels and clothesline A-Train. All four men end up fighting, Rhyno belly-to-belly suplexing the hairy heel. After Show rushes to his partner's defense with a clothesline, Nathan Jones runs out to attack his WrestleMania opponents. The heels quickly repel his attack, hammering him down until The Undertaker runs out for the save, knocking the monsters from the squared circle.

Backstage, Kurt Angle is looking for Brock Lesnar's locker room.

The Lugz Boot of the Week is Kurt Angle attacking Brock Lesnar's ribs last week. Afterwards, the Olympian confronts his WrestleMania XIX opponent in Lesnar's locker room. He says they are a lot alike. While they are both champions and winners, Kurt says Brock is "just a kid" with a big future. This Sunday, the Olympian tells Lesnar that his life is going to change forever when they raise the bar. Angle adds that they are the best in the business. Even if Brock ends his career this Sunday, Kurt knows he's done it all and can live with his legacy. The champion just wants to know if Lesnar is willing to put his career on the line at WrestleMania XIX because he won't hesitate to finish off the "next big thing". Brock says Kurt may look courageous entering his locker room, but they both know that Lesnar isn't going to jump him tonight. He's going to wait until it matters and that's this Sunday. The challenger agrees that they are going to raise the bar at WrestleMania XIX and he's going to bring everything he's got to beat Angle.

After the announcers preview WrestleMania XIX, we see footage of Vince McMahon training with his son, Shane, for his upcoming match.

In another twenty years in the making interview, "Mean" Gene Okerlund says Vince McMahon made wrestling what it is, but he's not the wrestler Hulk Hogan is. Okerlund gives the Hulkster the slight edge.

Chavo Guerrero Jr. (with Eddie Guerrero) def. Shelton Benjamin (with Charlie Haas). Like their partners earlier, the wrestlers open the match trading amateur holds. Things break down into a fight quickly before Chavo scores a two-count with a head scissors and dropkick. He then unloads with fists until Benjamin presses him high into the air. A clip gives the rookie a target and he works on Guerrero's left leg. When Chavo starts to fight back, Haas cheap shots him. Eddie gives chase, but he can't catch Charlie. Inside the ring, Shelton applies an Indian deathlock. Although Guerrero briefly escapes, the rookie goes right back to the hold. Eventually, Chavo punches his way free. He briefly applies a side headlock, but Benjamin escapes and dropkicks the babyface's injured knee. A stretch and leg drop on the joint follow. When Guerrero escapes, he surprises Shelton with a roll-up for a near fall. He also gets a two-count with an enziguri kick. When he tries to sunset flip the rookie, Charlie hops onto the apron to hold his man's hands. He pays courtesy of "Latino Heat" ramming Haas face-first into the ring post. Back up, Benjamin hammers Chavo until he runs into a drop toe hold and Guerrero roll-up for the three-count. Post-match, Chris Benoit and Rhyno look at Los Guerreros from the top of the ramp. Team Angle capitalize, hitting Chavo and Eddie with the WWE Tag Title belts. That sends the other babyfaces down the aisle for Rhyno to Gore Shelton while Benoit traps Haas in the Crippler Crossface.

The New Balance Slam of the Week is John Cena issuing a challenge to any rapper to freestyle battle him at WrestleMania XIX.

John Cena def. Rikishi. Cena makes his return from injury to slug Rikishi as he steps into the ring. Once Jimmy Korderas steps in, the big Samoan unloads with his own shots, driving John out to the floor. Rikishi makes the mistake of following him and gets whipped into the ring steps. The rapping heel then pulls free a section of barricade to ram the big Samoan into it for a two-count back in the squared circle. Cena follows up with a modified cross face chicken wing, but he can't properly apply it around the big babyface's body. Rikishi eventually fights free to clothesline and Samoan drop John. He teases a butt splash, but when the rapping heel hops up to his feet to avoid it, he does so into a thrust kick and corner splash. The big Samoan follows up with a Stinkface. He tries to finish off Cena with a Rump Shaker, but John counters with a pair of knees to the crotch. As he falls back, Rikishi knocks Korderas down to the mat. That lets the rapping heel grab his steel chain and blast the big Samoan's skull. Somehow, the big babyface just manages to kick out. Cena doesn't care, hoisting up Rikishi and impressing with a Death Valley Driver for the win. Post-match, John calls out Brock Lesnar, saying this is "basic thuganomics". When Brock doesn't come out, Cena goes to find him, "word life".

Fred Durst of Limp Bizkit talking about how special it is to perform at WrestleMania XIX plays.

The final twenty years in the making segment sees Arnold Schwarzenegger talking about how exciting WrestleMania is and credits Vince McMahon with creating Hulkamania. However, Arnold believes that the Hulkster will win their match and can't wait to see it.

Backstage, John Cena finds Brock Lesnar and attacks. The "next big thing" sees him coming and responds in kind until Kurt Angle blindsides the number one contender, shattering a two-by-four across his ribs to end the episode.

PPV: WrestleMania XIX
March 30, 2003
Seattle, WA
Announcers: Jim Ross, Jerry "the King" Lawler, Michael Cole, Tazz

The show opens with Ashanti singing "America the Beautiful" to shots of American troops ahead of a video package featuring the top superstars talking about how amazing WrestleMania is. The Rock calls it a "culmination of hard work" while Kurt Angle says this is the most important moment of his life. Afterwards, fireworks explode and JR hypes up his tenth WrestleMania. The *SmackDown!* announcers are just as fired up for this outdoor event.

Matt Hardy Version 1.0 (with Shannon Moore) def. Rey Mysterio (Cruiserweight Title match). As he has numerous Thursday night shows, Rey is out first to hype up the crowd. After popping up from the stage, Mysterio walks the long aisle for his WrestleMania debut. The heels follow, Matt Facts letting fans know that this is Hardy's fourth WrestleMania appearance and that he wonders how the WWE did the show without him. Shannon tries to distract the masked man, but he sees Matt's sneak attack coming and back body drops him over the top rope onto his MFer. A dive from the ring follows for a two-count. When he attempts a sunset flip powerbomb out to the floor moments later, Moore helps his mentor with a kick. That swings the momentum and Hardy scores a two-count with a side effect. The heels then take turns choking the challenger before Matt sets up for a Twist of Fate. At the last second, Rey counters with a roll-up for a near fall. When Mysterio leaps over him in a corner, the champion surprises him with a side effect for another two-count. He then grounds the high-flyer with a surfboard submission. It doesn't take the masked man long to fight free, but clubbing blows slows him again. Unfortunately, Hardy misses a corner charge and hits the ring post. The challenger follows up with a springboard butt splash for a two-count. Moments later, a tornado DDT gets him another near fall before he sets up for a 619. When he hits the ropes though, Shannon trips him and Matt capitalizes with a Twist of Fate. Somehow, the challenger kicks out at the last second. When Hardy tries to finish him off with a crucifix powerbomb from the bottom rope, Rey counters with a hurricanrana for a two-count. At the last second, Moore drapes his man's foot on the ropes. Mysterio has had enough and grabs the MFer. The champion tries another sneak attack, but the masked man moves and Matt hits Shannon. Rey follows up with a 619, but when he goes for the West Coast Pop, Hardy ducks. He then tosses the masked man onto the ropes, but Rey springs back onto his shoulders for a victory roll. Well-prepared, the champion drops down and holds the bottom rope for the three-count.

Backstage, the Miller Lite Catfight Girls arrive in a long limo to argue about which is the bigger match tonight, "Stone Cold" Steve Austin and The Rock or Vince McMahon and Hulk Hogan.

Afterwards, Cole replays footage from *Sunday Night Heat* of A-Train and Big Show laying out Nathan Jones.

Tony Chimel then introduces Limp Bizkit as the WWE's favorite band to play "Rollin" on the stage. Fred Durst puts in some work, heading to the ring and dancing around before The Undertaker rides his motorcycle down the aisle, an American flag on the back in a high octane entrance.

The Undertaker def. A-Train/Big Show. The heels come out together to Big Show's music, the announcers speculating that this will be the end of The Undertaker's undefeated streak. A-Train stops in the aisle to spit on the "Deadman's" bike to distract him for a giant sneak attack. The biker sees him coming and dodges his ambush ahead of a chokeslam to A-Train. Luckily, Show just manages to break up the cover. The Undertaker dominates the opening moments, giving the hairy heel Old School before Big Show trips him. A-Train capitalizes with a Derailer and Show follows up with a ram into the ring post. After he slams the biker onto the barricade, tearing off a section of padding, the giant shoves the "Deadman" back into the ring for a catapult into the middle rope and a near fall. Big Show tags in afterwards to trade shots with The Undertaker. When he tries to Chokeslam him, the biker counters with an armbar. He has to release it when A-Train makes the save, but the hairy heel gets trapped in an armbar too until the giant helps out. After the heels double-team the "Deadman", Show headbutts him and locks on an abdominal stretch. Already with the numbers advantage, the heels also cheat, A-Train grabbing his partner's hand for added leverage. The hairy heel soon tags in to apply his own abdominal stretch. When he doesn't cheat, The Undertaker reverses the hold. He follows up with a side suplex to put both men down on the mat. Unfortunately, when he runs the ropes, Big Show hits him, knocking him into an A-Train clothesline and two-count. The hairy heel then taunts the biker, saying he's not "such a big dog". The "Deadman" proves him wrong, coming back to life with a flurry of fists and a leaping DDT for a two-count. When the giant makes the save, Brian Hebner gives him the business and even shoves Show. The Undertaker does him one better, fighting both heels and crushing them in corners. He teases a chokeslam to the giant, but A-Train makes the save and eats a big boot. The biker follows up with a leaping clothesline to Big Show, but when he gets up, a hairy heel bicycle kick levels him. Show follows up with a Chokeslam. That brings Nathan Jones out. When Big Show rushes to meet him in the aisle, the "Colossus from Boggo Road" kicks him. He also kicks A-Train in the ring ahead of a Tombstone for the three-count to keep the "Deadman's" undefeated streak alive.

Backstage, Stacy Keibler and Torrie Wilson meet the Miller Lite Catfight Girls. They all love each other. Stacy has a marketing idea for the girls and they walk away to discuss it.

Afterwards, the *Raw* announcers tell the troops that they support them in Iraq and want them to get the fight over quickly. They then show footage of The Dudley Boyz helping Chief Morley and Lance Storm successfully defend their World Tag Titles earlier on *Heat*.

MUST SEE! Trish Stratus def. Jazz and Victoria (with Steven Richards) (Women's Title match). Victoria is out last for Jazz to hit Trish from behind and sneak attack the champion. Once she knocks the "black widow" from the ring, Jazz traps Stratus in a chin lock. The vixen answers with a string of fists and a corner boot. When she tries to go up to the top rope, Victoria trips her and takes the fight out to the floor. After handling both challengers, the "black widow" slingshot somersault leg drops Trish for a two-count before Jazz makes the save. She also scores her own near fall with a leg drop before Victoria breaks her cover. The heels decide to work together, delivering a double shoulderbreaker to Stratus before turning on each other. The champion nearly gets the win with a powerslam, but Jazz just kicks out. When she badmouths the challenger, Trish surprises Victoria with a roll-up for a two-count. The rivals then trade shots until Jazz hits the vixen from behind. A sit-out powerslam nearly gets Jazz the win, but when Victoria makes the save, the heels fight each other again. Stratus helps them, ramming their heads together. The "black widow" recovers first and holds Trish for a Jazz shot, but at the last second the vixen ducks and Jazz hits Victoria. Stratus capitalizes with a near fall roll-up to Jazz ahead of a Chick Kick. Once again, the "black widow" makes the save. Trish responds with a handstand head scissors out of the corner to the champion and chops. She also decks Jazz before knocking Victoria out to the floor. Jazz takes advantage of the opportunity, trapping the vixen in a single leg crab. When Stratus nearly reaches the ropes, Jazz turns her hold into an STF. The champion hops onto the apron to distract Jack Doan before Trish can tap out, allowing Richards to break the hold and toss Jazz out to the floor. Victoria and Stratus then trade roll-ups and tight pulls, the "black widow" exposing her butt before Jazz drops Trish with a chicken wing slam. The champion answers with a kick to the jaw, but misses her top rope moonsault. When Jazz tries to respond, Victoria back body drops her over the top rope. Steven tries to interfere again, but misses Stratus with a steel chair and hits himself. She follows up with Stratusfaction to him only to be caught and set up for a Widow's Peak. At the last second, Trish slips free and answers with a Chick Kick for the victory.

Backstage, Jonathan Coachman is in a tuxedo as he asks how excited The Rock is with over 54,000 people in attendance. The "Great One" couldn't care less about the people since they booed him and called him a sellout. He says they are right and that he has sold out every WrestleMania he's been in. Tonight, he's going to right a wrong. Yes, "Stone Cold" Steve Austin beat him the last two times they wrestled at WrestleMania, but no one cares about act one and act two. In Hollywood, all that matters is act three and he's going to make sure he ends the series beating the "rattlesnake". Once he does, The Rock says he will have finally done it all.

Team Angle def. Chris Benoit/Rhyno and Los Guerreros (WWE Tag Title match). Only Benoit and Rhyno have separate entrances for their team. Despite that, they win the opening six-man brawl. When Jimmy Korderas gets order, Chavo starts the action back dropping, suplexing, and dropkicking Haas. Charlie tags in "the Crippler" who runs into a Guerrero back suplex and Eddie slingshot somersault splash. Back up, Benoit responds with chops and fists until the former Radicalz collide. The man-beast tags in afterwards to powerslam "Latino Heat" for a near fall. Having almost watched his championship slip away, Benjamin tags in to elbow and club Rhyno's surgically repaired neck. Charlie joins him for a double dropkick and two-count before Chavo makes the save. Soon after, the "rabid wolverine" tags in for a snap suplex and back suplex, scoring a pair of near falls. When the man-beast returns, Haas clubs him again before Shelton tags in to knee the challenger. Rhyno answers with a corner spear for a one-count. Eddie tags himself in afterwards to dropkick and stomp the man-beast. When Benoit returns, Guerrero back suplexes him on his neck. He then heads upstairs, but "the Crippler" meets him for a superplex. Benjamin breaks up the cover before Haas breaks a Crippler Crossface. "Latino Heat" capitalizes with a brainbuster, but Charlie breaks that cover too. Chavo tags in afterwards to attack everyone until Benoit gives him a quartet of rolling German suplexes. Unfortunately, the "rabid wolverine" doesn't realize that Shelton tagged in on the fourth and he superkicks Benoit for a near fall before Eddie breaks the cover. Afterwards, he and "the Crippler" collide heads to put both men down. Benjamin capitalizes with a leg drop to Benoit moments later, but "Latino Heat" makes the save with a Frog Splash. Chavo tags in afterwards only to run into a Haas belly-to-belly suplex. Rhyno then illegally enters the ring to Gore both men before Korderas admonishes him. While Eddie drags the man-beast out to the floor, Shelton crawls over Chavo to score the three-count.

Backstage, the Miller Lite Catfight Girls take pictures with Stacy Keibler and Torrie Wilson. Everything is fine until Stacy and Torrie argue over who created WrestleMania, Hulk Hogan or Vince McMahon. When they walk off, the Catfight Girls continue the argument and agree to settle things in the ring and in bed somehow.

Afterwards, JR is happy to get back to wrestling and plays a video package for the upcoming Shawn Michaels/Chris Jericho match.

MUST SEE! Shawn Michaels def. Chris Jericho. As Jericho heads to the ring, the announcers talk about a film crew videotaping footage for a WrestleMania movie. Shawn then heads out firing confetti cannons into the crowd. After his lengthy entrance, the wrestlers trade takedowns, Michaels trapping Y2J in a head scissors before taking a break on top of the ropes. When he locks up again, he traps Jericho in a headlock. Y2J answers with a leg sweep, but is quickly driven to the mat with a side headlock. Following a Jericho roll-up and two-count, the heel slaps the "Heartbreak Kid". Shawn answers with a right hand and toss out to the floor for a baseball slide kick. Back in the ring, he connects with a top rope flying cross body block, but Y2J rolls through for a two-count. He follows up with a spinning heel kick to take control. That lets him punch and chop his one-time idol. When he goes for a running face slam, Michaels tosses the heel crotch-first onto the middle turnbuckle. The "Heartbreak Kid" follows up with a figure four leg lock, but it doesn't take Jericho long to turn over the hold. Although Shawn connects with a knee breaker, when he tries to reapply his hold, Y2J kicks him shoulder-first into the ring post. He then whips Michaels over the top rope, but the "Heartbreak Kid" skins the cat and head scissors Jericho out for a plancha. When he attempts a dropkick in the aisle, the heel steps back and answers with the Walls of Jericho. He works Charles Robinson's count before returning to the ring at the last second. Back at ringside, Y2J slams Shawn's back into the ring post ahead of a springboard dropkick and back suplex inside the squared circle. He then badmouths Michaels, telling him that he's better than the "Heartbreak Kid". A suplex afterwards gets him a two-count before he applies a chin lock with a handful of hair. Continuing to focus on the back, Jericho delivers a backbreaker for an arrogant cover and two-count. He returns to his chin lock, but this time he doesn't pull the hair. That forces Shawn to fight free and surprise the heel with a DDT to put both men down. Once they catch their breath, Y2J connects with a flying forearm and kip up. He wastes time flexing while Michaels kips up behind him for his own flying forearm and a back body drop. The "Heartbreak Kid" follows up with a top rope moonsault for a near fall. The two men trade two-counts and roll-ups afterwards before the heel tries to lock on the Walls of Jericho again. This time, Shawn kicks him off, but Jericho scores a two-count with a northern lights suplex moments later. After they fight over a backslide, Y2J rocks Michaels with a clothesline ahead of a running face slam. He also hits his Lionsault, but is slow to make the cover and only gets a two-count. Frustrated, he covers his opponent again, but still only gets a two-count. Frustrated, the heel stomps around and chops the "Heartbreak Kid" before countering a hurricanrana with the Walls of Jericho. Shawn reaches down deep and crawls to the ropes for the break. When Jericho tries to follow up, Michaels small packages him for a near fall. That sets off the heel again and he responds with a double underhook backbreaker. A top rope flying back elbow follows before Y2J tunes up the band to boos. He jukes and jives before connecting with his own superkick for a close two-count. More strikes follow from the heel until the "Heartbreak Kid" surprises him with a springboard forearm to the jaw. Shawn teases his own Walls of Jericho, but instead catapults Jericho face-first into the ring post for a near fall. Y2J answers with a shot to the back before taking the fight upstairs. Unfortunately, Michaels counters his back suplex attempt with a cross body block for a two-count. Afterwards, Shawn heads upstairs, but Jericho shoves Robinson into the ropes to crotch the "Heartbreak Kid". He tries to follow up with a superplex, but Michaels tosses him down to the canvas ahead of a flying elbow drop and big pop. With the fans cheering him on, Shawn tunes up the band. At the last second, Y2J ducks Sweet Chin Music and locks on the Walls of Jericho. The fans cheer as Michaels refuses to give up and crawls to the ropes once again. Jericho can't believe it, yelling at the referee that the "Heartbreak Kid" tapped out. When he turns back around, Shawn rocks him with Sweet Chin Music. He takes a while making the cover and that gives the heel just enough time to recover and kick out. Afterwards, he tries a corner whip, but Y2J reverses and whips him up and over the top rope hard. He tries to follow up with a back suplex, but Michaels flips free and rolls him up for the three-count to end this incredible confrontation. Post-match, Jericho cries in a corner while Shawn offers him a handshake. Y2J doesn't want a handshake. He hugs his former idol to a nice pop before turning the fans on him with a kick to the crotch. JR can't stand it.

Backstage, Sylvan Grenier enters Vince McMahon's locker room.

Inside the ring, Tony Chimel announces the attendance of 54, 097 fans before introducing Limp Bizkit again to perform "Crack Addict".

Afterwards, Jonathan Coachman introduces the Miller Lite Catfight Girls, Tanya Ballinger and Kitana Baker, to crawl around on an oversized bed for a pillow fight. Stacy Keibler interrupts. She says the only thing better than two girls is three and enters the "three-way". Torrie Wilson follows her out. She wants in too. She proceeds to strip off her and Stacy's shirts before spanking her. The Catfight Girls rip off each other's clothes too while Jonathan Coachman stands nearby saying it's "getting out of control". Things get worse when the girls roll over him and pull down his pants to reveal his tighty-whities. Forgetting about fighting each other, the girls turn on Coach and Keibler rolls him up for a Wilson three-count in this unofficial match.

A video package for the Booker T/Triple H match plays featuring Booker's past and Hunter not considering him a real challenger for the championship.

Triple H (with Ric Flair) def. Booker T (World Title match). Triple H is out first for this one, sporting purple trunks as he spits water at the crowd. Jerry says he's never run afoul of the law and he's a champion that the world can be proud of. JR doesn't agree, but talks about Booker's bad decisions and tough upbringing as he heads to the squared circle. There, he stares down Hunter and tells him that he's in trouble. When Helmsley tries to cheap shot him, the challenger unloads with his own stiff shots and a back body drop. A back elbow slows him, but "the Game" takes too long climbing the ropes and is arm dragged to the canvas. The fight then spills out to the floor where Booker T slams the champion's face into the ring post. After staring down Flair, the babyface returns to the ring to clothesline Triple H for a two-count. More fists follow before Booker misses a side kick and is back dropped out to the floor. When he tries to return, Hunter slams his face into the ring post. A shot into the ring steps follows as Helmsley seizes control. He wears down the challenger with stomps and fists ahead of a neckbreaker for a two-count. The fans are quiet as "the Game" punches Booker T ahead of a spinebuster and another near fall. He wakes up the crowd with a stiff corner clothesline for another two-count before blatantly choking the babyface. He responds with fists and chops, but the champion doubles him over with a knee to the gut. When he attempts a suplex, Booker slips free and DDTs him. Jerry continues taunting the challenger about his past, nearly forcing JR to curse as he says "the King" has driven it into the ground. Booker T catches a second wind with a twisting strike and near fall. When he sets up for the Scissors Kick though, Triple H briefly locks on a sleeper hold. Although the babyface escapes, he runs into a high knee and another near fall. A facebuster follows, but when he charges Booker afterwards, the challenger answers with a spinebuster for his own two-count. Although he runs into a corner boot, Booker T counters a second rope dive with a superkick for a near fall. Unfortunately, he misses a pair of Scissors Kicks and straddles the top rope. Ric takes advantage of Nick Patrick checking on Hunter to drop the babyface on the ring steps with a knee breaker. Lawler says he was trying to help him back into the ring, but JR doesn't buy it. When Booker does get back into the squared circle, Helmsley traps him in an Indian deathlock. Ross has never seen "the Game" use it and is shocked. It takes the challenger a while, but he eventually reaches the ropes for the break. JR says the damage has been done. Once he's free, the champion continues to target his leg, dropping a knee on it in a corner. Booker T can't even run into a corner on an Irish whip, collapsing to the canvas. When Triple H tries to give him another knee breaker, the babyface answers with a sunset flip for a near fall. Undeterred, Hunter sets up for a Pedigree, but Booker catapults him back into a corner and Patrick. The referee is back up quickly to count to two on a challenger roll-up. Booker T follows up with a back elbow and Scissors Kick, but he's slow to make the cover and only gets a near fall. When he tries to head upstairs,

"The Nature Boy" hops onto the apron. The babyface decks him and fights free of a Helmsley superplex attempt. He decks Flair one more time before flying off the top rope with a somersault leg drop onto "the Game". Unfortunately, he hurts his leg landing on the champion's face. By the time he makes the cover, Ric drapes Triple H's foot on the bottom rope for the break. It takes both men some time to get up, but Booker's leg gives away and he collapses for Hunter to Pedigree him. After taking several seconds crawling over, Helmsley gets the win with a hand draped on the challenger's chest.

Following a WWE Shop Zone ad, a video package plays for the upcoming Hulk Hogan/Vince McMahon match.

Hulk Hogan def. Vince McMahon ("Street Fight"). In what will be his final WrestleMania match and with Hulkamania on the line, Hogan comes out to "Voodoo Chile" instead of "Real American". Vince welcomes him with a slap to the face. That sets off the Hulkster and he tackles his boss and former friend for a flurry of fists and chokes. He follows up with boots until McMahon surprises the babyface with a back elbow and clothesline. Catching his breath, Vince punches and shoulder blocks Hulk in a corner. After he repeatedly punches Hogan, the WWE owner surprises everyone with a hammerlock. He softens up that arm to wrap it around the ring post twice. Afterwards, McMahon applies a Greco-Roman knuckle lock. The Hulkster starts to power up, but a kick to the gut drops him. The WWE owner can't keep Hulk down and he powers up once again only to get kicked right back down. Following a third kick to the gut, Vince takes the fight out to the floor and grabs a chair. Luckily, Hogan ducks his shot against the ring post and turns the tide with his own strikes. A thunderous chair shot to the skull follows, busting open the WWE owner. Fists follow in and out of the ring. When the fights spills back out to ringside, the Hulkster smashes McMahon twice with a chair. Vince manages to dodge his third shot, but Hugo Savinovich doesn't and is busted open. McMahon doesn't care, slowing Hulk with a low blow before busting him open too with a chair shot. Afterwards, he stomps and punches Hogan and sets up a ladder between the announce tables. As he clears the Spanish announce table, Vince blasts the Hulkster with a television monitor. He then sets the babyface on the edge of the table and heads up the ladder. After mocking Hogan's hand to ear celebration, he guillotine leg drops Hulk through the table. During the lull in action as McMahon recovers, trainers rush out to check on Hugo. Afterwards, Vince covers the Hulkster back in the squared circle for a pair of two-counts. The WWE owner can't believe it. Blood all around ringside, McMahon reaches under the apron and finds a steel pipe. He smiles sadistically as he returns to the ring to try to finish off Hulkamania. Instead, Hogan gives his grapefruits a low blow. With both men down, "Rowdy" Roddy Piper emerges from the crowd to kick Vince's butt and spit on the Hulkster for a big pop. He then grabs the pipe and taunts the WWE owner to get up. While he does so, Piper blasts Hulk with the pipe for boos. He then heads backstage while McMahon crawls over to the Hulkster for a near fall. When Brian Hebner tries to stop Vince from using the pipe again, the WWE owner attacks and tosses the referee out to the floor. That sees Sylvan Grenier running out to the ring followed by Mike Sparks. While they argue, McMahon hits Hogan with the pipe and leg drops him for a Grenier near fall. At the last second, the babyface powers out and hulks up. With the fans cheering him on, he absorbs fists, wags his finger, and decks Vince. He also punches and tosses Sylvan out to the floor. Three punches and a big boot follow to McMahon before the Hulkster Legdrops the WWE owner three times for a Hebner three-count and huge pop. Post-match, Shane McMahon walks out in a suit. Hogan glares at him and invites the son of the owner into the ring when Shane says he just wants to check on his dead. True to his word, he does just that while the Hulkster leaves the squared circle.

A video package plays for the upcoming "Stone Cold" Steve Austin/Rock match.

MUST SEE! The Rock def. "Stone Cold" Steve Austin. JR reminds everyone that The Rock has never beaten Austin at WrestleMania and he believes it's eating him alive. He'll get one last chance here. Once the bell rings, the two men trade shots before the "rattlesnake" teases an early Stone Cold Stunner. When the "People's Champ" retreats to the floor, "Stone Cold" follows and slams his face on the ring steps amidst fists and chops. He then clotheslines him over the *SmackDown!* announce table before slamming the "Great One" on the barricade. A hard whip into the ring steps follows before Austin finally takes the fight back to the squared circle to choke his longtime rival. A back suplex gets him a two-count afterwards. Whips back and forth across the ring follow. When the "Brahma Bull" reverses one, "Stone Cold" explodes out of the corner with a clothesline. He follows up with chokes until Earl Hebner admonishes him and The Rock capitalizes with a chop block. Another chop block follows on the floor before the "People's Champ" punishes the "rattlesnake" on the announce table. Focusing on the leg, the "Great One" stomps and slams it on the apron before whipping his hurting limb around the ring post. He can't keep Austin down and the "rattlesnake" fights back until the "Brahma Bull" clubs him and locks on a sharpshooter. JR reminds fans that "Stone Cold" has been trapped in the hold before back at WrestleMania 13. This time, he's not bleeding and reaches the ropes for the break. The Rock stays on the attack, punching Austin and threatening Hebner when he gets in the way. He then dons "Stone Cold's" vest and takes a drink of water. That wakes up the "rattlesnake" and he recovers for the wrestlers to connect with simultaneous clotheslines. They work Earl's count to nine before getting up for Austin to punch and Thesz press the "People's Champ". After flipping off the referee, "Stone Cold" drops an elbow onto the "Great One" for a two-count. Jerry believes the vest is bad luck and the "Brahma Bull" should take it off. He doesn't and gets a mudhole stomped in him before he explodes off the ropes with a leaping clothesline. Unfortunately, he wastes time celebrating and turns into a Rock Bottom for a "rattlesnake" two-count. Austin then motions for The Rock to get up, stalking him for a Stone Cold Stunner. At the last second, the "People's Champ" catches his foot and answers with a middle finger salute and his own Stunner for a near fall. Afterwards, he jacks "Stone Cold's" jaw until the "rattlesnake" surprises him with a Stunner for a close two-count. When Hebner gets in his way, Austin tosses him aside, but pays for that courtesy of a "Great One" low blow. He tries to follow up with a People's Elbow, but "Stone Cold" rolls out of the way and attempts another Stunner. This time, the "Brahma Bull" shoves him off for a spinebuster before finally hitting his People's Elbow, ripping off the vest in the process, for a near fall. He follows up with a Rock Bottom, but Austin kicks out again. The Rock can't believe it. Focusing, he squats down to set up for another Rock Bottom. Although "Stone Cold" fights free, the "People's Champ" quickly recovers and Rock Bottoms him again for another close two-count. Squatting again, the "Great One" waits for the "rattlesnake" to get up for a third Rock Bottom. That's the charm and finally the "Brahma Bull" gets the win in what will be Austin's last match for nearly twenty years. Post-match, The Rock shoves Hebner away and whispers something to "Stone Cold" before celebrating his victory. Austin then heads up the aisle to a standing ovation, the fans not realizing that they have just witnessed the end of an era.

A video package for the main event plays, the final few moments focusing on the fact that if anyone interferes on Kurt's behalf, he'll lose the WWE Title.

MUST SEE! Brock Lesnar def. Kurt Angle (WWE Title match). The champion is out first again, Lesnar following with his ribs bandaged. Inside the ring, the competitors stare each other down before Mike Chioda calls for the bell. The amateur stars trade holds early on, neither man able to get a true advantage as they repeatedly reverse and counter each other's moves. It's Brock's strength that flattens Kurt and has the Olympian rethinking his strategy. He elbows the challenger, but Lesnar catches his follow up attack with an arm drag. When he reaches the ropes, Angle clubs the "next big thing". Brock likes a good fight and he answers with his own strikes and a powerslam for a near fall. The champion responds with a German suplex, but Lesnar is right back up for a clothesline, chasing Kurt out to the floor. The challenger follows behind, but when they return to the ring, the Olympian catches him with a series of boots. Brock will not stay down, press slamming Angle before running into a boot on a corner charge. The champion follows up with a German suplex onto the top turnbuckle. That has the challenger writhing in pain as he rolls out to the floor. Kurt doesn't give him a moment to recover, punching him in and out of the ring ahead of a side suplex and near fall. He follows up with boots in a corner and a suplex for another two-count. Slowing the pace, the Olympian traps Lesnar in a reverse chin lock. It takes him quite a while, but the "next big thing" eventually picks up Angle and rams him into the turnbuckles for the break. The champion is right back on the attack with a belly-to-belly suplex and knee to the back. Another shot sends Brock out to the floor, but Kurt brings him back in quickly only to run into a spinebuster. Once both men catch their breath, the challenger picks up the pace with a string of strikes and his own belly-to-belly suplex. A second gets him a two-count. The Olympian is right back up, delivering four rolling German suplexes. He then dares Lesnar to get up and sets up for the Angle Slam. Instead, the "next big thing" slips free and hoists him up for an F5. Angle also escapes and applies an Anklelock. When Brock reaches the ropes, the champion drags him back to the center of the ring for a single leg crab. Continuing to focus on the back, Kurt hits the challenger with a running knee. When he attempts a second, Lesnar back body drops him out to the floor. He dodges a corner charge moments later to shoulderblock the Olympian. Angle responds with a release German suplex, flipping the "next big thing" completely over for another near fall. He also gets a close two-count with an Angle Slam. Back up quickly, Brock rolls up the champion for a two-count ahead of an F5 and another near fall. Cole says no one has kicked out of the F5 before. Kurt not only kicks out, but he quickly hooks another Anklelock. Somehow, the challenger manages to crawl to the ropes for the break. When he goes for another F5, the Olympian counters with a small package and two-count. He tries to follow up with an Angle Slam, but Lesnar escapes and hits another F5. Instead of going for the cover, the "next big thing" heads upstairs, confusing the announcers and Chioda. This almost proves to be a colossal mistake as he comes up just short on a shooting star press and nearly knocks himself out landing on his head. Despite that, he manages to kick out of Angle's subsequent cover at the last second. He then hoists the champion up for a third Angle Slam and the victory. Post-match, the competitors shake hands and hug before fireworks explode.

The PPV ends with a recap package of all the action.

WrestleMania XIX is a great show with very little to complain about. The Cruiserweight Title opener is a fast-paced affair and while only five and a half minutes, it's action-packed and showcases both Rey and Matt's talent. The Undertaker's handicap match is far less impressive. After removing Nathan Jones from the match last minute, the "Deadman" weathers the attack of two monsters to get another WrestleMania victory, one of his most forgettable. The women have a solid match as Trish manages to become just one of two challengers to win gold tonight. The undercard features short matches making even the WWE Tag Title match featuring six *SmackDown!* stars a bit of a disappointment. The action is great, it just would be nice to have more of it. Under nine minutes for six men, there's not enough time for anyone to showcase what all they can do and Team Angle escapes with the belts. Shawn and Jericho get plenty of time at over twenty minutes and they make the most of it with a fantastic back and forth match featuring high-flying, mat wrestling, and brawling. The final five minutes are spectacular and it's a true **MUST SEE!** contest. Triple H and Booker T isn't. The match itself is fine, if a bit long at eighteen minutes. Some of that time could go to the WWE Tag Title match. The problem is that after the build up to the match being questionably racist, Booker doesn't get his revenge. Instead, he gives Triple H another win. For the record, Hunter is the only heel to leave with his title at WrestleMania, and he's done it twice. The delayed pin after the Pedigree also makes Booker look weak. The story does not match the result here, but the match itself in a vacuum is solid. Hogan and McMahon then have a great brawl. They were never going to have much of a wrestling match, but brawling and weapons help to tell the story. Both men bleed, there's an appearance from "Rowdy" Roddy Piper, and Vince even dives off a ladder through an announce table. Considering their ages and the fact that neither is regarded as an in-ring technical wizard, this is as good as it gets. And sometimes it's good to have a great brawl. The WWE is like the circus in some respects. Some people come for the high-flyers and some like the elephants. In this case, fans get a nice nostalgic brawl. Afterwards, "Stone Cold" and The Rock have another fantastic match in their WrestleMania series. Considering that this is the last full-time match of Austin's career and that injuries have all but taken him out completely, the fact that he can even compete at this level is amazing. Even with hindsight it's impossible to tell he's injured. While it's another brawl, it's not the weapons and bloody mess that is the last match. Somehow, even in their third WrestleMania match, Austin and The Rock tell a fresh story that entertains in every moment. This is the end of an era and a **MUST SEE!** classic. The main event is also **MUST SEE!**. Brock and Kurt raise the bar on technical matches and the fans appreciate every minute. Both men break out all their best moves, show off their amateur skills, and brawl for a twenty-minute classic. It should be the beginning of the Brock Lesnar era, but things will take a sudden turn soon. Now, it's remembered as a great match and the night where Brock landed on his head. Despite that, it's an amazing match and caps off one of the WWE's greatest nights. With just one weak match—the Undertaker handicap match—this is one of the best WrestleManias in history. It doesn't surpass WrestleMania X-Seven, but it's up there. Other than one skippable match, everything else is enjoyable. Even the divas have a very good match considering the fact that the WWE still hasn't embraced female wrestling fully at this point. The celebrities look like they are having fun, the show moves at a brisk pace despite being four hours long, and the main event features a big title change in Lesnar's WrestleMania debut. All in all, this show is well worth taking the time to watch and enjoy.

Monday Night Raw

March 31, 2003
Seattle, WA
Announcers: Jim Ross, Jerry "the King" Lawler

The show starts with a video package of action from WrestleMania XIX to Limp Bizkit's "Crack Addict". After the four-minute video, the regular intro video plays and fireworks explode.

Backstage, The Rock checks his glasses and yells at a makeup artist not to touch up his face. Despite saying he doesn't need any makeup, the "People's Champ" soon asks for a touchup for "Rock Appreciation Night".

Afterwards, "Stone Cold" Steve Austin comes out to a big pop. He says he's always been an honest man and he got his butt kicked last night. After admitting that The Rock was the better man last night, "Stone Cold" says that doesn't mean he'll be the better man tonight. Since it's "Rock Appreciation Night", Austin offers to shake the "Brahma Bull's" hand if he'll come to the ring. Instead, Eric Bischoff steps onto the stage holding paperwork. He doesn't believe the "rattlesnake" wants to shake the "Great One's" hand because he's vengeful. "Stone Cold" admits that's true. Eric doesn't think Austin is going to be kicking butt any time soon because the general manager knows his secret. Bischoff reveals that the "rattlesnake" spent the night before WrestleMania XIX in the hospital. It turns out that Austin is more injured than anyone thought, Eric reading off his medical records. His doctor won't clear him to wrestle again due to his risk of serious injury. "Stone Cold" doesn't appreciate him reading his medical charts and he's not going to let anyone stop the "rattlesnake" from competing. Bischoff disagrees. "Due to medical reasons", he fires Austin. Tying into their history, Eric says he's sent a FedEx notice of termination to Steve's house. The announcers are stunned as we cut to a commercial break.

Following the break, "Stone Cold" Steve Austin scratches his head backstage.

Triple H (with Ric Flair) def. The Hurricane. As Triple H heads to the ring in red trunks, the announcers casually reveal that Goldberg has signed with the company and will appear at Backlash. Afterwards, the superhero comes out to give his mask to a boy in the crowd. Flair takes it away and stomps it. When The Hurricane runs out to stop Ric, Hunter attacks him from behind for an early advantage. Back in the squared circle, Helmsley devastates the superhero with a spinebuster. When he attempts a suplex, The Hurricane slips free for a neckbreaker. Moments later, he catches "the Game" with a pair of clotheslines and a shining wizard for a near fall. A tornado DDT also gets him a two-count. When he tries to follow up, "The Nature Boy" trips him, but pays courtesy of a baseball slide kick. Flair gets involved again, distracting Earl Hebner so he misses the superhero's chokeslam and subsequent cover. When he pulls The Hurricane out to the floor, the masked man decks Ric. He returns to the ring for a flying cross body block and two-count. The champion tries to answer with a Pedigree, but the superhero escapes and attempts his own Pedigree. Although Triple H fights free, the masked man drops him with an Eye of the Hurricane. At the last second, Hunter just manages to kick out. Moments later, he dodges an overcast and Pedigrees The Hurricane for the victory.

Backstage, Kane and Rob Van Dam talk. The "Big Red Machine" thinks it's better if they separate after losing their title match last night. RVD would be cool with that, but he says he's already gotten them a rematch tonight. The monster likes that, but knows there's a catch. The catch is that if the babyfaces lose they have to join the Bischoff administration. Kane can't believe Rob would sign them up for that without talking to the "Big Red Machine". Van Dam is sure they are going to win.

A Goldberg teaser plays. The fans are excited.

Scott Steiner def. Christopher Nowinski. Nowinski is wearing a protective face mask as he heads to the ring to say he might look a little weird now, but the people of Seattle always look weird. He asks Scott not to hit his face and waste thirty thousand dollars of work he had done to reconstruct it. Steiner says it was wasted money and chases the Harvard heel out of the ring. He immediately slams Nowinski's face onto the apron. Back in the squared circle, he clubs and clotheslines the Harvard heel. Following an elbow drop and pushups, "Big Poppa Pump" stomps and clubs Nowinski. The Harvard heel eventually turns the tide with a kick on a back body drop attempt and headbutt with his mask. He lands a few shots until he runs face-first into a corner boot. A belly-to-belly suplex follows for a near fall. A second drops Nowinski right on his head before Scott locks on the Steiner Recliner for the tap-out victory.

Backstage, Terri asks "Stone Cold" Steve Austin if what Eric Bischoff said was true. Austin admits that his "neck sucks" and that's the "bottom line". He wonders if she's happy. She's says no and walks away.

After a commercial break, Lawler is happy to talk about "Rock Appreciation Night", but JR is focused on Eric Bischoff. He calls him a "no good son of a bitch" and should burn for revealing "Stone Cold" Steve Austin's medical records and firing him.

Backstage, Bubba Ray Dudley explains to D-Von Dudley that he had to save the World Tag Titles last night or The Dudley Boyz would be back on the streets. D-Von says it sucks to be part of the heel administration, but Bubba says right now they have to play by the heels' rules. Chief Morley and Lance Storm interrupt. The chief tells them that there will be no outside interference in tonight's main event because he's adding the Dudleys to the World Tag Title match. However, it's going to be triple threat in name only because once the Dudleys help the champions eliminate Kane and Rob Van Dam, they'll lay down and give Morley and Storm the win. Afterwards, The Dudley Boyz will officially join the Bischoff administration.

Further backstage, Ric Flair interrupts Booker T getting taped up to mock the five-time champion. Booker has had enough and chokes "The Nature Boy", warning that if he ever gets in Booker T's way again, the five-time champion is going to finish him off once and for all.

A clip of Ashanti singing "America the Beautiful" last night plays.

Maven def. Rosey (with Rico). Despite showing plenty of courage, Maven can't match up to Rosey's power or the heels' numbers advantage early on. After Rosey clubs the babyface and Rico trips him, Maven surprises the big Samoan with a forearm. He then slips free of a side slam, but misses a dropkick that should send Rosey into Rico on the apron. Things go off the rails from there and everyone tries to figure out what to do. Maven nearly gets the win with a roll-up before immediately sunset flipping Rosey for a victory in a match that falls apart and never recovers.

Jerry "the King" Lawler serving as a guest photographer for a *Playboy* shoot plays before the announcers shill Torrie Wilson's issue.

Booker T def. Chris Jericho by disqualification. Pre-match, Jericho thanks Shawn Michaels for having one of the best WrestleMania matches ever with him. Y2J thinks Shawn should thank him too since the heel carried him and proved he was the better man. After he complains about being cheated last night, Jericho promises to take his frustrations out on Booker. The five-time champion has his own frustrations, limping down the aisle with his left leg bandaged. Before the bell rings, Y2J attacks the injured limb. After he drops down onto Booker T's leg multiple times, the babyface kicks Jericho out to the floor. That sets off the heel and he returns to threaten a Walls of Jericho. Booker stops him with a roll-up for a two-count. Afterwards, he flapjacks and kicks Y2J until Jericho surprises him with a running face slam. Unfortunately, he misses the Lionsault. That brings Ric Flair out, but Booker T sees him coming and chops him while Charles Robinson calls for the bell. Y2J joins the attack as Triple H slowly walks down the aisle to Pedigree the five-time champion. Flair then traps Booker in a Figure Four Leglock until Shawn Michaels runs out for the save, punching and clotheslining the heels. When he tunes up the band, Jericho cuts him off from kicking Hunter. Back in control, the three heels toss Booker T out to the floor ahead of a backbreaker to Michaels and Walls of Jericho. The five-time champion tries to make the save, but Helmsley knocks him down for an Indian deathlock, JR acting like it's the greatest hold of all-time as the babyfaces tap.

Jeff Hardy def. Steven Richards (with Victoria). The announcers hype The Hardy Boyz's book as Jeff heads to the squared circle. Richards follows to punch him, but is quickly driven from the ring with a double front kick. When Hardy tries to follow up with a barricade dive, Victoria pulls her man away. Back in the ring, the daredevil misses a whisper in the wind, opening the door for Steven to attack his arm with an armbar drop. Covered in Jeff's blue paint, Richards locks in an armbar. Hardy escapes with a jawbreaker. Building momentum, he clotheslines and mule kicks the heel for a two-count. When Victoria trips him, Steven tries to capitalize with a DDT. Luckily, the daredevil fights free and leg drops the heel's legs for a near fall. He follows up with a jawbreaker, his knees hitting Richards's chin. When he tries to head upstairs, the "black widow" grabs his boot. That brings out Trish Stratus to Chick Kick her before Jeff shoves Steven down to the canvas for a Swanton Bomb and the win.

Backstage, "Stone Cold" Steve Austin shakes hands with the crew as he leaves the arena.

A "Rock Appreciation Night" Moment shows The Rock making fun of the crowd, Hulk Hogan, and Jonathan Coachman.

Backstage, Test is on the phone telling someone that their magazine spread goes on sale tomorrow and they look hot. Stacy Keibler interrupts and the bodyguard hangs up quickly. He says it was a wrong number and gets defensive. To back him up, he turns to Goldust despite Stacy believing him anyways. While the "bizarre one" agrees with him, when his twitch kicks in he confesses that Test was talking to Torrie Wilson and wants to see her naked.

Further backstage, The Rock looks for "Stone Cold" Steve Austin. He says the "rattlesnake" can't leave on "Rock Appreciation Night". He notices how sad the crew looks and tells them that he's still here. While he doesn't know their names, he does offer to take them to a party. They like that, but get even more upset when he tells them that they'll have to wait outside the party.

A Backlash ad featuring Goldberg plays ahead of Tony Chimel announcing the WrestleMania XIX attendance last night.

MUST SEE! Kane/Rob Van Dam def. Chief Morley/Lance Storm and The Dudley Boyz (Elimination World Tag Title match). While the babyfaces are the only ones who come out to separate entrances, it's the

Dudleys that the announcers think are divided. The champions order them to go after Kane and RVD to start the match, but when they are driven from the ring, Morley and Storm give it a go. They are driven out too for a Rob over the top rope somersault splash. The "Big Red Machine" then impresses with a slingshot dive out onto the heels. Afterwards, Van Dam and D-Von lock up, the popular superstar staying a step ahead and scoring a two-count with a spinning heel kick. Both men tag their partners soon afterwards for Bubba to rake the monster's eyes and club him. Kane answers with a leaping clothesline, but misses an elbow drop. After Dudley cheap shots RVD, he tosses the "Big Red Machine" backwards to the canvas for a wassup drop, the chief of staff distracting Nick Patrick. The monster fights back and stuns D-Von with a side slam before tagging in Rob for a spinning dropkick. He continues kicking the heels, knocking down all four ahead of rolling thunder to D-Von. At the last second, the champions break up his cover. Once everyone else ends up outside the ring, Van Dam kicks Bubba down, but misses a Five-Star Frog Splash. The champions then whip Kane into the ring steps to take him out while Lance grabs a chair. Although Patrick grabs it, Morley has his own and teases knocking out RVD until D-Von takes the chair away. When the chief of staff yells at his half-brother, Bubba Ray tackles Morley to save him from a D-Von chair shot. That leaves no one to protect D-Von from Rob's spinning heel kick driving the chair back into Dudley's face for the three-count ahead of a commercial break.

Afterwards, Storm wraps Van Dam's leg around the ring post ahead of a pair of suplexes from the chief for a near fall before the "Big Red Machine" makes the save. The champions follow up with a double back elbow for another near fall while the announcers remind everyone that if the challengers lose, they'll have to join the Bischoff administration. Lance nearly gets RVD to tap out with a single leg crab, but the popular superstar crawls to the ropes for the break. He follows up with a kick and hot tag to the monster, Kane clotheslining and back body dropping the champions. He nearly gets the win with a side slam to the chief, but Morley just kicks out. Moments later, he runs into a tilt-a-whirl slam for another near fall. The "Big Red Machine" follows up with a top rope flying clothesline, but this time Storm makes the save. Rob follows up with a top rope flying kick. When Kane tries to Chokeslam him, Morley makes the save with a low blow ahead of a Lance leg lariat. The chief is stunned that the monster kicks out of his cover. Things get worse when the "Big Red Machine" counters a double back body drop with a double Chokeslam for a big pop. Van Dam then tags in to Five-Star Frog Splash Morley for the win.

Backstage, Eric Bischoff tells someone on the phone to keep following the show because he's got a big surprise and the "ink is still wet" on a new contract.

MUST SEE! After the final commercial break, The Rock heads to the ring for "Rock Appreciation Night". Lawler loves it, but JR is down in the dumps that "Stone Cold" Steve Austin is gone. The heel takes his time saying that he's "finally come back to Se…all the jabronis appreciate him". The "People's Champ" feels bad that Austin got fired and says that they put on a great performance last night. The "Great One" thanks Steve for a great match, but Ross doesn't believe him. He shouldn't as the "Brahma Bull" mocks "Stone Cold" for going down to three Rock Bottoms before asking who better than the "People's Champ" to beat the "rattlesnake" in his last match. Speaking of last matches, The Rock says that he's done it all and the fans booed him when he came back for them. As such, he's leaving. When the fans chant "Goldberg", the "People's Champ" is amused that they're chanting his accountant's name, "Ira Goldberg". The real Goldberg interrupts to a huge pop, walking out and standing in fireworks in a huge moment. The "Great One" squares off with him, but doesn't make a move as the fans loudly chant for the WCW superstar. Goldberg has one thing to say to the "Brahma Bull", telling him that he's next and Spearing The Rock. Calmly, the newly arrived superstar heads up the ramp, the fans continuing to chant his name to end the show.

SmackDown!

April 3, 2003
Spokane, WA
Announcers: Michael Cole, Tazz, Matt Hardy (briefly), Shannon Moore (briefly)

Like *Raw*, *SmackDown!* opens with a video package for WrestleMania XIX. Afterwards, the intro video plays and fireworks explode before Stephanie McMahon steps onto the stage. She congratulates her wrestlers on a great night Sunday before telling fans that Brock Lesnar and Kurt Angle will not be here tonight. While Kurt may be out months with a neck injury, Brock will be back next week. To decide who the number one contender will be to face him at Backlash, Stephanie has created an eight-man number one contender's tournament and the opening match is next.

The Undertaker def. Rey Mysterio (#1 Contender's Tournament match). The "Deadman" is out first to a big pop as he rides his motorcycle around the squared circle. Rey follows, popping out of the stage for another good cheer. A meeting of styles and future legends, Mysterio kicks and moves, dropkicking The Undertaker out to the floor. Once big boot from the biker puts the masked man down on the canvas. The "Deadman" follows up with a corner clothesline and fists until Rey responds in kind. He also adds in a jawbreaker, but The Undertaker cuts his momentum off with a hand around his neck. The masked man blocks his chokeslam with a tornado DDT and 619, but when he springs off the ropes for a West Coast Pop, the "Deadman" catches him. An impressive Last Ride follows for the win. Post-match, it looks like The Undertaker is going to hit Rey, but he helps him up and poses with an American flag.

Backstage, Vince McMahon tells a member of the crew to let him know when Hulk Hogan arrives.

After a commercial break, Matt Hardy heads to the ring alongside Shannon Moore and Matt Facts letting fans know that he was the only Hardy at WrestleMania this year and he's read his book twelve times. The heels join the announce table to watch the next match and provide guest commentary.

Brian Kendrick def. Jamie Noble (with Nidia). Jamie starts strong clubbing Kendrick and choking him in a corner. The rookie answers by knocking the redneck out to the floor and diving off the top rope onto him while the announcers talk about Matt's diet and new book. Back in the ring, Brian nearly gets the win with a top rope flying cross body block. When he attempts a charge, Noble catches him with a powerslam for his own near fall. Unfortunately, he takes too long climbing the ropes and Kendrick catches him. When he attempts a hurricanrana, the redneck counters with a sunset flip powerbomb. Moments later, he distracts Brian Hebner for Nidia to low bridge the rookie. Jamie tries to follow up with a baseball slide kick, but hits his girlfriend instead. Kendrick capitalizes with his Step Up Reverse Bulldog, called Sliced Bread #2 by Cole, for the victory. Post-match, Hardy and Moore attack Brian from behind. Once he's down, Matt challenges Brock Lesnar to a "champion versus champion" match next week. Brian returns afterwards to kick Shannon, but turns into a Twist of Fate. Cole thinks Hardy is crazy challenging Brock.

In a prerecorded vignette, Nunzio and The FBI tie up a man and steal electronics from his truck.

Still shots from the WrestleMania XIX WWE Title match are shown. Afterwards, we see footage of Brock Lesnar falling on his head and trainers checking on him after the PPV. Cole reveals that he suffered a concussion, but avoided a career ending injury.

A teaser for Piper's Pit returning next week plays.

Chris Benoit def. A-Train (#1 Contender's Tournament match). The hairy heel starts strong, elbowing and kneeing Benoit while the fans chant for him to shave his back. A-Train ignores them, but when he tries to outwrestle the "rabid wolverine", Benoit maneuvers him into a Crippler Crossface. Fortunately, the hairy heel rolls up "the Crippler" for a two-count ahead of briefly applying a camel clutch. Instead of waiting for the submission, A-Train slams Benoit for a two-count. He follows up with clubbing blows and a hard whip into the corner. Afterwards, the hairy heel traps his opponent in a reverse chin lock. It doesn't take the "rabid wolverine" long to fight free only to be tossed out to the floor. When he tries to sunset flip A-Train, the hairy heel stomps and slingshots him into the middle rope, called the decapitator by the announcers. A-Train doesn't go for the cover, waiting for Benoit to stand up and chop him. One knee stops him. When the hairy heel attempts a corner charge though, "the Crippler" moves and delivers a trio of German suplexes. A diving headbutt gets him a pair of two-counts, but afterwards he runs into a bicycle kick. When A-Train tries to follow up with a Train Wreck—called the Derailer by the announcers—Benoit counters with the Crippler Crossface. The hairy heel fights it, but can't escape and eventually taps.

Backstage, Stephanie McMahon interrupts her father on the phone to ask him how he's doing and what he's doing here. Vince says he's going to do something he should have done a long time ago. She hopes he doesn't do anything he'll regret.

In a prerecorded vignette, Sean O'Haire says laws are made to be broken.

John Cena def. Eddie Guerrero (#1 Contender's Tournament match). As Cena heads to the ring, Tazz shows him on the cover of the new issue of *Raw* magazine. Eddie then runs out only to see John club and choke him. The rapping heel is all offense, stomping "Latino Heat" ahead of a delayed vertical suplex and near fall. He then slows the pace with a bearhug. When Guerrero starts to fight back, Cena rams him into a corner and suplexes him for another two-count. He then returns to the bearhug, but this time Eddie headbutts free. He follows up with a drop toe hold onto the middle turnbuckle ahead of a flying forearm. Clotheslines and a trio of rolling suplexes nearly score "Latino Heat" the win, but John just kicks out. Guerrero follows up with a top rope missile dropkick, but once again the rapping heel kicks out of his cover. Moments later, Cena surprises Eddie with an electric chair drop. He grabs his chain, but "Latino Heat" dropkicks it out of his hand. After teasing using it, Guerrero goes upstairs for a Frog Splash. Although the rapping heel moves, Eddie rolls as he hits the mat to avoid any damage. Unfortunately, John hoists him up afterwards for his Death Valley Driver and the three-count.

Backstage, Hulk Hogan, his son, and Jimmy Hart arrive in a black limo. Nick wants to know where catering is.

Limp Bizkit performing The Undertaker's theme song at WrestleMania XIX plays. Tazz says he partied with Fred Durst after the show.

Torrie Wilson then heads to the ring for her "*Playboy* coming out party". She thanks the fans for their support and teases taking off her top as a sneak preview. The announcers are stunned when a cat sounds over the loudspeaker and Sable makes her return to the WWE for the first time since 1999. She has her own coming out party, telling everyone that she's back in the WWE where "the men want to see" her and the "women want to be" her. While she's proud of Torrie, Sable notes that some people don't think *SmackDown!* is big enough for both of them. Sable disagrees, promising they'll be best friends before giving Wilson a peck on the lips. Torrie doesn't like it, but the announcers do.

Team Angle def. Funaki/Tajiri. A non-title match, the champions start fast with Shelton slamming Funaki. Tajiri attacks from behind, kicking the champion's butt before the babyfaces mock him with jumping jacks. Although they get in several shots, a double back elbow drops Funaki and sees Haas tag in to challenge Tajiri. The "Japanese Buzzsaw" joins him with a leg lariat. Kicks follow to both champions, but when he sets up for the Buzzsaw Kick, Benjamin grabs his leg to save Charlie. Haas follows up with a back suplex for a two-count, swinging the momentum. A belly-to-belly overhead suplex follows before Team Angle hit their double-team leapfrog splash for a near fall. Shelton then slows the pace with a Boston crab. Funaki makes the save with a dropkick to the back. Afterwards, Tajiri ducks a double clothesline and hits a double handspring back elbow. Funaki then gets the hot tag to back body drop the champions ahead of a top rope flying cross body block to Charlie. When Benjamin makes the save, the "Japanese Buzzsaw" traps him in the Tarantula. Moments later, Funaki tries to finish off Haas with a second rope tornado DDT, but Shelton chop blocks him. Charlie follows up with the Haas of Pain for the tap-out.

Backstage, Nunzio leads The FBI to find The Undertaker, promising to have a sit down talk with the biker ahead of a *Sunday Night Heat* ad, the show now on TNN.

After a commercial break, Josh Mathews stops John Cena from leaving the arena. Cena raps as he talks about facing The Undertaker next week. While he knows he's the underdog, John says anything can happen on any given *SmackDown!*.

Speaking of The Undertaker, he mocks Nunzio and The FBI's accents. The heels want to talk about helping A-Train and Big Show attack Nathan Jones at WrestleMania XIX because of what he did to Palumbo last week. Nunzio hopes they can bury the hatchet. The biker thanks them for being direct. While he can appreciate that everyone has to face the consequence of their actions, The FBI's actions affected him at WrestleMania. Because of that, he's not going to bury the hatchet. The heels threaten the "Deadman", but Jones arrives to even up the odds a bit. Nunzio says they have a problem, but they are going to wait to settle their issue until the time is right. The Undertaker says the babyfaces aren't hard to find ahead of a Backlash ad featuring Goldberg.

Rhyno def. Big Show (#1 Contender's Tournament match) by disqualification. The final first round tournament match, Rhyno goes right after the giant with heavy fists. One big chop slows his momentum for Big Show to walk across the man-beast's back. More chops and a headbutt follow before Show tosses Rhyno halfway across the ring. The giant also mixes in chokes and fists until the man-beast starts to fight back only to run into a side slam for a near fall. Showing his nasty streak, Big Show removes a turnbuckle pad before headbutting and tossing over Rhyno again. Moments later, he misses a corner charge and hits the exposed bolt himself. The man-beast follows up with a pair of Gores to knock down the giant. Unfortunately, before he can get the three-count, A-Train runs out to stomp and bicycle kick Rhyno for the disqualification. Post-match, the hairy heel tells Show to "snap his neck". He tries to do so with a leg drop to the neck while A-Train holds Rhyno. Cole wonders what shape he'll be in next week ahead of another Piper's Pit teaser.

After a commercial break, Vince McMahon heads to the ring. He asks the crowd to be quiet so he can admit that he misjudged Hulk Hogan and the power of Hulkamania. He invites the Hulkster to come out so he can apologize to him. Hogan does so to a big pop. McMahon doesn't want to admit defeat, but he's a "realist" and accepts that Hulk beat him up Sunday night. He wants to "let bygones be bygones" and move on from their war. The Hulkster has his doubts and Vince doesn't blame him. However, if Hogan can forgive him, the WWE owner hopes they can be friends again one day. Afterwards, he offers Hulk his hand. The babyface doesn't accept. McMahon doesn't blame him. After thinking it over, the Hulkster offers his hand if Vince is serious. He seems to be and accepts to a nice pop. When he leaves the ring, Hogan stops his music to thank McMahon. Cole calls both men class acts. At the top of the ramp, the WWE owner thanks Hulk for the memories. He then shows his true nature, telling the Hulkster that he never loses and Sunday night was Hulk's last in a WWE ring. While Vince will honor Hogan's contract, he's going to pay him to stay at home. "As a billionaire", McMahon doesn't care what it costs him to make Hulkamania "rot". Without Hulk on television, Vince knows the fans will forget him. If the Hulkster has a problem with that, McMahon offers to meet him in the parking lot. Those are fighting words for Hogan and he follows behind. There, Vince is waiting at the end of two semitrucks by Hulk's limo. Before he can reach the WWE owner, police intercept him. Nick pleads with his dad to get in the car while McMahon threatens to kick his butt. The Hulkster eventually listens to his son and gets in the limo instead of fighting. Once he does, the WWE owner throws his bags in the trunk and tells Hogan to stay out of his life. Vince ends the episode letting everyone know that he never loses.

Monday Night Raw

April 7, 2003
Milwaukee, WI
Announcers: Jim Ross, Jerry "the King" Lawler, Jonathan Coachman

The show opens with a replay of The Rock threatening to retire before Goldberg arrives to Spear him last week. Afterwards, the intro video plays and fireworks explode ahead of the opener.

Trish Stratus def. Jazz (Women's Title match). The women open the match trading shots, Jazz getting the early upper hand. Trish answers with a string of kicks to knock the challenger out to the floor. She follows her out with a flying Thesz press off the apron and fists, but Jazz overpowers her and slams the champion into the apron for a two-count. Afterwards, she stretches out Stratus with a surfboard. Jerry calls it his favorite hold. It's not Trish's and she quickly escapes only to be double ax-handled ahead of a fisherman's buster suplex near the ropes. That saves the championship for Stratus as she reaches them for the break, but sees her locked in a single leg crab afterwards. Jazz follows up with an STF, but the vixen reaches the ropes for the break. Bleeding from the mouth, Trish comes back to life with a string of forearms and a Chick Kick for a near fall. Shots in a corner follow ahead of a handstand head scissors and another two-count. When she pulls the challenger back up, Jazz answers with a jawbreaker. It only briefly stuns the champion as she comes back to life quickly to hit Stratusfaction for the three-count despite Jazz's foot on the bottom rope.

Backstage, The Rock arrives and heads directly to Eric Bischoff's office to complain about Goldberg Spearing him. When Eric says that Goldberg isn't here yet, the "People's Champ" makes fun of him and promises to call him out later tonight. Bischoff likes it.

After a commercial break, Rob Van Dam reminds Kane that last week he didn't want to team up and now they are the World Tag Team Champions. He wonders how the "Big Red Machine" celebrated. The monster says he found a stinky skunk and took it to his basement. Rob thinks that's cool and both men agree that so long as Kane listens to RVD everything will be cool.

Further backstage, Theodore Long and Rodney Mack tell Jazz they saw what happened to her and she was a victim of circumstance. If she wants to back the Mack, Long promises no more bigotry will hold her down. She shakes his hand and walks away, Rodney wearing a Fat Albert jacket.

Even further backstage, The Rock finds Trish Stratus and asks if she's all "sweaty and wet" because of her match or because she's been thinking about the "People's Champ". She says it was the match, but he continues hitting on her until Jeff Hardy approaches from behind. The "Great One" wants to know who he is. When he says he's too busy to sign an autograph, Jeff says the last time he saw him he was busy getting his butt kicked. That sets off the "Brahma Bull" and he offers to kick Hardy's butt while Trish watches later.

Chief Morley def. Rob Van Dam. The chief overpowers RVD to start the match, driving him into a corner to punch and stomp the champion. Rob answers with a pair of clotheslines, chasing Morley back into a corner where he hides while Chad Patton holds the popular superstar back. When they tie up again, Van Dam briefly applies a side headlock before German suplexing the chief for a bridging two-count. Fists follow until Morley counters a back body drop attempt with a neckbreaker. The chief hits three consecutive suplexes afterwards, but only scores a two-count when he takes his time making the cover. He then slows the pace with a reverse chin lock. When RVD fights free, a knee to the gut cuts off his momentum. Moments later, Rob stuns the chief with a string of kicks ahead of rolling thunder. When he makes the cover, Lance Storm runs out and puts his man's foot on the ropes for the break. He also distracts Patton when Van Dam rolls up Morley. When RVD heads upstairs for a Five-Star Frog Splash, Lance grabs his foot. That gets him kicked down to the floor for a flying dive off the top rope. When Rob tries to get back in the ring, Storm grabs his foot for the chief to steal the win with a DDT. Post-match, the heels try to double-team Van Dam, but he gives them both low blows to escape.

Backstage, Booker T gets his leg taped up. When Shawn Michaels checks on him, Booker assures him that he's good to go for their tag team main event.

Shawn Michaels and Ivory visiting a naval base plays as the WWE continues to support the coalition in Iraq.

The Christopher Nowinski/Scott Steiner match never officially starts. Scott is out first, the Harvard heel following to say that "Big Poppa Pump" reminds him of America in being big and dominant. Nowinski believes that's what's wrong with America and that the country has become overconfident. He thinks forcing American views on other countries makes them wild and unpredictable. The fans boo that, setting off the Harvard heel. He argues that he's an American and has the freedom to express his views. Steiner disagrees, hopping out of the ring to pound Nowinski and slam him on the steel ramp. Afterwards, he locks him in the Steiner Recliner before heading backstage, the Harvard heel never even entering the squared circle.

Backstage, Goldberg arrives.

After a commercial break, the announcers talk about Goldberg and play a video package of his highlights in WCW.

Backstage, Christian knocks on The Rock's door and asks the "People's Champ" for a favor. When he asks for an autograph on his *The Scorpion King* DVD, the "Great One" is happy to do so. Although Christian says it's for a friend, apparently that friend has the same name as him. Once done, The Rock tells Christian that he doesn't take advantage of his skills and opportunity. He wants the heel to "seize the day" and own the room. Christian tells the "Brahma Bull" that he's the Canadian's favorite wrestler no matter what anyone says. When pressed, Christian says that people are saying that the "People's Champ" is afraid of Goldberg. That fires up The Rock and he heads to the ring, handing Christian his shirt and telling him not to smell it.

Further backstage, Trish Stratus gives Jeff Hardy a kiss for luck.

The Rock def. Jeff Hardy. Jeff races down the aisle second only to run into a string of Rock fists. When he gets cocky, the daredevil surprises the heel with a running cross body block. One big clothesline turns the tide and the "People's Champ" chokes and punches Hardy while the fans boo loudly. Once again, he gets cocky and dances. Although Jeff pays him back with shots, the heel once again cuts off his momentum. The "Great One" follows up with a Samoan drop for a near fall before running into a corner elbow and second rope flying dropkick. That puts both men down for a Nick Patrick five-count. When they get up, the daredevil punches and throat drops the "Brahma Bull" on the top rope. He follows up with a springboard moonsault and double leg drop to the groin. When he attempts a whisper in the wind though, The Rock sidesteps his attack. He tries to follow up with a back suplex, but Hardy flips free for a reverse twist of fate. Jeff gets a loud squeal when he takes off his shirt for his own version of the People's Elbow. The Swanton Bomb follows, but the "People's Champ" just manages to kick out of his cover. Back on his feet, the "Great One" answers with a DDT before kipping up for a Rock Bottom and the victory. Post-match, the "Brahma Bull" grabs a mic while the fans chant "Goldberg". The Rock invites him to "just bring it" for interrupting his "Rock Appreciation Night" last week. Goldberg doesn't make him wait, hurrying down the aisle to jaw with the "People's Champ". Despite talking a big game, the "Great One" backs down and tells Goldberg "nah" when asked about a match at Backlash. When he leaves, Christian tries to sneak attack the intense superstar, but is Speared. The "Brahma Bull" returns to try to ambush Goldberg, but quickly backpedals away once again when spotted.

After a commercial break, The Rock hurries out of the arena in just his trunks and a light jacket despite it snowing outside. When Terri asks him why he said no to Goldberg, the "Great One" says, "because".

The Dudley Boyz def. Kane. With their two-on-one advantage, the Dudleys attack Kane before the bell. The "Big Red Machine" easily repels them and scores a two-count with a side slam to D-Von. Dudley answers with a leaping clothesline before tagging in Bubba Ray. The monster meets him with a string of strikes until D-Von trips Kane from the floor and rams his groin into the ring post. Bubba follows up with elbow drops for a near fall. When the Dudleys attempt to double-team him, the "Big Red Machine" catches a second wind and slams them to the canvas before nearly finishing off D-Von with a top rope flying clothesline. Luckily, Bubba breaks up his cover. Afterwards, the monster teases a double Chokeslam, but The Dudley Boyz fight free to 3D him for the victory. Post-match, Bubba Ray tells D-Von to get the tables, but Rob Van Dam runs out for the save, punching and kicking the reluctant heels. When he heads upstairs for a Five-Star Frog Splash to Bubba, Lance Storm sprints out to trip him into a side slam. D-Von follows up with a chair shot to Kane's back when he tries to protect his partner. Chief Morley then delivers a Money Shot to RVD ahead of a Lance top rope missile dropkick into a chair back into the popular superstar's face. Still not done, the Dudleys 3D the "Big Red Machine" again.

Backstage, Test yells at Goldust for getting him in trouble with Stacy Keibler last week. He wants the "bizarre one" to "help a brother out" and tell her that the bodyguard doesn't want Torrie Wilson. After a commercial break, Goldust tells Keibler that he was the one looking at Torrie's *Playboy* last week. Unfortunately, he starts to stutter and bark again, revealing that Test has a copy in his bag under a Goldberg fake cover. Stacy takes offense and storms off while the "bizarre one" looks through the magazine.

Afterwards, "Stone Cold" Steve Austin's music plays and his truck drives into the arena, the fans and JR going wild. Unfortunately, it's Eric Bischoff dressed up like the "rattlesnake" mocking them. Jim calls it sick. Lawler tries to get his broadcast partner to calm down while Eric tells Austin that he misses him. Specifically, he misses the look on his face when Bischoff fired him. However, not everyone agreed with his decision. The general manager tells JR to get on the stage and say what he said last week to Eric's face. Jerry tries to stop him, but Ross doesn't back down. He wants to say something in his own defense. That's that he meant every word of calling Bischoff a "lousy son of a bitch". JR then quits to a mixed reaction. The GM says he can't quit because he's fired.

Goldust def. Steven Richards (with Victoria). "The King" is on commentary solo as the wrestlers trade shots ahead of a Richards neckbreaker. The heel follows up with stomps and a choke before scoring a two-count with a suplex. Coach finally joins the announce table to provide help while Goldust comes back to life with a bulldog and pair of clotheslines. A butt bump afterwards gets him a near fall before the "bizarre one" attempts to deliver Shattered Dreams. Although Steven fights free, he runs into a modified chokeslam for a near fall. When Goldust attempts to finish him off with the Curtain Call, Richards flips free and answers with a face slam for his own two-count. Victoria tries to find her championship belt to help, but forgets that she lost it. She tells Steven that she can't find it, distracting him for the "bizarre one" to score the win with a snap powerslam, called the Shock Treatment by Coach. Post-match, Victoria brings a chair into the ring, but Goldust slams the heels' faces together and celebrates.

Backstage, Chris Jericho and Triple H glare at each other. Ric Flair plays peacemaker, telling them that they have to bury the hatchet to finish off Booker T and Shawn Michaels. The heels agree to do so.

Sylvan Grenier, no longer a referee, joins Rene Dupree behind a news desk to tell WWE fans that they are coming to the WWE to prove that the French are not weak and teach everyone a lesson.

Booker T/Shawn Michaels def. Chris Jericho/Triple H (with Ric Flair). Everyone gets separate entrances here, Shawn out last to lead the babyfaces into the ring to brawl with their rivals. It's Michaels and Booker dominating early, the "Heartbreak Kid" hammering Jericho at ringside while the five-time champion clotheslines Triple H for a near fall. Together, the babyfaces work on Hunter's arm with armbars and strikes. When Y2J tags in, he gets more of the same until the heels trap Shawn in their corner. After absorbing a few shots, he fights off both men and flying forearms Helmsley. When he sets up for Sweet Chin Music, Jericho intercepts him for "the Game" to tease a Pedigree. Michaels also fights free, but when he escapes, Flair low bridges him ahead of a shot of a limo arriving backstage and a commercial break.

Afterwards, Triple H high knees Shawn. Y2J soon tags in to choke Michaels with his wrist tape. He follows up with elbows and flexes like the "Heartbreak Kid" ahead of a near fall. After chopping and choking Shawn in a corner, the heel whips him across the ring. Michaels responds with a springboard cross body block and two-count. One forearm puts him right back down before Hunter tags in to trade shots with his former friend. Changing tactics, Helmsley locks on a sleeper hold. It doesn't take the "Heartbreak Kid" long to reverse the hold, but "the Game" back suplexes free for a two-count. When Jericho returns, he badmouths Shawn ahead of a spinning heel kick. A running face slam follows before Y2J leaps into Michaels's knees attempting a Lionsault. Both men tag out afterwards for Booker to punch and forearm the World Champion. A flurry of chops and a back body drop have Triple H seeing stars before the babyface scores a near fall with a kick. He also gets a two-count courtesy of a DDT, but Hunter just kicks out. When Jericho tries to make the save, he runs into a flapjack. Booker T follows up with a spinebuster to Helmsley before clearing the ring and entertaining the fans with a spinaroonie. When the heels return, Y2J traps Booker briefly in the Walls of Jericho, but Shawn makes the save with Sweet Chin Music. Afterwards, Booker T tries to give "the Game" a Scissors Kick, but the champion sidesteps and sets up for a Pedigree. At the last second, Booker sweeps his legs and rolls over him for the three-count. Post-match, Flair chop blocks the five-time champion's injured leg. He and Triple H then target the babyface's leg until Michaels makes the save. Jericho follows him in with a vicious chair shot, busting open the "Heartbreak Kid". Afterwards, the heels handcuff Shawn to the ropes before The Hurricane runs out to try to help. He's quickly repelled and tossed out to the floor before Kevin Nash makes his surprise return. Hunter is stunned as Nash big boots Y2J and Ric. While Helmsley gets a sledgehammer, Kevin Jackknife Powerbombs Jericho. Before "the Game" can hit him, Nash grabs a chair and stares down Triple H, the champion retreating up the aisle to end the show.

SmackDown!
April 10, 2003
Chicago, IL
Announcers: Michael Cole, Tazz

The show starts with footage of Brock Lesnar arriving at the arena earlier and signing a woman's shirt ahead of the intro video and fireworks.

Brock Lesnar def. Matt Hardy Version 1.0 (with Shannon Moore). The new champion comes out first to a big pop. He's followed by the heels, Matt Facts revealing that Matt's book is a *New York Times* best-seller—"of course". His second Matt Fact says he's the longest reigning singles champion on the show. Inside the ring, Hardy shows off his belt for this non-title match. Lesnar kicks it aside. When Matt tries to grab the WWE Title, Brock clotheslines him back into a corner. Shannon has seen enough and distracts the "next big thing" and Brian Hebner for Hardy to blast Lesnar with a championship belt for an early two-count. Unfortunately, he runs into a back body drop over the top rope where the cruiserweight lands chin-first on the top turnbuckle. Despite that, Matt drops Brock's neck on the top rope ahead of a neckbreaker and chokes. Continuing to focus on the neck, Hardy leg drops him on the middle rope and rides Lesnar. The WWE Champion answers with an electric chair drop, Matt falling on the back of his head. Somehow, he avoids injury again. Soon after, Brock clotheslines Hardy three times and belly-to-belly suplexes him twice. When he attempts to powerslam him, Moore pulls his man off Lesnar's shoulder. Matt tries to capitalize with a Twist of Fate, but Brock fights free and F5s him for the win.

Ahead of a new Piper's Pit, "Rowdy" Roddy Piper talks about his first Piper's Pit with jobber Frankie Williams even though that's not actually the first installment. The announcers reminisce about the segment before replaying Vince McMahon telling Hulk Hogan that he's going to pay him to stay home last week. Cole and Tazz argue if that's fair.

Brian Kendrick/Torrie Wilson def. Jamie Noble/Nidia. Before the competitors come out, Sable heads out to sit at ringside with Torrie Wilson's issue of *Playboy*. That confuses Torrie when she heads to the ring. Once the heels are out, Noble blindsides Kendrick. When he tries to run the rookie into Nidia's boot, Brian reverses it. Cole doesn't think that's the first time he's tasted her foot. Despite that shot, Jamie quickly recovers to northern lights suplex Kendrick into the heel corner. Nidia tags in afterwards for a combination drop toe hold and diva dropkick for a two-count. Despite counting that cover, Jimmy Korderas eventually remembers the rules and orders Noble back in to side suplex the rookie on his head for a near fall. The redneck scores another two-count with a forearm to the back of the head before hooking a reverse chin lock. The fans chant for Torrie, upsetting Jamie and he slams Brian back down to the canvas ahead of a reverse neck vise. Kendrick doesn't stay in the hold for long, escaping with his reverse snap mare facebuster. An enziguri follows, but when he goes for Sliced Bread #2, Noble surprises him with a neckbreaker. The heels attempt to deliver a rocket launcher afterwards, but Brian rolls out of the way and tags in Wilson to chop and catapult Nidia into a neutral corner. When she runs the ropes, Jamie grabs her and gets slapped. Torrie follows up with a low dropkick to Nidia for a near fall. Sable watches as the heel rakes Wilson's eyes, but the diva answers with a clothesline. When Noble tries to give her a Tiger Driver, Kendrick makes the save with a top rope missile dropkick. Despite that, the redneck pulls Torrie off Nidia after a neckbreaker. Moments later, Nidia shoves Brian off the top rope when he threatens Jamie at ringside. Back in the squared circle though, Nidia misses a top rope flying cross body block and accidentally hits her boyfriend. Wilson capitalizes with a tornado DDT for the win, impressing Sable. The announcers and Torrie are confused as Sable applauds the winner.

Backstage, Chris Benoit congratulates Brock Lesnar on his win at WrestleMania XIX. He calls Brock a "warrior" and looks forward to facing him at Backlash. Rhyno thinks the "rabid wolverine" is overlooking him and says he's going to be the one competing for the title at Backlash. Lesnar wishes them both luck and hopes they beat each other down trying to get a WWE Title shot.

Chris Benoit def. Rhyno (#1 Contender's Tournament match). The partners take their time feeling each other out to start the match before Rhyno trips Benoit and traps him in a crisscross choke. He then applies an arm wringer before whipping "the Crippler" down to the canvas. Continuing to use wear down holds, the man-beast applies a headlock before running through Benoit for a two-count. He also gets a near fall with a vertical suplex. The "rabid wolverine" answers with a stiff clothesline before chopping Rhyno in a corner. The man-beast responds in kind, exciting the crowd in this hard-hitting match. Just when the fans get into it though, Rhyno slows the pace with a chin lock. It doesn't take Benoit long to fight free and knee the man-beast for a two-count. He tries to follow up with a dropkick, but Rhyno holds the ropes for "the Crippler" to crash and burn for a near fall. The man-beast once again slows the pace with a body scissors, but Benoit rolls onto him for a two-count. Back up, Rhyno hammers and belly-to-belly suplexes the "rabid wolverine" while the announcers talk about Kurt Angle having surgery this week. Although Benoit dodges a corner Gore, he can't avoid a spinebuster and near fall. When he attempts a corner whip, "the Crippler" reverses and elbows the man-beast. He follows up with a diving headbutt for an extremely close two-count, but when he tries to lock on the Crippler Crossface, Rhyno reaches the ropes. When Benoit tries to apply the hold moments later, the man-beast battles free only to be backslid for a three-count. Post-match, the intense superstars shake hands and hug.

Backstage, Sable enters Torrie Wilson's locker room and talks to her through the shower. She congratulates Wilson on her issue of *Playboy* selling almost as well as Sable's. The returning diva then takes her towel and invites Torrie to come get it.

Back at ringside, the crew sets up for Piper's Pit, but Vince McMahon comes out instead. While he heads to the ring, "Rowdy" Roddy Piper talks about his interview with "Superfly" Jimmy Snuka where he hit him with a coconut in another great Piper's Pit moment. Afterwards, Vince brags about sending Hulk Hogan home last week. He promises that the Hulkster will never appear on WWE television again. After dealing with one of his creations last week, McMahon is happy to "dust off" another after fourteen years and bring back Piper's Pit. That sees "Hot Rod" head to the squared circle. Vince continues doing the talking, introducing himself as Roddy's special guest. Piper takes offense, saying McMahon has short fingers and that no one made his career but "Hot Rod". The WWE owner wants him to chill out. Vince gives Roddy credit in creating Piper's Pit. He also gives him credit in creating an oversized gut. After he mocks Piper with fat jokes, McMahon offers to let "Hot Rod" join his "Kiss My Ass" club. Roddy has had enough and takes his turn insulting the WWE owner, calling him a "little nothing" who went belly up as a rock and roll promoter. He also tanked his bodybuilding federation, but his wig looks good. Any conversation about Vince's failures has to mention the XFL and that gets a cheer from the crowd. Piper says the only success McMahon has is the company his dad gave him. He calls Vince "Junior" and gets a reaction. While the WWE owner hates Roddy, they can both agree that they both hate Hogan, shaking hands and calling themselves two "sons of a bitch". When McMahon leaves the ring, Piper stops his music to give Vince credit. He tells him he did something "Hot Rod" never did, losing to the Hulkster at WrestleMania "1-2-3". Rikishi then heads to the ring with a coconut. He hasn't forgotten what Roddy did to Snuka. Piper backs down and takes away the coconut before Sean O'Haire ambushes the big

Samoan. After he smashes a wooden chair over Rikishi, "Hot Rod" offers to make the big babyface just like "Superfly" and smashes him with a coconut too while the announcers question what's going on.

Sylvan Grenier and Rene Dupree deliver another prerecorded vignette to warn the WWE that they are coming to right wrongs. They accuse America of destroying other cultures and they are going to make the USA pay.

Rey Mysterio/Tajiri def. Team Angle. As the champions head to the ring, the announcers reveal that Kurt Angle will have neck surgery tomorrow. Charlie Haas dedicates this match to him and asks the fans to pray for the Olympian. They don't. After Benjamin yells at the crowd, Tajiri heads to the ring with a new partner after the champions injured Funaki last week. While Rey watches on the apron, the "Japanese Buzzsaw" kicks and locks Haas in a Tarantula. Mysterio tags in at the same time to dropkick the helpless heel for a two-count before Shelton makes the save. Charlie answers with a throat drop on the top rope, but when Benjamin tags in, the masked man swings around him for a dropkick and arm drag. He then slides out to the ring to trip Haas, but his fun runs out when he hops onto the apron and a superkick for a near fall. The champions follow up with a double-team gutbuster for a Charlie two-count. He follows up with an abdominal stretch and knee to the gut. Moments later, he attempts an electric chair drop, but Rey drives him face-first to the canvas. Unfortunately, he lands on his knee and is slow to crawl to his corner to give Tajiri the hot tag. It doesn't matter as the "Japanese Buzzsaw" kicks Haas before scoring a two-count with a handspring forearm. The announcers are stunned that he didn't use an elbow. Benjamin isn't, making the save, but he misses a blind tag and catches a springboard butt splash. Luckily, Charlie makes the save with a clothesline. The champions try to follow up with a double-team attack, but Tajiri kicks Shelton down to the floor. Despite Haas powerbombing him, the masked man is back up quickly to take advantage of the "Japanese Buzzsaw" kicking Charlie into position for a 619 and springboard leg drop for the victory.

Backstage, The Undertaker tells Josh Mathews that John Cena's insults last week have fired him up. The biker demands respect and promises that tonight he's going to "beat up, bust up, and shut up" Cena.

Nathan Jones def. Bill DeMott. After teasing it twice, Jones finally makes his in-ring debut to punch the bully. DeMott is surprised, but responds with a takedown and front face lock. The rookie answers with a shot out to the floor. Although Bill staggers him with a throat drop on the top rope, when the bully returns to the ring, Jones lays him out with a Big Boot for the three-count.

Backstage, Nunzio and The FBI file a police report over some missing money in their lockers. They have an idea who did it and after a commercial break, Nathan Jones is taken to a precinct to answer questions. The Undertaker takes offense and says the cops are profiling his ex-con friend.

John Cena def. The Undertaker (#1 Contender's Tournament match). Cena is out first to rap about how strong he is and being the new guard. He warns The Undertaker that Paul Bearer better have an urn for him. He also insults Chicago, telling the city that he's going to leave them broken down like when Michael Jordan left. The biker then rides his motorcycle around the squared circle to a big pop. He takes some frustrations out on John, hammering the rapping heel against the ropes while the announcers note that the "Deadman" was supposed to get surgery on his injured elbow this week. Instead, he's here punching and chokeslamming Cena for a big pop. Unfortunately, John lands close enough to the ropes to drape his foot on them for the break. The Undertaker continues punishing him, choking and stomping the rapping heel into a commercial break.

Afterwards, the biker remains in control with elbows and a leg drop on the apron. A corner splash follows before the "Deadman" unloads on Cena with a flurry of fists. John finally turns the tide, taking advantage of Mike Chioda being out of position to hit The Undertaker with his chain. Afterwards, he whips the biker's injured elbow onto the top rope and barricade. A dropkick to the elbow follows before Cena stomps it on the ring steps. Back in the squared circle, John clubs the elbow, but the "Deadman" cuts off his momentum with a running charge and Old School. When he sets up for the Last Ride, the rapping heel twists free for an armbar drop and near fall. He continues targeting the injured elbow with an armbar, the fans chanting for The Undertaker. He hears them and answers with a hard punch. Cena won't stay down, attacking the elbow again. The biker won't give up either, dropping John with snake eyes and a big boot. When he attempts another corner charge, the rapping heel pulls Chioda into the path. That puts the referee down while Cena gives the "Deadman" a spinebuster. When he tries to hoist him up for a Death Valley Driver, the Undertaker fights free and gives him a Last Ride. Chioda is still down and The FBI capitalize, running out to attack the biker. Chuck Palumbo and Nunzio take turns blasting him with a chair before John crawls over to the "Deadman" for the three-count.

Monday Night Raw
April 14, 2003
Richmond, VA
Announcers: Jonathan Coachman, Jerry "the King" Lawler, Theodore Long (briefly)

Following the intro video, Kevin Nash comes out instead of fireworks exploding. While he's making his return, Jim Ross isn't, having quit last week. Nash says it's been a long time, but he's conflicted on being back. He's upset that his friends, Shawn Michaels and Triple H, are fighting each other. Kevin says they were supposed to be friends whether on top or on the bottom. That brings out Hunter as the announcers reveal that they will face each other in a six-man tag match at Backlash. Despite that, Nash and Helmsley hug. Kevin doesn't care what matches Eric Bischoff makes. While "the Game" is happy to see Nash, the champion tells him that he will never be friends again with Shawn and wants to slap him. Michaels comes out to get in Triple H's face. When Kevin steps in, the former friends continue arguing. Nash didn't come back for this and asks if they can get along. Hunter says they can't and Kevin has to make a choice between him and the "Heartbreak Kid". If Nash comes with him, Helmsley says he'll shoot straight with Kevin and he'll be Hunter's right hand man. On the other hand, if he sides with Shawn, "the Game" says Michaels will always be talking behind his back and stealing his spotlight. If Nash joins the champion, it's them against the world, but if he doesn't, Triple H will be against him. As Hunter leaves the ring, he reminds Kevin that the two of them have had their biggest successes without the "Heartbreak Kid".

Backstage, Stacy Keibler goes through Test's bag. She's disgusted by his tissues and dried up towel, but furious when she finds Torrie Wilson's issue of *Playboy*. The bodyguard bursts in to ask what she's doing before she storms off.

Chris Jericho def. Test (with Stacy Keibler). Despite their earlier argument, Stacy still accompanies Test to the ring. Jericho follows, the announcers talking about him participating in the Backlash six-man tag match alongside Ric Flair and Triple H. Inside the ring, he punches and stomps the bodyguard in a corner. Test responds in kind ahead of a hard clothesline. When he tosses the heel out to the floor, Y2J skins the cat only to return to a military press slam. The bodyguard tries to follow up with a corner charge, but Jericho moves and Test hits his shoulder. Keibler smiles. The bodyguard isn't smiling as Y2J works over his arm and Stacy autographs a fan's sign. Soon after, Jericho lands an armbar drop, but the fans are paying attention to the diva and chanting her name. Y2J doesn't help matters applying an armbar. Eventually, Test fights free and sidewalk slams the heel. Catching a second wind, he punches and tilt-a-whirl slams Jericho for a near fall. A full nelson slam also gets him a close two-count. When he goes for a powerbomb, Y2J sunset flips him for a two-count with his feet on the ropes. Stacy hops onto the ring steps for some reason and shows off her backside while the heel attempts to lock on the Walls of Jericho. Test manages to power out and shove Jericho into the corner ahead of a gut wrench powerslam. When Keibler shows off her backside again, the bodyguard gets distracted and Y2J capitalizes with a running face slam and Lionsault for the win. Post-match, Test yells at his girlfriend and drags the fan who Stacy signed an autograph for over the barricade to slap and shove around.

Backstage, Eric Bischoff says he's been getting calls and letters since firing "Stone Cold" Steve Austin and has no choice but to listen to the fans and do right by the "rattlesnake" tonight.

After a commercial break, Test complains about Stacy Keibler costing him a match. He's had enough of Stacy complaining about Torrie Wilson and compares the two. While he does well saying that her legs and face are better, when he stumbles talking about their chests, Keibler storms off. Test yells that "two out of three ain't bad".

Jazz/Victoria (with Steven Richards) def. Ivory/Trish Stratus. While the babyfaces come out united, the heels get separate entrances including Jazz's decidedly uninteresting saxophone music. Theodore Long accompanies her to the ring, but leaves to provide guest commentary as Victoria and Ivory start the match. It doesn't take Trish long to tag in and hurricanrana the "black widow" for a two-count. She follows up with forearms while Long complains about "the man" keeping Jazz down. When Stratus challenges Jazz to get into the ring, Victoria hits the champion from behind. Jazz then tags in for a double chicken wing slam. Unfortunately, she misses a corner charge and the vixen gets in a few shots until Jazz tosses her around for a two-count. The heel then decks the champion, but her body splash is met with a pair of knees. Ivory tags in afterwards to fight both heels and nearly get the win with a face slam to Jazz. Luckily, Victoria makes the save. Stratus tags in afterwards and kicks off a four-woman brawl while Long accuses all white people of being biased. Coach disagrees. When Ivory and Victoria end up outside the ring, Jazz slams Trish onto the canvas before locking on an STF for the tap-out victory.

Backstage, a crew member tells Goldberg that a "relative" wants to see him. It's Goldust and he barks and stutters as he welcomes the intense superstar to the WWE. The "bizarre one" has a gift for him, putting a blonde wig on Goldberg and calling them twins. Goldberg has pointed to this skit as a sign that his run was destined for failure, but it's such a small thing. The intense superstar actually looks cool as he calmly takes off the wig and tells the "bizarre one" to never do that again before walking away.

Following a shot of a conflicted Kevin Nash backstage, "Stone Cold" Steve Austin's music plays. Once again, it's Eric Bischoff taunting the crowd. He says the fans are too easy before telling everyone that Austin won't be forgotten. To help fans remember "Stone Cold", Eric shills Austin t-shirts like he's on an infomercial. He calls it a "farewell package" and fans can order the shirts through WWE Shop Zone. For the first person that orders, Bischoff offers to throw in a bottle of Jim Ross's barbecue sauce since he's gone too. Booker T has heard enough and interrupts. He's got a deal for the general manager, suggesting that he sign a WrestleMania XIX rematch pitting Booker against Triple H tonight.

Kane/Rob Van Dam def. Chief Morley/Lance Storm ("No Disqualification" World Tag Title match). While the champions come out separately, the challengers are unified as they march out just to see the babyfaces chase them from the ring. Despite there being no disqualifications, both teams honor the normal rules to start the contest. That means Lance and RVD start the action while their partners watch from their corners as Rob scores a two-count with a springboard cross body block. He also gets a two-count with a spinning kick before Kane tags in to stomp and punch the former champion. Storm tries to answer only to run into a big boot. When the "Big Red Machine" attempts an elbow drop, Lance moves and tags in Morley. He fares no better and the monster tosses around and clotheslines him in a corner. When he attempts a second charge, the chief boots and punches him. He attempts a fisherman's suplex, but Kane powers free. Storm rushes to his aid with a top rope flying clothesline. The heels follow up with a double suplex for a Lance two-count. When the "Big Red Machine" sits up, the Canadian clubs him in vain. The monster effortlessly hoists him up for a powerslam and tags Van Dam for a slingshot leg drop and near fall. Morley returns moments later to elbow RVD before running into a roll-up and two-count. Rob follows up with kicks and a corner choke, perfectly legal in this match. After Kane clubs the chief from ringside, Van Dam scores a two-count with a leg drop. He attempts a monkey flip, but Morley catches and drops him face-first onto the top turnbuckle. The former champion follows up with some pounding blows before RVD fights both heels and scores a two-count with another heel kick to the chief. When he runs the ropes, Storm hits Rob with a trashcan. That brings the "Big Red Machine" over to brawl with the heels. When he grabs the steps, Lance hits them with a trashcan ahead of a Morley two-count back in the ring and commercial break.

Afterwards, Storm briefly traps Van Dam in a chin lock. When the challengers attempt a double back body drop, the champion counters with a double DDT. Kane then gets the hot tag to clothesline both challengers and big boot Morley. A powerslam to Lance afterwards gets him a near fall. The "Big Red Machine" follows up with a top rope flying clothesline, but the chief breaks the cover. That brings RVD into the ring for the champions to trap their opponents in a corner. After Rob monkey flips Storm, the monster clotheslines Morley down for rolling thunder. That sends the chief rolling out to the floor for Kane to press slam Lance onto him. Van Dam follows with a somersault splash over the top rope. When the "Big Red Machine" tries to Chokeslam Morley, Bubba Ray Dudley runs out to attack the monster. He also gives RVD a Bubba Bomb. That brings out D-Von Dudley to yell at his half-brother. When Morley yells at D-Von and threatens to hit him with a chair, Bubba takes it away. The chief demands it back, but when he gets it, Rob kicks it into his face. The Dudley Boyz leave the heels for Kane to Chokeslam Storm. He then holds the chair in front of Lance's face for a coast-to-coast Van Daminator and the win.

Backstage, Triple H and Ric Flair question why Eric Bischoff would consider giving Booker T a World Title shot tonight. The Hurricane flies in to offer three reasons: Booker beat Hunter last week, he would have done so at WrestleMania XIX if not for Flair, and three, "what's up with that". Helmsley wants to know why he's here. The superhero is here for "truth and justice". "The Game" proposes a few matches for Booker T to earn a match tonight. Bischoff eventually settles on Booker and The Hurricane facing the champion and Ric in a tag match for a title shot. When "The Nature Boy" calls himself "jet-flying", the superhero interrupts to say that some people don't need a jet to fly before leaping off.

After a shot of NASCAR driver Elliott Sadler in the crowd, a video package of The APA at a military hospital in Washington, D.C., plays.

Unfortunately, The Rock couldn't be here in person tonight, but he is available via satellite in Hollywood to say hello to "West Virginia". The Virginia crowd doesn't like that. The "People's Champ" has a big announcement, debuting his new guitar. He promises to play it next week in Atlanta for an all-new concert. When Coach asks him why he declined to face Goldberg, the "Great One" says he has nothing to prove, and the intense superstar hasn't accomplished anything. He's not afraid of Goldberg. In fact, the "Brahma Bull" isn't afraid of anything. Eventually, he talks himself into agreeing to a match with the intense superstar at Backlash. The Rock promises that history will be made and makes fun of Goldberg's intensity.

After a commercial break, Christian calls The Rock. He compliments him on his previous promo and is looking forward to next week's concert. The Canadian knows the "People's Champ" will take care of Goldberg at Backlash because Christian took a Spear last week and only hurt himself laughing at how weak it was. However, he warns the "Great One" that there might not be anything left of Goldberg if he gets in his way tonight before saying that the "Brahma Bull" is his favorite wrestler too, implying that The Rock said the same thing to him.

Goldust def. Christian by disqualification. Christian updates his music a bit here, but it doesn't help him as Goldust starts fast clotheslining and punching him. That sends the Canadian out to the floor for a chair. Although the "bizarre one" stops him from using it, he can't block a low blow for a blatant disqualification. Christian follows up with a chair shot to the back for boos. Post-match, the Canadian hopes The Rock was watching because he just "owned the room". He then challenges Goldberg to take off his wig and face him. The intense superstar doesn't need an engraved invitation, marching out to counter a chair shot with a Spear. This week, Goldberg also Jackhammers Christian to a big pop.

After the announcers hype "The Rock Concert II", Scott Steiner and Christopher Nowinski head to the ring for a debate, Lawler moderating. Tonight's topic is "Operation: Iraqi Freedom". Nowinski is against it and speaks first. He's got his mask in case Scott gets out of line. He is against the USA invading other countries and wonders what's next. Will America invade countries with different viewpoints. Steiner rebuts that he's wrestled in many countries and the US is the best. "Big Poppa Pump" says terrorists started the war and the USA will finish it. He tells Nowinski, The Dixie Chicks, and anyone who doesn't support the troops to "go straight to Hell or France". The Harvard heel says his views are wrong and he's wasted his three minutes. That sets off Scott and he attacks Nowinski before Three-Minute Warning and Rico attack. With the numbers advantage, Rosey slams Steiner for a Jamal Flying Splash.

Sylvan Grenier and Rene Dupree return in a new segment to tell the WWE wrestlers not to be afraid of them just because they have a different viewpoint. Afterwards, Jerry wishes he could show footage of Jim Ross quitting last week, but Eric Bischoff forbids it. Instead, the announcers preview Backlash and thank Cold for the theme song, "Remedy".

Booker T/The Hurricane def. Ric Flair/Triple H. As Triple H heads to the ring, Shawn Michaels and Kevin Nash watch him from separate rooms. Booker opens the match hip tossing and clotheslining Flair. Ric answers with a kick and chops. The five-time champion likes to chop too and unloads with his own shots before slamming "The Nature Boy" off the top rope. Ric slows him with an eye gouge before Hunter tags in only to run into a spinebuster. The Hurricane joins him for a head scissors and clothesline for a near fall. Afterwards, Helmsley shows off his own spinebuster before tagging in Flair for the heels to chop the superhero in their corner. "The Game" returns quickly to back elbow The Hurricane for a two-count before Booker T makes the save. In control, the champion stomps the superhero and mocks his partner. The Hurricane takes advantage of the distracted Triple H and leg sweeps him. Booker gets the tag afterwards to chop "The Nature Boy" once again. He follows up with side kicks to both heels for a two-count on Ric before Hunter makes the save. Moments later, Helmsley counters a back body drop with a facebuster. The heels don't see the superhero tagging himself in to missile dropkick "the Game" ahead of a shining wizard kick to Flair. While Booker T and the champion fight at ringside, "The Nature Boy" stops The Hurricane climbing the ropes, crotching him. Booker returns to give Ric a Scissors Kick ahead of a spinaroonie. When Triple H drags the five-time champion back out to the floor, the superhero tries to give Flair the overcast, but "The Nature Boy" rolls out of the way. He then works on The Hurricane's leg while Hunter threatens to use a chair to finish off Booker. While the referee saves the five-time champion, Shawn Michaels runs out to give Ric Sweet Chin Music for the superhero to steal the win and earn Booker T a World Title shot next week. Post-match, Chris Jericho attacks Shawn while Helmsley Pedigrees The Hurricane. When "the Game" threatens to hit the "Heartbreak Kid" with a sledgehammer, Kevin Nash walks out and confronts his friend. Both men smile until Nash takes away the weapon. Booker ends up at the wrong place at the wrong time and Kevin decks him when he gets too close to Nash's back. Michaels tries to pay peacemaker, but Booker T decks him too, Coach claiming that both shots were accidents. Whether that's true or not, the babyfaces don't seem to be on the same page less than two weeks from their six-man tag match at Backlash.

SmackDown!
April 17, 2003
Norfolk, VA
Announcers: Michael Cole, Tazz

The show opens with a music video featuring action from the WWE Title #1 Contender's Tournament. Afterwards, the intro video plays and fireworks explode before the announcers tease tonight's tournament finals.

A-Train/Big Show def. Rey Mysterio/Tajiri. Always good to hype up the crowd, Rey pops out of the stage for the opener. Everyone gets separate entrances before A-Train clubs Mysterio down. When he attempts a sit-out powerslam, the masked man lands on his feet and dropkicks the hairy heel. Tajiri does too ahead of a pair of double dropkicks, the first not hitting at the same time. Despite those shots, A-Train runs through the babyfaces with a double clothesline. He can't keep Rey down and the babyface stuns him with a jawbreaker. When he runs the ropes for the 619, Show kicks Mysterio. He then tags in to try to crush the masked man's head and toss him back into a corner. He also tosses him out of the corner before walking over Rey. When the hairy heel tags back in, he delivers a pair of backbreakers and stomps Mysterio. He also applies a reverse full nelson and holds the masked man for a Big Show chop. Afterwards, a backbreaker drop scores A-Train a near fall. When he attempts to finish him off with a running powerslam, Rey counters with a tornado DDT. The "Japanese Buzzsaw" gets the hot tag afterwards to kick and handspring elbow the hairy heel for a two-count. He also dropkicks the giant off the apron before rocking A-Train with a Buzzsaw Kick. At the last second, Big Show breaks the cover and kicks off a four-man brawl. With one hand, Show press slams Mysterio high into the air. The hairy heel follows up with a bicycle kick to Tajiri for the win. Post-match, A-Train tries to give the "Japanese Buzzsaw" a Derailer, but Tajiri sprays his face with green mist. Although the giant chases him off, Rey surprises him with a 619 around the ring post, embarrassing Big Show.

After a commercial break, A-Train wipes his eyes while Big Show hammers a cage door and complains about falling on his butt. The giant doesn't like people laughing at him and promises to get a match with Rey Mysterio.

Afterwards, Cole is in the ring to introduce Brock Lesnar. Following footage of Brock landing on his head at WrestleMania XIX, Lesnar jokes that he was "feeling the pain". He says he was lucky to survive without serious injury. However, Brock knew that he had to bring everything he had to get the WWE Title back from Kurt Angle after the Olympian kicked out of his F5. Lesnar says they hurt and offers to give Cole one, but the announcer backs down. Despite suffering a concussion, Brock says he'd do it again to leave with the title. Lesnar then tells Angle that he took the "next big thing" to another level and he respects Kurt. John Cena interrupts to say that Brock doesn't respect the fans or the rapping heel. Cena calls him a liar because to get a concussion, "you need a brain". John warns Lesnar that WrestleMania is over and the rapping heel is the "new next big thing". While Brock might still think of him as a "Vanilla Ice wannabe", Cena warns him that he's going to beat him at Backlash. That brings Chris Benoit out to say John's problem is that he ignores the obvious. Before the rapping heel worries about facing Lesnar, he's got to get through "the Crippler" tonight. Benoit then tells him that you always respect the WWE Title even if you don't respect the man holding it. That sets off Brock and he wonders if the "rabid wolverine" respects him. While they argue, Cena demands respect. Lesnar offers to respect whoever wins the number one contender spot tonight and even shakes both men's hands. When he shakes Benoit's, John cheap shots "the Crippler" and runs away.

A Mr. America teaser plays.

Eddie Guerrero (with Chavo Guerrero Jr.) def. Jamie Noble (with Nidia). As Los Guerreros head to the ring, the announcers reveal that they'll finally get a WWE Tag Title rematch at Backlash. That brings Team Angle out for Shelton Benjamin to mock Eddie with a Mexican accent. Charlie Haas adds that the Guerreros' grandmother is the best housekeeper money can buy. That distracts "Latino Heat" for Noble to attack him from behind and score a two-count with a neckbreaker. The champions remain at the top of the ramp watching as Eddie comes back to life with fists and a European uppercut. A suplex afterwards gets him a two-count. Although Jamie counters his corner charge, Guerrero surprises him with a tilt-a-whirl backbreaker. The redneck answers with a pumphandle suplex for a near fall. When he sets up for a Tiger Bomb, "Latino Heat" slingshots him into the top turnbuckle. A back suplex follows, but when he goes upstairs, Nidia grabs his leg. Luckily, Chavo rushes to his uncle's aid and pulls the diva down for Eddie to block Jamie's attack and fling him to the canvas for a Frog Splash and the win. Post-match, "Latino Heat" compliments Team Angle's wrestling skills and them taking each other down all the time. Chavo jokes that they give a new definition to "you suck". Those are fighting words and the champions runs out to brawl with Los Guerreros. Unfortunately, the challengers are ready for them and drive off Team Angle.

A Backlash ad featuring Goldberg plays.

No longer sitting behind a desk, Rene Dupree and Sylvan Grenier warn Americans not to be afraid and promise to teach them a lesson while touring the United Nations building.

Afterwards, the announcers preview Backlash including a newly signed Big Show/Rey Mysterio match as well as Nathan Jones against Nunzio. We then get a video package for that feud. Cole also reveals that The Undertaker just had surgery on his injured elbow and should be back in a few weeks.

Filmed earlier today, Nathan Jones chokes Nunzio and accuses him of setting up the "Colossus of Boggo Road" last week. When The FBI rush to his defense, Jones takes care of them too.

Backstage, Sable interrupts Torrie Wilson stretching. She compliments Torrie getting out of the shower last week and asks Wilson to help her with her stuck dress zipper. She tries to seduce the diva when she removes her dress and says she has nowhere to change. One of the writers definitely has a fetish after the Torrie/Dawn Marie storyline. Wilson tells her to change wherever she wants and leaves Sable alone, topless.

After a commercial break, "Rowdy" Roddy Piper comes out to a big pop for another installment of Piper's Pit. He thanks the fans cheering his name, but calls the ones talking about him at home on their computers "cowards". He then replays hitting "Superfly" Jimmy Snuka with a coconut in 1984 as well as Rikishi last week after Sean O'Haire attacked the big Samoan. Piper promises more where that came from before introducing his new friend, O'Haire. Sean says it's an honor to be with a winner like "Hot Rod". He wants to learn from a mind that might be eviler than him, but he's "not telling you anything you don't already know". Snuka interrupts, stunning Roddy who hides behind his new friend. "Superfly" says they have a problem. Piper tells O'Haire he can take care of it and tells his protégé to leave the ring so he can deal with Snuka. "Hot Rod" rants that he doesn't need anyone to watch his back and claims to be the greatest wrestler of all-time. However, he wants to bury the hatchet with "Superfly" tonight and offers him his hand before trying to cheap shot Snuka. The legend sees him coming and answers with his own shots until Sean returns to big boot Jimmy's throat. That brings out Rikishi to hammer O'Haire until Piper threatens him with a chair. When the big Samoan turns to stop him, Sean kicks Rikishi down again. Cole calls the heels a lethal combination. Once they leave the ring, the big babyface warns O'Haire that he's in trouble at Backlash before challenging "Hot Rod" to a fight. Unfortunately, Sean holds back Piper from accepting that challenge.

Footage of Torrie Wilson at an autograph signing plays.

Torrie Wilson def. Nidia (with Jamie Noble). After the competitors come out, Sable heads down the aisle in skimpy referee attire, confusing Torrie. Nidia capitalizes with a northern lights suplex and clothesline, earning a pair of two-counts. Moments later, she tosses Torrie over the top rope, but Wilson lands on the apron and slams the heel's face into the top turnbuckle. A top rope flying cross body block follows for a near fall. Afterwards, Torrie chops and back body drops Nidia for another two-count. When she attempts a monkey flip, the heel holds her ground and sets Wilson on the top rope. Unfortunately, Torrie stays in control and lands a tornado DDT off the second rope. When Jamie tries to interfere, Sable baseball slide kicks him off the apron before making the three-count for Wilson.

Matt Hardy Version 1.0 (with Shannon Moore) def. Brian Kendrick (Cruiserweight Title match). This week's Matt Facts are that Matt "really likes his book" and his favorite sushi is "freshwater eel". Brian then sprints down the aisle for a pair of pinning predicaments and near falls before diving through the ropes to spear Moore. When he heads upstairs, Hardy dodges his flying attack and answers with a side effect to swing the momentum. He then scores a two-count with a clothesline before applying a full nelson while the announcers reveal that "Rowdy" Roddy Piper has accepted Rikishi's challenge and will face him next week. When the champion attempts a full nelson slam, Kendrick fights free and runs up the ropes for a face-first slam and near fall. Kicks follow ahead of his snap mare facebuster. Afterwards, he takes a page from his trainer's book and scores a near fall with a top rope flying elbow drop. When he goes for Sliced Bread #2 though, Matt shoves him off for a Twist of Fate and the victory.

Backstage, The FBI promise Nunzio that they are going to take care of Nathan Jones tonight.

An ad for the new Divas in Heat DVD plays before we get a replay of The APA visiting a military hospital.

Nathan Jones def. Nunzio. The heels are out first for Nunzio to attack Jones as he tries to step into the ring. Nathan responds with a big right hand and spinning kick. The Italian heel runs the ropes afterwards, running into a hanging choke. Nunzio has had enough and calls for help, but Jones fights off The FBI too while the referee calls for the disqualification. When he chases Nunzio out to the floor, Chuck Palumbo surprises him with a superkick. Johnny Stamboli follows up by slamming the ring steps down onto Nathan's leg. Cole says he brought it on himself attacking Chuck last month.

A Backlash ad featuring Goldberg and The Rock plays.

A Mr. America teaser featuring shots of US troops plays.

John Cena def. Chris Benoit (#1 Contender's Tournament Finals match). Pre-match, John promises to teach Benoit a lesson in respect and calls him a "Dynamite rip-off", referencing Dynamite Kid. "The Crippler" then rushes out to run through Cena and work on his arm. He also targets his leg before hooking a side headlock while Cole speculates that Nathan Jones may have a broken ankle. Benoit is all over the rapping heel with chops until John surprises him with a low blow while Brian Hebner is out of position. That gets Cena a near fall before he applies his own wear down hold, a reverse chin lock. It doesn't take the "rabid wolverine" long to fight free and chop his opponent. When he tries to German suplex him, the rapping heel surprises Benoit with a roll-up for a two-count. The babyface tries to answer with a Crippler Crossface, but John reaches the ropes and retreats to the floor. "The Crippler" follows him out with a flying dive through the ropes ahead of a commercial break.

Afterwards, Benoit scores a pair of two-counts before stretching Cena's arm. John answers with a boot and hot shot. Following a second drop on the top rope, the rapping heel nearly scores the win with a flipping face slam. He then slows the pace with a front face lock. The "rabid wolverine" escapes with chops, but a drop toe hold puts him on the middle turnbuckle. Cena follows up with a leg drop on Benoit's neck from the second rope. That scores him a two-count before he hooks a side headlock. This time, "the Crippler" forearms and back suplexes his way free. After working the referee's count to five, Benoit gets up to chop and suplex the rapping heel for a near fall. John answers with a spinning side slam for his own two-count before he loses his cool and chokes the "rabid wolverine". Benoit capitalizes on his frustration, stunning him with a forearm to the jaw. When he heads upstairs though, Cena dodges his diving headbutt and Oklahoma rolls "the Crippler" for a near fall. Right back up, Benoit traps the rapping heel in a Crippler Crossface, but John holds on long enough to reach the ropes for the break. Afterwards, the "rabid wolverine" hammers Cena's back before the two men tease their finishers. Ultimately, Benoit slips free of a Death Valley Driver to try to sunset flip the rapping heel. Instead, Cena sits down on him to score the victory and Backlash WWE Title shot.

Monday Night Raw

April 21, 2003
Atlanta, GA
Announcers: Jonathan Coachman, Jerry "the King" Lawler, Theodore Long (briefly), Christopher Nowinski (briefly)

The show opens with Ric Flair complaining about having to face Shawn Michaels, Kevin Nash, and Booker T this Sunday in a six-man tag match. He's even more upset that Triple H has to give Booker a World Title match tonight. Eric Bischoff is ecstatic with his booking. He's even happier that he has a special guest referee for the title match…Shawn Michaels. The general manager assures Flair that it will be great and he needs to take his frustrations out on someone else because Eric is just doing his job. Afterwards, the intro video plays and fireworks explode to kick off the episode.

Chris Jericho def. The Hurricane. After Lawler says that he still misses Jim Ross, Jericho tries to sneak attack the superhero before he removes his cape. Instead, The Hurricane greets him with an inverted atomic drop. He then blinds Y2J with the cape for fists, chasing the heel out to the floor. The superhero follows with a baseball slide kick before flying over the top rope with a springboard cannonball smash. A slingshot Oklahoma roll back in the ring gets him a near fall, but when he leaps up for a hurricanrana, Jericho powerbombs him to the mat. Y2J immediately follows up with the Walls of Jericho, but The Hurricane won't submit. Reaching down deep, he crawls to the ropes for the break. With the fans chanting that he sucks, the heel back suplexes the superhero ahead of a backbreaker. When he applies a chin lock, The Hurricane slowly fights free ahead of a tornado DDT. He follows up with a leaping clothesline and neckbreaker for a near fall. He tries to finish off Jericho with an overcast, but the heel dodges his neckbreaker to plant him with a running face slam. Unfortunately, Y2J also misses a big move, his Lionsault. Afterwards, the superhero rocks him with a shining wizard kick for a near fall. When he can't turn the heel over into the Walls of Jericho, The Hurricane catapults him onto the top rope. Jericho tries to respond with a flying attack, but the superhero catches him by the throat and chokeslams him. He tries to finish off the heel with the Eye of the Hurricane, but Y2J holds onto Jack Doan until he can trip The Hurricane for the Walls of Jericho and the tap-out victory. Post-match, Ric Flair runs down to attack the superhero and take out some frustrations with a Figure Four Leglock.

Backstage, The Rock arrives in a black stretch hummer. He's excited for his second concert tonight.

Rodney Mack (with Theodore Long) def. Unnamed Jobber ("Five-Minute White Boy Challenge"). Long interrupts Mack's terrible entrance music to "holla at ya playa". He says the WWE is holding Rodney down and the only way to get his man on television is to introduce his five-minute challenge against any white wrestler. Theodore then joins the announce table as Mack marches down to clothesline and club the jobber. Chokes and a backbreaker follow as Coach accuses Long of being racist. Theodore says he's not and the only thing he cares about is the "dollar bill". While the announcers argue, Rodney finishes off the jobber in under two minutes with a powerslam. Post-match, Long refuses to let Chad Patton raise his man's hand.

Backstage, Booker T confronts Shawn Michaels. Shawn says he's just as surprised as anyone that he's a referee tonight, but Booker knows that he's the odd man out in their six-man tag match with Kevin Nash this Sunday. Last week, Booker T says he accidentally hit Michaels, but the "Heartbreak Kid" superkicked him last year on purpose. As far as Booker is concerned, the superstars are now even. Shawn repeats that, but doesn't seem sincere.

After footage of Goldberg visiting the troops plays, Lita heads to the squared circle where Coach introduces her. She says it's been a long year while the fans chant her name. As she tells fans that she's cleared to start training again, Eric Bischoff walks out to interrupt. He says Coachman is doing a better job than Jim Ross and says Lita is amazing. He paws at her as he says she has "talent" that he wants to "expose". Since Lita is just getting cleared, it will probably be two months before she is ready to step back into the squared circle. To help her, Bischoff teases getting her some exposure like Torrie Wilson. Lita is proud of Torrie, but doesn't want to pose for *Playboy* unless it's her decision. Eric isn't sure she'd even make the magazine, telling her that he wants her to give him a private audition. When he threatens to take her job unless she does so, she tells him to "go to Hell" and walks out. Like JR and "Stone Cold" Steve Austin, Bischoff fires Lita for defying him.

Following a commercial break, Triple H complains to Ric Flair about tonight's main event. He doesn't care about facing Booker T, but says Eric Bischoff is screwing with him making Shawn Michaels the referee. The heels try to come up with a way to get some insurance for the match.

Scott Steiner/Test (with Stacy Keibler) def. Three-Minute Warning (with Rico). Christopher Nowinski joins the announce table to talk about his views on the war in Iraq and insult Scott. Steiner opens the match clubbing both Samoans. While he can belly-to-belly suplex Jamal, he can't lift Rosey before Rico sneaks into the ring to kick "Big Poppa Pump's" ribs. That swings the momentum and the heels turn the tide with strikes and a big splash for a near fall. Jamal also applies a bow and arrow submission before Rosey tags in to lock on a surfboard. Scott easily powers out and answers with a jawbreaker, but when he rolls for his corner and the tag, Jamal hits Test. Rosey follows up with a spinebuster to Steiner, but Jamal misses his top rope Flying Splash. That lets the bodyguard get the hot tag to clothesline and slam the Samoans. He impresses with a pumphandle slam to Jamal, but when he goes for the cover, Rosey tries to make the save. Unfortunately, he ends up splashing his own partner. Afterwards, Stacy tries to get Rico off the apron and gets kicked down to the floor. "Big Poppa Pump" comes to her defense and clubs the stylist while Test Big Boots Rosey. He sets up to finish off Jamal, but gets distracted by his partner checking on his girlfriend at ringside. Although Jamal crushes the bodyguard in the corner, Scott makes the save with a reverse DDT for the win.

After a commercial break, Test yells at Scott Steiner for stealing the glory in the previous match. He tells Scott to keep his hands to himself, but Stacy Keibler steps in to tell "Big Poppa Pump" thanks.

Further backstage, Kevin Nash interrupts Eric Bischoff on the phone bragging about firing Lita. Kevin wants to know what's going on with Eric making Shawn Michaels a guest referee tonight. Nash doesn't like being manipulated and doesn't want to be put in the middle of things. Bischoff tells him he can just pick a side and get out of the middle. Kevin doesn't like that either. He promises to pick the winning side...his.

Even further backstage, Terri asks The Rock what we can expect from the Rock Concert II. He says it will be the most entertaining night in sports entertainment history and he has a surprise. As he walks away, the "People's Champ" tells her not to look at his "booty".

After a commercial break, it's time for the Rock Concert II. Whether cheering or booing, the fans are exceptionally loud as the "People's Champ" heads to the squared circle with his guitar. Notably, there are far more cheers than boos. After teasing and taunting the crowd, he sings about Georgia being an "inbred hick state". When the fans start to chant "Goldberg", The Rock sings about kicking his butt and says he insisted that "Bill Goldberg came here tonight". He then invites out Goldberg, but instead it's Gillberg walking through sprinklers and acting a fool as he stomps down the ramp. His impression cracks up the "Great One". After the "Brahma Bull" says he looks to be in the best shape of his life, Gillberg grunts and screams for more laughs. The Rock then performs a parody of "The Devil Went Down to Georgia" to let everyone know he's going to kick the intense superstar's butt this Sunday. Gillberg dances around the ring and claps. When Goldberg arrives backstage on the Titantron, the "People's Champ" calls for security. On second thought, he realizes that he doesn't need any help and says Gillberg is in big trouble for making fun of Goldberg for years. When the "Great One" says the intense superstar doesn't have the guts to face him, Goldberg proves otherwise, storming down the aisle to a big cheer. The "Brahma Bull" doesn't care if he wants to fight Gillberg, but The Rock says he's not afraid of Goldberg and will fight him right now. The intense superstar storms into the ring, but he can't catch the "People's Champ". Instead, he manhandles security until Gillberg attacks from behind. When Goldberg hammers him, the "Great One" clubs him from behind and Rock Bottoms his Backlash opponent. That doesn't keep Goldberg down for long and he rushes out of the ring to chase the "Brahma Bull" backstage. There, The Rock hurries into his limo and hightails it out of the arena, Goldberg trying to chase behind in his muscle car. Unfortunately, something is wrong with his car and he sprints out of the arena, trying to outrun a hummer. When he leaves, the "People's Champ" emerges from the shadows, still in the building.

The Spike Dudley/Trish Stratus and The Dudley Boyz match never officially starts. Once the babyfaces come out, Chief Morley steps through the curtain to introduce their opponents and give the Dudleys a World Tag Title shot this Sunday. Inside the ring, Spike doesn't want anything to do with his half-brothers, but Bubba Ray kicks and powerbombs him immediately. Morley yells at D-Von to prove his loyalty and attack Trish, but it's Bubba squashing her in a corner. When the chief of staff tells them to put Stratus through a table, D-Von refuses. Bubba Ray argues with him until D-Von tells his half-brother to get his own table. Instead, Morley slides a table into the ring. Before the Dudleys can drive Trish through it, Kane and Rob Van Dam run out to fight the heels, chasing off The Dudley Boyz ahead of a Chokeslam to the chief of staff. When the champions follow the Dudleys out into the crowd, Jazz rushes out with Theodore Long to double chicken wing slam Stratus on the table laying on the canvas.

Backstage, The Rock tells a member of the crew to set up the ring for an encore.

After a commercial break, the camera catches Kevin Nash and Triple H talking in a stairwell and smiling.

Back in the squared circle, The Rock is ready for his encore. Before he can sing his final song, Goldberg rushes into the ring and tosses around the "People's Champ" inside and out of the squared circle. When he sets up for a Spear, Christian ambushes the intense superstar. The "Great One" waits until he's down to try to finish off Goldberg. Instead, the intense superstar clotheslines him ahead of a Spear to Christian. The "Brahma Bull" answers with a trio of chair shots to the head before wailing on his lower back repeatedly to leave Goldberg laying twice in the same episode.

After a commercial break and replay of the previous segment, the announcers preview Backlash.

Backstage, Kevin Nash knocks on Shawn Michaels's door and asks him to keep an open mind. Triple H then enters the "Heartbreak Kid's" locker room.

Booker T and Triple H (with Ric Flair) (World Title match) wrestle to a no contest. Shawn Michaels is out first as the special guest referee. Unlike in the Attitude era, he wears track pants alongside his referee's shirt tonight. The announcers aren't sure that he can call the match down the middle. They also wonder if Kevin Nash has chosen a side while the wrestlers jockey for position and trade strikes early on. Booker scores an early two-count with a flying forearm. A side kick and side slam also get him a pair of near falls. When he gets near the ropes though, Triple H tosses the challenger out to the floor. Ric tries to get involved but is dropped ahead of a slam on the barricade to Hunter. That brings out Chris Jericho to distract Booker T following a side kick. The distraction pays off as Helmsley knocks the babyface out to the floor ahead of a commercial break.

Afterwards, "the Game" has Booker trapped in a sleeper hold. It takes him a minute, but the challenger escapes by running Triple H into a corner. The champion answers with a spinebuster for a two-count. He follows up with a suplex and knee drop to the face for another near fall. Even when Booker T starts to fight back, Hunter drops him with a high knee for a series of two-counts. Frustrated, Helmsley chokes his opponent until the referee intervenes. Focusing back on the task at hand, "the Game" nearly scores the win with a neckbreaker. He goes back to the well afterwards, locking on another sleeper hold. Booker won't give up, reaching down deep to fight free and side kick the champion. Moments later, a second side kick has Triple H seeing stars. The challenger follows up with a series of fast-paced high-impact shots including a leg lariat when Hunter takes a risk and flies off the second rope. Following a suplex, Booker T nearly wins the belt with a missile dropkick, but Helmsley grabs the ropes at the last second to break Shawn's count. "The Game" quickly recovers to counter a back body drop with a facebuster ahead of a DDT and close two-count. Y2J doesn't like the count. When the babyface tries to answer with a Scissors Kick, the champion steps back and attempts to counter with a Pedigree. Booker also fights free to finally hit his finisher. Unfortunately, he has to knock both Flair and Jericho off the apron giving Triple H time to recover and kick out at the last second. Moments later, the challenger heads upstairs, but Hunter shoves the referee back into the ropes, tearing the "Heartbreak Kid's" breakaway pants and knocking Booker T down to the canvas for a near fall. When Ric argues with the special guest referee, the babyface back drops free of a Pedigree and Scissors Kicks the champion again. Before he can score the win, Y2J races into the ring to blast the babyface with the World Title. While Shawn doesn't see that, he does see the belt and refuses to make the count. When the heels take offense, Michaels decks Flair, tosses Jericho out to the floor, and gives "the Game" Sweet Chin Music. He tries to count to three for Booker afterwards, but "The Nature Boy" and Y2J recover to break up the count and end the match with a no contest. Before the heels can finish off Shawn, Nash hurries down the aisle to chase off Ric and Jericho. He helps Triple H up to his feet before turning to do the same to the "Heartbreak Kid". While his back is turned, Hunter makes Kevin's decision for him, low blowing the big man and storming out of the ring to end the episode. Nash promises him that he's dead.

SmackDown!
April 24, 2003
Nashville, TN
Announcers: Michael Cole, Tazz, John Cena (briefly)

John Cena def. Rhyno. Following the intro video and fireworks, Cena heads to the ring for a tune-up for his WWE Title match this Sunday. After Tazz shills him on the cover of the new issue of the *Raw* magazine, John runs down his list of accomplishments and promises to be the next WWE Champion in a promo where he doesn't rap for once. He promises to show footage that proves Brock Lesnar is a liar until Rhyno rushes down to trap the rapping heel in a side headlock. When Cena escapes, the man-beast clotheslines and tosses him out to the floor. John takes advantage of Rhyno sliding him back in first to attack the man-beast and target his injured neck with a leg drop off the second rope. He then stretches Rhyno's neck on the barricade with a reverse chin lock. That scores the rapping heel a near fall back in the ring before he applies an armbar and drives a knee into the man-beast's neck. Eventually, Rhyno fights free to punch and back body drop Cena. He follows up with a clothesline and a butterfly suplex for a two-count. John is right back up to double over the man-beast and snap mare slam him to the mat. A spinning side slam gets him a near fall moments later before he runs into a spinebuster. When Rhyno sets up for a Gore, the rapping heel moves and knees the man-beast's jaw. He quickly follows up with a roll-up for the out of nowhere victory.

Backstage, "Rowdy" Roddy Piper and Sean O'Haire enter the building to mess with the crew.

A Mr. America teaser plays. Tazz says he better be good.

Earlier today, Nunzio and The FBI tell Chris Benoit that he cost them money losing to John Cena last week. "The Crippler" tells them if they want to collect, Nunzio can do so in the ring. He accepts.

Backstage, Josh Mathews asks Sable about tonight's "Sable Invitational". Before she answers, she unzips her top and seduces the interviewer. She wonders if he has what she has before saying that she's the perfect judge for tonight's "hot body" competition.

After a commercial break, a video package of *SmackDown!* superstars visiting a naval base plays.

Chris Benoit def. Nunzio (with The FBI). As the heels head to the ring, we see footage of them injuring Nathan Jones last week. The FBI then distract Benoit for Nunzio to slingshot splash him from the ring. After the goons get in their shots, they shove "the Crippler" into the ring for a Nunzio two-count. He follows up with fists and chokes. It doesn't take Benoit, wrestling in a shirt this week, long to fight back with a string of vicious chops until Stamboli trips him. Nunzio capitalizes with a Sicilian slicer for a near fall. A forearm to the jaw and neckbreaker moments later nearly gets the Italian heel the win. When he wastes time arguing with Jimmy Korderas, the "rabid wolverine" rolls up Nunzio for his own two-count. Moments later, he holds the ropes to block a neckbreaker. Benoit follows up with an enziguri to finally slow the Italian heel. After catching his breath, "the Crippler" catches Nunzio with a forearm to the jaw and German suplex. Palumbo tries to make the save, but Benoit tosses Nunzio into him. After driving Stamboli into the ring post, the "rabid wolverine" counters Arrivederci with the Crippler Crossface for the tap-out win. Post-match, he puts Chuck in the hold too until Johnny makes the save and holds

Benoit for a Palumbo superkick. Stamboli powerslams him too before Nunzio slaps and badmouths "the Crippler".

Backstage, Funaki and Tajiri laugh as they repeatedly watch footage of Rey Mysterio knocking Big Show down with a 619 last week. That sets off the giant and he chases off the babyfaces before smashing their TV.

After Rey Mysterio heads to the ring for the next match, Matt Hardy Version 1.0 comes out in street clothes with a Matt Fact telling everyone that he only uses low fat salad dressing. Hardy takes this opportunity to introduce his newest MFer, Crash Holly, before joining the announce table.

Rey Mysterio def. Crash Holly (with Shannon Moore). Although Rey drives Moore from the ring, Holly capitalizes with a sneak attack before applying an armbar. Although Matt is at the announce table, he doesn't say anything as he scouts the competitors. He doesn't seem impressed when Mysterio head scissors Crash. When he attempts to deliver his body scissors bulldog, the MFer counters with a back suplex. He then briefly applies a hammerlock before shoving the masked man out to the floor for Shannon to hit him with Hardy's book. That only gets Holly a two-count back in the ring. When he attempts a whip into the corner, Rey reverses it and finally hits his bulldog. Picking up the pace, he scores a two-count with a springboard butt splash and tornado DDT. Crash slows his momentum with an eye rake, but accidentally runs into Shannon moments later. The masked man capitalizes with a 619 to Holly and back body drop off the apron to Moore. A slingshot leg drop afterwards gets Rey the win.

Backstage, John Cena hypes up A-Train and tells him that his match with Brock Lesnar isn't about winning or losing. He wants the hairy heel to injure Brock tonight before showing footage of Lesnar dropping A-Train on his neck with an F5. Fired up, the hairy heel promises that Brock will feel his pain.

Rikishi def. "Rowdy" Roddy Piper (with Sean O'Haire) by disqualification. O'Haire distracts Rikishi, also wrestling in a t-shirt this week, for a Piper low blow to open the match. This marks Roddy's first WWE match and first with the company in over seven years. "Hot Rod" follows up with a flurry of strikes until the big Samoan comes back to life with fists and a stomp to the gut. When Rikishi squashes his man in a corner, Sean hops onto the apron only to get decked. The big babyface teases giving Piper a Stinkface, but O'Haire makes the save with a clothesline to the back of the head for the disqualification. Post-match, Sean leaping side kicks Rikishi ahead of a reverse death valley driver.

A Backlash ad featuring John Cena and Brock Lesnar plays.

A Rene Dupree/Sylvan Grenier teaser plays. This week, the French heels are called La Resistance as they chastise America for trying to secure peace through war.

Afterwards, Sable heads to the squared circle to catcalls. She says since she's been back, everyone has told her that she's the sexiest diva on *SmackDown!*. Sable wants to size up her competition, but says that Torrie Wilson didn't accept the offer since she's feeling "fat" and hasn't hit the gym in a while. Since she's not here, Sable welcomes out Nidia and Dawn Marie for the "Sable Invitational". When Sable gives them fifteen seconds to disrobe, Wilson interrupts in a robe to a big pop. Nidia is up first to reveal her flowery bikini and dance around pathetically. The announcers can't help but laugh. Dawn follows with a bobcat print bikini for a better pop. Finally, Torrie puts a lollipop in her mouth and parades around in a red bikini, grinding against Sable. The veteran says there's a clear winner and calls the competition a tie between Nidia and Marie. While Wilson is willing to shake their hands, the heels attack her from behind, Sable taking her sucker and calling Torrie the only real loser tonight.

Backstage, Eddie Guerrero hypes up Chavo Guerrero Jr. in Spanish ahead of a *WWE Confidential* ad featuring Kurt Angle's recent neck surgery.

Shelton Benjamin (with Charlie Haas) def. Chavo Guerrero Jr. (with Eddie Guerrero). In a prerecorded promo, Team Angle dedicates their Backlash victory over Los Guerreros to Kurt Angle. Although Benjamin outwrestles him to start the match, Chavo chases him to the floor with a dropkick. Back in the squared circle, Guerrero chops the champion before scoring a near fall with a twisting senton splash off the second rope. Shelton answers with a lightning fast powerslam for his own close two-count. A superkick follows to the kidneys before Benjamin applies a chin lock. Luckily, Chavo is close enough to the ropes for a quick break. Shelton doesn't care, slamming the babyface for another near fall. Guerrero answers with a forearm uppercut and flapjack. Dropkicks to the face then score him a two-count before Benjamin slams him onto the turnbuckle. When he attempts a suplex, Chavo surprises the champion with an STF. Charlie tries to make the save, but Eddie cuts him off. Unfortunately, Brian Hebner is distracted yelling at "Latino Heat" while Haas drags his partner to the ropes for the break. Moments later, he kicks Chavo for Shelton to steal the win with a handful of tights and the ropes for the three-count. Post-match, Los Guerreros attack the champions before Eddie tosses his nephew into them with an elevated dropkick.

Backstage, John Cena warns Brock Lesnar that the pain will be coming from the A-Train.

Tajiri def. Big Show by count-out. As the giant heads to the ring, Rey Mysterio watches backstage. Tajiri cautiously enters the squared circle and tries to stay away from Show, but he can't stay away forever. Eventually, Big Show grabs him and flattens the "Japanese Buzzsaw" with a clothesline. He follows up with a press slam onto the top turnbuckle and vicious pair of chops. When he attempts a big boot though, Tajiri dodges and the giant crotches himself. The "Japanese Buzzsaw" follows up with a string of kicks, but his handspring back elbow is met with a big boot. When Big Show motions for a Chokeslam, Rey's music plays, but the masked man is nowhere to be seen. The distraction lets Tajiri kick Show until he leaps into a Chokeslam. This time, Mysterio sneaks out and tries to attack the giant from behind. When Show sees him, Rey runs off, Big Show following him only to be ran into the steel post for the count-out loss.

Backstage, Brock Lesnar squats a CO2 tank.

After a commercial break, Stephanie McMahon shows off her legs and backside. She says she's no Torrie Wilson, but that's what's great about America. She says bodies come in all shapes and sizes and she's proud to be an American. She's also ecstatic to announce that she's signed Mr. America to compete on *SmackDown!* next week. A teaser package then plays for the soon to be arriving superstar featuring iconic American imagery before the announcers preview Backlash.

Brock Lesnar def. A-Train by disqualification. Pre-match, John Cena comes out to insult Brock and provide guest commentary. Following a commercial break, Lesnar trips the hairy heel and holds him down with a front face lock. When A-Train powers out, the champion repeatedly rams him with shoulder blocks in a corner. The hairy heel is fired up and answers with clubbing blows before the two men trade shoulder blocks. Although neither man moves on their first two collisions, the third time they hit, both men fly back to the canvas. A-Train takes control afterwards, hammering Brock until the babyface clotheslines him down. A second clothesline sends the hairy heel down to the floor in front of Cena. When Lesnar gets distracted arguing with Cena, the hairy heel capitalizes with a bicycle kick to knock the babyface off the apron. That gets him a pair of near falls before he wails on the champion again. A decapitator catapult also gets him a two-count. Afterwards, A-Train stomps Lesnar and applies a chin lock. That gives John and Cole time to argue at the announce table before Brock eventually fights back up to his feet and escapes the wear down hold. Just when he starts to build up momentum, the two big man collide head-to-head. The hairy heel has a massive head and gets the better of the collision. Despite hitting Lesnar a few times, A-Train soon runs into a spinebuster. Soon after, the champion clotheslines and powerslams the hairy heel for a near fall. A pair of belly-to-belly suplexes follow, but when he goes for a third, A-Train answers with a headbutt and Derailer for a near fall. The rapping heel argues that Mike Chioda was out of position. While he complains, Brock recovers to F5 the hairy heel. Before he can get the three-count, Cena attacks for the disqualification. Softening up his opponent this Sunday, John hits him with his steel chain ahead of a Death Valley Driver. Afterwards, the rapping heel grabs the WWE Title and blasts the champion with it, busting him open.

PPV: Backlash

April 27, 2003
Worcester, MA
Announcers: Jonathan Coachman, Jerry "the King" Lawler, Michael Cole, Tazz

The show opens with a video package featuring Goldberg and The Rock. Afterwards, fireworks explode before the *Raw* announcers preview the action. They quickly give way to Cole and Tazz.

Team Angle def. Los Guerreros (WWE Tag Title match). The champions are out first, Haas carrying a picture of Kurt Angle to the ring after dedicating this title defense to their leader. Cole wonders how they'll do without Kurt for the first time in their careers at a PPV. Charlie doesn't look too good early on as Eddie outwrestles him and scores a trio of quick covers. When the fans chant for "Latino Heat", he gets them to cheer Chavo too. The younger Guerrero then tags in to flip over the top rope and lock up with Benjamin. Like his uncle, Chavo outwrestles Shelton and scores a quick cover. He then punches the champion and traps him in an arm wringer. When Eddie returns, he scores another two-count with forearms and fists. The challengers make quick tags and focus on Shelton's arm until Haas knees Chavo's back running the ropes. Benjamin capitalizes with a clothesline before "Latino Heat" proves that he'll cheat too, kneeing Shelton's back and illegally switching places with his nephew. After Chavo chokes the champion with the tag rope, he returns to the ring. While he distracts Jimmy Korderas, Eddie punches Benjamin at ringside for a Chavo two-count. A slingshot somersault splash follows from "Latino Heat" for a near fall. Instead of staying on top of him, Guerrero back suplexes Shelton and lets him tag Charlie. That proves costly as the champions quickly seize control, working over Eddie in their corner for a Benjamin two-count. Team Angle follows up with their double-team leapfrog splash for a near fall. Fortunately, Chavo breaks up the cover and saves his uncle. Haas continues the attack with clubbing blows and a reverse chin lock, but "Latino Heat" won't stay down, back suplexing his way free. When Eddie tries to race to his corner for the tag, Charlie catches and double leg slams him for another near fall before Chavo makes the save. Benjamin illegally switches places with his partner afterwards, but is stunned with a jawbreaker. Unfortunately, "Latino Heat" can't tag out before Shelton catches his foot and powerslams him for another close two-count. Continuing to wear down Guerrero, Benjamin applies another chin lock. When he tires of that hold, Haas returns to stomp and punish the challenger with a backbreaker. Eventually, Eddie surprises him with knees to the head and flies into his corner for the hot tag. Chavo has waited a long time to get his hands on the champions and he unloads with a flurry of fists and a brainbuster to Charlie for a near fall. Shelton immediately responds with a powerbomb, but "Latino Heat" recovers to missile dropkick him. He then suplexes Haas three times in a row for Chavo to crawl over him and score a close two-count. After Chavo knocks Benjamin off the ropes, he dropkicks Charlie for an Eddie Frog Splash. Unfortunately, he's not the legal man and Korderas spends time ordering him to get out of the ring. By the time he leaves, Shelton recovers and breaks up the cover. Moments later, he whips "Latino Heat" into the ring steps before tripping Chavo attempting to back suplex Haas. That lets Charlie land on the challenger and steal the win. Post-match, Team Angle celebrate beside Kurt's picture until Eddie back body drops his nephew out of the ring onto them. Los Guerreros then steal the title belts and head backstage where they talk about making their grandmother proud as they enter a green lowrider and celebrate. The horn even plays "La Cucaracha".

Further backstage, Torrie Wilson tells Test to stop calling her. She doesn't want him and Stacy Keibler is her friend. The bodyguard calls her a tease and says her pictures say that she wants him "real bad".

When she tries to walk away, Test grabs her and forcibly kisses the diva. As she manages to get away, Sable watches in the background.

Sean O'Haire (with "Rowdy" Roddy Piper) def. Rikishi. Piper is out first with a basket full of coconuts. He gets a good pop as he introduces the "new millennium wrestler". "Hot Rod" promises that O'Haire will teach Rikishi that everyone "pays the Piper". The big Samoan then marches out to chase off the heels. He goes right after Roddy, but sees Sean's sneak attack and tosses him into the ring steps and announce table. Finally inside the squared circle, the big babyface punches and Samoan drops O'Haire. Piper tries to help his man, but Rikishi sees Sean's sneak attack coming again and fights him off. Eventually, "Hot Rod" proves his worth, distracting the big Samoan long enough for his man to finally drop him. After Roddy chokes the big babyface, Sean clotheslines him and applies a neck wrench. The fans get really worked up about something in the crowd as O'Haire kicks Rikishi. When he attempts a Samoan drop, the big babyface fights free to crush the "millennium wrestler" in a corner. He tries to follow up with a Stinkface, but Sean kicks him away for Piper to tease hitting the big Samoan with a coconut. Luckily, Brian Hebner catches him and stops the legend. Both wrestlers follow up with simultaneous superkicks. Rikishi recovers first and stops "Hot Rod" from using the coconut again, finally paying back him back for his attack on "Superfly" Jimmy Snuka twenty years ago with a coconut shot to the head to bust open Piper. Unfortunately, O'Haire capitalizes on the distraction and scores the victory with a Reverse Death Valley Driver.

Backstage, Sable stops Stacy Keibler to tell her that Torrie Wilson is after Test. Stacy doesn't believe it, but Sable says that Torrie gave the bodyguard an advance copy of her *Playboy* magazine. She also says she saw Wilson kiss Test. That sets off Keibler.

Further backstage, Rob Van Dam is fired up. He says Chief Morley being the guest referee for their World Tag Title defense tonight is "not cool". He likes being a champion, but doesn't think there's any way that Morley is going to let them win. Kane promises that if they are going down, the entire Eric Bischoff administration is joining them.

Kane/Rob Van Dam def. The Dudley Boyz (World Tag Title match). Chief Morley is out first in referee gear, having assigned himself the job earlier on *Sunday Night Heat*. Jerry says he must not have confidence in the Dudleys winning on their own. Although the challengers come out together, they are on different pages as D-Von wants nothing to do with the Bischoff administration. The champions come out separately before Bubba Ray trades shots with RVD. The champion gets the better of the exchange with a spinning heel kick and two-count. When he attempts a corner attack though, Bubba clotheslines him to the canvas and tags in D-Von. He may not like the heels, but he wants to be a champion again and slugs Rob until he surprises him with more kicks for a two-count. "The King" thinks Morley would have counted three. Dudley takes that decision out of his hand before Kane tags in to absorb fists and big boot the challenger for a two-count. D-Von answers with a leaping clothesline for his own near fall. When Bubba Ray returns, the "Big Red Machine" clotheslines and punches him until his half-brother makes the save with a throat drop on the top rope. That scores Bubba a two-count, but he soon runs into a spinebuster and another near fall. Back in, Van Dam kicks the challenger down in a corner for a dropkick to the face. More kicks follow before he scores a two-count with a split legged moonsault. When he attempts a monkey flip, Dudley shoves him off for a sidewalk slam. He follows up with a cheap shot to Kane, the monster distracting the guest referee while The Dudley Boyz give RVD a wassup drop. The fans want tables, but instead they get a D-Von spinning back elbow and two-count. Afterwards, he slows the pace with a reverse chin lock. Bubba Ray then illegally enters the ring to dropkick Rob's face for D-Von to nearly score the victory. After the referee doesn't disqualify him, Bubba takes over with a neck vice and backward head slam. Moments later though, Van Dam rocks him with a kick to the jaw and tags in the "Big Red Machine" to fight both challengers. After clotheslining both men, he sidewalk slams D-Von for another near fall. Once he makes the save, Bubba Ray remains in the ring to double-team the monster. Even together, the Dudleys can't put Kane down and he drops them both before tagging in RVD to kick the challengers ahead of rolling thunder to Bubba. When he attempts to monkey flip D-Von, the challenger moves and answers with a neckbreaker off the second rope. The "Big Red Machine" makes the save with a top rope flying clothesline. Bubba tries to slow him, but the monster catches him by the throat and teases a Chokeslam until Morley low blows him. Bubba Ray follows up with a clothesline for a near fall. The referee has had enough of Kane and rolls him out of the ring. When he tries to clothesline RVD, the champion ducks and Morley hits Bubba. D-Von sees that and unloads on the referee with a flurry of fists. Unfortunately, Lance Storm races out to flying clothesline D-Von. Bubba Ray pays him back with a Bubba Bomb. The heels continue to turn on each other, Morley punching Bubba until the challengers 3D him. Afterwards, the "Big Red Machine" returns to Chokeslam Bubba Ray ahead of a Five-Star Frog Splash. Chad Patton quickly runs down the aisle for the three-count and big pop as the champions somehow retain the belts.

Backstage, Stacy Keibler enters Torrie Wilson's locker room and confronts her. Of course, there's a misunderstanding and Torrie admits that she kissed Test. That sets off Stacy and she shoves Wilson into the wall, the other divas arguing whether they should let the women fight or break it up.

MUST SEE! Jazz (with Theodore Long) def. Trish Stratus (Women's Title match). Pre-match, Long says tonight is about vindication. Jazz adds that she's "back and black…believe that". When Trish comes out, the announcers talk about trainers not wanting her to compete due to her injured back. Despite that, the champion surprises Jazz with a quick cover for a two-count. The heel answers with a backbreaker and heavy blows to the lower back. She follows up with her double chicken wing slam. When she attempts a powerslam, Stratus flips free and slams the challenger for a near fall. Jazz is right back on the offensive, taking her down for a running splash. Instead of trying to get the win, she wastes time trying to remove a middle turnbuckle pad. That costs Trish as Charles Robinson misses her backsliding the heel. Soon after, she attempts a corner handstand head scissors, but the challenger slams her to the canvas for a single leg crab. Despite the pain, the vixen escapes and puts Jazz in an STF. Before his man submits, Theodore pushes the bottom rope close to her for the break. Despite that, the champion remains in control, nearly scoring the win with a Chick Kick. The heel answers with a dropkick for her own near fall. When she attempts a back suplex, Trish flips free and surprises her with Stratusfaction. As she makes the cover, Long throws his shoe at the vixen. When she throws it back at him, Jazz surprises Stratus with a roll-up. Trish manages to kick out of that cover, but she can't a follow up roll-up as the heel grabs the ropes for added leverage and the victory.

Backstage, Booker T asks Shawn Michaels if he's ready. He is. So is Kevin Nash, but he wants Triple H all for himself.

Big Show def. Rey Mysterio. Ahead of the match, the announcers show footage of the wrestlers crossing paths recently. Show has come up short on those occasions and he's not happy as he storms down the aisle. Rey is much more cautious this week, slowly circling the ring until the giant chases him. When Mysterio slips away from him, Big Show kicks over the ring steps. He tries to enter the squared circle, but the masked man surprises him with a dropkick. Soon after though, Show slams Rey back into a corner before chopping him. Mysterio tries to retreat to the floor, but the giant pulls him back in by the head. Even though he escapes with a throat drop on the top rope, the masked man springboards into a backbreaker. Once Rey is down, Big Show stands on him before press slamming his opponent.

Although Mysterio lands on his feet, Show shoves him out to the floor. There, he grabs a chair and takes advantage of the giant flinging Mike Sparks out of the way to hit Big Show. The masked man follows up with a springboard senton smash and three 619s. When he goes for the West Coast Pop though, Show catches and Chokeslams him for the victory. Post-match, Sparks calls for EMTs to put Rey on a stretcher to protect his neck. Once he's strapped in, Big Show returns and swings him and his backing board against the ring post.

Backstage, Lilian Garcia interviews Chris Jericho, Ric Flair, and Triple H. She says Kevin Nash is going to be gunning for "the Game" after what he did to "Big Sexy" Monday night. Hunter isn't worried about him because he's got the best team at his side. Y2J promises to take care of Shawn Michaels while Flair threatens Booker T. When Lilian starts to walk away, Helmsley tells her that he's not done. After yelling at her for not doing her job, he promises to take care of business tonight.

Backstage, Stacy Keibler and Torrie Wilson continue fighting until a supply tub falls onto Stacy's head. Scott Steiner rushes over to help her and carries her down the hall until Test takes offense.

Brock Lesnar def. John Cena (WWE Title match). Following a video package for the match, Cena heads to the ring to rap about being a better champion than Bruno Sammartino. He references multiple former champions and wears a Yankees jersey to try to get his hometown crowd to turn on him. Instead, they chant that the "Yankees suck". Brock follows, a big bandage on his forehead. John isn't intimidated, attacking the champion immediately and driving him into a corner. Lesnar answers with a pair of backbreakers and a fallaway slam. Suplexes follow for an early babyface two-count. Brock then uses his impressive power to squeeze the rapping heel with a front face lock. A fisherman's suplex and press slam continue his dominant display before he clotheslines the challenger out to the floor. There, he whips Cena into the announce table and taunts him with the WWE Title. He continues his assault with knees until John reverses a whip into the ring steps. After slamming the champion's head two more times on the steel, busting him open, the rapping heel poses with the championship. Back in the squared circle, he scores a quick two-count. A side slam also gets him a near fall before he stomps and elbows Lesnar for another two-count. He tries to shoulderblock Brock out to the floor, but the champion holds the ropes and lands on the apron. Unfortunately, that gets him a flying leg drop on the back of the head as he lays on the ropes. The challenger follows up with a whip into the ring post for another near fall. Afterwards, he slows the pace with a chin lock. Even when Lesnar escapes, Cena stays on top of him with a DDT. Once again, the champion just kicks out before surprising John with a spinebuster to put both men down on the canvas. Although Brock is up first and lands a pair of knees, the rapping heel surprises him with a jawbreaker for another near fall. Afterwards, he applies a rear naked choke and body scissors. The fans start to chant for the challenger, but Tazz says he doesn't care about them. It takes him a while, but Lesnar powers up and rams Cena three times into the turnbuckles to finally break the hold. He follows up with his leg sweep clothesline. Two more clotheslines and a powerslam finally get the champion a near fall. Catching a second wind, he rams John into a corner ahead of another powerslam and two-count. The rapping heel tries to slow him by tossing the champion into Brian Hebner, but Lesnar holds up at the last second. That lets the challenger stun him with a low blow ahead of his snap mare neckbreaker for a near fall. He can't keep Brock down for long and the babyface drives him back hard into the corner, slamming Cena's neck into the top turnbuckle. John has had enough and grabs his chain, but Hebner stops him from using it. Lesnar capitalizes with an F5 for the victory.

Chris Jericho/Ric Flair/Triple H def. Booker T/Kevin Nash/Shawn Michaels. Following a video package for the match largely featuring Kevin Nash, everyone gets separate entrances, starting with the heels.

Shawn and Jericho open the match trading shots, roll-ups, and two-counts. Afterwards, Nash tags in to elbow and punch the heel. After he tosses him out to the floor, Kevin decks Flair and dares Triple H to enter the ring. Instead, he distracts his former friend for a Y2J sneak attack. It doesn't take Nash long to recover and toss him back out of the squared circle. Although Jericho skins the cat, Kevin is waiting to big boot him. Booker then tags in for his share of the fun, scoring a two-count with a spinebuster before chopping Y2J. He also gets a near fall with a flapjack before Jericho drives him back into the heel corner. Hunter tags in afterwards only to be kicked by the five-time champion. When he attempts a back body drop though, Helmsley answers with a facebuster. The two men then trade shots, Lawler continuing to make fun of Booker T's background until "the Game" plants him with a spinebuster. When Ric tags in, the babyface rolls to his corner to tag Michaels for fists and a back body drop. He also fights off the other heels before planting "The Nature Boy" with a flying forearm. After he kips up, he gives Flair Sweet Chin Music. Before he can make the cover though, Triple H Pedigrees him to put both legal men down. Ric is closer to his corner and tags in Jericho to elbow and taunt the "Heartbreak Kid" for a near fall. Hunter also wants a piece of his former friend, hammering him. When Shawn starts to fight back, Helmsley rocks him with a high knee. Luckily, Booker makes the save. Moments later, Michaels small packages "The Nature Boy" when he tries to apply a Figure Four Leglock for a two-count. Y2J quickly tags in to suplex his rival and trap him in a surfboard, targeting his back. Once he's slowed him, "the Game" returns and wraps the "Heartbreak Kid's" leg around the ring post. He then lures Booker T into the ring to distract the referee while the heels trap Shawn in their corner. Now focusing on the leg, Flair returns to stomp, stretch, and strike the limb. That wakes up Michaels and he responds with fists and an enziguri kick. When the wrestlers collide moments later, the "Heartbreak Kid" falls with his arm on Ric for a pair of two-counts. Both men tag out moments later for Nash to punch and elbow Triple H. He deals with the other heels when they try to make the save, clotheslining Flair out to the floor. A big boot follows to Jericho before he gives Hunter snake eyes and a sidewalk slam. Luckily, Ric makes the save. When he chops "Big Sexy", Kevin chases him back into Booker who takes their fight out to the floor. Y2J attacks Nash afterwards, but his running face slam is countered with a slam to the canvas. Before Kevin can Jackknife Powerbomb Helmsley though, Jericho makes the save with a top rope missile dropkick. Booker T returns to Scissors Kick the Canadian heel. He also knocks "The Nature Boy" down ahead of a spinaroonie. Afterwards, he chops Y2J at ringside while Michaels trades shots with Flair inside the squared circle. Kevin and Triple H are also outside the ring brawling, Nick Patrick roaming between the fights while Shawn slams Ric off the top rope. When he tunes up the band, Jericho makes the save with a running face slam. Flair capitalizes with the Figure Four Leglock, but the referee tells the heels that the "Heartbreak Kid" isn't the legal man. That doesn't save him from a Y2J Lionsault and Walls of Jericho. Outside the ring, Nash clears the announce table to prepare to Jackknife Hunter. Before he can get payback, he notices his friend in trouble and rushes to his defense, fighting both Y2J and "The Nature Boy". After he shoves Flair into Patrick, Kevin Jackknifes Jericho. Ever the opportunist, Helmsley grabs a sledgehammer and bashes Nash's skull while the referee recovers to steal the victory.

Back at ringside, the *SmackDown!* announcers replay Big Show's post-match assault on Rey Mysterio. They have no update on him and speculate on potential nerve damage. Tazz says there's no call for it.

Following a video package for the main event, Terri tells The Rock that he says he's done it all, but some people think Goldberg is going to beat him in just a few minutes. The "People's Champ" isn't impressed, mocking how stupid Bill is before talking about how strong he is. While the "Great One" admits that his Spear hurts, The Rock reminds everyone that his steel chair shots hurt worse and Goldberg is "next".

Goldberg def. The Rock. As The Rock heads to the ring, the announcers talk about how big this match is. Goldberg then makes his entrance, the camera following him backstage and as he steps through sparks on the ramp and heads to the ring where the "People's Champ" bails out to the floor. Coach says the "Great One" has done everything, but he's never beaten the intense superstar. After he hesitates to step into the squared circle, the "Brahma Bull" finally locks up with Goldberg. Bill heaves him down to the canvas. Despite that, The Rock says Goldberg is in trouble and ties up again. This time, the intense superstar flings him out to the floor. The "People's Champ" quickly returns to slap his opponent. Goldberg likes it and unloads with a flurry of shots, knocking the "Great One" back out. That's all the "Brahma Bull" can take and he threatens to leave. When Bill interrupts Earl Hebner's count, The Rock returns to throat drop him on the top rope. Despite that, Goldberg quickly recovers to Rock Bottom the "People's Champ". He sets up for the Spear, but the "Great One" takes his time getting up and dodges to the side, flinging Bill into the ring post and out to the floor. Some of the fans and Lawler love it. Jerry hopes to see the intense superstar tap-out when the "Brahma Bull" gets him back in the ring and locks on a sharpshooter. After he reaches down deep and crawls to the ropes for the break, The Rock shoves the referee out of the way for a low blow. He then sets up for a Rock Bottom, but Goldberg beats him to the punch with a Spear to put both men down. After he catches his breath, a shoulderblock and powerslam score Bill a two-count, but he's still favoring his injured shoulder. When he attempts a corner charge, the "People's Champ" meets him with a back elbow. He gets a big pop when he spears the intense superstar and kips up. Beaming, the "Great One" waits for Goldberg to stand up for a Rock Bottom. Somehow, Bill just manages to kick out of his cover. When both men get up, the "Brahma Bull" punches his opponent until Goldberg clotheslines him for boos. The fans come to life when The Rock answers with a spinebuster and People's Elbow for a near fall. The "People's Champ" can't believe it. Bill is actually up first, surprising the "Great One" with a Spear. As he sets up for a third, the fans chant for one more. He delivers after the "Brahma Bull" slowly stands up and collects himself. Not done, Goldberg picks up The Rock and spins him around with a Jackhammer for the three-count.

While some consider Backlash a horrible show, it's really an average B-show PPV after a hot WrestleMania. The WWE put all of their eggs in the main event basket and the rest of the card shows it with quick feuds and pairings. The opening WWE Tag Title match is fun as Team Angle can hang in the ring with anyone. Los Guerreros provide the storytelling and excitement, Eddie continuing to be a star even if he doesn't leave with the belt. Piper then does most of the storytelling in the Rikishi/O'Haire match before Sean gets what seems to be more of a fluke win with a nice finisher. While it makes sense to have the heels cheat, O'Haire being more dominant against another opponent would have helped his push. The World Tag Title match is fun too, with a lot of focus on the Bischoff administration despite Eric not being on the show. Jazz and Trish have a weak match with a neither doing a lot tonight. Rey and Show offer a David versus Goliath story, but it's hard to take Mysterio seriously as anything above mid-card when one Chokeslam out of nowhere destroys him. Yes, Big Show is huge, but he usually has to work for his finisher. Here, he absorbs three 619s and a chair shot to decimate Rey. The post-match angle doesn't help Mysterio's credibility. Brock and Cena don't set the world on fire in their match, but it's not bad. John shows flashes before Lesnar catches him with an out of nowhere F5 for the expected victory. It's a good PPV to give a new face a chance to shine. *Raw* doesn't even cart out a World Title match. Instead, six top stars have a fun and chaotic fight. It's harmless fun and keeps everyone in a good place moving forward. This is B-show PPV action at its best. Finally, Goldberg makes his WWE debut successfully and sets the table for future matches featuring signature moves, a little brawling, and little else. It works and the fans enjoy it, even if they side with The Rock too. The WWE tried to put Scott Steiner with a hated heel and the crowd turned on him. With Goldberg, he gets a wrestler willing to make his opponent look like a star and the fans still cheer the heel. You can't always predict WWE fans. Overall Backlash has decent action with little impact. For those on a time budget, the whole show is skippable, but there is some fun to be had if you have a few hours, particularly in the main event and tag matches.

Monday Night Raw

April 28, 2003
Boston, MA
Announcers: Jonathan Coachman, Jerry "the King" Lawler, Theodore Long (briefly)

Following the intro video and fireworks, Chris Jericho heads to the squared circle. Jerry says he wants to be called the "highlight of the night" now. Inside the ring, Y2J makes fun of "Rowdy" Roddy Piper's gut and says that if he can drag Piper's Pit out of retirement on *SmackDown!*, *Raw* needs their own talk show. He calls it the "Hi-Lite Reel". For his first guest, Jericho welcomes his "WCW friend", Goldberg. The intense superstar doesn't waste time walking out to the ring to sit on one of the bar top chairs for Y2J to compliment him for beating The Rock last night. However, Jericho says he's beaten the "People's Champ" multiple times. He then asks Bill why he never accepted his challenge to a match in WCW. When Goldberg threatens to fight Y2J right now, the Canadian heel tells him that this is a verbal confrontation. Using his verbal skills, Jericho wonders why the intense superstar Speared the "Great One" in the first place. Before he can answer, Christian steps through the curtain to proclaim himself the new "People's Champ" and question how it felt for Goldberg to be booed last night. Bill doesn't care about that. He says the fans can cheer or boo him, but he's going to destroy everyone in his way. When he offers to Spear Christian again, Y2J says no one is getting Speared tonight. The heels want to know why Goldberg is here since no one wants him in the WWE. The fans do, cheering for him as Christian brings out Three-Minute Warning, Steven Richards, and Victoria. The heel criticizes Bill for getting a PPV main event in his first match while Christian has been fighting for years. Goldberg invites them to do something about it and get in the ring. Christian hypes them up and leads everyone to ringside, but only Richards enters. Alone, he's no match for the intense superstar and is dropped with one Spear when he turns and realizes that no one accompanied him. After a commercial break, trainers help him backstage.

The Hurricane def. Chief Morley. As Morley heads to the ring, the announcers reveal that he has suspended The Dudley Boyz for their actions last night. Inside the ring, the wrestlers take turns mocking each other, The Hurricane wrapping his cape around his waist to pretend to be Val Venis. That makes the chief laugh and he even offers the superhero a handshake before trying to cheap shot him. Although The Hurricane spots that obvious ploy, Morley takes quick control and traps him in a front face lock. A slam and butterfly suplex follow before the chief briefly applies a chin lock. When the superhero fights free, Morley cuts off his momentum with a spinebuster for a pair of near falls. Continuing to share a move with Eddie Guerrero, the chief goes for a trio of suplexes, but on the third attempt, his opponent answers with the Eye of the Hurricane. He's too winded to go for the cover, but after catching his breath, The Hurricane stuns the chief with a neckbreaker. He tries to follow up with a shining wizard kick, but Morley ducks and counters with a sit out slam for a near fall. When he heads upstairs though, the superhero dodges a Money Shot and responds quickly with the overcast for the win.

Backstage, Ric Flair praises Triple H for his *Raw* magazine cover and calls him the greatest wrestler of all-time. If Flair believes it, Hunter says it must be true because "The Nature Boy" is a legend. Ric is confused why Helmsley wanted him in wrestling gear tonight. "The Game" has a surprise, telling his mentor that he wants more gold and tonight they are going to take it when they face Kane and Rob Van Dam for the World Tag Titles.

Rodney Mack (with Theodore Long) def. Unnamed Jobber ("Five-Minute White Boy Challenge"). Pre-match, Long criticizes Larry Bird and says no one would care about him if he was black. He then joins the announce table to watch Mack destroy another white jobber. He dominates the opening minute until the jobber makes a very brief comeback and attempts a second rope flying strike. Unfortunately, Mack catches and hammers him ahead of a Powerslam to finish the match off in just under two minutes.

Post-match, Long introduces "the woman who changed Backlash into Black-lash", Jazz. Balloons fall from the ceiling into the crowd as Jazz marches out to show off her belt while Trish Stratus watches backstage.

After a commercial break, Trish Stratus interrupts Eric Bischoff on the phone to ask for a rematch. He says there was a clause in their contract that said, "no rematch". Trish doesn't care. She says she'll do whatever it takes. Those are the kind of words that Bischoff likes. He offers to give her a World Title match next week if she beats him in a match tonight. However, if she loses, she has to spend "quality time" with the general manager. Stratus is sure that she'll beat him tonight.

Further backstage, Stacy Keibler continues to yells at Test. The bodyguard deflects, telling her that he knows she doesn't have eyes for Scott Steiner just like he doesn't like Torrie Wilson. Test just wants to move on from all of this, but he doesn't know how when Stacy signed him to a tag match alongside Steiner tonight. Keibler thinks it will be good for him. The bodyguard agrees to the match if she will start trusting him. Stacy "wants to".

Kane/Rob Van Dam def. Ric Flair/Triple H (World Tag Title match). Following separate entrances for everyone, Kane shoves around Flair. Ric does get in a chop, but the "Big Red Machine" answers with fists and a press slam. RVD then tags in only for "The Nature Boy" to poke his eyes. When Triple H tags in, Rob drives him from the ring to slingshot splash both heels. He continues going after Flair and pays courtesy of a Hunter clothesline. Backstage, Shawn Michaels calls Helmsley a "sitting duck" while talking on the phone ahead of a commercial break.

Afterwards, Kane slams "the Game" for a Van Dam slingshot leg drop and two-count. RVD follows up with a series of kicks for a nice pop before scoring another near fall with a twisting leg drop. When he runs the ropes though, Ric hits him. Although Rob decks "The Nature Boy", Triple H capitalizes with a spinebuster. Flair then tags in to stomp Van Dam in a corner and distract Earl Hebner while Hunter elbows the downed champion. Chops and fists follow from both challengers before Hunter scores a two-count with a high knee. Fortunately, the "Big Red Machine" makes the save. He only watches moments later when Ric illegally enters for a knee drop and another near fall. Afterwards, the heels continue to punish Van Dam in their corner, beginning to focus on the leg. Following stretches and leg locks from both men, "The Nature Boy" tries to apply a Figure Four Leglock. At the last second, RVD counters with a small package for a two-count. He then stuns Helmsley with an enziguri kick before giving Kane the hot tag. He proceeds to fight both challengers, crushing them in opposite corners with clotheslines. A sidewalk slam follows to "the Game" before he clotheslines him out to the floor. That leaves Flair alone for a "Big Red Machine" flying clothesline. Luckily, Triple H returns for the save. The heels then work on the monster's leg, Ric even applying a Figure Four Leglock before Rob returns with a flying kick to Hunter and rolling thunder to "The Nature Boy". Unfortunately, Helmsley grabs the popular superstar and DDTs him. He then Pedigrees Kane, but before he can win the titles, Kevin Nash's music plays and he marches out with a sledgehammer. "The Game" sprints off, retreating through the crowd and backstage. That leaves Flair alone for the "Big Rd Machine" to Chokeslam him ahead of a Five-Star Frog Splash and the three-count. Post-match, Triple H hops into a limo and speeds away after Nash smashes two of the windows.

Scott Steiner/Test (with Stacy Keibler) def. Christopher Nowinski/Rico. The announcers argue over whether Stacy can ever trust Test again as Scott hammers and suplexes Nowinski. Already bleeding, Steiner chases him out of the ring before working over Rico too. When he runs the ropes, the Harvard heel trips him for a stylist kick. Outside the ring, Nowinski whips "Big Poppa Pump" into the ring post. When Rico applies a sleeper hold, Scott back suplexes free. He tries to make the tag, but the bodyguard is on the floor arguing with his girlfriend. That lets the heels double suplex and elbow drop Steiner for a near fall. They follow up with clubbing blows and the Harvard heel mockingly does pushups until "Big Poppa Pump" catches him with a belly-to-belly suplex. Test finally gets the tag afterwards to destroy both heels. When he attempts a powerbomb, Nowinski slips free only to accidentally clothesline his own partner. Despite that, the stylist saves the Harvard heel moments and kicks the bodyguard. Test answers with a Big Boot, but runs into a Nowinski clothesline. Jerry says the match "needs subtitles" because the action is going so fast. Scott then scores the win with a reverse DDT. Post-match, the bodyguard takes offense to Keibler hugging Steiner. "Big Poppa Pump" doesn't care, dedicating the match to his freaks while his partner storms after his girlfriend. La Resistance interrupt to introduce themselves. The fans boo over them, but the rookies are undeterred. They have a problem with Scott telling everyone to "go to Hell or France" a few weeks ago. While most people would want to fight about it, Rene Dupree and Sylvan Grenier are "lovers". They want to talk it out, but when they enter the ring, they attack Steiner. He doesn't mind a fight and responds in kind until the rookies toss him into the ring steps. Back in the squared circle, they finish him off with a Double Flapjack for boos.

After a commercial break, Chief Morley tells Eric Bischoff that he's taken care of everything for the boss. That's good because Eric is planning to get "Stratusfied" later tonight.

Further backstage, Goldberg and Booker T talk. The five-time champion says Bill has always been "straight up" and he's gone through what the intense superstar is dealing with right now. It takes some time, but Booker is sure the fans will come around. Booker T adds that Christian doesn't speak for the locker room and welcomes Goldberg to the WWE.

Booker T def. Christian by disqualification. Before Booker heads to the ring, the announcers highlight some servicemen in the crowd. When the heel comes out, the five-time champion toys with him, clotheslining and side kicking him. Chops follow in a corner ahead of a back body drop and two-count. Christian changes tactics and takes the fight out to the floor to slam Booker T's head on the ring steps. A dropkick back in the squared circle gets him a two-count before he hooks a reverse chin lock. Following a backwards head slam, the heel taunts and chokes his opponent. An elbow drop gets him another two-count before he returns to choking the babyface. When he heads up to the second rope though, Booker catches and flapjacks him to put both men on the canvas for Charles Robinson's standing six-count. The five-time champion then comes back to life with a forearm, clothesline, and side slam for a near fall. Although he misses a Scissors Kick, Booker T still catches the heel with a spinebuster. Afterwards, he fights free of an Unprettier and finally delivers his Scissors Kick ahead of a spinaroonie. Unfortunately, that brings Three-Minute Warning and Rico out for the disqualification. The fans loudly chant for Goldberg as the heels squash Booker and slam him. Afterwards, the intense superstar finally comes out to kick and clothesline the Samoans. After he Spears Rico, Goldberg impresses with a Jackhammer to Jamal. Unfortunately, Christian hits him from behind and knocks him out to the floor where Rosey tries to whip him into the ring post. At the last second, Bill reverses the whip. He follows up with a Spear through the barricade, marking the first time someone has done so on WWE television in a moment that many superstars will copy in the years to come. The fans are shocked and absolutely enthralled by the move here tonight. Christian isn't, rushing backstage to get away from the intense superstar.

Eric Bischoff def. Trish Stratus ("No Disqualification" match). As Trish heads to the ring holding her ribs, ring crew puts up police tape over the broken section of the barricade. Pre-match, Bischoff asks if Stratus really wants to do this. Considering that if she wins she gets a Women's Title match, she does. However, if she loses, she'll have to spend the night with Eric. Despite him making this a "No Disqualification" match, the vixen wants a shot to regain her belt. She starts strong, answering Bischoff's mocking karate pose with a Chick Kick. Victoria then runs out to clothesline and moonsault her. Although Trish fights her off, she has no answer for Jazz attacking the vixen from behind. After manhandling her at ringside, including a double chicken wing slam, the Women's Champion does the same inside the squared circle. Eric eventually stops her assault. He wants Stratus conscious for what happens later. Stunned, there's nothing she can do to stop Bischoff from covering her for the three-count.

Post-match, Eric taunts the vixen as a black limo arrives backstage. Instead of being for the general manager, it's Linda McMahon. Bischoff is stunned when he sees her on the Titantron. The GM quickly changes his tune and calls for referees to help up Trish Stratus.

After a commercial break, Linda McMahon heads to the ring to the WrestleMania theme song. She says she's here on behalf of the board of directors and invites Eric Bischoff to come back to the squared circle to discuss his performance. He just can't catch a break from McMahons monitoring him. Eric says his previous segment with Trish Stratus was just a joke and his attempt to create "compelling television". In all honesty, he's more interested in "mature women". Linda calls him charming and says he makes her job too easy. She says his actions are "unprofessional, abusive, and harassing". While some board members don't think he's competent, Linda has reached an agreement to let Bischoff keep his job. He'll just have a co-general manager starting tomorrow that shares equal responsibilities. McMahon says he's more in-tune with the fans and "sensitive" before introducing the new boss, "Stone Cold" Steve Austin. The fans go bananas as the redneck stomps around to a massive pop. Eric can't believe it. Austin wants to know what Bischoff's thinking. The "rattlesnake" offers him a handshake, but Eric doesn't take it. He's not sure he can trust Steve, but he wants this to work. "Stone Cold" says when they shake hands they're partners and will get along. However, Austin says their partnership doesn't start until tomorrow and gives Bischoff a Stone Cold Stunner to a big pop to end the episode.

SmackDown!

May 1, 2003
Manchester, NH
Announcers: Michael Cole, Tazz

Ahead of the intro video and fireworks, footage of Big Show swinging Rey Mysterio against the ring post at Backlash plays.

Los Guerreros def. Matt Hardy Version 1.0/Shannon Moore (with Crash Holly). Despite losing last night, Los Guerreros come out with the WWE Tag Titles. The heels follow with Matt Facts asking if you've read Hardy's book and telling everyone that he invented Mattitude. Once the match starts, the babyfaces trap Shannon in their corner, double-teaming him and making quick tags. Focusing on the leg, Eddie wears down Moore until the MFer kicks him into the ropes and a Crash book shot to the back of the head. Hardy then tags in to choke and leg drop "Latino Heat" on the middle rope. Guerrero answers with a back suplex, but when he tags his nephew, Mike Chioda misses it dealing with Shannon. Chavo doesn't care, attacking the heels and then flying over the top rope onto Crash. Afterwards, Eddie fights the other heels and drives Moore from the ring to head scissors Matt off the top rope for a two-count. He tries to deliver his trio of suplexes, but Shannon returns for the save. The heels follow up with a combination Samoan drop and neckbreaker for a near fall. When Hardy pulls "Latino Heat" up for a Twist of Fate, Chioda escorts Moore back to his corner. Unfortunately, he misses Eddie shoving Matt into Chavo and a title belt shot. "Latino Heat" capitalizes with a Frog Splash for the win. Post-match, the heels attack the winners, but Shannon gets back body dropped onto Crash. That brings out Team Angle to take back their belts, but Los Guerreros see them coming and drive off the champions.

After a commercial break, Josh Mathews stops Stephanie McMahon outside Mr. America's locker room. He wants to know who the new superstar is, but Stephanie doesn't know. She signed him "sight unseen" to beat Eric Bischoff. Before she enters the room to meet him, Team Angle petition the general manager to get their belts back. McMahon says they shouldn't have lost them in the first place. However, she will make Los Guerreros give them the belts back later tonight. To settle things once and for all though, she's signing the two teams to a "Ladder" match at Judgment Day.

A Big Show/Rey Mysterio video package plays.

Backstage, Stephanie McMahon is horrified as she leaves Mr. America's locker room ahead of a teaser for the new superstar.

Big Show def. Funaki. Pre-match, Show says all he's heard all week is to pick on someone his own size. The giant says there's no one his size, but tonight he's picked an opponent bigger than Rey Mysterio. Funaki then marches out to punch Big Show's gut. It has no effect and Show hammers him back into a corner ahead of a toss all the way across the ring. When the interviewer retreats to the floor, the giant follows him out to press slam him back into the squared circle. As he tries to return, Funaki crotches Big Show on the top rope. A Tornado DDT follows, but the interviewer can't keep the big man down. Right back up, Show big boots Funaki, but picks up his head rather than take the pinfall. Instead, he hoists the babyface up for a Chokeslam, but slowly lowers him back to the canvas. Tazz thinks he's showing heart, but instead he clotheslines Funaki savagely for the victory.

Backstage, Stephanie McMahon is still in a daze and tells her staff that she needs a few minutes alone. That's all she'll get because Vince McMahon is on his way to the arena. Now, Stephanie is even more concerned.

After a commercial break, Big Show walks past WWE superstars. No one likes him except A-Train.

John Cena heads to the squared circle. He's in a bad mood after getting "robbed" at Backlash. He raps about busting open Brock Lesnar before the referee cost him the WWE Title. Brian Kendrick then comes out in a bucket hat and wearing a clock around his neck. The babyface tells Cena to call him "Spanky". He's tired of John lying, so he's got his own rap. Brian just needs a beat. When the rapping heel turns to Brian Hebner, everyone is surprised the referee can beatbox. While he surprises the announcers, Kendrick tells Cena that he got beat by Brock and gets the fans to wave their hands in the air. He also leads the crowd in a "Cena sucks" chant and scratches a record on John's head. That's all the rapping heel can take and he pounds down Kendrick ahead of a Death Valley Driver, now called the FU by Tazz.

Backstage, Nunzio and The FBI win money rolling dice with fans. When a fan is out of money, they kick him out of the room rather than give him an autograph.

Chris Benoit and Johnny Stamboli (with Chuck Palumbo/Nunzio) wrestle to a no contest. Outnumbered, Benoit takes the fight out to the floor to deck Palumbo. He then returns to chop and punch Stamboli. When he nears the ropes, Nunzio trips "the Crippler". That sends him back out to the floor. Although he misses the Italian heel, he does clothesline Chuck. Johnny capitalizes, wailing on Benoit before Palumbo finally gets his hands on him. "The Bull" tries to finish off the "rabid wolverine" with a press slam, but Benoit slips free and nearly hooks the Crippler Crossface. Luckily, Stamboli escapes and applies his own submission hold, a surfboard stretch. "The Crippler" refuses to submit and escapes with a backslide for a two-count. Moments later, he unloads with a string of running strikes and a snap suplex for a near fall. A German suplex follows before Benoit motions for a diving headbutt. First, he has to fight off the other heels before nailing Johnny. That brings Nunzio into the ring with a chair, but Rhyno has seen enough. He sprints out to Gore the Italian heel. Brian Hebner is also fed up, telling Tony Chimel that he's going to change the contest to a tag team match after a commercial break.

The FBI (with Nunzio) def. Chris Benoit/Rhyno. After the break, Rhyno wails on Palumbo until the heel surprises him with a shot to the head. When Stamboli tags in, the man-beast clobbers him too, Nunzio down and out at ringside following the earlier Gore. The babyfaces follow up with a double-team attack, but when Hebner gets Benoit out of the ring, Chuck nearly knocks Rhyno out with a Superkick for a near fall. The FBI then work over the man-beast in their corner while Nunzio starts to come to his senses. He sees Palumbo nearly get the win with a back suplex, but "the Crippler" makes the save. Back in, Johnny elbows the man-beast and tosses him out to the floor for a Chuck slam into the barricade and two-count. Focusing on the lower back, "the Bull" locks on a bearhug. Although Rhyno fights free, a Palumbo cheap shot puts him right back down. When he tags in though, the man-beast surprises him with a spinebuster. Benoit gets the hot tag afterwards to clothesline the heels and German suplex Chuck. The heel manages to block a second, but the "rabid wolverine" rolls him up for a near fall while Rhyno Gores Stamboli into the referee. While he figures out what's going on, Nunzio rolls over Benoit for Palumbo to steal the victory.

Backstage, Stephanie McMahon is trying to reach Vince McMahon and tell him not to come to the arena. She can't reach him, so she leaves a message while Brock Lesnar arrives despite the night off.

After a commercial break, Brock Lesnar heads to the ring to a big pop. He congratulates John Cena on a great fight at Backlash. However, Brock likes fighting and he's looking for one tonight with Big Show. He calls the giant "gutless" for what he did to Rey Mysterio and invites him to try to bully the WWE Champion. Show answers quickly, saying Rey got what he deserved. Big Show isn't afraid of Lesnar, but will only face him if the WWE Title is on the line. Brock offers him the shot, but Show doesn't want the match tonight, disappointing the fans.

A Mr. America teaser plays.

Team Angle def. Eric Stevens/John Walters. Pre-match, the champions set up a picture of Kurt Angle and put his gold medals on it before they get to work. Haas opens the match slamming and punching Stevens. The jobber answers with a roll-up, but that just makes the champion mad. After he pounds on Eric, Team Angle give him their double-team leapfrog splash. Benjamin then drives the jobber into his corner and dares Walters to enter the ring. When he does, Shelton knees and slams him. Back in, Haas works on the jobber's arm until John fights back. Benjamin cuts off his momentum with a shot to the back of the head. That brings in Stevens again for the champions to quickly drive him off ahead of an Inverted Atomic Drop and Superkick to Walters for the win.

Post-match, Team Angle demands that Los Guerreros return their gold. They don't have to wait long for the former champions to walk through the curtain. They feel bad about what they did and promise to never steal anything of Team Angle's again. Afterwards, they drop the belts on the canvas for the champions to reclaim them. When Los Guerreros leave though, Charlie taunts them. He says they'll never see the belts again and Team Angle are going to win the Judgment Day "Ladder" match. Chavo says they might be champions, but Los Guerreros are gold medalists, showing off their stolen gold medals.

Backstage, Sable puts her hand on Torrie Wilson's shoulder. That sets off the diva and she tells the legend that she doesn't want to team with her and she doesn't trust her after she told Stacy Keibler that Torrie kissed her boyfriend at Backlash. Sable says they can be great partners if Wilson "plays" with her. She adds that they "play for the same team" and Torrie doesn't want to cross her.

Dawn Marie/Nidia (with Jamie Noble) def. Sable/Torrie Wilson. Torrie is out last, the heels attacking her as she gets in the ring for a Nidia two-count. Wilson answers with a neckbreaker for her own near fall before Dawn Marie makes the save. When the babyface goes after her, Nidia clotheslines Torrie. It doesn't take Wilson long to recover, but she gets distracted by Dawn again and is kicked down. The heels then work on Torrie's left leg with repeated kicks and splashes. When Marie attempts a corner bomb though, Wilson rolls out of the way and crawls to her corner for the tag. Sable leans back and avoids the tag, playing mind games with her partner. Afterwards, she walks off the apron and watches as Dawn Marie catapults Torrie to the center of the ring for a single leg crab and the tap-out victory. Cole doesn't understand.

Backstage, Stephanie McMahon calls her dad and leaves a message that she'll meet him back at the hotel. Unfortunately, Vince McMahon arrives and is excited to meet Mr. America. He's proud of her signing the new superstar and is looking forward to seeing him. He's even heard he's seven feet tall.

After a commercial break, "Rowdy" Roddy Piper and Sean O'Haire head to the ring for Piper's Pit and the debut of Mr. America. "Hot Rod" has to respond to Chris Jericho's insult Monday night. Roddy says he's heard Y2J sing and watched him compete. He promises to call Jericho when Piper loses weight if Y2J will call him when he gets some talent. With that out of the way, "Hot Rod" is happy to introduce Mr. America. "Real American" plays as an obviously red, white, and blue masked Hulk Hogan steps through the curtain and plays air guitar. Tazz says he looks familiar. The fans love it as he tears off his shirt and Roddy goes wild. He says America is the "home of the brave, but not stupid". He knows Mr. America is Hogan. The fans do too, chanting for the Hulkster. The masked man responds to tell him something and call the accusation "ridiculous". Mr. America then offers to kick "Hot Rod's" butt from "sea to shining sea". He stands for everything that makes America great, but he is "not Hulk Hogan, brother". That brings out Vince McMahon. He's furious and stomps down the aisle as the fans boo him. He can't believe Hogan would do this. The WWE owner tells the Hulkster that he's going back home, but this time he's going with a lawsuit for breach of contract. Mr. America says Vince must have brain damage from the beating Hulk gave him at WrestleMania XIX because he's not Hogan and McMahon can ask the "American-maniacs". Vince won't stand for someone insulting his intelligence. Before he threatens him again, McMahon has a change of heart. He accepts that the masked man is Mr. America. As WWE owner, he has the power to fire him and does so. The masked man doesn't go anywhere because his contract says he can't be fired or suspended and there's nothing Vince can do about it. He adds, "God bless America" to a big pop. McMahon says he's going to prove the newcomer's identity when the heels rip off his mask. Mr. America stops them to ask what they are going to do when he drops the "twenty-four inch patriots" on them. Mr. America then fights off the heels and decks the WWE owner before tickertape rains throughout the arena, the masked man proudly waving Old Glory to end the show.

Monday Night Raw
May 5, 2003
Halifax, Nova Scotia, Canada
Announcers: Jonathan Coachman, Jerry "the King" Lawler, Jim Ross

The show opens with a graphic for the recently passed away Miss Elizabeth. We then see shots of the co-general managers, "Stone Cold" Steve Austin and Eric Bischoff, ahead of a video package featuring Austin's return last week. The intro video plays and fireworks explode before "Stone Cold" heads to the ring to a huge pop. He thanks Linda McMahon for giving him his new job. Since he's never done anything low profile, he promises to throw a beer bash celebration for himself tonight. He says he's got some problems with the way things have been ran on *Raw*. First and foremost is that someone got rid of the Intercontinental Title. He's going to fix that at Judgment Day with a battle royal for the vacant belt featuring anyone who held the championship previously on *Raw*. Before he can announce his second decision, Eric Bischoff and Chief Morley head to the ring, the fans loudly calling them names. Eric tells them to shut up before saying that he and Steve are equal partners. That means they should discuss matters together concerning the Intercontinental Title. Austin just wanted to do something to better the show, but Bischoff says he's the one who abolished the title. To be a team player, Eric agrees with the decision to bring back the belt. Bischoff has his own announcement, signing a World Title match between Triple H and Kevin Nash. "Stone Cold" likes it and agrees. The co-GMs are surprised that they are getting along and Eric says things might just work out. Austin wants to get back to his announcements and says he's hired someone, his "buddy and the best announcer in the WWE", Jim Ross. JR comes back out to a big pop, but Bischoff doesn't like it. Eric welcomes him back just to fire him again. The GMs then argue about whether he's hired or fired until the "rattlesnake" says he's trying hard not to lose his temper. The fans chant for him to lose it. Austin offers to settle things with a match. If "Stone Cold" wins, Ross stays, but if he loses, JR goes. Eric likes it, but says Linda won't let them lay a hand on each other. The GMs argue again, this time on whether Bischoff is scared. Chief Morley steps in to offer to wrestle on Eric's behalf. He doesn't want to wrestle Austin though. He offers to wrestle JR for his job. "Stone Cold" says that's stupid before Lawler volunteers to wrestle for his friend's job. That works for everyone and the GMs shake hands to make it official.

Jerry "the King" Lawler (with "Stone Cold" Steve Austin/Jim Ross) def. Chief Morley (with Eric Bischoff). While Morley wrestles in slacks, Jerry always commentates in his gear so he's ready to go. Unfortunately, the chief pounds him down in a corner to open the contest. When he turns to argue with Charles Robinson, "the King" attacks with clotheslines and fists for a two-count. Morley answers with a knee to the gut and his own strikes. Following a back body drop, the chief sets up for a second. Lawler counters with a Piledriver for a near fall. Afterwards, he misses a second rope flying elbow drop. Back up, Morley delivers a trio of suplexes ahead of his own second rope flying elbow drop and near fall. Following a string of heel fists, Jerry comes back to life with his own shots. When he tries to run the ropes though, Bischoff trips him. That sends Austin after his fellow GM, distracting Robinson. When Morley heads upstairs to finish off "the King" with a Money Shot, JR shoves him down for Lawler to steal the win. Post-match, Eric yells at his chief of staff and slaps him. Morley can't stand it. Once the heels leave, Coach heads to the ring where "Stone Cold" tells him he's done a good job and shakes his hand. Unfortunately, *Raw* only needs two announcers and Austin gives Coachman a Stone Cold Stunner.

After a commercial break, Chief Morley says he was screwed, but Eric Bischoff doesn't want to hear it. He's had enough of excuses and fires Morley, calling him "worthless". When the fired superstar walks by "Stone Cold" Steve Austin, the "rattlesnake" wants to know what's going on. He leads Morley back to Eric and says he has to be consulted on any firing decisions. Morley is briefly excited to be chief of staff again, but Austin fires him too.

JR is back at the announce desk and thanks Lawler before playing footage of Goldberg fighting Three-Minute Warning and chasing off Christian last week. Ross announces that Bill will have his *Raw* debut tonight against the Canadian heel.

Backstage, Scott Steiner and Test work out and flex ahead of their World Tag Title shot. Stacy Keibler plays peacemaker for the disgruntled pairing.

Kane/Rob Van Dam def. Scott Steiner/Test (with Stacy Keibler) (World Tag Title match). For once, the champions come out together. Their opponents don't. While RVD wants to taunt Scott, the challenger is more concerned with hammering the popular superstar. Rob answers with a kick and split legged moonsault for a two-count. He then takes the fight out to the floor for a slingshot splash. Back in the squared circle, Steiner catches his leapfrog for a modified powerslam and near fall. He follows up with an elbow drop and pushups, impressing Stacy. A belly-to-belly suplex afterwards gets him a two-count before Test tags in to elbow the champion in a corner. A clothesline follows for a near fall before the bodyguard hooks a reverse chin lock. When Van Dam escapes, the two men trade counters until RVD kicks Test and tags in Kane to clothesline both challengers. After he knocks "Big Poppa Pump" out to the floor, the monster heads upstairs for a flying clothesline to Test. Scott makes the save with a modified German suplex, but Rob answers with a top rope flying kick. The bodyguard then whips Van Dam into the ring post before pumphandle slamming the "Big Red Machine" for a near fall. Unfortunately, he misses a Big Boot. He manages to recover and full nelson slam Kane ahead of a top rope flying elbow drop, but RVD makes the save. When he tries to pumphandle slam him, Rob slips free and dodges a Big Boot that hits Steiner instead. The champions capitalize with a Chokeslam and Five-Star Frog Splash to Test for the three-count.

After a commercial break, Eric Bischoff complains about "Stone Cold" Steve Austin bringing in cases of beer and a desk into their office. Eric says they don't have the budget for beer, but Austin will pay for that himself. He then turns over a couch, Bischoff sitting on it, to make space for his desk. Eric isn't happy about the way things are working out. It gets worse when "Stone Cold" doesn't invite him to the beer bash.

Following another commercial break, Chris Jericho heads out to the ring to a nice pop from the Canadian fans. He's got a background set this week as he introduces the "Highlight Reel", renamed after last week. First, he makes fun of "Rowdy" Roddy Piper's weight again before entering the Intercontinental Title battle royal at Judgment Day. Y2J then talks about being the captain of the heel Backlash team where Triple H beat Kevin Nash "fairly and squarely". In response, Jericho says Nash acted like a "typical American" and broke Hunter's limo windows, showing footage from last week and Backlash. Kevin has had enough and marches out to tell Y2J to shut up. He wants a piece of his former friend and Jericho has a surprise for him, introducing the WWE Champion. Nash has heard enough from Y2J and tosses him out to the floor before tearing up the set and threatening Helmsley. Unfortunately, Jericho recovers and low blows "Big Sexy" before "the Game" smashes him with a chair. When he sets up to Pedigree his former friend on the chair, Kevin escapes with a back body drop. He then unloads with a series of fists and knees before clotheslining Triple H out to the floor. The former friends then brawl on the floor, Nash reversing a whip into the ring steps. Not done, he grabs the steps and slams them into Hunter's face, busting him wide open. JR says Helmsley has no backup since Ric Flair is in Australia. Following a shot from the title belt, WWE officials come out to try to stop Kevin. He decks them, including Terry Taylor. That distracts "Big Sexy" long enough for "the Game" to get a pole and slow his former friend with a shot to the back. More shots follow, but he can't keep Nash down, the big man tossing him into the set and leading him backstage where they fight at the Gorilla position. Triple H once again slows "Big Sexy", this time with a monitor shot. Kevin won't stay down, tackling Hunter into a rolling metal door. When the fight spills outside, Helmsley nearly gets run over by an SUV. "The Game" seizes the opportunity to commandeer the vehicle and speed away. Jerry wonders if it's a carjacking. After a commercial break, Jericho watches the carnage and smiles. "Stone Cold" Steve Austin asks if he's proud of himself and calls him a main event guy. As such, "Stone Cold" gives him a main event match next week against Nash. Y2J can't believe it and throws his water angrily.

After the announcers recap JR getting his job back earlier, they preview Judgment Day.

Booker T def. Lance Storm. Storm gets a nice pop waving the Canadian flag. He follows up with an eye gouge and fists, but Booker answers. When he attempts a roll-up, Lance rolls through and locks on a sharpshooter for a nice pop. Luckily, the five-time champion reaches the ropes for the break. After a leg lariat scores him a two-count, Booker T gets his own near fall with a spinebuster. He tries to follow up with a Scissors Kick, but Storm dodges only to be rocked by a side kick. Once the Canadian is down, Booker gets a nice pop for a spinaroonie. Unfortunately, he rises up into a superkick and near fall. Focusing back on the task at hand, Booker T responds with a flapjack and Scissors Kick for the victory.

Backstage, La Resistance approach Stacy Keibler. They say they are only here to talk. They don't understand why she's aligned with Test and Scott Steiner and offer to give her a job with the rookies.

La Resistance def. Spike Dudley/Tommy Dreamer. The rookies wear berets for their debut, the ECW superstars already in the ring waiting. Rene actually wrestles with his hat on until Dreamer whips him into the ropes. The babyfaces then work on his arm briefly until he slams Dudley to the canvas and tags in Grenier. The runt greets him with fists before sliding under Dupree's legs to slam him face-first on the apron. Rene pays him back moments later, pulling the ropes down for Spike to fly out to the floor. Back in the ring, Sylvan scores a two-count with a hard whip into a neutral corner. He then applies a reverse chin lock for boos. Following a double hip toss, Tommy breaks Grenier's cover. Back to the chin lock, Sylvan can't hold the runt down and he escapes to headbutt the rookie's gut. Dreamer then fights both men, stunning Dupree with a spinebuster before hitting both men with a combination DDT and neckbreaker. Dudley returns afterwards with a top rope double stomp to Sylvan's gut, but when he celebrates, La Resistance recover and answer with a Double Flapjack for the win. Post-match, Rene attacks with a kendo stick until Scott Steiner runs out to club the rookies. When they double-team him, Test runs out for the save, chasing off La Resistance.

After a commercial break, Eric Bischoff is on the phone complaining to Linda McMahon about "Stone Cold" Steve Austin being out of control. She tells him he needs to get along with his co-GM or resign. Eric isn't quitting and promises to raise the bar next week. Bischoff ends the phone call hitting on Linda.

Further backstage, Terri interviews Christian. He wants her to call him the "People's Champ" as "anointed by The Rock". Christian calls them his "Peeps" before telling Terri that he's not impressed by Goldberg on the cover of *WWE Magazine*. While the intense superstar might have Speared him, Christian says he's still standing and rips up the magazine, promising a new losing streak for Goldberg.

Jazz (with Theodore Long/Rodney Mack) def. Trish Stratus (Women's Title match). JR doesn't think it's fair that Jazz has Mack in her corner alongside Long. He thinks Trish will be great one day, but isn't sure she's ready for the champion. That seems true as Jazz slams and leg drops her early on, but Stratus won't let down her home country, responding with chops. When she attempts to deliver her handstand head scissors, the heel shoves her down. Theodore tries to use his shoe again, but slips on the apron hilariously. Jazz improvises with a powerbomb and her feet on the ropes for the cover, but only gets a two-count. Trish answers with Stratusfaction as Victoria runs out to distract Chad Patton. Stratus rewards her with a Chick Kick while Rodney slides the champion her belt to blast the vixen for the three-count.

The Christian/Goldberg match never officially starts. Christian is out first, waiting as the intense superstar debuts new black and white shorts. Despite being in Canada, Goldberg gets a nice reaction. He's followed by Rico and Three-Minute Warning, the stylist saying that they haven't forgotten about last week. Before Christian tears Bill apart, the trio want a piece of him. Rico advises Christian to get out of the ring, but he's already gone.

Goldberg def. Rico/Three-Minute Warning. The trio runs out to attack Goldberg, Jamal planting him with a Samoan drop. This is a good way to keep the fans from booing the intense superstar in Canada as the heels triple-team him. The crowd especially come to life when he recovers quickly to double Spear the Samoans ahead of a Jackhammer to Rico for the three-count.

Post-match, Christian hits Goldberg with a chair and runs into the crowd. Bill grabs a microphone, but before he can call out the Canadian, "Stone Cold" Steve Austin's music plays. It's time for his beer bash. When he walks around the ring, he notices the intense superstar and wonders if he has a problem with that. Goldberg does. The two men tease a confrontation that fans wanted for years during the Monday Night Wars. Unfortunately, it's not going to come to pass due to Steve's injuries. Instead, Austin says he knows Bill wants Christian and gives the Canadian to him next week in a "Steel Cage" match. When he starts to drink, the "rattlesnake" realizes that something is missing and gives Goldberg a pair of beers. JR never thought he'd see that. Two beers is hardly a bash, so four women bring trays of beers down the aisle before fans and members of the crew make their way out from backstage to join the bash. Austin is having so much fun that he swims through beer as the babyfaces drink to end the show.

SmackDown!
May 8, 2003
Halifax, Nova Scotia, Canada
Announcers: Michael Cole, Tazz, Spanky (briefly)

The show opens with a video package of events from last week involving Mr. America. After the intro video plays, Vince McMahon heads to the squared circle to say that he's going to present Hulk Hogan tonight. He hasn't had a change of heart in sending him home to rot. Instead, he's going to play the Hulkster via satellite from Tampa, Florida. Because he's not here, Mr. America won't be either. McMahon says that even the "mentally challenged" Canadians know that Hogan and the masked man are one and the same. The fans loudly chant that he "screwed Bret". Vince proudly admits it and says he'd do the same to everyone in the arena if he gets the chance. He then blames Stephanie McMahon for signing Mr. America and brings her out, cutting off her music. She says she heard all the hype and wanted to keep Mr. America from joining *Raw*. To do so, she signed a contract that says he can't be fired or suspended. The only way Vince can get out of the contract is by proving that Mr. America and the Hulkster are the same person. The WWE owner tells her to get thinking about ways to prove Mr. America's identity and kicks her out of the ring. He then welcomes in Hogan via satellite. Hulk doesn't like sitting at home and he hopes to return to action one day, possibly teaming up with Mr. America. The Hulkster really enjoyed watching the masked man punch McMahon last week. Vince can't believe he's keeping up the charade. Hogan agrees they both have mustaches and similar builds, but Hulk says his pythons are a little bit bigger than the newcomer's. To prove that they are different people, Vince invites Mr. America to appear here tonight. The Hulkster quotes George Washington to say he "cannot tell a lie" and thinks Mr. America may show up. McMahon would love to see it, promising to rip off his mask.

After a commercial break, a member of the crew stops Vince McMahon and tells him that Mr. America is in the building. Vince wonders if it's "April Fools" before shooing off the crewmember.

Eddie Guerrero (with Chavo Guerrero Jr.) def. Matt Hardy Version 1.0 (with Crash Holly/Shannon Moore). Matt Facts this week reveal that Hardy hates to get up before noon and eats slowly to savor his food. While Eddie takes the champion down in this non-title match, Chavo watches from ringside wearing gold medals around his neck. He's got plenty to enjoy as "Latino Heat" is all over Matt until the heel whips him into the second turnbuckle. That lets a bloodied Hardy get in a few shots, but they only wake up Eddie and he decks the champion as well as Moore. Unfortunately, Matt capitalizes on the distraction with a pair of side effects. Afterwards, "Latino Heat" briefly applies a sleeper hold, but Hardy slams him to the mat for a two-count. When he goes up to the second rope for his patented leg drop, Guerrero counters with a hurricanrana. Catching a second wind, he punches and suplexes Matt three times. When he heads upstairs though, Matt dodges a Frog Splash and nearly scores the win with an Oklahoma roll. He tries to follow up with the Twist of Fate, but "Latino Heat" shoves free. Despite that, Hardy knocks Eddie down for a second rope leg drop and near fall. When he pulls Guerrero up for an exploder suplex, "Latino Heat" surprises him with an arm drag and roll-up for the win. Post-match, Team Angle jump Chavo from behind and take back the gold medals.

Backstage, Big Show talks to Nunzio and The FBI while crew members carry equipment in front of them. At one point, Mr. America is obscured by a large piece of glass.

Spanky def. Jamie Noble (with Nidia). Pre-match, the former Brian Kendrick says he got his butt kicked last week for getting the crowd to say "Cena sucks". He does the same tonight before the heels enter and make out. Jamie starts slow, holding Spanky in a headlock. It doesn't take long for the babyface to escape and tease Sliced Bread #2. Unfortunately, Noble tosses him onto the apron for a throat drop on the ropes. Nidia gets in a few shots afterwards while John Cena watches backstage. An exploder suplex back in the squared circle nearly gets the heel the victory before he applies a neck vice. Spanky quickly fights free only to leap into a fireman's carry slam and single leg crab. When he escapes, the babyface steals a two-count with a roll-up, but is quickly clubbed back down. The redneck is the aggressor for most of the match, but Spanky eventually turns the tide with a single leg dropkick and enziguri for a near fall. Although Jamie answers with a powerslam for his own close two-count, when he sets the rookie on the top rope, Spanky shoves him down to the mat. He then attempts a moonsault, but lands on his feet when Noble moves. The redneck can't avoid Sliced Bread #2 for Spanky to get the win. Backstage, Cena hates it, but his tantrum is cut short by what looks to be Mr. America watching the video monitor.

Video of Big Show injuring Rey Mysterio at Backlash plays. The announcers say Rey is getting better and will appear on next week's show.

Backstage, Josh Mathews asks Brock Lesnar about teaming with Chris Benoit tonight against A-Train and Big Show. The WWE Champion says the babyfaces will handle their opponents "no problem". He then challenges Show to make their title match at Judgment Day a "Stretcher" match.

Further backstage, Funaki tells Vince McMahon that Mr. America is heading to the ring. Vince laughs and calls him an imposter. He then makes Funaki pour the WWE owner a cup of coffee.

After a commercial break, Vince and Stephanie McMahon watch backstage as Mr. America heads to the squared circle to a big pop despite being in Canada. Cole says the masked man has charisma while the fans chant "Hogan". When he speaks, Vince knows it's Hulk Hogan and sprints out of the office. Despite that, Mr. America assures fans that he's not Hulk Hogan and he watched him at WrestleMania. That inspired the masked man to take his vitamins, train, and say his prayers to become the superstar he is. He tells the Hulkster "thank you" before Mr. McMahon storms down the aisle. Circling the ring repeatedly, Vince says he's a man of his word and he promised to rip off the mask tonight. Instead of the WWE owner though, McMahon orders his daughter to come out and do it. When Stephanie enters the ring, Vince uses her to distract Mr. America while he gives him a low blow. He then tries to remove the mask, but he can't before the masked man recovers and knocks him back onto his daughter. While Vince checks on his daughter, Mr. America "hulks up" and decks the WWE owner before carrying Stephanie backstage. For those keeping track, this is another extended segment featuring Vince McMahon tonight.

After a commercial break, Vince McMahon is more concerned with finding Mr. America than checking on his daughter. Stephanie McMahon says the masked man didn't hurt her, Vince did. He puts the blame on Hulk Hogan and tells her that she'll be fine.

Torrie Wilson def. Dawn Marie. Sable is out first to watch the action from ringside. When the competitors come out, Torrie is too distracted by Sable and Dawn Marie capitalizes with a cheap shot. She tries to finish her off with a fireman's carry slam, but Wilson sunset flips her for the quick three-count. Post-match, Sable enters the squared circle and congratulates the babyface on breaking her "losing streak". The heel adds that she made the "Sable Invitational" to see who could compare to her.

Sable wonders if Torrie really thinks she can match up to her and challenges her to a bikini contest. In response, Wilson unzips her top, seemingly to accept the challenge.

A Kurt Angle video package highlights his perseverance even with a broken neck.

Team Angle def. Rikishi/Tajiri (WWE Tag Title match). The champions are excited to have their mentor's gold medals back and bring them and a picture of Kurt Angle to ringside for this title defense. Rikishi opens the match slugging Haas and knocking him from the ring. Shelton tries to make the save, but nearly gets squashed. Charlie does with a butt splash, but Benjamin makes the save. Tajiri then tags in to kick Shelton and nearly win the titles. When he runs the ropes, Haas clubs him into an exploder suplex. Charlie then tags in for a belly-to-belly suplex, but the "Japanese Buzzsaw" responds with a thrust kick to put both men down. When they tag out, the big Samoan punches and clotheslines both champions. A Samoan drop follows to Haas ahead of a belly-to-belly suplex for Benjamin. Not done, he squashes the champions in the same corner before chokeslamming Charlie. When he tries to give Shelton a Stinkface, Haas distracts Jimmy Korderas for his partner to low blow the big babyface. Tajiri then stuns Charlie with a handspring elbow. He also traps him in a Tarantula moments later, but can't finish him off. Instead, Team Angle respond quickly with a combination Inverted Atomic Drop and Superkick for the win. As they celebrate, Los Guerreros steal the gold medals and picture of Kurt.

Rhyno def. John Cena. Spanky joins the announce table to scout Cena and insult him. It's been a whirlwind few weeks for the rapping heel as he's dropped from vying for the WWE Title on PPV to a feud with Spanky. John continues to make the most of his time, rapping pre-match about beating Rhyno's butt so bad he'll look like he's "been on a prison tour". The man-beast then rushes out to hammer Cena for the early advantage. Boots follow, knocking the rapping heel out to the floor. There, the "Doctor of Thuganomics" rams him into the apron to swing the momentum and score a two-count. A suplex moments later also gets him a near fall before he applies a surfboard stretch. He can't keep Rhyno down and the man-beast answers with a flying clothesline for a two-count. Back and forth the action goes, John getting a two-count with his snap mare neckbreaker before Rhyno plants him with a spinebuster. When Cena goes after his chain, Spanky grabs it and distracts him long enough for the man-beast to roll him up for the victory. Post-match, John chases the rookie into the crowd before Rhyno tries to Gore the rapping heel at ringside. At the last second, Cena moves and the man-beast hits the ring steps, injuring his knee.

Backstage, Nunzio tells The FBI it's time to get to work.

After a commercial break, the announcers preview Judgment Day.

Backstage, Nunzio stops Brock Lesnar. He says that he was disrespectful to his friends A-Train and Big Show. Nunzio takes that personally, but Brock doesn't care, shoving the Italian heel aside. Nunzio takes offense and attacks him from behind, leading Lesnar into a trap where The FBI lock him in a room, a forklift blocking the door. Big Show and A-Train congratulate them on their work before the giant says shows the hairy heel a stretcher. It has Rey Mysterio's name crossed off already. He promises that Chris Benoit will leave on a stretcher tonight before Brock takes a ride at Judgment Day.

Big Show (with A-Train) def. Chris Benoit. Instead of a tag match, Benoit marches out to shove the giant. He doesn't move Show, but one big chop from the heel drops him. Back up, "the Crippler" answers with his own chops and a dropkick to the knee. Unfortunately, he quickly runs into a sidewalk slam. While Big Show stands on the Canadian, the announcers talk about how barbaric a "Stretcher" match is, noting that the last one was seventeen years ago between Andre the Giant and Killer Khan. Every bit of that is false. The last "Stretcher" match was Hulk Hogan versus Khan in 1987, sixteen years ago. The last time Andre and Khan had a stretcher match was 1981, twenty-two years ago. Either way, it's been a while. It's also a while before Benoit gets in any offense as the giant clubs him and locks on a bearhug, picking up the Canadian babyface and holding him up until he bites free. A jawbreaker follows, but one Show elbow stops him. Unfortunately, Big Show misses a leg drop, putting him on the mat for a dropkick. The "rabid wolverine" follows up with a top rope flying headbutt for a near fall. When Show tries to answer with a Chokeslam, Benoit traps him in the Crippler Crossface. Luckily, A-Train makes the save, grabbing the stretcher and threatening to use it. Although "the Crippler" meets him with a baseball slide kick into the hard plastic stretcher, when he tries to reapply his finisher to Big Show, the giant answers with a Chokeslam for the three-count. Post-match, the hairy heel gets revenge with a bicycle kick ahead of a second Chokeslam. Afterwards, the heels strap Benoit to the stretcher, but before Show can finish him off, Brock Lesnar returns to wail on both giants. Although he gives A-Train an F5, Big Show takes advantage of the distraction to clothesline and Chokeslam the WWE Champion. The giant ends the show roaring overtop of the downed Lesnar.

Monday Night Raw
May 12, 2003
Philadelphia, PA
Announcers: Jim Ross, Jerry "the King" Lawler, Theodore Long (briefly)

The show opens with Christian inside a steel cage for his match with Goldberg. The "new People's Champ" says no one wants to see him brutalized inside a cage and he's got a big photo shoot tomorrow. That brings out "Stone Cold" Steve Austin. The "rattlesnake" wants to know why he's out already because it's not time for his match. Christian says Austin told him he was "number one", but Austin was just flipping him off. Regardless, "Stone Cold" assures him that he will compete tonight. The heel has something to say in response. He doesn't think the "rattlesnake" should be jealous of him being the new "People's Champ" after The Rock beat Austin at WrestleMania XIX. Steve says he's trying hard to not lose his temper, but the fans want him to. Before he loses it, Rob Van Dam interrupts and the cage is raised to the ceiling. RVD announces that he's officially entering the Judgment Day Intercontinental Title battle royal. Since he's so great, Christian offers to give Rob his match with Goldberg tonight. He thinks the fans want to see it. They don't, preferring to see Goldberg destroy the heel. Van Dam gets a cheer when he asks the fans to give him an "RVD" if they think he'll win the Intercontinental Title this Sunday. Christian tries to get a "Christian Rules" cheer, but the fans boo him. Austin has heard enough and tells both men to stop stealing his material before telling the heel to get out of his ring. He's replaced by Kane. He says no one is going to stop him from winning the Intercontinental Title this Sunday. RVD hears him, but promises that he'll find a way to eliminate him if need be. "Stone Cold" detects some dissension, but he knows how to alleviate that and calls for some beer. Eric Bischoff interrupts to promise no beer bash tonight. Instead, he's going to raise the bar and he's starting right now with a World Tag Title match pitting the champions against a team they've never faced before and one of the greatest. The fans go wild when the Legion of Doom make a surprise return.

Kane/Rob Van Dam def. Legion of Doom (World Tag Title match). Hawk and Animal aren't quite as in shape as they used to be, but they still look good and the fans are into their return. Animal opens the match pounding RVD until the champion answers with a monkey flip and spinning heel kick. Hawk tags in soon afterwards to punch Rob, but he also gets knocked down with a spinning heel kick. After Van Dam gets a two-count, Hawk shoots up for a neckbreaker. Kane tags in moments later to clothesline and boot both challengers. Following a sidewalk slam to Hawk, he rocks Animal with a top rope flying clothesline. When he sets up for a Double Chokeslam, the Legion of Doom drive him from the ring. RVD picks up the slack with a flying kick and rolling thunder to Hawk, but Animal makes the save. He follows up with a big slam before hoisting Rob up for the Doomsday Device. Unfortunately, Van Dam ducks and Hawk crashes to the canvas ahead of a "Big Red Machine" big boot to Animal. The champions follow up with a Chokeslam and Five-Star Frog Splash to Hawk for the victory. Post-match, Hawk ends any chance of having one more run in the WWE by immediately hopping up and leaving the ring to end his final match with the company.

Backstage, Victoria and Steven Richards surround Trish Stratus. The "black widow" promises that she's going to take Trish's good looks away in their upcoming "Hardcore" match.

Following footage of Kevin Nash and Triple H fighting last week, a bandaged Hunter talks to Chris Jericho backstage. Helmsley says this Philadelphia arena is famous, but Y2J disagrees because all of the teams suck. "The Game" remembers this as the place that Nash tore his quad a year ago. Jericho also remembers tearing Triple H's quad. While the champion doesn't like that, he says Y2J made a career after injuring Hunter. He wonders how much he could do if he injures Kevin tonight.

In the parking lot, Goldberg arrives in a limo. He opens his door, but takes his time getting out. That saves his life as a car sideswipes the limo and hits the door.

After a commercial break, "Stone Cold" Steve Austin doesn't like Theodore Long calling him "playa". Long apologizes before offering to have Rodney Mack wrestle two men tonight. He wants to impress the co-general manager to get Rodney a shot at the Intercontinental Title this Sunday. He thinks it's time a black man gets a chance. "Stone Cold" agrees, but gives that spot to Booker T.

Rodney Mack (with Theodore Long) def. Ken Phoenix/Mike Phoenix ("White Boy Challenge" match). The jobbers get an introduction this week before Long joins the announce table to talk about his man while he destroys the Phoenix brothers. Ken taps out first to a cobra clutch. Mike doesn't last much longer, also tapping out to cobra clutch, the match lasting just one minute and thirty-one seconds.

After a commercial break, Jonathan Coachman asks Eric Bischoff about someone trying to run over Goldberg. Bischoff says there's no issue and Bill is fine. He then notices "Classy" Freddie Blassie. Unfortunately, he doesn't have time to hype his new book, blaming his former chief of staff for bringing him here tonight. Rico interrupts to ask the co-GM for help. Three-Minute Warning has become a joke and he wants to get their mojo back. That gives Eric an idea and he tells Blassie to follow him. The legend asks if he's going to hang himself.

Further backstage, Goldberg kicks equipment. He's fired up about almost dying. "Stone Cold" Steve Austin understands what it's like to get hit by a car and tells the intense superstar to get ready for his match so he can take out his frustrations on Christian.

Afterwards, Lilian Garcia introduces "Classy" Freddie Blassie. Eric Bischoff joins him on stage, telling Mrs. Blassie that she can go backstage after pushing her husband out in a wheelchair. Bischoff briefly promotes his book before telling the legend that he's only got about three minutes left. That sees Three-Minute Warning and Rico hop out of the crowd while Bischoff wheels Blassie down the aisle. He's helpless to stop them, but "Stone Cold" Steve Austin isn't. He says he wasn't consulted on this. Once he wheels Freddie out of the way, "Stone Cold" tells Eric that he reinstated The Dudley Boyz. Bischoff can't stand it, but Bubba Ray and D-Von run out to attack the heels and give Jamal a wassup drop. Austin stops them because Blassie has something he wants to say, "D-Von, get the tables". The fans love it. Rico doesn't as he stumbles into a 3D through the table. The "rattlesnake" and Dudleys then have a Philadelphia beer bash despite Eric's promise earlier.

Goldberg def. Christian ("Steel Cage" match). Christian brings a chair into the cage, but it's no normal chair. He tells the fans that it's the same chair The Rock used to beat up Goldberg last month. The intense superstar then heads to the ring to a good pop, stepping through sparks and smoke. Christian tries to stop him from entering the cage, but loses his chair. When the heel tries to climb out, Bill slams him to the canvas. He accuses Christian of trying to run him over in between fists and knees. Although Goldberg stops him from escaping through the door, the heel grabs his chair. He uses it moments later after slowing the intense superstar with a low blow. Repeated chair shots follow to give the new "People's Champ" the advantage. Instead of escaping, Christian makes a cover for a two-count. More chair shots follow before the heel tries to climb out. Once again Goldberg stops him, but Christian remains in control until he attempts to spear the intense superstar. At the last second, Bill sidesteps and the heel crashes hard into the cage, busting himself open. Goldberg capitalizes with a string of shots and whips into the cage. After slamming him face-first into the steel, the intense superstar Spears Christian to a big pop. He follows up with a Jackhammer for the three-count and big pop.

After a commercial break, Ric Flair stops "Stone Cold" Steve Austin and calls him the man. However, he says Triple H runs *Raw*. The Hurricane interrupts. He thinks Kevin Nash will beat down Hunter this Sunday. Flair doesn't like that, warning the superhero that he's going to get hurt if he runs his mouth. Austin tells them to shut up and settle it like men inside the ring right now. Ric doesn't have time to get changed, "Stone Cold" ringing an imaginary bell for this match that can only end inside the ring.

Ric Flair def. The Hurricane. Flair is always ready for a cheap shot and nails the masked man. The Hurricane answers with his own fists, the two men fighting out to the announcer's platform. When Ric gets the upper hand, he heads to the squared circle where the superhero pulls his pants down to reveal his bare butt. The Hurricane follows up with a leaping clothesline and back body drop, the veteran's pants ripped. The superhero doesn't give him a break, scoring a near fall with a top rope flying cross body block. When he tries to follow up, Flair pokes his eyes only to get slammed off the top rope. Although he escapes one chokeslam with a low blow, "The Nature Boy" wastes time strutting and walks into a second chokeslam. After The Hurricane struts, he scores a near fall with a shining wizard kick. That's as close as he'll get to victory as Ric chop blocks him before working on the left leg. He doesn't waste time, transitioning quickly to his Figure Four Leglock to score the tap-out victory. When he doesn't break the hold post-match, Triple H hurries out to talk sense into his mentor and tell him that he won. Hunter isn't a good guy though, pulling The Hurricane up for a Pedigree and boos.

Goldust/Scott Steiner/Test (with Stacy Keibler) def. Christopher Nowinski/La Resistance. As Scott and Test head to the ring, the announcers reveal that they will face La Resistance at Judgment Day. The heels then come out for Sylvan to accuse Americans of always looking for war. While they consider most Americans "barbarians", Rene says Nowinski has class. That brings the babyfaces out to brawl with the heels, Test starting strong and pummeling Dupree in the squared circle. Goldust then works on the Harvard heel's arm before rocking his face mask wearing jaw with a right hand. An inverted atomic drop and clothesline chase him off for Steiner to hammer Grenier. As usual, he elbow drops his opponent, but instead of going for the cover he mocks him with pushups. Afterwards, Test tags in to hit the heels until Nowinski throat drops him on the top rope. That finally swings the momentum and Rene whips the bodyguard into the ring post twice. When the Harvard heel returns, he works on Test's arm until he misses an elbow drop. That lets "Big Poppa Pump" tag in to attack all three heels and belly-to-belly suplex Dupree. When he tries to finish him off with a reverse DDT, Sylvan makes the save. Everyone joins the brawl, eventually clearing the ring for Scott to finish off Nowinski with a reverse DDT. Post-match, the bodyguard is upset when his girlfriend raises Steiner's hand in victory.

Backstage, Steven Richards pumps up Victoria ahead of her "Hardcore" match with Trish Stratus.

After a commercial break, the announcers preview Judgment Day, adding a Fatal 4-Way Women's Title match to the proceedings. Tazz and Michael Cole even get to join the announcers via satellite to preview *SmackDown!* this week and the brand's PPV matches.

Backstage, Terri asks Chris Jericho if he has any idea who tried to run over Goldberg. The heel says if he was going to take out Bill, he'd do it face-to-face like he's going to do Kevin Nash tonight. Then, Y2J is going to go on to Judgment Day and win back the Intercontinental Title.

Trish Stratus (with Tommy Dreamer) def. Victoria (with Steven Richards) ("Hardcore" match). When Richards threatens Trish, Dreamer runs out to join the vixen and chase Steven out of the ring. That leaves Stratus alone to slam Victoria to the mat before trying to get a weapon from one of the trashcans filled with weapons bound to the ring posts. Although the "black widow" stops her, Trish counters an electric chair drop with a sunset flip for a two-count. Moments later, she kicks a trashcan lid back into Victoria's face. Both women use the lid afterwards before the "black widow" slams Stratus on it for a two-count. When she grabs a second lid, Trish takes a cue from The Matrix and ducks for a Chick Kick. Despite that, Victoria soon regains control to choke the vixen with a leather strap. There's nothing Chad Patton can do about that, even though he counts and warns the "black widow" to stop. Eventually, the women fight on the ropes culminating with a Stratus hurricanrana to the canvas. When Richards tries to interfere, Trish throat drops him onto the top rope into a Tommy kendo stick shot. Afterwards, Stratus Chick Kicks Victoria again ahead of her own kendo stick shots and Stratusfaction for the victory.

Kevin Nash def. Chris Jericho by disqualification. Jericho attempts a sneak attack to start the match, but Nash catches him and knocks him down to the canvas. As JR says, Kevin is not much of a technical wrestler, so he opens the match punching and back body dropping the heel. Y2J goes after the leg to try to slow the big man, but he pays courtesy of several clubbing blows. A knee lift sends the heel out to the floor, but Jericho finally slows the big man with a throat drop on the top rope. By the time he returns to the ring though, Y2J leaps off the top rope into a two-handed chokeslam. Despite that, the heel chop blocks Nash down to the canvas. When he attempts to hook a figure four leglock though, Kevin kicks him into a corner and out of the ring. Jericho refuses to stay down, wrapping the big man's knee around the ring post. Like Y2J, Kevin is up quickly to surprise his opponent with a sidewalk slam. Neither man can string many moves together, Jericho locking on a sleeper hold only to be driven into the ropes ahead of a sidewalk slam. Y2J answers with a running face slam and Lionsault, but Nash kicks out at the last second. Frustrated, Jericho wastes time yelling at Earl Hebner before turning into a big boot and knee to the gut. When the big man sets up for a Jackknife, Triple H and Ric Flair run out to attack for the disqualification. Shawn Michaels follows, but Jericho hits him from behind. His momentary assistance allows Kevin to recover and fight all three heels. After clearing the WWE Champion from the ring, he big boots and Jackknifes Y2J. Shawn joins him to give Flair Sweet Chin Music before counting to three for Nash's foot on Jericho's chest. Helmsley attempts to sneak attack his Judgment Day opponent, but Kevin sees him coming and big boots the World Title back into his face. A Jackknife and another three-count follow. JR wonders if there's any way Hunter can stop Nash this Sunday while Michaels and the big man strike a classic two-man pose to end the episode.

SmackDown!

May 15, 2003
Baltimore, MD
Announcers: Michael Cole, Tazz

Following the intro video and fireworks, Vince McMahon storms down to the ring to say that there's no doubt in anyone's mind that Mr. America is Hulk Hogan. He adds that the masked man is "deceitful" and "greedy". After yelling at the crowd for interrupting him, Vince says Hogan is "double dipping" and drawing two paychecks. Even worse, he "batters women". McMahon then shows footage of Mr. America escaping Vince trying to remove his mask and knocking him back into Stephanie McMahon. The WWE owner says Stephanie is partially responsible for "bungling" the attempt to remove the mask. Instead of beating Mr. America to a "bloody pulp", Vince issues an open contract for someone or multiple people to face the masked man at Judgment Day. Afterwards, he promises to unmask Mr. America. Nunzio and The FBI interrupt to introduce themselves. Instead of the government—who Nunzio says McMahon has defeated—they are the Full Blooded Italians. The Italian heel has a video package of their greatest hits taking care of people. Johnny Stamboli says if they get the contract they'll be on Mr. America like "baked on ziti". Nunzio says he's not very smart, but Johnny is strong. Vince likes the idea of the trio taking care of his problem and heads backstage to talk to Nunzio about it.

Chuck Palumbo (with Johnny Stamboli) def. Rikishi. While Nunzio heads backstage with the WWE owner, he crosses paths with Rikishi and threatens him. That amuses the announcers. Inside the ring, Chuck hammers the big babyface. When the big Samoan starts to fight back, Stamboli distracts him. Unfortunately, Palumbo can't capitalize and accidentally decks his own partner. Moments later, Rikishi nearly finishes off Chuck with a belly-to-belly suplex. He tries to drag Palumbo away from the ropes, but Johnny holds onto his partner. When the big babyface argues with him, Chuck unloads with a Superkick. Rikishi responds with one of his own and a Samoan drop. He then squashes the heel in a corner, but when he goes for the Stinkface, "the Bull" hops onto the apron and distracts him. Although Stamboli takes a beating, Palumbo capitalizes and Superkicks the big Samoan for the win. Post-match, Brock Lesnar walks into the arena and charges the ring to F5 Chuck.

After a commercial break, Stephanie McMahon tells Brock Lesnar that he was "so impressive" taking care of The FBI. She hopes he brings the same aggression this Sunday for the first "Stretcher" match in over "seventeen years". She says he'll need it because it's the most barbaric match in WWE history.

A video package of Mr. America visiting wounded soldiers plays.

Afterwards, Torrie Wilson steps onto the stage to disrobe and show off a small blue bikini. She promises to wear something a little more revealing this Sunday.

Backstage, Stephanie McMahon sees flowers on her desk. She thinks they are from her dad, but when she reads the cards she realizes she's wrong. Vince McMahon enters at the same time to tell her that in spite of her bungling the unmasking last week, he forgives her. Stephanie thought he was apologizing to her, but instead it was Hulk Hogan and Mr. America who sent her the flowers. Vince can't stand it, smashing the vases after his daughter leaves the office.

Footage of Rey Mysterio arriving earlier today and signing autographs for excited fans plays.

Matt Hardy Version 1.0 (with Crash Holly/Shannon Moore) def. Tajiri (Cruiserweight Title match). This week's Matt Facts are that Hardy thinks Tajiri weighs too much to be a cruiserweight and that Matt can eat more sushi than him. The champion celebrates after just one arm drag. When the "Japanese Buzzsaw" does the same, Hardy hits him from behind. Tajiri is back up quickly though to walk across Matt's back and kick him. More kicks follow, but when he attempts an apron attack, Shannon grabs his foot. The champion takes advantage of the situation with a face-first suplex onto the top rope and side effect for a near fall. He follows up with an abdominal stretch and fists to the ribs briefly. When he attempts a crucifix powerbomb, Tajiri slips free and stuns the heel with a thrust kick. Catching a second wind, the challenger unloads with a flurry of kicks and a handspring back elbow. He follows up with a handspring kick to Moore ahead of a two-count on the champion. Moments later, the "Japanese Buzzsaw" locks on the Tarantula. When he sets up for a Buzzsaw Kick though, Crash hops onto the apron and takes the blow himself. Matt capitalizes with an immediate Twist of Fate for the win. Post-match, Hardy says he has the "Mattributes" to take care of Mr. America at Judgment Day. Tajiri answers with a flying dive off the top rope onto him and Shannon out on the floor.

Backstage, Eddie Guerrero puts a poncho and sombrero on Kurt Angle's picture as he talks to the injured Olympian. He says Kurt will be in his corner tonight. He almost feels like family to Eddie, so he puts a fake mustache and goatee on him. That makes "Latino Heat" feel right at home.

After a commercial break, Mr. America asks Stephanie McMahon how she's doing. She thanks him for the flowers and gives him a kiss on the cheek as she asks him to thank Hulk Hogan for her too.

Chris Benoit def. John Cena by disqualification. Pre-match, Cena offers to squash Mr. America in his customary rap before promising to take care of Benoit with his steel chain. "The Crippler" doesn't appreciate that, marching out to punch John ahead of a backbreaker and one-count. He then unloads with chops and kicks until the rapping heel takes advantage of Benoit turning his back to argue with Mike Sparks. After clotheslining the back of the "rabid wolverine's" head, Cena whips him into the ring post for a two-count. He then slows the pace with an armbar. When Benoit starts to get up, John whips him down by the hair ahead of another ring post toss and near fall. Focusing on the shoulder, he hammerlocks "the Crippler" and slams him on his arm. Fists to the jaw wake up Benoit and he unloads with more chops. A snap suplex follows before Nunzio and Johnny Stamboli run out to distract the "rabid wolverine". The rapping heel takes advantage, knocking Benoit out to the floor while Sparks orders The FBI to leave ahead of a commercial break.

Afterwards, Cena traps "the Crippler" in another armbar. When he escapes, John runs over him for another two-count. He also gets a near fall with a second hammerlock slam. Continuing to focus on the arm, the rapping heel stomps it and rams Benoit into the top turnbuckles for a near fall. When he goes for a third hammerlock slam, the "rabid wolverine" slips free and dropkicks him. A drop toe hold onto the middle turnbuckle follows ahead of a roll-up and two-count. He continues to build momentum with elbows and a German suplex. With the fans cheering him on, Benoit heads upstairs for a diving headbutt. Before he can get the three-count, Nunzio returns only to be tossed out to the floor. This time when John tries to capitalize with an FU, the babyface slips free and locks on the Crippler Crossface. Stamboli also returns to attack "the Crippler" for the disqualification. Rhyno follows him out, Goring "the Bull". Unfortunately, Nunzio smashes the man-beast with a chair. Afterwards, Spanky runs out for the save and hurricanranas John out of the ring before the other babyfaces clear house.

A video package plays for the WWE's recent United Kingdom tour.

Following a commercial break, "Rowdy" Roddy Piper and Sean O'Haire head to the squared circle for Piper's Pit. Once again, Mr. America will be their guest. Before the masked man comes out, Piper talks about Vince McMahon's open contract. While the wrestlers backstage want to suck up to the WWE owner and help their careers, "Hot Rod" wants a match with Hulk Hogan because he hates him. In fact, Roddy demands it. That brings out the flag waving masked man. He gives his flag to a "lucky fan" in the crowd before Mr. America tears off his good ripping shirt. Inside the ring, the masked man says he grew up watching Hogan kick Piper's butt and he'd love to do it at Judgment Day too. Roddy says the Hulkster never beat him "1-2-3". That might be true, but Mr. America says Piper has never beaten the masked patriot either. "Hot Rod" is tired of Mr. America and Hogan putting their hand to their ear. He's also tired of the fan waving the American flag over and over. Sean leaves to deal with the fan, but when the masked man tries to stop him, Piper cheap shots him. It doesn't take Mr. America long to "America up", according to Tazz, and big boot "Hot Rod". When he hits the ropes for a Legdrop, O'Haire trips him. He follows up with a trio of chair shots to the lower back before holding the masked man for a series of Roddy fists. He nearly takes the mask off before the fan limps into the ring to hit Piper with the flag. Unfortunately, Sean tackles him to the mat for "Hot Rod" to choke and punch the fan. When he yanks at the fan's leg, he pulls off his prosthetic. O'Haire wants nothing to do with that and leaves. Piper follows, clearly confused while the fans boo him loudly.

While Eddie Guerrero heads to the ring with his Mexican-garbed picture of Kurt Angle, the announcers reveal that Chavo Guerrero Jr. was injured over the weekend but as of now the "Ladder" match is still scheduled for this Sunday.

Backstage, Vince McMahon chastises "Rowdy" Roddy Piper and Sean O'Haire for attacking a fan. He warns them that they may face lawsuits. Sean pleads innocence and blames Roddy before McMahon tells them that he's going to make a decision that will affect their careers. Piper can't believe he was thrown under the bus, but O'Haire says he has to think about his future.

Shelton Benjamin (with Charlie Haas) def. Eddie Guerrero. Right back to the ring, Shelton powerslams Eddie before hooking a chin lock. When he heads up the ropes, "Latino Heat" hurricanranas him across the ring. Despite that, Benjamin is back up quickly to powerbomb Guerrero for a near fall. Eddie answers with a dropkick and pair of clotheslines. He follows up with a flurry of mounted fists and a trio of suplexes. That brings Charlie Haas out with a ladder. When "Latino Heat" wastes time arguing with him, Shelton capitalizes with a superkick for the three-count. Post-match, Team Angle try to hit Eddie with the ladder, but he dropkicks it back into them. Afterwards, he smashes Kurt Angle's picture over Benjamin's head.

Backstage, Vince McMahon believes that Sean O'Haire has legitimate concern for the kid who lost his leg earlier, but he doesn't think "Rowdy" Roddy Piper does. He says "Hot Rod" has a black heart and is the perfect man to deal with Mr. America this Sunday.

A *WWE Confidential* clip featuring Miss Elizabeth plays. It's not the usual highlights package for a recently passed superstar, but rather the WWE speculating on rumors about drug use and calling out Lex Luger who was dating Elizabeth and called 911 after her death. Thankfully, this segment has been removed from the Network.

After a commercial break, Sable comes out to preview her outfit for this Sunday's swimsuit competition. Tazz can hardly breathe as she writhes around and reveals a black bikini. Afterwards, the announcers preview Judgment Day. They return the favor from Monday night and let Jim Ross and Jerry "the King" Lawler hype *Raw*'s matches.

Backstage, Rey Mysterio talks to the announcers via video. He can't wait to get back in the ring and plans on winning back the Cruiserweight Title. For a moment, he thought his career was over after Big Show attacked him at Backlash. He was actually scared. Cole wonders if he would ever get back in the ring with the giant, but Rey doesn't know. Show answers for him, grabbing the masked man by the throat and carrying him out to ringside where he rips his shirt and chops his chest. Afterwards, Big Show slides the stretcher into the ring, but Mysterio catapults it into his face. A 619 follows before Rey goes upstairs only to have his flying cross body block caught and answered with a Samoan drop. When he sets up for a Chokeslam, Brock Lesnar runs out and tackles the giant. He follows up with a series of stretcher shots and an impressive F5. When he leaves the ring, Show yells at the WWE Champion. He forgets all about Mysterio and pays when the masked man bulldogs him to the canvas. That makes Big Show even madder and he fumes to end the show while Brock puts Rey on his shoulder to celebrate. Because of his size and despite Lesnar just F5ing him, Tazz says there's no way Show can lose this Sunday.

PPV: Judgment Day
May 18, 2003
Charlotte, NC
Announcers: Jim Ross, Jerry "the King" Lawler, Michael Cole, Tazz

Like prior Judgment Day PPVs, the show opens with creepy girls talking in unison and shots of the gallows before we see superstars like Triple H, Vince McMahon, and Kevin Nash in the intro video. Afterwards, fireworks explode to kick off the PPV.

"Stone Cold" Steve Austin heads to the ring to a big pop. He's excited to be in Charlotte, but isn't going to run his mouth. Instead, he's going to watch the show with the fans in the upper deck and enjoy some beer. He's already thirsty, so he has a beer with Tazz before heading up through the crowd to "redneck heaven".

John Cena/The FBI (with Nunzio) def. Chris Benoit/Rhyno/Spanky. Pre-match, Cena raps about joining The FBI family tonight. When the babyfaces come out, they chase the heels out to the floor. Spanky follows them, flying over the top rope onto his opponents. Back in the ring though, John hammers the rookie down. Spanky answers with an enziguri, but Palumbo illegally enters the ring to hammer him while Mike Sparks holds the other babyfaces back. The FBI capitalize with a double-team slam to give the heels the advantage. After they work over the babyface, Chuck scores a two-count before locking on a bearhug. Spanky won't give up, fighting free only to be clotheslined to the canvas. The rookie uses his speed to escape the heel corner moments later and give Benoit the hot tag. He and Rhyno take care of business, "the Crippler" suplexing The FBI while the man-beast clotheslines Cena out to the floor. Benoit follows up with a diving headbutt to Palumbo. When Nunzio illegally enters the ring, Rhyno Gores him. Although John returns to the ring to club the "rabid wolverine", Spanky surprises him with a top rope missile dropkick after blind tagging Benoit. He tries to finish off Chuck with Sliced Bread #2, but Nunzio grabs his leg and holds him for The FBI to score the win with The Kiss of Death, a combination backbreaker and Stamboli guillotine leg drop.

In his own skybox, a woman brings "Stone Cold" Steve Austin a hot dog. They are interrupted by Eric Bischoff wondering what's going on. He says that everything they have is supposed to be split fifty-fifty. When Austin gives him the hot dog, Eric reluctantly takes a bite. He also reluctantly accepts a beer from the worker. "Stone Cold" calls him a "sissy" for wanting his drink in a cup before smacking it and spraying beer everywhere as he says cheers.

La Resistance def. Scott Steiner/Test (with Stacy Keibler). Ahead of the match, we get a video package of La Resistance crossing paths with Scott Steiner. When the heels come out in berets, JR says "the King" should wear one too. Sylvan Grenier questions why the fans are booing them just because they are French. La Resistance blame the US government for promoting hatred of the French. Dupree opens the match slapping Test. The bodyguard responds in kind before hammering both heels and back body dropping Rene. Scott then tags in for more of the same. He also breaks out his elbow drop and pushups, but when he turns to deck Sylvan after he hits him running the ropes, Dupree capitalizes with a hotshot. Following shots from both heels, La Resistance double suplex Steiner for a Grenier two-count. He then applies a chin lock, but it doesn't take "Big Poppa Pump" long to fight free. Unfortunately, he runs into a corner boot and flying clothesline. When Rene tags back in, he leaps off the top rope into a belly-to-belly suplex. Both men tag out afterwards for Test to punch the heels and sidewalk slam Sylvan.

Although Dupree escapes a pumphandle slam, he can't escape a full nelson slam. The bodyguard then dons a beret to tease a Big Boot to Grenier, but Rene makes the save. All four men brawl afterwards, Scott belly-to-belly suplexing Sylvan ahead of a Test pumphandle slam. Unfortunately, Nick Patrick is distracted trying to get Steiner out of the ring. That brings Stacy up onto the apron and sees Grenier dropkick the bodyguard into her. When she falls off the apron, "Big Poppa Pump" catches her while Sylvan rolls up Test for a near fall. Things get worse moments later when Scott tags in only to see Test miss the heels and accidentally Big Boot him. Once La Resistance toss the bodyguard out to the floor, they finish off Steiner with a Double Flapjack for the victory. Post-match, Keibler checks on "Big Poppa Pump" until Test drags her away.

Backstage, Mr. America arrives. Gregory Helms is waiting to interview him and note that he's "not who he claims to be". The masked man argues that he's heard Helms is actually The Hurricane. Gregory says his sources are wrong and the two men agree that they aren't anyone else, wishing each other luck.

Further backstage, Eddie Guerrero tells Josh Mathews that since Chavo Guerrero Jr. isn't here tonight, he has the option of finding a replacement. "Latino Heat" says it wasn't easy to find anyone crazy enough to team with him, but he did so in Tajiri. The "Japanese Buzzsaw" laughs as he takes a gold medal and says that they "lie, cheat, and steal". Eddie then dedicates their match to Chavo.

MUST SEE! Eddie Guerrero/Tajiri def. Team Angle (WWE Tag Title "Ladder" match). As the babyfaces head to the ring, the announcers wish Chavo Guerrero Jr. well in his recovery from bicep surgery. The champions then attack, knocking Eddie into a tall ladder at ringside. That lets Team Angle double-team Tajiri inside the squared circle. After working him over, the champions rock "Latino Heat" with a double-team gutbuster. Even when the babyfaces try to respond with slingshot planchas, the champions manage to largely sidestep their attack. Once the challengers are back down, Team Angle set up a ladder in the center of the ring and climb up on opposite sides. That lets the "Japanese Buzzsaw" knock them both down with a handspring back elbow. After driving Benjamin from the ring, the babyfaces double baseball slide kick the ladder into Haas's groin. The challengers then introduce a second ladder and sandwich Charlie for an Eddie slingshot somersault splash. It hurts him too, but the sacrifice lets Tajiri set up a ladder and head up it. Unfortunately, Shelton is back up and drops the replacement babyface face-first onto the steel rungs. Guerrero recovers before Benjamin can climb up, but pays for his attack when the heel powerslams him onto a ladder propped up in a corner. Once Team Angle drive Eddie from the ring, they put the "Japanese Buzzsaw" onto one ladder for Shelton to dive off the second with a modified version of their leapfrog splash. Haas tries to grab the titles afterwards, but "Latino Heat" shoves the ladder over, dumping the champion on the floor. He then wedges a ladder in a corner only to see Benjamin reverse his Irish whip into the steel. Tajiri is back up though and kicks the champions repeatedly. He also uses the ladder to nail the heels' ribs before running through them at the same time. Once he knocks Shelton out to the floor, the "Japanese Buzzsaw" baseball slide kicks one of the ladders into him. He then traps Charlie in a Tarantula, but Benjamin makes the save smashing the challenger's skull with a ladder. Afterwards, Team Angle double-team Eddie. "Latino Heat" won't stay down, monkey flipping Shelton into Haas holding a ladder. He then chases off the champions and sets a ladder up. He can't even get up halfway before Team Angle return to fight with him. Guerrero doesn't quit either, fighting both men and tossing Benjamin to the canvas for a Frog Splash from the top of the ladder. Charlie tries to capitalize, heading up the ladder afterwards, but Eddie recovers and climbs up to punch the champion ahead of a sunset flip powerbomb off the ladder. "Latino Heat" goes back up the ladder, but Shelton grabs him from behind. Luckily, Tajiri comes to his partner's aid, spraying green mist between Guerrero's legs into the champion's face to blind him and allow Eddie to grab the gold to crown new champions.

In their skybox, Eric Bischoff says *Raw* should get Eddie Guerrero and Tajiri. He wants "Stone Cold" Steve Austin to call Eddie because "Latino Heat" won't take his calls. "Stone Cold" changes subjects and forces Eric to eat a hamburger and drink another beer. When Bischoff takes a sip, Austin opens the skybox window and criticizes his co-GM. With the fans cheering him on, the "rattlesnake" shows him how to drink. He then threatens to launch Eric out of the skybox if he doesn't start drinking.

Backstage, Terri asks Chris Jericho what he thinks his chances of winning the Intercontinental Title tonight are. He calls himself the "highlight of the night" before "Rowdy" Roddy Piper interrupts. Y2J tells him, slowly, that he's taken a wrong turn and the senior center is down the street. The two men then mock each other, Jericho wondering if Piper ate the fan's leg that he pulled off on *SmackDown!*. Despite being at odds, they both agree to rip their opponents to pieces tonight.

MUST SEE! Christian wins a 9-man Intercontinental Title Battle Royal.

Elimination Order	Wrestler	Eliminated By
1	Lance Storm	Kane
2	Kane	Booker T/Chris Jericho/Christian/Goldust/Test/Val Venis
3	Test	Booker T
4	Val Venis	Goldust
5	Rob Van Dam	Chris Jericho
6	Goldust	Booker T
7	Chris Jericho	Christian
8	Booker T	Christian
9	Christian	Winner

Ahead of the battle royal, JR tells fans that fifty-one competitors have held the Intercontinental Title in WWE history. We get to see several of those champions in a video package featuring former stars including Owen Hart. Afterwards, Howard Finkel introduces the first Intercontinental Champion, Pat Patterson, who comes out with the belt to present it to the winner of the match. Everyone is surprised that Val Venis follows, making his return after Chief Morley was fired. He says hello to the fans while Eric Bischoff throws a fit in his skybox. Once everyone else makes their entrances, the announcers wondering if Christian making his debut five years ago at this event is an omen and criticizing Booker T being the only non-former champion in the ring, the wrestlers turn on Kane. He doesn't go down without a fight, tossing Storm out first before everyone else gangs up on him. Once they eliminate the "Big Red Machine", the monster proves to be a poor sport and returns to attack and Chokeslam the competitors, including his tag team partner. Booker takes advantage, tossing out Test before Goldust eliminates Venis. Christian tries to eliminate RVD, but he lands on the apron only to see Y2J springboard dropkick him out to the floor. Thanks to the lightning fast eliminations, we are already down to four men. It's the heels seizing control with Jericho missile dropkicking the "bizarre one" and back suplexing him. He and Christian then try to eliminate Goldust, but Booker T makes the save. He pays courtesy of a flashback. When the heels attempt a double back body drop, the "bizarre one" drops down for fists to each man's jaw ahead of a double bulldog. The babyfaces then set up the heels for Shattered Dreams. Goldust hits both men before Booker side kicks Jericho. He follows up with a spinaroonie, but the "bizarre one" tries to capitalize and eliminate him. At the last second, Booker T reverses his whip for the elimination. Despite the betrayal, both babyfaces laugh. Booker doesn't laugh for long as the heels club and double suplex him. JR wonders if they can trust each other. So long as they can work together to wear down the five-time champion, it seems like they'll do that. Together, they nearly eliminate Booker, but he manages to hold onto the top rope and fight free of their attack. He's still outnumbered and hammered in a corner until he dodges a clothesline to punch and chop the heels. Booker T tries to eliminate Y2J, but the heel skins the cat and returns. With blood trickling down his nose, he watches Christian reverse DDT Booker. When he tries to follow up with a Lionsault, Christian shoves him out to the floor. That sets off Jericho and he pulls at the barricade while Christian laughs and pummels the five-time champion. Soon after, Booker T comes back to life with a flying forearm, spinning kick, and flapjack. Christian answers with a handful of hair and backward head slam. When he attempts a baseball slide kick against the ropes, Booker moves and the heel hits Chad Patton. That means there's no referee to see Booker T toss Christian out to the floor. Despite Booker's music playing, Christian grabs the Intercontinental Title from Patterson and decks him. He then returns to the ring where he bashes Booker's face with the gold. Afterwards, he spots Patton just getting up and shoves Booker T over the top rope to officially win the Intercontinental Title. The announcers can't believe it, but Jerry says the referee's decision is final. JR doesn't think Booker deserves all of this bad luck.

Backstage, Sable tells Torrie Wilson not to be nervous about their upcoming bikini contest. Torrie isn't, but Sable says she's never lost one. She then borrows Wilson's baby oil and rubs it onto her leg. Back at ringside, Tazz reveals that Lawler offered him a lot of money to host the bikini competition, but the thug turned him down. The *SmackDown!* announcers then display the tale of the tape ahead of a video package for the upcoming competition. Afterwards, Wilson dances behind a white screen as Lilian Garcia sings her theme song. Following that extended entrance, Sable comes out for Tazz to explain the rules of the contest. He gives each woman time to shake their butts, Sable going first in a tiny bikini. She grinds around quite a while, impressing Cole on commentary and making "the King" hyperventilate. Torrie then reveals her black bikini with pink bunnies. Both women get good pops so Tazz polls the audience one more time. Before the fans can decide a winner, Wilson strips down to an even skimpier bikini to get the victory. To make sure there are no hard feelings, Torrie kisses her opponent, dropping Tazz to a knee.

In the skybox, Eric Bischoff is drunk and struggling to eat or drink. "Stone Cold" Steve Austin tells him to eat more to absorb the alcohol. When Eric says he can't eat them, Austin gives him some pickles. Unfortunately, they are red hot jalapenos so "Stone Cold" pours some more beer in Bischoff's mouth to cool him down.

Backstage, "Rowdy" Roddy Piper is still upset about Chris Jericho. Sean O'Haire tells him not to worry about him and focus instead on Mr. America. Vince McMahon interrupts to ask if they understand what tonight means to him. The WWE owner calls Piper "the chosen one" and says without him there would be no Hulkamania or "Ruthless Aggression". After Roddy beats down Mr. America, McMahon promises to unmask him. Afterwards, we se footage of "Hot Rod" ripping off a fan's leg Thursday night.

Mr. America (with Zach Gowen) def. "Roddy" Roddy Piper (with Sean O'Haire). The heels are out first, followed by Mr. America bringing a chair into the squared circle to chase off Piper and O'Haire. Afterwards, he says the chair is for a "real American" and introduces Zach to be in his corner tonight. When the bell rings though, the heels double-team Mr. America in front of Jimmy Korderas. After a few seconds, they do some normal heel cheating, Roddy distracting the ref for Sean's cheap shots. They don't keep the masked man down for long, Mr. America coming back to life to mount Piper in a corner and pull up his mask to bite his head. Unfortunately, no one gets a good look at him. When he leaves the squared circle to choke O'Haire at ringside with his weight belt, Roddy dives out onto the masked man. He gets in a few shots before Mr. America whips him back. Unfortunately, O'Haire is back up and throat drops him onto the top rope into a Sleeper Hold. It takes him a minute, but the masked man "Americas up" and unloads with a string of fists and a big boot. When he sets up for a Legdrop though, Vince McMahon marches out to distract him and the referee. "Hot Rod" capitalizes with a low blow. Vince then hands O'Haire a pipe and distracts the referee. When Sean tries to blast Mr. America though, the masked man ducks and O'Haire hits Piper. Mr. America follows up with a Legdrop for the three-count, Gowen holding back Mr. McMahon from breaking the cover. Post-match, the winner flexes and motions for the heels to kiss his butt.

Backstage, Stephanie McMahon and Triple H cross paths. In an awkward moment, she tells her ex-husband to be careful. Afterwards, a video package plays for the upcoming World Title match.

Kevin Nash def. Triple H (World Title match) by disqualification. Shawn Michaels is out first, followed by "Big Sexy" to a good pop. Ric Flair gets an even bigger reaction before Triple H enters last. Nash greets him and his purple trunks with a flurry of fists in the shortened aisle before the bell. When Flair and Michaels start to fight, Earl Hebner orders them backstage despite the WWE heavily promoting them being involved in the match. Kevin briefly takes the fight into the ring, but following a back body drop the friends turned enemies fight out on the floor again. When they return to the squared circle, the challenger connects with a big boot and trio of elbow drops. Hunter answers with an eye gouge before shoving the referee. Moments later, Helmsley drops "Big Sexy" with a swinging neckbreaker. Fists follow in a corner, but "the Game" can't keep Nash down. He responds with his own fists and shoves Hebner also. When Earl grabs his hair, the challenger threatens him before composing himself only to see the champion miss "Big Sexy" and accidentally deck the referee. With the official down, Triple H gives Nash a low blow. He then pulls off the top turnbuckle pad, but Kevin avoids a shot into the exposed steel to sidewalk slam Hunter. A big boot follows, but when he picks up Helmsley to snake eyes him, "the Game" slips free and rams "Big Sexy's" head into the bolt for a Pedigree and near fall. He tries to Pedigree Nash a second time, but the challenger back body drops Triple H over the top rope to escape. At ringside, the champion grabs a sledgehammer, but Hebner stops him from using it. He pays when Hunter hits him with the weapon for the disqualification. Post-match, Kevin unloads with a big boot and snake eyes onto the exposed bolt. Not done, he Jackknifes "the Game" before spotting the sledgehammer. Luckily, WWE officials grab the champion and carry him up the aisle. Unfortunately, Nash follows and continues his assault, knocking down Flair when he tries to intervene. He even shoves the "Heartbreak Kid" down before Jackknifing Hunter through the *Raw* announce table by the entrance. As trainers attend to Helmsley, JR says that you hate to see anyone, including "the Game", treated like "Big Sexy" did him.

Back in the skybox, "Stone Cold" Steve Austin applauds Kevin Nash's initiative as the waitress brings in a tray of buffalo wings. Eric Bischoff has had enough and throws up out of the skybox onto the fans. Austin offers to clean him up, pouring beer on his co-GM before we get another shot of Eric vomiting.

Jazz (with Theodore Long) def. Jacqueline and Trish Stratus and Victoria (with Steven Richards) (Women's Title match). Richards trips Trish for the heels to attack her to open the match. When Jacqueline helps Stratus clear the ring, the two babyfaces lock up. This time, Victoria trips the vixen and pulls her out to the floor for a whip into the ring post. Inside the ring, Jacqueline suplexes Jazz for a two-count, but the "black widow" makes the save. She follows up with a spinning slam for a near fall, but this time the champion makes the save ahead of a double chicken wing slam to both women. Trish recovers and returns to clothesline Jazz for a near fall. Unfortunately, the champion catches her Chick Kick and applies an STF. Jacqueline takes her time making the save. In fact, she waits so long that

Victoria stops her. Jacqueline traps her in a single leg crab while Stratus pulls her way to the ropes for the break. Afterwards, the champion breaks Jacqueline's submission hold and locks the "black widow" in another STF. This time, Trish makes the save with a dropkick. Moments later, she ducks a clothesline with a Matrix move to Chick Kick Jazz for a near fall. Jacqueline and Victoria join the fight, battling in one corner for Stratus to toss both heels to the canvas with handstand head scissors. When she attempts to give Victoria Stratusfaction, the "black widow" tosses her out to the floor. She tries to follow up with a Widow's Peak to the other babyface, but Jacqueline slips free for a northern lights suplex. Unfortunately, Jazz makes the save with a big splash followed by a DDT to Jacqueline for the win.

Brock Lesnar def. Big Show (WWE Title "Stretcher" match). Following a video package for the feud, Tony Chimel explains that the only way to win this match is to put the opponent on a stretcher and wheel them past a yellow line in the aisle. Show then comes out with a stretcher, the announcers wondering if he can lose this match due to his size. He tries to hit the champion with the weapon, but Brock ducks and uses the stretcher himself to knock the giant out to the floor. There, he hits him with the hard plastic until Big Show knocks the weapon free and headbutts Lesnar. The challenger then sets up the stretcher against the ring post, but when he tries to slam the "next big thing" onto it, Brock slips free and rams the gurney into Show. Despite that, the giant quickly recovers to slam the champion and hit him with the stretcher again. Back in the squared circle, Big Show Chokeslams Lesnar. Afterwards, he puts the "next big thing" on the stretcher for a big leg drop. Once he's out, the challenger drags Brock to the apron and onto a gurney. He makes it halfway up the aisle before the champion kicks his way free. Despite that shot, Show knocks him off the stretcher and past the yellow line, Cole letting everyone know that he has to be on the stretcher to lose. Instead of putting him on it, Big Show beats Lesnar with the stretcher. The "next big thing" responds in kind, wailing on the giant in the aisle. He then grabs a camera cable and chokes out Show. Unfortunately, the cable ends up saving the challenger because it keeps Brock from dragging him past the yellow line. When both men get back up, the champion uses the stage set to swing up and kick Big Show. He follows up with a big spear, the announcers speculating on him playing professional football. That's a little bit away, so Lesnar slams the giant onto the stretcher. When he tries to run Show over with the gurney, the challenger grabs it and rams the "next big thing" back into the apron. He follows up with a slam against the ring post. More stretcher shots follow, but Brock won't give up, knocking Big Show off the apron and onto a gurney. With the giant down, the champion heads backstage. Rey Mysterio takes this opportunity to enter the ring to 619 Show. The challenger answers with a vicious clothesline. He then motions for a Chokeslam, but Lesnar returns on a forklift to distract him. Mysterio takes advantage, hopping onto Big Show's back to try to choke him out. When he flings the masked man off, the "next big thing" flies off the forklift with a cross body block to a big pop. Corner shots and a suplex follow before Brock hoists up the giant for an F5. Afterwards, the champion puts the stretcher on a pallet and backs up the forklift with Show on it to retain the championship.

Judgment Day is an okay PPV that just feels like it's there. Just three weeks after Backlash, it's impressive the WWE could build the show they did. The opener has no build, but is a fun four-minute six-man tag match. Including Nunzio, four minutes isn't enough for seven men, but it's not enough to be bad either. La Resistance's PPV debut is worse, but at just six minutes, it's another match that doesn't have time to be awful. That's good because no in the match is putting on classics at this point. The "Ladder" match is very good and having everyone legal at all times promises a lot of fun action and spots. It's the best match of the night and the only **MUST SEE!** contest. Christian winning the belt is big, but the battle royal flies by with five men eliminated in the opening minutes. After that, it's a four-man match featuring familiar rivals before Christian surprises everyone with the victory. Torrie and Sable fill time afterwards. If you enjoy bikini contests, this is for you. If you don't, skip it. You can also skip all of the Austin/Bischoff vignettes, culminating in Eric spewing beer on some fans. There's nothing of note that happens and it's a shame that the WWE wasted so much time on their antics in unfunny skits. Mr. America and Piper are far past their primes, but with under five minutes of action and outside the ring antics, the match doesn't feel long. That's pretty much a trend all night. Even the World Title match only gets seven and a half minutes. Even more egregious is the WWE pushing Shawn and Flair being in Nash and Triple H's corners only to see them evicted from ringside before the contest officially starts. The match itself is a good brawl and it's obviously what the WWE was hoping for with Scott Steiner and Hunter. The fans don't turn on Kevin and he looks legitimately pissed as he stalks after and destroys "the Game" before Helmsley gets himself disqualified to set up a future match. The women of *Raw* then have a four-way match with some good action. Like the opener, four women plus two men outside the ring have a hard time fitting a match in with just five minutes, but it also prevents the action from dragging. Jazz winning is good as she continues to be the dominant female on the roster while Jacqueline taking the loss protects both Trish and Victoria. Finally, Lesnar and Show beat on each other for fifteen minutes. Big Show isn't having technical masterpieces, but he does entertain with a brutal battle that sees both men hitting each other with the stretcher repeatedly. Brock really gets the fans on their feet after he drives a forklift down the aisle for a flying cross body block. This is right up there with the "Ladder" match for most entertaining of the night. Ultimately, Judgment Day isn't bad, but it's not great either. The WWE wastes a lot of time outside the ring with the *Raw* co-GMs as well as Sable and Torrie's bikini contest (technically in the ring). However, that keeps the matches from dragging and makes for an entertaining three hours. It's a fast view and there's nothing that's terrible. However, it's not great either making this a middle of the road PPV that you can mostly skip without missing too much.

Monday Night Raw
May 19, 2003
Greenville, SC
Announcers: Jim Ross, Jerry "the King" Lawler, Theodore Long (briefly)

Following the intro video and fireworks, "Stone Cold" Steve Austin heads to the ring to say he had a great time at Judgment Day. While he had fun drinking beer, eating food, and watching great matches, Austin was less happy to share his skybox with Eric Bischoff who made a fool of himself. "Stone Cold" shows him doing that, playing multiple angles of Eric puking on the crowd. The "rattlesnake" says Bischoff isn't here tonight because he's got a hangover. The show must go on and Austin is happy to guarantee satisfaction at June's Bad Blood PPV, a *Raw* exclusive show presented by "Stone Cold". Austin then changes course and promises to find out who tried to run over Goldberg last week. When he does, the "rattlesnake" will give Bill a match against the assailant tonight. The co-general manager changes topics again, this time talking about Triple H. That brings the World Champion limping down the aisle, accompanied by Ric Flair. Austin doesn't have time for his music and "stupid water" spit. "Stone Cold" isn't happy with how Helmsley retained his title last night, hitting Earl Hebner with a sledgehammer. Because of that and the fact that Hunter is a bully, Austin signs him to a title defense tonight. "The Game" argues that he's injured and has some stroke. The "rattlesnake" has even more stroke, guaranteeing Triple H that he will wrestle tonight. However, he'll let him pick his own opponent so long as they are a former heavyweight champion. After thinking it over, Hunter agrees to wrestle tonight...against his friend, Flair. Austin doesn't like that while Ric is confused.

The Dudley Boyz def. Three-Minute Warning (with Rico). Good guys again, the Dudleys go right after the Samoans to start the match. Unfortunately, when D-Von runs the ropes, Jamal low bridges him for Three-Minute Warning to take control. That includes a Rosey leg drop and Samoan double headbutt. Afterwards, Jamal gets a two-count with a knee drop. Rosey illegally enters the ring moments later for a superkick, scoring Jamal a near fall. When Jamal goes up to the second rope for a corner bomb, Dudley answers with a pair of knees. Bubba Ray gets the hot tag afterwards to elbow and cross body block Rosey off the second rope for a two-count. He then fights both heels while JR shills "Classy" Freddie Blassie's autobiography. Although Rosey rocks Bubba with a clothesline for a two-count, D-Von rushes to his partner's aid and the Dudleys double suplex the Samoan. A wassup drop follows before Bubba Ray tells D-Von to get a table. Unfortunately, Jamal baseball slide kicks it into his face. That leaves Bubba against two men again, culminating in a Jamal pop-up Samoan Drop. Luckily, Charles Robinson remembers that Rosey is the legal man. While he argues with Jamal, Rico slides a table into the ring. Jamal sets D-Von onto it and heads upstairs for a Flying Splash. At the last second, D-Von moves and the Samoan crashes through the wood. A 3D follows to Rosey for The Dudley Boyz to score the victory. Post-match, Rico yells at his clients. He's had enough and tells them that he's "leaving" in the goofiest manner possible. Other than a *Heat* match, this marks the end of Three-Minute Warning's run.

After a commercial break, Eric Bischoff is nearly passed out in a chair. "Stone Cold" Steve Austin says they have a show to run and don't have time to rest. Austin says the secret is for Bischoff to have a drink to beat his hangover. Unfortunately, just the smell of beer makes Eric throw up on a picture of himself. When "Stone Cold" leaves their office, Kevin Nash confronts him. Austin tells "Big Sexy" that he's the number one contender for the World Title and he'll get a shot at the winner of the Ric Flair/Triple H match.

Speaking of, Ric Flair tells Triple H how honored he is to get a match with "the Game" tonight. Hunter stops him. Helmsley says he picked him so the World Champion can have an easy night and recover from the injuries he suffered last night. Triple H walks Flair through how their match will go with Ric laying down for "the Game".

After a commercial break, Chris Jericho heads to the ring for a new installment of the Highlight Reel. This week he introduces the "Jeritron 5000", a small flatscreen television, to show footage of Christian "screwing him" last night to win the Intercontinental Title. That brings out the new champion with a new short haircut. Jericho calls him a "new man", but is mad that Christian slapped him in the face. However, Y2J would have done the same thing and loves it, hugging the new champion. Christian thanks him and his Peeps for making him the new "American Idol". Jericho jokes that he's not even American. Some people think that Christian won under questionable circumstances, Y2J showing footage of the champion being eliminated while the referee was down and out. Christian says Booker T doesn't deserve the championship because he doesn't have the champion's charisma or "cool haircut". Jericho thinks Booker looks like a pineapple. When Christian continues bragging, Rob Van Dam interrupts. He says the champion is trying to make changes, but everyone knows he still sucks. RVD wants Christian to give everyone what they really want and give Van Dam an Intercontinental Title shot. The champion tells him no before the heels attack. That brings out Kane to save his tag team partner and chase off the Canadians. "Stone Cold" Steve Austin interrupts to say that he respects what Christian did to get the belt. However, he also likes a good fight and he sees one in the ring, signing all four men to a World Tag Title match after the ring crew clears the Highlight Reel from the squared circle.

Kane/Rob Van Dam def. Chris Jericho/Christian (World Tag Title match) by disqualification. After a commercial break, Jericho and Van Dam trade shots. When Christian tags in, wearing street clothes instead of wrestling gear, Rob kicks him down and tags in Kane to punch and stomp the new Intercontinental Champion. The "Big Red Machine" follows up with a powerslam for a two-count before flinging Christian from the ring. He follows up by press slamming Y2J onto his own partner before whipping Van Dam over the top rope for a somersault splash onto both heels. Back in the ring, the monster sidewalk slams Jericho ahead of an RVD rolling thunder and near fall. The champion follows up with kicks and shoulder blocks, but when he goes for a monkey flip, Christian holds his partner. Y2J capitalizes with a second rope missile dropkick before the new "People's Champ" tags in to choke the popular superstar with his shirt. He then slows the pace with a reverse chin lock. When Rob fights free, Christian rocks him with a reverse backbreaker for a two-count, but Kane makes the save. Y2J tags in afterwards to leg drop Van Dam on the ropes and cover him with a foot on the chest. The heels take turns stomping RVD before Christian powerslams him for another near fall. He returns to choking the popular superstar before Jericho tags in to apply his own chin lock. Eventually, Rob elbows free only to run into a spinning heel kick. Moments later, Van Dam nearly steals the win with a small package, but Y2J just kicks out. When he tags in Christian though, RVD fights off the heels and tags in the "Big Red Machine" to kick Christian and toss Jericho out to the floor. He follows up with a two-handed chokeslam to Christian, but misses an elbow drop. Despite that, the monster sits up and grabs the heel for a Chokeslam. Luckily, Y2J distracts him climbing the ropes. He pays when Kane shoves Christian back into the corner to crotch Jericho. A top rope flying clothesline from the "Big Red Machine" follows to the Intercontinental Champion, but Y2J makes the save. Van Dam returns afterwards to knock Jericho from the ring ahead of a Chokeslam to Christian. When RVD tries to follow up with a Five-Star Frog Splash, Y2J shoves him off the ropes and into the barricade. The monster answers with a powerslam, but when he sets up for the Chokeslam, Christian low blows him. A Lionsault follows, but Kane just manages to kick out of Christian's cover. Frustrated, the heels grab chairs and shove the referee aside for the disqualification. Before they can give the "Big Red Machine" a conchairto, Booker T runs out for the save, chasing away Jericho and side kicking Christian to a big pop. Afterwards, Booker celebrates with a spinaroonie.

Backstage, Shawn Michaels stops Ric Flair and talks to him "man-to-man". Shawn says that "The Nature Boy" cannot lay down in the ring because he's the "measuring stick". Michaels adds that wrestlers are only as good as their last match. Ric wonders if the "Heartbreak Kid" really thinks he can beat Triple H. Shawn does, telling Flair he's the only one who has to believe it.

Rodney Mack (with Theodore Long) def. Spike Dudley ("White Boy Challenge" match). Pre-match, Long says the heels haven't had much opposition in the "White Boy Challenge" and offers an opportunity for anyone to give Mack a fight. Dudley answers, but he's steamrolled through the opening two minutes as Theodore heads to the announce table to provide guest commentary. When Spike tries to fight back, Rodney slams him to the canvas for a two-count. Unfortunately, thirty seconds later he misses a shoulderblock and falls out to the floor. Halfway through the match, the runt flies off the top rope onto Mack on the floor. Back in the squared circle, he nearly steals the win with a roll-up. A second roll-up gets him a two-count before he slams Rodney's face to the mat despite missing him by several feet on his bulldog attempt. When he tries to follow up with a Dudley Dog, Mack counters with a powerslam. Dudley holds onto the rope to try to last the full five-minutes and win the challenge, but Rodney pulls him back and locks him in a cobra clutch, called the Black Out, with a minute left. Although Spike holds on until the last second, Dudley finally taps out.

The Castrol GTX WWE Rewind is Victoria slamming Trish Stratus over the top rope last night. JR says Trish is banged up after busting open her mouth and isn't here tonight.

After the announcers talk about Ric Flair facing Triple H later, "Stone Cold" Steve Austin yells in Eric Bischoff's ear with a megaphone. He then pounds on a trashcan lid and blares the megaphone to mess with the hungover co-GM. Austin says the real way of getting over a hangover is "female entertainment". Bischoff isn't in the mood, but "Stone Cold" insists and invites Mae Young and The Fabulous Moolah into the office. Eric has had enough of them and kicks them out of the office, noting that they stink.

After a commercial break, Ric Flair dons a robe and gets ready for his match later.

La Resistance def. Scott Steiner/Test (with Stacy Keibler). Scott and Test open the match arguing about who will start for their team and La Resistance capitalize, attacking them from behind. After Dupree whips Steiner into the ring steps, Stacy checks on him while the heels double back suplex the bodyguard for a near fall. They take turns hammering him until he rocks Rene with a Big Boot. When he attempts to pumphandle slam Sylvan, the heel slips free and shoves Test into "Big Poppa Pump". That stuns both men and Grenier capitalizes by rolling up the bodyguard for the win. Post-match, Scott and Test shove each other and fight over Keibler. She's had enough and storms off.

Backstage, "Stone Cold" Steve Austin enters an "interrogation room", according to the small piece of cardboard in the window. JR then shows the results of a WWE.com poll that says The Rock is the most likely suspect to have attempted to run over Goldberg last week.

After a commercial break, "Stone Cold" Steve Austin interrogates Lance Storm. He wants to know where he was in 1989. Lance wants to know what that has to do with anything, but Austin is just checking if he'll lie. When pressed, Storm says it was an accident and the gas got stuck on his rental car.

He blames his mistake on being Canadian and driving on the "wrong side of the road". "Stone Cold" know that Canadians drive on the same side of the road and doesn't buy it. While Storm says it was someone else's idea, the "rattlesnake" doesn't care. He tells Lance to head to the ring for his match with Goldberg.

Further backstage, Ric Flair is fired up as he yells at Triple H, telling him that he's not laying down in Greensboro. "The Nature Boy" says he's had thousands of tough matches like Hunter had last night and he always showed up. Tonight, Flair wants to see if he's still got it and is going to take Helmsley to the limits. "The Game" doesn't like that.

Goldberg def. Lance Storm. Bill doesn't care if it was an accident or not that Lance tried to run him over. He proceeds to destroy the Canadian, kneeing and slamming him as soon as he gets into the ring. A Spear follows before Goldberg Jackhammers Storm for the victory. The announcers speculate on who put Lance up to trying to run over the intense superstar. Goldberg does his own interrogation, choking Storm until he says it was Chris Jericho behind the attack.

After a commercial break, Jonathan Coachman follows Chris Jericho out into the parking lot to ask him about what Lance Storm said. Y2J admits that he told Storm to run over Goldberg. Next week, Jericho promises to do it face-to-face himself.

Triple H def. Ric Flair (World Title match). Flair is out first, JR calling it like Mickey Mantle getting one more at bat. Triple H follows, too injured to even spit water. When Hunter offers his mentor a handshake, Ric fakes him out. That sets off Helmsley and he corners "The Nature Boy". When he mockingly offers a "woooo", Flair slaps and chops him. One back elbow from the heavily bandaged champion slows Ric's attack. "The Nature Boy" quickly recovers and takes the fight out to the floor to suplex "the Game". Back in the ring, a second suplex gets him a near fall, but the champion answers with a spinebuster. He follows up with chokes and a whip up and over the top rope. Shockingly, Ric runs along the apron and climbs the ropes to finally hit a top rope flying ax-handle. More fists follow before Flair struts and chop blocks Triple H. Lawler can't believe that Mantle is about to hit a homerun. He does so with his Figure Four Leglock, drawing a big pop from the fans. Despite the fans cheering on "The Nature Boy", Hunter manages to reach the ropes for boos. The two men then trade strikes in a corner, Helmsley taking advantage of Nick Patrick pulling Ric back for a hard right hand. He follows up with a sleeper hold, but Flair pushes him back into a corner, squashing the referee. "The Game" answers with a facebuster, but when he grabs the World Title, "The Nature Boy" ducks his shot and pokes the champion's eyes. He then lands his own title shot for an extremely close two-count. Once again, he struts and sets up for the Figure Four. This time Triple H kicks him into the corner to escape. He follows up with a back body drop and Pedigree for a surprisingly competitive victory. Post-match, Kevin Nash strides out, chasing off Hunter who retreats up the ramp with his World Title. "Stone Cold" Steve Austin congratulates him before telling Helmsley that he's got a match with Nash at Bad Blood for the championship inside the Hell in a Cell. "The Game" is horrified to end the show, but Kevin loves it.

SmackDown!
May 22, 2003
Greensboro, NC
Announcers: Michael Cole, Tazz, Rey Mysterio (briefly)

The show opens with a video package of Mr. America beating "Rowdy" Roddy Piper at Judgment Day despite Vince McMahon's interference. Afterwards, the WWE owner storms out onto the stage to say he's in a foul mood. He says he hasn't been happy with all the mistakes Stephanie McMahon has been making as the general manager. While she'll keep the job, Vince says tonight he's taking over to deal with Mr. America and end the mistakes. A new intro video and song, "I Want It All", then plays ahead of the fireworks.

Eddie Guerrero/Tajiri def. Team Angle (WWE Tag Title match) by disqualification. After losing the belts at Judgment Day, Team Angle tries to get them back two weeks before Kurt Angle's return. They don't have any luck early on as Tajiri fights off both heels. When Eddie tags in, he gets a nice pop. Haas greets him with some shoulders, but a leaping arm drag and head scissors have the challenger seeing stars. The "Japanese Buzzsaw" returns afterwards to kick and chop Charlie until the heel tackles him to the canvas. He can't follow up as Tajiri kicks him and tags in Guerrero to suplex both heels. When Shelton misses a clothesline, "Latino Heat" runs him out to the floor. Haas joins him ahead of a "Japanese Buzzsaw" somersault plancha and commercial break.

Afterwards, Eddie tries to triple suplex Benjamin, but Charlie tags in to sunset flip Guerrero before he can deliver his third. When the heel can't take Guerrero down, Shelton follows up with a neckbreaker off the second rope to swing the momentum. Haas hits his own neckbreaker and nearly wins back the titles, but "Latino Heat" just kicks out. Unfortunately, he's trapped on the heel side of the ring and Benjamin powerslams him for another near fall. Charlie also gets in several shots before planting Eddie on the top rope. Guerrero fights back, hitting both heels and shoving Haas to the canvas for a Frog Splash. At the last second, the former champion counters with a pair of knees for another two-count. Staying on the offensive, he delivers a backbreaker before locking on the Haas of Pain. Fortunately, Tajiri makes the save with a dropkick to the back of the head. Despite that, the challengers remain in control, Shelton locking on an abdominal stretch. When Mike Chioda turns around to deal with the "Japanese Buzzsaw", Haas illegally switches places with his partner. Even when "Latino Heat" escapes, Charlie double leg slams him for a near fall. A double-team leapfrog splash follows, but Tajiri breaks up the cover. Soon after, Eddie shows signs of life with a string of fists and kicks. He follows up with a top rope arm drag and head scissors to Team Angle before the "Japanese Buzzsaw" tags in to kick down Shelton. A handspring elbow and tornado DDT follow, but Haas makes the save. That brings Guerrero over to tackle Charlie out to the floor. Unfortunately, when Tajiri hooks Benjamin in the Tarantula, Haas makes the save. Shelton follows up with a Dragon Whip, but before Chioda can make the three-count, "Latino Heat" hits him with a chair weakly. He then tosses the weapon to Charlie so that when the referee stands up he sees Haas holding the chair and disqualifies him. Team Angle can't stand it.

After the announcers show footage of "Rowdy" Roddy Piper pulling off Zach Gowen's prosthetic leg, Cole reveals that Stephanie McMahon will interview the fan later. Speaking of Stephanie, she stops her father backstage and asks Vince McMahon if he's okay. The WWE owner is just tired of mistakes.

After a commercial break, Vince McMahon heads out to the squared circle. He says he was disappointed with Judgment Day since it wasn't the end of Mr. America. Vince is still ranting about mistakes and says tonight instead of someone having to "pay the piper", "Rowdy" Roddy Piper will have to apologize to the WWE owner. That brings out "Hot Rod" and Sean O'Haire. Reluctantly, Piper apologizes only to be slapped. When McMahon calls him "sniveling" and tries to slap him again, Roddy stops him. He warns Vince not to touch him again. That sets off the WWE owner and they tease a fight until Sean steps in between them. He knows they all want revenge and offers to face Mr. America tonight. McMahon likes that idea, but tells Piper that if his protégé doesn't win, "Hot Rod" is fired.

John Cena def. Spanky. Pre-match, Cena calls Spanky a pale imitation of himself and tries to get the fans to end his rap by cursing for him. The babyface then runs out to attack John, but one big shot puts the cruiserweight down on the canvas. A snap suplex moments later gets the rapping heel a two-count. Showing ruthless aggression, Cena hammers Spanky and rams his head into the middle turnbuckle for a near fall. Tazz says he uses his "smashing" style to wear down his opponents. He also adds in a delayed vertical suplex for a two-count. Just when he looks done, the rookie responds with fists and an enziguri for his own near fall. That's as close as Spanky will get to a win as John levels him with a shoulderblock before scoring the victory with an FU.

Still shots of Brock Lesnar beating Big Show in their "Stretcher" match are shown.

Backstage, Johnny Stamboli is impressed with how good he looks in a magazine. Nunzio tells him to focus on Brock Lesnar. Johnny is sure he'll knock the "People's eyebrow" off him. Chuck Palumbo tells him he's facing Brock, not The Rock. Nunzio interrupts to say that when you face one member of The FBI, you face them all.

Chris Benoit def. Matt Hardy Version 1.0 (with Crash Holly/Shannon Moore). Rey Mysterio heads out first to provide guest commentary and scout the Cruiserweight Champion. Matt Facts reveal that Hardy likes his steaks medium well and has more teeth than Benoit. "The Crippler" follows to slap the champion's hand hard and attempt to lock on an early Crippler Crossface. When Hardy reaches the ropes, Benoit pulls him back to the center of the ring for a whip to the canvas. Rey reveals during this time that he is cleared to compete in the ring once again before the "rabid wolverine" hooks an armbar. When he transitions into a hammerlock, Matt elbows free. Benoit responds with chops and a German suplex. That brings Moore and Holly into the ring to distract Brian Hebner for a Hardy low blow. A side effect follows for a near fall before the champion grounds "the Crippler" with a neck wrench. When Benoit escapes, Matt traps him in a sleeper hold. It doesn't take the "rabid wolverine" long to reverse the hold, but a side slam gets Hardy a two-count. He also gets a two-count with a leg drop on the middle rope, using the bottom rope for added leverage on his cover. Continuing to focus on the neck, a neckbreaker gets the champion another near fall before he hooks a front face lock. Eventually, Benoit drives him back into a corner to escape, but Matt drops him quickly for a second rope leg drop and two-count. When he sets up for the Twist of Fate, the "rabid wolverine" shoves him free for both men to connect head-to-head off the ropes. They work Hebner's count to eight before trading fists. Benoit gets the better of the exchange and scores a near fall with a backbreaker. Although Hardy blocks a German suplex, "the Crippler" catapults him into the ring post ahead of a back suplex. Benoit follows up with a top rope diving headbutt. When that brings Moore onto the apron, Mysterio knocks him down ahead of a 619 to Holly. Inside the ring, the "rabid wolverine" escapes another Twist of Fate attempt and scores the tap-out victory with the Crippler Crossface. Post-match, Matt has had enough of Rey. He tells him that he's going to be the one laughing when Shannon and Crash beat up the masked man. However, if Mysterio can beat them, he'll give him a Cruiserweight Title shot.

Rey Mysterio def. Crash Holly/Shannon Moore (with Matt Hardy Version 1.0). Following a commercial break, Rey dodges a Moore corner charge that sees the MFer hit the ring post hard. He then knocks Crash into position for a 619, but Shannon trips him for the save. Moments later, Holly back body drops Mysterio out to the floor where Moore tosses him into the ring post. The MFers follow up with a double press slam for a two-count. When they attempt a double suplex, the masked man counters with a double DDT to put everyone down. After they catch their breath, Rey punches and kicks the heels ahead of a bombs away splash to Holly. A springboard cross body block gets him a two-count, but tweaks Mysterio's groin. He's slow to follow up a low corner dropkick, but despite the pain, he puts Moore down onto the ropes for a 619 and West Coast Pop for the three-count. Not done, he also has to beat Crash, but does so quickly, countering a powerbomb with a hurricanrana for the win. Post-match, WWE officials carry Rey backstage while Matt attacks his MFers and leaves them laying with a side effect to Holly and Twist of Fate for Shannon. Thankfully, Mysterio avoids a serious injury here.

After a commercial break, Stephanie McMahon sits down with Zach Gowen and apologizes for his treatment last week. She then asks him about losing his leg at eight years old. Zach says it was tough, but his mom helped him through it. That's good because he says he doesn't have much of a relationship with his father. Stephanie notes that Gowen received a "Make-a-Wish" because his cancer was so serious. Zach says it would have been to meet Hulk Hogan, but he passed on the wish because he knew he was going to live. McMahon wonders what's next for him. Gowen says it's to be a professional wrestler and he hopes to one day step into the ring. Stephanie says, "anything can happen in the WWE". Vince McMahon doesn't agree, glaring at a screen backstage.

Following another commercial break, Vince McMahon tells Mr. America that if he loses his match tonight he'll have to take a lie detector test next week. The masked man says he's not losing and he's not taking a test. Vince tells him he will because if Mr. America doesn't, Zach Gowen will never get a shot to wrestle in the WWE or anywhere. With his back to the wall, the masked man accepts. Once again, McMahon rants about proving that Mr. America is a fraud. The storyline is fine and it's goofy fun, but the WWE focusing so much on it with such a talented roster is becoming overkill.

Brock Lesnar def. Johnny Stamboli (with Chuck Palumbo/Nunzio) by disqualification. Brock's WWE Title run is a perfect example of the WWE spending too much time on Vince McMahon and Mr. America. His appearance here seems like an afterthought. He's out first and doesn't know which member of the trio he'll face. He doesn't care, attacking them all, but he's outnumbered and stomped down until "the Bull" officially starts the match. He doesn't get in much offense before Lesnar rams him into opposite corners and clotheslines Johnny. A big fallaway slam brings Nunzio onto the apron for the champion to fling him into the ring. Palumbo capitalizes on the numbers advantage, ramming Brock's shoulder into the ring post before clotheslining him down on the floor. That lets Stamboli unload with a string of boots for a two-count. A second whip into the ring post stuns Lesnar ahead of a shoulderbreaker and pair of two-counts. Continuing to focus on the arm, "the Bull" applies an armbar. He soon transitions into a cross arm breaker, but Tazz disagrees with that strategy. He doesn't think anyone should try to outwrestle the champion. Brock isn't worried about proving his amateur acumen, picking up Johnny with one arm and slamming him to the canvas. A belly-to-belly suplex follows, but when he picks up Stamboli for an F5, the other heels attack for the disqualification. Chuck lays out the "next big thing" with a Superkick while Nunzio grabs a chair. Before he can use it, The Undertaker makes his return to attack The FBI and fling Nunzio out of the ring. Lesnar is back up soon afterwards for the babyfaces to clear the squared circle to a big pop.

After a commercial break, Sable heads to the ring to brag about being on the cover of the new *Raw* magazine and not Torrie Wilson. Once she's done hyping up her photoshoot, Sable heads over to the announce table to tell Tazz that she is "the diva". Standing on the announce table in front of him, Sable says it's not fair that the fans didn't get to vote for her Sunday. She wonders if the thug really thinks she should have won, posing provocatively. Sable then mocks him for being "premature" in making a decision before pouring water on Tazz. While that fires him up, the thug quickly composes himself as Sable walks away.

Backstage, Vince McMahon talks to "Rowdy" Roddy Piper and Sean O'Haire. The WWE owner is looking forward to Sean beating Mr. America tonight so he can force the masked man to take a lie detector test next week. Vince doesn't need to remind the heels that "Hot Rod" will be fired if O'Haire loses. One way or another, McMahon says he'll be happy at the end of the night.

Sean O'Haire (with "Rowdy" Roddy Piper) def. Mr. America (with Zach Gowen) by count-out. Zach accompanies Mr. America once again and holds his American flag while the masked man tears off his good ripping shirt. When the heels come out, O'Haire shows off his power flinging Mr. America down to the canvas twice. The masked man answers with a shove of his own before unloading with right hands and a clothesline. More fists and chops follow before Mr. America crushes Sean in a corner. When he runs the ropes, Piper grabs the patriot's leg allowing O'Haire to take control with a slam and kicks for a two-count. A kick to the face also gets him a near fall before Sean hooks a sloppy chin lock. Roddy wants the timekeeper to ring the bell and end the match since his career is on the line. He nearly gets his wish, but Mr. America just manages to keep his arm up on Mike Chioda's third check. Unfortunately, he then runs into a superkick and two-count. That wakes him up and the masked man Americas up to punch O'Haire and "Hot Rod". He follows up with a big boot and Legdrop, but Piper pulls Mr. America off his protégé before the referee can count to three. Vince McMahon's music plays afterwards as the WWE owner brings police officers down to ringside. He wants them to arrest Gowen for trespassing tonight and assaulting Mr. McMahon at Judgment Day. The WWE owner even takes away Zach's cane, calling it a weapon. When Mr. America leaves to check on his friend, Chioda counts him out. Roddy celebrates having a job while Vince laughs. When the masked man goes after the WWE owner, "Hot Rod" hits him with a chair. The show ends with McMahon telling Mr. America "goodbye".

Monday Night Raw

May 26, 2003
Mobile, AL
Announcers: Jim Ross, Jerry "the King" Lawler, Trish Stratus (briefly)

The show opens with a two and a half minute video package featuring Ric Flair challenging Triple H last week. Afterwards, the intro video plays and fireworks explode before Shawn Michaels heads to the ring to introduce "The Nature Boy", calling him the "greatest heavyweight champion of all-time". Shawn says he's waited eighteen years to tell Ric how great he is and how much Flair means to the "Heartbreak Kid". While Michaels thinks "The Nature Boy" is the greatest of all-time, he's got to know how he measures up to him and challenges his idol to a match tonight. Ric tells him that he's already passed the torch to Shawn and it would an honor to face him tonight. That brings out Hunter. He says he's the one who told Flair six months ago that he needed to go back to being the man he is and look where "The Nature Boy" is now. The champion wants Flair to fall back in line with him. Ric says Helmsley is the greatest wrestler alive today, but it was Michaels who woke him up last week and showed him who he was. "The Game" gets furious, saying he's the one who brought Flair back and Ric does not want to go against him. Before "The Nature Boy" can respond to his threat, Eric Bischoff comes out. The co-general manager says that he was under the weather last week and "Stone Cold" Steve Austin took advantage of him. Tonight, Eric is going to throw his weight around and show what he can do. While he'd love to see Shawn and Flair wrestle one-on-one, he says that match is too big for a town like Mobile. Instead, he signs the two to meet at "Eric Bischoff presents Bad Blood". They will be in action tonight as well, but instead of facing each other, they are going to team up to wrestle Triple H in a handicap match. While the duo like that, Hunter is none too happy.

Booker T def. Test (with Stacy Keibler). As Test heads to the ring, the announcers reveal that Stacy has agreed to manage both Scott Steiner and the bodyguard separately since they can't get along. Booker starts fast here, knocking Test down, but the bodyguard responds with a hotshot on the top rope. Once in control, he elbows and kicks the five-time champion in a corner. Keibler applauds. She also applauds a stiff clothesline for a two-count. Test changes tactics afterwards and hooks a reverse chin lock. It doesn't take Booker T long to escape and respond with a hook kick to swing the momentum. That sees him flying forearm and suplex the bodyguard for a two-count. When he goes for a Scissors Kick though, Test moves only to be side kicked down ahead of a spinaroonie. The bodyguard dodges a second side kick, but Booker slips free of his pumphandle slam to throat drop him on the top rope ahead of a missile dropkick. A back body drop out to the floor follows, but when the five-time champion attempts a baseball slide kick, Test pulls Stacy into his path. The announcer's can't believe it, but it nearly earns the bodyguard the win as he clubs Booker T from behind and pumphandle slams him back in the ring for a near fall. When he sets up for a Big Boot, Steiner runs out to help Keibler and distracts Test long enough for Booker to recover and steal the win with a Scissors Kick. Post-match, Scott carries Stacy backstage.

Also backstage, "Stone Cold" Steve Austin is happy to see Booker T "coming around". Triple H interrupts to mock his black eye. Austin says he slipped in the shower. Hunter tries to butter him up, telling the co-GM that he's doing a great job and has a great shirt, but "Stone Cold" tells him his handicap match is still on. That sets off Helmsley and he yells at the "rattlesnake" accusing him of always wanting to be "the Game" and letting Eric Bischoff bully him. Despite that, Austin says the "match is still on".

Val Venis def. Steven Richards (with Victoria). Trish Stratus joins the announce table to provide guest commentary and for Lawler to promote her *Flare* magazine cover. Val then comes out to say hello to the ladies and tell everyone that the rumors are true and he's starting his own film company. He'd like to offer Victoria a job, but Richards interrupts and cheap shots "the big Valbowski". When he applies a chin lock, Jerry hits on Stratus and shills WWE.com. Soon after, Venis comes back to the life with a back body drop and knees to the gut. A sit-out powerbomb nearly gets him the win, but Steven just kicks out and surprises the adult star with a DDT for his own near fall. When he runs the ropes though, Val catches him with a spinebuster. He follows up with the Money Shot for the victory.

After a commercial break, Jonathan Coachman talks to Kevin Nash. "Big Sexy" says that Triple H's "world is unraveling" with Ric Flair turning against him and Nash getting ready to take the World Title in less than three weeks. Tonight, Kevin is looking forward to watching Helmsley get his butt kicked.

Further backstage, Terri tries to interview Christian, but he interrupts her to talk about his hair and make fun of Mobile. The Intercontinental Champion says the fans creep him out and asks Terri to find him a "Diet Tab". Goldust walks in to stutter as he calls the heel a "dictator". Booker T joins his friend to sandwich Christian and call him a "chump". Booker promises at Bad Blood he's going to win the Intercontinental Title for the first time.

Even further backstage, Eric Bischoff talks to "Stone Cold" Steve Austin about signing Ric Flair to face Shawn Michaels at Bad Blood. Austin likes the match, but says that he is the one presenting the PPV. The co-GMs argue, Bischoff taking offense to "Stone Cold" offering Bad Blood to the military for free. The two men can't get along and argue until they agree to some type of competition at the PPV.

For Memorial Day, Lilian Garcia sings "America the Beautiful". La Resistance interrupt, tired of the display of patriotism. Sylvan Grenier calls America a land of "barbarians" who could learn a lot from the French. That brings out "Stone Cold" Steve Austin to toss Grenier from the ring and give Rene Dupree a Stone Cold Stunner. He's got some French for the heels as they retreat, flipping off La Resistance. Afterwards, Austin talks about Memorial Day and drinking beer. He then invites Lilian back into the ring to sing a duet and drink beer. "Stone Cold" can't help but pour beer on her for a nice pop before slapping hands with the fans as he heads backstage.

Also backstage, Ric Flair stretches for his match, unaware that a masked man in a button down shirt is watching him.

Goldust def. Christian. Despite this being a non-title match, JR reveals that Christian didn't even want to compete tonight. Before he locks up with Goldust, the champion kisses his belt. He then corners the "bizarre one" for fists and kicks. Goldust responds with a big boot and bulldog. When he attempts a cross body block, Christian ducks and the "bizarre one" falls out to the floor. The champion capitalizes with a series of chokes, JR noting that he doesn't care if he gets disqualified. He proves it, ripping at Goldust's face while Jim makes fun of Christian's haircut. When he attempts a leapfrog, the "bizarre one" answers with an inverted atomic drop and clothesline for a two-count. He tries to finish off the champion with a Curtain Call, but Christian flips free and reverse DDTs him for his own near fall. When he attempts a leg drop on the middle rope, Goldust moves and the champion hits the ropes hard. The "bizarre one" capitalizes with fists, but Jack Doan prevents him from delivering Shattered Dreams. Despite that, Christian runs into a powerslam afterwards for Goldust to score the win. Post-match, the champion rushes out to grab his title and hug it as he retreats backstage.

Rodney Mack (with Theodore Long) def. Bubba Ray Dudley ("White Boy Challenge" match). Once again, Long is looking for a "white boy". He gets more than he asked for tonight when Bubba Ray answers to run over Mack and chop him in a corner. Rodney answers with his own clubbing blows. The fans want a table, but Dudley gives them a sunset flip for a near fall. When Mack traps him in a chin lock, JR takes the opportunity to reveal that "Classy" Freddie Blassie is in the hospital and wishes him well. Soon after, Bubba clubs and German suplexes Rodney for a two-count. A Bubba Bomb also gets him a near fall before Dudley goes after Theodore. While Chad Patton is distracted trying to get Long to calm down, Christopher Nowinski sneaks into the ring to blast Bubba Ray with his face mask for Mack to steal the win.

Backstage, Eric Bischoff apologizes on behalf of his co-GM to La Resistance for "Stone Cold" Steve Austin's earlier attack. Since Rene Dupree is unable to compete, his eyes glazed over, Bischoff gives Sylvan Grenier a chance to compete tonight against Rob Van Dam in a "Flag" match and earn a World Tag Title match.

While Chris Jericho gets makeup applied for his Highlight Reel, a video package plays featuring Goldberg destroying Lance Storm last week for trying to run him over two weeks ago. After he takes a beating, Lance confesses that Y2J put him up to trying to finish off Goldberg.

Further backstage, Triple H confronts Ric Flair. "The Game" says he's changed, but Flair says he's still the same "kiss stealing" superstar. He warns Hunter that very few become great and he's looking forward to their match. When Ric walks away, Helmsley quietly threatens him.

Sylvan Grenier (with Rene Dupree) def. Rob Van Dam (with Kane) ("Flag" match). French and American flags are hung on opposite sides of the ring for this match. The only way to win is to climb the pole and claim the superstar's respective flag. Instead of going for the flag early on, RVD takes the fight out to the floor to dump Grenier on the barricade for a twisting leg drop off the apron. When he tries to get his flag afterwards, Sylvan cuts him off and pays courtesy of a heel kick and rolling thunder. Rene then attacks Kane, slamming him into the ring steps with a drop toe hold. Unfortunately for the heel, Rob sees him and slingshots out onto him. Grenier tries to capitalize and grab his flag, but Van Dam returns to dropkick him out to the floor. While Jack Doan checks on Sylvan, Dupree drops RVD from behind. Grenier follows up with a whip into the ring post, but Rob tosses him off the ropes before he can reach his flag. When Van Dam attempts to give him a flying cannonball smash, Sylvan moves and RVD hits the referee. That means Doan misses Rob retrieving the flag to win the match. While Jack is down, La Resistance attack Van Dam until the "Big Red Machine" makes the save. Unfortunately, Dupree grabs the American flag and drives the pole into the monster's throat. He then hangs the flag back up into position ahead of a La Resistance Double Flapjack to RVD. The referee finally stirs just in time to see Sylvan grab the French flag for the victory. JR can't believe this would happen on Memorial Day.

After a commercial break, it's time for the Highlight Reel. Chris Jericho comes out to say that his show is the biggest in the world and he's going to prove it not only tonight with Goldberg, but also next week when he welcomes back The Rock. As for tonight, Y2J tells Bill that he did try to take him out two weeks ago, but he did it for the entire WWE because no one wants the intense superstar around. Jericho says they used to be friends, but Goldberg's ego got in the way. When Y2J requested a match with the intense superstar, Bill felt Chris wasn't a big enough star to step into the ring with him. That led to Jericho leaving WCW and becoming the first ever Undisputed Champion. Y2J says he's done everything he wanted in wrestling except beat Goldberg. To fix that, Jericho challenges him to a match at Bad Blood. That brings out Bill to chase the heel off his own set. The intense superstar dares him to get back in the ring, but Y2J isn't going to do that until he accepts his challenge. That's fine with Goldberg and he's happy to face Jericho at Bad Blood. Bill adds that Y2J's "nothing but an ass". Jericho can't believe he called him that and threatens to beat the intense superstar out of the squared circle. When he hops onto the apron, Goldberg slams him into the ring. Unfortunately, Y2J is ready for him and sprays something into Bill's eyes ahead of a heel spear. Before Goldberg can recover, Jericho sprints off, the damage done. During the commercial break, he sprints out of the arena to his car, but it won't start. Instead, he runs off again, Terri trying to get a word with him.

Triple H def. Ric Flair/Shawn Michaels. Kevin Nash watches backstage as Shawn starts the match clotheslining Triple H. Hunter answers with a string of fists, but Michaels responds in kind, dropping the champion again. When he sets up for a back body drop, Helmsley counters with a facebuster and side backbreaker. A hard whip into the corner follows moments later, but when "the Game" sets up for a Pedigree, Flair distracts him long enough for the "Heartbreak Kid" to back body drop free. He follows up with Sweet Chin Music, but is too injured to make the cover. Instead, he slowly crawls to his corner to tag Ric. "The Nature Boy" proves he's the dirtiest player in the game, decking his own partner. While he pummels him, the masked man attacks Nash backstage. Soon after, Triple H Pedigrees Shawn for the three-count. Post-match, the heels continue attacking Michaels until Kevin rushes down the aisle to slug Flair and Hunter. The masked man brings a chair out to attack him again. Although Nash fights him off, Helmsley grabs the chair and blasts "Big Sexy" to finally put him down. Afterwards, Ric removes Randy Orton's mask, Lawler ominously warning that he's back. The show ends with Flair trapping Michaels in a Figure Four Leglock while "the Game" chokes Kevin with the chair.

SmackDown!
May 29, 2003
Pensacola, FL
Announcers: Michael Cole, Tazz

Once again, the show opens with a video package featuring Vince McMahon and Mr. America. Due to the masked man's loss last week, he'll have to take a lie detector test tonight. Afterwards, the intro video plays and fireworks explode.

Nidia (with John Cena) def. Torrie Wilson. Sable serves as the guest ring announcer for this match. When she asks Tazz if he missed her, he says he did "like a rash". The diva then introduces Torrie as weighing too much before telling Nidia that they need to get together to discuss fashion. As the heels head to the ring, the cameras catch Zach Gowen a few rows back in the crowd. He's got a good seat to watch Wilson chop Nidia. The heel responds with her own chops and a suplex for a two-count. Although Torrie fights back with more chops, she hurts her knee leapfrogging Nidia. The heel takes advantage, attacking and stretching out the babyface's knee. Mike Sparks tries to step in, but Nidia ignores him to wrap the knee around the bottom rope. Wilson has to take matters into her own hands, tackling the heel and rolling around with her on the canvas and over Sparks. The referee loves it and celebrates in a corner while Noble distracts Torrie. Nidia capitalizes, rolling up the babyface for the three-count. Post-match, Tazz hits Jamie from behind before Sable tosses a pitcher of water onto the announcer to get the last laugh.

Backstage, Vince McMahon arrives. His limo driver wants to move the car after the WWE owner exits to get out of the handicap space, but Vince tells him to stay put because he won't be long.

After a commercial break, Stephanie McMahon tests the lie detector. While she's happy to answer her name, when the detectives ask her if she's ever cheated on her taxes she takes the connectors off and says it's working just fine.

Backstage, Team Angle head to the ring for their WWE Tag Title rematch. With Kurt Angle returning next week, they know they have to get the belts back tonight.

Further backstage, Eddie Guerrero is impressed by Tajiri's attire. The "Japanese Buzzsaw" is trying to fit in with Guerrero and dress like him. He's even got some car keys for "Latino Heat", telling him that they "lie, cheat, and steal" when questioned how he got them. Eddie says they grow up so fast.

Eddie Guerrero/Tajiri def. Team Angle (WWE Tag Title match) by disqualification. The champions are out second in a lowrider pickup truck, but when they pose for the crowd, Team Angle attack. Desperate to get the belts back before Kurt Angle's return next week, the challengers take early control, Haas back body dropping Eddie. When he tosses him out to the floor, Shelton takes some cheap shots and shoves "Latino Heat" back into the squared circle. Benjamin joins him, kneeing and elbowing the champion. When the challenger attempts to press slam him, Guerrero counters with a dropkick. Tajiri tags in afterwards for a head scissors and roll-up all around the ring for a near fall. After he dropkicks Shelton down, the champion applies a side headlock. It doesn't take Benjamin long to fight free before both men connect with simultaneous kicks ahead of a commercial break.

Afterwards, Tajiri dropkicks Benjamin, but Charlie illegally enters the ring to grab the champion's leg and hold him for a Shelton kick to the knee. Haas focuses on the knee afterwards, leg dropping it and applying an Indian deathlock. Following a knee breaker, Benjamin returns to ax-handle the "Japanese Buzzsaw's" injured joint. He applies his own leg lock, trying to force the submission. The challengers then alternate single leg crabs. With the fans chanting for Eddie, Charlie drags Tajiri to the heel corner for a Shelton slingshot attack. When Benjamin tries to deliver another knee breaker, the champion escapes with a spinning head scissors to give Guerrero the hot tag. He fights both men, monkey flipping them into each other before tossing Shelton out to the floor. That leaves Eddie alone to give Haas his trio of suplexes. Afterwards, "Latino Heat" heads upstairs, kicks Benjamin off the apron, and nails Charlie with a Frog Splash. Luckily, Shelton recovers and breaks up the count. Team Angle answers with an Inverted Atomic Drop and Superkick for their own near fall before the "Japanese Buzzsaw" makes the save. Soon after, Eddie counters a double-team attack with a double DDT. Tajiri returns afterwards to chop and enziguri kick Haas. He tries to follow up with a tornado DDT, but Charlie counters with a northern lights suplex. At the last second, "Latino Heat" breaks the cover. Moments later, he back body drops Shelton out to the floor. After the "Japanese Buzzsaw" kicks Haas, Eddie dives off the top rope out onto Benjamin. That leaves Tajiri alone in the ring with a bad knee. Charlie capitalizes with the Haas of Pain. When the bell rings, Haas celebrates, but Brian Hebner says he never called for the bell. Instead, it's Guerrero ringing the bell to trick the challengers. It gets worse for Charlie as Eddie enters the ring and tosses him a title belt before collapsing to the mat. When Hebner turns around, he sees the weapon in Haas's hand and disqualifies him.

Out in the crowd, Josh Mathews interviews Zach Gowen. He's moved up to the front row and shows off his ticket. The fan is nervous to watch Mr. America take the lie detector test next, Zach's future in the masked man's hands.

After a commercial break, Vince McMahon heads to the ring where the lie detector test is set up and two men wait to administer it. The WWE owner crows about watching Mr. America fail the lie detector test tonight so he can fire both him and Hulk Hogan on the same night for breach of contract. Before he welcomes out Mr. America, Vince notices Zach Gowen in the crowd. He says after he fires the masked man, he'll be just like Zach "without a leg to stand on". Mr. America then comes out lacking his usual enthusiasm. He doesn't say a word as McMahon mocks him while the fans chant "USA". After getting hooked up, the masked man answers that he is Mr. America and employed on *SmackDown!*. Vince doesn't want to wait through these questions and demands that the expert ask if he's Hulk Hogan despite the detective saying that there's a method to the testing. Before he answers, the masked man takes a drink of water. McMahon has heard enough and asks if Mr. America is Hulk Hogan. He says, "no". It turns out he's telling the truth. Vince can't believe it, but the fans love it. McMahon has the expert asks the question again, but Mr. America passes once again. As his music plays, Vince blames the detectives for messing up. To prove that anyone can pass the test, McMahon agrees to take it himself. He rants that lie detector tests are not admissible in court before telling the expert to ask him anything. After he answers his name and that he's the chairman of the WWE, Mr. America takes the microphone to ask if Vince is the "biggest asshole" on Earth and a "sick, perverted, power hungry freak". McMahon says no, but he fails the test. He continues failing when he says he's a businessman who does things for the fans. Ultimately, he only passes when he says he does everything for himself. He also fails when he says he's not a pervert, something that only gets funnier in hindsight. He continues failing when he talks about how recently he lusted over Torrie Wilson and looked at her pictures. He also fails when he says he doesn't think about Mae Young before finally passing the test to say that he hates Hulk Hogan. The masked man says this proves that he's telling the truth and McMahon is a liar. When the WWE owner tries to hit him, Mr. America beats him to the punch and poses.

After a commercial break, Vince McMahon throws a fit in Stephanie McMahon's office. He blames her for hiring the detectives and bringing in the lie detector equipment. Vince also blames her for hiring Mr. America. She wonders if he wants her to take a lie detector test. McMahon tells her not to get cute and promises things will change for the better next week.

Sean O'Haire (with "Rowdy" Roddy Piper) def. Chris Benoit. Although Piper accompanies his man to the ring, he doesn't follow him very closely. Pre-match, "Hot Rod" looks for Zach Gowen in the crowd before Benoit heads to the squared circle. There, O'Haire muscles him back into a corner and wails on "the Crippler". Benoit answers with a dragon screw leg whip and chops. He can't keep Sean down and the bigger superstar responds with a string of kicks and a ground and pound assault. He then slows the pace with a reverse chin lock. When the "rabid wolverine" starts to fight free, O'Haire tries to stop him with a spinning heel kick, but Benoit ducks and DDTs him. Once both men catch their breath, "the Crippler" German suplexes the heel for a two-count. A neckbreaker also gets him a near fall. When he runs the ropes moments later though, Roddy grabs his foot. He leads Benoit on a chase around and into the ring where the "rabid wolverine" locks "Hot Rod" in a Crippler Crossface. Piper ends up sacrificing himself for Sean to steal the win with a kick to the back of Benoit's head and handful of tights.

Ahead of his Cruiserweight Title match next week, footage of Rey Mysterio earning that shot last week plays. He then talks to the announcers via video backstage. The masked man says he pulled his groin last week and he's hurt, but he's not about to miss his chance to represent his people on the west coast next week and destroy Matt Hardy Version 1.0. Matt interrupts to say that the fans can chant "619" all night long, but nothing will stop him from injuring Rey even more. Mysterio isn't scared, but he should be as Hardy doubles over the masked man with a low blow to his injured groin.

A teaser plays for Ultimo Dragon.

The Basham Brothers def. Rikishi/Spanky. The Bashams also make their debut here, the announcers knowing nothing about the brothers. They look similar with their shaved heads and black leather pants. Rikishi doesn't care which one he's fighting, tossing them around before Spanky tags in to forearm Doug for a two-count. Unfortunately, Danny trips the babyface to swing the momentum. Once they get control, the heels punish Spanky in their corner with a string of strikes, Doug scoring a two-count with a scoop slam. When he applies a neck wrench, the announcers wish "Classy" Freddie Blassie well. Rikishi returns soon afterwards to fight both men and Samoan drop Doug. He then squashes the Bashams in a corner to deliver a tandem Stinkface. When Spanky tries to return to attempt a monkey flip, Doug slams him to the mat and Danny pushes his brother's butt with his foot for added leverage and the three-count. Other than some heel antics, the Bashams don't particularly look impressive inside the ring for their debut.

Backstage, Vince McMahon finds his limo hooked up to a tow truck. He yells at his driver to take care of things before getting into the vehicle. Zach Gowen knocks on the window with his cane and tells Vince that parking in a handicap zone is illegal. The tow truck then drives off, McMahon sitting inside the limo.

Big Show/The FBI (with Nunzio) def. Brock Lesnar/The Undertaker. The babyfaces are out first, separately, to big pops. When The FBI come out, Nunzio says there will be a handicap match tonight, but he's not going to be in it due to The Undertaker tossing him over the top rope last week. However, he found a "suitable replacement" and welcomes out Show. The babyfaces aren't intimidated and the biker makes his return to the squared circle pounding Palumbo until he runs into a back elbow and clothesline. The "Deadman" responds with his own leaping clothesline moments later ahead of an Old School strike. Afterwards, Brock tags in to hammer and belly-to-belly suplex Chuck. The heel manages to surprise him and ram the champion back into the heel corner, but Stamboli lets him leave and clothesline "the Bull". A suplex follows before The Undertaker tags back in for a big boot and elbow drop. After that gets him a two-count, the biker slams Johnny, but misses a second elbow drop. It doesn't hurt him as he quickly recovers for a leaping DDT and two-count before Palumbo makes the save. Big Show then tags in, but he wants Lesnar. The champion doesn't make him wait, tagging in to shoulderblock and knee the giant. Show absorbs his shots and responds with a chop and headbutt. After he scoop slams the "next big thing", Big Show attempts a leg drop, but Brock moves and answers with a shoulderblock. He tries to finish off the giant with an F5, but when he picks him up, Stamboli enters the ring only to run into a spinebuster. The distraction works as Show Chokeslams Lesnar when he turns around. At the last second, the "Deadman" breaks Mike Chioda's count. The FBI continue their assault, pummeling the champion at ringside. Soon after, Chuck kicks Brock's face before Big Show slams him into the ring post. That brings The Undertaker over to chase off the heels with the ring steps. Following a two-count, Palumbo unloads with a discus punch and tags in "the Bull". Lesnar greets him with a clothesline before slowly crawling to his corner for the tag. The biker hits and clotheslines all three heels ahead of snake eyes to Stamboli. A big boot and clothesline send Chuck out to the floor before The Undertaker traps Show in Taking Care of Business. When Lesnar rushes to his defense to fight The FBI, Nunzio takes advantage of the referee's back being turned to hit the biker with a steel chair. The "Deadman" doesn't even go down, turning to chokeslam the Italian heel. Unfortunately, Chuck responds with a Superkick and clothesline, but misses Brock getting the blind tag. Lesnar immediately F5s both FBI members one after another, but turns into a giant Chokeslam for the three-count.

Monday Night Raw
June 2, 2003
San Diego, CA
Announcers: Jim Ross, Jerry "the King" Lawler

The show opens with The Rock arriving backstage to a nice pop. He promises the "most electrifying night in *Raw*" and is already fired up as he jokes with the cameraman about filming his butt and the show being live ahead of the intro video and fireworks.

Ivory/Jacqueline/Trish Stratus def. Jazz/Molly Holly/Victoria (with Theodore Long). While Jerry drools, the heels attack and drive everyone from the ring but Trish. Victoria nearly scores the quick victory with a spinning fireman's carry slam, called the Spider's Web by Lawler. After Stratus kicks out, she ducks a clothesline with her Matrix move to see the black widow hit Molly. Once those two women end up at ringside, Ivory dives off the top rope onto them. Unfortunately, Jazz clotheslines and slams the vixen back in the ring for a two-count. Knees to the back soften her up for a double chicken wing slam. Afterwards, Jazz cheap shots Ivory and distracts Charles Robinson for Holly and Victoria to trap Trish in a combination Boston crab and camel clutch. Despite that, Stratus comes back to life moments later with a neckbreaker to the Women's Champion. Jacqueline then tags in to toss around Jazz. Ivory tags in soon afterwards to flying cross body block the champion off the top rope for a two-count before the black widow makes the save. Jacqueline tries to make her pay with a superplex, but Victoria shoves her down to the mat. Before she can get off the ropes, Trish catches the black widow with her handstand head scissors. Ivory follows up with a face slam to Jazz for the three-count.

In the parking lot, Goldberg arrives in his sports car. Jonathan Coachman tries to get a word from him, but the intense superstar shoves him aside ahead of an ad for JR's new cookbook.

After a commercial break, Stacy Keibler and Test argue. She's had enough of him and tells him "it's over". The bodyguard disagrees, telling her that she is "contractually obligated" to him. When she slams her locker room door in his face, Test seethes.

Back at ringside, The Hurricane steps through the curtain for his upcoming match. Instead, Randy Orton attacks him from behind and tosses the superhero backstage. Triple H, Ric Flair, and Orton then head to the squared circle to boos. Flair tells Shawn Michaels that he was honored that the "Heartbreak Kid" called him the greatest. However, Ric can't say the same and tells everyone that he never passed the torch to Michaels. Instead, "The Nature Boy" reminds everyone that he lost a match to Hunter and now is passing the torch to him, bowing to "the Game". After Flair beats and outsmarts Shawn at Bad Blood and Helmsley leaves Kevin Nash bloodied, Ric promises to make Michaels his "bitch". That brings out the "Heartbreak Kid" to admit that he took a risk confessing his admiration for Flair last week and "The Nature Boy" made him pay. Unlike Ric, he doesn't need to brag about his accomplishments. He also doesn't need someone to pass him the torch because Shawn says he took it when everyone "went south". At Bad Blood, Michaels promises to show that "Space Mountain", one of Flair's favorite things to call himself, is a broken down ride and prove that he's the best in the business. Triple H challenges him to bring his torch into the ring and take care of things now. When he starts to walk down the ramp, Nash joins his friend. They aren't alone, The Hurricane returning to hit Randy with a chair from behind before the Two Dudes with Attitudes chase off Hunter and Ric.

Scott Steiner (with Stacy Keibler) def. Steven Richards. After the babyfaces head to the ring and Stacy stretches stepping through the ropes twice, Test heads out to the ramp to watch them and distract Scott. Richards capitalizes with a sneak attack, but doesn't keep "Big Poppa Pump" down for long. Instead, Steiner clotheslines, belly-to-belly suplexes, and elbow drops the heel. Test just smiles as he watches his former partner drive Steven face-first into the mat for the victory. Post-match, Eric Bischoff storms down to the ring. He reminds Keibler that she's contractually obligated to manage Test. To settle things, he's signing a Bad Blood match between Scott and the bodyguard for Stacy.

After a commercial break, JR has the unfortunate duty of announcing that "Classy" Freddie Blassie just passed away.

Backstage, Eric Bischoff tells "Stone Cold" Steve Austin that they are starting to work well together and brags about the match he just signed. Austin is fine with Scott Steiner and Test wrestling at Bad Blood, but he wants to focus on tonight's show too. That's why he's signing a six-man tag match pitting Evolution against Kevin Nash, Shawn Michaels, and The Hurricane. Eric likes it. With that out of the way, Steve wonders if Bischoff has thought about their competition at Bad Blood. Instead of a wrestling match, they agree to have a "redneck triathlon". Despite shaking hands and agreeing to the match, "Stone Cold" warns his co-general manager that they aren't friends.

Further backstage, Terri interviews Goldberg. He's waiting to get his hands on Chris Jericho. Unfortunately, Y2J isn't even in the building right now. Instead, he's in the parking lot where he dumps a gallon of paint onto Bill's freshly painted vintage car. That sends Goldberg out to the parking lot to speed after the heel, driving his yellow paint covered black car away in pursuit.

After a commercial break, Christian steps in for Chris Jericho to host the Highlight Reel. He calls it the "first edition of the Peep Show" before introducing The Rock. Despite leaving as a heel, he gets a very good pop. The "People's Champ" congratulates Christian on taking advantage of his opportunities, but before he answers his questions, he's got something to say. Unfortunately, the Intercontinental Champion interrupts his "finally, The Rock…" catchphrase. Christian says he's replaced the "Great One". The "Brahma Bull" wonders if he's on crack because there's only one "People's Champ". When he threatens to slap around the heel, the fans go wild. Christian takes offense to The Rock calling his dad a "ho", telling him that he's actually a pediatrician. He then claims that the fans love him and asks them to chant for the Intercontinental Champion. They don't. The "Great One" follows up, heading into the crowd to poll the people. They go bananas hugging him and confirming that the "Brahma Bull" is the real "People's Champ". He tells Christian that there's only one, but when he tries to deliver another catchphrase, Y2J interrupts. He tells The Rock to come back and answer his questions quickly because he doesn't have much time. Since he's never been Speared by Goldberg before, he asks the "Great One" how it feels. When the "Brahma Bull" says it hurts, that's all Jericho needs to hear and he wants to leave. The Rock stops him and threatens to beat up Y2J. Instead, Christian attacks him from behind. The two heels then double-team the "People's Champ" until Booker T makes the save. While he fights with Christian at ringside, the "Great One" comes back to life with a leaping clothesline and spinebuster. The People's Elbow follows, chasing off Jericho. Afterwards, Christian rolls back into the ring and a Rock Bottom. Once the heel is down, the "Brahma Bull" invites Booker to give Christian a People's Elbow. The two men shake hands afterwards, but Booker T stops The Rock from leaving the ring. He wants the "People's Champ" to give everyone a sneak peek of his new move…the "Rockaroonie". The "Great One" can't quite figure out how to do it, so the five-time champion gives him a lesson. Afterwards, the "Brahma Bull" drops down in his leather pants and entertains with a Rockaroonie to end this fun segment.

After a commercial break, Chris Jericho and Christian try to leave the arena, but "Stone Cold" Steve Austin stops them.

Rene Dupree (with Sylvan Grenier) def. Kane (with Rob Van Dam). After Grenier defeated RVD last week, Kane gets a chance to try to even the series. He starts fast tossing around and clotheslining Dupree until Sylvan trips him near the ropes. That lets Rene kick the "Big Red Machine" ahead of a second rope flying clothesline. Unfortunately, he dances around to celebrate and pays courtesy of a sidewalk slam and top rope flying clothesline. When Grenier climbs onto the apron to distract the monster, Rob comes to his partner's aid with a top rope flying kick. Unfortunately, he misses Sylvan with a follow up attack off the apron and crashes hard to the floor. That leaves Kane alone against two men. Although he initially fights them off, when he tries to Chokeslam Grenier off the apron, the heel holds onto the ropes long enough for Dupree to low blow the "Big Red Machine" and steal the win.

Post-match, "Stone Cold" Steve Austin marches down to the ring to "dismiss" Van Dam. Alone, Austin wants to know what the monster is doing. He's been watching Kane and he's not impressed. "Stone Cold" wonders where his fire is, mocking him for getting rolled up for a three-count. He asks if Kane cares about anything. Steve tries to make him mad, shoving the "Big Red Machine". He continues to needle him, stomping on his boot and even putting Kane's hand around the general manager's throat. When the monster walks away, Austin shoves him and puts the monster's hand on his throat again. The "Big Red Machine" refuses to Chokeslam him until "Stone Cold" calls him weak. That fires up the monster and he nearly Chokeslams the boss before shoving him aside. Steve has had enough and gives him a Stone Cold Stunner, confusing the announcers.

Backstage, Triple H smiles as he leaves the officials' locker room. After a commercial break, Hunter tells Ric Flair and Randy Orton that he's got a plan to end Shawn Michaels and Kevin Nash tonight and make sure that there's no "Hell in a Cell" match at Bad Blood.

Further backstage, Chris Jericho and Christian are in a hurry to wrestle Booker T and Goldust so they can leave the arena.

Booker T/Goldust def. Chris Jericho/Christian. The heels don't waste time, Christian walking out with Jericho to Y2J's music. Chris is nervous and constantly looking around for Goldberg. Inside the ring, Booker goes right to work knocking down and slamming Christian for a two-count ahead of a commercial break.

Afterwards, Jericho has Booker T trapped in a surfboard stretch. When he fights free, Christian hits him running the ropes for a Y2J spinning heel kick. Luckily, Goldust makes the save when Jericho goes for the cover. Christian then enters the squared circle to dropkick the five-time champion before leaping into a flapjack. That lets the "bizarre one" get the hot tag to punch and inverted atomic drop the Intercontinental Champion. He also nails Jericho when he enters the ring ahead of a double DDT to the heels. With the match well in hand, he sets Christian up for Shattered Dreams, but takes too long delivering the blow and Y2J forearms him. Booker gets the tag afterwards to trade roll-ups with Christian, the heel holding the ropes for a near fall. Moments later though, the champion accidentally hits Jericho, knocking him off the apron before turning into a Scissors Kick and the three-count. Post-match, Y2J hits both babyfaces with the Intercontinental Title. When he tries to give them another shot, Charles Robinson grabs the belt while Goldberg sprints down the aisle. He tries to Spear the heel, but

Jericho sees Bill coming and shoves the referee into the intense superstar's path. Afterwards, the heels sprint off while trainers load Robinson onto a stretcher.

After a commercial break, the officials complain to the general managers about Triple H's recent actions. Since he keeps attacking them, they refuse to referee the "Hell in a Cell" match. Luckily, "Stone Cold" Steve Austin knows a man "crazy" and "sick" enough to officiate the contest.

Randy Orton/Ric Flair/Triple H def. Kevin Nash/Shawn Michaels/The Hurricane. Everyone gets separate entrances for this match, Nash coming out last to chase off the heels. Orton and Michaels start the action, but Shawn wants Flair. After tossing his shirt at him, the "Heartbreak Kid" gives The Hurricane a blind tag to dropkick Randy from behind and toss him out to the floor. When he returns, the superhero gets a two-count before Orton answers with his own dropkick. Triple H tags in afterwards to punch and whip around the masked man. The Hurricane answers with arm drags and a tag to Shawn. When he teases tagging Kevin, Hunter knocks the "Heartbreak Kid" down. Despite that, Michaels punches all three heels until Ric chop blocks him. That turns the tide and Evolution capitalize, Randy tagging back in to target Shawn's knee. Helmsley does the same, slamming the "Heartbreak Kid's" knee onto the canvas. When "The Nature Boy" tags in, he stomps Shawn in a corner and threatens the referee for trying to make him break. Michaels tries to fight back, but a knee breaker puts him down for Flair to quickly apply a Figure Four Leglock. Fortunately, Nash makes the save with a big elbow drop. Afterwards, the "Heartbreak Kid" stuns Ric with an enziguri before giving "Big Sexy" the hot tag. He goes to work punching, slamming, and clotheslining all three heels. When Kevin lowers his straps and sets "the Game" up for a Jackknife, a bloodied Flair makes the save with chops. Nash makes him pay, chasing Hunter and Ric from the ring before The Hurricane tags in to catch Orton with a top rope flying cross body block and shining wizard kick for a near fall. When he connects with the overcast, "The Nature Boy" makes the save. After the superhero hammers him, Helmsley returns to surprise the masked man with a Pedigree. That lets Randy cover The Hurricane and score a very bizarre victory. For some reason, Earl stops his count at the last moment to check if the superhero's shoulder is down then calls for the bell without actually counting to three. This has to be on Hebner as the show is almost out of time and it's unlikely The Hurricane was supposed to kick out after a Pedigree. Maybe someone was supposed to make the save, but it doesn't look like it. The announcers are just as confused as the fans who take offense and let Earl know about it. JR and Lawler say Helmsley has the officials intimidated. Post-match, the babyfaces get a measure of revenge when Kevin Nash Jackknifes the World Champion to end the episode standing tall despite the loss.

SmackDown!
June 5, 2003
Anaheim, CA
Announcers: Michael Cole, Tazz

Following the intro video, "Rowdy" Roddy Piper and Sean O'Haire head to the squared circle for Piper's Pit. "Hot Rod" says he has a "special" guest tonight. When he repeatedly says "special", O'Haire wonders if he's special. Piper knows he is, telling him that he'll be a champion one day, but his "special" guest tonight is Zach Gowen. Instead of Mr. America's fan, it's Vince McMahon who storms down the aisle. He says he was blinded by his hatred of Hulk Hogan and Mr. America and was wrong about Gowen. Now, Vince sees Zach as a "true American success story". That's why McMahon is going to give him a chance to earn his dream—a WWE contract. That brings out Gowen and Mr. America to "Real American". The masked patriot starts to speak, but the WWE owner cuts him off. He doesn't want to hear from Mr. America and knows that he cheated the lie detector test. Most importantly, Vince doesn't need to hear from the masked patriot because he has nothing to do with Zach getting a job. Only Mr. McMahon can offer him that opportunity and he'll do so next week in an arm wrestling match. When Mr. America accepts, thinking the offer is for him, Vince corrects him. He says it will be the WWE owner arm wrestling Zach for a contract. O'Haire then distracts Mr. America for Piper to drop down behind Gowen and McMahon to push him down. From the aisle, Vince says Zach has the same chance as a "one-legged man" in a butt-kicking contest to beat him next week.

A Kurt Angle Classic moment featuring Milk-o-mania plays.

The Undertaker def. Chuck Palumbo (with Johnny Stamboli/Nunzio). Tazz expects a slugfest. Instead, Palumbo hooks a side headlock before running into a pair of arm drags and a wrist lock. Finally, Chuck unloads with fists to match Tazz's prediction. That plays to The Undertaker's strengths and he answers with a leaping clothesline and Old School. Unfortunately, the FBI distract him long enough for Palumbo to recover and deliver a spinebuster. A big punch then sends the biker out to the floor for Stamboli and Nunzio to stomp. Joining his allies at ringside, Chuck slugs the "Deadman" before scoring a two-count back in the squared circle with a delayed vertical suplex. When The Undertaker starts to fight back, Palumbo answers with a sleeper hold. The biker escapes with a back suplex. Afterwards, the two men trade fists, the "Deadman" getting the upper hand. He follows up with a DDT and corner clotheslines before leveling Chuck with a big boot. Once again, the FBI distract The Undertaker, but this time the biker recovers quickly to chokeslam Palumbo out of nowhere for the three-count. Post-match, he decks Nunzio and sets him up for the Last Ride. Unfortunately, Chuck makes the save with a Superkick before the heels triple-team the "Deadman". Despite the numbers advantage, The Undertaker boots a chair back into Nunzio's face and chases off The FBI to a nice pop.

After playing footage of Big Show and Brock Lesnar crossing paths last week, the commentators announce that the rivals will meet next week for the WWE Title.

A video package plays for "Classy" Freddie Blassie's recent passing.

Eddie Guerrero/Tajiri def. The Basham Brothers. The champions head to the ring in a lowrider while the announcers talk about this being a big opportunity for the Bashams to earn a title shot in the near future. Although Doug starts strong, Tajiri quickly knocks him down and knee drops him before both men tag out. Eddie gets the better of Danny, giving him a trio of suplexes. When Doug tries to help his brother, Guerrero drops both heels with a combination head scissors and arm drag. Unfortunately, he can't continue to fight both men at the same time and the brothers eventually knock him down for Danny to score a two-count. Cole reveals that Team Angle are out on a "sick day", coincidentally on the same night as Kurt Angle's return. Eventually, "Latino Heat" surprises Danny with a side suplex to crawl to his corner and make the hot tag. The "Japanese Buzzsaw" unloads with kicks and a handspring elbow. After knocking Danny off the apron, Tajiri DDTs Doug for a near fall. Luckily, Danny makes the save, but gets trapped in the Tarantula. While Brian Hebner tries to break that hold, Eddie Frog Splashes Doug. A Buzzsaw Kick follows for the "Japanese Buzzsaw" to score the three-count.

Another Kurt Angle Classic Moment sees him singing "Jimmy Crack Corn" and playing guitar with "Stone Cold" Steve Austin. After a commercial break, Kurt heads to the ring to a big pop. Even he seems excited by the reaction, asking the sound guys to replay his music just so the fans can chant "You Suck" appreciatively for him. Following another good pop, Angle says he's back after two months of rehab. The Olympian is surprised that he had support and encouragement from an unlikely source. Before he can reveal who, Big Show walks out to say that he doesn't care and Kurt hasn't earned his respect. If Angle wants to be the champion again, he'll have to wait in line and pray that Show gives him a title shot after he beats Brock Lesnar next week for the WWE Title. However, the giant warns him that he might put Kurt in a hospital permanently, getting right into the Olympian's face. Kurt tries to give him a breath strip before climbing onto the second rope to look down at Big Show. Angle gets very aggressive, reminding the giant that the last time they wrestled Kurt beat him for the WWE Title. He also won an Olympic gold medal and competed in the WrestleMania XIX main event with a "broken freakin' neck". When Show doesn't back down, the Olympian steals a page from "Stone Cold" Steve Austin and asks the crowd if they want to see him kick Big Show's butt. Before they can lock up, Lesnar marches to the ring. The giant is willing to wait until next week to meet him and walks away, telling the champion "not now". That leaves Kurt and Brock in the ring, the Olympian saying he wouldn't be surprised to see Show beat the "next big thing" for the WWE Title. Lesnar doesn't agree and tells Angle that once he's done with the giant, he'll give him a shot at the championship. The Olympian appreciates that. He also appreciates that Brock checked on him in the hospital and he earned Kurt's respect. Angle tells him thanks before they shake hands and hug to another nice pop.

An Ultimo Dragon teaser plays.

John Cena def. Chris Benoit. Cena wears a Lebron James high school jersey to the ring as he makes fun of the Cruiserweight division for being small and uninteresting. When he also mocks Benoit for being small, "the Crippler" marches out to hammer and chop the rapping heel. He nearly locks on an early Crippler Crossface, but John rolls him out to the floor for a whip into the ring post. After scoring a two-count, he hooks a reverse chin lock until Benoit chops free. A snap suplex afterwards gets him a near fall. Cena tries to answer with an FU, but the "rabid wolverine" counters with a DDT and top rope diving headbutt for another close two-count. He tries to follow up with a series of German suplexes, but the rapping heel fights back until he runs into Mike Sparks. That lets John slow Benoit with a low blow, but when he grabs his chain, Rhyno runs out to stop Cena. Unfortunately, he ends up decking "the Crippler" with the chain when he tries to hit the rapping heel. John capitalizes, stealing the win with a groggy three-count. Post-match, the man-beast checks on Benoit while Cena celebrates.

Rikishi/Torrie Wilson def. Jamie Noble/Nidia. As the heels head to the ring together unlike the babyfaces, Tazz wishes his wife a happy birthday. Cole has a gift for her, Jim Ross's cookbook. The male competitors then show off their women, Torrie getting a big pop. When Nidia slaps Rikishi, he shoves her down to the canvas before Wilson unloads with chops and a clothesline in a corner. That knocks the heel down into position for a Stinkface, Torrie teasing it before tagging in the big Samoan to also threaten Nidia. Luckily, she comes to her senses and tags in Noble to dropkick and stomp the big babyface. Although he gets in several shots, one chokeslam puts him down and crawling to his corner for the tag. After Nidia badmouths Rikishi, Wilson tags in to clothesline and kick the heel again. A top rope cross body block nearly gets her the win, but when it doesn't, Jamie trips Torrie to briefly swing the momentum. Luckily, the big Samoan rescues his partner and slams Nidia to the canvas before tossing Noble out to the floor. When Nidia collapses in a corner, Rikishi gives her a Stinkface. Horrified, the heel flails around and runs into a Wilson neckbreaker for the three-count.

Following the tale of the tape for tonight's Cruiserweight Title match, we see Rey Mysterio's kids, including Dominik, in the crowd. Afterwards, Josh Mathews asks Rey about his injured groin. Mysterio says he's ready. This is the reason he came to the WWE and tonight he's bringing the Cruiserweight Title home to the "west coast". That gets him a big pop. Eddie Guerrero interrupts wearing the masked man's shirt. He speaks in Spanish as he tries to fire up Rey and wants him to make the west coast proud. However, Guerrero gets serious and tells Mysterio not to even think about coming back to the locker room without the gold.

Further backstage, Stephanie McMahon chastises her father for shoving down Zach Gowen. She says no one deserves a contract more than Zach and she wants to give him one now. Vince warns her that if she does, she'll be fired. He then introduces his daughter to her new assistant...Sable. Stephanie wants to know what position she's qualified for. Mr. McMahon says she's qualified for "a number of positions". The *SmackDown!* general manager can't believe he'd hire her after Sable sued the company for sexual harassment. Vince says his daughter is just jealous of Sable's looks.

MUST SEE! Rey Mysterio def. Matt Hardy Version 1.0 (with Crash Holly/Shannon Moore) (Cruiserweight Title match). Matt Facts reveal that Hardy is taller than Rey and he despises traffic. When Mysterio comes out, he stops to bump heads with his six year old son. Inside the ring, the champion uses his strength advantage to drive the masked man into a corner, but Rey answers with a quick roll-up and near fall. Matt responds with a clothesline to the back of the head and chokes. The MFers try to help, but Brian Hebner admonishes them. Soon after, Mysterio comes back to life with chops and a snap mare. A slingshot dropkick and splash nearly crown a new champion, but Hardy just kicks out. The challenger tries to follow up with another slingshot attack, but Matt answers with a forearm to the jaw, knocking Rey out to the floor. There, Crash and Shannon stomp him until the referee orders them to head backstage. While the champion argues with Hebner, Mysterio capitalizes with a springboard senton splash out to the floor ahead of a commercial break.

Afterwards, the masked man slips free of a crucifix powerbomb, but the referee is out of position and misses Hardy unloading with a low blow. He follows up with a single leg crab until Rey reaches the ropes. When the champion goes back for the leg, Mysterio kicks him into position for a 619, but is too injured to deliver his signature move. Moments later, he kicks Matt down, but is slow to climb the ropes and gets knocked into the tree of woe. Hardy tries to capitalize with a corner spear, but the masked man moves and Hardy hits the post. Although he catches the challenger's second rope moonsault, Rey swings around and plants the heel with a tornado DDT for a near fall. He also gets a two-count with a second rope bulldog. The champion quickly answers with a kick to the knee and slam, but takes too much time setting up for his second rope leg drop. Mysterio meets him on the ropes, but pays with a second rope side effect for a near fall. The masked man answers with a small package and his own close two-count. He then steals a page from Matt's playbook with a twist of fate, but takes too long making the cover and Hardy just kicks out. Despite his injured leg, the challenger follows up with the 619. He tries to give Matt a West Coast Pop too, but the champion catches him. The masked man won't relinquish the momentum, taking Matt out to the floor with a hurricanrana. That sends Hardy over to grab the Cruiserweight Title. Hebner follows him and argues with the champion while the MFers return to give the challenger a double modified gourdbuster. Matt capitalizes with a top rope guillotine leg drop, but somehow Rey just kicks out. Frustrated, Hardy hammers the challenger before setting up for the Twist of Fate. At the last second, Mysterio sweeps his legs and rolls through for the three-count to crown a new champion. Post-match, Dominik joins his father in the ring to celebrate the win.

Monday Night Raw
June 9, 2003
Miami, FL
Announcers: Jim Ross, Jerry "the King" Lawler, Test (briefly), Theodore Long (briefly)

The show opens backstage with Triple H demanding to know who the special guest referee is for his match this Sunday from "Stone Cold" Steve Austin. The "rattlesnake" says he'll tell Hunter and everyone when he's ready. However, he gives him a clue when he tells "the Game" to "have a nice day". That gives Helmsley pause ahead of the intro video and fireworks.

Goldberg def. Rosey. Wearing black and white trunks, Goldberg walks from his locker room to the squared circle, the fans chanting his name. Jerry wouldn't want to be in Chris Jericho's shoes this Sunday when he faces the intense superstar. Rosey then heads to the ring with footage of Bill Spearing him through the barricade six weeks ago. Before the two men lock up, Jericho's music plays and he steps onto the stage with a chair to watch the action. Despite the distraction, Goldberg clubs and dropkicks the Samoan. Rosey answers with a Samoan drop ahead of a pair of corner splashes. When he attempts a third, Bill moves and knees him before building up steam and clotheslining the heel out to the floor. That brings Y2J running down the aisle to try to hit the intense superstar with his chair. Fortunately, Goldberg sees him coming and kicks the Canadian heel down. When he sets up for a Spear, Rosey attacks Bill from behind. It doesn't take the intense superstar to recover from the clubbing blow to Spear the Samoan and impress with a Jackhammer for the win.

Rob Van Dam def. Rene Dupree. Footage of "Stone Cold" Steve Austin trying to motivate Kane and giving him a Stone Cold Stunner plays as RVD heads to the squared circle. Dupree then comes out waving his French flag for boos. Rob greets him with a step over heel kick and split legged moonsault to chase off the rookie. At ringside, Van Dam drops Rene onto the barricade for his twisting leg drop. Back in the squared circle, the heel begs off, but RVD remains on the attack until he runs his shoulder into the ring post. Once in control, Dupree stomps Rob's shoulder and stretches it until Van Dam back flips off the second rope and kicks the rookie down. He follows up with rolling thunder, but misses a Five-Star Frog Splash. When Rene tries to capitalize though, RVD surprises him with a roll-up for the victory. Post-match, Sylvan Grenier runs out to join his partner stomping Rob. While La Resistance plants Van Dam with a Double Flapjack, the announcers wonder where Kane is, noting that he's in the building.

After a commercial break, Eric Bischoff has created a roulette wheel for his redneck triathlon with "Stone Cold" Steve Austin this Sunday. He spins the wheel to reveal that one of the events will be a pie-eating contest. He wonders what kind of pie they'll have, but Austin calls him stupid. He says it's the type of pie that The Rock likes and wonders if Eric likes that too. Bischoff is game if "Stone Cold" is. Instead of spinning the wheel two more times, the co-general managers agree to save the mystery. Speaking of mystery, Eric wonders who the "Hell in a Cell" special guest referee will be this Sunday, asking Austin if it's "bang, bang". The "rattlesnake" tells him he'll just have to wait to see.

The announcers show footage of "Classy" Freddie Blassie's final *Raw* appearance before a video package plays of WWE superstars, including Vince McMahon, talking about how much they loved Blassie.

Backstage, Rob Van Dam finds Kane sitting quietly by himself. RVD wants to know where he was and tells him to get his head on straight. When he says what "Stone Cold" Steve Austin said last week might have been true, the "Big Red Machine" storms off.

Ivory/Trish Stratus def. Jazz/Victoria (with Theodore Long). While the babyfaces come out together, the heels make separate entrances, JR noting the Hell in a Cell cage hanging above the squared circle. Inside the ring, Long wants to talk to Jazz, but she says the time to talk is over. Despite that, she tells Ivory that she got lucky last week and the champion is coming for her. Ivory answers with a kick and slam. Trish then tags in for a double flapjack. When the vixen lowers her head for a back body drop though, Jazz kicks her and tags in Victoria for a series of fists. Stratus answers with a pair of roll-ups and kicks, a Chick Kick nearly getting her the three-count, but the Women's Champion makes the save. Soon after, Ivory head scissors the black widow out to the floor. Trish follows up with a back body drop out of the ring to Jazz and baseball slide kick. While they fight at ringside, Victoria whips Ivory off the top rope by the hair. She follows up with shoulder blocks and chokes in the heel corner. When Jazz returns, she double arm suplexes the babyface three times for a near fall. A sit-out powerslam follows before the black widow tags back in for a slingshot somersault leg drop and another close two-count. She even bites Ivory before hoisting her up for the Spider's Web. This time, Stratus makes the save. Although Ivory stuns Victoria with a jawbreaker, Jazz illegally dropkicks the babyface and prevents her from tagging out. When she tags in and tries to follow up, Ivory surprises the champion with a roll-up out of nowhere for another pinfall victory over the heel.

Backstage, Christian practices a spinaroonie. Chris Jericho doesn't want to know what he's doing. He's ready to get out of the arena. Y2J says he's got Goldberg fired up and exactly where he wants him. If Jericho sees him before Bad Blood, he might just take care of the intense superstar.

Following a shot of Miami Dolphins players in the crowd, we see footage from the WWE touring the UK.

Scott Steiner (with Stacy Keibler) def. Lance Storm. After the wrestlers are introduced, Test steps through the curtain to distract Scott and provide guest commentary. Lance capitalizes with a spinning heel kick and reverse chin lock, the bodyguard saying that Stacy is "all right" and he can do better. Soon after, Steiner comes back to life, powerslamming the Canadian heel. He follows up with an elbow drop and pushups, sending Test to ringside to pull Keibler up the aisle. "Big Poppa Pump" spots him and leaves the ring to play tug-of-war with his manager. Storm capitalizes, hitting Scott from behind ahead of a springboard flying splash and near fall. Steiner immediately answers with his Falling Facebuster for the win. Post-match, the bodyguard gives him a Big Boot before grabbing a chair and wailing on "Big Poppa Pump". When Stacy pleads for him to stop, Test corners her and questions if he's not good enough for her. With the fans insulting him, the bodyguard comes to his senses and apologizes. He says she doesn't have to be his girlfriend anymore, but this Sunday he's going to make her his "whore". He then forcefully kisses her. When she tries to slap him, he catches her hand and squeezes it hard.

After a commercial break, the Hell in a Cell is lowered for "Stone Cold" Steve Austin to announce the special guest referee for this Sunday's World Title match. It's not a big surprise as fans have been chanting his name since last week, but Mick Foley comes out to a big pop. He's happy to be the official this Sunday and talks about his time in the Cell. While he suffered injuries previously in the Cell, Foley says all he has to do this Sunday is count to three. That brings out Triple H. He expected to see Mick tonight and calls him just like the fans, an "ordinary guy". Hunter taunts the hardcore legend, telling him that he made him an "ordinary guy" when he retired Foley. Mick agrees, but says "the Game" never kept him down. Once again, he tells everyone that he just needs to use his right hand to count to three at Bad Blood. The World Champion knows that Foley has suffered a number of chair shots so he's going to make his words very simple. He tells Mick to reconsider serving as the referee this Sunday or before the end of the night, Triple H is going to take him out.

Randy Orton (with Ric Flair) def. The Hurricane (with Shawn Michaels). Flair is out first to introduce Orton, the young heel imitating Ric's strut. When The Hurricane comes out he thinks better of facing the heels alone and gets Shawn to join him. That sets off "The Nature Boy" and distracts Randy for a superhero ambush. When he goes for the Eye of the Hurricane though, Orton answers with a side slam. Unfortunately, he runs into a corner elbow and string of clotheslines. The Hurricane follows up with a top rope flying cross body block and near fall, but misses an Overcast. Randy can't capitalize and is stunned by an inverted atomic drop and shining wizard. When Ric breaks up the cover, Michaels rushes over to attack his Bad Blood opponent, busting him open. Flair responds with a whip into the ring post, stunning the "Heartbreak Kid" long enough for Orton to debut a new finisher, a Diamond Cutter that he will rename the RKO, for the victory. Post-match, Randy delivers a second Cutter. When Ric joins his stablemate in the ring, Shawn recovers and attacks the heels, busting "The Nature Boy" up even more.

Backstage, Spike Dudley asks Mick Foley if he really needs to referee "Hell in a Cell". He tells him to think about his family. Mick appreciates his concern and promises to take it under advisement.

After a commercial break, a camera catches Triple H berating Eric Bischoff. Unfortunately, we can't hear what he's saying.

At ringside, Jerry "the King" Lawler introduces Booker T for the first spinaroonie contest. Christian follows to boos. Ahead of their Intercontinental Title match this Sunday, the wrestlers have one last face-to-face confrontation. To kick off the contest, Booker wants to see a "King-a-roonie". Lawler tries, but runs horizontally on the canvas like a member of the Three Stooges. Christian calls it brutal before doing the running man and robot ahead of his spinaroonie, ending up staring seductively at the crowd. Booker T thinks that was pathetic and wants to show the champion how to do it. The heel tries to cheap shot him with the Intercontinental Title, but the five-time champion sees him coming and ducks. He then chases off the heel with a side kick and promises to take the belt this Sunday before showing the fans a true spinaroonie for a nice pop. Christian gets the last laugh, hitting Booker when he tries to step through the curtain to send a message ahead of this Sunday.

Rodney Mack (with Theodore Long/Christopher Nowinski) def. D-Von Dudley (with Bubba Ray Dudley). Theodore Long stops to join the announcers and provide guest commentary once again. For once, Mack is not competing in a "White Boy Challenge". D-Von starts strong, punching and bulldogging the rookie. Rodney answers with some clubbing blows and a nerve pinch. After complimenting Nowinski and saying he'll be good as long as he "backs the Mack", Long says that Dudley is "brown" and not black like Rodney. Mack continues to try to knock D-Von out with his nerve pinch until the babyface comes back to life with clotheslines and a neckbreaker. When D-Von plants the heel with a flapjack, Christopher hops onto the apron to distract him. Rodney capitalizes with a sidewalk slam for a near fall. He tries to follow up with a powerslam, but Dudley slips free to reverse DDT the heel. That sends Theodore down the aisle to distract Nick Patrick. While the referee's back is turned, The Dudley Boyz give Nowinski a 3D when he tries to attack D-Von. Unfortunately, Mack takes advantage and locks his opponent in the Black Out for the win.

Backstage, Terri reminds Goldberg about everything Chris Jericho has done to him ahead of their match this Sunday. Bill tells her that Y2J is next at Bad Blood. Jericho gets to him one more time, hitting him with a chair out of nowhere.

Further backstage, "Stone Cold" Steve Austin is looking for Mick Foley. He wants to know what's wrong with the hardcore legend and asks if he's afraid of Triple H. Austin is embarrassed of him and wants to know if Mick is going to be the referee this Sunday or not. He's got two minutes to think about it as we cut to a commercial break before the World Champion heads to the squared circle.

After the commercial break, the Hell in a Cell lowers and Triple H heads to the ring. He wants to know if Mick Foley is going to make the right decision and invites the hardcore legend to tell him if he's going to bow out of the match or get knocked out of it. Mick says he's going to return to his "normal ordinary life". Hunter thinks that's the right decision. However, Foley isn't going to return to his "ordinary life" until next Monday because he's going to officiate this Sunday's "Hell in a Cell" match. Mick admits that Helmsley has always been just a little better than him and he's afraid that "the Game" will attack him in the parking lot, his motel, or his home this week. Instead of depriving the fans of that fight, Foley offers to take his beating right here tonight and rushes into the cage to trade fists with the World Champion. Fueled by adrenaline and the crowd, Mick punches and knees Triple H in a corner. When they head to the floor though, Hunter whips his rival into the ring steps. He follows up with chair shots to the guest referee's back and head. When Helmsley storms off, Foley counts to three and tells "the Game" that he has a lot more butt to get kicked. That sends the champion back to the squared circle to Pedigree Mick onto a chair. Once again, Triple H storms up the aisle only to see Foley count to three again. The fans love it while Hunter seethes and removes his shirt. This time, Randy Orton and Ric Flair join Hunter attacking Mick. Kevin Nash and Shawn Michaels follow to even the odds. While Shawn deals with Flair and Orton, Nash and Helmsley trade fists. Kevin wins the exchange and stuns the champion with a big boot. A Jackknife Powerbomb follows before Foley counts to three when "Big Sexy" covers Helmsley. Jerry says that's all Mick has to do this Sunday.

SmackDown!

June 12, 2003
Orlando, FL
Announcers: Michael Cole, Tazz

The show opens with a two-minute recap of Rey Mysterio winning the Cruiserweight Title last week. Afterwards, the intro video plays and fireworks explode.

Rey Mysterio def. Matt Hardy Version 1.0 (Cruiserweight Title match). Matt enacts his rematch clause quickly and refuses to take the blame for his loss. Instead, he blames Crash Holly—making his last appearance before passing away in this series—and Shannon Moore, attacking them backstage before marching out, his sole Matt Fact stating that he's too handsome to wear a mask. Marching down the aisle, Hardy attacks Rey, but gets mesmerized by the championship. Mysterio capitalizes with a string of shots until the challenger nearly regains the belt with a side neckbreaker. When he heads to the top rope, the masked man stops his attack and answers with a flying bulldog. Matt responds with a side effect, but the action goes back and forth, Rey rolling up the challenger for a near fall. He follows up with a springboard senton for another two-count, but Hardy reverses and gets another near fall. When the champion attempts a leapfrog though, he pulls his groin and is slow to follow up. Although he gives Matt the 619 and a springboard leg drop, he's slow to make the cover and the challenger just kicks out. Moments later, Hardy swings the momentum with a crucifix powerbomb out of the corner for a near fall. When he attempts to finish off Rey with a Twist of Fate, Mysterio holds onto the ropes to escape. As Matt hits the back of his head on the canvas, the masked man immediately follows up with a modified West Coast Pop off the top rope for the victory.

After a commercial break, "Rowdy" Roddy Piper and Sean O'Haire have a table set up with Mexican and Japanese items and food for their guests on Piper's Pit this week, Eddie Guerrero and Tajiri. Eddie wonders if he has a loaded burrito like the coconut he used on "Superfly" Jimmy Snuka. "Hot Rod" has too much respect for them to do that. He'd like Guerrero to let O'Haire hold a title belt since he'll be the next champion. While "Latino Heat" refuses, Tajiri accepts some sushi in exchange. O'Haire refuses to give the belt back and wonders what Eddie is going to do about it. That fires up the champion and he wants to fight, but the "Japanese Buzzsaw" holds him back. When Roddy offers to drink tequila with him, Tajiri sprays it into his eyes and the champions attack to regain their belts and leave the heels laying.

Backstage, Sable is on Stephanie McMahon's computer looking for Zach Gowen's contract. While she didn't find it, she did see that Stephanie is bringing back the US Title. McMahon doesn't trust her and says that she knows she's up to no good. Sable pleads innocence and says she just wants to help.

Billy Gunn def. A-Train. Torrie Wilson serves as the guest ring announcer. As she comes out, the announcers hype the upcoming Divas Contest where fans can compete to become a WWE diva. She mocks A-Train's back hair before introducing Billy, making his return following rotator cuff surgery. He's back using his "Mr. Ass" gimmick, but the hairy heel isn't impressed, hammering him down. Torrie is, watching and licking a sucker at ringside as Gunn comes back to life with fists and a corner splash. When he motions for the Famouser, A-Train surprises him with a bicycle kick. He then motions for the Derailer, but Billy fights free and scores the victory with a Famouser. Post-match, Wilson spanks Gunn's butt and asks him to respond in kind. He does so to a nice pop, the announcers wondering how he got so lucky.

Footage of Brock Lesnar arriving earlier today and the fans warmly greeting him plays.

The Subway WWE Smack of the Night is The Undertaker fighting off The FBI and Nunzio.

The Undertaker def. Johnny Stamboli (with Chuck Palumbo/Nunzio). After taking care of Palumbo last week, The Undertaker continues his feud with the FBI. He wastes little time hammering Stamboli down to start the match ahead of a corner clothesline. When he sets up for the Last Ride, the other heels distract the biker. He joins them outside, ramming Chuck into the announce table before threatening to chokeslam Nunzio off the apron. Luckily, Johnny saves him. Although he pays with a jawbreaker on the top rope, Stamboli recovers quickly to save Nunzio as he crawls under the ring with a baseball slide kick. Palumbo follows up with a Superkick ahead of a slingshot leg drop from "the Bull" for a near fall. He also gets a close two-count with a delayed vertical suplex. Johnny tries to finish off the "Deadman" with a twisting top rope guillotine leg drop, but The Undertaker moves. The two men then trade counters until the biker rams Stamboli back into Chuck on the apron. Once he's down, the "Deadman" finishes off "the Bull" with a Last Ride for the three-count. Post-match, he goes after Nunzio, but Palumbo makes the save. Back in the squared circle, The Undertaker absorbs Chuck's blows and drops him with a leaping clothesline and chokeslam. When he sets up for a second Last Ride, Nunzio makes the save with a chair shot to the skull.

Backstage, Mr. America pumps up Zach Gowen for his arm wrestling match.

After a commercial break, Stephanie McMahon heads to the ring to oversee the upcoming arm wrestling contest. She reminds fans that if Zach Gowen defeats her father, he'll get a *SmackDown!* contract. When Stephanie tries to introduce Zach, Sable comes out instead. The general manager doesn't want to hear why she's out there, taking away the microphone to introduce Gowen, walking with a cane, and Mr. America. Vince McMahon follows to boos. While the fans don't like him, the announcers are impressed with his massive arms. Mr. America tells him that he's "fighting the wrong battle" because Hulk Hogan is back home and Vince really wants the masked patriot. He challenges McMahon to arm wrestle him instead, but the WWE owner says no. He signed on to arm wrestle Zach. Sable has her own thoughts, whispering into McMahon's ear. On second thought, Vince will arm wrestle Mr. America, but if the WWE owner wins, the masked patriot has to leave the arena. That's fine with Mr. America and he locks up with McMahon. Toying with Vince, the masked patriot flips him off. Sable grabs his hand as soon as he starts to get the advantage, accusing Mr. America of cheating. Stephanie threatens to disqualify her father if Sable touches another competitor. Vince tells Sable to stay out of things and locks back up with the masked patriot. This time when the WWE owner starts to lose, Sable flashes Mr. America, distracting him long enough for McMahon to steal the win and kick the masked patriot out of the building. Mr. America is incensed. Vince dares him to lay a had on the WWE owner. If he does, McMahon promises that Gowen will never get a WWE contract. When the masked patriot reluctantly backs down, Vince tells Sable and Stephanie to head backstage before he deals with the WWE hopeful. McMahon is so confident that he agrees to compete with his left arm. Although he initially toys with Zach, Vince can't put him away and the fan nearly puts his hand down. At the last second, McMahon kicks Gowen's prosthetic leg out from under him and steals the win. Afterwards, Vince gets in his face and asks Zach if he's going to cry since his dream went up in smoke. He then kicks Gowen out of his ring. Despite the fans loudly booing him, Vince happily celebrates his tainted victory.

After the lengthy segment and a commercial break, we get a replay of Vince McMahon cheating Zach Gowen. Backstage, Mr. America tries to console him while Big Show tells the fan to "forget it".

The Basham Brothers (with Shaniqua) def. Chris Benoit/Rhyno. Linda Miles returns in black leather with a riding crop as Shaniqua, the Bashams' new manager. It doesn't make a difference as Rhyno clubs Doug to start the match. When he runs the ropes though, Danny knees him and Doug nearly steals the win with a neckbreaker. Afterwards, he applies a reverse chin lock, but it doesn't take the man-beast long to fight free and back suplex Basham. Benoit gets the tag afterwards to hit both men and suplex Doug for a two-count. Rhyno recovers to side suplex Danny and take the fight out to the floor while "the Crippler" German suplexes Doug. When he heads upstairs, Shaniqua trips Benoit and he misses his diving headbutt. Despite that, he locks Doug in a Crippler Crossface until Danny makes the save. The man-beast follows him in, fighting with Danny again. In the chaos, the "rabid wolverine" grabs Danny for a German suplex while Rhyno tries to hit Basham. At the last second, Danny ducks and the man-beast hits his own partner. Doug follows up with a leg lariat to Benoit for the three-count. Post-match, "the Crippler" yells at his partner.

After a commercial break, Rhyno tells Chris Benoit that he made a mistake backstage, but "the Crippler" doesn't want to hear it. He says he made that mistake two times in a row. The man-beast says if he wanted to hit Benoit he'd do it right now, but he respects Chris. The "rabid wolverine" isn't buying it.

John Cena def. Funaki. Pre-match, Cena says the fans love him and accuses Cole of chasing after boy bands. When he makes fun of Funaki's tight shorts, the wrestler turned announcer turned wrestler steals a cheer to call him ugly. He follows up by doing the robot. That fires up John and he steamrolls Funaki, hammering him ahead of a quick FU for the decisive victory.

The JVC Tower of Power Extreme Blast of the Night is Kurt Angle and Brock Lesnar agreeing to a future match last week. Kurt then heads to the squared circle. He said it was great returning last week and he's looking forward to tonight's WWE Title match to find out who he'll face for the championship. Before then, he wants to talk to Team Angle, inviting them to enter the ring. When they do so, he shakes hands with them and says he understands why they didn't call him when he was in the hospital. He knows they are world class athletes, but he doesn't know why they called in sick last week. Charlie Haas and Shelton Benjamin say they are sick of being in Angle's shadow and he let them down when he wasn't in their corner for their title defense. The Olympian is sick too…sick of them whining. He wonders if they turned into "Team Wah-ngle". Kurt tells them that they have to get back to business and plan their next move. Haas is tired of Angle. Charlie calls him a loser and says the former champions are tired of hearing the fans chant "you suck". Kurt says they don't deserve to hear that and the fans chant that because the Olympian earned their reaction. When Angle mentions breaking up Team Angle, Charlie says they aren't disbanding the team. Instead, they are making a change in leadership and he's taking over alongside Benjamin. Kurt disagrees. As the founder and current leader, he kicks them both out of Team Angle to a big pop. Instead of chanting that they suck, he gets the fans to sing goodbye to his former tag team, Shelton and Haas throwing a fit as they head backstage.

Ahead of the main event, we see the tale of the tape for Big Show and Brock Lesnar.

During the break, Charlie Haas and Shelton Benjamin attack Kurt Angle backstage and leave him laying.

MUST SEE! Big Show and Brock Lesnar (WWE Title match) wrestle to a no contest. Brock charges the challenger as soon as the bell rings, driving him back into a corner. He can't hold him down for long and

Show knocks the champion to the mat for an early two-count. Chops follow until the giant misses a clothesline and falls out to the floor. Lesnar follows, hammering Big Show at ringside. When he attempts a whip into the ring steps, the challenger reverses it. Back in the squared circle, Show absorbs a string of kicks to score a near fall with a sidewalk slam. He then applies a single leg crab, surprising Tazz. Although Brock escapes, Big Show stays on the offensive until he misses a corner charge. That lets the champion land a string of forearm shots and a big German suplex. He tries to finish him Show with an F5, but Lesnar's ribs are too injured and he collapses to the canvas. The giant responds with a big clothesline, but when he tries to Chokeslam Brock, the "next big thing" slips free. Despite that, Show flattens him for a leg drop and near fall. Afterwards, he finally hits his Chokeslam, but somehow, the champion just kicks out. The challenger sets up for another one, but wants to assure that he finishes him off and tries to take Lesnar to the top rope. Instead, Brock crotches him and sets up for a huge superplex. When they hit the mat, the ring collapses and the fans go bananas in a unique spot that has Mike Chioda stunned and the wrestlers out cold for a no contest. Having never seen this, the fans express their shock while the referee calls for assistance, the show ending with trainers and officials helping the competitors as replays of this innovative moment in WWE history are shown. Cole simply ends the show telling the fans "good night".

PPV: Bad Blood

June 15, 2003
Houston, TX
Announcers: Jim Ross, Jerry "the King" Lawler

The show opens with a video package featuring *Raw*'s top rivalries, Eric Bischoff and "Stone Cold" Steve Austin getting a lot of attention. Afterwards, fireworks explode to kick off the PPV.

Christopher Nowinski/Rodney Mack (with Theodore Long) def. The Dudley Boyz. As the Dudleys head to the ring, we see Nowinski questioning D-Von earlier tonight on *Heat*. He wonders why the "white brother" is always telling D-Von to get the table. That gives Dudley pause. Here, Mack and D-Von tie-up and trade fists. The babyface gets the upper hand with clotheslines for an early two-count. Christopher tags in afterwards to cheap shot Bubba Ray. That brings Bubba into the ring to chase after the metal facemask wearing Harvard heel. Dudley stays away from his reconstructed nose to punch Nowinski's gut until Long distracts him. That swings the moment and Christopher finally gets in a little offense. It's very little as Bubba answers with his own shots and a back elbow. When Rodney tries to help his partner, Dudley spots him coming and whips Mack into the Harvard heel. The Dudley Boyz work together afterwards with a clubbing shot and splash for a near fall. When D-Von backs into a corner though, Rodney trips and pulls him back into the ring post. He follows with hammering blows and a reverse chin lock. Dudley tries to fight back, even decking Nowinski before turning into a spinebuster. Christopher tags in moments later to score a two-count with a body splash. Unfortunately, he misses a second rope elbow drop and Bubba Ray returns to run through the Harvard heel. He also knocks down Mack when he illegally enters the ring before dropping Nowinski with a sidewalk slam for a two-count. The fans want tables, but instead Bubba boots Christopher's face ahead of a second rope dive. While D-Von fights with Rodney at ringside, the Harvard heel tries to use his mask to knock out Bubba Ray. Luckily, Dudley dodges and holds a returning Mack for a wassup drop. When Bubba tells his half-brother to get the tables, Long questions D-Von. That gives him pause and Rodney knocks D-Von out to the floor. Although Bubba Ray drops Mack, he turns into a Nowinski mask shot for the heels to steal the victory.

Footage of Eric Bischoff and "Stone Cold" Steve Austin spinning a wheel to determine that the first fall in their "Redneck Triathlon" will be a pie-eating contest plays. The second will be a burping contest, as spun on *Sunday Night Heat*. After footage of both spins are shown, Terri reveals that the competitions have flipped. Up first, Eric and Steve trade burps backstage. Bischoff's is really chunky and dry. "Stone Cold" lets out a majestic burp that definitely sounds piped in. Eric responds with his own, not quite as good belch. Poor Terri is stuck between the burps, Austin saying that his second attempt was "a little wet". Bischoff gets one last attempt and it's the most disgusting yet. With his back against the wall, "Stone Cold" reaches down deep and lets loose a titanic roar, clearly fake. Steve calls Eric a "worthy competitor" while Bischoff tells the "rattlesnake" to see a doctor.

Scott Steiner def. Test. Stacy Keibler's managerial services are on the line here as Test heads to the squared circle first. Scott follows before Stacy comes out alone to show off her underwear as she stretches out her legs over the ropes. When the bodyguard pulls her down from the apron, Steiner tries to dive onto him. He slips and misses, symbolic of his run with the WWE. Recovering quickly, "Big Poppa Pump" clubs Test until the heel hides behind Keibler. He takes advantage of her distraction, whipping Scott into the ring steps hard. The bodyguard follows up with hammering blows while the fans let him know that he sucks. He doesn't care, slamming Steiner and mocking him with pushups. He also blows Stacy kisses, but that only disgusts her. When the bodyguard applies a reverse chin lock, Keibler tries to wake up "Big Poppa Pump" by pounding the canvas. It works and he fights free before catching a diving Test for an overhead slam. A modified Samoan drop follows before Scott wails on the bodyguard in a corner. Test answers with a full nelson slam out of nowhere for a near fall. When he attempts a Pumphandle Slam, Steiner flips free. He also ducks a Big Boot ahead of a reverse DDT and two-count. The bodyguard responds with a Pumphandle Slam and his own near fall. Afterwards, he tries to remove a turnbuckle pad, but Stacy hops onto the apron to distract him. She almost gets knocked down when "Big Poppa Pump" charges Test from behind, but the babyface holds up at the last second. Unfortunately, he eats a Big Boot and another near fall. When Test heads to the floor to get a chair, Keibler tries to stop him. She gets thrown down to the floor, but when the bodyguard tries to use the chair on Scott, he misses and the weapon bounces off the top rope and back into his face. Steiner follows up with his Falling Facebuster for the win. Post-match, "Big Poppa Pump" watches as Stacy steps through the ropes before lifting her up onto his shoulder.

Backstage, "Stone Cold" Steve Austin and Eric Bischoff talk. The "rattlesnake" needs to use the bathroom before they compete in the second leg of the "Redneck Triathlon". Eric thinks he's disgusting, but before Steve heads to the restroom, Bischoff wants to show him something. It's a quartet of attractive girls for the upcoming competition. "Stone Cold" is impressed and wants to go first. Eric also wants to go first. While Austin says his co-general manager is being selfish, he agrees to let him go first so long as Steve gets to pick the "flavor" of pie that Bischoff will eat. That's fine with Eric because he says it's all quality.

Booker T def. Christian (Intercontinental Title match) by disqualification. Booker is the early aggressor, running through and tossing around the champion. He then traps Christian in a side headlock, even scoring a two-count before the heel fights his way free. Unfortunately, he immediately runs into a back body drop and near fall. A spinebuster also almost crowns a new champion and sends Christian out to the apron. There he slams the back of Booker T's head onto the ropes before whipping his face into the ring steps for a two-count. Afterwards, the champion applies his own reverse chin lock. When he attempts a dive off the second rope though, he leaps into a flapjack. Fists and a leaping cross chop follow ahead of a sidewalk slam and near fall. Booker also gets a two-count with a side kick. Keeping up the pressure, the challenger nearly gets the win with a hotshot and reverse DDT. Booker tries to answer with a roll-up, but Christian rolls through and holds the ropes for a two-count. A uranage also gets him a near fall before Booker T surprises him with a roll-up for his own close two-count. When he ends up on the apron moments later, the five-time champion surprises his opponent with a Scissors Kick and top rope missile dropkick for another near fall. He follows up with a side kick and spinaroonie for a good pop. He tries to score the win with a second Scissors Kick, but the heel grabs his belt and heads up the ramp to get counted out. Jack Doan isn't going to let that happen, grabbing the house mic to tell the champion that if he doesn't return to the ring, he'll forfeit the championship. That brings Christian back down the aisle to deck Booker T with the gold for the blatant disqualification. JR calls it the "coward's way out".

Following a shot of Kevin Nash getting ready backstage, Lawler is in the ring to introduce "Stone Cold" Steve Austin and Eric Bischoff for the second leg of the "Redneck Triathlon". "Stone Cold" cuts off "the King" to remind everyone that he gets to pick Eric's "flavor" for the pie-eating contest. However, before he picks from Bischoff's girls, he remembers that Eric said he liked mature women. While Steve believes the girls backstage are gorgeous, Austin wants to give Bischoff a mature option. That's, of course, Mae Young with The Fabulous Moolah in tow. "Stone Cold" applauds while Eric is disgusted and horrified. JR says he has to go first and if he loses this leg of the competition, he loses the triathlon. Despite that, Bischoff refuses to participate, Mae chasing him around the ring. Austin claims victory and questions Eric's guts. Before Jerry can make it official, Bischoff has a change of heart and kisses Young. He wants Steve to top that, but the "rattlesnake" says this is a pie-eating contest. While Eric complains, Mae gives him a low blow and bronco buster with a fish in her underwear. Once he's done, Bischoff wants "Stone Cold" to beat that. Instead, Austin forfeits the competition and gives Young a Stone Cold Stunner to tie up the "Redneck Triathlon". The fans in attendance laugh, but this isn't good.

Backstage, Kane looks at himself in a mirror, JR wondering what "Big Red Machine" will show up tonight. That will be more than he did Monday night when the heels attacked his partner.

Further backstage, Sylvan Grenier tells Jonathan Coachman that this is a big night for La Resistance, but it's a shame they have to have it in Texas. After he makes fun of the president, Rene Dupree praises the president of France before the heels head to the squared circle.

MUST SEE! La Resistance def. Kane/Rob Van Dam (World Tag Title match). While the challengers come out together, the champions continue to enter separately. Individually, the babyfaces are much better than their opponents, RVD proving that early on with a string of attacks to Dupree until Grenier cheats and throat drops him on the top rope. Sylvan then tags in to elbow drop Rob for a two-count. JR doesn't like La Resistance, telling the fans that they think they are better than everyone else. Rene tries to prove it, returning to apply a chin lock and pull Van Dam's hair. The champion answers with a kick and tag to Kane who fights both challengers, rocking Grenier with a big boot before tossing Dupree out to the floor. When Rene tries to return with a cheap shot, the "Big Red Machine" answers with a two-handed chokeslam. A sidewalk slam to Sylvan nearly gets him the win before he heads upstairs for a flying clothesline and two-count. At the last second, Rene makes the save. The challengers remain in the ring together, rocking the monster with a modified double neckbreaker. Kane answers with a double clothesline before tagging in RVD. While he catches Dupree with a top rope flying attack, Grenier pokes the "Big Red Machine's" eyes at ringside. Rob tries to rush to his partner's aid, but his somersault splash over the top rope hits Kane instead. La Resistance immediately capitalize with a Double Flapjack to Van Dam for the three-count to crown new champions and stun JR.

Ahead of the Chris Jericho/Goldberg match, a video package plays for their feud.

Goldberg def. Chris Jericho. After Jericho enters the ring, a member of the crew knocks on Goldberg's door and the intense superstar makes his way to the squared circle through smoke and sparks. Y2J hops out to the floor to make Bill wait. Goldberg has had enough waiting and charges Jericho when he returns, tackling him out to the floor. Back in the squared circle, he catches a cross body block for a front slam. The intense superstar then flings Y2J back into a corner before tossing him around the ring. Jericho doesn't just roll over, answering with fists and clotheslines until he runs into a back elbow and press slam crotch-first onto the top rope. A side kick sends the heel out to the floor where Bill slams him on the barricade. He tries to finish off Y2J with a Spear against the barricade, but Jericho moves at the last second and Goldberg bursts through the security wall. While he checks on him, Charles Robinson holds Y2J back from attacking the injured superstar, but the heel eventually slips past him to punch and missile dropkick the bleeding babyface. Focusing on the injured right shoulder, Jericho stomps and stretches Bill's arm. The intense superstar responds with a shoulderblock for boos. The fans cheer when Y2J answers with an armbar takedown. Unfortunately, when he attempts a springboard attack, he leaps into a kick to the gut. Unable to use his shoulder, a back kick flattens Jericho, but the heel answers with a second armbar drop for a near fall. With a few fans chanting that "Goldberg sucks", Y2J flattens him with a dropkick. A running face slam and Lionsault afterwards nearly gets Jericho the win, but the intense superstar just kicks out. The heel goes back to the well with a running face slam, but when he attempts a second Lionsault, Bill catches and slams him. A Spear follows, but when he attempts to Jackhammer Y2J, the heel holds his ground and rakes the referee's eye. While Robinson tries to clear his vision, Jericho gives Goldberg a low blow before locking him in the Walls of Jericho. The intense superstar won't submit and powers out before driving Y2J to the canvas with a second Spear. This time, Bill powers up Jericho and Jackhammers him for the victory. Post-match, Goldberg confronts a Jericholic wearing a Tigger costume in the crowd.

Backstage, Eric Bischoff and "Stone Cold" Steve Austin spin the wheel for the final contest in the "Redneck Triathlon". When it lands on a singing contest, Eric is ecstatic. He knows Steve stinks at singing. Terri agrees. Although "Stone Cold" offers to spin again, Bischoff promises to humiliate the "rattlesnake" in front of his home state.

Ric Flair def. Shawn Michaels. Following a video package for the rivalry, JR talks about the competitors dominating the eighties and nineties, respectively. When they finally lock up, Ric gets too cocky and Shawn trips him to walk across "The Nature Boy's" back and slap him. Flair can't stand it, but he can't do anything about it as Michaels knocks him out to the floor for a slingshot splash from the squared circle. When they return to the ring, the "Heartbreak Kid" drops Ric with a shoulderblock followed by a side headlock. Flair chops his way free only to receive his own string of chops and fists. Eventually, Earl Hebner steps in for the break, distracting Shawn for a "Nature Boy" chop block. Once in control, Ric focuses on the injured joint, kicking and stretching it while mixing in some stiff chops. Flair doesn't soften up the babyface for long, quickly applying a Figure Four Leglock and nearly getting the three-count with Michaels's shoulders on the mat. It takes him some time to reach the ropes, but he eventually grabs them. After arguing with Hebner, "The Nature Boy" goes back to work until the "Heartbreak Kid" stuns him with an enziguri kick. Despite that, Ric recovers first to chop Shawn in a corner. Michaels responds with chops and a back body drop before running into a back elbow. Flair tries to follow up with a top rope attack, but the "Heartbreak Kid" catches and slams him to the canvas. He then tunes up the band, but "The Nature Boy" catches his foot for a roll-up and two-count. After kicking out, Shawn briefly applies his own figure four, but a thumb to the eye stops him. Ric tries to capitalize with a back suplex, but Michaels flips free for a roll-up, sandwiching Earl in the corner. That makes him a little groggy for a pair of two-counts and the heel pulling his opponent's trunks. Moments later, Flair goes back upstairs only to collide heads with the "Heartbreak Kid". Shawn gets the better of the exchange and recovers to superplex "The Nature Boy" off the second rope. Instead of going for the cover, Michaels sets up a table at ringside. Placing Ric on the table, the "Heartbreak Kid" pummels him until Randy Orton appears out of nowhere only to get Sweet Chin Music. Shawn follows up with a splash off the top rope, driving Flair through the table. "The Nature Boy" howls in agony and bleeds from his back as Michaels shoves him into the ring for a near fall. Ric retreats to a corner and catches both the referee and "Heartbreak Kid" with a low blow. Despite that, Shawn is up quickly to rock Flair with a flying forearm ahead of a top rope diving elbow drop. With the fans cheering him on, Michaels tunes up the band and delivers Sweet Chin Music right before Orton blasts the babyface with a chair. As soon as Randy rolls "The Nature Boy" onto Shawn, Hebner recovers to give Flair the groggy three-count.

Afterwards, Eric Bischoff heads to the ring, still trying to spit the taste out of his mouth. He is happy to lip synch along with his entrance theme. "Stone Cold" Steve Austin interrupts from the Titantron. He wants to hear Eric sing live. Bischoff is fine with that, but he can't sing. "Stone Cold" says he sucks, but since he can't do any better, Austin offers to spin the wheel again. Instead of spinning it, Steve turns it to "Pig Pen Fun". Conveniently, there's a pigpen at ringside for the competitors to try to toss each other into the pen. If Eric runs off, "Stone Cold" deputizes all of the fans to throw Bischoff back into the arena. Mattress Mack gets the honors, catching the co-GM and throwing him over the barricade before Austin comes out to stomp a mudhole in Bischoff. He follows up with a Stone Cold Stunner before leading Eric up the ramp to toss him off the stage and into the pigpen. While he rolls around in the muck and mud, JR announcers "Stone Cold" as the winner of the "Redneck Triathlon". The "rattlesnake" celebrates with some beers and the fans cheering him.

While the Cell is lowered over the ring, a video package plays for the main event.

Triple H def. Kevin Nash ("Hell in a Cell" World Title match). Nash is out first, followed by the champion in blue. Finally, the special guest referee, Mick Foley heads to the ring to jaw with Triple H. After Hunter cheap shots Kevin, one boot puts him down. The challenger briefly takes the fight out to the floor before returning to the squared circle to punch and club Helmsley. "The Game" answers with a throat drop on the top rope and his own fists. Nash shoves him back into the referee and the canvas. Fists, knees, and elbows follow from "Big Sexy" before the fight spills out to the floor again. There, Kevin rams the champion into the ring post and cage. Following more whips into the cage and a back body drop on the floor, the challenger scores a two-count with a sidewalk slam in the squared circle. He also gets a near fall with an elbow drop before grabbing a steel chair and ramming it into Triple H's gut. A hard shot to the back follows, sending Hunter rolling back out to the floor. Nash remains on the hunt, slamming Helmsley back into the cage and whipping him into the ring steps. He tries to finish off "The Game" by flinging the steps at his head, but the champion just moves out of the way and swings the momentum. Jerry calls it a "wakeup call". Triple H takes it, unloading with shots and slamming the challenger's face into the steps. Although Kevin teases a Jackknife on the floor, Hunter grabs the cage and lands on his feet, punching "Big Sexy" down. He then opens up a toolbox and nails Nash's thigh and head with a hammer. Foley has seen enough and takes away the hammer. When Helmsley takes offense, the special guest referee shoves him down. "The Game" gets focused back on the task at hand, pummeling the bloodied challenger and raking his head against the Cell. He then grabs a screwdriver and runs it across Kevin's forehead. Still not done, he finds a barbed wire wrapped two-by-four and nails "Big Sexy". When he attempts a second shot, Nash beats him to the punch and takes away the weapon to blast the champion's skull. That busts Triple H open too. After propping up the two-by-four on a turnbuckle, the challenger crushes Triple H in other corners before dropping him face-first onto the barbed wire with snake eyes for a near fall. Lawler says Mick loves this. He has a great spot to watch Kevin toss the steel steps into the ring. When he tries to pull Hunter back into the squared circle, the champion smashes him with a wooden crate. Helmsley then grabs his sledgehammer, but Foley stops him from using it. "The Game" knocks him down and grabs the ring steps, but when he tries to use them, "Big Sexy" surprises him with a drop toe hold for another near fall. Nash tries to finish off his former friend with a chair shot, but the champion kicks his thigh. Triple H follows up with a pair of chair shots, one each for the challenger and referee. Busted open, the blood wakes up Foley and he responds with a Mr. Socko assisted Mandible Claw. Kevin tries to follow up with a shot from the steps, but Hunter moves and "Big Sexy" hits Mick. Things get worse for him when Helmsley knocks Nash into Foley, flinging the referee off the apron and into the cage. Despite that, he recovers quickly as the challenger snake eyes "the Game" onto the barbed wire two-by-four ahead of a Jackknife powerbomb. Somehow, the champion just manages to kick out. After everyone catches their breath, Triple H crawls to the sledgehammer and blasts Kevin. A Pedigree follows for the three-count. Foley isn't happy about it, but he reluctantly makes the count for Hunter to retain his championship. Post-match, Randy Orton and Ric Flair head to the ring while Helmsley lays barely conscious on Nash's chest.

The first brand exclusive PPV in WWE history is just okay. It's so strange that the WWE went from having so much talent in 2001 and 2002 to now featuring matches on PPV that would be weak on weekly television. The opener between the Dudleys and Rodney Mack and Christopher Nowinski is a perfect example. There's no real feud other than Nowinski trying to drive a wedge between the half-brothers on *Heat*. Considering they reunited not that long ago and the fans didn't want to see D-Von solo, that's a bizarre angle. The match isn't any better and is very forgettable. Test and Steiner then punch and stretch each other in a match that's more about Stacy Keibler than either man. This is kind of the end for both. They'll remain in the company into next year, but this is really their last major storyline as both have flamed out, Scott after a lackluster debut against Triple H and Test after numerous failed storylines. Both have tons of potential, although in Steiner's case he's already had a tremendous career, but just don't catch on with fans in the era. Booker and Christian have another decent match with a heel ending seeing the champion intentionally get himself disqualified. It's not amazing, but it keeps both doing something. Booker has cooled down since the WWE didn't have him beat Helmsley at WrestleMania XIX, but he still makes Christian look like a big deal locking up with him. La Resistance then take the World Tag Titles in a boring match other than the moments RVD is in the ring. This is a good result for a bad pairing with La Resistance moving on to be the heel champions and hopefully inject some life into the *Raw* tag division while Kane and Van Dam move into the next phase of their story. While the WWE needs more talent across the board for the brand split, the tag division in particular is really exposed as La Resistance is the best of the bunch on *Raw*. Goldberg and Y2J have a good match. Jericho takes a beating, but he gets in some shots before doing the honors for the intense superstar. This is as good as could be hoped for and both men come out of it just fine. It's a good match, but nothing memorable. Flair and Michaels also have a good match. If Ric was younger, they'd tear the roof off the building. It's still good and both men utilize good psychology to build to the ending. Orton's involvement mars the contest some, but this is a fun match between two masters. Finally, Triple H and Nash have a match far better than would be expected. The "Hell in a Cell" stipulation helps to cover for their weaknesses. Instead of a punch and kick affair, they get to add in weapons for built in high spots. Foley also helps keep the action moving and it's a brutal brawl featuring a lot of blood. It's not the best wrestling match or even "Hell in a Cell" match, but everyone does their job well and it's entertaining. Ultimately, that's my review for Bad Blood. It's not the greatest PPV, but it's entertaining. If you start at the end of the World Tag Title match and see the new champs, the rest of the show is enjoyable. However, that means the first half is skippable. In an era where you can go back to the Network and watch whatever you want for one low monthly price, that's not a big deal. However, in 2003, having to pay for half a PPV is not a good deal and keeps this from being a recommended PPV. It's fine. There are some enjoyable moments—none of which involve Austin and Bischoff in what absolutely is a waste of time—but by and large there are many other shows, some this year, more deserving of your time and attention.

Monday Night Raw
June 16, 2003
Dallas, TX
Announcers: Jim Ross, Jerry "the King" Lawler

Following the intro video and fireworks, Mick Foley heads to the ring to a big pop. He's carrying a copy of his new book, *Tietam Brown*, as he thanks the fans for their support. Despite saying that he was going back to his "ordinary life", Foley is hanging around this week and next at Madison Square Garden before going back home. Tonight, he tells the fans how much he enjoyed jamming Mr. Socko down Triple H's throat last night. When he starts to talk about how good getting into the ring last night made him feel, Evolution head to the ring with new music. Jerry says Mick should be leaving the ring. Instead, he hangs around while Randy Orton calls him a loser and tells everyone that not only did Hunter beat Kevin Nash last night, but he also retired Foley. On top of that, Ric Flair proved last night that he was the greatest of all-time by beating Shawn Michaels. The fans tell Randy that he sucks. Orton ignores them to tell Mick that if he plays his cards right, he might get to join Evolution when they present an open contract for their fourth member. Foley mockingly says all he wants is to be a "Four Horsemen wannabe". He then mocks Randy for showing everyone nothing but how to sit at home and whine about an injured arm. Until Orton shows him something, Mick says he's "just a sixteen year old boy" and doesn't deserve to be in his ring. The fans love it. Randy doesn't care. He tells the hardcore legend that he doesn't have to sleep in his car to get ahead or mutilate his body—removing his shirt—because he's a "third generation superstar". Orton calls hardcore wrestlers like Mick "extinct" and wishes that Helmsley never retired Foley so he could wrestle him. While he might be retired from wrestling, Foley dares Randy to fight him right now. When he attacks the hardcore legend, Mick comes to life and fights all three members of Evolution, "the King" yelling that he's retired and can't do that. Unfortunately, he's outnumbered and Orton drops him with his Cutter. Before Evolution can finish off the hardcore legend, Maven and Al Snow run out to chase off the heels.

Backstage, Eric Bischoff yells at Mae Young and The Fabulous Moolah. He is livid that Mae embarrassed him last night. To pay her back for putting her crotch in his face, Eric signs the eighty year old Mae to a match tonight.

A teaser video plays for Gail Kim.

Ivory/The Dudley Boyz def. Christopher Nowinski/Jazz/Rodney Mack (with Theodore Long). Although the heels run out for a fight, the babyfaces quickly chase them from the ring. Bubba Ray then press slams Ivory out onto Nowinski before chopping Mack in a corner. He fights all three heels until he elbows Christopher's metal face mask. That hurts his elbow and Rodney capitalizes with an armbar drop. The Harvard heel then tags in for a northern lights suplex and two-count. When he locks on an armbar, Dudley fights free and plants him with a Bubba Bomb. He can't tag in D-Von because Mack pulls him face-first onto the apron. Instead, Ivory hammers Jazz and drives her face into the canvas. Unfortunately, Charles Robinson is distracted by Long on the apron. That kicks off a six-person brawl, D-Von hitting Rodney with a top rope flying clothesline. After dumping Christopher, the Dudleys hold Mack for an Ivory wassup drop. A 3D follows to the Harvard heel, but when they size up Jazz, Mack makes the save. The men then all fight outside the ring while Ivory rolls up the Women's Champion for the victory. Post-match, the heels go wild while JR reminds everyone that Ivory has beaten Jazz three times in a row.

The announcers hype up Evolution offering an opportunity for a superstar to join them here tonight. JR and Lawler try to get the fans to vote online on who they think will seize the opportunity ahead of an ad for Ross's new cookbook.

After a commercial break, Rob Van Dame tells Kane that they need to get on the same page for their World Tag Title rematch tonight. The "Big Red Machine" doesn't understand why he's talking to him about getting on the same page because the monster didn't mess up last night. As far as Kane is concerned, if they don't win back the belts tonight, they'll go their separate ways.

A video package plays showing action from Bad Blood.

Backstage, Mick Foley thanks Al Snow for helping him earlier. Snow calls Randy Orton a "punk". Maven agrees and he's going to do something about it. He just got a match from "Stone Cold" Steve Austin with the heel. Foley tells him that he won't be alone.

After a commercial break, Evolution watch a television monitor backstage. The announcers wonder if they've made their decision on who will join them yet.

Garrison Cade def. Lance Storm. Storm is followed by "Stone Cold" Steve Austin carrying a blanket and pillow. The co-general manager repeatedly calls Lance "boring" before telling the heel that he hasn't slept in a while. The only thing he can think that will definitely put him out is Storm wrestling. He continues to chant boring as Cade surprises Lance with a dropkick ahead of a wrist lock. When the Canadian fights free, Austin lays down and says this match is more boring than he thought it would be. That sets off Storm and he rocks the rookie with a leg lariat. When he applies a key lock, "Stone Cold" starts to snore. Steve calls watching a Lance match a "nightmare". Unfortunately, it's happening and Austin calls Storm the "most boring" wrestler he's seen. That sets off the Canadian heel and he yells at the GM until Garrison rolls him up for the shocking upset. Even with "Stone Cold" involved, this is a weird way to get someone over.

Booker T/Goldberg def. Chris Jericho/Christian. Booker doesn't even wait for his partner to come out, attacking Christian before the bell. When the heels get the upper hand, Goldberg runs out to chase off Christian and press slam Jericho onto him at ringside ahead of a commercial break.

Afterwards, a bloodied Y2J runs from Goldberg and makes Christian step into the squared circle with the intense superstar. The Intercontinental Champion attempts to cross body block him but gets caught for a front slam. A neckbreaker follows before he traps an illegally entering Jericho in a bearhug. He then fights both heels before tagging the five-time champion to chop Christian and drop him with a side kick for a near fall. When Y2J tags in moments later, Booker T chops him too. Eventually, Christian stuns the babyface with a cheap shot while he runs the ropes. He follows up with a backward head slam on the ropes, impressing Evolution backstage. They also enjoy seeing the heel choke Booker before Jericho tags in for a string of elbows and a two-count. Before he can score the win, Goldberg makes the save. Christian returns afterwards to hook a reverse chin lock. It doesn't take the five-time champion long to start to fight free, but the heel pulls his hair to cut off his momentum. When Y2J traps Booker T in the Walls of Jericho moments later, Bill again makes the save. This time, Booker capitalizes with a spinebuster to tag in the intense superstar. He rushes into the ring to give his rival an inverted atomic drop and spinning heel kick. After pummeling Christian, Goldberg whips Jericho into him to knock the heel off the top rope and down to the floor. He follows up with a press into a powerslam to Y2J, but

Christian recovers in time to break his cover. That gets him knocked out to the floor ahead of a pumphandle fallaway slam to Jericho. When he tries to finish off Y2J with a Spear, Christian pulls his partner out of the way. That sees Bill hit his shoulder on a turnbuckle. Fortunately, Booker T has recovered and returns to knock Christian back out to the floor ahead of a Scissors Kick to Jericho. He tries to entertain with a spinaroonie, but Christian returns with a top rope attack. At the last second, Booker counters with a side kick. Unfortunately, he then turns into a sloppy spot where Jericho goes for a running face slam but the five-time champion is positioned wrong. Pros, the two men adjust on the fly for a modified facebuster. Y2J follows up with a Lionsault, but Goldberg returns afterwards to Spear the heel. While the ref tries to get him out of the squared circle, Christian brings his Intercontinental Title into the ring. Unfortunately, Booker takes it away and bashes the champion's skull for the three-count.

A video package of last night's pie-eating contest plays. Afterwards, Eric Bischoff storms down the aisle and yells at the fans before serving as the guest ring announcer for the next match.

The Mae Young (with The Fabulous Moolah) and Test match never officially starts. As Eric orders Mae to get in the ring, the announcers wonder if he can make her compete. She looks ready for a match, but isn't so confident when Test is announced as her opponent. Luckily, "Stone Cold" Steve Austin interrupts to say that he wasn't consulted on this match. While he'll let Bischoff have his contest, he's appointing a special guest referee. It's Scott Steiner. When Scott and Stacy Keibler step through the curtain though, Test grabs Young and Pumphandle Slams her. JR is disgusted as trainers and officials load Mae onto a stretcher.

Backstage, Jackie Gayda helps Rico get ready by spraying body glitter on him. JR is stunned by his over the top antics and look.

While Mae Young is stretchered backstage, "Stone Cold" Steve Austin tells a worker to get him Kane and Rob Van Dam.

Rico (with Jackie Gayda) def. Spike Dudley. Having moved on from Three-Minute Warning, Rico takes a page from "Adorable" Adrian Adonis with an outlandish look and makeup. JR calls him "unique". Spike doesn't care what he looks like, rolling him up after a flying head scissors for a near fall. Although he delivers a second head scissors, when he attempts a third, the stylist drops him on the top rope to swing the momentum. Rico follows up with stomps and chokes, ignoring Jack Doan's instructions. While the fans chant "boring", the stylist elbows Dudley repeatedly until he leaps off the second rope into a clothesline. Spike follows up with fists and a headbutt to the gut before pinning Rico with a half-nelson roll-up. Moments later, he connects with a top rope diving stomp. Just when it looks like he's going to get the win, Jackie climbs onto the apron and distracts him with a seductive pose. Rico capitalizes, whipping Spike throat-first into the ropes ahead of a Heel Kick for the win.

Backstage, "Stone Cold" Steve Austin chastises Kane and Rob Van Dam. Steve wants to see the "Big Red Machine" be a monster. Since they are in America and not France, Austin wants them to win back the World Tag Titles tonight for their country.

Randy Orton (with Ric Flair) def. Maven (with Mick Foley). With Lawler singing his praises, Orton takes Maven down with amateur moves early on. The babyface answers with a series of dropkicks, chasing Randy out to the floor. There, Ric helps him recover. When Maven follows Orton out, the heel capitalizes, catching him when he tries to return to the squared circle with a DDT off the middle rope. Soon afterwards, he scores a near fall with a float over suplex before hooking a reverse chin lock. It takes him a while, but Maven eventually fights free only to see Randy slam him back to the mat. JR jokes that he certainly didn't pull the bald superstar's hair. Orton follows up with a dropkick, but when he attempts a back body drop, the babyface counters with a DDT. Both men are slow to get back to their feet giving the announcers time to speculate on who will join Evolution tonight. "The King" thinks it will be Kevin Nash. While he makes his pick, Maven comes back to life with fists and elbows before scoring a near fall with a flying bulldog off the second rope. When he heads upstairs, Flair shakes the ropes to crotch him. That brings Foley over to deck "The Nature Boy" and tease using Mr. Socko. Luckily, Orton makes the save. That nearly costs him as Maven surprises the heel with a top rope flying cross body block for a near fall. He tries to follow up with a suplex, but Randy slips free and plants him with a Cutter for the victory. Post-match, Mick gives both heels a Socko-assisted Mandible Claw.

The announcers reveal that the fan favorite to join Evolution is Test. JR says he'd fit perfectly ahead of a Vengeance ad featuring Kurt Angle.

La Resistance def. Kane/Rob Van Dam (World Tag Title match) by disqualification. The challengers are out second, separately, to either regain the titles or split apart for good. Kane tries to get the belts back quickly, punching Dupree when he starts to dance and choking Sylvan when he illegally enters. After he tosses both champions out to the floor, the "Big Red Machine" tags in RVD to dive over the top rope onto the heels. Jerry compares him to Crush from *Finding Nemo* as he gives Rene a twisting leg drop on the barricade ahead of a commercial break.

Afterwards, the momentum has swung and Grenier has Rob trapped in a surfboard stretch. When he escapes, Dupree puts him down and applies a reverse chin lock. The champions take turns stretching and hammering the popular superstar ahead of a Sylvan neckbreaker and near fall. Afterwards, he returns to the surfboard stretch. This time, Van Dam kicks free and immediately tags in Kane to squash both heels. Following a big boot to Grenier and back body drop to Rene, the "Big Red Machine" attempts a top rope double flying clothesline, but the champions move out of the way. They briefly double-team the monster only to see RVD surprise Sylvan with a cross body block. Kane follows up with a sidewalk slam to Dupree. The challengers show good teamwork with a "Big Red Machine" two-handed choke followed by a Rob top rope flying kick to Grenier. He nearly gets the win moments later with a standing moonsault. When he hits rolling thunder though, Rene returns and surprises Van Dam with a death valley driver. The monster answers with a top rope flying clothesline. He tries to follow up with a Chokeslam, but Sylvan grabs his mask and distracts him. La Resistance follow up with a double chokeslam on the floor. That leaves RVD alone against two men and the champions attempt to capitalize, tossing him down to the canvas ahead of a Double Flapjack. As he falls though, Rob counters with a double DDT to nearly win the belts back from Grenier. He tries to follow up with a Five-Star Frog Splash, but Dupree shoves him out to the floor onto Kane. That sets off the monster and he whips Sylvan into the ring steps before rocking Rene with a steel chair for the disqualification. Post-match, the "Big Red Machine" decks Nick Patrick too while Grenier hits Van Dam with a title belt. Kane chases after the champion, throwing him into the ring for another chair shot ahead of a Chokeslam.

Post-match, Triple H heads to the ring. He offers to make the "Big Red Machine" a star and give him a spot in Evolution. With Kane on their side, Hunter says Evolution would be unstoppable. "Stone Cold" Steve Austin interrupts. He believes Helmsley only wants the "Big Red Machine" on his side because "the Game" knows the monster is a threat to his championship. Austin gives him another offer, a World Title shot next week. Eric Bischoff emerges to get the last word. He tells Kane he can have his match, but if he loses next week, he'll have to unmask. The monster responds by grabbing both Triple H and Steve by the throat, but he only Chokeslams Hunter to make his decision.

SmackDown!
June 19, 2003
San Antonio, TX
Announcers: Michael Cole, Tazz

The show opens with replays of Big Show and Brock Lesnar breaking the ring last week. Afterwards, the intro video plays and fireworks explode. The announcers then let fans know that Show and Lesnar will have an "Unfinished Business" WWE Title match later tonight to settle things.

The Undertaker def. Nunzio (with The FBI). After beating Chuck Palumbo and Johnny Stamboli the last two weeks, The Undertaker takes on the leader of the team tonight. Just like in his previous matches, The FBI distract him early on for the biker's opponent to sneak attack him. Unfortunately, Nunzio is quickly driven into the ring post to put him down. The "Deadman" wastes no time motioning for a chokeslam. When The FBI hop onto the apron to distract him, The Undertaker shoves Nunzio into them. He then chokeslams the Italian heel over the top rope onto his friends. He follows up with a Last Ride for the easy victory. Post-match, The FBI attack again, Stamboli dropping the biker with a low blow. The APA make a surprise return, Bradshaw sporting blonde hair as they run out to chase off the heels.

Backstage, Bill DeMott and Brian Kendrick tell Zach Gowen that they're sorry he got screwed out of a contract last week. Zach appreciates that and heads to Stephanie McMahon's office. Unfortunately, she's not in, but Sable is. While he's willing to wait out in the hall, Sable insists he joins her. Other than a few *Velocity* matches, this ends Bill DeMott's time on television.

A Big Show/Brock Lesnar Timeline video clip shows the giant beating Brock at Survivor Series last year.

Chris Benoit def. Rhyno (US Title Tournament match). Kicking off the US Title Tournament, the friends who have had issues of late get a chance to lock up. Before they do so, Stephanie McMahon steps onto the stage to hype the upcoming *SmackDown!* exclusive PPV, Vengeance, and show off the new US Title. Early on, the friends trade armbars. Benoit gets the upper hand and traps the man-beast in a hammerlock. Rhyno answers with a roll-up for a quick cover. Back up, "the Crippler" attacks the arm again until the man-beast rams him into a corner. Afterwards, the wrestlers trade fists and chops before Rhyno misses a corner charge and hits his shoulder against the ring post ahead of a commercial break.

Afterwards, Rhyno pounds Benoit down ahead of a single leg crab. The "rabid wolverine" responds with chops and a back elbow, but the man-beast won't stay down. Showing off his power, he reverse powerbombs Benoit onto the top turnbuckle for a near fall. He also almost gets the win with a stiff clothesline. Following another clothesline and two-count, Rhyno powerslams "the Crippler" for another near fall. Changing tactics, he tries to twist Benoit's head off his shoulders. Although the "rabid wolverine" surprises him with a roll-up and near fall, a clothesline puts Benoit back down for a reverse chin lock. The fans are not enamored with his slow pace and start to boo. The man-beast doesn't endear himself to the crowd by taunting them. Eventually, "the Crippler" escapes with a jawbreaker. He follows up with shoulder blocks and a suplex for his own two-count. When he sets up for a German suplex, Rhyno holds the ropes and responds with a spinebuster. After that only gets him a near fall, Benoit finally hits a German suplex. A top rope diving headbutt nearly gets him the win, but the man-beast just kicks out. Soon afterwards, he answers with a DDT to put both men down through Mike Chioda's standing nine-count. Once back up, Rhyno tries to Gore the "rabid wolverine", but Benoit sidesteps. Despite that, the man-beast still nails "the Crippler" with a double ax-handle to the back of the head for a near fall. He tries to follow up with a scoop slam, but Benoit slips free and locks on the Crippler Crossface for the tap-out victory. Post-match, Rhyno takes offense to his friend not breaking his hold faster.

Backstage, Sable attempts to seduce Zach Gowen. She tells him that she saw him looking at her when she flashed Mr. America last week and puts his hand on her chest. Zach is stunned.

An Ultimo Dragon teaser promises his debut next week in Madison Square Garden.

Rey Mysterio def. Kanyon. Making a rare appearance, Kanyon powers Rey back into a corner only to see the Cruiserweight Champion show off his speed with a head scissors. When he attempts a dive out to the floor on the heel, Kanyon catches him for a face-first wheelbarrow suplex on the barricade. The fans let him know that he sucks. Despite that, he remains in control, scoring a near fall with a backbreaker. When he attempts a corner charge though, Mysterio moves. Kanyon quickly recovers and counters a springboard attack with a northern lights suplex. He tries to follow up with a superplex, but the masked man fights free, knocking the heel down for a flying butt splash off the ropes. The champion follows up with a snap mare and slingshot kick to the face. A twisting moonsault afterwards gets him a two-count, but when he leaps up for the West Coast Pop, Kanyon answers with an electric chair drop and near fall. He tries to follow up with a suplex on the apron, but Rey fights free to leg drop the heel back into the ring in a unique spot. A 619 and West Coast Pop follow for the three-count.

Another Big Show/Brock Lesnar Timeline moment shows Lesnar giving the giant an F5 to help Kurt Angle beat him for the WWE Title.

The former Team Angle debut new music and maroon and silver attire as they head to the squared circle. Tazz explains it is an homage to their respective colleges. They refuse to apologize for their actions last week. Charlie Haas even says that if Kurt Angle wants to do something about it, they can wrestle next week. The Olympian doesn't want to wait a week, marching out now to tell them that leaving Team Angle might be the best thing they ever did. He believes they might even be the "world's greatest tag team". The only thing he takes offense to is the words "next week". He says "next week" is for "crybabies". He dares either of them to wrestle him right now.

Kurt Angle def. Charlie Haas (with Shelton Benjamin). Charlie accepts the invitation and is quickly slammed to the canvas for a reverse chin lock. When Haas escapes, Kurt tosses him around, the fans chanting for the Olympian. He follows up with a key lock and overhead throw. Charlie finally gets in a little offense, arm dragging Angle ahead of his own wear down hold, a wrist lock. The two men then trade takedowns and holds, the fans chanting for Kurt. When he fights free, the Olympian catapults Haas out to the floor. Shelton fires his partner up and he returns to slap Angle. That's a big mistake as Kurt unloads with fists and a cross body block for a near fall. A big back body drop follows, but before he can finish off Charlie, the heel whips him out to the floor. Benjamin makes an impact, tossing the Olympian into the ring steps. While Brian Hebner sends Shelton backstage, Haas stomps and slams Angle's face into the steel steps ahead of a commercial break.

Afterwards, Charlie chokes Kurt in a corner. He focuses on an arm afterwards with a hammerlock until Kurt monkey flips free. He follows up with a leg sweep to put both men down through Hebner's eight-count. That lets the Olympian catch his breath before he connects with a cross body block and belly-to-belly suplex for a near fall. A German suplex follows, but instead of going for the cover, Angle lowers his straps. He tries to deliver the Angle Slam, but Haas slips free to German suplex the returning superstar. Charlie tries to deliver an Angle Slam of his own, but Kurt counters with an arm drag into the Anklelock. Although Haas quickly escapes the submission hold, the Olympian immediately follows up with an Angle Slam for the win. Post-match, Benjamin runs back out to assault the winner. Together, the former Team Angle drop Angle with a combination Inverted Atomic Drop and Superkick. When they apply tandem anklelocks, Brock Lesnar runs out to chase the heels away.

Another Big Show/Brock Lesnar Timeline clip shows the giant Chokeslamming Brock through the announce table.

Backstage, Sable pins Zach Gowen down onto Stephanie McMahon's desk. He tells her that he wants her with some bad acting as she removes her top. Unfortunately, Sable says he's not a real man and that he'll never have her. Vince McMahon then bursts in to call him a freak and chase off Gowen.

Billy Gunn (with Torrie Wilson) def. Jamie Noble (with Nidia). As the babyfaces head to the ring, the announcers talk about rumors that they are together. The heels are definitely a couple, mocking their opponents and spanking each other. Once the bell rings, Noble surprises Billy with a headlock. The fans loudly chant for Torrie as Gunn chases the heel out to the floor. There, he continues punching him only to see Jamie dropkick his knee back in the ring. Focusing on the knee, Noble stretches it and drives Billy down in a corner with an innovative drop for a two-count. Afterwards, he applies a side leg lock, nearly keeping Gunn's shoulders down for a three-count. Eventually, Billy punches free ahead of a tilt-a-whirl powerslam. Catching a second wind, he unloads with more fists and a press slam. Unfortunately, his knee gives out and Jamie rolls up "Mr. Ass" for a two-count. Gunn tries to answer with a Famouser, but Nidia trips him. That brings Wilson over to attack the heel. While Billy breaks it up, Noble recovers and attempts a flying attack from the ring. Unfortunately for the redneck, Gunn moves and Jamie crashes onto the floor. Back in the squared circle, Billy soon hits the Famouser for the victory.

Another Big Show/Brock Lesnar Timeline clip shows Lesnar beating the giant in a "Stretcher" match.

Sean O'Haire (with "Rowdy" Roddy Piper) def. Eddie Guerrero (with Tajiri). The babyfaces are out first in a bigger lowrider this week. They get a big pop before the heels head to the ring. Piper is carrying a bottle of tequila as he accompanies his man. He proves his worth, distracting Eddie for Sean to press slam him for the early advantage. Stomps and fists follow before O'Haire scores a two-count with a kick to the chest. He then locks on a reverse bearhug while Roddy drinks tequila at ringside and slams a WWE Tag Title belt on the announce table. Eventually, "Latino Heat" swings the momentum by dropkicking Sean's knee. A pop up dropkick moments later puts the heel down for a top rope missile dropkick to the back of the knee. When he heads upstairs, Piper grabs Guerrero's leg and distracts him long enough for O'Haire to recover and dodge a Frog Splash. Afterwards, "Hot Rod" spits tequila into Tajiri's eyes while Sean scores the win with a Reverse Death Valley Driver, called the Prophecy by Cole.

After a commercial break, Vince McMahon praises Sable's performance earlier humiliating Zach Gowen. He offers to thank her with a kiss, but that's just a start. Hopping onto the desk, he mocks Zach before inviting Sable to show him how bad she can be. Stephanie McMahon bursts in to kick Sable out of the office and say she's sorry she's done terrible things for her father. However, she refuses to let him mistreat Gowen like he did her. Showing some real emotion, Stephanie calls Zach her "last bastion of hope" and she hopes Vince knows that he's about to lose the only person who ever really cared about him. That gives Mr. McMahon pause as Stephanie storms away, having shown the only real acting ability in this series of vignettes. Stephanie gets knocked a lot, but this is good.

The final Big Show/Brock Lesnar Timeline clip shows the wrestlers breaking the ring last week again.

Brock Lesnar def. Big Show (WWE Title match) by disqualification. Brock climbs up the ropes to start the match. He dares Show to come after him, but when he does, Lesnar leaps over him and knocks the giant out to the floor. There, he rams Big Show into the ring post. The challenger answers with his own string of strikes, a stiff chop in the corner sending Lesnar rolling out to the floor. Show makes a mistake letting him recover and the "next big thing" capitalizes with a throat drop on the top rope. The giant answers with a sidewalk slam and chokes. Dominating the action, Big Show headbutts and slams Brock. The champion responds with a string of shoulder blocks in a corner, but one clothesline puts him back down. Afterwards, the challenger slows the pace with an abdominal stretch. Lesnar escapes by twisting Show's hand only to run into a big boot and leg drop. The giant tries to replicate last week's big moment and superplex the "next big thing" again, but Brock knocks him down to the canvas for a flying clothesline. The champion follows up with a German suplex, but when he picks Show up for an F5, Charlie Haas and Shelton Benjamin run out to attack the champion for the disqualification. Big Show follows up with a Chokeslam. That brings out Kurt Angle to attack his former tag team. After he takes care of them, the giant Chokeslams him as well. Finally, Mr. America hurries down the aisle to punch and big boot Show. He motions that he's going to slam the giant, but Haas and Benjamin attack the masked patriot for the save. Like Kurt, he fights them off only to see Big Show Chokeslam him too, the show ending with the giant standing tall.

Monday Night Raw
June 23, 2003
New York City, NY
Announcers: Jim Ross, Jerry "the King" Lawler

Following the intro video and fireworks, the announcers are excited to be back in Madison Square Garden.

Christian/Test def. Booker T/Scott Steiner (with Stacy Keibler). Stacy is none too happy watching Test's entrance. Once everyone is in the ring, Booker punches and slams Christian for an early two-count. The bodyguard takes his turn in the ring, surprising the babyface with a clothesline. He can't keep Booker T down for long and he tags in Scott to fight both heels, slamming Christian over the top rope to the floor at one point. He then chops and clubs Test in a corner to Keibler's delight. She doesn't like when her ex-boyfriend kicks Steiner and nearly steals the win with his feet on the ropes. When Stacy gets on the apron, the bodyguard drives "Big Poppa Pump" into her. Despite that, Scott recovers in time to fight off Christian trying to use the Intercontinental Title. Unfortunately, he then turns into a Big Boot for Test to steal the win. Post-match, the bodyguard laughs as the referee checks on Keibler's injured ankle.

Ahead of his World Title match with his mask on the line, we see a shot of Kane looking into a mirror. A thought bubble materializes showing his 1997 debut. The announcers then ask fans to vote, continuing to plug that feature on WWE.com, on whether the "Big Red Machine" will win the belt or unmask.

Maven def. Christopher Nowinski (with Theodore Long). Pre-match, Long talks about injustices heaped on Nowinski. Theodore knows that Christopher lost *Tough Enough* due to discrimination over his intelligence. When Maven sprints out, the Harvard heel stomps and clotheslines him. He tries to follow up with a suplex, but the babyface slips free and steals the quick win with a roll-up. This marks the end of Nowinski's career due to concussions. He'll become a major figure in CTE research afterwards.

After a commercial break, Chris Jericho heads to the ring for the Highlight Reel. The announcers have no idea who his guest will be. Y2J opens up the segment by insulting the New York crowd. At least, he says, he tells the truth unlike "Stone Cold" Steve Austin. He then plays footage of Austin calling Lance Storm "boring" last week before welcoming out his fellow Canadian as his guest. While the fans chant that he's boring, Lance reads a prepared statement to say that no one is more interesting than him and if fans want a show they should go to the circus. As he speaks, "Stone Cold" sends crew members out to take down the Highlight Reel. Austin says he has to do something because the heels are boring the fans. Jericho believes he's just jealous that Y2J beat him and The Rock on the same night. The co-general manager tells him to shut up. He was trying to motivate Storm last week, but if he took it the wrong way, Austin doesn't care. Instead, "Stone Cold" signs a match for the heels to do something about it.

The Dudley Boyz def. Chris Jericho/Lance Storm. Although the Dudleys have the element of surprise, the heels attack them to start the action. It doesn't take the babyfaces long to turn the tide and crush their opponents in a corner before tossing them out to the floor. Chad Patton finally gets order as Bubba Ray slams and elbow drops Storm for a two-count. He follows up with a sidewalk slam for another near fall. When he runs the ropes though, Y2J trips him for a Lance baseball slide dropkick. Jericho tags in afterwards to distract the referee while Storm chokes Bubba. Y2J follows up with a leg drop on the middle rope and back suplex. Lance returns afterwards for more chokes and "boring" chants. He answers with a leg lariat for a two-count before applying a reverse chin lock. It doesn't take the babyface long to escape and sunset flip Storm for a near fall. Jericho returns afterwards to chop Bubba and roll him into the Walls of Jericho when Dudley tries to respond with a Samoan drop. Luckily, D-Von makes the save, but his half-brother pays courtesy of a string of Lance kicks. He then applies a sleeper hold for another "boring" chant. Jerry says it would be ironic for him to put Bubba Ray to sleep like he does the fans. Luckily, Dudley side suplexes free and gives D-Von the hot tag. He proceeds to give Storm a neckbreaker ahead of a powerslam to Jericho. Y2J doesn't stay down for long, recovering to break the cover after D-Von gives Lance a second rope neckbreaker. That gets Jericho a double flapjack before the Dudleys give Storm a wassup drop. Although Bubba tells D-Von to get the tables, Y2J returns to dropkick Bubba Ray out to the floor. D-Von tries to answer with a reverse DDT, but Lance surprises him with a springboard clothesline for a near fall. Afterwards, the heels make a mistake and Storm accidentally knocks Jericho off the apron when he tries to hold D-Von. The Dudleys capitalize with a 3D to Lance for the victory.

Another Kane memory shows Batista unmasking him five months ago and the monster running away.

Backstage, Randy Orton reads a passage from Mick Foley's *Tietam Brown*. Ric Flair doesn't think Foley knows anything about romance. However, tonight, Evolution's focus has to be on making sure Triple H retains the World Title.

La Resistance def. Sgt. Slaughter/The Hurricane. Pre-match, the champions sing the French national anthem to boos. The Hurricane can't believe they would disrespect America and New York City. He has an American partner ready to "beat up maggots", Slaughter joining him for a "USA" chant. After the heels kiss each other's cheeks, the Americans attack. The superhero takes the fight out to the floor to dive off the top rope onto Sylvan while Slaughter slams and elbows Dupree, still wearing his shiny robe. The patriot follows up with a back body drop before locking on the Cobra Clutch. Luckily, Grenier makes the save with a double ax-handle. Unfortunately, that just makes Slaughter mad and he puts him in a Cobra Clutch too. While Jack Doan gets Grenier out of the ring, Rene seizes the opening and blasts the patriot with a title belt to steal the win.

As Kane stares into a mirror, another memory shows "Stone Cold" Steve Austin calling him out two weeks ago.

After a commercial break, "Stone Cold" Steve Austin heads to the ring to a big pop. He congratulates Madison Square Garden on being the home of WrestleMania XX before fireworks explode around the event's logo on the stage. Afterwards, Austin welcomes out Mick Foley. Before he goes on his book tour, Steve stopping Mick to tell him that he wants an autographed copy, the "rattlesnake" has something for him. Foley backs away, expecting a Stone Cold Stunner. "Stone Cold" laughs, but that's not his surprise. Instead, he invites former ECW superstars like Rob Van Dam and Tommy Dreamer to come out carrying a framed Hardcore Title. Before he presents it to Mick, Austin plays a video package documenting Foley's career and hardcore moments. "Stone Cold" the calls him the "toughest SOB" there is and gives him the belt. Mick jokes that he forgot how good he was. That brings out Vince McMahon in a surprise *Raw* appearance. He wants to say something to the hardcore legend. Personally, Vince is disgusted to see Foley back in the ring since he promised the WWE owner that he'd never return. From a business standpoint though, McMahon tells him thank you and shakes Mick's hand. That's not good enough for the hardcore legend and he hugs Vince. Foley then admits that he had a tear on his cheek watching his career retrospective. He also gets a cheap pop saying it's great being back in New York City with so many great performers "and Al Snow". The hardcore legend talks about sitting in the crowd watching "Superfly" Jimmy Snuka compete as a kid. Foley believes that he gave just as much back to the WWE and he's glad that the fans gave him a good reaction for his brief return. He quotes Frosty the Snowman to promise that he'll "be back again someday". JR says there'll never be another like Foley.

Kevin Nash/Shawn Michaels def. Randy Orton/Ric Flair. After the babyfaces make separate entrances, Evolution come out together to Orton's music. Shawn opens the match hammering Flair until he turns his back to hit Randy. That lets Ric drop him with a chop and tag in the young superstar. Kevin greets him with a sidewalk slam for a two-count. A stiff clothesline follows, but Nash misses an elbow drop allowing "The Nature Boy" to tag in and chop him. "Big Sexy" absorbs his shots to punch and elbow Flair. He drives both heels out to the floor before tagging in Michaels to slingshot dive out onto them ahead of a commercial break.

Afterwards, the "Heartbreak Kid" punches and rolls up Flair, but Orton makes the save in the heel corner with a clothesline from the apron. He then tags in to punch and stomp Shawn. Following a hard whip into the corner, Michaels imitating "The Nature Boy" as he flips over, Randy plants the veteran with an armbar drop. Focusing on the arm, Orton holds the babyface down with a key lock. Ric joins the attack moments later, kneeing the "Heartbreak Kid's" knee and arm. When Shawn starts to fight back, he misses Randy getting a blind tag to break up a backslide and apply a hammerlock. Eventually, Michaels escapes and surprises the young heel with a cross body block. Afterwards, the two men collide to put them both down on the canvas. After they work Nick Patrick's count to nine, both men tag out for Nash to big boot the heels. He gets a good pop when he lowers his straps, but when he sets up Orton for the Jackknife, Flair makes the save with a low blow. Somehow, Kevin recovers quickly to double clothesline both heels. The "Heartbreak Kid" then tags back in to punch and back body drop the heels. He tunes up the band, but Ric blocks Sweet Chin Music. Despite that, Shawn tosses Randy out to the floor and slams "The Nature Boy" to the canvas. A top rope flying elbow drop follows as Nash deals with Orton at ringside. Once again, Michaels tunes up the band, this time dropping Ric with Sweet Chin Music for the three-count.

Footage of how tonight's main event came to be last week plays. The WWE.com poll predicts that Kane will win the World Title. JR isn't so sure.

During the commercial break, Mick Foley signs his book for Vince McMahon. When Randy Orton and Ric Flair storm past, Mick tells Ric that he had a good match. That sets off "The Nature Boy" and he brawls with Foley. While the hardcore legend fights him off, he's outnumbered and Orton smashes a bottle on Foley's head before kicking him down a stairwell. Vince finally calls for help. Specifically, he needs a janitor to clean up a mess.

Goldberg def. Rodney Mack (with Theodore Long) ("White Boy Challenge" match). Pre-match, Long says he's going to be happy tonight because his undefeated superstar will beat another "white boy". That brings out Goldberg to a big pop. Rodney doesn't wait for him to enter the ring, running up to fight Bill in the middle of his entrance sparks. The intense superstar loves a good fight and answers with a Spear on the ramp. He then leads Mack to the ring for a Jackhammer and the twenty-six second victory. The Madison Square Garden crowd has waited a long time to cheer Goldberg and they do so loudly here.

Backstage, Rob Van Dam tells Kane to kick some butt. He knows the title is the "Big Red Machine's". When RVD leaves the room, the monster smashes his mirror.

A WrestleMania Recall moment sees Triple H giving Stephanie McMahon a Pedigree.

Triple H (with Ric Flair) def. Kane ("World Title versus Mask" match). The monster is out second to pummel and back body drop Triple H. Sporting blue trunks, Hunter tries to answer, but Kane overpowers and chokes him. He then takes the fight out to the floor and whips Helmsley into the ring steps after threatening Flair. Not content to fight at ringside, the "Big Red Machine" clotheslines "the Game" into the crowd to hammer him in the front row. When they return to ringside, Ric distracts Earl Hebner for the champion to bash the monster's head with a steel chair ahead of a commercial break.

Afterwards, Triple H plants Kane with a spinebuster, but the challenger sits up. The two men then trade fists. Despite Hunter giving him a DDT and neckbreaker, the "Big Red Machine" continues to sit up. He invites Helmsley to punch his jaw before unloading with his own haymakers. Corner clotheslines and a powerslam follow for a near fall. Even after running into a boot moments later, the monster quickly recovers to sidewalk slam "the Game". He follows up with a flying clothesline, but the wrestlers sideswipe Hebner. Things get worse for him when the champion dodges a big boot, but the referee doesn't. While he's down, "The Nature Boy" tries to hit Kane with the World Title, but the challenger beats him to the punch and bashes Triple H's head with the belt. That brings Chad Patton out to count the cover, but Hunter just kicks out. The challenger can't stand it and tosses Patton out to the floor. Helmsley capitalizes with a low blow and Pedigree. By the time Earl rolls over for a groggy count, the "Big Red Machine" just kicks out. He then back drops free of a Pedigree and Chokeslams Flair. When "the Game" sets up for another Pedigree, the monster catapults him into Flair. He then motions for a Chokeslam to the champion, but Randy Orton sneaks out to low blow him ahead of a Cutter. Triple H follows up with another Pedigree to finally score the three-count.

Post-match, Eric Bischoff storms onto the stage and demands that Kane unmasks. Before he can, Evolution attack the "Big Red Machine". That brings Rob Van Dam out for the save, the former champions punishing Orton with a combination Chokeslam and Five-Star Frog Splash. Once the heels are gone, the monster teases removing his mask. Conflicted, he stomps around the ring before finally peeling off his mask and most of his hair to reveal a half shaved head covered in black marks. Lawler wonders if he's human as Kane surprises RVD with another Chokeslam to end the show.

SmackDown!

June 26, 2003
New York City, NY
Announcers: Michael Cole, Tazz, Rey Mysterio (briefly)

The show opens with a video package featuring Vince McMahon, Sable, Stephanie McMahon, and Zach Gowen. Afterwards, the intro video plays and fireworks explode for this Madison Square Garden show.

John Cena def. Orlando Jordan. Josh Mathews serves as the ring announcer tonight, introducing Cena to come out to claim that he's bigger than Madison Square Garden and will main event WrestleMania XX. He brags about all he's accomplished in his first year with the WWE. To commemorate his debut, John invites any rookie to step into the ring with him. When Jordan comes out, the rapping heel isn't impressed. Neither is Billy Kidman, sitting in the crowd with two women. Orlando doesn't care what people think, punching Cena and powerslamming him for a two-count. He also surprises John with an enziguri kick, but when he grabs the rapping heel's collar, Cena elbows him down. John tries to follow up with an FU, but Jordan flips free and dropkicks him out to the floor. He then heads up to the top rope for a flying cross body block, but the rapping heel rolls through and steals the win. Post-match, Cena stomps the rookie and FUs him. That brings out The Undertaker to chase off John and pat Orlando's ribs.

The APA/The Undertaker def. Nunzio/The FBI. After a commercial break, The Undertaker locks up with Palumbo. Chuck surprises him with a shoulderblock before running into a drop toe hold. The two men then trade shots, the biker dropping his opponent with a leaping clothesline. He follows up with Old School before decking Stamboli illegally entering the squared circle. The distraction lets Palumbo stomp the "Deadman" down before tagging in Johnny. He continues the assault until he lowers his head for a back body drop and eats a DDT. Fortunately, Nunzio breaks up The Undertaker's cover with a dropkick. Ron Simmons, no longer Faarooq even with The APA's return, tags in to show off his power with a spinebuster, but is outnumbered and The FBI slam him together for a Chuck two-count. More stomps follow before Nunzio tags in to try to punch the brawler. Although Simmons stops his assault, the heels continue to cheat and attack Ron from behind before Palumbo illegally switches places with the Italian heel to lock on a camel clutch. He tries to add extra punishment by jumping on Simmons's back, but the brawler turns and knees his groin. Bradshaw then gets the hot tag to wail on Chuck and "the Bull". After he gives Stamboli a fallaway slam, Nunzio tries to sneak attack him with a diving attack, but the big Texan catches him. Palumbo stops him from delivering a second fallaway slam with a Superkick, but the "Deadman" makes him pay with a chokeslam. Although Stamboli clotheslines The Undertaker out to the floor, he turns back into a Clothesline from Hell for Bradshaw to score the victory.

An Ultimo Dragon teaser plays for his debut tonight.

After a commercial break, Jamie Noble gives a woman an autograph outside. She wanted directions to the subway. When she storms away, an attorney stops Noble and Nidia. Jamie pleads innocence, referencing a girl in Alabama. The attorney doesn't have a subpoena, but rather a check from Noble's rich Aunt Lucille. After inheriting over eight hundred thousand dollars, the redneck tells Nidia to kiss the attorney to celebrate.

A WrestleMania Recall moment plays footage from the first WrestleMania.

Backstage, Sable apologizes to Vince McMahon for Stephanie McMahon finding them in a compromising condition last week. However, she wants Vince and runs her hands all over him. Despite her attempts, McMahon tells her "not tonight" because he has something he has to do.

Matt Hardy Version 1.0 def. Rikishi (US Title Tournament match). This week's Matt Fact is that Hardy has better abs than Rikishi. As Matt gets in the ring, Tazz shills him on the cover of the new issue of the *WWE Magazine*. The big Samoan starts fast with a kick to the gut and DDT for a near fall. A corner clothesline follows, but before he can give Hardy a Stinkface, the heel slides out to the floor. There, he drives the big babyface back into the ring post twice for his own two-count. When he applies a surfboard submission, Rikishi powers out and clotheslines Matt to the canvas. He tries to follow up with a belly-to-belly suplex, but Hardy headbutts free. He can't escape a second and is driven hard to the mat. Afterwards, the big Samoan punches Hardy ahead of a Rikishi Driver and near fall. It's been a while since he used that move and apparently it's lost some of it's effectiveness. When he climbs the ropes for a Rump Shaker, Matt counters with a pair of knees to the groin. A Twist of Fate afterwards nearly gets him the win, but Rikishi just kicks out. Frustrated, the heel removes a turnbuckle pad, but runs into a side kick. When the big babyface tries to follow up with a corner splash, Hardy moves and Rikishi hits the exposed steel. A Twist of Fate follows for Matt to score the win.

After a commercial break, Josh Mathews asks Billy Kidman how it feels to be back. He tells his girls to wait for him as he stands up to say that it's not so good watching his friends doing what he loves. Billy believes he should be the Cruiserweight Champion and can't wait to get back in the squared circle.

Eddie Guerrero/Tajiri def. "Rowdy" Roddy Piper/Sean O'Haire (WWE Tag Title match). O'Haire and Guerrero open the match trading shots. Eddie gets the upper hand with a back elbow ahead of a slingshot somersault splash. Tajiri then tags in to chop and kick the heel. His handspring back elbow doesn't knock down O'Haire, but a stiff kick does for a two-count. The "Japanese Buzzsaw" tries to follow up with a Tarantula, but Piper blocks it with a boot. Sean capitalizes with a slam before "Hot Rod" tags in to score a two-count. He doesn't stay in the ring long before O'Haire returns to kick and choke the champion. When he attempts a running powerslam, Tajiri escapes with a reverse bulldog slam. That lets both men tag out and Roddy trade shots with Guerrero. Sean doesn't care about the rules, returning and kicking "Latino Heat". Eddie responds with a dropkick, but Piper knocks down the champion. Afterwards, Jimmy Korderas is distracted and misses the "Japanese Buzzsaw" spewing mist into "Hot Rod's" eyes. A throat drop on the top rope follows before Guerrero scores the three-count with a Frog Splash. This match ends Piper's run after he makes some controversial comments about the industry in an HBO interview.

The finish and post-match antics from last week's WWE Title match replay. Due to the interference, we get tonight's six-man tag main event.

Afterwards, Vince McMahon heads to the squared circle. He invites Stephanie McMahon and Zach Gowen to join him. He speaks to his daughter first and apologizes for using her to help close business deals when she was seventeen. While he's clear to point out that he didn't do it personally, he can't help feel guilty for "deflowering" her. He then turns to Zach and says he's always wanted to be someone like Gowen who flies free. Mr. McMahon wants Zach to accept his apology, but the fans says no. Vince demands he accepts his apology, but Gowen refuses. He isn't intimidated by the WWE owner and says he's faced things in his life that would make McMahon cry. The fan refuses to be treated like a joke anymore. Zach spits on Vince's apology and says the only thing he will accept is a contract. The

WWE owner is happy to give him one under one condition. He wants Gowen to join a "special club" and pulls down his pants for the fan to kiss his butt. Vince doesn't have all night and tells his daughter to get Zach to kiss his butt for the contract. With no other option, Gowen drops to a knee, but instead of kissing the boss's butt, Zach low blows him. Stephanie loves it.

Ultimo Dragon def. Shannon Moore. Rey Mysterio pops out of the stage and heads to the announce table to scout the debuting superstar. Billy Kidman is also scouting his fellow former WCW cruiserweight. Inside the ring, the silver and white clad masked man trades arm wringers with Moore. He then picks up the pace and back elbows Shannon out to the floor. When he runs the ropes for a diving attack, the heel moves, but Dragon stops himself. Despite avoiding a big mistake, Moore slams and elbow drops the debuting superstar for a two-count. He then applies an arm lock and clubs Ultimo Dragon down to the canvas. The masked man answers with a jumping heel kick. A back leg sweep and twisting kick follow for a near fall. Afterwards, he back body drops Shannon out to the floor for an Asai moonsault, named after Dragon. That gets him a two-count back in the squared circle. Moore tries to answer with an attack off the second rope, but the masked superstar counters with a jawbreaker. He immediately follows up with a Backflip Reverse DDT for the victory. Post-match, Rey shakes Ultimo Dragon's hand while Kidman half-heartedly applauds.

Big Show/Charlie Haas/Shelton Benjamin def. Brock Lesnar/Kurt Angle/Mr. America. The babyfaces get separate entrances, Cole exclaiming that Mr. America has had a lot of big moments in Madison Square Garden. Tazz corrects him, reminding everyone that this is his debut in the arena. Cole adds that the masked patriot will be in action next week too, but he won't as Hulk Hogan will walk away from the WWE after this show, ending his Mr. America run. The fans don't know that or their Hogan chants would be even louder. After everyone enters, the fans chant "USA". Tazz is confused because everyone is American. Eventually, Kurt locks up with Haas and drives him into a neutral corner. He shows off his amateur skills with a series of holds before picking up the pace and tossing around both Charlie and Benjamin. A big back body drop follows to Haas, but eventually the tag team gets the upper hand with their superior numbers, double dropkicking Angle. When Charlie leaves the ring, Angle regains control, hammering Shelton. Once again, the fans chant for Hogan before Kurt cross body blocks Benjamin. Mr. America gets a big pop when he tags in to hit the heel tag team and choke Shelton. Brock joins the masked patriot for a double clothesline before slugging his former college teammate. The WWE Champion nearly gets the win running over Benjamin, but he just kicks out of his cover and tags in Haas. He doesn't fare any better, Lesnar press slamming him before tagging back in Mr. America. He continues his pounding assault before scoring a near fall with a back suplex. When Brock returns, he shoulder blocks and suplexes Charlie ahead of a commercial break.

Afterwards, the champion remains in control, knocking Shelton out to the floor before hoisting Haas up for an F5. Before he can hit his finisher, Benjamin hits him from behind and the tag team follows up with their double-team leapfrog splash. That finally brings Big Show into the ring to slam and choke Lesnar. Brock answers with his own big shots, but can't slam the giant and is driven back to the mat. When Big Show continues his assault, the champion surprises him with a German suplex to send both men crawling to their corners for tags. Kurt is rested and ready for a fight, attacking and suplexing his former tag team before trapping Haas in an Anklelock. Fortunately, Show makes the save with a boot to the back of the head. Lesnar rushes to his partner's aid, driving Big Show out to the floor while Shelton knocks Mr. America off the apron. The heel tag team tries to finish off the Olympian as the giant knocks down Brock at ringside, but Angle ducks a superkick that flattens Charlie. Kurt follows up with a leg sweep to Benjamin before giving the masked patriot the tag to pummel the giant. He also decks Haas, but when he goes for a big boot, Show holds the ropes. That kicks off a six-man brawl, the Olympian

Angle Slamming Charlie while Lesnar F5s Shelton. Big Show responds with a double Chokeslam to the babyfaces. That leaves Mr. America to punch and big boot the giant. Before he can score the win with a Legdrop, Vince McMahon drags Zach Gowen through the curtain and throws him down for a boot to the gut. The masked patriot tries to help his friend, but Show grabs and Chokeslams him for the three-count. Post-match, Vince says Zach can't cut the mustard as a wrestler and decks him until Stephanie McMahon runs out to shield Gowen. That gives Mr. McMahon an idea. He gives Zach a chance to earn a WWE contract next week in a handicap match where he'll team with Stephanie to face Big Show. The *SmackDown!* general manager can't believe it.

Monday Night Raw

June 30, 2003
Buffalo, NY
Announcers: Jim Ross, Jerry "the King" Lawler

A video package of Kane unmasking last week plays ahead of the intro video and fireworks.

Inside the ring, Chris Jericho welcomes everyone to "*Raw* is Jericho" and the Highlight Reel. While everyone has been talking about Kane lately, Y2J says he's not about the ugly. That's why his guest tonight is the lovely Stacy Keibler. She's accompanied by Scott Steiner who removes her garter for some reason. Jericho enjoys her legs, but didn't invite Steiner and tells him to hit the bricks. Scott says he stays or kicks Y2J's butt. The heel doesn't want to fight and destroy his expensive set, claiming that it can pay everyone's salary in the arena for three years. Instead, Jericho shows some of Keibler's pictures in *Stuff* magazine. Y2J wonders why she's with "King Arthur", making fun of Steiner's chainmail headgear. He promises he could make her happy, but Stacy disagrees. She loves being with "Freakzilla" and has only heard how "small" Jericho is. Y2J isn't laughing as he introduces his next guest, Test. While "Big Poppa Pump" turns to see him, Jericho attacks, but the heels are quickly driven from the ring. Before Steiner can tear up the set, Eric Bischoff interrupts. He tells fans that "Stone Cold" Steve Austin isn't here tonight and he's running the show solo. To showcase his power, he signs Jericho and Test to face Scott and Keibler tonight. JR says that's not fair.

The Goldberg/Lance Storm match never officially starts. After a commercial break, Lance Storm is in the ring talking over the fans to claim that he's not boring. He reads a statement to define boring until Goldberg interrupts, stepping through sparks and fireworks to a big pop. Before he gets in the ring, Rodney Mack attacks the intense superstar from behind. Bill doesn't waste any time responding, Spearing the now once defeated superstar. Lance wants nothing to do with Goldberg and runs away, the referee following him before the intense superstar gives Mack a Jackhammer.

Backstage, Eric Bischoff talks to Kane, wearing a towel over his head. Eric tells the "Big Red Machine" that it's Rob Van Dam's fault that he had to unmask last week. However, Bischoff loves that he got big ratings last week for the unmasking and wants the monster to head to the ring and show off his face again. Kane doesn't want to, even when the general manager offers him a World Title shot. Since the "Big Red Machine" won't take the opportunity, Eric gives the title shot to RVD. He also warns the monster that if he doesn't go out and show his face, he will be fired.

MUST SEE! Gail Kim wins a seven-woman Women's Title battle royal.

Elimination Order	Wrestler	Eliminated By
1	Ivory	Molly Holly
2	Jazz	Unable to compete
3	Molly Holly	Victoria
4	Jacqueline	Victoria
5	Trish Stratus	Gail Kim/Victoria
6	Victoria	Gail Kim
7	Gail Kim	Winner

Gail Kim makes her debut tonight, dressed like Neo from *The Matrix*. Her entrance video also has nods to that film. When Jazz comes out, she attacks Ivory while JR reveals that "Stone Cold" Steve Austin isn't here due to food poisoning. Molly nearly gets eliminated first courtesy of an Ivory back body drop, but lands on the apron and returns to catapult Ivory to the floor. Kim and Jacqueline then team up on Holly while Victoria slams Trish. At this point cameras and the announcers notice that Jazz is hurt and holding her shoulder from an earlier kick by the "black widow". Officials help her backstage despite her never being thrown over the top rope. Molly joins her quickly when Jacqueline kicks her onto the apron for a Victoria forearm to the jaw. The "black widow" gets another quick elimination, tossing Jacqueline out right after Holly. Down to three women, Gail and Trish team up on Victoria. When Kim gets knocked down, Stratus tries to slam the "black widow" over the top rope. She manages to hang on and even block a handstand head scissors to toss Trish out to the apron. When Gail attacks Victoria, the "black widow" drops her and slingshots the rookie into Stratus for another elimination. In control, Victoria shoulder blocks and clotheslines Kim. When she attempts a fallaway slam though, the rookie counters with an arm drag. She then counters a powerbomb with a head scissors to toss the "black widow" out to the floor to capture the Women's Title in her first televised match in the WWE.

Booker T and Christian (Intercontinental Title match) wrestle to a draw. When Booker tries to enter the ring, Christian attacks him from behind before the bell rings. He continues his assault at ringside until the challenger reverses a whip into the ring steps. He follows up with a flurry of fists, the wrestlers brawling into the crowd. Eventually, WWE officials swarm the competitors, JR telling the fans that Booker T is tired of getting screwed.

After a commercial break, referees finally get order and the wrestlers fight in the ring, Booker scoring a two-count with a back body drop. The champion answers with a backward head slam on the top rope. He follows up with a choke on the ropes, JR calling him the luckiest Intercontinental Champion of all-time. He's more than just lucky here, dropkicking the challenger for a two-count before applying a reverse chin lock. Even when Booker T fights free, Christian drops him with a neckbreaker for a near fall before returning to his chin lock. Eventually, the babyface fights free to rock the champion with a spinning heel kick. When he tries to follow up with a side kick, Christian moves and Booker crotches himself on the top rope. A reverse backbreaker afterwards gets the champion a two-count before he returns to his chin lock. Once again, the challenger fights free only to be slowed with a back elbow. When Christian attempts a second rope flying attack, Booker T answers with a spinning heel kick. Catching some momentum, he clotheslines and suplexes the champion for a near fall. A spin kick also gets him a two-count before Christian pokes his eye. Despite that, Booker rolls him up for another near fall. Moments later, the men counter each other's finishers before the champion rolls up the babyface with a handful of tights for a close two-count. Booker T answers with a flapjack and spinaroonie. When Christian attacks afterwards, the challenger knocks him out to the apron for a Scissors Kick. He tries to follow up with a top rope attack, but the champion hits the ropes to crotch him. Christian follows up with a superplex, but as they hit the canvas, Booker hooks the champion's legs for the three-count. Booker T's music plays briefly before Eric Bischoff steps onto the stage to correct the referee's decision. Replaying the superplex, Eric shows both men's shoulders down and declares the match a draw.

Backstage, Rob Van Dam confronts Kane. He can't believe he turned down a World Title shot or that he Chokeslammed RVD last week. Rob especially can't believe that the "Big Red Machine" won't address the fans tonight. Van Dam admits that he told Eric Bischoff to get the monster to unmask because Kane doesn't need it. The fans will accept him anyways. The "Big Red Machine" says he hates the fans. Rob hopes he doesn't hate RVD when he wins the World Title tonight. When he walks away, Kane says he does.

Chris Jericho/Test def. Scott Steiner/Stacy Keibler ("No Disqualification" match). JR is livid about this match, yelling at "the King" to look at Stacy's concerned face and not her legs for once. Luckily, she's got Scott on her side. He starts the match shoving down Jericho and flexing. Elbows and clubbing blows follow before Steiner scores a two-count with a powerslam. Despite being in a glorified handicap match, "Big Poppa Pump" stops to do pushups after an elbow drop. When Test tags in, Scott wails on him too. He follows up with a northern lights suplex prompting the bodyguard to ask for a timeout. Steiner doesn't give it to him, but when he runs the ropes, Y2J hits him from behind and whips the babyface into the ring steps. That turns the tide and Test stomps, punches, and chokes his rival. He also taunts Keibler before tagging in Jericho to assault "Big Poppa Pump" as well. When the bodyguard returns, he clotheslines Scott in a neutral corner. Making quick tags, Y2J returns and hooks a reverse chin lock. It doesn't take Steiner long to elbow free and belly-to-belly suplex the heel. "Big Poppa Pump" also hammers Test when he tags back in before press slamming Jericho onto him. The bodyguard tries to sneak attack Scott with a Big Boot, but he moves at the last second and Test crotches himself. Stacy makes things worse for him shaking the ropes. Afterwards, Steiner gets a two-count with a reverse DDT, but Y2J breaks the count. When Jack Doan takes offense, Jericho throws him to the canvas. While the heels stomp "Big Poppa Pump", the referee calls for the bell. Eric Bischoff disagrees. He's not letting this contest end like that, making it a "No Disqualification" match. Scott doesn't waste any time, belly-to-belly suplexing the bodyguard, but Y2J answers with a chair shot to knock out "Big Poppa Pump". Test then makes Keibler tag into the match to give her a Pumphandle Slam for the three-count.

Rico (with Miss Jackie) def. Maven. Now called Miss Jackie, Gayda accompanies the lime green wearing superstar to the squared circle. Once the match starts, Rico pinches his opponent's butt. Maven gets serious with an arm wringer, but the stylist flips out of the hold. Miss Jackie loves it and rubs her nose on her man's. Afterwards, Rico tries to give the babyface a key, but Maven won't take it. Continuing to mess with his opponent's head, he sits on his face and kisses the babyface's cheek. When Maven chases Rico around the ring, Jackie trips the babyface and holds his leg for an elbow drop. Rico follows up by skipping around the ring with Chad Patton before twirling into a kick to the gut. When Maven tries to answer, Jackie trips him again for the stylist to unload with kicks and make a provocative cover for a near fall. Afterwards, he leaps off the second rope into a slam into the corner. Clotheslines and a spinning heel kick follow before Maven attacks the groin with an inverted atomic drop. When he teases a stomp to the midsection, Jackie grabs her man and holds onto him. Despite that, the babyface bulldogs Rico off the second rope, but Miss Jackie puts her man's boot on the rope to break Maven's cover. She continues to get involved, shoving the babyface off the top rope moments later for Rico to score the win with a Spin Kick.

Randy Orton (with Ric Flair) def. Tommy Dreamer. A friend of Mick Foley, Dreamer hurries out to get some revenge for the hardcore legend. Instead, Randy slows him with a collar and elbow tie-up, the two men rolling out to the floor. There, they trade fists, Tommy getting the upper hand until Orton drop toe holds him into the ring steps. A European uppercut and shots to the head follow. When Dreamer tries to fight back, a dropkick puts him down for a near fall. Seemingly on his last legs, Tommy surprises the young heel with a hotshot. Catching a second wind, he back body drops Randy ahead of a sit-out spinebuster for a near fall. Unfortunately, he misses a second rope diving elbow drop. It doesn't come back to cost him as he surprises Orton with a DDT, but before he can get the three-count, Flair drapes his man's foot on the ropes. That sends Dreamer out to the floor to grab a kendo stick. Unfortunately, he can't catch "The Nature Boy" and Ric lures him into the ring for an RKO, called such by JR, for the win. Post-match, Flair puts Tommy in the Figure Four Leglock while Randy bashes him with the stick.

Backstage, Eric Bischoff asks Rob Van Dam if he's ready for his title match tonight. He's more focused on Eric taking advantage of Kane and exploiting his face for ratings. Bischoff tells him to take his aggression out on Triple H tonight rather than the general manager.

After a commercial break, Eric Bischoff tells Terri to go find out Kane's state of mind. She doesn't want to, but when the general manager threatens to fire her, the interviewer reluctantly complies.

La Resistance def. Spike Dudley/The Hurricane. The heels come out first, the only champions not to put their belts on the line tonight. When the babyfaces come out, Dupree dances around to taunt the superhero. The Hurricane answers with takedowns and his own dance before Spike tags in for a top rope flying head scissors. A neckbreaker to Sylvan moments later gets the runt a two-count. He follows up with shots to the face and a head scissors pull into the top turnbuckle. The fans are not impressed, chanting "boring". "Stone Cold" Steve Austin let the genie out of that bottle. Soon after, the wrestlers pick up the pace, Grenier back body dropping Dudley out of the ring to the floor. When he returns, the champion nearly scores the victory before wrenching his neck. Spike responds with a bulldog and tags in the superhero to punch the heels and toss Rene out to the floor. That lets him get a near fall with a top rope flying cross body block to Sylvan. A neckbreaker follows before Dudley returns with a double stomp and two-count. After Dupree makes the save, all four men fight, La Resistance knocking The Hurricane out to the floor to block a chokeslam. They then counter a runt Dudley Dog with a Double Flapjack for the win.

Backstage, Terri hesitantly enters a storage area looking for Kane. He's already gone.

Triple H (with Ric Flair) def. Rob Van Dam ("Falls Count Anywhere" World Title match). Triple H goes right after RVD, hammering him down in a corner. Trying to put away the challenger quickly after a series of title defenses lately, Hunter scores an early one-count with a high knee. Rob answers with a spinning heel kick and his own fists. Following a monkey flip, Van Dam scores a two-count with a back kick. More near falls follow, including one after a dropkick, before the challenger takes the fight out to the floor for a baseball slide kick. After ramming Helmsley's face into the apron, RVD hits a moonsault off the second rope to put both men down and bring Ric running to ringside ahead of a commercial break.

Afterwards, Rob is back on the attack, stomping and kicking "the Game" in a corner until the champion clips his knee. Once he's down, Triple H distracts Jack Doan while Flair wraps Van Dam's knee around the ring post. Hunter continues the assault, slamming the injured joint onto the apron and chop blocking him. After dropping an elbow on RVD's knee, Helmsley applies an Indian deathlock. It takes him a while, but Rob eventually crawls to the ropes for the break. Although he reaches them, he also receives a Ric cheap shot before "the Game" hooks a figure four leglock. The heels cheat, Flair pulling the champion's hands for added pressure. Van Dam reaches down deep to turn over the hold and force the break. Afterwards, he surprises Triple H with a kick to the jaw to put both men down. Following another kick, the challenger nearly wins the title with a springboard cross body block. Riding the momentum, a dropkick gets RVD another two-count, as does a split legged moonsault until Ric breaks the cover. Rob has had enough and flattens Flair with a spin kick. Back in the ring, he counters a Pedigree with a slingshot into the top turnbuckle. A Five-Star Frog Splash follows before "The Nature Boy" breaks the count with a shot from the World Title. As soon as the bell rings, Eric Bischoff refuses to let a World Title match end in disqualification and makes this a "No Disqualification" match too. Helmsley tries to take advantage of the situation, but Van Dam kicks a chair back into his face. When he tries to toss "the Game" back in the ring, Eric tells the challenger that it's "Falls Count Anywhere" too. That brings out Randy Orton to attack the challenger, but RVD fights him off. He also takes care of Ric before chasing the champion up the aisle. There, he counters another Pedigree attempt, this time with a back body drop on the steel stage. Van Dam immediately follows up with rolling thunder, but Triple H just kicks out. Afterwards, Flair and Orton provide another distraction for Hunter to bash Rob's skull with the title belt. He quickly follows up with a DDT on the stage to successfully retain the World Title.

Post-match, Kane bursts through the curtain and teases Chokeslamming Van Dam. At the last second, the mask-less and now bald monster shoves RVD aside and Chokeslams Bischoff off the stage to a big pop. The show ends with the "Big Red Machine" glaring angrily into the camera.

SmackDown!
July 3, 2003
Rochester, NY
Announcers: Michael Cole, Tazz

The show opens with a video package featuring Vince McMahon and Zach Gowen. Afterwards, Vince promises to seal the fate of Mr. America tonight before teasing the main event seeing his daughter and Zach facing Big Show in the "first ever handicap match".

Rey Mysterio def. Nunzio (Cruiserweight Title match). Rey pops out of the stage to a big cheer, Billy Kidman watching from the crowd. Although The FBI try to accompany Nunzio, Mike Chioda intercepts them and orders the heels to head backstage. That evens the odds and the champion knocks down the Italian heel before surprising him with a roll-up for an early two-count. He follows up with a head scissors into an armbar to send the challenger out to the floor. Mysterio joins him with a flying rolling senton. Back in the squared circle though, Nunzio catches him on the top rope only to get thrown to the canvas. When the masked man tries to follow up, the challenger catches and slams him for a near fall. A face-first slam also gets him a close two-count before the Italian heel slows the pace with a surfboard. Although Rey escapes and rolls up Nunzio, the challenger regains control with a sidewalk slam. Following that near fall, he grounds the champion with a reverse chin lock. Mysterio refuses to give up, but the Italian heel plants him with a backbreaker. A leg scissors frees the masked man to tornado DDT his opponent. After working Chioda's count to four, Rey punches and flapjacks the challenger. He follows up with a springboard butt splash and standing moonsault for a near fall. Unfortunately, he then runs into a corner knee and second rope elbow to the back of the head for a two-count. The champion responds with a head scissors out to the floor, knocking out Nunzio. He's actually playing possum to distract the referee while The FBI nail Mysterio from behind. That gets the Italian heel a near fall before The APA run out to brawl with the heels. Inside the ring, Rey head scissors Nunzio into position for a 619 and springboard leg drop for the three-count. Post-match, Kidman hops into the ring to celebrate with the champion.

After a commercial break, Brock Lesnar and Kurt Angle are eating in catering and argue when a woman says, "hey, champ". A friendly rivalry, the men compare resumes and debate who will win at Vengeance. When Brock walks away, Kurt takes a drink of milk and tells the woman that he's the champ. Lesnar returns and pats his back, forcing him to spit milk on the woman, cracking up the announcers.

Chris Benoit/Rhyno def. The Basham Brothers (with Shaniqua). Pre-match, Shaniqua slaps her men with her riding crop. Once the babyfaces come out, all four men brawl until Danny tosses Benoit out to the floor. Doug and Rhyno then trade shots, the man-beast crushing Basham in a corner. When Danny enters, the man-beast clubs him down for a Boston crab. Doug tries to make the save with a clothesline, but misses. Rhyno doesn't, knocking him off the apron only to turn into an enziguri kick. Danny follows up with a blatant choke, working Jimmy Korderas' count before tagging in Doug for a twisting elbow off the second rope and near fall. The heel follows up with clubbing blows before Danny returns for a pair of elbows and a two-count. Eventually, the man-beast answers with a back suplex. When the Bashams try to double-team him, Rhyno ducks and they collide. "The Crippler" then tags in to German suplex Danny. Doug saves him from a second before all four men fight. Benoit briefly traps Danny in the Crippler Crossface, but Doug makes the save. The man-beast quickly knocks him from the ring for the "rabid wolverine" to score a two-count with a German suplex and top rope diving headbutt. After Doug makes the save again, Danny returns the favor and trips Rhyno before he can Gore his brother. The Bashams try to finish off Benoit, but Rhyno intercepts Doug with a Gore before Chris forces Danny to tap-out to the Crippler Crossface. Post-match, Shaniqua stares at "the Crippler". Benoit wants nothing to do with her.

Backstage, Stephanie McMahon nervously asks her father if he really wants her to face Big Show tonight. She says Vince McMahon can't really compare her having to step into the ring to Stephanie getting Zach Gowen to give him a low blow last week. He provides a famous quote to say, "spare the rod and spoil the child". She argues she's not a child, but he thought she was daddy's little girl and wishes her luck.

After a commercial break, Sable tells Stephanie McMahon that she can't believe Vince McMahon is making her get into the ring. She wishes the boss luck, but if anything happens, promises to take care of *SmackDown!*.

In a prerecorded vignette, Jamie Noble tells Nidia that despite being rich they have to be smart. However, he's got them a luxury car to ride around in and bought new sunglasses. Nidia has also made a purchase, getting a faux fur coat. Now that he has money, Jamie tips their driver. When Nidia walks away though, Noble takes back his cash.

Backstage, The Undertaker tells Orlando Jordan that he's going to have to earn his respect and victories in the WWE. However, John Cena attacking him last week "doesn't fly". The biker tells Jordan that he's going to have to earn back his respect and do something about it. Cena interrupts wearing Lakers gear. He tells Orlando not to let the "Deadman" brainwash him. John then tells The Undertaker that Cena is a veteran now and the biker needs to stay out of his business. When the rapping heel walks away, the "Deadman" says everyone has to learn the hard way.

Billy Gunn (with Torrie Wilson) def. John Cena (US Title Tournament match). Pre-match, Torrie shakes her butt before Cena raps and calls out The Undertaker. He quickly transitions to Billy, saying he'd rather feel up Chuck than wrestle. That sets off Gunn and he unloads with fists and clotheslines for a pair of early two-counts. The rapping heel quickly slides out to the floor to regroup, but Billy follows behind and slams him into the barricade. When he tries to follow up, John reverses a whip into the ring post to finally swing the momentum. Once in control, he repeatedly stomps the babyface ahead of a suplex and two-count. A reverse chin lock slows the pace briefly before Cena hammers Gunn down again. Following another two-count, the rapping heel yells at Mike Sparks. He gives him a dirty look when he doesn't get the win off a sidewalk slam before applying another chin lock. This time, Billy fights free and powerslams John. After catching his breath, he punches and slams Cena face-first to the canvas for a near fall. Unfortunately, he misses a corner splash and the rapping heel nearly gets the win with a flipping facebuster, called the throwback. When he grabs his chain, the "Deadman" rides his bike down to the squared circle to distract him. That lets Gunn recover and small package John for the win.

Backstage, Brock Lesnar and Kurt Angle laugh and shove each other. Their friendly rivalry sees them shoving each other harder and harder until Kurt challenges the WWE Champion to a pushup contest. Lesnar offers to go first, each man agreeing to do 300 pushups. Brock struggles on the last few, but gets the job done. After he collapses on the floor unable to even lift his arms, the Olympian calls him the winner and leaves Lesnar writhing.

MUST SEE! Charlie Haas/Shelton Benjamin def. Eddie Guerrero/Tajiri (WWE Tag Title match). Tajiri opens the match elbowing and kicking Haas. He briefly follows up with a headlock, but Charlie outwrestles him and turns it into an overhead hammerlock. When the champion regains control, he tags in Eddie. Shelton joins him, "Latino Heat" targeting his arm. Benjamin has an amateur background too and reverses a hold before Guerrero surprises him with a dropkick. When Haas illegally enters the ring, Eddie powerslams him ahead of a head scissors and headlock takedown to the challengers. Unfortunately, Charlie quickly recovers and tags in to slow the champion with a backbreaker. A float over suplex afterwards gets him a two-count before he rakes Eddie's face in the ropes. He attempts to follow up with a corner attack, but Guerrero counters with a back elbow and twisting belly-to-belly suplex. The "Japanese Buzzsaw" gets the hot tag afterwards to kick both challengers and drive Haas to the canvas with a reverse bulldog for a near fall. He tries to follow up with a hurricanrana, but Shelton holds his partner up before leveling Tajiri with a springboard clothesline. Somehow, that only gets Charlie a near fall, as does a double-team slam ahead of a commercial break.

Afterwards, Benjamin remains in control, trapping the "Japanese Buzzsaw" in an abdominal stretch. "Latino Heat" inadvertently distracts Brian Hebner allowing Haas to illegally switch places with his partner. For once, the referee listens to a wrestler and orders Charlie back to his corner. Unfortunately, Shelton returns and hammers down Tajiri. Haas then tags in to whip the champion hard into a corner for a two-count. When he punches the "Japanese Buzzsaw", Guerrero illegally enters the ring only to see Hebner intercept him. Soon after, the challengers score a near fall with a double-team leapfrog splash before "Latino Heat" makes the save. When the referee admonishes him, Eddie holds onto the tag rope for a nice pop. Moments later, Tajiri rocks Benjamin with a thrust kick. Guerrero gets the hot tag afterwards to clothesline and dropkick the heels. He follows up with a snap suplex to Shelton, but Charlie stops him from delivering a second. That gets him a pair of suplexes instead. When he tries to head upstairs, Benjamin intercepts "Latino Heat" and superplexes him. The "Japanese Buzzsaw" responds with a handspring back elbow. He tries to follow up with a baseball slide kick, but Shelton moves and the two men fight at ringside while Haas crawls onto Eddie for a close two-count. Guerrero answers with a tilt-a-whirl backbreaker, but Benjamin makes the save. Shelton continues the punishment, suplexing "Latino Heat" over the top rope leaving Tajiri alone against the challengers. He shows why he's a champion, kicking Benjamin's face before locking Charlie in a Tarantula. When Eddie tries to fly over him with a Frog Splash, Shelton moves at the last second. He quickly follows up with a kick that sends the "Japanese Buzzsaw" face-first onto the lowrider. Guerrero can't believe it. He stares in horror at his partner on the hood, allowing the challengers to pin him with an Inverted Atomic Drop and Superkick. The announcers are impressed that they won back the belts without Kurt Angle.

Backstage, Zach Gowen stretches until Big Show stands on his prosthetic leg. The giant laughs that Zach's only got one leg left.

After a commercial break, Eddie Guerrero is still at ringside and horrified to see his partner writhing on the lowrider hood. When he approaches Tajiri, "Latino Heat" shoves him aside and exclaims, "my car".

A Mr. America video package plays.

Afterwards, Eddie Guerrero attacks Tajiri and slams him through the windshield of his lowrider. That sees the "Japanese Buzzsaw" stretchered off during the break.

A-Train def. Orlando Jordan. The hairy heel storms down to the squared circle to hammer and shoulderblock Jordan. A scoop slam and big splash afterwards gets him a two-count. All offense, A-

Train delivers his decapitator slingshot before crushing Orlando in a corner. Manhandling the rookie, the hairy heel also applies a reverse full nelson until Jordan slips free for a roll-up and two-count. That makes A-Train mad and he tries to follow up with a bicycle kick, but Orlando moves and the big man crotches himself on the top rope. The rookie follows up with an enziguri and flying forearm for a near fall. One shot to the kidneys slows Jordan for the hairy heel to deliver a Derailer for a very close two-count. A-Train wastes time afterwards arguing with Jimmy Korderas and nearly pays as Orlando surprises him with a drop toe hold. Unfortunately, he misses his follow up top rope flying cross body block and the hairy heel answers with a Train Wreck for the victory.

Backstage, Big Show stops Stephanie McMahon in a hallway and smells her hair. He hopes she doesn't get hurt in the ring because there are "so many other ways" he'd like to hurt her. Afterwards, Vince McMahon reminds the giant that Stephanie is his daughter and invites Show to watch his upcoming announcement about Mr. America.

This week's WrestleMania Recall moment is Alice Cooper accompanying Jake "the Snake" Roberts at WrestleMania III and putting Damian on Jimmy Hart.

Back at ringside, Sable accompanies Vince McMahon to the ring. There, Vince tells everyone that he promised he would expose Mr. America as Hulk Hogan. To do so, he's got footage from Madison Square Garden after last's week show went off the air. In it, the Hulkster raises his mask to reveal that he is in fact the masked patriot. The fans chant for Hogan, but McMahon says he's sitting at home. To make it official, Vince says he's been waiting for a long time to tell Hulk that he's fired. He does so now to boos. The WWE owner then turns his attention to Zach Gowen, telling everyone that he could have had a WWE contract last week if he would have just kissed Vince's butt. McMahon knows all the fans would. Since Zach didn't take the easy way, Vince is making the upcoming handicap contest a "No Holds Barred" match. Finally, the WWE owner tells everyone that at Vengeance, Brock Lesnar will defend the WWE Title against both Kurt Angle and Big Show before Vince takes a seat at ringside.

Stephanie McMahon/Zach Gowen def. Big Show ("No Holds Barred" match). Show is out first, Stephanie following with a terrified look on her face. Zach comes out last, Cole saying he's overcome so many odds to get here. He won't back down now with a contract on the line, getting in the giant's face only to be slugged down. When Big Show follows Gowen out to the floor, Stephanie leaps onto his back. She can't do much to stop Show and he slams her on the floor before pulling off Zach's prosthetic leg. With just one leg, Gowen kicks the giant and dives over the top rope onto him. Unfortunately, Big Show catches and press slams him back into the ring. He also press slams Stephanie into the squared circle, Vince McMahon and Sable watching at ringside. When Show picks up his daughter, Vince finally climbs onto the apron. However, he just wants an up close view of the giant Chokeslamming her. Zach doesn't, pulling Mr. McMahon off the apron and attacking Big Show. The giant answers with a stiff clothesline and Chokeslam at the WWE owner's request. Stephanie has had enough and slaps her father. Vince is all fed up and orders Show to Chokeslam her. Before he can, Kurt Angle runs out to give the giant a low blow and trap him in the Anklelock. Before he can break his ankle—Cole pleading with him to do so—the WWE owner saves Big Show with a chair shot to Kurt's back. Brock Lesnar sprints out afterwards and hoists up Vince for an F5, but Show returns the favor and saves him with a big boot. The giant tries to use the chair, but Gowen kicks it back into his face ahead of an Angle Slam. Lesnar adds an F5 before Zach dropkicks the WWE owner out to the floor. Gowen follows up with a top rope moonsault onto Big Show for the three-count and a WWE contract.

Monday Night Raw
July 7, 2003
Montreal, Quebec, Canada
Announcers: Jim Ross, Jerry "the King" Lawler

The show opens with a video package featuring Kane, including him Chokeslamming Eric Bischoff off the stage last week. Afterwards, "Stone Cold" Steve Austin heads to the squared circle to a huge pop. He's glad to be back after having food poisoning last week. The only good thing that happened for him last week was watching Eric get thrown off the stage. That leaves Austin alone this week and he's ready to get the action started.

MUST SEE! Booker T def. Christian (Intercontinental Title match). As Booker heads to the ring, JR points out that he's been screwed over more times than anyone can count. Lawler thinks it should be his last shot at the title. When Christian comes out, he says he's better than the challenger and refuses to step into the squared circle with him. "Stone Cold" interrupts to say that the belt can change hands tonight on a count-out or disqualification. The champion refuses to enter the ring to make it official, so Austin throws him in to settle that problem. Once the bell rings, Booker T repeatedly punches Christian. When the champion tries to flee, the babyface follows him out and tosses him back into the ring even though he doesn't have to win the belt. There, Christian gets in a few shots before Booker plants him with a sidewalk slam for a two-count. The two men then trade strikes, the challenger getting the upper hand until the heel stuns him with a face drop onto the top turnbuckle and near fall. A backbreaker moments later gets Christian a two-count before he applies a chin lock. Even when Booker T fights free, the champion drops him with a knee to the gut for another near fall. Soon after, the babyface surprises his opponent with a flapjack, but when he motions for the spinaroonie, Christian boots him hard. Despite that, Booker recovers quickly and drops the heel with a Scissors Kick for the three-count. Unfortunately, Chad Patton realizes the champion's foot was on the ropes and orders the match to continue ahead of a commercial break.

Afterwards, Christian is back in control with a chin lock. Although the challenger fights free and rolls up the heel, Christian levels him with a dropkick for a near fall. The champion follows with fists until Booker T powerslams the heel to put both men down. The babyface recovers first to elbow and hotshot Christian on the top rope. A new champion is nearly crowned thanks to a Book End, but the heel just kicks out. He also kicks out of a roll-up before Booker rocks him with a heel kick. When the challenger heads upstairs, the heel punches him into straddling the top turnbuckle. Despite that, Booker T recovers to slam Christian face-first to the canvas for a missile dropkick and close two-count. He follows up with a spinaroonie, but when he goes for a second Scissors Kick, the champion shoves Patton into the babyface to low blow Booker for a near fall. Christian has had enough and grabs the Intercontinental Title. Unfortunately, he misses the challenger with it. Booker T doesn't miss, nailing the champion with another Scissors Kick to finally win the Intercontinental Title.

Backstage, Nick Patrick interrupts "Stone Cold" Steve Austin talking to Mark Jindrak. Nick leads the co-general manager backstage where Tommy Dreamer is out cold and bleeding. Bubba Ray Dudley tells the "rattlesnake" to take care of his best friend.

Footage from the 1997 "Montreal Screwjob" plays ahead of Shawn Michaels appearing on the Highlight Reel later tonight.

Rosey (with Theodore Long/Rodney Mack) def. The Hurricane. Pre-match, Long complains about the powers that be keeping him and his team down, noting injuries to Jazz and Christopher Nowinski. To replace them, he's signing Rosey and asks him to "knock a white boy out". While he talks, Jonathan Coachman tries to figure out who attacked Tommy Dreamer. Bubba Ray Dudley has a good idea who it was. We'll have to wait to see who as The Hurricane marches down to offer Rosey a handshake. When the Samoan doesn't accept it, the superhero punches him until Mack grabs his foot while he runs the ropes. That swings the momentum, Rosey hammering the masked superstar until he misses a corner charge. The Hurricane capitalizes with an overcast before knocking Rodney off the apron with a Shining Wizard. He tries to follow up with a top rope attack, but Rosey grabs him for a Samoan Drop and the win. Post-match, Theodore orders the winner around, but Rosey doesn't like that, shoving Long into a corner to squash him. That sets off Mack and he assaults the Samoan before helping his manager.

Backstage, Bubba Ray Dudley accuses Randy Orton and Ric Flair of attacking Tommy Dreamer earlier. Randy says he was busy drinking a protein shake. "Stone Cold" Steve Austin stops Dudley from doing anything crazy to tell him to get a tag team partner and he can face Evolution later. When Austin interrogates the heels, Miss Jackie runs up to get the GM to check on Rico.

After a commercial break, a wounded Rico tells "Stone Cold" Steve Austin that Kane left him barely conscious.

Gail Kim/Val Venis def. Steven Richards/Victoria. Kim helps her partner remove his towel before spanking his backside. Victoria doesn't appreciate the pre-match antics and chokes Gail ahead of a press slam. The new Women's Champion answers with a cross body block for a two-count. A head scissors and monkey flip also get her a near fall. When she chops the "black widow" into the heel corner, Richards makes the blind tag. Val spots it even if Gail doesn't, tagging in to clothesline Steven and drive him to the canvas with a uranage after Kim slaps him. When the adult star runs the ropes though, Victoria trips him for a Richards DDT and near fall. He briefly follows up with a sleeper hold, but Venis escapes with a sit out slam. Afterwards, the women return to the ring for the "black widow" to attempt a powerbomb. Unfortunately, Kim punches her opponent down to the canvas. When Steven tries to make the save, he accidentally elbow drops his own partner. "The big Valbowski" rewards him with a spinebuster. While he deals with Richards at ringside, Gail scores the win with a Hurricanrana.

Backstage, Test interrupts Trish Stratus stretching. He says since he's single, he's going to give her the first chance to "hook up" with him. When she says no, the bodyguard grabs her and tells the vixen that he doesn't take no for answer. Kevin Nash doesn't care what he takes, challenging him to a match.

After a commercial break, Chris Jericho heads to the ring for the Highlight Reel. The Canadian gets a big pop before he shows footage on the Jeritron 5000 of Shawn Michaels "screwing" Bret Hart at the 1997 Survivor Series here in Montreal. The fans want Bret and so does Y2J. He promises to make Shawn face the music and address the situation. The fans are not happy to see him, insulting Michaels as he heads to the squared circle. While he claims that he's apologized to everyone else, he hasn't apologized to the people of Montreal. He does so now, with a caveat. He's mostly sorry that Montreal is still stuck in 1997 and cares about what happened at Survivor Series. When the fans chant that he "screwed Bret", the "Heartbreak Kid" wants to know what their point is. He had a job and did it. Jericho has had enough and curses Shawn, drawing a big pop. Michaels says he's trying to help the people of Montreal move on, even offering to let them boo him for beating Y2J at WrestleMania this year. When Jericho says that they are never going to forget, the "Heartbreak Kid" calls him Captain Canada. The fans love that, but

Shawn wonders if Chris is such a proud Canadian why does he live in Florida. Michaels offers to wrestle him tonight, but Y2J isn't going to wrestle in Montreal due to the terrible economy. That's why he moved to the United States in the first place. Instead of wrestling tonight, Jericho offers to wrestle the "Heartbreak Kid" in Hollywood in two weeks. When he tries to get the fans to chant "Hollywood", they boo. Y2J tells them "screw you" and walks away.

Backstage, Jonathan Coachman asks "Stone Cold" Steve Austin how he's going to stop Kane's rampage. The GM promises to take care of things. When he enters his office, the "Big Red Machine" is waiting to talk to him. After a commercial break, we find out that's about the monster quitting. Austin calls him "pathetic" for threatening to quit. He's also not happy that Kane is attacking superstars backstage. He wants him killing them in the ring. After what the "Big Red Machine" did to Eric Bischoff last week, "Stone Cold" promises the fans will cheer him if he stays.

Test def. Kevin Nash. Nash opens the match elbowing and kneeing the bodyguard before clotheslining Test out to the floor. When he follows him out though, the bodyguard shoves Kevin into the ring post as JR insults Hillary Clinton. The heel proceeds to stomp "Big Sexy" in the ring and remove a turnbuckle pad until Trish Stratus runs out to try to save Nash. Instead, Test shoves her into Kevin and gives "Big Sexy" a Big Boot for the three-count. Post-match, the bodyguard pulls Stratus out face-first onto the floor before whipping her into the barricade.

Backstage, Terri interviews the new Intercontinental Champion. Booker T says his smile is bigger than ever because he's the "first-time Intercontinental Champion". He's feeling so good that he invites Terri and Montreal to celebrate with the new champion. She's okay with that and leaves with Booker.

Chris Jericho def. Mark Jindrak. Y2J is all over Jindrak, slapping, dropkicking, and slamming his face into the canvas to start the match. JR considers Mark a future champion. He avoids an early loss with a pair of knees to counter a Lionsault. Afterwards, he shows flashes of talent with a back body drop and dropkick, but misses a corner splash. Jerry says he'll make "rookie mistakes", ignoring the returning superstar's time with the company during the Invasion. Despite getting dropkicked out to the floor, Jindrak recovers quickly to whip the heel into the ring steps. Moments later, he scores a two-count with a tilt-a-whirl slam back in the ring. He also gets a near fall with a springboard clothesline out of a corner. When Y2J tries to answer with a dropkick, Mark catches and slingshots him into a corner for a near fall. With the fans chanting "boring", Jericho shoves the babyface out to the floor. When he tries to get back in, Y2J low blows him ahead of the Walls of Jericho for the tap-out victory.

After a commercial break, the announcers shill the new issue of the *WWE Magazine* focused on the late "Classy" Freddie Blassie.

Molly Holly def. Trish Stratus (#1 Contender's match). Trish is limping as she heads to the ring in her lingerie-like outfit. Molly capitalizes, slamming her to the mat and choking her with her coat. All "the King" and the fans care about is nudity. Holly silences them with a flipping snap mare for a two-count before wrenching the vixen's neck. Although Stratus fights free, a swinging neckbreaker puts her down for a two-count. Molly keeps her down on the canvas, raking her face and choking Trish. When the heel attempts a handspring corner attack, the vixen surprises her with a roll-up for a near fall. More two-counts follow on roll-ups before Stratus unloads with a string of chops. One snap mare puts Trish back down. Holly follows up with a shoulderbreaker before applying an inverted camel clutch for the tap-out victory.

Backstage, Kane surprises "Stone Cold" Steve Austin as he looms behind him. Austin wants to know if he's going to head to the squared circle with the GM or quit. The "Big Red Machine" just says he'll do it.

Bubba Ray Dudley/Rob Van Dam def. Randy Orton/Ric Flair. Since D-Von Dudley is out tonight due to personal reasons, as relayed by Lawler, RVD helps Bubba and takes care of the heels to start the match. Eventually, Flair distracts Rob long enough for Orton to surprise the popular superstar with his unique backbreaker. Ric then tags in to pummel Van Dam. When RVD shows signs of life, Randy tags back in to dropkick him for a two-count. Rob answers with a stepover heel kick, but can't tag out before "The Nature Boy" returns to trap him in the Figure Four Leglock. Luckily, Van Dam reaches the ropes. When Ric tries to reapply the hold, RVD surprises him with a small package for a near fall. Orton tags in moments later only to catch a spinning heel kick to the jaw. Bubba Ray finally gets the tag to clothesline both heels and trade chops with Flair. Back body drops follow before Dudley gets a two-count with a sidewalk slam to "The Nature Boy". Randy pays for breaking up the cover courtesy of a neckbreaker. Bubba then elbows and squashes Ric in a corner, even atomic dropping Orton into his partner. Flair tries to head upstairs to turn the tide, but Bubba Ray slams him to the canvas. Soon after, RVD tags back in to catch "The Nature Boy" with a top rope flying kick. Once again, Randy makes the save and pays, this time with a slam out to the floor. There, he grabs Rob's foot to prevent him from splashing Ric until Spike Dudley runs out and knocks Orton down. Van Dam capitalizes with a Five-Star Frog Splash onto Flair for the win.

After the final commercial break, "Stone Cold" Steve Austin heads back to the squared circle. He tells the fans they can cheer or boo Kane before introducing the "Big Red Machine". The crowd gives him a big pop. "Stone Cold" says the fans don't care what he looks like and it's time for the monster to rise higher than he ever has in the WWE. Both Austin and Rob Van Dam have been trying to motivate him and now he's ready to take the next step in his career. The GM is even more impressed watching footage of Kane Chokeslamming Eric Bischoff off the stage last week. When "Stone Cold" says that was funny, the "Big Red Machine" gets upset. He thinks the "rattlesnake" is making fun of him and attacks. After the monster gets in several shots, Austin responds in kind and drives Kane's face into the ring post. He follows up with a chair shot to the skull, busting the monster open five years too late for their "First Blood" match. The GM follows up with a Stone Cold Stunner, but when he turns his back to celebrate with a beer, the "Big Red Machine" sits up and Chokeslams him to end the show.

SmackDown!

July 10, 2003
Toronto, Ontario, Canada
Announcers: Michael Cole, Tazz

The show opens with a video package for Zach Gowen earning a WWE contract last week ahead of the intro video and fireworks.

Afterwards, Kurt Angle heads to the ring to a big pop. He says he lost the WWE Title three months ago and in less than three weeks, he's going to win it back. However, he knows it's going to be tough beating both Big Show and Brock Lesnar. Despite that, he refuses to lose and promises to come back to Toronto with championship gold. Instead of his Vengeance opponents, John Cena interrupts. The rapping heel says the real main event of the PPV is going to be him versus The Undertaker. He also accuses Angle of making him sick, drawing a small but noticeable pop. Kurt didn't think it was possible, but he says he found "someone in the company whiter" than he is. The Olympian then tells John that Angle is multitalented and "likes to kick it freestyle". When he steals the rapping heel's hat, Cena tells him that he can't see him. John doesn't think he's on his level, his next rap confusing Kurt. Despite that, the Olympian invites Brian Hebner into the ring to beatbox for him. Angle proceeds to provide his own rap. He doesn't have much flow, but it's highly entertaining. When John says he didn't "major in thuganomics", Kurt hugs him. He says Cena needs a lesson in "huganomics". He then warns the rapping heel that if he messes with him, John will tap. Before they come to blows, Show marches down the aisle. He distracts the Olympian long enough for Cena to hit him from behind and give Angle an FU. Big Show follows up with a Chokeslam, Cole saying that he's making a statement.

Billy Kidman/Rey Mysterio def. The APA and The Basham Brothers (with Shaniqua) and The FBI (with Nunzio) (#1 Contender's match). Chuck opens the match hammering Simmons in this one fall to a finish match. Ron answers with a powerslam, but Stamboli breaks his cover. Afterwards, Danny Basham tags in for The APA to hammer him, Bradshaw wearing a shirt in the ring. When he nears the ropes, Kidman makes his return to the ring, tagging himself into the action. He greets Danny with a dropkick before Doug illegally enters to tilt-a-whirl slam him. Rey leaps to his partner's defense with a top rope flying senton splash. "The Bull" then gives the masked man a press slam gutbuster before Simmons decks him. Palumbo helps his partner with a spinebuster. Chaos reigns as all four teams brawl around ringside. The APA and The FBI soon brawl backstage leaving Mysterio and Billy to catch the Bashams with a pair of flying dives ahead of a commercial break.

Afterwards, we see footage of The APA and The FBI brawling, Cole revealing that both teams have been eliminated. Inside the ring, Doug tries to put Rey out with a reverse chin lock. When Danny tags in, Mysterio surprises him with a bulldog. Kidman gets the hot tag afterwards to bulldog Doug and enziguri kick Danny out to the floor. He tries to finish off Doug, but the heel surprises him with a powerslam for a near fall. When he picks up Billy for a powerbomb, the returning superstar answers with a facebuster. He tries to head upstairs, but Shaniqua grabs his foot. Rey returns afterwards to head scissors Danny out to the floor. Luckily, he returns to break the count when Kidman gives Doug a Shooting Star Press. After tossing a returning Mysterio out to the floor, Danny plants Billy with a reverse DDT for Doug to nearly get the win. Danny then tags in only to see Kidman stun him with a jawbreaker. The masked man tags in afterwards to hit a 619 and a springboard leg drop, called Dropping the Dime by Cole, for the three-count.

Backstage, trainers check on Kurt Angle. Brock Lesnar enters to make fun of Kurt and ask how he's going to be able to win the WWE Title at Vengeance if he can't deal with Big Show alone. When Lesnar tells him not to worry about it and they'll take care of the giant together, Angle says it's every man for himself at Vengeance. Brock understands, but he's still in a good mood and jokes with the trainer that the Olympian needs more ice because his head is swollen.

Following a shot of the NBA's Vince Carter in the crowd, the announcers replay Stephanie McMahon and Zach Gowen beating Big Show last week. That earns Zach a WWE contract and he heads to the ring to sign it. Stephanie is already in the squared circle and hugs him. Afterwards, Gowen said his dream came true last week when he pinned Show and he thanks the fans and all the people that helped him get here. As soon as he signs his contract, Vince McMahon and Sable head to the squared circle to claim that the WWE owner is proud of Stephanie and Zach. Vince is also proud to announce that tonight Brock Lesnar will pay for helping Gowen when he faces Big Show, Charlie Haas, and Shelton Benjamin in a handicap match. Mr. McMahon isn't upset with Zach because now he works for the WWE owner. That means Vince can fire him if he crosses the boss. He'll give him the chance to do so without repercussions at Vengeance when Gowen steps into the ring with Mr. McMahon. Vince warns Zach that he might have beaten cancer, but he won't beat the WWE owner. Out of nowhere, Sable smashes Stephanie with a clipboard before the heels head backstage.

After a commercial break, Vince McMahon tells Sable that he is proud of her. Before they can kiss, Stephanie McMahon charges the diva and topples her over a couch. While WWE officials, including Fit Finlay, pull Stephanie back, Vince signs the women to a match at Vengeance.

Chris Benoit/Rhyno def. Matt Hardy Version 1.0/Shannon Moore. This week's Matt Facts are that Hardy lost his virginity at seventeen and has never worn earrings. He'll also lock up with Benoit next week in a US Title Tournament semifinals match. Instead of "the Crippler" though, it's Rhyno opening the match hammering the heels. Eventually, Matt illegally enters the ring while Brian Hebner is distracted to chop block the man-beast. He follows up with a side effect, but Benoit breaks up the cover. He doesn't bother following a Moore swinging neckbreaker. It doesn't cost him as Rhyno just kicks out. Shannon remains on the attack, choking the man-beast with his own arm. When he starts to fight free, the MFer clotheslines him to the mat. Unfortunately, he then runs into a face slam onto the top turnbuckle. Afterwards, the "rabid wolverine" gets the hot tag to snap suplex both heels. He follows up with German suplexes to put both men down ahead of a top rope diving headbutt to Moore. Before he can score the three-count, Hardy spins Benoit around for a Twist of Fate. Rhyno sees him and comes to his partner's defense, Goring Matt before Shannon crawls over to "the Crippler". Before he can score the three-count, Benoit rolls over and locks on the Crippler Crossface for the tap-out victory.

After a commercial break, Kurt Angle tells Brock Lesnar tonight's going to be a tough night. Brock says that's why he's the champ. Angle promises to watch his back because he doesn't want Lesnar complaining that he lost at Vengeance only because he wasn't one hundred percent.

Eddie Guerrero def. Ultimo Dragon (US Title Tournament match). Eddie is out solo in a lowrider tonight after attacking Tajiri last week. Pre-match, he wishes the "Japanese Buzzsaw" a speedy recovery. The fans chant for Guerrero as he says he has a bit of a temper problem. However, Eddie blames Tajiri for what happened because he touched his lowrider. From now on, "Latino Heat" promises to take care of himself and he's entered the US Title Tournament to do so. Dragon then comes out to arm drag Guerrero. The announcers are really looking forward to this one and the wrestlers don't disappoint with a fast opening exchange. The masked man has the early advantage, kicking and driving Eddie out to the floor. When he returns, "Latino Heat" attacks Dragon's arm and suplexes him onto his shoulder. He then transitions to the back with a backbreaker before the masked man back body drops him out to the floor. That nearly causes Guerrero to fly into his lowrider. At the last second he holds up. He does so again following a baseball slide kick. When Dragon hops onto the apron, Eddie pulls him face-first onto the canvas, but misses his slingshot somersault splash back in the ring. The two men then trade counters until the masked man hurricanranas "Latino Heat". He follows up with a kick to the gut, but Guerrero catches his springboard moonsault off the second rope and rolls through for the three-count. In fairness, the finish isn't perfect, but both men are pros and roll through to the planned ending.

Backstage, Billy Gunn and Torrie Wilson sneak around and make out, giggling as they pass Dave Hebner.

Billy Gunn/Torrie Wilson def. Jamie Noble/Nidia. Billy opens the match overpowering Noble and pounding on him for a two-count. Jamie answers with kicks and an eye rake before tagging in Nidia. Gunn wants a piece of her, but has to tag in Torrie to clothesline the diva due to the match rules. Nidia answers with her own clothesline for a two-count, but lowers her head too soon for a back body drop. Wilson takes advantage of her mistake with a swinging neckbreaker. When Noble makes the save, Billy drives him out to the floor for Torrie to score the victory with a DDT.

Post-match, Jamie grabs a microphone to tell Wilson that she got lucky but will never be as beautiful as Nidia or as good in bed. To find out, Noble offers her ten thousand dollars. Torrie tries to slap him, but he blocks her hand and crushes it. That brings in Gunn to tackle and punch the redneck. Once Billy doubles him over, Wilson DDTs Jamie too. Nidia wants nothing to do with her, but Torrie pulls off her shorts for some reason, sending the heel out to the floor to cover herself with her faux fur coat.

Backstage, Kurt Angle accompanies Brock Lesnar down the hall until an assistant rushes up to tell the Olympian that Vince McMahon wants to see him right now.

After a commercial break, the announcers preview Vengeance.

Big Show/The World's Greatest Tag Team (Charlie Haas/Shelton Benjamin) def. Brock Lesnar ("Falls Count Anywhere" match). Before Tony Chimel introduces the competitors, he announces that he was just informed that this is now a "Falls Count Anywhere" match. When Haas and Benjamin are introduced, Shelton tells Chimel that they will now be called "The World's Greatest Tag Team". Following a commercial break, Lesnar is in the ring trading holds with Charlie. Despite being outnumbered, he press slams Haas. Benjamin tries to make the save, but gets press slammed over the top rope onto his own partner. Brock isn't done, spearing Show before fighting with the WWE Tag Team Champions at ringside. After handling both of them, he returns to the ring where Charlie briefly slows him with a choke in a corner. The WWE Champion answers with a running slam into the corner. When he tries to run the ropes afterwards, Shelton low bridges Brock. The giant follows up with a chair shot to the back for a Haas near fall at ringside. Back in the squared circle, Charlie back suplexes the WWE Champion for another two-count. Big Show is in afterwards, headbutting and clubbing Lesnar. Brock tries to fight back, but Show slows him with a leg drop. He then puts the WWE Champion into position for his partners to deliver their double-team leapfrog splash. A double slam follows before Benjamin applies a reverse bearhug, squeezing Lesnar's ribs. When Show distracts Jimmy Korderas, Charlie slips into the ring to kick Brock and trade places with his partner. Lesnar tries to fight back, but runs into a dropkick and near fall. Back in, Big Show applies his own bearhug. Eventually, the WWE Champion shows signs of life and fights free. Although the giant tries to stop him with a Chokeslam, Brock escapes and tosses over Show with a belly-to-belly suplex. That sends Big Show rolling out to the floor where Lesnar rams him into the ring post. Unfortunately, The World's Greatest Tag Team rushes to his defense. They can't keep the WWE Champion down and he gives Haas an F5 inside the squared circle. An overhead release belly-to-belly suplex follows to Benjamin putting all three heels down. With the fans cheering him on, Brock clears the announce table. When he sets the ring steps in front of the table, Shelton runs over to attack Lesnar. The WWE Champion sees him coming and rams Benjamin into the ring post. Afterwards, he picks up Shelton and tries to give him an F5 off the steps. Unfortunately, Big Show recovers and kicks the babyface. He pays for it when Brock slams his face onto the ring steps. Not done yet, he pulls Big Show up onto the steps and teases an F5 through the table. Before he can lift the giant, Show recovers and answers with his own finisher, Chokeslamming the WWE Champion through the announce table to score the victory with a foot on Lesnar's throat. Tazz wonders where Kurt Angle was as WWE officials check on Brock to end the show.

Monday Night Raw
July 14, 2003
Indianapolis, IN
Announcers: Jonathan Coachman, Jerry "the King" Lawler

The show opens with a video package featuring "Stone Cold" Steve Austin and Kane.

After the intro video and fireworks, Chris Jericho is in the ring already for the Highlight Reel. He says things have to change in the WWE because people are getting attacked in the locker room. Even Y2J, the self-professed toughest guy in the company, is a little worried. At least he was until Eric Bischoff made his return earlier. Jericho then welcomes out Eric, sporting a neck brace. After Y2J compliments his toughness, Bischoff says there was no way he was going to stay at home and let "Stone Cold" Steve Austin run his show into the ground. To get things under control, Eric has banned Kane from the arena tonight. However, the co-general manager says the "Big Red Machine" will be on the show with a special sit down interview in Stamford, Connecticut, with Jim Ross later. Bischoff also has special footage of him from last week, showing Kane tossing Rob Van Dam through a fake wall before heading to the ring on the Jeritron. Jericho is glad that the monster won't be here tonight because no one knows what he'll do. Y2J tries to speak on behalf of Austin, but that brings out "Stone Cold" to tell the Canadian heel to shut up. He turns to his co-GM and says he was going to take care of Kane tonight, probably by kicking his butt. That doesn't sit well with Eric. He says Steve is making things worse and getting people beat up like Tommy Dreamer and RVD last week. In fact, Bischoff blames the "Big Red Machine's" recent attacks on Austin riling him up. "Stone Cold" is riled up too and he wants to take his frustrations out on somebody, threatening Eric. While the fans want to see that, Steve says Bischoff isn't worth it and turns to leave. Jericho tells him to keep walking because no one wants him and he doesn't know what to do. When the Canadian heel calls him a failure, Austin drops him with a Stone Cold Stunner. Afterwards, the announcers preview the show.

Kevin Nash/Scott Steiner/Trish Stratus (with Stacy Keibler) def. Steven Richards/Test/Victoria. While the babyfaces all get separate entrances, the heels are united. Inside the ring, Scott wants Test, but he gets Richards instead. Steiner quickly takes his frustrations out on him, clubbing and belly-to-belly suplexing Steven. Following his elbow drop and pushups, "Big Poppa Pump" chases the bodyguard around the ring before tagging in Stratus. She surprises Victoria with her Matrix dodge and a Chick Kick. Before she can score the win though, the "black widow" picks her up for an assisted hotshot alongside Test. The bodyguard then tags in and mocks the vixen. He wastes too much time and she unloads with a string of forearms before running into a vicious shoulderblock. Once again, Test mocks her and Scott, doing pushups and jumping jacks. Victoria then tags in for a slingshot suplex and near fall. When she misses a clothesline, Trish answers with a neckbreaker before both women tag out. Nash nearly gets his hands on the bodyguard, but he shoves the "black widow" into "Big Sexy". When he teases slamming her, Richards rushes to her defense only to eat a big boot ahead of a Jackknife for the three-count.

Backstage, Chris Jericho complains to Eric Bischoff about "Stone Cold" Steve Austin Stunning him. They both agree it's not right. When Bischoff says he's never heard of a company policy that would allow that, Y2J gets a bright idea.

Maven def. Lance Storm. Pre-match, Storm reads a statement from his lawyers to warn fans that if they chant "boring" during his matches he will seek legal action. Maven interrupts to a nice pop, rushing down to tie up with the heel and work on his arm. Lance briefly turns the tide with a chin lock, the fans chanting "boring" for his offense. When he attempts a hip toss, the heel slips and the fans get on his case even more. That seems to fire him up and he clotheslines and chokes the babyface before yelling at Chad Patton. He's so mad that he even tears off his elbow pads before stretching Maven's arm and neck at the same time. The babyface escapes with a roll-up for a two-count, but Lance regains control with a back elbow and his own near fall. Once again slowing the pace with a chin lock, Storm gets under the fans' skin. The announcers agree that it's boring. Soon after, Maven comes back to life with a string of clotheslines and a spinning heel kick for a two-count. A back body drop moments later sends Lance out to the floor where the babyface catches him with a slingshot kick. When he tries to follow up with a top rope flying cross body block, the two men roll through, Maven ending up on top for a near fall. Storm answers with a jawbreaker and superkick for his own close two-count. With the announcers insulting him, Lance rolls through on a sunset flip and locks on a Single Leg Crab. Although the babyface reaches the ropes for the break, Storm refuses to release the hold. Maven takes matters into his own hands, sitting up and pushing his weight back onto Lance to steal the win.

In Stamford, Connecticut, Jim Ross tells his crew that tonight we're going to find out if Kane is really a monster.

Afterwards, La Resistance heads to the ring to celebrate Eric Bischoff's return. Since he was gone last week, "Stone Cold" Steve Austin kept them off the show. Now, they are back. Rene Dupree also wants to celebrate Bastille Day and sing the French national anthem. The fans loudly boo over him. When Sylvan Grenier takes the microphone, The Dudley Boyz and Spike Dudley interrupt. Bubba Ray and D-Von have heard enough and run to the ring to shut up the World Tag Team Champions. Although the heels get in a few shots, the Dudleys quickly recover and chase Sylvan off ahead of a 3D to Dupree. While the heels retreat, Bubba says their song sucked and he wants to sing the US national anthem. The fans join him, Spike proudly waving the American flag. Of the three, only D-Von can sing.

Randy Orton/Ric Flair/Triple H def. Spike Dudley/The Dudley Boyz ("Elimination" match). Evolution come out together, the fans cheering for Flair as he opens the match with Bubba. Dudley gets the early advantage with a series of chops and a back body drop. That sends Ric after Spike on the apron. The runt joins him in the ring, slapping "The Nature Boy". Afterwards, the two men trade strikes, Dudley getting the upper hand ahead of a back body drop and dropkick. Unfortunately, Ric slows him with an eye gouge. When Orton tags in, Spike attacks his arm until Randy also pokes his eyes and dropkicks him out to the floor. Outside the ring, Flair attacks the runt before tagging in to pummel him in the squared circle. Triple H tags in moments later to punch Dudley briefly. When Orton tags back in, he misses a dropkick allowing D-Von to tag in and attack all three heels, scoring a two-count with a neckbreaker. He follows up with a leaping clothesline for another near fall. He then slams Randy into position for a Spike top rope double stomp. That kicks off a six-man brawl. Once everyone else leaves the ring, the runt tries to finish off Orton with a Dudley Dog, but the heel surprises him with an RKO for the first elimination. Despite having the numbers advantage, the heels can't slow Bubba Ray and he drives Ric and Hunter from the ring. The babyfaces follow up with a Dudley Device to Randy before squashing the other heels in a corner. Once they drive Helmsley back out to the floor, Bubba elbows and slams Flair into position for a wassup drop. Fortunately, "the Game" returns for the save. Unfortunately, he pays when the Dudleys slam him and finally hit their wassup drop. Afterwards, Randy rushes into the ring only to get a 3D. Before D-Von can get the three-count, "The Nature Boy" pulls Earl Hebner out of the ring. While the referee admonishes him, Triple H smashes D-Von with the French flag for Orton to score another elimination. That leaves Bubba Ray alone against three men. He does his best, pounding Ric down before ordering D-Von to get a table. He tries, but Jack Doan and Charles Robinson run out to stop him ahead of a commercial break.

Afterwards, Bubba has turned around a Figure Four Leglock, putting the pressure on Flair's legs. It forces Ric to release the hold and trade shots with Dudley. That plays to the babyface's strengths and he gets the upper hand before tackling Hunter when he illegally enters the ring. Randy tags in afterwards for Dudley to keep up the attack, but he's outnumbered. Helmsley nearly takes advantage with a Pedigree while Ric distracts Hebner, but Bubba counters with a low blow and Bubba Bomb. Unfortunately, Orton rushes to his leader's defense. "The Nature Boy" does too when Bubba puts "the Game" on a table at ringside and heads upstairs to splash him from the top rope. While Ric distracts the referee again, Triple H returns to the squared circle to Pedigree Dudley. Afterwards, Randy, bleeding from the mouth, crawls over to cover Bubba Ray for the win, scoring all three eliminations for his team. Survivors: Randy Orton/Ric Flair/Triple H.

Backstage, Eric Bischoff is surprised to see Rob Van Dam here tonight. RVD is mad Kane's in Connecticut because he wants him in the ring. Eric understands and signs Rob a match with the "Big Red Machine" next week. When Bischoff warns him that "Stone Cold" Steve Austin has created a monster in Kane, Van Dam says Austin didn't do it. RVD started it and he's going to finish it next week.

Backstage, Chris Jericho leads a meeting with *Raw* heels. He's also brought Tommy Dreamer in to join Rico as perfect examples of what Kane has been doing. Y2J blames "Stone Cold" Steve Austin and wants everyone to sign his petition to get rid of the "rattlesnake". Rico is the first to sign.

Rodney Mack (with Theodore Long) def. Rosey. Pre-match, Long calls "Stone Cold" Steve Austin a "cracker snake" and says he was happy to sign Chris Jericho's petition. While he'd love to be the new co-general manager, he's too busy leading "Players Incorporated". Instead, Theodore proposes that Snoop Dogg serve as Austin's replacements. The heels like it backstage, but Tommy Dreamer isn't cheering in the background. When Rosey comes out, he steamrolls Mack down for a leg drop. Rodney answers with an eye rake and fists. He can't keep the Samoan down for long and Rosey responds with a corner splash. When he hoists Mack up for a Samoan Drop, Rodney's foot hits Nick Patrick and briefly blinds him for Long to low blow Rosey. Mack capitalizes with a roll-up for the win. Post-match, the lights go out and The Hurricane flies off the top rope to missile dropkick Rodney.

Backstage, Chris Jericho tries to get Evolution to sign his petition. With their signatures he knows Linda McMahon will get rid of "Stone Cold" Steve Austin. Triple H says life will be easier without Austin and signs.

Booker T def. Christian (Intercontinental Title match). Christian rushes out to try to win back the Intercontinental Title, but Booker easily repels his attack, punching and slamming him down for a two-count. A side kick brings the fans to their feet. When the babyface heads to the apron to attempt a maneuver, the challenger whips Booker T into the ring post. He follows up with a whip into the ring steps for a two-count. Unable to get the pin, he chokes and stomps the babyface. Booker responds in kind until he runs into a knee to the gut and another near fall. Christian then slows the pace with a reverse chin lock. Although the champion escapes, a neckbreaker puts him down for a two-count. When the challenger takes too long celebrating, Booker T surprises him with a spinning heel kick. Fists and a spinebuster follow for a near fall. Unfortunately, the babyface inadvertently runs into Chad Patton, stunning him before Christian plants Booker with an Unprettier. By the time Nick Patrick sprints down to the ring, the champion just manages to kick out. He responds moments later with a Book End for his own near fall. Following a spinaroonie, Booker T attempts to hit his Scissors Kick. At the last second, Christian dodges and rolls up the babyface. Grabbing the ropes, the challenger holds on for the three-count. Post-match, Patton slides back into the ring to tell Patrick what just happened. Nick doesn't want to change his decision, bringing out "Stone Cold" Steve Austin with Jack Doan to restart the match. Booker capitalizes with a quick roll-up for a close two-count. While Christian escapes that pin, he can't avoid a Scissors Kick and the champion scores the three-count. Post-match, the heel shoves Doan. When the referee shoves him back, Christian decks and stomps Jack. That sends Austin to the ring to stomp a mudhole in the heel ahead of a Stone Cold Stunner. Jerry says he doesn't feel safe.

Backstage, Eric Bischoff is exasperated watching a television. He says "Stone Cold" Steve Austin is nailing his own coffin before his phone rings. It's "Linda".

After a commercial break, Kane gives Jim Ross a present in Stamford, Connecticut.

Gail Kim def. Molly Holly (Women's Title match). The champion opens the match working on Molly's arm, but the heel flips free. Gail shows off her own agility with a flipping arm drag from the ropes, but Holly surprises her with another flip, scoring a two-count with a neckbreaker. Another two-count follows as Molly hammers down the champion before raking and pulling at her cheeks. Kim scores her own near fall with a roll-up, but a clothesline puts Gail back on the canvas. Holly capitalizes with a choke on the ropes, but when she goes for a tilt-a-whirl slam, Kim counters with a spinning head scissors. A Hurricanrana moments later stuns Molly for the champion to score another victory.

Ahead of their interview, Kane wants Jim Ross to open his present. Inside is a gas can. The "Big Red Machine" warns JR that if he makes fun of him one time, the monster is going to set him on fire.

After a commercial break, Jim Ross assures Kane that he will not make fun of him. He wants to help everyone understand where the "Big Red Machine" is coming from and plays a video package of his recent events. JR asks his reaction. Wearing a black towel over his head, the monster says it causes him anger. He's angry that Rob Van Dam and "Stone Cold" Steve Austin were supposed to be his friends but want him to relive his horrific past where his face was burnt. Ross interrupts. He says that in the few times that he's seen Kane's face he didn't have any scars. The monster disagrees. He says his therapists told him the same thing. JR believes he needs help and needs to tell stupid people not to tell him how to live his life. Jim believes the fans support him. The "Big Red Machine" call the people liars. That sets off the monster and he threatens JR. Before he can lay a hand on Ross, Austin heads to the ring to tell the monster that no one is making fun of him. They want to help Kane. The "Big Red Machine" says the only way to help him is to feel what he feels. He wants JR to feel his pain and slams him on the floor to pour gasoline on the interviewer. Despite protests from the crew, Kane sets Jim on fire. Eventually, the crew manages to put him out, but the damage has been done. "Stone Cold" is stunned in the ring until Eric Bischoff comes out to ask if the "rattlesnake" is proud of himself. Eric says it wasn't the "Big Red Machine" who set JR on fire, but Austin. Bischoff reveals that he just talked to Linda McMahon and next week she will fire him inside the ring. That's not enough for Eric as he damns "Stone Cold" to Hell to end the show.

SmackDown!
July 17, 2003
Columbus, OH
Announcers: Michael Cole, Tazz

Following a replay of Big Show Chokeslamming Brock Lesnar through the announce table last week, the intro video plays and fireworks explode. Afterwards, Vince McMahon power walks out to the ring to insult Zach Gowen. The WWE owner says Zach only won his WWE contract due to help from Brock and Kurt Angle. To teach them a lesson, Mr. McMahon signed Lesnar to a "Falls Count Anywhere" match against Big Show and The World's Greatest Tag Team. The WWE Champion learned his lesson last week and tonight Kurt is going to do the same in the same match. Before Vince can continue, Brock interrupts and steps into the ring. McMahon warns him not to cross the boss. Lesnar doesn't want to cross him. He wants to fight him in a match tonight. The WWE owner isn't afraid and tells Brock he's on to a good pop. The cheers turn to boos when he says, "just not tonight". Vince only wants to face Lesnar when he's at his best. To help him get there, Mr. McMahon gives Brock the night off. He tells the WWE Champion to go home and stay out of Angle's match tonight or he'll be stripped of his belt. Lesnar doesn't like it and lets Vince know before heading backstage.

Chris Benoit def. Matt Hardy Version 1.0 (with Shannon Moore) (US Title Tournament match). This week's Matt Facts are that Matt's beard is much cooler than Benoit's and Hardy only tans wearing a sock. Inside the ring, the "rabid wolverine" tries to lock on a quick Crippler Crossface, but the heel retreats to the ropes. Benoit retains control, stretching and chopping Matt. When Hardy tries to rake his eyes, "the Crippler" ties him up in the ropes and stomps the heel. While Brian Hebner attempts to free him, Shannon attacks Benoit from behind and drops him with a neckbreaker for a Hardy two-count. Matt follows up with wear down holds, including a surfboard stretch. When he goes for the Twist of Fate, the "rabid wolverine" counters with a backslide for a near fall. Forearms and elbows follow ahead of a snap suplex. That brings Moore into the ring, but Benoit escorts him out with a suplex over the top rope ahead of a Crossface. Luckily, Matt is close enough to reach the ropes for the break. Sporting a busted nose, Hardy shifts gears and connects with a series of side effects. Unfortunately, he misses a top rope diving headbutt to put both men down. They work the referee's count to nine before "the Crippler" unloads with fists and a pair of German suplexes. When he goes for a third, Matt grabs the ropes only to be dropped face-first on the apron. Finally hitting his third German suplex, Benoit heads upstairs but misses his own diving headbutt. Hardy tries to capitalize with his second rope flying leg drop, but the "rabid wolverine" meets him on the ropes. Matt has one last move in mind, but when he attempts to drive Benoit to the canvas with a second rope side effect, the babyface counters into a falling Crippler Crossface for the tap-out victory.

After a commercial break, Vince McMahon is on the phone in Stephanie McMahon's office. Stephanie expected to see him there. He expected her too and says that Sable has the night off. However, she sent Stephanie a present—a bottle of Midol. Stephanie slaps it away.

Further backstage, Brock Lesnar storms out of the arena. Kurt Angle follows him. He can't believe Brock is just going to leave. Lesnar doesn't have a choice, just like Angle last week. Brock warns the Olympian that he's in for a fight tonight and he wants Kurt at one hundred percent at Vengeance so he doesn't have any excuses. Angle says he never makes excuses.

Ultimo Dragon def. Jamie Noble. Although Nidia accompanies Jamie to the ring, when he apologizes to Torrie Wilson for offering her ten thousand dollars last week, his girlfriend takes offense. Noble says Torrie is worth way more and promises to give her twenty-five thousand dollars to sleep with him. That sends Nidia off in a huff before Ultimo Dragon heads to the ring to sweep the redneck's leg and drive him out to the floor. There, the masked superstar catches Noble with an Asai moonsault. Back in the squared circle, he attempts a flying attack only to catch a dropkick to the chest. Jamie tries to finish him off with a Tiger Bomb, but Billy Gunn and Torrie step onto the ramp to distract him for a Dragon roll-up and the win.

Filmed in a cemetery, John Cena says The Undertaker is "full of crap" and drives around hitting on priests. Cena raps that the biker is a fake and a "dead issue". He promises to pee on the "Deadman" just like he does a grave in this prerecorded vignette.

Filmed earlier today, The APA invite Brian Kendrick to a "Bar Room Brawl" at Vengeance. After Ron Simmons questions Bradshaw about his new blonde hair, the tag team gives Kanyon an invitation too. He tries to get out of match, but they refuse to let him miss it. Bradshaw then has a great idea, proposing that The APA makes everyone pay them to kick their butts at Vengeance.

Billy Kidman/Rey Mysterio def. Los Conquistadores. Instead of all gold outfits, Los Conquistadores sport black masks and trunks this week. Kidman is all over the first, a man with a blonde mullet. When Rey tags in, the other Conquistador, showing dark hair, hits him running the ropes. It doesn't take the number one contenders long to turn the tide, Billy knocking the dark-haired masked man down for a Mysterio senton. The blonde Conquistador makes the save ahead of a neckbreaker to Kidman for a near fall. After knocking Rey off the apron, the blonde Conquistador picks up Billy for a powerbomb. While he holds him, Mysterio knocks his partner off the apron to prevent a double-team move while Kidman hurricanranas the newcomer onto the second rope for a 619. Billy follows up with a Shooting Star Press to the blonde Conquistador for the win while Rey baseball slide kicks the other Conquistador on the floor. For the record, the blonde Conquistador is future superstar Rob Conway.

After a commercial break, Vince McMahon heads back to the ring to introduce Sable in his skybox. He calls her a predator who tears apart her prey. He then continues his tirade on Zach Gowen. Vince believes Zach makes people uncomfortable having to look at his deformity. He promises to do what Mother Nature couldn't and finish off Gowen at Vengeance. John Cena interrupts, upsetting the WWE owner. John isn't here to talk about The Undertaker. Instead, he raps about how much McMahon is going to destroy Zach. He ends his rap telling everyone that the only thing better than a one-legged wrestler is being able to walk. Vince loves it and even tells the rapping heel "word life" before the "Deadman" rides his bike around the squared circle. John stops that by tossing the steel steps into the way. When the biker gets in the ring, Cena attacks only to be driven off with a big boot.

The Rhyno and Sean O'Haire match never officially starts. Now solo, O'Haire comes out to cheap shot Rhyno. The two men then brawl at ringside. When Sean gets the upper hand and chokes the man-beast with a camera cable, The APA come out to give both men invitations to their Vengeance "Bar Room Brawl". O'Haire takes offense and attacks Bradshaw. When Ron Simmons attacks him, Sean spots Rhyno running up for the Gore and moves, the man-beast nailing Simmons instead. The big Texan takes up for his partner, hammering Rhyno while O'Haire heads backstage, promising to see everyone at Vengeance.

In her skybox, Sable acts like a diva and demands that the waitress chills her drink.

Eddie Guerrero def. Billy Gunn (with Torrie Wilson) (US Title Tournament match). Once again Eddie drives a lowrider to the squared circle. Billy gets a big reaction when he brings out Torrie in a short dress. Inside the ring, he overpowers "Latino Heat" initially, Guerrero trying to pick up the pace only to run into a powerslam for a two-count. Gunn follows up with a delayed vertical suplex for another near fall. Eddie changes tactics and unloads with a string of forearms and elbows ahead of a leaping snap mare and his own two-count. He then slows the pace with a neck twist. With Wilson cheering him on, Billy side suplexes free. That gets him a one-count when he finally rolls over onto "Latino Heat". Despite that cover, Guerrero retains control, elbowing and stretching Gunn. This time, Billy elbows free and plants Eddie with a hip toss into a modified brainbuster. Afterwards, he sits "Latino Heat" on the top turnbuckle, but misses a corner splash. When he hits the ring post, Guerrero capitalizes with a top rope missile dropkick and near fall. Gunn refuses to stay down and slams Eddie to the canvas before motioning for the Famouser. When he rebounds off the ropes though, "Latino Heat" dropkicks his knee. He follows up with a single leg crab, but Billy reaches the ropes. Soon after, "Mr. Ass" attempts a suplex, but his knee is too weak and Guerrero counters with his own suplex. Following a second, Eddie heads upstairs, but misses a Frog Splash. Gunn capitalizes with a One and Only slam, but "Latino Heat" just grabs the ropes for the break. When he motions for the Famouser, Jamie Noble runs out with a steel chair. Although Mike Sparks intercepts him and takes the chair, Billy is distracted long enough for Eddie to shove the babyface into the referee. He then bashes Gunn's skull with the chair before dropping it between them and collapsing to the canvas. When Sparks turns around, both men are down on their backs. Miraculously, "Latino Heat" recovers first and pins Billy to steal the win.

In the skybox, Josh Mathews asks Sable's thoughts about facing Stephanie McMahon at Vengeance. She says she'd do anything for Vince McMahon including taking out his daughter. Speaking of, Stephanie poses as a waitress and pours a drink on Sable. She pays for that as the heel absolutely destroys her and slams her face into a tray of food. When Josh tries to intervene, Sable rocks him with a hard slap. That lets Stephanie recover and she repeatedly slams Sable's head on the floor until security separates them.

Kurt Angle def. Big Show/The World's Greatest Tag Team ("Falls Count Anywhere" match). Once everyone is in the ring, Show knocks Angle down with a big boot. His teammates then double-team Kurt until Mike Chioda restores order. The Olympian capitalizes, punching Shelton onto the top rope and driving Charlie into his groin. When Benjamin falls off the ropes, he lands on Haas's groin too. That leaves the giant alone to wail on Angle. As soon as Kurt shows signs of life, Shelton trips and hits him with a trashcan lid for Big Show to get a two-count. Outside the ring, Show whips the Olympian into the ring steps. Charlie follows up with a chair shot for a near fall at ringside. After press slamming Angle back into the ring, Show chops the babyface before missing a charge against the ropes and falling out to the floor. Kurt then German suplexes his former teammates to put everyone down. The giant is up first. He spots the ring steps and remembers last week, setting the stairs up in front of the announce table. Before he can use them, the Olympian slams him into the steel and grabs a chair to blast him ahead of a commercial break.

Afterwards, The World's Greatest Tag Team is back on the attack, stomping and tossing around their former leader. When Benjamin whips Charlie toward Angle though, the babyface back drops Haas into the crowd. He follows him in, punching Charlie and using the fans to separate him from the other heels. When he hooks Haas in an Anklelock though, Shelton finally arrives to make the save. That gets him tossed into a steel guardrail. Kurt tries to follow up with another Anklelock, but Big Show makes the save this time with a big headbutt. He then leads the Olympian to the entrance way and teases a Chokeslam. Before he can lift him, Angle answers with a low blow. Unfortunately, Haas and Benjamin are back on the attack, pounding him down and leading the babyface to the squared circle. There, Charlie tries to use a trashcan lid, but the babyface takes it away and repeatedly hammers the heels. Show returns afterwards only to be chop blocked. Before he falls all the way to the canvas, the giant clotheslines Kurt to put everyone down again. Zach Gowen isn't down, racing down the aisle and removing his prosthetic leg before he dropkicks all three heels. He doesn't keep Big Show down for long and the giant recovers to toss Zach to the canvas. When he teases another Chokeslam, the Olympian makes the save. Moments later, he impresses with an Angle Slam to Show. He follows up with an Angle Slam to Shelton before trapping Haas in the Anklelock again. Once again, Big Show makes the save. When he leads Angle out to the floor, Show misses a clothesline and hits the ring post. Gowen follows up moments later with a flying cross body block off the top rope, but the giant catches him and tosses the rookie into the crowd. The distraction gives Kurt time to grab the ring steps and drive them into Show, knocking him into the crowd too. Although The World's Greatest Tag Team double-teams him, when they set up for their Inverted Atomic Drop and Superkick combination, the Olympian catches Benjamin's foot and whips him around to kick Charlie. Afterwards, he forces Shelton to tap-out with an Anklelock and scores the improbable victory. Post-match, Angle celebrates and helps Zach backstage, the fans loudly cheering while Big Show seethes.

Monday Night Raw
July 21, 2003
Los Angeles, CA
Announcers: Jonathan Coachman, Jerry "the King" Lawler, Triple H (briefly)

The show opens with a video package featuring "Stone Cold" Steve Austin and Kane. After the "Big Red Machine" sets Jim Ross on fire, Eric Bischoff promises that Linda McMahon will fire Austin tonight. The intro video then plays and fireworks explode to kick off the episode. Afterwards, Eric is in the center of the ring. He says he may not like JR, but no one deserves to be set on fire and he blames "Stone Cold". Linda interrupts to tell Bischoff that the "rattlesnake" is not to blame for Jim getting fired, Kane is. While she can't understand why Ross hasn't pressed charges, the "Big Red Machine" is still under house arrest. However, house arrest still allows him to work and he'll be here later tonight to face Rob Van Dam. The co-general manager changes tunes and is glad the monster will compete tonight. He's not even worried about JR. he just wants to see "Stone Cold" fired. That brings Austin out to a big pop. He refuses to apologize for anything, and if Ross isn't going to press charges on Kane, he's going to kick the "Big Red Machine's" butt personally. Bischoff thinks that's the problem and wants Linda to go ahead and fire him. That's not why she's here, but there is a problem with the general manager's office. While she appreciates the job he's done, Steve can't beat up WWE superstars. Eric loves it and gets in the "rattlesnake's" face until McMahon says that he can't attack anyone unless physically provoked. That backs up Bischoff. Austin understands the situation he's in, but he needs to think about it. Linda warns him that if he steps down, she'll have no choice but to give Eric complete power. She can't wait long for Steve to decide, giving him just a week to make a decision and the night off tonight. When Bischoff taunts him and sings goodbye, McMahon gives him the night off too. That leads to "Stone Cold" singing goodbye to him too before drinking beers with Linda.

Molly Holly/Victoria (with Steven Richards) def. Gail Kim/Trish Stratus. The babyfaces open the match working together to hip toss and elbow drop Molly for a Trish two-count. The vixen follows up with chops until Victoria pulls her hair from the apron. Holly capitalizes with a handspring back elbow for a near fall. Afterwards, she slams Stratus into position for a "black widow" slingshot somersault leg drop from the apron and her own two-count. She tries to finish off Trish with a Widow's Peak, but the vixen counters with a head scissors. A Chick Kick follows to Molly before Kim tags in for a flying cross body block despite momentarily slipping. She slips again moments later attempting a step up attack and pays with a backbreaker. When Victoria gets into the ring and distracts the referee attacking the Women's Champion, Stratus returns to toss Holly off the top rope with a handstand head scissors. Gail capitalizes with a Hurricanrana, but the "black widow" makes the save and removes the champion's top for a big pop from Lawler. Kim is incensed and tackles Victoria before Trish ducks a Molly clothesline with her Matrix move. Unfortunately, when she tries to follow up with a Chick Kick, Holly ducks and the vixen hits her own partner. After the "black widow" drags Stratus out to the floor, Molly scores the win.

Afterwards, the announcers talk about Jim Ross. Jerry accuses Coach of not caring, but he argues that.

Backstage, Eric Bischoff and "Stone Cold" Steve Austin argue about getting the night off. Eric blames the "rattlesnake". Austin blames Bischoff for putting WCW out of business and flips him off.

Randy Orton (with Ric Flair) def. Val Venis. Pre-match, Orton says he made a name for himself tossing Mick Foley down a flight of stairs and pinning three men last week. He adds that he's always been a lady killer, but now he's giving himself the nickname, "Legend Killer". As Val heads to the ring, Triple H joins the announce table for guest commentary. While he praises Randy, the adult star attacks his arm. Hunter also jokes about Jim Ross. Even Lawler doesn't appreciate that and hesitantly tells "the Game" so while Venis punches, elbows, and slams Orton. Ric helps his man turn the tide, grabbing "the big Valbowski's" leg for Randy to dropkick him. Despite that, Val comes back to life with clotheslines and a sit-out slam for a near fall. Impressively dominant, the adult star plants the "Legend Killer" with a spinebuster. When he heads upstairs, Flair distracts Jack Doan and Venis long enough for Orton to recover and dodge a Money Shot. He immediately capitalizes with an RKO for the victory. Post-match, Triple H heads to the ring to put an Evolution shirt on Randy and claim that no one can stop them. Goldberg refutes that claim. He marches out to a big pop to tell the World Champ that he's next. Evolution circles the intense superstar, but he doesn't back down. He wants a fight, but Hunter doesn't give it to him, calling off his allies to say that they'll meet on the champion's terms.

After a commercial break, Randy Orton is fired up and wants Goldberg for calling them out. Ric Flair and Triple H try to calm him down. They say that they do things on their time and Randy has a job to do tonight. The announcers wonder what that is.

The WrestleMania Recall moment is footage from this year's Chris Jericho/Shawn Michaels match.

MUST SEE! Chris Jericho def. Shawn Michaels. As Jericho opens the match targeting Shawn's arm, Jerry is all over Coach's case. He doesn't think he likes or respects Jim Ross and is trying to steal his job. Michaels slows Y2J's attack flinging him out to the floor. When he returns though, the heel traps his opponent in a side headlock. Once again, the "Heartbreak Kid" tosses Jericho off. Jerry dares Coachman to call the match a "slobberknocker". Instead of a brawl, the two men trade roll-ups and pinning predicaments for two-counts before Shawn traps Y2J in a headlock. When Jericho escapes, Michaels shoulder blocks him and reapplies his hold. Eventually, the heels shoves him into the ropes for a back elbow to turn the tide. Fists and a backbreaker follow. After mocking and elbow dropping the "Heartbreak Kid", Y2J scores a two-count. Frustrated, he flings Shawn out to the floor and taunts the crowd. When the babyface attempts to return, Jericho helps him with a suplex from the apron. Moments later, he tries to toss Michaels over the top rope. Although he spots the "Heartbreak Kid" skinning the cat and punches him, he misses a springboard attack and falls out to the floor. Shawn follows with a moonsault out of the ring. Back in the squared circle, a flying cross body block gets the babyface a two-count. Both men exchange fists afterwards while Ric Flair rushes down the aisle. Michaels slides out and punches him before returning to the ring for Y2J to trap him in the Walls of Jericho ahead of a commercial break.

Afterwards, "the King" blames Coach for the abrupt commercial break. He says Jim Ross would never do that. During the break, Shawn escapes his opponent's finisher only to be back dropped over the top rope to the floor. There, Flair chokes him with his jacket before Jericho slams the babyface's back on the ring post. A flying elbow back in the squared circle nearly gets the heel the victory. Michaels answers with a cross body block, but he can't hold Y2J down. Right back up, Jericho hammers him before heading upstairs only to leap into a dropkick to the chest. That puts both men down. Earl Hebner barely counts, giving the wrestlers time to get up and the "Heartbreak Kid" to catch a second wind with a tilt-a-whirl backbreaker. He follows up with a flying forearm and kip up before clotheslining the heel. Although Shawn teases his own Walls of Jericho, he catapults Y2J into a corner for a roll-up and two-count. Jericho responds with a northern lights suplex and his own near fall. A running face slam follows, but when he goes for the Lionsault, Michaels rolls out of the way. Luckily, Y2J lands on his feet and hits the Lionsault moments later for a pair of close two-counts. When he attempts to charge the babyface afterwards, Shawn answers with a powerslam for his own near fall. The heel responds with a hard whip into the corner to set up Michaels for a top rope back suplex. Fortunately for the "Heartbreak Kid", he latches onto the top rope and shoves Jericho down for a top rope flying elbow drop and pop. He then tunes up the band, but Y2J ducks Sweet Chin Music. Hebner does too, enabling the heel to give Shawn a low blow while the referee is out of position. Frustrated, Jericho grabs a chair, but the babyface kicks it back into his face with Sweet Chin Music. This time, the referee is fast to count both men down, Ric distracting him at the last second to stop the count. Earl is fed up with Flair and goes out to the floor to confront and eject him. While he does so, Randy Orton sprints out to give Michaels an RKO on the chair. That lets Y2J crawl over to the babyface and score an extremely close two-count. Afterwards, the heel traps Shawn in the Walls of Jericho in a corner. Although he reaches down deep and crawls across the squared circle, Jericho pulls the "Heartbreak Kid" back to the center of the ring to force the tap-out and end this incredible match.

Following a recap of Linda McMahon giving the co-GMs the night off, Lance Storm is in the ring to read a statement. He says it will sell him to the Hollywood elite, including Rob Reiner sitting in the crowd. Unfortunately, he's interrupted by Kane's arrival backstage, the monster in shackles and escorted by police. Afterwards, a video package of divas entertaining the troops in the Middle East last week plays.

Booker T def. Test (Intercontinental Title match). Booker opens the match punching and elbowing Test for a quick cover. The bodyguard answers with a thumb to the eye. While he stomps the babyface, Christian watches intently backstage. Inside the ring, the competitors trade shots, the challenger crushing Booker T in a corner. Afterwards, he mocks Scott Steiner doing pushups and jumping jacks. The champion answers with a clothesline and side kick for another near fall. The two men then miss kicks, Test straddling the top rope. A side kick nearly gets Booker the win, but the bodyguard just kicks out and responds with a clothesline for another near fall. He tries to steal the win holding onto the ropes, but the babyface still kicks out. While the challenger wastes time arguing with Chad Patton, Booker T recovers and plants him with a spinebuster. Unfortunately, he wastes time motioning for the spinaroonie. Test capitalizes with a boot to the jaw, but Steiner steps onto the apron with Stacy Keibler to distract the bodyguard when she strips off her skirt and straddles "Big Poppa Pump". While the challenger fumes, Booker rolls him up for a two-count. A Book End follows for the victory. Post-match, the champion celebrates with a spinaroonie.

After a commercial break, wrestlers talk about Kane. The Hurricane tells Rosey that the "Big Red Machine" isn't the man he used to know. The superhero stops himself when he realizes that Rosey is a "superhero in training". Goldust interrupts to spell out that that would make Rosey the "S.H.I.T.".

Kane and Rob Van Dam wrestle to no contest. After the police lead Kane to the ring and unshackle him, a video package plays for the "Big Red Machine". RVD then sprints down the aisle to dropkick the monster out to the floor. He follows him with a flying tackle off the top rope. Fired up, Rob moonsaults Kane off the barricade, but the "Big Red Machine" quickly recovers and flings Van Dam face-first into the ring post. A slam on the steps follows. The monster doesn't care about winning the match, leading RVD up the ramp to hammer him on the stage. After he decks Nick Patrick, Kane teases Chokeslamming Rob off the stage. Luckily, WWE officials including Arn Anderson run out to try to stop him. Although RVD kicks his way free, the "Big Red Machine" remains on the offensive and slams Rob. Afterwards, he decks John Laurinaitis and Arn before threatening a terrified Linda McMahon. With the fans buzzing, the monster tries to Chokeslam Linda. Luckily, Lawler makes the save. It just gets him knocked down before Kane Tombstones Linda on the stage to end the episode.

SmackDown!
July 24, 2003
Fresno, CA
Announcers: Michael Cole, Tazz

Following a recap of Zach Gowen helping Kurt Angle defeat Big Show and The World's Greatest Tag Team last week, the intro video plays and fireworks explode. Stephanie McMahon then heads to the ring to take back *SmackDown!* since Vince McMahon is back home taking care of Linda McMahon. Stephanie's first act is to make competitive matches tonight including a six-man tag main event. She then threatens Sable ahead of their match this Sunday until John Cena interrupts. He apologizes, but says he had a dream about Stephanie last night. He proceeds to make innuendos about her before offering Stephanie twenty dollars to rip off Sable's top. When he says no one is looking and offers to spank her, Stephanie dares him to do so. He does to a big pop before Sable interrupts from the Titantron to play footage of her attacking the general manager last week. She conveniently edits out the part where Stephanie attacks her back. Sable tells the GM that she needs to take care of Linda because Sable will be taking care Stephanie's daddy. That sends the boss backstage looking for Sable.

Billy Kidman/Rey Mysterio def. Matt Hardy Version 1.0/Shannon Moore. Matt Facts this week reveal that Mattitude "is considered sacred in Japan" as well as that Hardy defeated Rey and Billy at consecutive PPVs. Tonight, he trades amateur holds with Mysterio. When they pick up the pace, Rey rocks Matt with a boot in a corner and face-first slam to the canvas. Kidman then tags in for a slingshot leg drop from the apron and two-count. Moore tags in afterwards and runs away from the babyface, luring Billy into a Matt clothesline off the second rope. Hardy then returns to score a near fall with his own leg drop. While he distracts Mike Chioda, Shannon throat drops Kidman on the top rope. A neckbreaker afterwards gets Matt a two-count. Moore also gets a near fall with a swinging neckbreaker before applying a submission hold where he stretches Billy's arm across his own face. When Kidman escapes, Hardy hits him running the ropes before tagging in to lock on a surfboard stretch. It doesn't take Billy long to fight free and drive the heel face-first to the mat with a step up bulldog. Although Shannon gets the tag first, Kidman kicks him back to tag in Rey. He enters with a springboard flying senton. A dropkick to the face follows before Mysterio counters a Matt wheelbarrow suplex with a bulldog. When he heads upstairs, Moore grabs the masked man but gets knocked onto the ropes with a head scissors. Fortunately, Hardy saves his partner from a 619 by tripping Rey. He pays with a slingshot kick, but Mysterio turns into a spinning heel kick. He's also got a partner watching his back and Billy delivers a sit-out slam, called the BK Bomb by Tazz. Matt is back up and takes Kidman down with a side effect followed by a sit-out powerbomb to Rey. That gets Shannon a near fall, but Mysterio just kicks out. Afterwards, he flips free of a back suplex to kick Moore and tag back in Billy. He flies into the ring with a cross body block, but Chioda misses his cover trying to get the masked man out of the ring. He also misses Hardy saving his partner with a top rope guillotine leg drop. Once again, Shannon gets a two-count. This time, Rey makes the save before dumping Matt to the floor with a head scissors. When Kidman dropkicks Moore onto the middle rope, Mysterio rocks him with a 619. He then springboard moonsaults Hardy while Billy scores the win with a Shooting Star Press onto Shannon.

Backstage, Stephanie McMahon finds Sable and attacks her on top of a limo, ripping off her top before the heel manages to climb into the car and lock the door. Undeterred, Stephanie tries to break a window with a steel bar, but Vince McMahon stops his daughter. She wants to know why he's not home with Linda McMahon. Vince tells her to worry about her match with Sable instead of Linda before she ends up incapacitated like her mother.

Billy Gunn (with Torrie Wilson) def. Jamie Noble. Pre-match, Jamie says Nidia isn't here because she's sick and not because of his offer to Torrie. Noble wants to know what her price is, raising his offer to a hundred thousand dollars. That sends Billy rushing down to the ring to punch and hip toss suplex him. When Mike Sparks backs the babyface off, Jamie tosses him out to the floor for a baseball slide kick. Boots and fists follow at ringside until Wilson checks on her boyfriend. The redneck loses his focus and chases her around the squared circle. When she leads him into the ring, Billy is ready and waiting to catch him with a swinging uranage for the three-count. Post-match, Noble wants a rematch because he claims he's better than Gunn in every way, including "in bed". Torrie is so confident in her man that she'll sleep with Jamie next week on *SmackDown!* if Noble beats "Mr. Ass" this Sunday.

Video of *SmackDown!* superstars touring the far east this week plays.

Backstage, The APA invite A-Train to compete in their "Bar Room Brawl" this Sunday. He hopes they have backup and wants to know who else will compete. When Ron Simmons says Doink the Clown will be there, the fans boo. The hairy heel is more upset that the Easter Bunny is going to compete. He hates him. Steve Lombardi is looking for an invite. The APA tell him if he can prove he's the Brooklyn Brawler and make an impact tonight they'll let him into the brawl. Lombardi really wants to get his hands on Doink because he hates clowns.

In a prerecorded vignette, John Cena stands inside a burning pentagram to call out The Undertaker. He's not afraid of him and wants to get his hands on the "Deadman" this Sunday.

After a commercial break, Eddie drives a lowrider to the squared circle. When he gets out of the vehicle, "Latino Heat" notes a smudge on the front bumper and cleans it up with some spray. He gets a good pop when he says hello to the fans and talks about competing for the US Title this Sunday. Guerrero tells everyone that he'll be wrestling his best friend and talks about their history together. That brings out Benoit, Eddie surprising him with a hug. "The Crippler" hugs back. Despite him acting like a heel, the fans cheer Guerrero's name. Once they stop, Benoit notes that "Latino Heat" hasn't called him in months. The "rabid wolverine" wonders how many best friends Eddie has and isn't about to let his guard down this Sunday. Guerrero admits that Benoit caught him because "Latino Heat" can't stand him. He's jealous that "the Crippler" gets all the attention and he's been in Benoit's shadow. At Vengeance, he promises to prove he's number one. The "rabid wolverine" doesn't want to wait until this Sunday, but Eddie says they are doing things on his schedule now. When Benoit turns his back though, Guerrero tries to attack him. "The Crippler" easily repels him, but when he follows "Latino Heat" out to the floor, Eddie sprays him with cleaner. Once he's down, Guerrero stomps him to cheers until Rhyno runs out for the save. The man-beast dare Eddie to get back in the ring for a match right now.

Eddie Guerrero def. Rhyno. After a commercial break, the match has already begun and Eddie takes control with a head scissors and fists. Rhyno answers with a back elbow and reverse powerbomb onto the top turnbuckle for a two-count. Afterwards, the man-beast hammers "Latino Heat" down before applying a reverse chin lock. When Guerrero fights free, a clothesline puts him back down for a Rhyno two-count. The man-beast soon returns to his hold following a scoop slam. When Eddie escapes with a northern lights suplex and scores a two-count, the fans briefly pop. They quiet as Rhyno answers with a Crippler Crossface. Luckily, "Latino Heat" reaches the ropes for the break. Afterwards, he tosses the man-beast out to the floor. Guerrero follows with a slingshot splash before ramming Rhyno's head into the ring post. A slingshot somersault splash gets him a near fall afterwards. Standing on the man-beast's hair, "Latino Heat" draws another cheer. Tazz says he has no idea what that feels like. He knows what a reverse chin lock feels like and so does Rhyno when Eddie applies it. The man-beast doesn't stay in the hold long, escaping and scoring a two-count with a shoulderblock. He also gets a near fall with a spinebuster. He tries to finish off Guerrero with a top rope attack, but "Latino Heat" catches him climbing and follows him up for a hurricanrana off the top. Somehow, the man-beast just manages to kick out of his cover before Brian Hebner can count to three. Moments later, he surprises Eddie with a belly-to-belly suplex. When he sets up for the Gore, Guerrero shoves Hebner into his way. Fortunately, Rhyno holds up at the last second, but "Latino Heat" capitalizes with a low blow. Before the referee turns around, Eddie pretends he received a low blow too. After catching his breath, Guerrero dropkicks the man-beast and steals the win with his feet on the ropes.

The APA def. The FBI (with Nunzio). As The APA head to the ring, we see the brawlers handing out invitations in the desert earlier this week. When a thirsty serviceman asks if they have water, they say they have plenty of it and leave him to roast. Afterwards, The FBI sneak attack the brawlers. Unfortunately, Palumbo accidentally Superkicks his own partner. With Johnny Stamboli down, Bradshaw levels Chuck with a Clothesline from Hell for the win. Post-match, Nunzio pays for getting into the ring courtesy of a big Texan boot to the jaw and APA double spinebuster. Brooklyn Brawler then runs down the aisle to smash the winners with a steel chair. He's followed by The Basham Brothers, A-Train, and Sean O'Haire who assault the downed brawlers.

Backstage, Vince McMahon interrupts Zach Gowen getting ready for his match. Zach is startled and threatens to hit the WWE owner, but Vince says he's not the kind of guy to hit someone from behind. He's looking forward to mauling him this Sunday. While McMahon doesn't feel sorry for him losing his leg, Vince tells him that he'll give the fans a real reason to feel sorry for Gowen this Sunday. Zach calls him sorry. The WWE owner doesn't like that, but before he does anything rash, Brock Lesnar and Kurt Angle appear to chase off McMahon.

Big Show/The World's Greatest Tag Team def. Brock Lesnar/Kurt Angle/Zach Gowen. Kurt and Benjamin open the match trading amateur holds. When the Olympian gets the upper hand with an overhead belly-to-belly suplex, Haas illegally enters and receives a back body drop. His distraction allows Shelton to clothesline Angle, but when Charlie returns, Kurt traps him in an armbar. When Haas fights free, the Olympian hip tosses and clotheslines him for a two-count. Brock then tags in to hammer the heel, but Charlie surprises him with a dropkick. Despite that, the WWE Champion is up quickly to toss the heel overhead with a belly-to-belly suplex. Gorilla press slams follow to both WWE Tag Team Champions before Lesnar slams Zach onto them. A snap suplex afterwards puts Haas down for a Gowen slingshot leg drop and near fall. Afterwards, Benjamin rushes to his partner's defense with a vicious clothesline. Big Show then tags in to chop Zach in a corner. He tries to follow up with a Chokeslam, but Angle clips his knee for the one-legged wrestler to score a two-count. Kurt and Brock then double-team the giant, knocking him out to the floor. While the babyfaces fight with The World's Greatest Tag Team in the ring, Vince McMahon walks out and smashes a chair on Gowen's leg. Angle and Lesnar finally notice their partner down after dropping Shelton and Charlie inside the ring. While WWE officials help Zach backstage, we take a commercial break.

Afterwards, Kurt hammers Show, the babyfaces now at a man's disadvantage. Cole shows things are even worse for the Olympian with footage of the giant slamming Brock against the ring post during the break. He somehow climbs back up to his corner to watch as The World's Greatest Tag Team take turns hammering Angle. A high elevation back suplex nearly gets Haas the victory. Afterwards, he attacks both babyfaces before tagging in Benjamin for the champions' double-team leapfrog splash and a two-count. Show returns afterwards to chop and vertical suplex Kurt. He also shows his wrestling acumen with a single leg crab, but he doesn't sit all of his weight back onto the Olympian. That lets Angle escape and roll up the giant for a near fall. One shot puts him back down and Charlie tags in to give his former leader an overhead belly-to-belly suplex. When he misses a clothesline though, Kurt answers with a leg sweep. Unfortunately, Shelton illegally helps his partner, kicking the Olympian down for a Haas near fall. Benjamin continues to get involved, hitting Angle when he starts to fight back. Afterwards, Shelton tags in to trade shots with Kurt. The Olympian finally fights free of the heel corner and gives Lesnar the hot tag. He rocks Big Show with a forearm before the WWE Champion tosses around The World's Greatest Tag Team with a pair of overhead belly-to-belly suplexes. When he focuses too long on Benjamin, Show recovers and boots him. He attempts to finish off Brock with a Chokeslam, but Lesnar slips free and suplexes the giant. Angle then tags in to knock The World's Greatest Tag Team off the apron and trap Big Show in the Anklelock. He might get the tap out, but Lesnar stops Haas from making the save and accidentally swings the heel around on an F5 attempt, Charlie's legs hitting Kurt's head. It stuns him long enough for Show to recover and Chokeslam the Olympian for the three-count.

Post-match, Brock returns and smashes Big Show repeatedly with a steel chair. He then finally gives Haas the F5. Afterwards, Angle comes to his senses and questions the WWE Champion. When Lesnar pulls away, Kurt slaps him. That sets off the champion and the two men trade counters until Show double Chokeslams them to end the show standing tall ahead of this Sunday's triple threat WWE Title match.

PPV: Vengeance

July 27, 2003
Denver, CO
Announcers: Michael Cole, Tazz

The show opens with a video package of WWE superstars talking about their dreams with pictures of them as kids and their actions in the ring leading them to this moment. In contrast, Vince McMahon says everything is about control and he and Sable are going to dominate the show. Afterwards, a lot of fireworks explode to kick off the PPV.

MUST SEE! Eddie Guerrero def. Chris Benoit (US Title Tournament Finals). Eddie is out first in a red lowrider. Benoit then marches out looking for revenge after getting cleaner sprayed in his eyes. He's also looking to win the US Title, Mike Chioda explaining the rules to both men. He wants a handshake, but doesn't get it. Instead, the two men trade tie-ups, "the Crippler" chasing Guerrero from the ring with a shoulderblock. When he returns, "Latino Heat" stuns Benoit with his own shoulderblock. Afterwards, they lock up for a test of strength, but the "rabid wolverine" turns it over into a game of mercy. Eddie changes strategies and chops his former friend before the two men kick off an exchange of roll-ups and near falls. Evenly matched, they also trade arm drags, Guerrero chasing Benoit out to the floor. When he returns, "Latino Heat" slows him with a side headlock. When "the Crippler" escapes, the two men trade counters, culminating in a Benoit shoulderbreaker. He quickly follows up and tries to lock on the Crippler Crossface. By the time he does so, Eddie reaches the ropes for the break. He tries to retreat to the floor for a breather, but Benoit follows him out with a dive through the ropes. Back in the squared circle, the "rabid wolverine" slams his opponent to the mat and locks on a half nelson submission hold, focusing on Guerrero's shoulder. He follows up with boots and slaps. That riles up "Latino Heat", but that's what Benoit wants and he chops and rolls up the fired up heel. Eddie answers with a back elbow and top rope hurricanrana for a near fall. A back suplex also gets Guerrero a two-count. Despite the fans chanting that he sucks, "Latino Heat" starts to get cocky, kicking, chopping, and trapping "the Crippler" in an armbar. Benoit answers with his own chops before taking Eddie upstairs for a top rope back suplex. That takes almost as much out of the "rabid wolverine" as it does Guerrero and both men work the referee's count to seven before Benoit rolls over his opponent for a near fall. He follows up quickly with a pair of German suplexes. Although "Latino Heat" avoids a third, Chris traps him in the Crippler Crossface. Luckily, Eddie reaches the ropes with his foot for the break. Swinging the momentum, he delivers a pair of suplexes, but instead of hitting a third, he places Benoit on the top rope for a superplex to once again put both men down. A wicked smile on his face, Guerrero heads upstairs for a Frog Splash, but the "rabid wolverine" rolls out of the way. Although "Latino Heat's" forearm still hits his shoulder, Benoit is able to recover first and powerbomb Eddie. He follows up with the Crippler Crossface again, but Guerrero reaches the ropes once more for the break. Afterwards, he rams "the Crippler" back into Chioda. While the referee is down, "Latino Heat" smashes Benoit with the US Title and Frog Splashes him. Somehow, the "rabid wolverine" still manages to kick out following a groggy two-count. Grabbing the belt again, Eddie smashes Chioda this time. He then drops the belt on Benoit and lays down, trying to trick the referee. Unfortunately, Mike is out cold and doesn't wake up. "The Crippler" does, coming back to his senses to lock Guerrero in the Crossface again. Although he taps out, there's no referee to see it. When "Latino Heat" grabs the belt again, Benoit ducks his shot and German suplexes the heel. He then heads upstairs for a diving headbutt, but Eddie pulls the referee into the way. While he's down, Rhyno runs out to a big pop. Those cheers turn to boos when he Gores the "rabid wolverine". Guerrero doesn't know why the man-beast did that, but he takes advantage of the situation with a Frog Splash for the victory.

Backstage, Stephanie McMahon enters her father's office. She's not happy to see him. Vince McMahon tells her to lose the attitude because this has been a rough week for the family. When he talks about Linda McMahon, Stephanie gets upset and doesn't think he cares about his wife. Vince promises to deal with Kane tomorrow night on *Raw*. To make his daughter happy, Mr. McMahon says he bought Stephanie flowers. She thinks the display is nice. Unfortunately, the roses are for Sable. Instead, Vince has some cheap dry daises for his daughter.

Jamie Noble def. Billy Gunn (with Torrie Wilson). Ahead of the match, a video package plays for this rivalry featuring Torrie offering to sleep with Jamie on *SmackDown!* if he wins tonight. Noble is out last with a briefcase. He says it's filled with toys and lotions that Wilson will need for their night. That sends Billy out to the floor to kick it into his face. Gunn is all over the redneck until he misses a corner splash and gets driven out to the floor. There, Jamie dives onto "Mr. Ass". Although he catches him, Billy's knee gives out and he drops to the floor. While Noble focuses on the knee in and out of the ring, Nidia makes her way to ringside in her faux fur coat. Despite the pain, Gunn drops his opponent with a One and Only slam. That puts both men down, Torrie checking on her man while Nidia remains emotionless. "Mr. Ass" recovers first and scores a two-count with a hip toss neckbreaker. He tries to deliver a Famouser, but he can't leap high enough with his bad knee. Instead, he gets a near fall with a neckbreaker. When he heads upstairs, he takes too long climbing due to his knee and Jamie DDTs him from the top rope for his own close two-count. At the last second, Nidia puts Billy's foot on the ropes for the break. That sends Noble out to argue with his girlfriend. Wilson runs over to argue with him too, but Jamie grabs and forcefully kisses her. That gets him slapped by his girlfriend and Torrie too. Afterwards, Gunn drags the redneck back into the ring, but Noble dropkicks his injured knee. When he runs the ropes, Wilson grabs his leg and climbs onto the apron. Jamie makes her pay, driving Billy into his girlfriend moments later before rolling up "Mr. Ass" and stealing the win with a handful of tights. While Torrie stares horrified, Nidia retreats backstage.

Also backstage, Funaki tries to interview The APA about Brooklyn Brawler attacking them Thursday night. The brawlers don't care about that, inviting the interviewer to compete in the "Bar Room Brawl" too. As he tries to decide what to wear, the Easter Bunny hops past.

Bradshaw defeats Brooklyn Brawler and Brother Love and Chuck Palumbo and Conquistador Dos and Conquistador Uno and Danny Basham and Doink the Clown and Doug Basham and Funaki and John Hennigan and Johnny Stamboli and Kanyon and Matt Cappotelli and Matt Hardy and Nunzio and Orlando Jordan and Ron Simmons and Sean O'Haire and Shannon Moore and Spanky and The Easter Bunny (22-man "APA Invitational Bar Room Brawl"). Several wrestlers are already hanging around the makeshift bar beside the stage before Hardy enters, his Matt Facts revealing that he hates bar fights. Brother Love and Doink follow. The APA are out last, Bradshaw leading everyone in a toast and a round of beers. He's ready for a fight, but Brother Love interrupts and asks for a moment of love. He adds that just because he loves everyone doesn't mean he likes The APA. He then preaches a message and asks for forgiveness before hitting Los Conquistadores with a stool. A brawl, Ron Simmons hits people with a barrel while Spanky is tossed through a table. Palumbo soon smashes Orlando Jordan with a piece of lumber before Ron hits the heel with a stool. Brawls continue everywhere, Funaki preferring to drink beer instead. Sean O'Haire stands on the bar and dares The APA to fight him, smashing them with pool cues. After Shannon Moore flies off the stage onto Love, the reverend shoves him through a glass window. He also smashes Sean with a plant, ending his time on the main shows, before Bradshaw tosses the Easter Bunny through a window. Brooklyn Brawler hits the big Texan with a cookie sheet, but Bradshaw answers with a stool shot. Afterwards, Hardy drinks a beer and leg drops The Basham Brothers off the bar onto a table. It doesn't break so he dives onto them a second time, this time the leg breaking instead of the wood. Once Bradshaw lays out Funaki with a stool, Brother Love offers to drink a beer with The APA. Bradshaw takes it before smashing a glass on the reverend's head. Mike Sparks and Tony Chimel declare the big Texan the winner because he's the "last man standing" despite Simmons standing right beside his partner. Why weren't they both winners?

Backstage, Jamie Noble smells Torrie Wilson's *Playboy* magazine. Jamie's copy is well worn. He's happy to show it to a worker and tell him that this Thursday he'll get to touch Torrie. The man wonders what Nidia thinks. Noble says she'll get over it.

The World's Greatest Tag Team def. Billy Kidman/Rey Mysterio (WWE Tag Title match). Rey and Benjamin open the match trading shots and counters. The masked man gets the upper hand with a spinning head scissors before tagging in Billy to dropkick the champion for a two-count. He also delivers his own head scissors before Shelton drives him to the canvas with a backward head slam. Haas tags in afterwards only to receive a leaping fist and two-count. Frustrated, Charlie hammers Kidman and chokes him on the ropes. When he attempts a leg drop, the challenger moves and tags in Mysterio for a springboard leg drop and two-count. He tries to follow up with a bulldog, but Haas slams Rey to the canvas for a near fall. Showing off his strength, he whips the masked man hard into a neutral corner ahead of a slam for another two-count. Benjamin also gets a near fall with a big press slam before slowing the pace with a reverse chin lock. When he attempts a corner charge moments later, the two men trade counters again, Mysterio rolling out of a powerbomb to dropkick the champion. Billy returns afterwards to dropkick both heels and back body drop Charlie. A BK Bomb gets him a two-count, but when he attempts another head scissors, the champions catch him and set up for their leapfrog splash. Before they can hit it, Rey pulls Shelton out to the floor. Benjamin returns the favors moments later, blocking a 619. When the champions end up outside the ring, Kidman follows them out with a Shooting Star Press off the middle of the top rope. By the time Billy gets Haas back in the ring, the champion just kicks out of his cover. Soon after, Shelton sneak attacks Kidman and rams him into the ring post. That gets Charlie another near fall. Working together, Benjamin slams Billy onto Haas's knee. Shelton follows up with a modified bow and arrow. He then rolls it around into a regular version of the hold, but Kidman flips free and gets a two-count. He can't tag out before Benjamin drags him back to the champions' corner. When Charlie returns, he continues to focus on the challenger's lower back until he flings Haas out to the floor. By the time he makes the tag, Mike Chioda is distracted by Shelton and forces Mysterio back to his corner. He also misses the champions double-suplexing Rey. After Charlie scores a two-count, Benjamin tags in for his own near fall courtesy of a powerbomb. When he sets up for a second, Billy counters with a face-first slam. Mysterio finally gets the hot tag to fight both champions, rocking Shelton with an enziguri kick before ducking a Haas attack that sees the champion fall out to the floor. Soon after, the masked man nearly wins the belts with a big DDT, but Benjamin just kicks out. Charlie tags in afterwards only to be kicked into position for a 619. Rey follows up with a springboard senton, but Chioda is busy trying to get Kidman out of the ring and misses the cover. Shelton capitalizes with a kick to the masked man's head for Hass to score another near fall. When he tries to follow up, Mysterio stuns him with a jawbreaker. Afterwards, Billy tosses his partner up to hurricanrana Charlie off the top rope. Somehow, the champion still just kicks out. The fans don't like it. They really don't like Benjamin stunning Kidman with a Dragon Whip kick. The champions follow up with a double-team move where Haas Powerbombs Mysterio while Shelton hits the masked man with a Flying Clothesline to score the three-count.

Sable def. Stephanie McMahon ("No Count-out" match). Following a brief video package setting up this match, Stephanie heads to the ring to a solid pop. The announcers are impressed with how excited the crowd is tonight. They've certainly seen some good action to get them in the mood. While this match lacks the technical skills of the earlier title contests, Stephanie brings the intensity tackling Sable on the ramp. She follows the heel around the ring and through the crowd, clotheslining Sable. When they get in the squared circle, the heel surprises the general manager with a dropkick to the head for a two-count. Sable follows up with a string of kicks. Pulling Stephanie out of the corner, the heel slams her to the mat for another near fall. McMahon answers with forearms to the stomach, but one kick drops her for Sable to grind over her opponent. When Brian Hebner says something, Stephanie rolls up the heel for her own two-count. That sets off Sable and she slaps and chokes McMahon until she runs into a back elbow. Stephanie then mounts and punches the diva. A hair whip nearly gets the general manager the victory, but Sable just kicks out and rolls out to the floor. There, McMahon slams her into the apron and grabs a chair. Fortunately, Hebner grabs it and stops Stephanie from hitting the heel. Despite that, McMahon remains in control, repeatedly slapping Sable for a two-count back in the ring. She also rakes her face across the canvas ahead of a snap mare. Kicks to the backside follow, but when Stephanie chokes Sable in a corner, the referee physically intervenes. That doesn't stop McMahon from pulling at the heel's top, nearly exposing her. This time, Hebner stops the general manager. While he removes his shirt to cover up Sable, A-Train rushes out and runs over Stephanie. Sable immediately makes the cover to steal the victory. Post-match, officials help McMahon from the ring.

The Undertaker def. John Cena. Following a video package featuring the wrestlers looking for respect, Cena heads to the ring to say he leads the old school. He promises to eat The Undertaker alive and take his bike. He's going to have a hard time because the "Deadman" leaves his motorcycle at the top of the ramp. Inside the ring, John refuses to give the biker respect, slapping him. The Undertaker responds with a flurry of fists. After chasing off Mike Chioda, he decks the rapping heel and knocks him out to the floor. Outside the ring, the biker continues to punish Cena. When the "Deadman" slides in to break the ref's count, John grabs a bottle of water and spits it into The Undertaker's face. That sets off the biker and he rams John into the ring post before removing a section of the barricade covering. Instead of using it, he punches the rapping heel and gives him a leg drop on the apron. Elbows, fists, and boots follow before the "Deadman" scores a two-count. He also briefly applies a key lock, absolutely dominating the match. Old School and a chokeslam follow, but instead of taking the victory, The Undertaker lifts Cena's head as Chioda counts to two. He tries to finish off John with a Last Ride, but the rapping heel hops free and DDTs the biker. He then unties a turnbuckle pad and stomps the "Deadman". Cena can't get the pad off completely and pays when The Undertaker punches him back into the corner and squashes him. When the biker attempts a second charge though, John finally pulls the pad off and the biker hits the exposed steel. Despite that, the "Deadman" keeps fighting until the rapping heel knocks him off the apron and into the exposed section of barricade. Fists and kicks follow, The Undertaker coughing up blood. Cena focuses on his ribs, ramming his shoulder into them until the biker drops John with a clothesline. That gets him a close two-count. John tries to answer, but the "Deadman" slips free of his slam to lock on Taking Care of Business. Fortunately, the rapping heel is close enough to the ropes to reach them for the break. He follows up with a spinebuster for a near fall. He also gets a two-count courtesy of strikes to the injured ribs. When The Undertaker gets up, he catches a second wind and clotheslines his opponent for another near fall. As he picks up Cena for a Tombstone though, the rapping heel slips free. He tries to finish off the biker with an FU, but the "Deadman" counters with a big boot and leg drop for a close two-count. Back on the attack, The Undertaker wails on and chokes John. When the biker shoves the referee aside, Cena grabs his chain and hits the biker's ribs. An FU follows, but John can't keep the "Deadman" down for a three-count. Frustrated, he repeatedly punches The Undertaker's ribs and face, yelling about respect as he mounts him in a corner. That proves costly as the biker capitalizes on his positioning, delivering a Last Ride for the victory.

A video package plays for Zach Gowen. In it, he talks about losing his leg and dreaming about being a WWE superstar. Afterwards, footage of Zach and Vince fighting over the last month, Mr. America removed from the storyline, plays to set up the next match.

Vince McMahon def. Zach Gowen. While Brian Hebner goes over opening instructions, Zach hands him his prosthetic leg. Vince isn't impressed, forcing the rookie back into a corner. The WWE owner toys with him, shoving Zach back into corners and slamming him to the canvas. After riding Gowen, McMahon body slams the rookie. When he attempts another, Zach slips free only to run into a clothesline. Instead of going for the cover, Vince chokes and pounds on Gowen in a corner. The rookie answers with elbows and a back body drop to the floor. He follows him out with an Asai moonsault for a nice pop. When the WWE owner returns to the ring, Zach surprises him with a guillotine leg drop to the back of the head for a near fall. Vince answers with a leg lock, the rookie writhing in agony. He then kicks and slams Gowen on his knee. Cole is disgusted that McMahon won't go for the victory. Instead, he tries to take away Zach's other leg, wrapping it around the ring post. A single leg crab follows, but the rookie won't tap out. He reaches down deep and crawls to the ropes for the break. That just gets him slammed to the canvas before Gowen attacks the WWE owner's leg. He slows him with a series of kicks before leaping over Vince to dropkick him. He follows up with a string of fists and pulls McMahon crotch-first into the ring post. He repays Vince's earlier attack, wrapping the WWE owner's leg around the post twice. Cole says he's trying to even up the odds. Afterwards, Zach flies off the top rope with a sloppy bulldog. A second rope missile dropkick looks better and puts McMahon down in position for a moonsault and near fall. Vince has had enough and slides out to grab a chair, but Hebner intercepts it. When the WWE owner shoves him out to the floor, Gowen kicks the chair back into McMahon's head, busting him wide open. Despite the blood absolutely pouring from Vince's head, he dodges a top rope twisting somersault splash and covers Zach for the three-count. Even after taking the loss, the fans still cheer Gowen as the referee gives him back his prosthetic leg.

Backstage, Josh Mathews asks Eddie Guerrero if his win is tainted by Rhyno's interference. Eddie says, "a win is a win", and Chris Benoit paid for having friends. That's why Guerrero says he doesn't have or need friends.

A video package plays for the upcoming WWE Title match, focusing on Kurt Angle's injured neck and new friendship with Brock Lesnar.

MUST SEE! Kurt Angle def. Big Show and Brock Lesnar (WWE Title match). Brock and Kurt open the match hammering Show, but the giant fights them both off, chasing the Olympian out to the floor. He immediately Chokeslams Lesnar and nearly gets the win before Angle makes the save. When he tries to German suplex Big Show, the giant knocks him down with his backside. He tries to follow up with a final cut, but Kurt counters with an Anklelock. Show refuses to stay down, shoving him aside and scoring another near fall with a leg drop. That brings the champion back into the ring to make the save. Lesnar follows up with a string of shoulders and a flying forearm off the second rope. He then tries to hoist up Big Show for an F5, but the giant counters with a final cut for a near fall. That brings the Olympian back into the ring with a pair of trashcan lids. The babyfaces take turns hammering Show with them before a double shot finally puts him down. When they try to double suplex the giant, he answers with a suplex to both men. He teases a double Chokeslam, but the babyfaces work together to chokeslam him. When Brock goes for the cover, Angle breaks it. That kicks off an argument between the friends, Lesnar clotheslining Kurt. He follows up with an F5, but the Olympian rolls over to the ropes so he can't be pinned. Brock doesn't care, hoisting up Show for a second F5. At the last second, Angle pulls Mike Chioda out to the floor to break his count. That sees the champion leave the squared circle and whip Kurt into the ring steps and post. Big Show tries to attack Lesnar, but the champion stuns him with a throat drop on the ropes. He doesn't stay stunned for long, surprising Brock with a clothesline and elbow drop for a two-count while the Olympian bleeds at ringside. He can't do anything as Show clubs the champion and sets him up in a corner. Eventually, Angle starts to stir and tries to stop the giant only to see Big Show shove him to the floor. Lesnar capitalizes with an impressive running powerbomb. Before he can score the win though, Kurt blasts him with a pair of chair shots. The Olympian then covers Show for a near fall. Afterwards, he blasts the giant with the chair too. When he attempts a second shot at ringside, Big Show kicks the chair back into his face. He then clears off the Spanish announce table. He tries to Chokeslam Angle through it, but Kurt slips free and counters with an Angle Slam through the table to a big pop. Unfortunately, this isn't a "Falls Count Anywhere" match. After a few seconds, Angle and Brock return to the ring to trade shots. The champion wins the exchange and hoists up the Olympian for an F5. Wisely, Kurt grabs the top rope to block it. Lesnar responds by tossing the Olympian out to the floor. There, Angle whips an also bloodied Brock into the ring steps. Another shot on the steps follows before the two men return to the squared circle for Kurt to German suplex his fellow babyface. A second German suplex sees the champion completely flip around as he falls to the canvas. That scores the Olympian a near fall. Afterwards, he lowers his singlet straps and goes for an Angle Slam. At the last second, Lesnar slips free and scores a two-count with a spinebuster. He then applies the Brock Lock briefly before transitioning into a half nelson submission. It nearly gets him the victory, but Show returns to leg drop the champion and cover both men for a two-count. A double Chokeslam follows, but only gets the giant a near fall on Lesnar. When he covers Angle, Brock makes the save. Big Show sets up for another Chokeslam, but the champion blocks it with a low blow. Afterwards, Kurt punches Lesnar and dodges a corner charge to see the champion hit his shoulder on the ring post. Angle capitalizes with an Anklelock. When Show tries to make the save, the Olympian Angle Slams him. An Angle Slam follows to Brock for Kurt to score the three-count and win the WWE Title for the fourth and final time.

Vengeance is a fantastic PPV and shows the stark difference in talent up and down the roster between *Raw* and *SmackDown!*. Very few matches fail to exceed expectations and the show starts with a fantastic US Title match. Benoit and Guerrero are always good, and they have another classic in the longest match of the show at nearly twenty-two minutes. Noble and Gunn isn't as good or as long, lasting just long enough for Jamie to steal the win and set up the next part of this storyline. It's nothing special, but it gets the job done. The "Bar Room Brawl" is also short and entertaining, if a bit confusing. Why does Bradshaw get the win knocking down Brother Love if Ron Simmons is still standing? If The APA won, that would make sense. The WWE Tag Title match is another fun fast-paced match. Different than the opener, this features more aerial acrobatics and a near fall that has the fans absolutely on the edge of their seats. The McMahons then bring the show down. First, Sable and Stephanie have a catfight that sees them slapping and pulling each other's hair for most of their six-minute match. While Cena and The Undertaker have a good brawl to bring back the crowd, Vince then pummels Zach for nearly fifteen minutes. When Gowen starts to show signs of life, he accidentally gouges the WWE owner with a chair and the match anticlimactically ends following a missed top rope attack. Fifteen minutes is too long for this, but the same could be said for their weekly segments. Luckily, the title match overdelivers. Brock and Kurt are amazing in the ring and Show fulfills his part as the monster heel. There are a number of false finishes and big spots before Angle regains the WWE Title just a few months after neck surgery. Vengeance has only a few stumbles, and even they aren't terrible, on the way to being one of the WWE's best PPVs. This is a home run for *SmackDown!*'s first exclusive PPV.

Monday Night Raw

July 28, 2003
Colorado Springs, CO
Announcers: Jonathan Coachman, Jerry "the King" Lawler, The Dudley Boyz (briefly)

The show opens with a video package featuring Linda McMahon giving "Stone Cold" Steve Austin the night off and issuing an ultimatum that if he wants to remain the co-general manager he has to stop attacking superstars. Sending him home comes back to haunt her when Kane Tombstones her later in the show. Afterwards, the intro video plays and fireworks explode to kick off tonight's episode.

Afterwards, Vince McMahon steps onto the stage in casualwear to call out Kane. He's not calling him out because he's a good husband though. He's doing it because the "Big Red Machine" is an animal and McMahon is a man. Tonight, Vince has no idea what he's going to say or do, but he will unleash Hell.

Booker T/Scott Steiner (with Stacy Keibler) def. Christian/Test. Booker opens the match punching and chopping Test. When Christian hits him running the ropes, the Intercontinental Champion decks him too. Unfortunately, he pays courtesy of a bodyguard shot. Christian then tags in to slam and choke Booker T. Back in, Test punches his one-time tag team partner before walking into a side kick. When Steiner gets the tag, the bodyguard retreats to the floor and tags Christian. The fans are all over Test's case as Scott knocks down Christian and elbow drops him. Following some pushups, he punches and chops the heel. A press slam follows, but he gets distracted taunting the bodyguard and Christian ambushes him. Once "Big Poppa Pump" is down, Test tags in to club his rival and mock him with pushups. Scott responds with a belly-to-belly suplex for a two-count before Christian makes the save. That kicks off a four-man brawl, Booker and Test getting knocked out to the floor. Steiner helps Christian out of the squared circle with a belly-to-belly toss before joining him outside the ring. After ramming the heels' heads together, "Big Poppa Pump" pounds on the bodyguard. Christian makes the save for the heels to drop Scott wrist-first onto the ring steps ahead of a commercial break.

Afterwards, Test does jumping jacks and mocks Steiner. When "Big Poppa Pump" starts to fight back, the bodyguard locks him in a sleeper hold. The two men exchange elbows before Scott catches a Test dive off the second rope to toss him overhead. Both men tag out afterwards, Booker chopping and back body dropping Christian. When the bodyguard recovers, the champion takes turns kicking both men and celebrating with a spinaroonie. Test tries to make him pay, grabbing him for a pumphandle slam. Luckily, Booker T escapes and dodges a Big Boot that hits Christian instead. Steiner follows up with his Falling Face Slam to the bodyguard opening the door for Booker to score the win with a Scissors Kick to Christian.

Filmed over the weekend at the SummerSlam kickoff party, Eric Bischoff announces the *Raw* main event for the PPV pitting Goldberg against Triple H for the World Title.

Goldberg def. Steven Richards. Richards attacks Goldberg as soon as he slides into the ring before Lilian Garcia can finish his introduction. The intense superstar doesn't care, pressing Steven high into the air and dropping him down for a spinebuster. With the fans going wild, Goldberg Spears and Jackhammers Richards for the easy victory. Post-match, Triple H, Ric Flair, and Randy Orton applaud Bill's win. However, Hunter says Steven isn't the World Champion. Goldberg invites him to step into the ring right now, but Helmsley says he's not going to ruin Bill's reputation by beating him up tonight. Flair excitedly yells at the intense superstar, praising the World Champion. Goldberg invites him to step into the ring himself. Before he can, Eric Bischoff rushes out to say that he's not going to give away a match like that without the proper promotion. Instead, he'll let them wrestle next week. That's fine with Bill. He warns Ric that he's next.

Val Venis def. Rico (with Miss Jackie). Val is out first, but the stylist interrupts his pre-match shtick. That frustrates the adult star, but a spank to the backside infuriates him. When Venis grabs him around the waist, Rico backs up closer to him, confusing "the big Valbowski". Eventually, Val gets serious and dropkicks the stylist out to the floor. When he follows him out, Jackie distracts the adult star for a Rico cheap shot. A double ax-handle off the second rope back in the squared circle scores the heel a two-count, as does a snap suplex. Rico stays on the attack with kicks in a corner, but when he leaps up for a hurricanrana, Venis powerbombs him to slow his assault. After catching his breath, "the big Valbowski" clotheslines and slams the stylist with a uranage for a near fall. He also gets a close two-count with a fisherman's suplex. The stylist refuses to stay down, surprising him with a leg sweep. Unfortunately, he runs into a spinebuster afterwards. When Val heads upstairs, Jackie tries to save her man but gets kicked down to the floor ahead of a Money Shot to Rico for the three-count.

Backstage, Eric Bischoff tells crewmembers that Kane is here and they need to get away. After everyone clears out, officers back up a van with the "Big Red Machine" inside. Eric says no one is allowed to open the door until Vince McMahon gives the order to let him out.

After a commercial break, Chris Jericho heads to the ring for the Highlight Reel. Before he welcomes out his guest, Y2J brags about making Shawn Michaels submit last week for the first time in his career. He plays a clip of that multiple times before welcoming out Randy Orton, a man who dislikes the "Heartbreak Kid" too. Randy gives Chris a hug and an Evolution t-shirt. Jericho wishes he could do the same, but all his shirts are sold out. The heels then talk about Orton's new finisher. Although he didn't need any help, Y2J wonders why Randy interfered in his match last week. The "Legend Killer" says he had to make a name for himself. Orton isn't the only guest tonight. Shawn also comes out to tell Y2J that he didn't get the job done alone last week. He then turns to Randy and tells him that if he was paid for every time he beat a punk like Orton, he'd be a millionaire. Michaels stops when he realizes that he's already a millionaire and promises to finish off Randy before his career gets started. Jericho takes offense to being ignored. The "Heartbreak Kid" offers to step into the ring with Y2J again tonight, but Jericho turns down his offer. He says he'd face anyone else in the arena before wrestling Shawn tonight. Orton then tries to attack Michaels. Although he handles the heels solo for a few seconds, eventually the numbers get to him. As Randy and Jericho stomp his friend, Kevin Nash rushes down the aisle to even the odds. He says his name isn't Shawn Michaels and challenges Y2J to a match right now.

Kevin Nash def. Chris Jericho by disqualification. Joined in progress after a commercial break, Kevin punches the heel until Jericho spits in his face. That fires up "Big Sexy" and he makes the mistake of running into a back elbow. He also runs into a corner boot moments later. Y2J struggles to put him down, leaping into a two-handed choke off the ropes. Eventually, he cuts the big man down to size with a chop block. Afterwards, he works on Kevin's knee with elbow drops. When Nash gets up, Jericho chops him before returning to the knee with a series of strikes. He also wraps "Big Sexy's" leg around the ring post before applying a leg lock. Eventually, Kevin shoots him off into the ring post ahead of a sidewalk slam for a near fall. Once more, Y2J attacks the leg, ducking a big boot and kicking Nash. He follows up with a running face slam, but hurts his knee when Kevin avoids a Lionsault. "Big Sexy" capitalizes with a big boot, but when he sets up for a Jackknife, Jericho low blows him for the disqualification. Post-match, Y2J tries to apply the Walls of Jericho, but Nash is too big. Instead, he removes a turnbuckle pad, but Kevin stops him from using it too. When Jericho grabs a chair, "Big Sexy" kicks it back into his face, busting him open. A flurry of fists follow before Nash snake eyes him onto the exposed steel bolt twice. Still not done, he flings the heel out to the floor and tears off some padding from the barricade. Before he slams him on it, Kevin also whips Y2J into the ring steps. He tries to end the heel's career, picking up the ring steps to use as a weapon, but Jericho escapes into the crowd.

Backstage, Rosey tells The Hurricane that he doesn't like hearing people call him a "superhero in training" after Goldust tells him what the acronym spells. The superhero is just excited to have him as his protégé. Rosey would like to get a mask, but The Hurricane says he's not ready for that. He might give him a half-mask and beach towel for now, but one day he'll be a real superhero and able to fly. When the superhero leaps away, Rosey practices flying himself, but he can't get off the ground.

Further backstage, officers open Kane's van door, but Eric Bischoff yells at them and makes them close it until he's ready for the "Big Red Machine" to be free. Afterwards, the Stacker2 Burn of the Week is Kane injuring Rob Van Dam. The announcers reveal that he could be back as soon as next week before offering a positive injury update for Jim Ross.

La Resistance def. Garrison Cade/Mark Jindrak (World Tag Title match). The Dudley Boyz join the announce table to provide guest commentary for this match and insult La Resistance. They don't care who wins so long as they get a title shot afterwards. Early on, it looks like the rookies will score the upset as Cade handles both champions before tagging in Jindrak for a double dropkick. Following a Mark corner splash, Garrison atomic drops Rene into Sylvan. The fans want tables. Instead, they get Dupree swinging the momentum with a hotshot onto the middle rope. Grenier then tags in pummel the dazed Cade. Following his own atomic drop, Rene tags in to clothesline the rookie. When Jindrak breaks the cover, Sylvan teases using the French flag. That sends the Dudleys down to ringside and prompts WWE officials to stop them ahead of a commercial break.

Afterwards, Cade escapes a Dupree sleeper hold with a side suplex. Mark gets the hot tag afterwards to dropkick the heels and nearly score the win with a flying cross body block to Grenier. The rookies follow up by whipping the champions into each other before Garrison picks up Rene for a Jindrak dropkick. When they attempt to do the same to Sylvan, Dupree trips Mark. After Grenier tosses Cade out to the floor, the champions successfully defend their titles with a Double Slam to Jindrak. Post-match, The Dudley Boyz head back to the ring to stop La Resistance from continuing their attack. Although they initially dominate the champions, when Rene gets the French flag, he bashes both Dudleys' skulls.

Backstage, Eric Bischoff is ready to release Kane, but he wants the officers to have their tasers ready.

MUST SEE! Molly Holly def. Gail Kim (Women's Title match). Molly opens this rare women's main event slamming Gail to the canvas. The champion answers with a roll-up and two-count. When she attempts a top rope arm drag, Holly shoves Kim out to the floor. That gets the challenger a two-count moments later. Molly follows up with a pair of suplexes for another near fall. Showing off her wrestling ability, Holly locks on a bow and arrow. She tries to follow up with a sidewalk slam, but the champion counters with a spinning head scissors. Moments later, she counters a handspring back elbow with a boot to the backside. Gail nearly scores the win with a string of roll-ups and a spinning head scissors. Chops and shoulder blocks in a corner follow, but when she heads upstairs, Holly shoves the champion back to the canvas for a Molly Go Round and the victory.

After a commercial break, Vince McMahon heads to ringside. He waits for officers to lead Kane down the aisle in shackles. Vince says it would be too easy to take care of him now and orders the officers to remove the chains. After they do so, McMahon orders the "Big Red Machine" to get into the squared circle. The two men have an intense stare down before the WWE owner asks who Kane thinks he is. Vince calls him a "French fried freak" and "Frankenstein" for touching Linda McMahon. He also calls him a "monster" who is remorseless. A smile forms on Mr. McMahon's face as he thinks about what his monster could do for him. "Stone Cold" Steve Austin has heard enough. He storms out to a big pop to say that he's going to stay on as the co-GM. While he's happy about that, he's not happy that he can't do anything unless provoked. Austin hopes the "Big Red Machine" provokes him tonight and dares the monster to do something. Instead, Kane just laughs and backs up. He's not going to make it that easy on the "rattlesnake". Since "Stone Cold" can't touch the "Big Red Machine", Shane McMahon steps through the curtain, focused intently on the monster. Inside the ring, he immediately charges Kane and clotheslines him over the top rope. When Vince stops him from punching the "Big Red Machine", Shane decks his own father. He then follows the monster up the aisle to smash him three times with a steel chair, the final shot knocking Kane off the stage through tables and production equipment. Despite the fall, the "Big Red Machine" sits up and laughs to end the episode.

SmackDown!

July 31, 2003
Colorado Springs, CO
Announcers: Michael Cole, Tazz

Following shots of Kurt Angle winning the WWE Title at Vengeance, the intro video plays and fireworks explode. Afterwards, the new champion heads to the ring to a big pop and "USA" chant. He says he could come out and give everyone a sob story, but he wonders if there was ever really any doubt that he was going to win. Getting serious, Kurt says it's an honor and a dream come true being the champion for the fourth time. That brings out Brock Lesnar to take the microphone. He knows how much winning the belt means to Angle, but it means a lot to the former champion as well. That's why Brock is challenging the Olympian to a rematch. The fans want to see it. Kurt hedges, saying there's a lot to consider including all the people backstage who deserve a shot. Angle is still just playing around and immediately tells Lesnar that he's on. That brings Vince McMahon powerwalking down the aisle. He calls the new champion "something" and makes fun of Kurt for waving at the fans and kissing babies. Despite the fact that Angle just offered to give Brock a rematch, Vince says the Olympian begged him not to sign that contest earlier today. Kurt argues that he never said that. Mr. McMahon continues to say that he admires Angle being the type of person who will stab someone in the back. While the WWE owner won't give Lesnar a return match, he wants to test the new and former champions' friendship by putting them in a tag match tonight. A SummerSlam ad featuring Brock giving a shark an F5 then plays.

Rey Mysterio (with Billy Kidman) def. Shelton Benjamin (with Charlie Haas). After coming up short trying to take the WWE Tag Titles at Vengeance, Rey slaps and mocks Shelton tonight. One hard whip into the ring post slows the masked man. Haas also gets involved, working on Mysterio's arm until Billy runs over to chase him away. Back in the squared circle, Benjamin scores a two-count with a shoulderbreaker and scoop slam. When he applies a hammerlock, Rey leaps up and snap mares the heel into the ring post. Kicks and fists follow before the masked man gets a near fall with an enziguri kick. He also gets a two-count with a pop-up seated senton. The two men trade counters afterwards until Shelton plants Mysterio with an armbar drop. Afterwards, he slows the pace with an arm lock and camel clutch. When Charlie pulls the ropes back, Brian Hebner admonishes him. He doesn't see Haas trip Benjamin, but Kidman does. While he takes care of Charlie, Rey stuns Shelton with a 619. Although the heel blocks the West Coast Pop when the masked man leaps onto his shoulders, Mysterio has more tricks up his sleeve and spins around for a victory roll and the three-count.

After winning a night with Torrie Wilson by beating Billy Gunn at Vengeance, Jamie Noble is in a hotel room and already in his underwear. He's got a briefcase full of toys to show her, but it makes her nauseous. As she runs to the bathroom, Jamie says he has all night.

Afterwards, Chris Benoit heads to the ring looking for payback after Rhyno cost him the US Title at Vengeance. Instead, the man-beast appears on the Titantron to tell Benoit that he did this to himself and he was never a real friend. Rhyno calls him a joke and sends out a replacement for the match.

Chris Benoit def. Doink the Clown. Doink circles the ring spraying silly string and tossing out a balloon animal. Benoit has had enough and leaves the squared circle to hammer him at ringside. A vicious clothesline and side suplex follow inside the ring. All over the clown, "the Crippler" chops him ahead of a top rope back suplex. Not done, Benoit goes back upstairs for a diving headbutt before scoring the tap-out victory with the Crippler Crossface. Post-match, the "rabid wolverine" tells the man-beast it's time to come out and get his beating. Rhyno appears on the Titantron to tell Benoit that you don't always get what you want. He's leaving and calls "the Crippler" the joke tonight.

Back at the hotel, Torrie Wilson finally leaves the bathroom when there's a knock on the door. Jamie Noble doesn't want any room service. The knocking doesn't stop so Noble has to answer the door. Instead of room service it's Nidia who jumps onto her boyfriend. She says tonight isn't about Jamie and Torrie, but rather Noble and Nidia. Wilson looks disgusted.

After a commercial break, Brock Lesnar asks Kurt Angle if he talked to Vince McMahon earlier. The Olympian did, but he argues that all he said was Vince needed to keep in mind his investment in both men. If Brock wants a rematch, Kurt says he'll give him one and has an idea how to make it happen.

Eddie Guerrero def. Tajiri (US Title match). Pre-match, Eddie rides a lowrider to the ring as usual, but tonight the hydraulics aren't working. Disgusted, "Latino Heat" checks the car only to find Tajiri in the trunk. The "Japanese Buzzsaw" gets a measure of revenge spraying Guerrero with green mist before the bell. Eddie claims he can't wrestle because he can't see. Mike Chioda doesn't care if he can't see, telling Tony Chimel that if the champion doesn't get in the ring, he'll forfeit the belt.

After a commercial break, "Latino Heat" is in the ring and Tajiri is all over him, kicking and rubbing his forearm across Guerrero's face. When Chioda pulls the challenger back, Eddie takes advantage with a shot to the eyes. He gets in a few shots before the "Japanese Buzzsaw" pounds him down into the tree of woe for a baseball slide kick to the face. That gets Tajiri a two-count before the champion slams his face into the turnbuckle. The fight continues on the floor, "Latino Heat" ignoring the referee's instructions to keep up the assault. Eventually, Chioda gets Guerrero back in the ring. That gives the challenger time to catch his breath, but a back elbow and slingshot somersault splash from the apron nearly scores Eddie the win. The champion follows up with a chin lock. When Tajiri starts to fight back, Guerrero slams him to the canvas and heads upstairs. Unfortunately for him, the "Japanese Buzzsaw" reaches down deep and meets his former partner to superplex him to the canvas. Despite that, "Latino Heat" is up first to punch and kick the challenger. Tajiri answers with a monkey flip, chasing Eddie out the floor. The "Japanese Buzzsaw" follows him and flings the champion into the ring steps. When he tries to return to the squared circle, Tajiri stuns him with a baseball slide kick. Slaps follow before the challenger scores a two-count with a kick to the head. Guerrero tries to fight back, but a handspring back elbow flattens him. Although the "Japanese Buzzsaw" follows up with a tornado DDT, he's spent and works the referee's count to five before rolling onto "Latino Heat" for a near fall. From their knees, the former partners trade fists, Tajiri winning the exchange with a dropkick and another close two-count. Eddie answers with a pair of suplexes, but when he goes for a third the challenger escapes and locks on the Tarantula. He tries to finish off the champion with a Buzzsaw Kick, but Guerrero grabs Chioda and holds him to low blow kick the "Japanese Buzzsaw". While the referee argues with "Latino Heat", Tajiri sets up to spray green mist. Unfortunately, Eddie ducks and the "Japanese Buzzsaw" blinds the referee. While Chioda is down, Tajiri kicks the champion. He then wastes time checking on the referee. Guerrero takes advantage, hitting the challenger with the US Title. He then flushes out Chioda's eyes with water before scoring the victory with a Frog Splash.

From *WWE Confidential*, a video package for Zach Gowen plays. In it, he talks about losing his leg as a child and overcoming adversity.

Shannon Moore (with Matt Hardy Version 1.0) def. Zach Gowen. Zach is out first to a good pop while Moore follows with Matt Facts revealing that Hardy's favorite season is summer and he's "twice the man" Gowen is. Once the bell rings, Shannon shoves down the babyface and mocks him. Zach answers with an arm drag and dropkick. He tries to score the quick win with a tornado DDT, but Moore counters with a northern lights suplex onto the top turnbuckle. Following a two-count, Gowen tries to fight back only to see Matt trip him running the ropes. Shannon gets a two-count with a swinging neckbreaker afterwards. The rookie responds with a leg lariat and second rope missile dropkick for his own near fall. A moonsault also surprises Moore for another close two-count. After he drops Shannon with a spinning neckbreaker, Hardy has seen enough and hops onto the apron. Zach knocks him off with a clothesline but pays when Moore rolls him up for the victory. Post-match, Matt attacks Gowen from behind, planting him with a side effect and Twist of Fate.

John Cena def. Orlando Jordan. As Cena heads to the ring, Cole says he arrived at Vengeance. John then raps about sending The Undertaker home with an injury while the rapping heel is still standing. Cena demands a rematch next week and accuses the biker of being a coward and hooking up with Jordan. That brings Orlando out to jack John's jaw. The rapping heel answers with his own fists and a sternum-first suplex onto the top rope. Stomps and knees to the ribs follow, stunning the rookie. Even when Cena misses a corner charge, he's right back on the attack choking and clubbing Jordan for a near fall. Orlando tries to fight back, but John is dominant tonight, hoisting him up for an FU and the three-count.

Back at the hotel, Torrie Wilson has been drinking while Jamie Noble and Nidia finish up in the bathroom. Jamie says the couple has done everything two people can do and invites Wilson to join them. Before she makes a decision, Billy Gunn knocks on the door. Noble assures him that he never touched Torrie. He can't keep his hands off Nidia and the couple starts fooling around again, disgusting and entertaining the babyfaces.

After a commercial break, Brock Lesnar interrupts Vince McMahon on the phone. He wants to earn his way to a WWE Title shot by beating Vince next week. McMahon refuses to be intimidated. He'll think about giving Lesnar a return match, but accepts Brock's challenge. Tonight, he warns the former champion not to turn his back on Kurt Angle.

Back at the hotel, Jamie Noble and Nidia are laying together in their bed under the covers. Also under the covers are Billy Gunn and Torrie Wilson beside them.

Inside the squared circle, Sable brags about beating Stephanie McMahon Sunday night. Following footage of A-Train helping her, Sable says it's good to have friends in high places. She promises to see Vince McMahon later before introducing the hairy heel for the main event.

Brock Lesnar/Kurt Angle def. A-Train/Big Show. As usual when Brock comes out Tazz exclaims, "here comes the pain". He's followed by the WWE Champion, Cole wondering if Vince McMahon is trying to drive a wedge between them or if there's more to the story. Inside the ring, A-Train flings around Kurt and says he wants the belt. The Olympian answers with an arm drag before running into a shoulder and corner crush. When the hairy heel attempts a second charge, Angle dodges and hooks an Anklelock. Unfortunately, A-Train is too rested and kicks the champion into the babyface corner. The former champion tags in to absorb a series of strikes and powerslam the hairy heel for a two-count. When Kurt returns, A-Train muscles him up for a backbreaker. He makes the mistake of hitting Lesnar instead of following up and receives a series of fists from the Olympian. Unfortunately, Angle then tries to run the ropes only to run into a giant big boot. The hairy heel follows up with his own big boot for a near fall.

Finally tagging in, Show scores a two-count with a leg drop before Brock makes the save. The champion pays for the assist courtesy of headbutts and a stiff chop. Although Kurt shows signs of life with another string of fists, a sidewalk slam puts him back down for a Big Show two-count. A-Train returns afterwards to choke and slam the Olympian. He also gets a near fall, this time with a big splash, before Lesnar breaks the cover. The champion takes advantage of the assist, dropping the hairy heel with an Angle Slam. Brock gets the hot tag afterwards to belly-to-belly suplex A-Train twice. When he picks him up for an F5, the giant makes the save with a kick. He then tags in and attempts another kick. Lesnar catches it and F5s Show. While impressive, the F5 takes a lot out of Brock and he falls back into his corner where Kurt blind tags his way into the match and steals the three-count. Post-match, Lesnar takes offense and F5s Angle. Mr. McMahon interrupts to tell Brock that he'll meet him in a "Steel Cage" match next week. To make things interesting, he signs a special guest referee for the contest…Kurt Angle.

Monday Night Raw

August 4, 2003
Vancouver, British Columbia, Canada
Announcers: Jonathan Coachman, Jerry "the King" Lawler, Triple H (briefly)

A video package featuring "Stone Cold" Steve Austin, Vince McMahon, and Kane plays to open the show. It also shows Shane McMahon's return to the WWE last week, knocking the "Big Red Machine" off the entrance stage ahead of the intro video and fireworks. Shane then heads to the squared circle where he promises to kick the monster's butt. That brings Eric Bischoff out to the ring to say that he feels for the younger McMahon. Eric promises that if he had been in the arena the night Kane Tombstoned Linda McMahon, the co-general manager would have stopped him. Bischoff still remembers getting Chokeslammed off the stage by the "Big Red Machine" and would love nothing more than seeing Shane get revenge on the monster. Unfortunately, he can't sign them to a match. Eric reveals that Vince called him and said that Kane will face Rob Van Dam at SummerSlam. Shane doesn't care about SummerSlam. He wants the "Big Red Machine" tonight. Unfortunately, Bischoff reveals that Vince is upset that his son hit him and wants the younger McMahon escorted out of the building. The co-GM isn't going to have him thrown out. He offers to let Shane leave on his own. The younger McMahon tells Eric that he's not impressed with his calm tone and Bischoff disgusts him. He's not leaving unless the co-GM makes him. Eric tries to be the nice guy. He says he's the boss because he controls his emotions, but Shane is pushing him. Bischoff has two words for him if he keeps pushing the boss— "black belt". Before the two men come to blows, Austin heads to the squared circle to a big pop. "Stone Cold" tells Shane that he heard his co-GM and McMahon needs to get out of the ring. The "rattlesnake" warns Shane that Eric would kick his butt if they were to fight. When McMahon doesn't leave, Austin reminds him that Bischoff has been talking about loving mature women and Linda. That fires up Shane and "Stone Cold" offers to give him a match with Eric tonight. Bischoff says they aren't allowed to touch the superstars, but McMahon isn't a contracted wrestler. Shane wants the match, but Eric isn't so sure. However, after thinking it over, he agrees to meet McMahon in a "No Holds Barred" fight.

Bubba Ray Dudley (with D-Von Dudley) def. Rene Dupree (with Sylvan Grenier). When Dupree dances, Bubba clotheslines and hammers him. Sylvan makes the difference early, tripping Dudley and double-teaming him while D-Von inadvertently distracts Charles Robinson. A slam follows for a Rene two-count before he locks on a bearhug. It doesn't take Bubba Ray long to fight free and respond with a swinging neckbreaker. A clothesline moments later gets the babyface a two-count. The two men then trade counters until Dudley scores another near fall with a second rope flying cross body block. He tries to finish off the rookie with a Bubba Bomb, but Dupree fights free and gets a two-count with a spinebuster. When he tries to use the French flag, Grenier enters the ring and attempts a clothesline too, doubling up the cheating. Unfortunately, Sylvan accidentally clotheslines his own partner. While Robinson gets Grenier out of the ring, D-Von busts open Rene's skull with a flag shot. A Bubba Bomb afterwards gets Bubba Ray the victory.

Backstage, Ric Flair brags to Randy Orton about Triple H having a beautiful therapist in his room all last night. Eric Bischoff interrupts. He needs to talk to the World Champion.

Footage of the WWE's Ruthless Aggression tour in Australia last week plays.

Randy Orton def. Scott Steiner (with Stacy Keibler). Lawler wishes he was Scott as Stacy bends over and steps into the squared circle. Afterwards, Randy heads to the ring and says he can feel the tension in the arena. He thinks more people want to see his nipples than Keibler's. Steiner immediately hammers Orton into a corner in response. The "Legend Killer" answers with a dropkick, chokes, and fists. While the fans chant for Stacy, Randy wrenches "Big Poppa Pump's" neck. That gives the announcers a chance to talk about Jim Ross and his recovery from injury. While Coach says he might return next week, the replacement announcer tells JR to take his time recovering. Although Scott escapes a chin lock and belly-to-belly suplexes Orton, when they head to the floor, the "Legend Killer" shoves Keibler into Steiner. That lets him regain control with a clothesline. More fists and chokes follow inside the ring until "Big Poppa Pump" stuns the heel with a jawbreaker and powerslam, nearly scoring the victory. Ax-handle blows and chops have Randy seeing stars before Scott drops an elbow on the heel and mocks him with pushups. Getting serious, Steiner belly-to-belly suplexes Orton from the middle rope. That brings Test down to ringside for "Big Poppa Pump" to hammer him. The bodyguard's distraction pays off though as the "Legend Killer" catches Scott with an RKO out of nowhere for the victory.

Backstage, Eric Bischoff is fired up. He wants to know if he and Triple H have a deal. The World Champion tells him to calm down before agreeing to the deal.

After a commercial break, The Hurricane tells Rosey that he's not quite ready to be a superhero. Christian interrupts to ask what his power is—eating a stack of cheeseburgers? He also makes jokes about injuring Booker T and wants to know what makes The Hurricane think he can beat Christian tonight. The superhero says he has his powers. When the heel walks away, Rosey reveals a box with "S.H.I.T." written on it. It's the costume he made. The Hurricane says he's not ready, but the Samoan plans to prove him wrong.

Further backstage, Eric Bischoff tells Rodney Mack that he needs to plan ahead. "Stone Cold" Steve Austin interrupts to find out what Eric promised Triple H. Bischoff laughs that he made Hunter's SummerSlam main event World Title defense against Goldberg a "No Disqualification" match and there's nothing "Stone Cold" can do about it.

Christian def. The Hurricane. The superhero is all over Christian with an early head scissors. He follows up by chasing the heel out to the floor for a flying somersault senton over the top rope. Back in the squared circle, The Hurricane teases a chokeslam, but Christian elbows free. Unfortunately, he runs into a leaping clothesline for a superhero two-count. When he tries to finish off the heel with a shining wizard kick, Christian ducks and scores the victory with a handful of tights. Post-match, Chad Patton wants to review the footage, but Christian attacks and chokes the superhero until Rosey marches out in an orange and purple costume, his shirt saying "Super Hero In Training". He's also sporting a white cape and mask as he plants the heel with a side slam to save his mentor. Afterwards, The Hurricane poses with his sidekick, making sure to get Rosey to stand behind him.

After a commercial break, Kane arrives in the back of a police van.

Goldberg def. Ric Flair by disqualification. Although Triple H accompanies Ric through the curtain, the World Champion immediately heads to the announce table to provide guest commentary. Afterwards, Goldberg begins his march from backstage through the curtain and warns Hunter that he's next. Inside the ring, Flair badmouths the intense superstar. Bill doesn't budge. When they lock up, Goldberg shoves him down while Helmsley reveals that he suffered a groin injury tangling with the intense superstar last week. "The Nature Boy" might be lucky with just a groin injury with Bill press slamming and tossing around the legend. When Goldberg works over Ric in a corner, Earl Hebner tries to get order. He just ends up distracting the intense superstar for Flair to chop block him. "The Nature Boy" follows up with a string of strikes, but they only make Bill mad. He responds with a pair of punches, each dropping Ric. A back body drop does as well. Following a powerslam, Goldberg stalks Flair until the heel pokes his eyes. He tries to go upstairs, but the intense superstar recovers quickly to slam him off the top rope. When he sets up for a Spear, Randy Orton sprints out to hit him with a chair from behind for the disqualification.

Post-match, Ric and Orton work over Bill, "The Nature Boy" doubling him over with a low blow before "the Game" steps into the ring to hit his SummerSlam opponent with a sledgehammer. Before he can do so again, Shawn Michaels runs out for the save. Unfortunately, he's followed by Chris Jericho who gets a big pop from the Canadian crowd. Kevin Nash isn't as fondly greeted as he runs out to narrow the odds and chase off the heels. "Stone Cold" Steve Austin has seen enough. He heads to the announce table to talk about the SummerSlam main event. While he can't take away the Triple H/Goldberg World Title match, he can change it. Change it he does when he adds Y2J, Orton, Michaels, and Nash to the contest inside an Elimination Chamber. With the match made, Austin tells the wrestlers to resume beating the tar out of each other.

After a commercial break, Terri interviews Pat Croce at ringside. He shills the second season of *Slamball* after the show. Afterwards, Chris Jericho tries to attack Kevin Nash and Shawn Michaels inside the ring and pays for it courtesy of a Nash Jackknife.

Backstage, trainers, Randy Orton, and Triple H check on Ric Flair. Eric Bischoff knows that this is a bad time, but he's got to know if the deal is still on with "the Game". Hunter tells him that it is if Eric fixes the SummerSlam main event. When Bischoff says he can't, Helmsley tells him he can't help him.

Trish Stratus def. Molly Holly (Women's Title match) by disqualification. The new champion starts fast slamming and suplexing Trish. She nearly gets the win with a northern lights suplex, but Stratus just kicks out. Afterwards, the vixen gets her own series of near falls dodging a corner charge and kicking off a trio of roll-ups. A head scissors out of the corner and dropkick also nearly crowns a new champion for the second straight week. When Holly tries to charge her, Trish dodges with her Matrix move. That sees the champion fly out to the floor where Stratus dives onto her. When she punches Molly at ringside, Victoria runs out to attack the vixen and slam her on the floor for the disqualification. Victoria seems to hurt her leg, limping around the ring before Holly joins her to stomp Trish. That brings Gail Kim down the aisle to toss out the heels, Jack Doan making sure to check on the "black widow". Once the heels are gone, Gail helps up her fellow Canadian only to deck her ahead of a double leg slam. The announcers are confused about what's going on.

Backstage, Shane McMahon tries to fight his way into Kane's vehicle, but officials stop him.

Further backstage, Lance Storm finally accepts that he's boring. He needs some help and knows the perfect person to ask—Goldust. The "bizarre one" says they are going to have a lot of fun.

Back at the police van, Eric Bischoff rushes over to tell the officers that "Stone Cold" Steve Austin is on a rampage and has taken several people down. When they run off, Eric shakes the keys to the van and smiles.

Rob Van Dam def. Chris Jericho. The announcers continue to argue, Lawler accusing Coach of not caring about RVD or Jim Ross's injuries. While they fight, Rob takes the early advantage with a string of kicks and a monkey flip. Following a two-count, Jericho pokes the popular superstar's eyes to turn the tide. He follows up with chops, but misses a corner charge and flies head-first into the ring post. After he falls out to the floor, Van Dam misses a top rope dive and hits the barricade instead. Y2J capitalizes with a slam on the floor and back suplex inside the squared circle. A series of elbow drops afterwards gets him a near fall. In complete control, Jericho continues working over RVD and scores a two-count with a knee to the gut. He also gets a near fall with a flashback. When Chad Patton only counts to two, Y2J yells at him. He then takes his frustrations out on Rob, pummeling him. Moments later, he tries to suplex Van Dam back into the squared circle from the apron, but the popular superstar counters with a suplex out to the floor to put both men down. Despite that fall, Jericho recovers first and dropkicks Van Dam. He tries to follow up with a corner charge, but RVD answers with a back elbow and springboard kick. A step over back kick has Y2J seeing stars and Rob repeatedly charges him until Jericho moves and tries to lock on his submission finisher. The fans cheer loudly until Van Dam counters with a roll-up for another near fall. Jericho answers with an enziguri kick for his own close two-count. When he attempts to deliver his running face slam though, RVD moves and catches the Canadian with a spinning heel kick. He tries to finish off Y2J with rolling thunder, but Jericho moves and scores his own two-count with a roll-up. Y2J follows up with a stiff clothesline, but misses the Lionsault. Rob responds with another spinning heel kick. When he leaps onto the top rope, Jericho dodges the Five-Star Frog Splash and scores an extremely close two-count with an Oklahoma roll. He tries to follow up with a corner charge, but misses. Despite that, he counters a hurricanrana attempt by dropping his weight down onto Van Dam and locking on the Walls of Jericho. Unfortunately, the popular superstar is close enough to the ropes for the break. After he shoves the referee, Y2J's springboard attack is countered with a RVD dropkick to the jaw. Van Dam immediately capitalizes with a split legged moonsault for the victory. Post-match, Jericho claims that his loss is a conspiracy against him and blames Kevin Nash for injuring him earlier tonight. He calls Nash "stupid" and says he can't treat "Mr. Canada" like that. Y2J makes it his mission to ruin Kevin's life, challenging him to a "Hair versus Hair" match.

Backstage, Eric Bischoff is smiling and Kane is missing from the back of the police van.

Eric Bischoff def. Shane McMahon ("No Holds Barred" match). Eric is out first, carrying a karate pad with him. Inside the ring, he gets a crew member to hold the pad and shows off his power with a series of stiff kicks. Shane follows, both men wrestling in jeans. Bischoff is also wearing a leather jacket as he kicks McMahon to start the fight. Shane responds by tackling the GM and peppering him with fists. That brings Kane down the aisle. McMahon is ready and waiting for him, wailing on the "Big Red Machine" before grabbing a cord to choke him. It doesn't take the monster long to sling Shane over his shoulder and big boot him. He follows up with a slam into the ring post and barricade. Not done yet, Kane moves the ring steps over and Tombstones McMahon onto them. Once Shane is out, the "Big Red Machine" slides him back into the ring for Bischoff to score the three-count. Jerry treats Eric winning this match as the biggest thing that's ever happened. So does Bischoff, mocking Shane and pinning him again before heading to the announce table to high five the announcers.

SmackDown!

August 7, 2003
Kelowna, British Columbia, Canada
Announcers: Michael Cole, Tazz, Matt Hardy Version 1.0 (briefly), Shannon Moore (briefly)

The show opens with a video package featuring Brock Lesnar, Kurt Angle, and Vince McMahon setting up tonight's "Steel Cage" match between Brock and the WWE owner with Angle as the special guest referee.

Chris Benoit and Eddie Guerrero wrestle to a no contest. As Eddie rides his lowrider to ringside, the announcers reveal that Stephanie McMahon is out again tonight due to injuries she suffered at Vengeance. Benoit then marches out to a big pop from the Canadian crowd. The former friends turned rivals take their time feeling each other out tonight. When they lock up for a test of strength "the Crippler" gets the upper hand until "Latino Heat" escapes with a unique head scissors. Benoit responds with some stiff chops until Guerrero pokes his eyes. He follows up with a boot rake across the "rabid wolverine's" face. A back elbow and slingshot somersault splash from the apron follow for a near fall. The US Champion tries to apply a cross arm breaker afterwards, but Benoit holds onto his own wrist to block the hold. That gets him a back suplex and near victory for Eddie. Afterwards, "Latino Heat" applies an armbar, the announcers noting that injuring the arm takes away "the Crippler's" finisher. To prevent that, Benoit comes back to life with a string of shots and a tilt-a-whirl backbreaker for a near fall. Although Guerrero blocks a German suplex, he can't stop the "rabid wolverine" from kneeing him ahead of a powerbomb and big pop. Benoit tries to follow up with a top rope diving headbutt, but Rhyno runs out to shove him off the top rope. The champion attempts to capitalize with a Frog Splash, but "the Crippler" moves at the last second. Afterwards, Benoit dives out of the ring to brawl with the man-beast while Tajiri hops into the ring and attacks Eddie. Sgt. Slaughter has seen enough. He orders Mike Chioda to waive off this contest and signs a tag match so the four-men can work out their issues.

Chris Benoit/Tajiri def. Eddie Guerrero/Rhyno. After a commercial break, Benoit traps Rhyno in a quick Crippler Crossface, but "Latino Heat" breaks it just as fast. The heels then take turns working over "the Crippler", Guerrero scoring a two-count with a top rope hurricanrana before Tajiri makes the save. When the US Champion misses a shot off an Irish whip, Benoit dropkicks his leg. Both men tag out afterwards for the "Japanese Buzzsaw" to fight both heels. After chasing off Eddie, he rocks Rhyno with a handspring back elbow. "Latino Heat" returns to a series of chops and kicks. Although the man-beast helps his partner, he quickly gets trapped in the Tarantula. This time, Guerrero makes the save with a baseball slide dropkick. Once in control, Rhyno stuns Tajiri with a backbreaker before applying a sharpshooter. Although the "rabid wolverine" makes the save, Eddie takes advantage of the ref's back being turned to illegally switch places with his partner and apply a single leg crab. Eventually, the "Japanese Buzzsaw" crawls to the ropes for the break while the fans chant that "Latino Heat" sucks. Tajiri follows up with a head scissors but can't reach his corner for the tag before the heels double-team him. While the man-beast distracts Chioda, Guerrero chokes his former partner. Afterwards, Rhyno scores a near fall with a scoop slam and falling headbutt. The "Japanese Buzzsaw" tries to fight back, but the man-beast hammers him down before tagging back in the champion for a flurry of fists. When he attempts a corner charge though, Tajiri elbows and back body drops him out to the floor. Rhyno tries to stop him from tagging out, but accidentally knocks the "Japanese Buzzsaw" into his partner and knocks "the Crippler" off the apron. The man-beast then powerbombs Tajiri. When he tries to finish him off, the "Japanese Buzzsaw" sprays green mist into his eyes. Benoit follows up with a German suplex before Eddie Frog Splashes Tajiri. Unfortunately, he's not the legal man and the "rabid wolverine" forces "Latino Heat" to tap to the Crippler Crossface.

Backstage, Josh Mathews interviews Kurt Angle. When he mentions some rumors, Kurt tells the interviewer not to talk about rumors. The Olympian has heard some rumors about Mathews that involve scotch tape, a banana, and other items that keep him up at night. Angle doesn't like rumors and he's going to deal with them concerning Brock Lesnar tonight. Despite how he's been acting, Kurt says Brock is still his friend.

Nunzio def. Zach Gowen. Pre-match, Matt Hardy and Shannon Moore head to the announce table to provide guest commentary. Matt Facts reveal that Matt puts ketchup on his fries one at a time and is a better commentator than Cole. Hardy then talks about his issues with Zach before The FBI try to accompany Nunzio to the ring. Fortunately, Mike Sparks orders them to head backstage before Gowen takes the Italian heel down to the canvas. It doesn't take Nunzio long to turn the tide while Matt calls Zach a "freak" and says he doesn't deserve to steal Hardy's camera time. Inside the ring, Gowen surprises the Italian heel with a falling face slam to nearly score his first singles victory. Instead, Nunzio just kicks out and comes back to life with a stiff clothesline for his own near fall. Afterwards, he chop blocks the rookie for another two-count before hooking a reverse chin lock. Unfortunately, he misses a leg drop on the ropes and crotches himself. Zach capitalizes with a moonsault to put both men down. Once he catches his breath, Gowen scores a pair of two-counts with a leg lariat and second rope guillotine leg drop. When he heads back upstairs, Matt distracts the referee for Shannon to attempt to attack the rookie. Instead, Zach dives onto him with a flying back elbow. Unfortunately, Nunzio takes advantage of the distraction, scoring the victory with a double front kick off the second rope. Post-match, Hardy stomps Gowen and gives him a Twist of Fate to a chorus of boos.

After a commercial break, The Undertaker interrupts Vince McMahon sitting with Sable on his lap. The biker says he thought he'd seen how low Vince can go after thirteen years, but he can't believe he'd send A-Train after his daughter at Vengeance just to help Sable get the win. The "Deadman" warns that if he was in McMahon's family, he'd take care of him. Vince starts to threaten The Undertaker but Funaki interrupts to tell him that something is going on with Brock Lesnar. The WWE owner rushes out of the room to find Brock unconscious on the ground. McMahon wonders what's going on before noticing Kurt Angle standing around. Vince smirks as he looks at Angle.

John Cena def. The Undertaker. Pre-match, Cena says it's okay that he lost to The Undertaker at Vengeance because he's still standing. He proceeds to insult the biker into a commercial break. Afterwards, the "Deadman" rides his bike around the ring while footage of A-Train running over Stephanie McMahon at Vengeance plays. Once the bell rings, The Undertaker slams and punches John. A leg drop nearly finishes off the rapping heel, but he just kicks out. Eventually, Cena shows signs of life raking the biker's eyes and choking him in a corner. The "Deadman" answers with a big clothesline. He then focuses on John's shoulder, driving it into the top turnbuckle. Fists and shoulder blocks follow before the "Deadman" brings the fans to their feet when he signals for Old School. The rapping heel has him well-scouted and fights free of his arm lock, hammering The Undertaker. One shot from the biker puts him right back down before the "Deadman" locks on an armbar. Showing off his power, he picks up Cena by the arm, continuing to apply pressure to the rapping heel's injured joint. When he lifts John up by the arm again, The Undertaker flings him down to the canvas. He then finally hits Old School for a big pop and near fall. The biker is right back on his arm, applying a key lock before punching Cena out to the floor. He follows behind, continuing this one-sided attack and demanding respect. The "Deadman" only briefly returns to the ring to break Brian Hebner's count before resuming his attack. Taking John back into the squared circle, The Undertaker puts him on the top rope for a superplex. When the biker hits the canvas though, he reinjures his ribs and writhes on the floor ahead of a commercial break.

Afterwards, Cena shoves the "Deadman" back into the ring for a two-count. Finally on offense, John clubs The Undertaker's injured ribs and head briefly. The fight spills back out to the floor where the rapping heel dives off the apron into the biker's arms to be rammed into the ring post. That gets the "Deadman" a two-count back in the squared circle. Still injured, he lowers his head too soon and Cena locks him in a body squeeze. John follows up with his leaping snap mare, called the throwback. That's not enough to keep The Undertaker down and he answers with a big boot and elbow drop for a near fall. Snake eyes follow, but when he goes for a second big boot, the rapping heel ducks and responds with a spinebuster for his own two-count. Afterwards, the two men trade punches. The biker gets the better of the exchange and clotheslines Cena hard to the canvas. He then sets John up for the Last Ride, but the rapping heel hops free. The "Deadman" is still on the attack, shoving Cena back into the referee ahead of a chokeslam. Unfortunately, there's no one to count his cover. There's also no one to see A-Train running out to attack The Undertaker. Although the biker initially fights him off, the hairy heel is fresher and quickly recovers to bicycle kick the "Deadman". A backbreaker follows before A-Train drags John onto The Undertaker for a groggy two-count. Spitting up blood, the biker lifts the rapping heel up for a Tombstone, but Cena slips free and finally scores the victory with an FU.

Jamie Noble (with Nidia) def. Doug Basham (with Shaniqua/Danny Basham). The happy couple are out first with footage from their hotel room last week with Torrie Wilson and Billy Gunn playing. Shaniqua then leads Doug down the aisle and hits him with her cat of nine tails. That motivates Basham and he wails on Noble, nearly getting the early victory with a springboard elbow drop. He also gets a near fall with a dropkick to the back of the redneck's head. Another close two-count follows courtesy of a back suplex before Basham knees Jamie's head. Although Noble answers with a leg whip, Doug counters a crucifix drop with a slam to the canvas for another near fall. An overhead hammerlock follows before Jamie escapes with a back suplex. He then scores his own two-count with a roll-up. A swinging neckbreaker also almost gets him the victory before he heads upstairs for a top rope flying elbow drop. Unfortunately, Danny hops onto the apron to distract the redneck. Noble knocks him off, but nearly pays when Doug catches him with a kick. The heel tries to follow up with a suplex, but Jamie rolls him up for the victory. Post-match, Shaniqua pulls Nidia off the apron, smashing her face onto the canvas. Sore losers, The Bashams double-team Noble, leveling him with a combination clothesline and leg sweep. That brings Gunn out for the save, clotheslining and chasing off the brothers.

Backstage, Josh Mathews chases down Kurt Angle to tell him that many people think he was the one who attacked Brock Lesnar and gave him a concussion. Kurt pleads innocence. He says he'd like to talk to Brock, but he knows he'll be fired up and is going to give him time to cool down.

Charlie Haas (with Shelton Benjamin) def. Rey Mysterio. After Rey beat Shelton last week, Haas is looking for revenge. Billy Kidman isn't here to watch his back because he's on his honeymoon. Coincidentally, Torrie Wilson is out this week too. Billy not being here costs the masked man as Benjamin distracts him for Charlie to take control and punish Mysterio in a corner. After he stretches Rey in the ropes, Haas argues with Mike Chioda while Shelton cheap shots the masked man. That gets the heel a two-count before he locks on a bearhug. He quickly follows up with a torture rack backbreaker. After dropping to his knees, Charlie gets another two-count. Soon after, he runs into a pair of knees and a drop toe hold onto the middle turnbuckle. Mysterio is slow to climb the ropes though and pays courtesy of a right hand to the jaw. When Haas tries to follow up with a corner splash, Rey moves and the heel hits his head on the ring post. The masked man switches gears and lands a springboard rolling senton. Low dropkicks afterwards get him a near fall. Rey isn't afraid to throw punches either ahead of a springboard twisting cross body block and another two-count. An enziguri puts Charlie into position for the 619, but first the masked man jumps onto his back. Afterwards, he hits his 619 but Haas dodges the West Coast Pop. He immediately puts Mysterio down on top of his head as he locks on the Haas of Pain for the tap-out victory.

Brock Lesnar and Vince McMahon ("Steel Cage" match) wrestle to a no contest. As the cage is lowered over the ring, we get a replay of Brock being laid out earlier. Despite that, the babyface heads to the squared circle. Before he makes his entrance, Kurt Angle leaves the WWE owner's office and heads to ringside to serve as the special guest referee. Vince follows, but Kurt refuses to shake his hand. Cole wonders if this is all a setup to get Lesnar. If it is, Brock doesn't care, shoving McMahon down twice before hoisting him up for an F5. Unfortunately, Lesnar immediately passes out and falls to the canvas. Vince wants the referee to check on his opponent before he covers the babyface. Angle refuses to count the cover and signals for help. That sets off the WWE owner and he shoves Kurt. When he slaps the WWE Champion, McMahon pays courtesy of an Anklelock. While Vince taps out, Brock kips up to save the boss with an F5. He then helps Mr. McMahon up, the two men laughing while the announcers realize that this was all a setup. Lesnar proceeds to whip Angle back and forth into the cage and rips off his referee's shirt. Vince then brings Brock the WWE Title and tells him it's his. The former champion uses the belt to smash Angle's already bloodied forehead. Still not done, Lesnar press slams the Olympian into the cage before standing with his boot on Kurt's face in victory.

Monday Night Raw

August 11, 2003
Moline, IL
Announcers: Jonathan Coachman, Jerry "the King" Lawler, Jim Ross

Following the intro video and fireworks, Eric Bischoff heads to the ring to get Lilian Garcia to announce him as the winner of his match last week with Shane McMahon again. He then shows footage from that match, including Kane Tombstoning Shane on the ring steps. Afterwards, Eric claims he has respect for every McMahon except Shane. He says he's only here because of his name, unlike Bischoff who crawled from the bottom to the top of the industry. Suddenly, Jim Ross's music plays and he interrupts. Coach had heard he was in no condition to work. The co-general manager had heard the same thing. JR accuses Eric of setting him up. He knows Bischoff put him in the position where the "Big Red Machine" hurt him. Ross knew what he was getting into in this business so he's not going to sue Kane. However, he is going to sue Bischoff for everything he's got. The GM changes tunes immediately and tells Coach to get out of JR's seat. Before he does, "Stone Cold" Steve Austin comes out to a big pop. He's glad to see Jim back. Since he knew there was going to be problems between Eric and Ross, Austin had a contract drawn up earlier. In exchange for JR dropping his lawsuits, Bischoff has to face an opponent of Jim's choosing. Eric doesn't want to face Shane again, but when pressed says he'll beat him one more time. He's feeling especially cocky after the "Big Red Machine" Tombstoned McMahon last week, assuming that he'll be at less than one hundred percent. He then signs the contract despite "Stone Cold" telling him to read it. He doesn't need to. Once he's done, Steve tells him that Shane is in no condition to wrestle tonight. Instead, Bischoff will face Kane. Eric stares wide-eyed and stunned while "Stone Cold" celebrates with a drink.

Miss Jackie/Rico def. Scott Steiner/Stacy Keibler. The heels are out second, Rico copying Stacy's backside showing ring entrance. He then tries to flirt with Scott, but "Big Poppa Pump" wants nothing to do with him and clubs the stylist. A belly-to-belly suplex and elbow drop follow. When Steiner does a series of pushups, Jackie tags in. Keibler is happy to trade slaps and roll-ups with her. Jerry loves it. After the heel chops her, Stacy gets serious with a heel kick and her own chops. When she runs the ropes though, Rico kicks her. That only stuns her for a few seconds before the women connect with simultaneous clotheslines. Before Keibler can tag her partner, Test rushes out to attack Scott and drag him into the crowd. That leaves Stacy alone for the stylist to throat drop her on the top rope ahead of a Jackie leg drop and the win. Post-match, Steiner has had enough. Cursing, he challenges the bodyguard to one last match to settle things. Test has no problem accepting his challenge, but not for tonight. He wants to wait until next week, but only if Stacy is on the line. Keibler accepts.

Backstage, Ric Flair complains to Randy Orton about "Stone Cold" Steve Austin putting him in another match with Goldberg. Even worse is that if Evolution interferes, they'll be suspended for thirty days. Triple H walks in with even bigger problems having to face five men at SummerSlam with a torn groin. Randy corrects him. He's only defending against four guys because Orton will be there to help him. The "Legend Killer" promises Hunter will leave with the championship at SummerSlam. Helmsley likes that. Tonight, he promises everyone is going to stop screwing with Evolution.

After a commercial break, Kane arrives in the back of a police van.

The Dudley Boyz def. La Resistance by disqualification. The Dudleys are out first waving the American flag for this non-title match. The champions follow, marching out for a four-man brawl. Sporting new attire, La Resistance don't fare well in the brawl. Unfortunately, once Bubba Ray tosses Dupree out to the floor, the champion grabs Old Glory and smashes both babyfaces with it for the disqualification. Post-match, the champions drink and pour French wine onto the Dudleys before draping them with the American flag.

After a commercial break, Goldust interrupts Molly Holly to say they both have an affinity for gold. He wants to introduce her to someone special "and not boring". It's Lance Storm in a Goldust wig and face paint. He struggles to impersonate the "bizarre one", stuttering as he tells her congratulations on her "huge ass-ass-ass-ass-ascension". After she slaps him, Goldust leads his protégé to a special party.

Further backstage, Kevin Nash tells Shawn Michaels that his hair isn't going anywhere when he locks up with Chris Jericho. More importantly, Nash plans on taking the World Title at SummerSlam in the "Elimination Chamber" match. Shawn disagrees. Goldberg also disagrees. He thanks both babyfaces for their help last week before telling them that he's leaving with the title at SummerSlam. Michaels wouldn't have him thinking any other way.

MUST SEE! Christian surprises everyone coming out with the Intercontinental Title to Booker T's music. The announcers reveal that Christian won the belt last night in Des Moines and Booker will be recovering at home for a while. The new champion says to celebrate he's going to defend his title against an opponent who is perfect for the debut of *Raw* on the newly renamed Spike TV.

Christian def. Spike Dudley (Intercontinental Title match). That sends Spike running down the aisle to punch, trip, and slap the champion. He also runs on top of him in a corner for a nice pop. Christian slows him with a poke to the eyes and slam on the top rope. After knocking the challenger out to the floor, the heel helps him back in only to kick him ahead of a gutbuster. Following a few punches, the champion finally scores a two-count. When he attempts a suplex though, Dudley shifts his weight and rolls up Christian for a near fall. The runt tries to swing the momentum, but another punch and abdominal stretch slows him. Even when Spike escapes, the champion slams him down to the mat by the hair. When he attempts a leg drop on the middle ropes though, Dudley moves and comes back to life with an inverted atomic drop and bulldog. That nearly gets him the win, as does a battering ram headbutt to the gut. When a tornado DDT only gets him a near fall, Spike heads upstairs. Christian meets him with a shot to the gut but is slammed down for a double stomp before he can superplex the challenger. When the runt sets up for a Dudley Dog though, the champion whips him hard into a corner before planting Spike with an Unprettier for the win.

Backstage, Kane is released from the police van. Before the officers unshackle him, Eric Bischoff runs up to take credit for freeing the "Big Red Machine" last week. He says they make a great team and offers to lay down in the ring for the monster tonight. Kane tells him they are doing things the monster's way tonight.

Eric Bischoff def. Kane by count-out. Pre-match, JR returns to the announce table. Coach isn't excited to give him his headset, but does so reluctantly before Bischoff heads to the ring. Ross says he's about to get what he deserves. Police officers then escort Kane down the aisle and unshackle him. Eric lays down like he said he would. The "Big Red Machine" doesn't want the pinfall, picking him up in position for a Chokeslam, but instead of driving him to the canvas, the monster lets him go and leaves the squared circle for the count-out loss. Everyone is confused. Post-match, Kane grabs Lilian Garcia's microphone and tells the fans that he knows they want him to destroy the GM. The "Big Red Machine" is sick of doing what other people want and is only going to do what he wants. Eric loves it. When the monster changes his mind and goes after Bischoff, Rob Van Dam runs out to attack his former partner and SummerSlam opponent. Unfortunately, he misses a dive off the top rope out to the floor and hits the barricade. When Kane grabs a chair though, RVD kicks him and drives it into the "Big Red Machine's" head. The monster pays him back moments later, dodging a Five-Star Frog Splash and smashing Van Dam's skull with the chair.

Molly Holly def. Gail Kim and Trish Stratus (Women's Title match). While Trish heads to the ring, Terri asks Gail why she attacked Stratus last week. Kim angrily says that the interviewer finally wants to talk to her. Tonight, she's going to show everyone exactly who the rookie is. Gail is out last. By the time she comes out, the vixen has already dropped Holly and goes after Kim. She almost wins back the title with a spinebuster, but the rookie just kicks out. That sees her run into a Thesz press and fists. When Stratus attempts a head scissors in the corner, Gail tosses her out to the apron where Molly pulls Trish face-first onto the canvas. Kim follows up with a slingshot splash, falling face-first to the floor. She still gets enough of Stratus to stun her while the fans tell the rookie that she messed up. Despite that, the heels work together to double-suplex the vixen. Holly then ties Trish into the tree of woe for a Gail running dropkick. Before she can hit Stratus though, the champion clotheslines Kim for the win. The announcers are impressed that she outsmarted the rookie.

Backstage, Ric Flair warns Randy Orton that Goldberg and "Stone Cold" Steve Austin are going to make Evolution so mad that someone is going to get hurt. Triple H interrupts to say that Eric Bischoff is so ecstatic with his recent wins that he told Evolution they can do whatever they want tonight. While Eric can't cancel Ric's match, he did allow them to add a special guest referee…Randy Orton. Flair is so excited that he chops Orton, stunning the "Legend Killer".

A prerecorded vignette plays of Rosey, Super Hero in Training, helping an elderly woman across the street. When the protégé spells his title, the woman slaps him. The Hurricane flies in to tell him that no good deed goes unpunished.

Backstage, "Stone Cold" Steve Austin congratulates Eric Bischoff on his earlier win. Bischoff says it's difficult being as good as he is and sometimes perfection is a burden. Austin tells him that he'll get a chance to prove how good he is in his next match. Eric doesn't believe that he should have another match. Unfortunately, he didn't read the contract close enough. Since he won his match, Bischoff will now go on to SummerSlam to face Shane McMahon.

The WrestleMania Recall moment this week is Jim Ross's WrestleMania debut at WrestleMania IX.

The Hurricane def. Rodney Mack. Mack is out solo tonight. Jerry tells fans that Theodore Long is on an extended cruise but should be back next week. Rodney doesn't need him early on, surprising the superhero with a big powerslam. He follows up with a vertical suplex, bringing The Hurricane back into the ring from the apron, for a near fall. Chokes and a bearhug follow, the heel rag dolling his opponent. When the superhero fights free, he connects with a cross body block and right hands. He tries to chokeslam Mack, but the heel escapes only to run into a clothesline. When Rodney tries to answer with a corner charge, The Hurricane moves and scores the victory with a top rope flying cross body block. Post-match, Mack attacks the winner from behind, bringing Rosey down the aisle to chop and slam the sore loser.

A video package for the upcoming "Elimination Chamber" match plays.

After a commercial break, it's time for the Highlight Reel. After challenging Kevin Nash to a "Hair versus Hair" match, Chris Jericho clarifies that he's only putting his beard hair—of which he has none right now—up against Nash's locks. The fans boo, but Y2J says he's a "huge rock star" and can't "lose his mojo". Kevin has heard enough and walks down the aisle with a silver briefcase. He says Jericho is looking at things all wrong. Instead of losing his hair, Y2J should see it as updating his tired look and getting a makeover. "Big Sexy" shows some hairdo options for a shaved Jericho including a Kid and Play style cut. Y2J fake laughs and calls Kevin a "funny guy". The heel thinks it will be really funny when he eliminates Nash at SummerSlam and wins the World Title. When Jericho calls him "Nash Hole", Kevin stands up and tells him that he's looking forwards to eliminating Y2J in the "Elimination Chamber" match. He's also going to take all of his hair off, not just his beard. Jericho can either accept the challenge or "Big Sexy" will kick his butt and shave his head right now. With no other option, Y2J accepts the match next week. When Nash turns to leave though, Jericho gives him a preview with a sneak attack. Kevin answers with a sidewalk slam. Following a clothesline out to the floor, "Big Sexy" stalks the heel and teases giving him a haircut with some hedge clippers. Fortunately, Y2J grabs a fire extinguisher from under the ring and sprays Nash to escape.

Goldberg def. Ric Flair ("No Count-out, No Disqualification" match). After the announcers preview the *Raw* portion of SummerSlam, Randy Orton heads to the ring to serve as the guest referee in shorts that would make Shawn Michaels blush. He passes something to Flair before Goldberg makes his entrance trek. Inside the ring, the intense superstar glares at the referee until Ric blasts him with brass knuckles. Even that blow and a fast count can't score "The Nature Boy" the win. Another fast count after a side suplex gets Ric another two-count. A chop afterwards wakes up Bill to press slam and back body drop the legend. A powerslam follows before Randy gives him one of the slowest counts ever for just a two-count. The count remains slow following a clothesline. After that gets him a two-count, Goldberg threatens Orton while Flair gets a chair. Even that doesn't slow the intense superstar for long and he chokes both Evolution members until "The Nature Boy" gives him a low blow. The Figure Four Leglock follows, the referee continuing to try to fast count Bill. When Goldberg reaches the ropes, Randy stomps him and drags the intense superstar back to the center of the ring. After the referee pulls on Ric's arms for added pressure, the legend finally releases the hold to chop Bill and clip his knee. That still doesn't keep Goldberg down and he clotheslines both heels. Back body drops follow before the intense superstar sets up for a Spear. The referee saves his mentor, taking the Spear himself. It doesn't help much as Bill Spears Flair afterwards. Shawn Michaels then runs down the aisle to give Randy Sweet Chin Music. After Goldberg Jackhammers "The Nature Boy", Shawn uses the unconscious referee's arm to count the three and give the intense superstar the victory.

SmackDown!
August 14, 2003
St. Louis, MO
Announcers: Michael Cole, Tazz, Eddie Guerrero (briefly), Chris Benoit (briefly)

Following the intro video and fireworks, Vince McMahon heads to the squared circle to boos. He says he has the honor of introducing a man the fans thought they knew, but they don't. He wants to introduce "the real Brock Lesnar". After listing some of Brock's accomplishments, Vince calls him "an animal". He shows how sadistic and cunning he can be, playing footage from last week's main event and Lesnar turning on Kurt Angle. While Kurt is at home recovering tonight, the WWE owner promises he'll face the music next week. McMahon then introduces Brock, Cole claiming he's been brainwashed. The newly turned heel says that Angle is not his friend, though he used to be. Lesnar only considers someone his friend when he can use them and the Olympian is no longer useful. When the fans boo him, Brock says they suck like Kurt. Vince then announces that Angle will defend the WWE Title against Lesnar at SummerSlam. That brings Stephanie McMahon down the aisle, making her return after suffering injuries at Vengeance from A-Train. Vince says she learned her lesson at the PPV. She learned that he'd do anything to help Sable beat her. Mr. McMahon admits that he sent the hairy heel to the ring, but he had his reasons. She wonders if he was intimidated by her power and she won't take a backseat until he fires her. As far as Stephanie is concerned, her father is a "piece of garbage". Vince tells her he doesn't take that from any man, "much less a woman". He considers Stephanie a tremendous disappointment and calls her his worst investment as a general manager. On second thought, Mr. McMahon believes marrying Linda was his worst decision. When Stephanie tries to slap him, Brock catches and squeezes her arm. Vince stops his new friend from hurting her. He's saving that honor for A-Train, signing his daughter to a match with the hairy heel tonight.

The World's Greatest Tag Team def. Billy Kidman/Rey Mysterio (WWE Tag Title match). Kidman opens the match head scissoring and arm dragging Haas. When forced into the champions' corner, he fights both heels until Shelton kicks his knee. Afterwards, the champions work on Billy's knee. It doesn't take the challenger long to snake eyes Benjamin and tag in Rey to fly around the ring and drive Charlie face-first to the canvas with a bulldog. Shelton tries to answer with a slingshot suplex, but the masked man counters with a neckbreaker for a near fall before Charlie makes the save. Moments later, Haas knees Mysterio into a T-bone suplex. Kidman immediately rushes over to his partner's defense, breaking Benjamin's cover and cross body blocking Charlie on the floor. That leaves Rey to give Shelton a hurricanrana from the top rope for a two-count ahead of a commercial break.

Afterwards, Billy leg drops Benjamin onto the middle rope, but when the masked man tries to hit him with a 619, Haas back body drops him out to the floor. That hurts Mysterio's knee and Charlie tags in to stomp, club, and choke Mysterio. Instead of working on the knee, he boots Rey's ribs before Shelton tags back in for a double-team gutbuster and two-count. Realizing his partner is in trouble, Kidman makes the save. Keeping up the punishment on the ribs, Benjamin traps the masked man in a bearhug. When Mysterio fights free, a knee to the gut drops him for a near fall. Right back to the midsection, Shelton traps Rey in an abdominal stretch. Eventually, the masked man flips free and covers Shelton for a two-count. Despite that, The World's Greatest Tag Team remains on the offensive with their double-team leapfrog splash for another near fall. When Charlie puts him on the top rope though, Mysterio knocks him down to the canvas and attempts to follow with a flying dive. Unfortunately, Haas leaps up and counters with a knee strike to the ribs. Billy is back in for the save once again before the champion applies a twisting armbar. This time, Rey flips free and dropkicks Charlie. Once again, he can't make the tag, but Kidman saves him from a cover. Moments later, the masked man arm drags and dropkicks Benjamin. Billy desperately reaches for the tag, waiting for Mysterio to crawl to him to clothesline and dropkick the champions. A head scissors and headlock takedown follows before he tosses Shelton out to the floor and nearly wins the titles with a BK Bomb to Charlie. When he turns and baseball slide kicks Benjamin, Haas capitalizes with a belly-to-belly suplex. Rey makes the save, Dropping the Dime for a Kidman near fall. Afterwards, the challengers block a World's Greatest Tag Team Inverted Atomic Drop and Superkick, the masked man head scissoring Shelton out to the floor. While he does so, Charlie gives Billy a spinebuster for his own near fall. He tries to follow with a superplex, but Mysterio saves his partner with a sunset flip powerbomb. A Shooting Star Press follows, but Mike Chioda is distracted watching Rey give Benjamin a 619. By the time he turns around, Haas just kicks out. Chioda then has to stop Mysterio when he kicks Shelton and takes a title belt from him. While the referee takes the belt from Rey, Benjamin superkicks Kidman for Charlie to steal the win.

Danny Basham (with Shaniqua/Doug Basham) def. Billy Gunn (with Torrie Wilson). Despite this being a singles contest, Billy fights both Bashams to start the match, in and out of the ring. Once Mike Sparks gets order, Gunn punches and hip toss neckbreakers Danny for a near fall. Shaniqua tosses Torrie into the ring afterwards, distracting the referee and Billy for The Basham Brothers to rock Gunn with a combination Leg Sweep and Clothesline, called the Ball and Gag by Tazz, for the win. Post-match, the Bashams clothesline "Mr. Ass" again and corner Wilson for Shaniqua. The dominatrix pulls her to the center of the ring for a slam. When the Bashams resume their attack on Gunn, Jamie Noble and Nidia run out for the save. Unfortunately, Doug clotheslines Jamie while Shaniqua slams and stands on Nidia. A Doug spinebuster to Noble follows before Shaniqua powerbombs Nidia to finally end the assault.

Backstage, Bradshaw tries to convince Ron Simmons that Shaniqua is really Shelton Benjamin in drag. Ron isn't sure, but knows that there are a lot of people needing protection. He wonders if they should reopen their agency. Bradshaw doesn't know about that, but he does know that Shaniqua is a man.

Further backstage, Big Show leaves Vince McMahon's office smiling.

Big Show def. The Undertaker by count-out. The Undertaker is out first, riding his motorcycle around the ring to a nice pop. Cole reveals that he'll face A-Train at SummerSlam. Show then comes out, one of the few men who can fling the biker down to the mat. While he clubs the "Deadman", the announcers talk about The Undertaker's injured ribs. They don't slow him here as he recovers to clothesline the giant twice. He then escapes a Chokeslam and drives Big Show to the canvas with a Fujiwara armbar. Luckily, the giant is tall enough to reach the ropes for the break. The biker follows up with a leaping DDT for a two-count before booting Show out onto the apron. A leg drop follows before the "Deadman" delivers Old School. Even that can't keep Big Show down and he rocks The Undertaker with a sidewalk slam. Clutching his ribs, the biker gives the giant a target and he capitalizes with a string of knees and forearm shots. The "Deadman" won't stay down, answering with fists, but a clothesline flattens him for a two-count. Show follows up with an elbow to the back before standing on The Undertaker's injured ribs. The biker keeps fighting back, trading fists with the giant. A leaping clothesline helps the "Deadman" win the exchange ahead of a leg drop and near fall. Lowering his straps, The Undertaker pounds Big Show in a corner ahead of a pair of body splashes. The biker then sets up for his own chokeslam, but Show shoves the referee aside before punching the "Deadman's" ribs. He then whips The Undertaker into Brian Hebner, dropping him on the canvas while the giant runs over the biker. When he tries to follow up with a big boot, the "Deadman" ducks and Big Show straddles the top rope. The fight then spills out to the floor where the two men trade shots before Show slams The

Undertaker's face on the ring steps. He tries to follow up with a slam into the ring post, but the biker slips free and shoves the giant into the steel instead. The fight then heads into the crowd, the "Deadman" unloading with a series of fists and a clothesline back over the barricade. Before he can follow him back to ringside, A-Train breaks a two-by-four over his SummerSlam opponent's ribs. That gives Big Show time to crawl back into the ring and score the count-out victory.

During the commercial break, trainers check on The Undertaker's injured ribs. He can barely breathe.

Tajiri def. Rhyno. Eddie Guerrero drives his lowrider to ringside pre-match and hugs Tazz before providing guest commentary. Chris Benoit follows, looking for his own hug. He says it's an honor to sit next to the US Champion. They will face off alongside this match's competitors for the championship at SummerSlam. When Tajiri comes out, the man-beast clubs and clotheslines him. A suplex nearly gets him the win while Guerrero claims that he never tapped out last week. He says he was smashing a cockroach. Inside the ring, the "Japanese Buzzsaw" scores his own two-count with a stiff kick before locking on the Tarantula. Unfortunately, he misses a Buzzsaw Kick and Rhyno powerbombs him. The man-beast tries to finish off Tajiri whipping him shoulder-first into an exposed turnbuckle bolt, but when he goes for the Gore, the "Japanese Buzzsaw" moves and Rhyno hits the steel instead. A Buzzsaw Kick afterwards scores Tajiri the victory. Post-match, "the Crippler" follows Eddie to the lowrider, looking for a ride. Although they argue initially, "Latino Heat" agrees to show off his vehicle. Benoit wants him to make the hydraulics go, bouncing up and down until Eddie storms off.

John Cena def. Zach Gowen. Pre-match, Cena raps to say that this is ridiculous. He says he handled The Undertaker's Last Ride while Zach can't handle the "last stand". He adds that Gowen is the perfect three-legged race partner. Despite John's insults, the rookie keeps his cool and surprises the rapping heel with an attack targeting his injured shoulder. That fires up Cena and he runs through Zack before hammering him. Gowen tries to answer with his own fists, but a huge back body drop stuns him. John teases an FU, but drops the rookie to drag him to the ropes. He tries to give him an FU off the middle rope afterwards, but Zach counters with an armbar drop. Gowen follows up with a dropkick to the injured shoulder and bulldog for a close two-count. When he heads upstairs for a flying cross body block though, Cena catches him and rolls through to finally hit his FU and score the victory.

Backstage, A-Train corners Stephanie McMahon. He says he was paid a lot of money to hurt her at Vengeance, but he would have done it for free. He forces her to run her hand over his hairy chest, warning her that he likes women who like it rough.

During the commercial break, Matt Hardy attacks Zach Gowen from behind. Cole is fired up about it.

Backstage, Spanky argues with Orlando Jordan. Apparently, they are betting on whether Spanky can chug chocolate syrup. When he slams a bottle on the table, it sprays onto Vince McMahon. That fires up the WWE owner and he wants to know who Spanky is. McMahon tells him that he's going to pay for his jacket. Spanky isn't impressed, calling him "Vince", and reminding the WWE owner that he talked about bad investments earlier tonight. The plucky babyface says that he forgot one, reminding Vince about the XFL. That's all Mr. McMahon can take and signs Spanky to a match next with Brock Lesnar.

Spanky def. Brock Lesnar by disqualification. The cruiserweight isn't intimidated and runs out to attack Brock. Despite his enthusiasm, the heel tosses him around and triple powerbombs Spanky. Tazz wants Brian Hebner to ring the bell now. Instead, he watches as Lesnar tosses aside a member of the crew and takes his chair. After chasing off the referee, Brock smashes his opponent's skull with the chair for the disqualification. More shots follow before Lesnar wipes his opponent's blood on his chest and hair. Still not done with him, the heel picks Spanky up overhead and hurls him into the ring post, the fans suitably impressed. With Vince at his side, the announcers believe carnage like this will continue. During the break, Spanky is stretchered backstage.

A-Train def. Stephanie McMahon ("No Count-out" match). Pre-match, Vince McMahon warns that the ring may get even bloodier during this match before introducing Sable to serve as the special guest ring announcer. She introduces Stephanie as the woman that she beat at Vengeance. When she gets in the ring, McMahon tries to get to Sable, but Mike Chioda holds her back while the diva announces that this match will have no count-outs. Afterwards, Stephanie finally gets her hands on Sable, pounding her until A-Train walks out smirking. She slaps him, but that only makes him mad and he tosses her across the ring. Vince and Sable love watching the hairy heel crush Stephanie in a corner. Afterwards, Mr. McMahon acts like an emperor and puts his thumb down for his daughter. A-Train tries to finish her off, putting her on his shoulders until The Undertaker walks down the aisle to brawl with the hairy heel. Unfortunately, when he gets the upper hand, Big Show hurries out to club the "Deadman" from behind and hit his ribs with a steel chair repeatedly. Once the biker is under control, A-Train returns to the ring to give Stephanie a corner bomb for the three-count. Post-match, Vince kisses Sable overtop of his downed daughter to end the show.

Monday Night Raw
August 18, 2003
Grand Rapids, MI
Announcers: Jim Ross, Jerry "the King" Lawler, Ric Flair (briefly), Triple H (briefly)

Following the intro video and fireworks, Chris Jericho is in the ring for the Highlight Reel. He's already in wrestling attire for his upcoming "Hair versus Hair" match. Y2J promises that he's going to beat Kevin Nash and make him "Big Daddy Bald" before regaining the World Title at SummerSlam. He says the belt was stolen from him last year and he blames Shawn Michaels. Jericho then welcomes out the "Heartbreak Kid" as his guest this week. He gets a big pop, but Lawler doesn't understand why Shawn keeps agreeing to be his guest since it never turns out well for anyone. Y2J asks if lightning will strike twice at SummerSlam for Michaels to win the belt in the "Elimination Chamber" again. Before Shawn can respond, Jericho cuts him off and says he's out of time. However, Y2J claims that he's a fair man. While he has to leave to get ready for his match, he invites Evolution to come out and serve as his guest hosts. Triple H speaks first, accidentally telling Michaels that only they understand the "Evolution Chamber". He calls it that a second time while telling everyone that he lost the most in the first "Elimination Chamber" match last year at Survivor Series. This time, Hunter promises that the "Heartbreak Kid" will be the one spending time in a hospital bed afterwards. Shawn immediately attacks him, but he's outnumbered and slowed with a Ric Flair low blow. That brings out Kevin Nash, sporting bleach blonde hair, to deck all three heels. When Evolution stomps him down, Goldberg runs out for the save. He manages to toss both Randy Orton and Flair out to the floor, but when he tries to Spear Helmsley, "the Game" moves and Bill Spears Nash.

Backstage, Test tells Stacy Keibler that he made some mistakes when they were together before. Once he wins her back in his match with Scott Steiner tonight, he promises to treat her even worse.

Molly Holly def. Trish Stratus (Women's Title match) by disqualification. As Trish heads to the ring, we hear prerecorded words from the vixen. She says Gail Kim has a problem with her, but Stratus is pushing that aside tonight to win back the Women's Title. Molly tries to prevent that, working on Trish's arm until the vixen answers with a Thesz press and fists. Back up, Holly regains control with a clothesline ahead of an arm wringer and two-count. A sloppy side slam follows. Things don't get any better when the champion picks up Stratus for a shoulderbreaker, nearly dropping her before delivering the move for another two-count. When she heads upstairs, Trish brings Molly down with a handstand head scissors. A dropkick and chops follow before Stratus plants the champion with a spinebuster. That brings out Kim for Trish to knock her off the apron. Unfortunately, she misses a top rope flying cross body block and Holly capitalizes, making the cover until Gail breaks that up for the disqualification. Post-match, Kim attacks the champion until WWE officials separate them.

Backstage, "Stone Cold" Steve Austin interrupts Evolution. He notes how happy they are with what they did to Shawn Michaels. Since he needs a main event tonight, he signs Randy Orton to face Goldberg. The "Legend Killer" hopes things don't break down. To stop that from happening, Austin agrees to be the special enforcer.

After a commercial break, Shane McMahon steps out onto the stage. He announces that there will not be a match between him and Eric Bischoff at SummerSlam. That's because he's planning on finishing off the co-general manager tonight as soon as Eric gets here. He's also waiting for Kane to get here and has a special present for him…a can of gasoline.

Backstage, Goldust tells Lance Storm that the key to not being boring is to be unpredictable. When asked, Lance says the most unpredictable thing he's ever done is return a videotape without rewinding it. That disgusts the "bizarre one" and he tells Storm to enter the women's locker room and say the most disgusting things he can think of.

Test def. Scott Steiner (with Stacy Keibler). Test is out first for this match with Stacy's managerial services on the line. Scott rushes out after him, but the bodyguard is waiting to punch and stomp him until Steiner responds with a powerslam. He takes his turn hammering and chopping his rival. A belly-to-belly suplex puts Test down afterwards for more fists and a two-count. More fight than wrestling match, "Big Poppa Pump" wails on and elbow drops the bodyguard ahead of some pushups. When he attempts a corner charge, Test elbows him and sets up for a Big Boot. Unfortunately, Scott ducks and the bodyguard hurts himself, stumbling around the ring unable to put weight on his knee. Steiner lets Jack Doan step in and check on Test before calling for trainers. That sends Chris Brannan down to the ring to check on the bodyguard's knee. He curses as officials check on him. Unsure of what to do, Keibler and "Big Poppa Pump" confer on the apron until Test boots Scott right in the face. Doan is okay with the ruse, immediately counting the bodyguard's cover for the win. Post-match, Test leads Stacy backstage, the diva frustrated while the bodyguard crows.

After a commercial break, La Resistance head to the ring with the announcers informing fans that they'll defend the World Tag Titles at SummerSlam against The Dudley Boyz. After what they did to them last week, the champions ask for a moment of silence for the Dudleys. At ringside, the heels call out a serviceman in the crowd and ask how many people he killed last year. It's Rob Conway who has recently wrestled as a Conquistador. When they slap and mock him, WWE security steps in until the Dudleys run out to chase off the champions. Bubba Ray and D-Von then invite the serviceman to get into the ring with them, the fans chanting "USA". Bubba thanks him for his service and lets him wave the American flag. Unfortunately, when they turn their back, the serviceman hits them with the flag. The announcers are quick to say that he's not a real serviceman as La Resistance return to give the number one contender's a pair of Double Slams. Afterwards, the French sympathizer drapes the American flag on the Dudleys and holds up the French flag. JR wants to know who he is when he spits on the flag.

Backstage, Chris Jericho nervously looks at his hair.

Chris Jericho def. Kevin Nash ("Hair versus Hair" match). The announcers wonder if Nash getting Speared earlier will affect him here. It doesn't seem to early on as he elbows and back body drops Jericho for a two-count. When Y2J attempts a top rope attack, Kevin catches him by the throat and slams him to the canvas for a near fall. The heel finally gets in some offense with a dropkick to the knee and kicks to the injured joint. Nash answers with a back body drop out to the floor, but misses his follow up attack and hits the ring post hard. Jericho capitalizes with a baseball slide kick and top rope missile dropkick for his own two-count. Unable to get the win, Y2J removes a turnbuckle pad. Earl Hebner spots it and tries to tie it back on while Kevin rolls up the heel. By the time Hebner turns around, Jericho just kicks out. He responds with a series of strikes for another near fall. Fists and chops follow in a corner, but when Y2J attempts a charge, "Big Sexy" moves and answers with a clothesline for a two-count. He also gets a near fall with a sidewalk slam. Jericho responds with a roll-up, but he's too close to the ropes and Nash easily escapes. After he escapes a second roll-up, Kevin clotheslines Y2J for another near fall. When he attempts a corner charge, Jericho boots him ahead of a running face slam and Lionsault. The heel is a little slow to make the cover and "Big Sexy" just manages to kick out. Afterwards, Y2J locks on the Walls of Jericho, but Nash won't submit. Slowly, he crawls to the ropes for the break, Jericho believing that he won. By the time he stops arguing with the referee, Y2J runs into a Jackknife Powerbomb. Luckily, he drapes his foot on the bottom rope to save his hair. Right back on the attack, Kevin gives him a big boot. When he sets up for a second Jackknife, Jericho waves his arms out and hits Hebner's eye. He capitalizes on Earl being blinded to give Nash a low blow. Not done yet, Y2J knocks Kevin out with a brass knuckles shot. Post-match, Jericho grabs some scissors and starts chopping away at "Big Sexy's" hair, running off when he wakes up.

In a prerecorded vignette, Rosey hops onto the screen to help a young girl get her cat out of a tree. When she asks how he can repay her, The Hurricane flies in to explain that superheroes save the day not for rewards, but to help. While he does so, the cat attacks Rosey and he slams it against the tree before flinging it far into the distance. Rosey immediately rushes over to his mentor and tells him that there's more crime that needs their attention, the superheroes flying off to leave the girl looking for her cat.

Rosey (with The Hurricane) def. Rodney Mack (with Theodore Long). Long says he was off for a few weeks "living large" and taking cruises, but now he's back to teach some lessons. Mack then welcomes Rosey in with a string of strikes. The super hero in training tries to respond in kind, but Rodney overpowers him, knocking the large man onto the middle rope. When Theodore attempts to distract the referee, The Hurricane pulls him off the apron. That distracts Mack for Rosey to come back to life with a Samoan drop and palm strike to the chest. Following a corner crush, the super hero in training scores the win with a Spinning Side Slam.

After a commercial break, Linda McMahon addresses the WWE from her home office in Connecticut. She tells JR that she is continuing to recover from Kane's heinous attack but will not require surgery. While she talks about how traumatized she's been her doorbell rings incessantly. It's Eric Bischoff and he sneaks in to laugh about Shane McMahon looking for him back in Michigan. With no one else there, Eric rubs Linda's arm and says she looks exceptional. She wants him to leave, but he isn't going anywhere. After he stops her from using the phone to call security, Bischoff tells Linda that he's going to "please her". Most importantly, he wants to hurt Shane for ruining WCW. He promises to break his legs this Sunday. When Linda tries to slap him, Eric hammerlocks her arm and tells her not to fight him before forcing a kiss on her. During the commercial break, Shane rushes out of the arena to try to get home.

Christian and Rob Van Dam (Intercontinental Title match) wrestle to a no contest. The champion starts fast and mocks RVD after a shoulderblock, stealing his pose. Rob responds with a monkey flip and smirk. Back up, Christian stomps Van Dam in a corner. When he attempts a whip across the ring, RVD reverses it and nails him in a corner. Unfortunately, he hits the ring post on his second charge for a heel two-count. Christian then targets his shoulder, dropping it onto the top rope before applying an arm wringer. The fans try to cheer Rob to life when the champion applies an armbar. Christian silences the crowd with an armbar drop and another mocking pose. While Van Dam does surprise him with a springboard cross body block, the heel is right back on the attack, stomping RVD. The fans get under Christian's skin telling him that he sucks, but it only fuels him to give the popular superstar a gutbuster for another two-count. Afterwards, Rob starts to fight back, rocking the champion with a spinning heel kick. A second kick and clothesline have the heel seeing stars before Van Dam scores a near fall with a third kick. When he goes for rolling thunder, Christian counters with a pair of knees for his own two-count. The two men then trade counters and escapes, RVD accidentally kicking Nick Patrick. The champion capitalizes with a reverse DDT, but when he tries to give the challenger a conchairto, Rob answers with a spinning heel kick into a chair driving it back into Christian's face. He immediately hits a Five-Star Frog Splash afterwards before Kane marches down the aisle. Van Dam meets him with a baseball slide kick with a chair. When he attempts a suicide dive afterwards, the "Big Red Machine" swings the discarded chair to knock out RVD and carry him backstage, this match ending in a no contest.

After a commercial break, Test tells a reluctant Stacy Keibler that she has to do what he says. She is none too happy having to dance for Rico and Steven Richards, but does so.

Further backstage, Kane has Rob Van Dam tied up and douses him in gasoline. The "Big Red Machine" warns his former tag team partner that he can take him out at any time. He taunts Rob with a matchbook, teasing the popular superstar and telling him that no one is coming to help him. Luckily, the monster says the fans want to see Van Dam burn and Kane isn't going to do what they want.

Goldberg def. Randy Orton. "Stone Cold" Steve Austin is out first to serve as the special enforcer. When Orton heads to the ring, Ric Flair and Triple H join the announce table to insult Goldberg. The intense superstar doesn't care about them, marching out from his locker room to chase off Randy. Eventually, he catches the "Legend Killer" with a stiff clothesline. While Orton turns the tide with a dropkick and clothesline out to the floor, Hunter says he can count on Randy to help him retain the World Title this Sunday. Tonight, the "Legend Killer" whips Bill hard into the ring steps for a two-count. Moments later, he slows the pace with a chin lock. Goldberg powers out with a judo toss. A kick to the midsection and press slam follows. Catching a second wind, the intense superstar press slams Orton. He tries to follow up, but Randy pokes his eyes. Blinded, Bill shoves the "Legend Killer" into the referee. When he makes the cover, Austin makes the count for him. He only gets to two before Orton kicks out. Goldberg follows up with a leg lock, but that sends Ric down the aisle to pull the "rattlesnake" out to the floor. That's provocation for "Stone Cold" and he attacks "The Nature Boy". When Randy tries to stop him, Austin hits him too. The intense superstar capitalizes with a Spear to Orton before Steve gives Flair a Stone Cold Stunner. Goldberg then scores the victory with a Jackhammer, "Stone Cold" making the three-count. Post-match, Helmsley glares at Bill from the top of the stage. While Goldberg threatens him, Kevin Nash slips into the ring to pay back the intense superstar with a Jackknife. "The Game" loves it. He doesn't love Shawn Michaels giving him Sweet Chin Music. Finally, Chris Jericho hits Shawn with a chair and grabs the World Title. He tells Nash that he's bald and this Sunday Y2J will be the champion.

SmackDown!
August 21, 2003
Detroit, MI
Announcers: Michael Cole, Tazz

The show opens with a video package featuring Brock Lesnar turning on Kurt Angle and joining forces with Vince McMahon two weeks ago. Afterwards, the intro video plays. Instead of the usual fireworks, Angle's music plays and his entrance fireworks kick off the episode. Inside the ring, Kurt tells Lesnar that he warned him he was going to take the WWE Title at Vengeance and that's what he did. The Olympian thought Brock could appreciate that the belt meant everything to him, but apparently he's not the man Angle thought he was. Kurt isn't going to cry about it or make a deal with Vince. Instead, he's going to kick Lesnar's butt at SummerSlam. However, he doesn't want to wait until this Sunday. He wants to fight him tonight. Or he wants Mr. McMahon. In fact, he'll take them both on at the same time. That brings out the WWE owner to tell everyone that he doesn't care what the Olympian wants or even what the fans want. Vince only cares what he wants. And what he wants is not to fight Angle tonight. He's also not going to sign Lesnar to a match with Kurt tonight. The Olympian can't stand it and curses the WWE owner, nearly drawing him into the ring. Before he locks up with the WWE Champion, Vince stops himself and says that he's not playing by Angle's rules. Instead, Kurt is playing by McMahon's rules and if the Olympian touches Vince or Brock tonight he will be immediately suspended and forfeit his SummerSlam match. However, he's going to give him a match after all tonight…against Big Show. Angle calls the WWE owner "stupid". He doesn't want a match. He wants a fight and he's going to have one right now, rushing up the aisle to punch the giant and give him a low blow. Once Show is down, Kurt hits him with the championship belt before Vince gets WWE officials to pull him off the giant.

After a commercial break, Big Show is still in pain and tearing up Vince McMahon's office. The WWE owner tells him to take his frustrations out on Kurt Angle later tonight in a "Street Fight".

Rey Mysterio (with Billy Kidman) def. Matt Hardy Version 1.0 (with Shannon Moore). After Rey pops out of the stage, Matt Facts reveal that Hardy has never lost his phone and his pants are "hipper" than the masked man's. Now that the heel is over the cruiserweight weight limit, this is a non-title match. With nothing to lose, Mysterio flips over Matt and dropkicks his face. Shannon tries to get involved, but Kidman stops him. He can't stop Hardy from poking Rey's eyes, but the masked man tosses him out to the floor soon afterwards for a dive off the ropes. When he attempts a springboard attack back into the ring, Matt catches and knocks him down. Moore tries to follow up with a chair shot, but Mysterio rolls out of the way and the MFer hits the canvas instead. Billy rushes over to help and takes away the chair, but Brian Hebner catches him with the weapon and orders him backstage ahead of a commercial break.

Afterwards, Hardy whips Rey into the ring post for a two-count. When he attempts to give him snake eyes, the masked man slips free and heel kicks Matt. Unfortunately, Mysterio's shoulder is too injured and he's slow to get up, Hardy planting him with a side effect for a near fall. The heel then slows the pace with a hammerlock, the fans telling him that he sucks. When he tries to show them that he doesn't with a powerslam, Rey counters with a tornado DDT to put both men down. Eventually, the wrestlers get up and trade shots, the masked man tossing Hardy over with a hurricanrana. A springboard seated senton moments later nearly gets him the win, but Matt just kicks out. He tries to give the champion a side effect, but Mysterio fights free only to be slammed with a reverse side effect. Following a two-count, Hardy puts Rey on the top rope, but the masked man knocks him back for a moonsault and his own near fall. More fists follow before Mysterio trips Matt onto the middle rope. He does the same to Moore when he illegally enters the ring. When he tries to give the MFer a 619, Hardy saves Shannon with a clothesline. He attempts to finish off Rey with a Twist of Fate afterwards while Hebner gets Moore out of the ring, but the masked man shoves him back into the ropes where Zach Gowen hurries out to hit Hardy with his cane. Mysterio follows up with a 619 and West Coast Pop, Matt landing on his head for the three-count.

After a commercial break, Brock Lesnar enters Vince McMahon's destroyed office. Vince says Big Show is going to take his aggression out on Kurt Angle later. Since Lesnar is a high level athlete, he thinks he needs a match too. Mr. McMahon gives it to him with Zach Gowen tonight. The heel promises to snap Zach's good leg.

A video package of A-Train injuring Stephanie McMahon last week plays.

From the crowd, Zach Gowen's mother tells Cole that she's proud of her son and doesn't understand why Brock Lesnar would want to hurt him.

The Basham Brothers (with Shaniqua) def. Billy Gunn/Jamie Noble (with Nidia/Torrie Wilson). The babyfaces don't even wait for the Bashams to get in the ring, attacking them at ringside. Inside the squared circle, Billy gives Doug a tilt-a-whirl slam. When he attempts a corner splash though, Shaniqua pulls her man out of the way for Danny to illegally switch places with his brother and clothesline "Mr. Ass". The Bashams then stomp and hammer Billy ahead of a double flapjack and Danny two-count. Doug returns moments later to wail on Gunn before attempting to whip Danny into Gunn in a corner. Luckily, "Mr. Ass" moves and drops Doug with a clothesline. A cutter follows to Danny before Jamie gets the hot tag. The fresh man, he clotheslines both Bashams and back suplexes Doug. A swinging neckbreaker and top rope flying elbow drop gets the redneck a pair of near falls on Danny before he traps the heel in a front face lock. Fortunately, Doug makes the save. When Billy knocks him out to the floor, Jamie rolls up Danny, but Shaniqua pulls Noble off to break the count. Nidia and Torrie take offense, but the dominatrix double clotheslines them. Although Danny baseball slide kicks Jamie, Gunn gives him a Famouser. Doug answers with a shot to the back of "Mr. Ass's" head with the cat of nine tails for the brothers to steal the victory.

Backstage, Brock Lesnar warns Zach Gowen that after their match he won't have a leg to stand on. We then see a video package of Brock destroying Spanky last week.

Zach Gowen def. Brock Lesnar by disqualification. Zach is out second to give his mom a kiss and put his prosthetic leg in a corner. Once he's in the ring, Brock hops out to the floor to glare at Mrs. Gowen. He offers to shake her hand, but she won't. When he turns around, Zach dives over the top rope onto him. Unfortunately, one knee doubles over the rookie. Instead of following up, Lesnar taunts Zach's mom. Gowen stops him with a shot from his prosthetic. Once again, the heel easily repels his attack and shoves Zach into the ring. With the rookie's mom watching anxiously, Brock gives him back-to-back powerbombs. Instead of making the cover, Lesnar tosses Gowen back out to the floor and grabs a chair. Right in front of Zach's mom, the heel smashes him with a steel chair for the disqualification. He then repeatedly headbutts Gowen's bloody skull. Still not done, he hoists up Zach and F5s his leg against the ring post. With Mrs. Gowen screaming, Brock smashes the rookie's leg with a chair before giving him a second F5 against the steel post. Finally, Zach's mom hops over the guardrail and checks on her son, the rookie wearing a crimson mask for his first singles victory in the WWE. Cole hopes Lesnar gets broken bones this Sunday while trainers stretcher Gowen backstage. Brock doesn't let him go peacefully, tossing the rookie off the stretcher and carrying it back into the ring where he shows off all the blood on it. Cole wonders what sickness is controlling Lesnar. Even Tazz is disgusted by him.

A-Train/John Cena def. Orlando Jordan/The Undertaker. Cena is out first in a somber mood. He's just pretending to care about Zach Gowen before making fun of him and Detroit. Once everyone is out, The Undertaker slams John to the mat and hammers his ribs. The rapping heel answers with a kick to the gut and low bridge when the biker charges him. Unfortunately for Cena, the "Deadman" surprises him with a throat drop on the top rope followed by Old School for a two-count before A-Train makes the save. When Orlando tags in, John back body drops him. Jordan impresses by landing on his feet for a roll-up and two-count. The hairy heel then tags in and suckers the rookie when he says he wants The Undertaker. When Orlando turns his back, A-Train clubs him, but misses a corner charge. The rookie answers with a DDT before tagging in the biker to give Cena snake eyes. He then hammers both heels and teases a chokeslam to John. When the hairy heel tries to make the save, the "Deadman" big boots him. He follows up with Taking Care of Business to the rapping heel. A-Train tries to make the save with a steel chair, but Jordan nails him with a flying forearm. The hairy heel answers with a Derailer before turning into an Undertaker chokeslam. Cena capitalizes with a spinebuster for a near fall. Afterwards, he grabs a chair, but the biker beats him to the punch with a shot to the midsection. He attempts to finish off John with a Last Ride afterwards, but A-Train smashes the rapping heel's chain into the "Deadman's" ribs for Cena to steal the win.

After a commercial break, Sable stops A-Train backstage. She calls him impressive and rubs her hands on his hairy chest. Sable tells the hairy heel that Vince McMahon wants her to personally thank him for taking care of Stephanie McMahon last week and gives him a hotel room key.

Eddie Guerrero/Rhyno def. Chris Benoit/Tajiri. The heels are out first in Eddie's lowrider. Tazz says he rented one just like it last week. When Benoit comes out, he wants to shake "Latino Heat's" hand. Guerrero tries to kick him instead, but his foot gets caught for a dragon screw. Eddie answers with chops, but a back body drop and press slam put the US Champion right back down. Changing tactics, he hides behind Brian Hebner to cheap shot one of his three opponents this Sunday for the title. He then tags in one of his other opponents this Sunday for Rhyno to hammer down the "rabid wolverine" and score a two-count with a diving headbutt. After Tajiri makes the save, Benoit traps the man-beast in a Crippler Crossface. Fortunately, Guerrero makes the save with a dropkick to the face. Eddie follows up with a cross body stretch and neck vice. Although "the Crippler" elbows free, "Latino Heat" gives him a trio of suplexes before heading upstairs. Benoit is right back up to meet him for a superplex. Both men tag out afterwards for Tajiri to kick and elbow Rhyno. He follows up with a head scissors to Guerrero before trapping the man-beast in a Tarantula. The "rabid wolverine" follows up with a top rope diving headbutt to Eddie, but when he holds Rhyno for a Buzzsaw Kick, the man-beast ducks and Tajiri hits his own partner. Rhyno capitalizes with a Gore to the "Japanese Buzzsaw" for the three-count. Post-match, Benoit traps the man-beast in a Crippler Crossface. "Latino Heat" seizes the opportunity to blast "the Crippler" with the US Title. When Rhyno gets up and celebrates his win with Guerrero, Eddie hits him too. The fans chant for "Latino Heat" as he starts to leave only to think better of it and blast Tajiri too.

Kurt Angle def. Big Show ("Street Fight"). Kurt is out first and he waits to sneak attack Show as soon as he steps through the curtain. Unfortunately, the giant weathers his attack and flings the Olympian back into the ring post. Big Show then shoves a table into the squared circle, Cole reminding everyone that anything goes here. Inside the ring, the Olympian lands a few fists, but one big punch drops him. Show follows up with a slam onto the table laying on the canvas. The giant then scores a two-count with a leg drop before chopping Angle hard twice in a corner. Once the champion is dazed, Big Show props up the table on him, but Kurt shoves it back into his face at the last second. An Angle Slam follows for a near fall. Back on his feet, the Olympian hammers his opponent until Show boots him out to the floor. While he sets up the table, Angle grabs a chair and smashes the giant's back. When he attempts a second shot, Big Show punches the chair back into his face. He then tries to powerbomb the champion through the table, but Kurt grabs the chair and smashes his face for another near fall. A third shot from the chair sends Show tumbling out to the floor, but he doesn't stay down for long. Instead, he headbutts and slams the Olympian onto the barricade. Afterwards, he sets up the steps in front of the announce table. Before he can use them, Angle applies a testicular claw. Although it hurts, the giant punches his way free and teases a Chokeslam off the steps. Instead, the champion fights free and rams Big Show into the ring post. He attempts a fourth chair shot, but Show catches him and teases a Chokeslam. Unfortunately, Kurt rolls free and traps the giant in an Anklelock. It takes him a few seconds, but Big Show manages to kick free of the hold. The Olympian remains on the offensive, ramming his opponent face-first onto the announce table. He then grabs a chair and puts it under him for a leg drop onto the announce table for a close two-count. After he shoves Show back into the squared circle, the champion pulls the table to the center of the ring for an Angle Slam and the victory. Post-match, Brock Lesnar steps onto the stage to stare down Angle and motion for the belt three days before their SummerSlam title match.

PPV: SummerSlam

August 24, 2003
Phoenix, AZ
Announcers: Jim Ross, Jerry "the King" Lawler, Michael Cole, Tazz

The show starts with the United States Marine Color Guard standing at attention on the stage while Lilian Garcia sings the national anthem. Afterwards a video package featuring the top storylines plays with an Irish voiceover talking about the bells tolling for the competitors. Finally, fireworks explode to kick off the PPV.

La Resistance def. The Dudley Boyz (World Tag Title match). The Dudleys are out first waving Old Glory for a big pop. Following video of what started this feud, the champions step through the curtain waving the French flag. The challengers meet them in the aisle, hammering both men in and out of the ring. D-Von nearly gets disqualified when he chokes Dupree with his own jacket. Eventually, the heel forces Dudley back into La Resistance's corner for both champions to pummel him. D-Von answers with his own strikes and a leg drop to Sylvan for a two-count. Afterwards, Bubba Ray tags in to chop and tie Grenier to the tree of woe. Once he's upside down, Bubba stands on his crotch. Rene illegally enters the ring afterwards, but the Dudleys chase him and his partner off for another solid pop. When they return, Sylvan cheap shots Bubba Ray for Dupree to score a one-count with a suplex. He follows up with chokes and a double shoulderblock alongside Grenier. That gets Sylvan a two-count. Back in, Rene punches and traps Bubba in a bearhug. Although Dudley escapes and decks Grenier, a spinebuster puts him down for a two-count before D-Von makes the save. Moments later, Bubba Ray plants Sylvan with a Bubba Bomb. D-Von tags in afterwards to fight both champions, chasing Grenier off with a neckbreaker before scoring a near fall with a powerslam to Dupree. A leaping clothesline follows, but when he tries to attack Sylvan on the apron, the heel grabs him. Unfortunately, D-Von ducks Rene's clothesline and he hits his own partner. Luckily, Grenier recovers in time to break up Dudley's cover. La Resistance follow up with their Double Slam, but D-Von somehow kicks out. Bubba returns afterwards to clothesline both heels at the same time and elbow Dupree. A wassup drop follows to Sylvan. The challengers then give Rene a 3D, but Grenier just interrupts Nick Patrick's count, grabbing his foot. While the referee and Bubba Ray chase after Sylvan, a cameraman blasts D-Von with a camera for Dupree to steal the win. Post-match, the cameraman hits Bubba with the camera too. That brings Spike Dudley out only to get hit with a camera as well before the cameraman removes his hat to reveal that it was Rob Conway all along. Post-match, Jonathan Coachman stops the Dudleys and says they have to admit that La Resistance were clever. Bubba Ray calls him a French sympathizer and promises to do whatever it takes to get back the World Tag Titles.

Backstage, Christian introduces himself to Eric Bischoff. The co-general manager knows who he is, surprising the Intercontinental Champion. He thought if Eric knew who he was he'd make sure he had a match tonight. The GM tells him that it's "Stone Cold" Steve Austin's fault that Christian isn't on the show. The heel thought that was the case. Before he leaves Bischoff alone, Christian wants to know what happened between Eric and Linda McMahon Monday night. The GM promises to tell everyone later.

The Undertaker def. A-Train (with Sable). Following footage of A-Train targeting The Undertaker's ribs in recent weeks, the biker rides out to ringside. The announcers are then surprised by Sable accompanying A-Train to the ring. The "Deadman" is surprised by the hairy heel's hammering attack until The

Undertaker counters a back body drop with a leaping DDT for a two-count. Shots and a leaping clothesline follow before the biker heads upstairs for Old School. When he attempts a charge near the ropes, A-Train low bridges him. Outside the ring, the hairy heel drives the "Deadman's" injured ribs into the ring post for a two-count. Kicks and forearms to the ribs follow, A-Train wisely targeting his opponent's injury. Afterwards, a vertical suplex nearly gets the hairy heel his biggest win. When A-Train headbutts and punches The Undertaker, he wakes up the biker. Unfortunately, the hairy heel has plenty of fight in him and counters a sleeper hold with a side suplex. Despite that fall, the "Deadman" unloads with a flurry of fists ahead of snake eyes. Both men then connect with clotheslines at the same time to put them down for a Brian Hebner five-count. Although A-Train is up first, The Undertaker beats him to the punch. A big boot and leg drop follow for a two-count. When a leg drop in the center of the ring doesn't get him the win, the biker hits one on the apron as well. Corner crushes and clotheslines follow before the "Deadman" sets up for a Last Ride. When he tries to lift the hairy heel, A-Train shoves The Undertaker back into the referee ahead of a Derailer. Hebner is a little groggy and only counts to two when he spots the cover. Afterwards, the biker accidentally hits the referee again, putting him down while A-Train lays out the "Deadman" with a bicycle kick. He tries to follow up with a chair shot, but The Undertaker kicks the weapon back into his face. Once again, Hebner is slow to make the count and only gets to two before the hairy heel kicks out. Afterwards, the biker picks up A-Train for a Tombstone, but the hairy heel slips free. Unfortunately, he misses a clothesline and is chokeslammed to the mat for the three-count. Post-match, the "Deadman" pulls A-Train back into position for a Last Ride, but Sable stops him, rubbing The Undertaker's chest. He isn't seduced and clutches the diva by the throat, holding her in place for Stephanie McMahon to hurry out and tackle her rival. After she gets in a few shots, A-Train drags Sable out to the floor, the heels retreating while Stephanie applauds the "Deadman".

Afterwards, Jonathan Coachman asks fans in the crowd who they think will win the "Elimination Chamber" World Title match.

Shane McMahon def. Eric Bischoff ("Falls Count Anywhere" match). Following a video package for the match, Eric heads to the ring to kiss and tell. Before he does so, he wonders why Vince McMahon is running around "eating hamburger when (he has) filet mignon at home". Bischoff says it's not a matter of what happened, but how much before complimenting Shane's genes. That brings the younger McMahon out to punch and kick the black belt. A fight instead of a wrestling match, Shane takes the battle out to the floor to clothesline and kick the GM. He wisely rolls into the ring to break Charles Robinson's count before returning multiple times to ringside to toss around and wail on Bischoff. Following his shuffle dance, Shane decks Eric and slams his face on the *SmackDown!* announce table. Out of nowhere, Jonathan Coachman makes the save with a chair shot to the back. The announcers can't believe it. While the referee wants to call for the bell, Bischoff stops him. He makes this a "Falls Count Anywhere" match and tells Coach to whip McMahon into the ring steps. That gets the GM a near fall. After admitting that Shane is a tough rich kid, Eric orders the production crew to turn off JR and Lawler's mics so Coachman can call the action. He proceeds to mock McMahon and Ross, stealing the latter's catchphrases as he holds Shane for a series of Bischoff kicks. Eventually, McMahon fights back, knocking down Coach and planting Eric with a DDT. When Coachman saves his boss with a low blow, "Stone Cold" Steve Austin marches down the aisle. Coach tells him that he doesn't work for the "rattlesnake" and only listens to Bischoff. He also knows that Steve can't touch him unless Coachman physically provokes him and he's not going to do that. Unfortunately, Shane shoves him into the co-GM and Austin is free to punch and stomp the newly turned heel. McMahon also gets in a few shots before "Stone Cold" dumps Coach on the floor and gets the announcers' microphones turned back on. Austin tries to leave, but Shane picks up Eric and forces him to slap the "rattlesnake". That's enough provocation for Steve and he gives his co-GM a Stone Cold Stunner. That should be enough for

McMahon to score the victory, but he takes Bischoff out to the floor and puts him on the Spanish announce table. Afterwards, he finally scores the win with a flying elbow drop off the top rope. Post-match, "Stone Cold" drinks beer with the winner.

Backstage, Ric Flair explains to Randy Orton that his only job tonight is to make sure Triple H leaves the "Elimination Chamber" match with the World Title. Randy understands that, but starts to ask, "what if". "The Nature Boy" tells him there are no "what ifs". Hunter enters to say the same thing. When Helmsley walks away, Ric reminds Orton about the task at hand. Randy gets it.

Eddie Guerrero def. Chris Benoit and Rhyno and Tajiri (US Title match). The champion is out last in a green and purple lowrider to a nice pop. He wants nothing to do with the competitors though, watching from ringside as Benoit tosses Tajiri out to the floor and Rhyno hammers "the Crippler". When Benoit traps the man-beast in an early Crippler Crossface, Eddie finally enters the ring for the save. He rolls right back out to watch as Tajiri kicks Rhyno and covers the "rabid wolverine". Once again, "Latino Heat" makes the save. He does so a third time when the man-beast clotheslines the "Japanese Buzzsaw". This time, Benoit catches him and all three challengers hammer Guerrero. When Tajiri tries to cover him, the alliance fades and Rhyno fights with "the Crippler". When the man-beast gets the upper hand, he spears Eddie in a corner ahead of a powerslam. Benoit makes the save and scores a two-count with a snap suplex to the man-beast. When the "Japanese Buzzsaw" makes the save, the "rabid wolverine" back suplexes him for a near fall. "Latino Heat" again makes the save, the fans chanting his name as he suplexes Benoit out to the floor. That leaves him alone with Tajiri for the "Japanese Buzzsaw" to deliver a monkey flip and tilt-a-whirl backbreaker. Fortunately, Rhyno breaks Mike Sparks' count and slams the "rabid wolverine" back into a corner. Moments later, he superplexes Guerrero from the second rope, but Tajiri breaks his cover. Following some kicks to the man-beast's ribs, the "Japanese Buzzsaw" gets a near fall. Benoit tries to ambush Tajiri, but receives a handspring back elbow instead. Afterwards, Rhyno back suplexes "Latino Heat" for a two-count. Eddie answers with a head scissors to toss the man-beast out to the floor. He can only watch as Guerrero head scissors "the Crippler" off the top rope for another near fall. All four men trade shots afterwards before Eddie traps the "Japanese Buzzsaw" in the Lasso from El Paso. Benoit traps Rhyno in the Crippler Crossface right beside him. When Tajiri reaches the ropes for the break, "Latino Heat" attacks the "rabid wolverine" only to be trapped in his own Crippler Crossface. This time, the man-beast and "Japanese Buzzsaw" break the submission hold before Rhyno tries to powerbomb Tajiri. Although the "Japanese Buzzsaw" flips free he can't follow up and runs into a spinebuster for a close two-count. After the other challengers chase the man-beast out to the floor, Benoit and Tajiri trade German suplexes. The "Japanese Buzzsaw" nearly gets the win with a bridging German suplex before locking "the Crippler" in a Tarantula. While the referee is distracted, Eddie grabs the US Title. It saves him when Rhyno Gores him, but hits the title belt. "Latino Heat" tries to follow up with a Frog Splash, but Tajiri kicks him down to the floor. Benoit then knocks the "Japanese Buzzsaw" down into the tree of woe before giving the man-beast a top rope diving headbutt. At the last second, Tajiri makes the save. While he head scissors himself and "the Crippler" out to the floor, Guerrero gets the win with a Frog Splash onto Rhyno.

Footage of Brock Lesnar injuring Zach Gowen Thursday night plays. We then see footage of Matt Hardy Version 1.0 mocking Zach and taking a forfeit victory earlier tonight over him on *Heat*. Afterwards, a video package plays for the upcoming WWE Title match.

Kurt Angle def. Brock Lesnar (WWE Title match). Mike Chioda tries to get the former friends to shake hands before the bell, but neither does. Once the match starts, Brock drives the champion back into a corner. Kurt answers with a takedown, showing off his amateur skills. He follows up with a headlock takedown, but the challenger has his own amateur skills and quickly escapes. Lesnar then shows off his power, flinging the Olympian down to the canvas twice. Angle gets under his opponent's skin, shoving him back into a corner before chasing him out to the floor with a trio of arm drags. That frustrates Brock and he threatens to toss the ring steps into the squared circle. Instead, he flings them aside, threatens Tony Chimel, and walks away with the WWE Title. The champion follows after him, brawling with the heel in the aisle. Shots to the knee and a head slam on the barricade follow before Kurt takes the fight back to the ring for a belly-to-belly suplex and two-count. Lesnar answers with a press slam over the top rope to the floor. The challenger doesn't give the Olympian time to recover, whipping him into the ring post before taking the fight back to the squared circle. There, he stomps and tosses Angle overhead with a belly-to-belly suplex for a two-count. The champion refuses to stay down, surprising Brock with a roll-up for a two-count. The challenger responds with a tilt-a-whirl backbreaker for another near fall. Changing tactics, Lesnar hooks Kurt in a body scissors and chin lock. Although the Olympian fights free, one knee to the gut slows him for a backbreaker. The heel follows up with stomps and chokes in a corner until Angle punches and cradles him for a near fall. Right back up, Brock clotheslines the champion ahead of a cradle suplex and his own close two-count. Keeping up the pressure, he shoulder blocks Kurt in a corner and clubs him down. More shoulders to the ribs follow until the challenger misses a corner charge and hits his shoulder on the ring post. That gives the Olympian a target and he attacks the shoulder repeatedly. Picking up the pace, Angle hits a flying forearm ahead of a trio of rolling German suplexes for a near fall. Lesnar answers with an overhead belly-to-belly suplex. When the champion tries to respond with an Angle Slam, the heel counters with a spinebuster for a two-count. He then hoists Kurt up for an F5, but the Olympian counters with a tornado DDT for another near fall. Dropping his straps, Angle stalks the challenger and finally delivers an Angle Slam. At the last moment, Lesnar just kicks out. The champion puts his straps back up before immediately lowering them again to apply an Anklelock. Cole wants him to break the heel's ankle for Zach Gowen. Instead, Brock kicks Kurt into the referee. When he tries to pick up the Olympian, Angle surprises him with a reverse bearhug. He then reapplies the Anklelock. The challenger crawls to the ropes for the break, but there's no referee to make the champion break his hold. Eventually, Lesnar taps out, but Chioda is still down. That means he also misses Vince McMahon running out to hit Kurt with a steel chair to break the hold. While the fans insult Vince, he cheers on Brock giving the Olympian an F5. At the last second, Angle just kicks out of the referee's groggy count. Both the challenger and McMahon are frustrated. When Lesnar attempts a second F5, the champion flips free and reapplies his Anklelock. Although the heel reaches the ropes multiple times, Kurt keeps pulling him back to the center of the ring until he taps out. Post-match, Vince tries to hit the Olympian with a chair again, but Angle sees him coming this time and answers with a series of kicks and an Angle Slam on the chair sitting on the canvas. Tazz says someone needs to help McMahon, but Cole asks, "who cares".

Ahead of the next match we see members of the Arizona Diamondbacks in the crowd. Jamie Koeppe is also in the crowd, the winner of the first "Diva Search". Other than a photoshoot, she won't do anything with the WWE.

Kane def. Rob Van Dam ("No Holds Barred" match). Following a video for this feud, Howard Finkle announces that this is now a "No Holds Barred" match. The announcers believe that favors Kane. He looks strong early on, clotheslining and slamming RVD out to the floor. There, Rob catches him with a boot and moonsault off the barricade. He can't keep the "Big Red Machine" down though. After tossing Van Dam's face into the ring post, the monster tries to bring a ladder into the squared circle. Before he does, RVD drives it into his face. He follows up with a kick, but Kane catches him by the throat when he goes for rolling thunder. Despite that, Rob kicks the "Big Red Machine" back into the ropes and drives him back to the floor with a flying cross body block. There, the monster regains control, whipping Van

Dam into the ring steps. He then moves those steps, but doesn't use them. Instead, he takes the fight back to the ring where RVD stuns him with a kick to the head. A springboard kick and leg drop afterwards gets the popular superstar a one-count. When he hops back onto the top rope, Kane shoves him off and out to the floor. There, the "Big Red Machine" nearly knocks his head off with a ladder shot. That gets him a two-count back in the squared circle. Afterwards, the monster clubs and chokes his opponent. Chad Patton tries to count for the choke, but there are no disqualifications here. After threatening the referee, Kane clotheslines and stomps Rob. While he continues his assault, JR ignores the match and jokes that Vince McMahon is having a rough birthday. Eventually, Van Dam slows the "Big Red Machine" with a kick, but is driven back out to the floor where the monster attempts to finish him off with a top rope flying clothesline. At the last second, RVD dodges. It's only a temporary reprieve as Kane surprises Rob with a DDT on the floor moments later. He tries to use the ring steps afterwards, but Van Dam counters with a drop toe hold. After the "Big Red Machine's" head bounces off the steps, RVD dropkicks him into the crowd. The monster answers with a thumb to the eye, but when he tries to climb back over the railing, Rob kicks him and Kane straddles the barricade. Van Dam follows up with his twisting leg drop off the apron before grabbing a chair. Instead of using it, he levels the "Big Red Machine" with a spinning heel kick back in the ring. Afterwards, he covers the monster with the chair and hits it with rolling thunder. Somehow, Kane sits up. He doesn't after RVD dropkicks the chair into his face. He then heads upstairs for a coast-to-coast corner dropkick. JR says he hit, but the "Big Red Machine" moves and rolls out to the floor to escape. While Lawler clarifies that Rob missed, the monster drags a stunned Van Dam out to the floor for a Tombstone on the base of the steps for the win.

Backstage, Terri asks a bloodied Eric Bischoff how he feels as trainers check on him. He calls her stupid and kicks the interviewer out of the room. When she leaves, Linda McMahon enters. Eric stutters when he sees her. She doesn't have any words for him…just a stiff slap.

Further backstage, Triple H stares at the World Title. Ric Flair tells him that he's not saying goodbye to the belt. He's just letting someone else hold it for a short time because Hunter is the best in the world and will retain tonight. Afterwards, a video package plays for the "Elimination Chamber" match.

Triple H (with Ric Flair) def. Chris Jericho and Goldberg and Kevin Nash and Randy Orton and Shawn Michaels ("Elimination Chamber" World Title match).

Entry	Wrestler	Elimination Order	Wrestler	Eliminated By
1	Shawn Michaels	1	Kevin Nash	Chris Jericho
2	Chris Jericho	2	Randy Orton	Goldberg
3	Randy Orton	3	Shawn Michaels	Goldberg
4	Kevin Nash	4	Chris Jericho	Goldberg
5	Triple H	5	Goldberg	Triple H
6	Goldberg	6	Triple H	Winner

After Howard Finkel goes over the rules, Randy Orton heads to the squared circle. That means he'll get to sit in one of the pods while the first two competitors wrestle. Kevin Nash will too, walking out with a new short haircut. Despite losing a "Hair versus Hair" match, Nash just got a nice haircut instead of being shaved bald. Triple H follows, sporting long black shorts to help with his groin injury. Ric Flair accompanies him, but can't help in this match. Goldberg is next, walking out from his locker room to a big chant. The announcers predict that he'll leave tonight with the World Title. Chris Jericho and Shawn Michaels draw the short straws here, continuing their rivalry to open the match. Shawn starts fast with a back elbow and springboard cross body block, but Y2J rolls through for a two-count. The fans don't care about them, chanting for Goldberg as they trade two-counts. Jericho gets frustrated at one point and slaps Michaels. "The Heartbreak Kid" responds in kind ahead of a back body drop. Y2J tries to answer with the Walls of Jericho, but Shawn rolls him up for a near fall. Right back up, Jericho surprises the babyface with a running face slam. Although Michaels dodges a Lionsault, the heel lands on his feet and clotheslines the "Heartbreak Kid". Afterwards, Orton's number is called and he bursts free from his pod to nearly eliminate Shawn with a top rope flying cross body block. A dropkick chases Michaels out to the steel at ringside before Jericho attacks the "Legend Killer". Randy answers with his backbreaker for a two-count. Back in, the "Heartbreak Kid" punches both heels, but lowers his head too soon for a back body drop and is rocked with an enziguri kick from Y2J. After that gets him a two-count, Orton dropkicks his fellow heel. They continue fighting on the steel at ringside courtesy of a Jericho back body drop over the top rope. While Shawn catches his breath, Y2J slams Randy on the steel. He then returns to the ring to catch Michaels's dropkick and lock on the Walls of Jericho. Before the "Heartbreak Kid" can submit, Nash's number is drawn and he steps out of his pod to hammer both heels. He focuses on Jericho, repeatedly slamming his head into the cage. While he rakes the Canadian heel's face across the steel, the "Legend Killer" pummels Shawn. Kevin makes the save with a sidewalk slam and two-count. Afterwards, he helps Michaels up only to clothesline him for a near fall. A big forearm shot follows before Nash turns his attention back to Jericho. When he pulls the bloodied superstar in for a Jackknife, the "Heartbreak Kid" drops his friend with Sweet Chin Music for Y2J to roll Kevin up for the first elimination. Afterwards, it's time for Triple H to enter the ring, but Shawn rocks him with Sweet Chin Music, laying out the champion before he can even leave his cell. He's lucky because Nash goes on a rampage, giving Orton and Jericho Jackknifes. He also rams Randy's head into Michaels's before finally leaving the chamber and the WWE for several years. Also bleeding now, the "Heartbreak Kid" crawls back into the squared circle to cover Orton and Jericho, but he only gets a pair of two-counts. Soon after, all three men trade fists until the countdown starts again to introduce Goldberg. For some reason, the WWE gives away the entrance order in this match with all four men in pods exiting them in the same order they entered. Regardless, the fans cheer loudly as Bill hits all three standing superstars. Showing off his strength, he presses Randy up into the air and drops him with a powerslam. A double clothesline follows to Shawn and Y2J before the intense superstar Spears the "Legend Killer" for a three-count. Jericho immediately capitalizes with a top rope missile dropkick, but Bill kicks out of his cover and press slams the heel into the chamber wall. When Michaels attempts an ambush, Goldberg drives him hard into a corner before leaving the ring to Spear Y2J through the plexiglass of a pod. That leaves only the "Heartbreak Kid" standing and he stuns the intense superstar with a top rope flying elbow drop. He tries to follow up with Sweet Chin Music, but Bill ducks and Spears him as well. A Jackhammer follows for Goldberg's second elimination, Hunter just starting to come to his senses. He can only watch as the intense superstar Spears and Jackhammers Jericho for another elimination. That leaves just two men in the match. That doesn't mean Flair can't help his man and he pulls the plexiglass back in front of Helmsley and flips off Bill. Goldberg doesn't care, kicking through the door to wail on "the Game". For some reason, Earl Hebner wants him to stop. The intense superstar doesn't listen, hammering and raking the champion's bloodied forehead across the chamber. He follows up with a clothesline on the steel before taking the fight back into the ring, the fans still loudly cheering for the challenger. When he tries to Spear Triple H, Hunter surprises Bill with a sledgehammer shot—courtesy of "The Nature Boy" sliding it into the ring—to steal the victory. Post-match, Orton returns to the ring to help Ric hold Goldberg for a series of sledgehammer shots from "the Game". The heels continue their assault on the bloodied superstar, handcuffing him to the chamber. No one comes to his aid as Hemsley smashes him with the sledgehammer one more time and tells Bill that he'll never get the World Title.

The sixteenth SummerSlam is a good show with solid matches, but no title changes or major moments. Not every PPV needs a standout moment or title change, but it's arguable that the major PPVs do. Thankfully, SummerSlam 2003 is entertaining in its own right. The opening tag match is decent. La Resistance work as a heel act cheating to win and they do that here. The match doesn't stand out from other recent *Raw* contests, but it's not bad. The Undertaker and A-Train then have a nice big man brawl. The biker is really working hard at this point and he's having some good matches. The hairy heel doesn't get a lot of credit, but he knows what he is and holds up his end of the match. Again, it's not much different than a weekly match, but it keeps both men in the spotlight. Shane and Bischoff don't have a good match, but Coachman turning heel is at least interesting and leads to "Stone Cold" getting involved for a nice pop. McMahon has had far better matches than this one, but Eric isn't the type of competitor Shane has faced in the past. With outside interference and one of the most popular superstars of all-time getting involved though, this match manages to entertain. The US Title match does that and more. While a little chaotic, all four men hit their signature moves and get to showcase why they are part of a solid *SmackDown!* roster. Despite being a heel, the fans love Eddie's cheating and he manages to continue to draw pops for innovative moments. The action is good, but it would be nice to have a little more than eleven minutes considering the talent level. Kurt and Brock get plenty of time at just over twenty-one minutes. The longest match of the show, it's a fun WrestleMania XIX rematch. A little slow to start, the wrestlers build to a nice finish. Their WrestleMania clash is better, but this is definitely a great contest and well worth seeing. The slow opening and Vince's interfering just keeps it from **MUST SEE!** status. Kane and RVD follow up with a nice brawl. This is definitely better than a *Raw* match and a nice ending to their rivalry. While it remains to be seen what the storyline does for Van Dam, it definitely makes the "Big Red Machine" a top-level monster again. *Raw* really needs high-level heels as Jericho and Triple H have been carrying that banner for a while now. Finally, the main event is entertaining, but hampered by Helmsley's injury. Hunter's injured groin largely keeps him on the sidelines for the "Elimination Chamber" match. Shawn and Y2J handle the heavy lifting with some good wrestling to start the contest. They then make Orton look like a million bucks before Nash enters and shows that he's at his best when he's tiptoeing the line between babyface and heel. Goldberg is easily the biggest star of the match, the fans loudly cheering for him as he destroys three men before Triple H cheats to retain the title. Bill has said that Goldust putting a wig on his head early in his run killed his character, but that's nowhere close to the truth. The fans are absolutely on Goldberg's side here and have been for the last few months. The real question is whether the WWE should have put the championship on him here tonight. The fans certainly wanted to see it and would have elevated SummerSlam 2003 to a much more prominent place in wrestling history. As it is, this is a very fun show with a lot of good-to-great matches. There's nothing that you absolutely have to see to understand where the WWE is going, but SummerSlam 2003 is a solid three hours of entertainment.

Monday Night Raw
August 25, 2003
Tucson, AZ
Announcers: Jim Ross, Jerry "the King" Lawler, Jonathan Coachman (briefly)

Ahead of the intro video and fireworks, a video package plays showing a bloodied Goldberg limping out of the Elimination Chamber. Afterwards, the intense superstar heads to the squared circle. Despite being injured, Bill says the World Title is his and he wants Triple H tonight. That brings out Evolution to the stage. JR jokes that everyone is there except the sledgehammer. Hunter removes his shirt and says that he is better than Goldberg in every way. He claims that he proved it last night by beating all five top contenders. The intense superstar warns Helmsley that he's going to come after him every night at the arenas, "the Game's" home, and even in his dreams until the champion gives him a World Title shot. Bill says that he'll beat him to death when they meet again. Triple H wants to know what makes Goldberg think he's any different than Rob Van Dam, Kane, Kevin Nash, or anyone else who came along before him. Fired up, Hunter vows to prove that he's the better man at Unforgiven. However, Helmsley wants Bill to put his career on the line and not in some cheap way where he goes to a "second rate show like *SmackDown!*" and "runs through their paper champion". The intense superstar isn't afraid and accepts.

Trish Stratus def. Gail Kim. Trish is out first, but Gail is waiting to ambush her at ringside before the match. When they get in the squared circle, Kim drives the vixen's face into the canvas for a near fall. She then hooks a tight chin lock. It's so tight that she retains it even when Stratus tries to escape with a side suplex. Although Trish eventually escapes with a snap mare, Gail is right back to the hold, transitioning into a modified dragon sleeper. This time, the vixen flips free and drives the heel to the mat. Catching a second wind, Stratus surprises Kim with a spinebuster for a near fall. Chops and a Chick Kick follow for another close two-count. Gail then attacks Trish's eyes, but walks into Stratusfaction out of nowhere for the vixen victory. Post-match, Molly attacks the winner from behind and rams her face into the railing. She then heads to the ring to glare at a nervous Kim.

Eric Bischoff talking last night about sleeping with Linda McMahon replays. The announcers reveal that Linda will be the guest tonight on the Highlight Reel.

After a commercial break, Molly Holly chokes Gail Kim backstage. Holly says that she brought Kim to the WWE to help her eliminate Trish Stratus and they need to get on the same page or Kim can leave. Gail agrees to work with the Women's Champion.

Mark Henry/Rodney Mack (with Theodore Long) def. Garrison Cade/Mark Jindrak. Pre-match, Long says he's expanding his group and he's got the perfect man for the job…Henry. After the "World's Strongest Man" lumbers down the aisle, stunning the announcers, Theodore asks for a couple of white boys to offer up a challenge. Mack greets Cade with some quick fists, but a dropkick offers the rookie a brief respite. Rodney responds with a stiff clothesline and hammering blows while Jerry tries to explain to JR what a player is. Once Garrison escapes a chin lock with a side suplex, Jindrak tags in to dropkick and inverted atomic drop Mack. He follows up with a springboard top rope cross body block, drawing Mark into the ring to stomp Jindrak and toss Cade out to the floor. Afterwards, he catches a second Jindrak springboard cross body block and Front Slams him to the canvas for the win despite being the illegal man.

Backstage, Lance Storm accuses Goldust of setting him up last week. The "bizarre one" says he should be happy because it led to Storm forming a "healthy relationship", but Lance isn't happy to have "Mini-Dust" humping his leg. Rosey interrupts to ask about a commotion in the ring. Storm is dealing with his own stuff and doesn't have time. When the super hero in training asks a member of the crew if she knows anything, she says there is a man in the ring with a gun. Rosey runs off to stop him, but when The Hurricane asks the crewmember about it afterwards, we learn it's actually a t-shirt gun.

During the commercial break, Rosey interrupts a worker shooting t-shirts into the crowd. After the super hero in training gives him a Spinning Slam, The Hurricane runs out to tell him about the error of his ways and ask, "what's up with that?"

Backstage, Terri asks "Stone Cold" Steve Austin about Jonathan Coachman turning heel last night. The "rattlesnake" is happy to recap what happened during the Shane McMahon/Eric Bischoff match including Coach attacking him and getting his butt kicked. Austin adds that he doesn't understand why Eric slapped him last night. It left Steve no choice but to give him a Stone Cold Stunner. Wearing sunglasses and a hat to cover up his injuries, Bischoff interrupts to argue with his co-general manager. He says "Stone Cold" wasn't provoked by anyone last night. Austin asks if he's calling the "rattlesnake" a liar. Eric doesn't want another fight so he moves on, warning Steve to stay out of his business tonight when Bischoff awards Coachman the *Raw* Employee of the Month award.

La Resistance/Rob Conway def. Spike Dudley/The Dudley Boyz. Following footage of him interfering in last night's World Tag Title match, Conway takes the microphone to call the fans ignorant and say "our country" is more concerned with policing the world than taking care of itself. Afterwards, Spike steps through the curtain to distract the heels for the Dudleys to sneak attack them. After all three Dudleys get in some shots, Bubba slams Sylvan for a Spike top rope double stomp. He can't keep Grenier down though and the heels hotshot the runt in their corner. When Rob tags in, Spike surprises him with a battering ram to the gut and Dudley Dog. Instead of making the cover, he tags in Bubba Ray to elbow and slam the champions. He also dodges a Sylvan sneak attack that hits Dupree. Things break down from there, D-Von joining the fight to 3D Rene. Spike gives Grenier a Dudley Dog afterwards before Bubba press slams the runt over the top rope onto Dupree at ringside. While Charles Robinson is distracted watching all that action, Conway blasts Bubba Ray with a title belt to steal the win.

After a commercial break, Chris Jericho is in the ring for the Highlight Reel. He starts it by mocking Goldberg before replaying footage of Eric Bischoff kissing Linda McMahon last week. Y2J believes Eric's story about what happened in Connecticut, but he offers Linda a chance to tell her side of the story. She calls Bischoff a liar who has to face the consequences of his actions. She'd love to fire him, but is sure that her husband would just rehire the co-GM just to stick it to their son. Speak of the devil, Vince McMahon heads to the squared circle. Jericho is ecstatic to have him on the Highlight Reel. Vince largely ignores him to say that Mr. McMahon is the boss and he has decided that there will be no punishment for Eric. The WWE owner says he was the one who invited Bischoff to their house. He also claims that Vince is the only victim in the WWE and that's because of his marriage to Linda and her giving him terrible kids. Linda says he needs help while Jerry wonders if this is the place for them to air their dirty laundry. Mr. McMahon tells her the only help he needs is dealing with their kids. Vince understands how Kane feels now since his kids turned on him like the fans did the "Big Red Machine". Shane McMahon interrupts to tell Vince that he and Kane are a lot alike because they are both "monsters". When he tells the WWE owner to "rot in Hell", Y2J takes up for the boss. He tells Shane not to talk to his father like that or to interrupt his show. Shane isn't worried about him, but he should be. When he gets in Vince's face, Jericho nails the younger McMahon with the microphone, cutting him ahead of a flashback. Although Mr. McMahon pulls Y2J off his son, the WWE owner tells Shane that he's going to get a chance for revenge later tonight when he wrestles Jericho.

Randy Orton (with Ric Flair) def. Maven (with Shawn Michaels). After the wrestlers feel each other out and go for dropkicks at the same time, Randy surprises the babyface with his backbreaker. He follows up with a string of fists and uppercut forearms for a near fall. A hard whip into a corner also gets him a two-count. Maven refuses to stay down, fighting back until Orton rakes his eyes and dropkicks him for a pair of two-counts. That brings Flair onto the apron to distract Jack Doan. When Michaels hops up and complains, Ric cheap shots the babyface. That brings Shawn over to drop "The Nature Boy" with Sweet Chin Music. Afterwards, Maven dodges a dropkick and punches the "Legend Killer". Although Randy slips free of a suplex, the babyface shoves him off when he attempts an RKO for a dropkick and near fall. A top rope flying cross body block also gets him a two-count. Unfortunately, his follow up charge is countered with a drop toe hold onto the middle rope. Orton capitalizes with an RKO, but picks up Maven's at the count of two to mock the "Heartbreak Kid" and tune up the band. Sweet Chin Music follows for Randy to score the three-count. Post-match, Shawn glares at the winner, JR claiming that using his finishing move is a total lack of respect.

After a commercial break, Eric Bischoff brings out Jonathan Coachman and gives him the *Raw* Employee of the Month award. The announcers mock his hat, Jerry saying it looks dumber than Ross's. Inside the ring, Coach says he didn't want to hurt anyone last night. He claims he was just doing his job and didn't deserve "Stone Cold" Steve Austin attacking him. He then turns his attention to JR, mocking him before Eric shows footage of Jim taking back his job two weeks ago with a scowl. Coachman says he worked hard to carry the ball and keep the show going, but JR didn't appreciate it. One day, Coach promises that Jim will apologize to him, but tonight he wants Austin to do it first. Instead, Christian walks to the ring. He says Coachman may deserve an apology, but no one deserves an apology more than him. He blames the "rattlesnake" for keeping him off SummerSlam and trying to keep him off tonight's episode. That brings "Stone Cold" out to a big pop with something in his back pocket. Austin tells Coach he couldn't carry JR's jockstrap and won't apologize to him. However, he does have something for Jonathan, reaching into the envelope in his pocket to reveal his middle finger. When Coach makes fun of the announcers, "the King" interrupts to offer to stick Coachman's plaque up his butt. Christian has had enough and yells at everyone, but "Stone Cold" tells him to shut up. If the Intercontinental Champion wants action, Austin gives it to him with a match against Lawler for the belt.

Christian def. Jerry "the King" Lawler (Intercontinental Title match). Coach fills in for "the King" here, yelling at JR and demanding an apology. Ross doesn't give it to him and offers him some lessons on how to commentate while the champion punches and chokes Jerry. While Christian applies a reverse chin lock, the announcers argue about their hats, Coach wondering if Jim is going to "get racial". He's actually pretty entertaining as a heel here. Eventually, Lawler comes back to life with fists and a back body drop for a two-count. When Christian tries to answer with an Unprettier, "the King" pokes his eyes and rolls him up for another near fall. Christian responds with a back elbow, but when he heads upstairs, he's slammed to the canvas for a falling fist drop. A second fist drop follows before Coachman interrupts the cover and pulls Lawler out to the floor. Jerry has had enough and chases after Coach until the newly turned heel leads him back into the squared circle for a Christian roll-up and three-count.

As Shane McMahon heads to the ring for his match, Kane lurks in the shadows.

After a commercial break, Jonathan Coachman interviews Christian, asking him how he beat Jerry "the King" Lawler tonight. The Intercontinental Champion says he lures his opponents into a false sense of security before stealing away the victory. When he goes off to celebrate with his "peeps", "Stone Cold" Steve Austin informs Coach that he'll have a match next week with "the King".

Chris Jericho and Shane McMahon wrestle to a no contest. Shane is out first and greets Jericho with a string of fists. Y2J answers with a back elbow and kick to the face. Unfortunately, when he attempts a charge near the ropes, McMahon back body drops him out to the floor. The babyface follows up with a flying clothesline off the ring steps. He then hammers Y2J in front of Lilian Garcia before returning to the squared circle for a top rope attack. Before he flies, Kane's music plays and distracts Shane for Jericho to recover and springboard dropkick him out to the floor ahead of a commercial break.

Afterwards, there's still no "Big Red Machine", but Jericho is dominating the action chopping McMahon. When he attempts a springboard attack though, Shane answers with a kick to the gut and DDT for a near fall. A flying back elbow and fists follow before he scores another close two-count with a clothesline. Y2J responds with an enziguri kick. After he mocks the babyface with a shuffling dance, Jericho plants him with a running face slam. Unfortunately, his Lionsault is met with a pair of knees. McMahon tries to follow up with a top rope attack, but Jericho kicks the referee back into the ropes to crotch Shane. A superplex follows to put both men down and bring Kane out. Y2J and Earl Hebner want nothing to do with him, bailing out of the ring and ending this match in a no contest.

Post-match, Kane Chokeslams Shane. Instead of continuing the assault, the "Big Red Machine" walks through the crowd and leaves McMahon alone. The babyface refuses to let the sneak attack stand and follows the monster backstage and out into a receiving bay. Kane is waiting to ambush him and slam Shane against a concrete wall. Having set up McMahon perfectly, the "Big Red Machine" reveals several gas cans and pours them into a dumpster. He then sets it on fire. The announcers beg for someone to help Shane before the monster tosses him into the flames. Instead, McMahon helps himself, kicking Kane into the fire and telling him to "burn in Hell" to end the episode.

SmackDown!
August 28, 2003
El Paso, TX
Announcers: Michael Cole, Tazz, Kurt Angle (briefly)

MUST SEE! Following the intro video and fireworks, Eddie Guerrero gets a big pop as he drives a sports car turned lowrider into the parking lot. He tosses the keys to a worker to park it before making his way through his hometown crowd to the squared circle. The fans are electric for his entrance and he hugs his family and Tazz as he heads to the ring. Cole tries to get a hug too, but Eddie puts a sombrero on his head instead. While it helps that he's back home, the pops "Latino Heat" has been getting has shot him up the card and made him an undeniable star in recent weeks. With the fans hanging on his every word, he tells a story about his great great grandmother telling people back in her day that she belongs here in America. Eddie jokes that that was the first ever Guerrero lie. He also tells the story of the first time Guerreros cheated with his grandmother beating up a woman and switching their citizenship tests. She then celebrated by riding a donkey. The fans love it, but they are not happy when John Cena comes out to question "Latino Heat's" sexuality. Cena tells Eddie that he doesn't belong here and he stole his green card. John doesn't understand how he's the US Champion when he's not even a citizen. Guerrero doesn't appreciate him making fun of his people and warns the rapping heel that he's got twelve thousand homies in attendance watching his back. Eddie wants to know if he thinks he's better than "Latino Heat". Fired up, Guerrero challenges Cena to a fight. John won't accept unless the US Title is on the line. That's fine with Eddie. John warns him that after he takes his belt, he's taking his sister too. "Latino Heat" has one other thing to offer him...his fist. With the fans going bananas, Guerrero knocks Cena out of his jersey and drives him from the ring. He then wears the jersey and taunts John. The rapping heel attempts to sneak attack him moments later, but Eddie knows every dirty trick and throws him out to the floor. He then shows off his rapping skills, warning Cena that he "lies, steals, and cheats" and no one can withstand his "Latino Heat" in an amazingly hot opening segment.

Rey Mysterio def. Nunzio (Cruiserweight Title match). Jimmy Korderas refuses to let The FBI accompany Nunzio to the ring tonight, ordering them backstage for Rey to take the challenger down early on. Nunzio answers with a clothesline for a two-count, but can't build any momentum as the masked man dropkicks him from the ring for a corkscrew splash over the top rope. Mysterio tries to get the quick victory with an early 619, but the Italian heel moves and counters with a wheelbarrow suplex onto the barricade for a near fall. He then slows the pace with a surfboard stretch. The champion has a unique escape, rolling back into a bulldog. A springboard splash afterwards gets Rey a two-count. Nunzio also gets a near fall with an atomic drop onto his butt followed by a dropkick to the face. The masked man continues to innovate, planting the challenger on the second rope with a forward leg sweep ahead of the 619. When he goes for the West Coast Pop though, Nunzio counters with a powerbomb for a near fall. The two men then trade roll-ups before the Italian heel puts Mysterio on the top rope for a back suplex. Unfortunately, the champion fights free and shoves Nunzio down to Drop the Dime on him for the victory.

Chris Benoit def. A-Train (with Sable). Despite giving up plenty of size, Benoit goes right after the hairy heel with a series of chops. A-Train answers with a toss and shoulderblock before slamming "the Crippler" onto the top rope. He then knocks him off with a hard kick, sending Benoit out to the floor. The hairy heel stays on top of him with a series of kicks and a whip into the apron ahead of a gourdbuster lift into a gutbuster for a near fall. When he attempts to deliver snake eyes, the "rabid wolverine" slips free and clubs A-Train. It doesn't have much impact and the hairy heel knocks him back down before removing a turnbuckle pad. Afterwards, Benoit comes back to life with a German suplex and top rope diving headbutt for a near fall. He tries to counter a Derailer with the Crippler Crossface, but A-Train shoves him back into the exposed corner bolt. Afterwards, the Derailer gets him a near fall and sets off the hairy heel. After yelling at Mike Sparks, he charges "the Crippler", but Benoit moves and A-Train stuns himself hitting the exposed bolt. The "rabid wolverine" immediately locks on the Crippler Crossface for the tap-out victory despite the hairy heel's feet being under the ropes and hanging out of the ring.

Backstage, a worker tells Eddie Guerrero that someone messed up his lowrider.

After a commercial break, A-Train shoves Chris Benoit backstage and says he can't beat the hairy heel. When "the Crippler" starts to respond, Rhyno Gores him through a door. A-Train taunts him before Mike Sparks arrives to offer help.

In the parking lot, someone has stolen one of Eddie Guerrero's tires. He questions The APA and Funaki, but they don't know anything. When The FBI laugh about it, Eddie decks them until the babyfaces pull him back.

After a commercial break, an angry Brock Lesnar heads to the squared circle. He yells at the crowd and tells them to shut up. All week he's heard people taunting about tapping out. That prompts the fans to chant that he tapped out, making him even madder. Brock says it was a mirage and he never tapped out. Lesnar calls it a miracle that Kurt Angle beat him. The raving heel says he'll never be done with Kurt and challenges him to another match. The Olympian interrupts from the Titantron, calling Brock a baby. Angle says he was like Lesnar before, whining and crying every time he lost. However, the WWE Champion learned from the fans. Specifically, he learned that they don't care about whining; they want action. He offers to beat up Brock right now and make him tap again. Instead, The Undertaker heads to the squared circle. He tells Lesnar that he had his shot at the belt and tapped out. Now, the biker says Brock is at the back of the line and it's been a long time since the "Deadman" had a title shot. He then warns Lesnar that he's trespassing. Big Show has heard enough. He tells both men that he's inflicted more punishment on Kurt than anyone in the WWE and deserves a title shot. The Olympian finally comes out to address his challengers. He's not sure who he'd like to face. While he'd like to make Brock tap out again, it would be an honor to make The Undertaker tap out as well. However, he agrees that Show has caused him more pain and suffering than anyone…mostly from his body odor. Angle wants someone to decide who will get the next title shot. That's Stephanie McMahon's cue to head to the ring and sign a triple threat number one contender's match tonight.

Backstage, Josh Mathews asks John Cena if he messed with Eddie Guerrero's lowrider. The rapping heel says the crime rate in El Paso is ridiculous and Eddie has plenty of enemies. When it comes to messing with a man's ride, Cena says he never crosses that line.

Eddie Guerrero def. John Cena (US Title match) by disqualification. Despite Cena's claims, he carries Eddie's tire to ringside. He says "Latino Heat" isn't the only one who can "lie, cheat, and steal". Guerrero then runs out to attack him, busting open John when he rams his head into the ring steps. Inside the squared circle, Eddie kicks and elbows the challenger ahead of a slingshot somersault splash. Chops and fists follow, the fans chanting for their hometown hero. He attempts to entertain them with his trio of suplexes, but the rapping heel slips free for a side suplex. Although Brian Hebner stops him from using his belt, Cena levels "Latino Heat" with a stiff clothesline. Guerrero answers with a dropkick to the face. That sends the challenger rolling out to the floor. He plays possum until the champion follows him, hitting Eddie's knee. Despite that, "Latino Heat" slams his face onto the announce table. He then slides the tire into the ring. While the referee struggles to get it out of the squared circle, Guerrero grabs a chair and blasts John's back. Afterwards, the champion suplexes Cena into position for a Frog Splash, but the rapping heel rolls out of the way at the last second. Once he catches his breath, John shoulder blocks Eddie out to the floor ahead of an abrupt commercial break.

Afterwards, the challenger tries to squeeze the life out of "Latino Heat'. When Guerrero escapes, Cena powerbombs him for a near fall. A delayed vertical suplex also gets him a two-count, the champion's mother concerned in the crowd. Frustrated, the rapping heel chokes Eddie before applying a bearhug. "Latino Heat" refuses to give up, fighting free to pummel and back suplex John for his own near fall. The challenger answers with a back body drop, but when he picks up Guerrero for an FU, the champion counters with a head scissors takedown. Eddie follows up with a throat drop on the top rope, but Cena falls back into Hebner. It saves the rapping heel because the referee is too slow to make his count after a Frog Splash and John just kicks out. When Guerrero pulls him up for a trio of suplexes, Cena blocks the third with a low blow for the disqualification. Post-match, the rapping heel wraps his hand in a steel chain and busts open "Latino Heat" with a shot to the skull. After flinging Hebner from the ring, John chokes Eddie with the chain. His mother can't watch, but Cena isn't done. He brings the tire back into the squared circle and drops Guerrero onto it with an FU. Afterwards, John holds up the US Title.

The Undertaker def. Big Show and Brock Lesnar (#1 Contender's match). Kurt Angle joins the announce table to say that he'll face the winner of this match next week and mock Tazz for picking Brock to beat him at SummerSlam. Inside the ring, the heels work together to punish The Undertaker, but after Show suplexes him, Lesnar tries to steal the win. The heels almost come to blows, but the giant lets Brock's actions go and clotheslines the biker out to the floor. When Lesnar hits him from behind, Big Show has had enough and answers with his own shots. Brock responds with an overhead belly-to-belly toss, but the "Deadman" breaks up his cover. He then clotheslines both heels and big boots Lesnar. A leaping clothesline follows to Show ahead of snake eyes to Lesnar. When he tries to answer with an F5, the giant boots Brock down first. Now it's Big Show fighting both men and teasing a Chokeslam for The Undertaker. At the last second, the biker counters with a Fujiwara armbar. When Lesnar makes the save, he and the "Deadman" battle out to the floor. There, The Undertaker slams Brock's face into the ring post before Show hits the biker with a steel chair. Lesnar tries to use it afterwards, but the giant punches it back into his face ahead of a commercial break.

Afterwards, Big Show and the "Deadman" trade big boots, Brock laid out from a giant chair shot. Show gets the upper hand briefly and scores a two-count with a leg drop, but The Undertaker answers with another armbar. Before he can tap out, Lesnar makes the save. That gets him a chokeslam from the biker. Before Mike Chioda can make the three-count, Big Show yanks him out to the floor. The "Deadman" ends their argument, slamming Show's head onto the announce table, but when they enter the ring, the giant Chokeslams The Undertaker. Brock breaks up the cover afterwards, but pays courtesy of a Big Show chop. Despite Kurt telling fans how much that hurts, Lesnar recovers quickly and suplexes Show for a two-count. The biker makes the save this time and fights with both men before turning into an F5. The giant stops Brock from scoring the win, kicking his head before Chokeslamming him for a near fall. Frustrated, Big Show slams Lesnar into a corner and climbs the ropes, Angle teasing a Chokeslam from the top. Instead, the "Deadman" makes the save and whips Brock across the ring. When he attempts another Irish whip, Lesnar reverses it and crotches the giant. He then heads upstairs for a superplex, but The Undertaker slips under him and gives Brock the Last Ride for the win.

Monday Night Raw
September 1, 2003
Lafayette, LA
Announcers: Jim Ross, Jerry "the King" Lawler

The show opens with a video package featuring Shane McMahon knocking Kane into a burning dumpster last week ahead of the intro video and JR revealing that the monster isn't dead.

Jonathan Coachman def. Jerry "the King" Lawler. JR is on commentary solo here as Lawler gets his hands on the freshly turned heel. Coach wears a Texas football jersey to mock Ross. He also mocks "the King" inside the ring, dancing around until Jerry jacks his jaw. The fans are firmly behind Lawler here, chanting his name as he punches and slams Coachman. The heel slows the pace with a side headlock, but "the King" back suplexes him to escape. That brings Al Snow out to tell Coach to "stop this nonsense". His *Sunday Night Heat* commentating partner, Al tells Coachman that he can't win. He doesn't listen, returning to the squared circle for Lawler to trap him in an armbar. Snow offers to throw in the towel for him if Jerry will let go of his partner. He does so, but Coach doesn't want his help and shoves his broadcast partner. When "the King" leaves the ring to continue the attack, Al slams his head into the ring post for Coachman to steal the win after an elbow drop back in the squared circle.

Backstage, Terri rushes up to talk to Shane McMahon about what happened last week with Kane. She reveals that when the dumpster fire was put out last week, the monster was gone. Shane hopes he's still burning. She warns McMahon to be careful.

After a commercial break, Eric Bischoff celebrates with Al Snow and Jonathan Coachman. "Stone Cold" Steve Austin interrupts. He wants to know if Coach is proud of himself. Steve promises to do something special just for Coachman. He then heads to the squared circle where the Highlight Reel set is up, but Chris Jericho is nowhere to be found. That's a good thing as "Stone Cold" tears down the set and tells the crew to raise up the Jeritron 5000. He's tired of hearing that he's JR's "boy" just because they have always dealt with each other with respect like men. To prove that Ross is a man, Austin signs him to a match with Coach at Unforgiven. He's not done signing matches, adding Randy Orton against Shawn Michaels. While he's not adding to the main event, since Goldberg's career is on the line, the co-general manager signs him to a six-man tag match tonight for the fans in attendance to see him one more time. Finally, Chris Jericho storms down the aisle to confront the "rattlesnake". Wearing black pleather clothing, Y2J tells Austin that no one cancels his show. He's even madder that "Stone Cold" isn't talking about his Unforgiven match. Jericho demands an apology and wants Steve on his hands and knees. Instead, the GM flips him off. Before they come to blows, Christian marches out and demands respect. He also wants an apology from Austin. "Stone Cold" tells him to keep waiting. However, since both heels want some action, he signs them to a match. Even though he doesn't have any gear, Y2J is fine with facing anyone in the back. The heels promise to kick anyone's butt in their way. Unfortunately, the GM is signing them to fight each other.

Christian def. Chris Jericho (Intercontinental Title match). After a commercial break, the fans are loudly chanting "boring" before the friends finally lock up. Lawler joins the announce table as Y2J skins the cat only to run into a back elbow and Christian's fists. The challenger answers with a double leg sweep and near fall with his feet on the ropes. The champion can't believe he'd cheat and argues with his friend before shoving and slapping him. The match soon devolves into a fight, Jericho whipping Christian up and over the ring steps. Back in the squared circle, Y2J unties a turnbuckle pad. While Earl Hebner tries to put it back on, unsuccessfully, Jericho chokes the champion with his wrist tape. Christian soon responds with a clothesline and reverse backbreaker. Chokes follow before the champion misses a charge and guillotines himself on the ropes. Although he recovers first, Y2J nails him with a flying forearm only to run into a corner elbow and reverse tornado DDT off the middle rope for a near fall. When Christian heads all the way upstairs, Jericho shoves the referee back into the ropes to crotch the champion. A top rope hurricanrana follows and nearly crowns a new champion. After arguing with Hebner, Y2J delivers a running face slam, but leaps into a pair of knees attempting the Lionsault. When Christian tries to capitalize with an Unprettier, the challenger rolls through and tries to turn over his friend into the Walls of Jericho. Unfortunately, the champion holds onto the ref and rolls up Jericho for a two-count. Y2J attempts to answer with a springboard forearm, but hits the ref instead. While he's down, Christian grabs his belt, but the challenger ducks his shot and delivers a flashback for a near fall. He also almost gets the win with a roll-up holding the ropes, but Earl spots the cheating. When he kicks Jericho's hand off them, Christian rolls up the challenger and steals the win, also holding onto the top rope.

After a commercial break, "Stone Cold" Steve Austin tells Shane McMahon that he thinks it would be best if Shane left the arena tonight. McMahon isn't worried about Kane, telling him to "bring it on".

Following footage of Triple H and Goldberg in the SummerSlam "Elimination Chamber" match, JR interviews "the Game" via video. Standing backstage, Hunter is tired of hearing about the intense superstar and calls him "all hype". He thinks he's just a marketed superstar of what someone thinks a wrestler should be, but Helmsley says he's the real deal. The World Champion promises to end Bill's "plague on wrestling" at Unforgiven. Goldberg stops him, stepping right next to Triple H. He tells Hunter he's going to give him a preview of what he's in for at Unforgiven tonight, warning him that that's not a threat, but a promise.

Gail Kim/Molly Holly def. Ivory/Trish Stratus. The heels sneak attack their opponents before the bell. When they try to trap Ivory in their corner, she slugs both women until Gail tosses her out to the floor. There, Holly rams Ivory's back into the apron for a two-count. Kim follows up with a backbreaker and stretch. When the Women's Champion tags in, Ivory surprises her with a roll-up, but Gail makes the save with a dropkick. Focused, Holly slams the babyface and distracts Charles Robinson for Kim to choke her. The rookie gloats about her cheating and pays when Ivory knocks her off the apron. Trish then gets the hot tag to rock Holly with a Thesz press and fists ahead of a Matrix dodge and Chick Kick. Before she can score the win, Gail breaks her cover. She helps out again moments later when she blocks a handstand head scissors to slam Stratus to the canvas alongside Molly for the three-count. Post-match, the heels double DDT Ivory for good measure.

Backstage, Shane McMahon asks his father what he's doing at the show. Vince McMahon tells him that he's concerned about his son's welfare and he's heard something bad is going to happen. The WWE owner wants to clear the air between the two in case something happens. When he tries to hug his son, Shane shoves Vince aside and heads to the ring.

After a commercial break, Shane McMahon steps into the squared circle. He says if something bad is going to happen to him, he'd rather let it happen right here and right now. After a few seconds of nothing, Eric Bischoff steps through the curtain. Shane jokes that if Eric is the worst that happens to him it won't be a bad night. Unfortunately, he's not as Kane's music plays and he ambushes McMahon. After hitting him with the ring steps, the "Big Red Machine" handcuffs Shane's hands around the ring post and traps his feet behind the steps. The monster then tosses water onto him before pulling out a pair of jumper cables. He attaches them to a battery and makes it spray sparks. Luckily, Rob Van Dam runs out for the save, repeatedly wailing on Kane with a steel chair. Afterwards, he removes the cables from McMahon's groin before he dropkicks the chair back into the "Big Red Machine's" face. A second kick into a chair to the face follows, finally driving off the bloodied monster. During the commercial break, Shane is stretchered backstage for help.

After a commercial break, Eric Bischoff tries to calm down Kane. He tells him that he can have Rob Van Dam inside a steel cage next week. That makes the "Big Red Machine" smile.

La Resistance def. Rosey/The Hurricane. The superhero opens the match arm dragging Rene before he tags in Rosey. Unfortunately, Nick Patrick misses it as well as Sylvan illegally entering the ring to inverted atomic drop The Hurricane ahead of a Dupree clothesline. The champions then dominate this non-title match, Grenier trapping the superhero in a bearhug. It takes him a few seconds, but The Hurricane fights free and slams Sylvan to the canvas before finally giving Rosey an official tag. The super hero in training proceeds to hammer and toss around both heels, scoring a near fall with a body splash to Grenier. Although Rene makes the save, Rosey clotheslines both men ahead of a Hurricane top rope flying cross body block to Sylvan. Following another Dupree save, the heels toss Rosey out to the floor. That leaves the superhero alone to tease chokeslamming Grenier. Unfortunately, Rob Conway runs out and blasts The Hurricane with a title belt for Sylvan to steal the win. Post-match, Rosey gives Conway a Spinning Side Slam, but Rene nails the super hero in training with the belt. After Grenier tells him to get the tables and Dupree sets one up, The Dudley Boyz run out to chase the champions out of the ring. They tease giving Rob a 3D through the table, but La Resistance pull him from the squared circle.

Backstage, Terri tells Maven that tonight may be the biggest night of his career when he teams up with Goldberg and Shawn Michaels. The babyface can't believe he's in the main event of *Raw* alongside some of the best in the industry. He feels good and thinks this might be his time, but Ric Flair and Randy Orton interrupt. "The Nature Boy" tells him that he has a lot of talent, but he's not good enough to join Evolution. Randy promises to prove tonight that "the Evolution has passed (him) by".

After a commercial break, Shawn Michaels finds Maven in his locker room. The "Heartbreak Kid" notices that he looks nervous and feels in over his head. Shawn says he is probably in over his head and doesn't deserve this. Maven disagrees quickly. That's exactly what Michaels wants to hear and is looking forward to teaming up with the babyface.

Backstage, Theodore Long complains to "Stone Cold" Steve Austin about Mark Henry and Rodney Mack getting bumped off the show tonight. Austin says there's no conspiracy. He needed time and had to bump someone. He then spots Rob Van Dam and asks if he's ready for his match next week. RVD is, but he doesn't want to wait until the end of the show to get his hands on Kane. He wants their match to open next week's *Raw*. "Stone Cold" doesn't think it's a good idea, but agrees to Rob's request.

Further backstage, Stacy Keibler complains about having to carry Test's bags this week and being mistreated. The bodyguard tries to calm her down, reminding her that they used to be a great team. To make her feel more comfortable, Test tells Stacy that they'll go to the ring to her music.

Stacy Keibler/Test def. Steven Richards/Victoria ("No Disqualification" match). Stacy and Test are out first. She's shocked when Lilian Garcia says this will be no disqualification. The bodyguard feigns ignorance too. Inside the ring, he takes offense to Richards touching his partner and hammers down the heel. Afterwards, he holds Steven for Keibler to tag in and slap him. Just when she starts smiling, Victoria grabs her from behind and punishes Stacy. Richards returns afterwards and teases a pumphandle slam, but Test makes the save. He then cheers on his valet, but when she nears their corner, the bodyguard hops off the apron to watch their opponents pummel Keibler. He even tries to hold Stacy for a Victoria slap, but the babyface ducks and the "black widow" hits Test. Frustrated, he pumphandle slams Richards only to turn into a low blow Victoria kick. Back up, Steven clotheslines Keibler before Scott Steiner runs out to hammer him and grab the "black widow". The bodyguard tries to ambush Steiner with a Big Boot, but Scott moves and Test knocks out Victoria for Stacy to steal the win. Post-match, "Big Poppa Pump" chops and clubs Richards when he tries to attack Keibler. While he belly-to-belly suplexes him, the bodyguard pulls Stacy backstage.

Goldberg/Maven/Shawn Michaels def. Randy Orton/Ric Flair/Triple H. After Evolution comes out together, the babyfaces get separate entrances, culminating in Goldberg. Shawn opens the match, still wearing his hat, hitting Orton. Maven then tags in to dropkick the heel for a two-count. When Randy recovers, he tags in Ric to chop and punch the babyface. Maven isn't intimidated and decks Flair before tagging back in Michaels. They trade shots, JR calling it a moment. The "Heartbreak Kid" doesn't just get the advantage over Ric, fighting all three members of Evolution and chasing them out to the floor for a springboard cross body block. The fans want Goldberg to tag in, but Shawn remains on the attack until "The Nature Boy" pokes his eyes and gives him a low blow. Afterwards, Triple H tags in to stomp his former friend's groin and mock the intense superstar. Orton returns moments later to punch, stomp, and choke Michaels. When Ric returns, the "Heartbreak Kid" trades shots with him again. Shawn tries to crawl away and tag out, but Hunter returns to stomp him ahead of a backbreaker for a two-count. Randy also gets a near fall with a back suplex. The heels know what they are doing, trapping Michaels in their corner and making a series of quick tags, no one staying in the ring long. Eventually, Helmsley traps his former friend in an abdominal stretch, the "Legend Killer" grabbing his hand for added pressure. When Earl Hebner catches the heels cheating, he kicks "the Game's" hand and the "Heartbreak Kid" hip tosses free. Ric then returns to trade chops with Shawn, the babyface getting the upper hand. Unfortunately, Flair grabs his leg before he can tag out and Orton returns to punch and dropkick Michaels for a pair of two-counts. The "Heartbreak Kid" will not quit, continuing to fight with the heels to no avail. Once again he gets close to his corner, but Triple H stops him with an elbow drop. When he wastes time taunting Goldberg, Shawn surprises the champion with a flying forearm. Both men then tag out for the fans to erupt as Bill punches, kicks, and slams the heels. Following a military press and front slam to Randy, the intense superstar Spears Flair. Hunter returns to ambush Bill, but he only gets in a few shots before Goldberg clotheslines him down. When he sets up for a Spear, Randy makes the save. He pays with his own stiff Spear. Staring at "the Game", Bill Jackhammers the "Legend Killer" for the victory.

SmackDown!

September 4, 2003
New Orleans, LA
Announcers: Michael Cole, Tazz

Following a video package showing The Undertaker winning a WWE Title shot tonight, the intro video plays and fireworks explode.

The World's Greatest Tag Team def. The APA (WWE Tag Title match). The champions rush down to attack the brawlers, frustrated that Bradshaw keeps saying that Shaniqua is Shelton in drag. Although the challengers meet their initial surge, the heels isolate Faarooq—repeatedly called that instead of Ron Simmons tonight—and deliver their double-team leapfrog splash. Haas follows up with a bearhug, Cole noting that all four men were college All-Americans. When Charlie attempts a top rope dive, the brawler catches and slams him to the canvas ahead of the hot tag. Bradshaw explodes into the ring, hammering both men. Following a neckbreaker to Haas, he gives Benjamin a fallaway slam. A big boot follows before the big Texan powerbombs Charlie for a near fall. The APA then double shoulderblock Shelton. Afterwards, the heels toss Bradshaw out to the floor only to see Faarooq give Haas a spinebuster for a near fall. When he sets up for the Dominator, Benjamin makes the save with a superkick. Fortunately for the challengers, the big Texan breaks his cover. He tags in moments later to big boot Shelton for another close two-count. Afterwards, he nearly wins the titles with a Clothesline from Hell, but Charlie drapes his partner's boot on the bottom rope to save the championships. When Bradshaw goes after Haas, the champion hits him with a title belt for a Benjamin roll-up and the victory.

In the parking lot, Eddie Guerrero waxes his lowrider while Vince McMahon arrives with Sable and Big Show. After they exchange pleasantries, Brock Lesnar confronts the WWE owner. He wants to know what's going on. He's barely heard from Vince since SummerSlam and now he's riding around with the giant and Sable. McMahon hasn't wanted to talk to him since he tapped out. When Lesnar starts to yell at him, the WWE owner leads Brock back to his office. After a commercial break, Vince yells at Lesnar and slaps him. He is embarrassed of Brock and says he's really a "monster". That fires up Lesnar and he grabs the boss by the collar before realizing that Vince is only trying to get him to unleash the monster.

Afterwards, John Cena heads to the ring to question if Eddie Guerrero is waxing his car because it's dirty or because he's trying to stop Cena from stealing it. John then shows footage of him giving "Latino Heat" an FU last week before claiming that he owns Eddie. That brings out Guerrero in his lowrider. The rapping heel doesn't back down, but he should because Eddie is all over him in and out of the squared circle. Thinking quickly, Cena grabs the discarded US Title and blasts "Latino Heat" with it. Afterwards, he steals Guerrero's lowrider and drives backstage and out of the arena.

Following a commercial break, Eddie Guerrero complains to Stephanie McMahon, but she says John Cena isn't coming back tonight. However, she'll give Guerrero any match he wants with the rapping heel next week. Eddie chooses a "Latino Street Fight" in the parking lot.

Chris Benoit def. A-Train. The only non-championship match of the show, Benoit chops the hairy heel to open the contest. A-Train answers with heavy shots and a corner elbow to drop "the Crippler". Focusing on Benoit's injured back, the hairy heel tosses him around and clubs his ribs. Afterwards, he applies a camel clutch, his knee driven deep into the "rabid wolverine's" back. Yelling at his opponent,

A-Train tells him that he didn't win last week and can't beat him. He tries to prove his point with a double underhook suplex, but Benoit just kicks out. While the fans chant for him to shave his back, A-Train locks on a bearhug. Instead of waiting for the submission, the hairy heel drives his opponent into the corner. He makes a mistake when he attempts a corner charge and misses. That lets "the Crippler" catch his breath and impress with a trio of German suplexes. His back slows him though as he heads up the ropes and misses a diving headbutt. A-Train capitalizes with a Train Wreck, but when he makes the cover, Mike Sparks spots Benoit's body under the ropes. This week he calls for the break, frustrating the hairy heel. While he argues with the referee, the "rabid wolverine" recovers and attempts to trap his opponent in the Crippler Crossface. A-Train tries to fight him off, accidentally knocking Sparks down for Rhyno to run out and attempt to Gore his former friend. At the last second, Benoit moves and the man-beast hits the hairy heel instead for "the Crippler" to steal the win.

In a prerecorded promo, The Undertaker admits that Kurt Angle is the best wrestler in the world today, but he's going to keep on his feet. There, he plans to wail on the Olympian ahead of a Last Ride or Tombstone. After promising that he'll never tap out, the biker warns Angle that he's coming for him.

Filmed earlier today, Nidia and Torrie Wilson try on bikinis and practice dance moves. Afterwards, the redneck rubs oil on her new friend. She starts on her back, but quickly moves down to her backside.

In another prerecorded promo, Kurt Angle says that he's honored to wrestle The Undertaker tonight. Despite that respect, he promises to make the biker tap and leave New Orleans the WWE Champion.

Backstage, Stephanie McMahon tries to get into her office, but Big Show holds the doors shut. Vince McMahon tells his daughter that she can have the office back in a minute, but Brock Lesnar is taking care of business, the giant even struggling to hold back the pounding against the door.

Kurt Angle and The Undertaker (WWE Title match) wrestle to a no contest. The Undertaker is out first, the announcers noting his taped wrist. It doesn't slow him early on as he shoves Kurt down to the canvas. The Olympian answers with a front face lock, but the biker powers out to shoulderblock Angle. The two men trade amateur holds, the "Deadman" getting the upper hand with a short arm scissors. The champion knows how to counter just about every hold and rolls him over for a two-count before tackling The Undertaker for another quick count. Afterwards, Kurt applies an overhead hammerlock, but the biker powers out and wrings his arm ahead of Old School. The Olympian responds with a pair of German suplexes and a double leg tackle for a near fall, but the "Deadman" answers with a vicious right hand to finally seize control. Once he has the upper hand, the challenger elbows and leg drops Angle on the apron. Afterwards, he drives the champion back into the ring post ahead of a commercial break.

Following the break, The Undertaker is still in control, stomping Kurt in a corner. The Olympian won't stay down, fighting back and locking on a sleeper hold. It takes him some time, but the biker escapes with a side suplex. He tries to lock on Taking Care of Business, but Angle slips free and belly-to-belly suplexes the "Deadman" for a one-count. The challenger is right back on the attack, crushing the champion twice in a corner ahead of snake eyes and a big boot. Instead of going for the cover, The Undertaker motions for a leg drop, but Kurt moves and traps him in an Anklelock. It doesn't take the biker long to kick free only to be driven to the mat with an Angle Slam for a near fall. The Olympian lowers his straps ahead of a second Angle Slam, but this time the "Deadman" slips free and chokeslams the champion for his own near fall. Afterwards, the challenger sets up for a Last Ride, but Kurt rolls through and sunset flips him into an Anklelock. Instead of tapping out, The Undertaker counters with his own submission hold, a Fujiwara armbar. Once again, the Olympian has the answer, returning to his

Anklelock. This time, the biker pulls Angle in and traps him in a triangle choke. The champion is close to the ropes, but he starts to fade, Mike Chioda checking his arm. Before he passes out, Kurt extends his foot onto the bottom rope for the break. The "Deadman" tries to follow up with a big boot, but the Olympian dodges and applies an Anklelock in the ropes. When the referee forces the break, the challenger capitalizes with a throat drop on the top rope. He then hammers Angle, bleeding under the eye, and badmouths him. The champion answers with his own shots before running into a big boot. When The Undertaker attempts another chokeslam, Kurt counters with another Anklelock. The biker refuses to tap out and flips the Olympian away ahead of a chokeslam. He follows up with a Last Ride before Brock Lesnar runs out to ruin this incredible match with chair shots to both competitors. After smashing the "Deadman's" ankle with the chair, he bashes Angle's skull with the WWE Title.

During the commercial break, The Undertaker limps backstage where Michael PS Hayes tries to help him. The biker initially refuses the aid, but needs officials to help him walk.

Also backstage, trainers check on Kurt Angle's busted eye.

Footage of Tazz hosting a pre-show "Bourbon Street" bikini contest plays. Although Sable, Dawn Marie, and Nidia impress, Torrie Wilson's skimpy bikini gets her the win. Afterwards, Shaniqua runs out to clothesline Dawn Marie and Torrie, and press slam Nidia over the top rope.

Backstage, Bradshaw complains that The APA had the WWE Tag Titles. The brawlers complain that they lost to a pair of kids. The big Texan has a surprise for Faarooq to cheer him up...the returned APA door. He also won a butler in a game of poker. Bruce delivers drinks to the brawlers, putting The APA back in business.

The Lugz Boot of the Week is Rey Mysterio Dropping the Dime on Nunzio.

Rey Mysterio def. Tajiri (Cruiserweight Title match). The wrestlers cut a blistering pace to open the match, tripping and tackling each other before stopping to shake hands. During the lull, Cole reveals that The Undertaker has been taken to a medical facility. Afterwards, Rey head scissors the challenger, using Brian Hebner's shoulders for a boost. When he attempts a springboard attack, Tajiri catches him with a kick. Despite that, the masked man knocks down the "Japanese Buzzsaw" into position for a 619. Fortunately, the challenger moves and takes the fight out to the floor to wrap Mysterio's arm around the ring post. Back in the squared circle, Tajiri attempts to hit his handspring back elbow, but the champion counters with a spinning heel kick to put both men down ahead of a commercial break.

Afterwards, the "Japanese Buzzsaw" drives Rey's arm into the canvas with an armbar drop. He then slows the pace with a hammerlock until the masked man tosses him out to the floor. After he catches his breath, Mysterio flies through the ropes to tackle the challenger. When they return to the ring, Tajiri unloads with a string of fists in a corner, but misses a kick and hits the turnbuckle. That stuns him for the champion to connect with a bulldog and near fall. He tries to follow up with a springboard flying butt splash, but the "Japanese Buzzsaw" rolls through for a two-count. Afterwards, he grounds Rey again with an armbar. Although he rolls out of the hold, the challenger drops the masked man with a kick to the injured arm for a near fall. Tajiri follows up with a Tarantula, but misses his Buzzsaw Kick afterwards. Mysterio capitalizes, dropping him into position for a 619, but springboards into a boot and Michinoku driver for another near fall from the "Japanese Buzzsaw". When he attempts a corner charge, the champion locks him in his own Tarantula. A roll up afterwards gets Rey a two-count. Tajiri answers with more stiff kicks before the two men fight on the ropes. The masked man gets the upper hand there, shoving the challenger down for a West Coast Pop and the three-count. Post-match, the wrestlers shake hands, but Tajiri is just suckering Mysterio and sprays green mist into his face.

After the final commercial break, Vince McMahon and Big Show head to the ring. The WWE owner says it's too bad that there was controversy in the WWE Title match earlier. To end all controversy on who should be the champion, Vince signs an hour long "Iron Man" match between Kurt Angle and Brock Lesnar in two weeks. He then introduces Brock in a skybox. The heel thanks McMahon for slapping him and reminding Lesnar who he is. Brock then reveals that he found Zach Gowen and has him in the skybox. The babyface is gagged and in a wheelchair as Lesnar asks him how he's doing. Brock promises to show everyone what kind of monster he can be and wheels Zach away. That's to a flight of stairs. He teases tossing Gowen down them, but instead knocks him down onto the concrete. Lesnar wants to show Vince exactly what kind of monster he can be, punching Zach's injured leg. While he tries to crawl away, Brock tells the babyface that his wheelchair is magical because it flies. Because he's a nice guy, Lesnar chokes Gowen with his shirt so he doesn't feel a thing before he shoves him down the stairs. Even Mr. McMahon is stunned inside the ring as Brock laughs and stares down at his handiwork to end the episode.

Monday Night Raw
September 8, 2003
Huntsville, AL
Announcers: Jim Ross, Jerry "the King" Lawler

Kane def. Rob Van Dam ("Steel Cage" match). Following the intro video, Kane heads to the ring for this feud match. As soon as RVD steps into the cage, the "Big Red Machine" assaults him. Rob is prepared and answers with a flying kick. A series of kicks follow until Van Dam attempts a cross body block. That's when the monster catches and slams him into the cage. While he smiles at his handiwork, Jerry notes his burns and bandages. They don't stop him from hammering RVD and throwing him back into the cage, cutting open his brow. Chokes and a side slam follow before Kane whips the popular superstar back into the cage. When he attempts a slam into the cage, Rob slips free and dropkicks his former tag team partner into the steel. It doesn't take the "Big Red Machine" long to recover and slam Van Dam to the canvas. He tries to finish him off with a powerbomb, but RVD fights free only to run into a big boot. The monster then heads upstairs, but Rob catches him with a kick, crotching Kane on the ropes. A cross body block against the cage follows before Van Dam attempts to climb out. When the "Big Red Machine" tries to stop him, RVD answers with a kick and rolling thunder. Afterwards, he heads back up the cage, but the monster sits up and catches his boot. The two men then fight on the top rope, Rob kicking Kane back to the canvas for a Five-Star Frog Splash. At the last second, the "Big Red Machine" moves and Van Dam crashes hard onto the mat. The monster follows up with an alley-oop reverse powerbomb and slams into the cage. After mocking RVD's taunt, Kane slams his former partner one more time against the steel. The force breaks the cage and propels Rob out to the floor for the victory. Just seconds into his music playing, Eric Bischoff interrupts. He says the only way to win is by pinfall or climbing over the cage or through the door. Since Van Dam did none of those, Eric orders the match to restart following a commercial break.

After the break, Kane slams Rob into the cage and taunts him. He even lets Van Dam crawl to the entrance door only to slam it onto his head. When RVD starts to climb out, the "Big Red Machine" follows him up the cage and Chokeslams the popular superstar off the top rope for the three-count. Post-match, EMTs hurry down the aisle to help Rob while Kane celebrates his victory with flames atop the stage.

After a commercial break, EMTs stretcher Rob Van Dam backstage while the announcers play footage of Goldberg dominating Evolution last week. Eric Bischoff interrupts at the top of the stage again. Before "Stone Cold" Steve Austin delivers his "State of *Raw*" address, Eric has a few things he wants to say. First, he signs an Unforgiven match pitting Kane against Shane McMahon. He then changes JR's match with Jonathan Coachman at the PPV to a tag match adding "the King" and Al Snow to the sides. Bischoff says he's doing it because Ross and Lawler "suck". Not only will the regular announcers have to wrestle at Unforgiven, but their jobs are on the line because the winners will be the *Raw* announce team going forward. Finally, the co-general manager plans to get his money's worth out of Goldberg before his career ends at Unforgiven. To do so, he signs him to a tag match against Triple H tonight, both men getting mystery partners.

Backstage, Goldust tries to hype up Lance Storm for his match with Rico. He tells him to take a deep breath, but Lance doesn't want to do it. At the "bizarre one's" prodding, Rico imitates Goldust and barks before heading to the ring.

Lance Storm (with Goldust) def. Rico (with Miss Jackie). Pre-match, Rico tells Lance that he'll always be boring. Storm answers with a right hand before Goldust gets the fans to chant that "Rico sucks". Afterwards, Lance suplexes the flamboyant superstar, but Rico quickly recovers to punch Storm and poke his eyes. An arm drag neckbreaker follows for a two-count while the announcers curse Eric Bischoff and complain about putting their careers on the line at Unforgiven. When Rico slows the pace with a reverse chin lock, Lance comes back to life with a series of strikes and a leg lariat. He tries to head upstairs afterwards, but Miss Jackie climbs onto the apron to distract him. She ends up regretting it when he kisses her and springboard missile dropkicks the flamboyant superstar for the win. Post-match, Storm dances around, surprising the announcers.

Backstage, Triple H stops Eric Bischoff in the hall. "The Game" wants to know who his and Goldberg's surprise partners are going to be tonight. Bischoff says that wouldn't be much of a surprise. Hunter wants it to be a surprise that makes him happy, because if he's not happy, Eric won't be happy. Helmsley pats the GM's shoulder and warns him that he wouldn't want the wrong person getting hurt.

Gail Kim/Molly Holly def. Jacqueline/Trish Stratus. After Ivory failed to help her get revenge last week, Trish brings out Jacqueline. She starts the contest arm dragging and rolling up Molly for a two-count. That brings Gail into the ring for Jacqueline to arm drag her too. She follows up with forearms to the jaw and a kick to the back. Afterwards, a low dropkick gets the babyface a two-count before Holly makes the save. When Stratus tries to get into the ring, she distracts Chad Patton for the heels to double DDT Jacqueline. Instead of taking the victory, Gail makes the unconscious Jacqueline tag the vixen. That's a mistake as Trish pounds on both heels and back body drops Kim. When she goes for Stratusfaction, Molly runs into her path only to see the vixen take both opponents down with a combination head scissors and headlock takedown. She tries to follow up with a cross body block, but the heels catch her and toss Trish over the top rope. That scores Kim the three-count back in the squared circle. Post-match, she slaps Stratus ahead of another double DDT.

After a commercial break, "Stone Cold" Steve Austin heads to the ring for his "State of *Raw*" address. First, he tosses the podium out of the squared circle, claiming that he doesn't need it. He then circles the ring as he talks about the Unforgiven World Title match. Since Goldberg is putting his career on the line, Austin wants to make sure Triple H doesn't get himself disqualified or counted out. To do that, he is adding a stipulation that if Hunter loses by either disqualification or count-out, Bill will win the World Title. After apologizing about how tight his shorts are, claiming he's been on a high alcohol diet, "Stone Cold" turns his attention to Kane and Shane McMahon. While he'd love to attack the "Big Red Machine" for his actions last week, Steve is bound by Linda McMahon's rule that he can't touch the superstars. He thinks that sucks and so does the crowd. Before he can continue his address, Christian makes his way to the squared circle. He says what really sucks is that he gets no respect and his "Peep-ulation" agrees. "Stone Cold" thinks they all suck. Despite the fans taunting him, Christian believes he should get his own talk show, especially after beating Chris Jericho last week. He proposes that they replace the Highlight Reel with "The Peep Show". That brings out Y2J. When the Intercontinental Champion calls his show "stale", Jericho pounds on him and clotheslines Christian from the ring. The fans like that and so does Austin. Y2J doesn't want him patronizing him because Chris thinks the "rattlesnake" is "full of crap" and a "bully". Jericho isn't done insulting him, calling him a "failure as a general manager and a human being". Y2J is really fired up that he's going to cancel the Highlight Reel, but Steve doesn't want to do that. He likes the segment. With that out of the way, Austin offers to drink a beer with Jericho, but the heel isn't stupid. He knows that the "rattlesnake" can't touch him if he doesn't provoke "Stone Cold". Instead of provoking him, he asks the crowd to give him a "doo wa diddy diddy dum diddy do" if they want him to drink a beer. A few do. Austin considers it the stupidest catchphrase he's ever heard, but still tosses Y2J a beer. When he misses it, "Stone Cold" has a great time stepping in close and softly tossing a second beer to the heel. He even tosses him a third before the two men share a drink. Unfortunately, Jericho pats the GM on the shoulder to celebrate. That's enough provocation for Austin to give Y2J a Stone Cold Stunner for a nice pop.

La Resistance/Mark Henry/Rob Conway/Rodney Mack def. Rosey/Spike Dudley/The Dudley Boyz/The Hurricane. The ten men open the match brawling until the babyfaces clear the ring. Afterwards, D-Von press slams Spike onto La Resistance. On the other side of the squared circle, The Hurricane flies onto Mack and Henry. A wassup drop follows to Dupree before all of the babyfaces shove each other and call for tables. Unfortunately, they only set one up at ringside before Mark attacks the Dudleys. Inside the ring, Rosey double clotheslines Conway and Rene. The runt tags in afterwards, but catches a Rene knee to the back to turn the tide. Once the heels have control, Henry tosses Spike out of a corner only to miss his leg drop on the ropes and fly out to the floor, hurting himself. That lets The Hurricane tag in and slam Rob to the canvas. The superhero and Bubba then take turns punching Rene before a ten-man brawl erupts again. In the chaos, Rosey and The Hurricane give Dupree a combination Samoan Drop and neckbreaker. Fortunately, Conway makes the save and gives the superhero a neckbreaker after Rosey misses a corner charge. The Dudleys reward the French sympathizer with a 3D, but Mack catches D-Von with a spinebuster. Bubba Ray immediately gives Rodney a Bubba Bomb before turning into a Henry Front Slam and the three-count. Post-match, Sylvan hits the babyfaces with his title belt. Once everyone else is down, the champions Double Slam Spike over the top rope towards the table. Unfortunately, they don't throw him far enough and his skull clips the table. While officials check on him, La Resistance finally break the table, Double Slamming The Hurricane through it.

Backstage, Al Snow and Jonathan Coachman mock the announcers. Eric Bischoff is glad they are having a good time, but watching the previous match gives him an idea for an Unforgiven contest. At the PPV, he signs a six-man tag "Tables" match between all three Dudleys and La Resistance and Rob Conway. Al and Coach love it. They hope the GM loves their surprise later tonight. Before they can give him a clue what it is, Gail Kim enters the room and sits on Eric's lap. She has a proposition for him and Bischoff wants privacy to hear it.

After a commercial break, Terri asks Triple H about Goldberg. The World Champion continues to claim that Bill is nothing but hype. Tonight, he plans to leave the intense superstar "a bloody mess".

After the announcers preview Unforgiven, Shane McMahon joins them via video from WWE studios in Stamford, Connecticut, to talk about his match with Kane. Eric Bischoff interrupts. He says after all Shane and the "Big Red Machine" have done to each other, a normal match won't do. Bischoff claims that this is not personal as he makes the Unforgiven contest a "Last Man Standing" match. McMahon isn't happy about it, telling Eric, "screw you". Bischoff jokes that that's what he just did to Shane.

After a commercial break, Gail Kim tells Molly Holly that Eric Bischoff gave them what they want and it didn't take as long as she thought. While she works on tying on her top again, Molly is happy to announce that next week they are going to finish off Trish Stratus.

Scott Steiner def. Steven Richards (with Victoria). Test and Stacy Keibler are out at ringside to watch Scott manhandle Richards. That includes a slam in the corner and clubbing blows until Victoria trips "Big Poppa Pump". Steven capitalizes with a neckbreaker for a near fall. When he applies a camel clutch, Steiner stands up and tosses the heel onto the top rope. Chops and a belly-to-belly suplex follow. After a clothesline and elbow drop, Scott mocks Richards with pushups. That brings the "black widow" onto the apron. Steiner brings her into the ring, whipping her over the top rope. While Charles Robinson tries to get her out, Test slips into the squared circle and full nelson slams "Big Poppa Pump". That nearly gets Steven the win, but Scott just kicks out. When Richards tries to finish him off with a Stevie Kick, Steiner catches his boot and answers with his Falling Face Slam for the three-count. Post-match, "Big Poppa Pump" says it's a shame that Stacy isn't with him anymore. He challenges the bodyguard to one more match for Keibler. Test is willing to accept that challenge at Unforgiven, but if he wins, he wants Steiner to join his group too. After the bodyguard licks Stacy, Scott accepts.

After a commercial break, Al Snow and Jonathan Coachman are in the ring. They show doctored images of JR on the screen, offering him some ideas for what he can do after he loses at Unforgiven. The best shot is Jim as Jabba the Hutt. When he takes offense, Coach challenges Ross to do something about it. That sends the announcers down to the squared circle, Jerry serving as his partner's backup. Coachman calls him a "worthless loser" and slaps his hat off. When he doesn't respond, Coach says he hates someone that's spineless. JR has had enough and decks the loudmouthed heel. When Snow tries to help his partner, "the King" cuts him off. Al decides to wait until Unforgiven to fight him and turns to check on his partner. When he does so, Jim kicks Snow's butt and shoves him out to the floor. He tries to return, but Jerry decks him to end the segment with a nice pop.

Backstage, Terri asks Goldberg if he knows who his partner is tonight. The intense superstar doesn't and doesn't care. Bill admits that Triple H has beaten a lot of people, but he's never beaten Goldberg. Bill warns "the Game" to "believe the hype".

After the final commercial break, Goldberg heads to the ring for the main event. Once Triple H makes his entrance, Eric Bischoff steps onto the stage to say he's thought a lot about what Hunter told him earlier and no one threatens the boss. He then introduces Helmsley's partner, Ric Flair. For Bill, Eric gives him Randy Orton.

Goldberg/Randy Orton and Ric Flair/Triple H wrestle to a no contest. JR calls this a setup as Goldberg fights three men, including his own partner. Earl Hebner can only watch as Evolution decimate the intense superstar and the cage is lowered. When Orton slides to the floor to get a chair, Goldberg comes back to life with a double clothesline to Ric and Hunter. He then Spears Randy, but Triple H gets the discarded chair to bust open Bill in a sickening shot. Having fulfilled his earlier promise, Helmsley whips Goldberg back and forth into the cage before Flair chokes the intense superstar. With Orton and "The Nature Boy" holding Bill, "the Game" badmouths him and tells Goldberg that he'll never get the World Title. Triple H tries to punctuate his attack with a Pedigree, but Bill falls first. The intense superstar picks him back up and hits a much better looking Pedigree to end the show standing tall over his Unforgiven challenger.

SmackDown!
September 11, 2003
Birmingham, AL
Announcers: Michael Cole, Tazz

For the two year anniversary of 9/11, the show opens with a brief graphic saluting the heroes and victims of the terror attacks. Afterwards, the intro video plays and fireworks explode.

Nunzio/Tajiri def. Billy Kidman/Rey Mysterio. Nunzio attacks Rey from behind to open the match, but the masked man quickly recovers and turns the tide with a head scissors. Kidman then tags in to swing the Italian heel into a Mysterio dropkick. The heels respond with their own double-team dropkick before Tajiri gets a two-count on Billy with a suplex. A knee drop also gets him a near fall, but the champion breaks the cover. Back in, the Italian heel lowers his protective pad to drop a knee on Kidman too. A jawbreaker follows, but the babyface responds with a dropkick to put both men down. The "Japanese Buzzsaw" gets the tag first and knocks Rey off the apron. Although Billy answers him with a back suplex, he has no partner to tag. Tajiri tries to capitalize with a tornado DDT, but Kidman counters with his BK Bomb. The masked man then gets the hot tag to springboard cross body block the "Japanese Buzzsaw" for a two-count. An arm drag into a roll-up also gets him a near fall before all four men fight. In the chaos, Mysterio gives Tajiri a 619 to the back. When he attempts a second to the face after Billy slingshot dives onto Nunzio at ringside, the "Japanese Buzzsaw" dodges and scores the win with a Buzzsaw Kick. Post-match, Tajiri hits the champion with his own belt.

Backstage, Vince McMahon orders flowers for Zach Gowen and compliments Big Show's suit. Stephanie McMahon isn't happy about what happened to Zach last week. Vince claims that Brock Lesnar "went into business for himself" and he never wanted Brock to do that to Gowen. Stephanie doesn't believe her father. She says everything Lesnar does is "downright criminal". Brock interrupts her, but the general manager isn't intimidated. She reminds him that he tapped out to Kurt Angle, but Lesnar is looking forward to winning back the WWE Title next week. He just wants a tune-up match tonight and proposes that he face Kurt, The Undertaker, and Zach all in one match. Unfortunately, none of them are here. Brock still wants a fight. He's already wrestled with Show, Vince, and even Sable apparently. That just leaves Stephanie in the room that he hasn't faced. Mr. McMahon isn't so sure about that match, but thinks about the ratings. Big Show says they would be big. Vince isn't heartless. He tells his daughter that she can get out of the match if she just quits her job. She walks off to think it over.

The Lugz Boot of the Week is Shaniqua attacking Dawn Marie, Nidia, and Torrie Wilson last week. Afterwards, Nidia tells Torrie that even if she doesn't like Dawn, Wilson needs to talk to her. The babyface tries to talk sense into Marie, but Dawn refuses to let Shaniqua manhandle them.

Dawn Marie and Shaniqua wrestle to a no contest. Shaniqua relies on her physique to get a reaction and it works. When Dawn enters the ring, the *Tough Enough* winner clotheslines her. A slam on the barricade follows before Shaniqua whips Marie into the ring steps. Back in the squared circle, the dominatrix tries to use a chair, but Nidia and Torrie Wilson run out for the save, Mike Sparks throwing out this match. Although Shaniqua drops Nidia, Torrie gets the chair and finally knocks her down for the other divas to escape.

Backstage, Sable taunts Stephanie McMahon and tells her that she'll be mangled if she steps into the ring with Brock Lesnar. However, if Stephanie quits, Sable is sure Vince McMahon will find someone capable to serve as the new general manager.

Chris Benoit def. Rhyno. Although the man-beast starts fast clubbing his former friend, Benoit trips him and nearly locks on the Crippler Crossface before Rhyno reaches the ropes. "The Crippler" remains on the attack with a snap suplex and chops in a corner. The man-beast only slows him with a thumb to the eye ahead of a throat drop on the middle rope. While Benoit tries to recover at ringside, A-Train runs out and slams him into the ring post ahead of a pair of near falls and a commercial break.

Afterwards, Rhyno scores a two-count with a superplex off the middle rope. Chokes and stomps follow before the man-beast ties up the "rabid wolverine" in the tree of woe for kicks and a shoulderblock. That gets him another near fall. Switching gears, Rhyno locks on a sharpshooter. Reaching down deep, Benoit crawls to the ropes for the break, but a clothesline puts him back down. When the man-beast wastes time celebrating, "the Crippler" catches his breath and applies his own sharpshooter. Rhyno also reaches the ropes, but Benoit keeps up the attack with a German suplex. When he heads upstairs, the man-beast meets him and attempts a second superplex. This time, the "rabid wolverine" counters with a sunset flip powerbomb for a near fall. Back up, Rhyno responds with a spinebuster to put both men down. He tries to follow up with a Gore, but Benoit counters with a Crippler Crossface for the tap-out.

Backstage, The APA plays cards with some mid-carders. Matt Hardy is insulted with how they treat their butler, Bruce. Shannon Hardy then enters with orange juice, but Matt is upset that he doesn't remember his Matt Fact that Hardy likes extra pulp. When The APA take offense, Matt challenges them to a tag match tonight. Once everyone walks away, Bradshaw and Faarooq toast the 9/11 American heroes.

In the parking lot, John Cena walks around in a Chicago Bears Brian Urlacher jersey as he swings his chain around. Brian Hebner tells the rapping heel that he can use anything he wants in the "Parking Lot Brawl".

The Maxim Cool Color of the Night is John Cena giving Eddie Guerrero an FU onto a tire.

Eddie Guerrero def. John Cena ("Latino Parking Lot Brawl"). Instead of a ring, cars are set up in a circle in the parking lot. WWE superstars surround the ring of cars as Cena raps about Eddie "sitting on his stick shift". "Latino Heat" then drives his vehicle into the circle before trading shots with John. The rapping heel gets the early upper hand, tossing Guerrero onto a hood. Eddie responds in kind before teasing a suplex off a car. Fortunately, Cena reverses the attempt and suplexes "Latino Heat" onto the car roof. He then gets a lawnmower out of the back of a van and starts it. When he tries to run him over, Guerrero moves. John isn't done with grabbing weapons. He also gets a shovel from the back of the van, but Eddie dodges it too and slams a car door into the rapping heel. Afterwards, he chokes Cena with a seatbelt before opening the trunk of the car. Unfortunately, it's John slamming him into the trunk and closing it. When he pounds on the trunk and tries to get Hebner to count his victory, "Latino Heat" pops it open into the rapping heel's face. Despite that, Cena scores the first two-count with a whip into a windshield, shattering it. He also gets a near fall slamming Eddie in between a car door. The two men then take turns ramming each other's faces through the car's windows. That gets John another close two-count. "Latino Heat" refuses to give up, shoving the rapping heel back into a car. When Cena tries to drive away, Guerrero slams his head into a steering wheel repeatedly and burns him with a cigarette lighter. He takes a big risk and pays for it moments later though when he charges John only to be back dropped onto another hood for a near fall. Bloodied, the rapping heel tries to get the win with an FU, but Eddie flips free and hip tosses Cena onto another hood. Chavo Guerrero Jr. then makes his return, smashing a hubcap over John's head before "Latino Heat" scores the win with a Frog Splash on a car. Post-match, Los Guerreros celebrate their victory and drive away from the bloodied Cena.

The APA def. Matt Hardy Version 1.0/Shannon Moore. Matt Facts this week reveal that he rarely uses turn signals and his entertainment system requires five remote controls. Inside the ring, Moore attacks Faarooq from behind and flexes. A second back attack sets off the brawler and he hammers Shannon down for a quick cover. Matt then tags in only to run into a powerslam. Bradshaw joins his partner for a double shoulderblock before scoring a two-count with a suplex. Clubbing blows follow until Hardy pokes his eyes. Shannon then returns only to leap into a fallaway slam. When Matt tries to help his MFer, the big Texan rocks him with a big boot. He recovers in time to break up a cover when Bradshaw elbow drops Moore. Moments later, he saves Shannon again with a top rope flying clothesline to block a powerbomb. That nearly gets the heels the victory, but it's as close as they'll come because the big Texan explodes up for a Clothesline from Hell to Moore for the win. Post-match, Bruce is happy to bring out a silver platter filled with beer for the winners.

A video package for Brock Lesnar plays ahead of his "Iron Man" match with Kurt Angle next week.

After a commercial break, Vince McMahon introduces "the next WWE Champion", Brock Lesnar. Once he's in the ring, Vince says it's decision time for Stephanie McMahon. She either wrestles Brock or quits her job. Stephanie refuses to quit and heads to the ring. Vince can't stand it. He says she's defying him and Lesnar will break her in half. She slaps her father, setting off Brock. When he corners her, Stephanie low blow kicks Lesnar. She also gives Vince a low blow before trying to run away. Unfortunately, Brock catches her and tosses Stephanie hard into the barricade. He threatens to hit her with the ring steps afterwards while Vince stares wide-eyed. Fortunately, the GM dodges the steps and runs backstage. Lesnar follows behind, Mr. McMahon struggling to stand up while holding his injured "grapefruits". When Brock returns, he's got Stephanie on his shoulders. She calls for her dad, but it's Kurt Angle who saves her from an F5 against the ring post. Vince tries to help Lesnar, but the Olympian decks him before whipping Brock twice into the post. He then chases off the heels, flinging the ring steps after them. Angle wants Lesnar right now, but he'll have to wait until next week because this episode is only an hour and a half for UPN to hype one of their new shows, *The Mullets*, with a special airing.

Monday Night Raw
September 15, 2003
Columbia, SC
Announcers: Jim Ross, Jerry "the King" Lawler, Al Snow (briefly), Jonathan Coachman (briefly)

The show opens with Triple H happily walking around backstage. Eric Bischoff is also happy to greet him. The co-general manager says he's a betting man and when it comes to career ending matches, he's betting on "the Game". Hunter appreciates that and wants to do something special for Goldberg's last night on *Raw*. He wants to throw him a going away party and invites Bill to join him in the ring when he shows up. Afterwards, the intro video plays and fireworks explode to kick off the episode.

Inside the ring, Chris Jericho and Christian are protesting "Stone Cold" Steve Austin. Carrying picket signs, the heels call Austin a failure and want him fired. Christian complains that not only was he kept off SummerSlam, but he doesn't have a match for Unforgiven either. The heels try to lead the crowd in a "'Stone Cold' must go" chant, but the fans don't join them. Instead, they cheer as the "rattlesnake" heads to the squared circle. He wants to clarify that the heels are holding up his show to try to get him fired. Austin then explains to Jericho that he attacked him last week because Y2J assaulted him and hurt his feelings. The co-GM believes the heels both deserve a butt kicking, but he's not allowed to do so unless physically provoked. The fans and "Stone Cold" don't like that. Fired up, Steve tells Christian that he makes him sick whining all the time. He can stop whining because Austin has a match for him. He will defend the Intercontinental Title at Unforgiven. Instead of telling him who he'll face, the GM calls out the heels and wonders who is going to provoke him. Jericho steps up, but quickly backs down and tells Christian to do it. He also fires himself up to get in "Stone Cold's" face, but he doesn't take the shot. Instead, Y2J interrupts to ask for the Intercontinental Title match at the PPV. Austin will give it to him if he beats his opponent tonight, a man "who doesn't whine or complain". That brings Rob Van Dam out with a bandage on his head to a big pop.

Chris Jericho and Rob Van Dam (Intercontinental Title #1 Contender's match) wrestle to a double disqualification. While he poses on the ropes, Christian tries to sneak attack RVD. The popular superstar sees him coming and knocks him out to the floor before Y2J ambushes Rob. Van Dam quickly dumps him out of the ring as well with a back body drop. Not done yet, he leaps over the top rope onto both heels with a flying somersault splash to put everyone down ahead of a commercial break.

Afterwards, RVD ducks a flying forearm and scores a near fall with a standing moonsault. He also gets a two-count with a hurricanrana, but when he heads upstairs, Christian shoves Rob off the ropes and down onto the entrance ramp. Jericho capitalizes with a whip into the ring steps before taking the fight back into the squared circle where he applies a reverse chin lock and pulls Van Dam's hair. The announcers wonder who Christian would rather face as RVD comes back to life, countering a springboard attack and following up with heel kicks and rolling thunder for a near fall. A slingshot leg drop afterwards sees him guillotine Jericho on the apron. Back in the ring, a flying martial arts kick nearly gets the popular superstar the victory. When he attempts to monkey flip Y2J though, the heel lands on his feet and attempts to lock on the Walls of Jericho. Although RVD escapes with a roll-up, Jericho answers with a flashback for a two-count. More chops follow as the announcers talk about this possibly being their last night on *Raw* as well as Goldberg's. Inside the ring, Rob accidentally knocks down Jack Doan before Y2J plants Van Dam with a running face slam. RVD has his opponent well-scouted and counters a Lionsault with a pair of knees. Jericho returns the favor with a pair of knees on a

Five-Star Frog Splash. That brings Christian into the ring to hit both men with the Intercontinental Title and shrug. After a groggy Doan throws out the match, "Stone Cold" Steve Austin returns to tell the champion that since he interfered, he'll face both Jericho and Van Dam at Unforgiven for the title.

A video package of Goldberg beating Hulk Hogan in 1998 for the WCW Title plays.

Rob Conway (with La Resistance) def. Spike Dudley (with The Dudley Boyz). Despite wearing a neck brace after being tossed onto a table last week, Spike is forced to compete here. When the heels come out, the Dudleys fight the champions into the crowd. That leaves the runt alone for Conway to blindside him and pull at his brace. A neckbreaker then gets him a quick three-count. Post-match, Rob sets up a table inside the squared circle and powerbombs Spike through it.

Backstage, Eric Bischoff insincerely says that he feels bad for Spike Dudley. He then asks Al Snow and Jonathan Coachman if they are going to provide more carnage and entertainment this Sunday. They plan on it and have a great idea. Before they reveal what it is, a worker delivers a note to the GM that says he has two half-naked women in his office.

After a commercial break, Eric Bischoff sees that the women in his office are none other than Mae Young and The Fabulous Moolah, the latter wanting a match tonight for her eightieth birthday. "Stone Cold" Steve Austin joins the trio to tell Eric to give her a good luck kiss. When he refuses, Mae kisses him instead. Once the women walk away, Austin jokes that Young likes Bischoff.

The Fabulous Moolah (with Mae Young) def. Victoria. To celebrate her eightieth birthday, Moolah comes out to a good hometown pop. Victoria isn't a fan, slamming her down and punching Young off the apron. While she badmouths Mae though, Moolah rolls up the "black widow" for the three-count. Post-match, Victoria hammers the women until Randy Orton runs out and pulls her off Moolah. He says she's out of her mind and Moolah doesn't deserve this on her birthday. Orton calls her a legend before introducing himself as the "Legend Killer". An RKO to the birthday girl follows to boos.

Another Goldberg video clip plays, this time featuring him giving Big Show, as The Giant, a Jackhammer.

Mark Henry/Rodney Mack (with Theodore Long) def. Goldust/Lance Storm. Lance has new rap music as he dances down the aisle. Once the heels are out, he outwrestles Mack, stunning him with a jawbreaker ahead of a dropkick and quick cover. Rodney answers with a string of forearms and a scoop slam, but lowers his head too soon for a back body drop and gets kicked. Fortunately, Henry takes up for his partner and clubs Lance as he runs the ropes. Afterwards, Mark clubs Storm into his own corner for Goldust to tag in to punch and kick the "World's Strongest Man". Despite all his blows, Henry answers with a Front Slam out of nowhere, called The World's Strongest Slam, for the victory. This match ends another Goldust WWE run, though he will seemingly be behind some cryptic messages later in the year.

Backstage, Ric Flair and Triple H congratulate Randy Orton on what he did to The Fabulous Moolah. He plans to join their celebration soon, but has a few things he has to do first. That includes staring down Maven and accusing Shawn Michaels of using people as a "steppingstone". This Sunday, he plans to use Shawn as a steppingstone. Michaels sees a lot of himself in Orton—both men stopping for a loud commotion off camera—before the "Heartbreak Kid" slaps Randy and tells him he better get the job done at Unforgiven.

Filmed earlier today, The Hurricane tries to teach Rosey how to fly, but the super hero in training doesn't get it. Instead, he calls for a cab. While the driver hangs up on him for spelling out his acronym, Terri spots Gail Kim and Molly Holly entering the arena. Molly reveals that thanks to Gail seducing Eric Bischoff last week, tonight the heels will face Trish Stratus in a handicap match.

Afterwards, Eric Bischoff heads to the ring to moderate a contract signing for Shane McMahon and Kane's "Last Man Standing" match this Sunday. On top of the contract, Eric is going to make them sign release forms that will not hold his administration liable for whatever happens at Unforgiven. The "Big Red Machine" is out first and signs his contract before igniting the turnbuckles. Shane follows. Before he signs the contract, he tells the monster that Bischoff might have signed this match to end McMahon's career, but the babyface is going to be the last man standing this Sunday. Kane tries to intimidate him by tossing aside the table, but Shane is ready for him and delivers a series of low blows before grabbing a chair and wailing on the stunned "Big Red Machine". Afterwards, McMahon puts the monster on an announce table, JR confused why it's even there considering the *Raw* announcers commentate from beside the stage. Regardless, Shane uses it to deliver a top rope flying elbow drop onto Kane for a big pop. Jerry says this is just a sample of what's going to happen at Unforgiven. Despite all the punishment he just received, the "Big Red Machine" sits up and stares at McMahon as he walks up the aisle.

Another Goldberg video shows him beating The Rock at Backlash.

Gail Kim/Molly Holly def. Trish Stratus. Outnumbered, Trish goes after both women, culminating in a double throat drop on the top rope. She then scores a two-count with a dropkick before unloading with a series of kicks to Molly. A handstand head scissors follows, but Holly slows the vixen by tossing her throat-first onto the middle rope. Gail then tags in to stomp and slam Stratus. JR says it's not fair. Whether it's fair or not, Kim scores a two-count with a second rope guillotine leg drop. Molly tags back in afterwards for a handspring back elbow and her own near fall. When she attempts a charge, Trish surprises the Women's Champion with a spinebuster for a close two-count. Unfortunately for her, Holly has a partner to tag and work with to deliver a double-team backbreaker for another near fall. Gail only stays in long enough to kick the vixen before tagging her partner for the Molly Go Round and three-count. Post-match, the heels kick and slap Stratus ahead of a double DDT. JR calls them "witches". They aren't done yet, placing Trish on a chair and holding another over her face until Lita makes a surprise return to DDT Molly and powerbomb Kim. The fans love it, especially when she rips off her shirt and gives Holly a twist of fate. Afterwards, she helps Stratus backstage.

After a commercial break, Gail Kim and Molly Holly complain to Eric Bischoff about Lita's attack. Eric doesn't understand why she's here since he fired her. "Stone Cold" Steve Austin interrupts to say that he hired her back and has signed a tag match this Sunday between the heels, Lita, and Trish Stratus. Gail can't believe she "slept with the wrong co-GM".

At ringside, Jonathan Coachman and Al Snow come out to JR and "the King's" music, respectively, mocking their Unforgiven opponents. They take a seat behind the broken announce table at ringside and have the crew cut off the regular announcers' microphones to call the upcoming match.

Val Venis def. Test (with Stacy Keibler). While the heel announcers mock their Unforgiven opponents, Stacy reluctantly follows Test to the ring. She doesn't make her customary entrance, disappointing the crowd. When Val blows her a kiss, the bodyguard hits him from behind and stomps the adult star. He then gives Keibler a chair and tells her to sit down and shut up. She doesn't, pounding on the mat to wake up Venis. That fires up "the big Valbowski" and he slips free of a pumphandle slam to sit-out powerbomb Test for a two-count. When he heads upstairs, the bodyguard kicks Charles Robinson into the ropes to crotch Val. Test follows up with a pumphandle slam, but when he goes for the cover, Stacy pulls him off the adult star. She then leads the bodyguard around the ring on a chase, bringing out Scott Steiner. When Venis gets back up, he dodges a Test Big Boot to see the bodyguard crotch himself on the top rope. Keibler makes things worse shaking the ropes up and down ahead of a "big Valbowski" uranage for the win. Post-match, Steiner tosses the bodyguard from the ring before Test pulls his valet backstage with him.

Afterwards, Jerry heads to the ring to challenge Snow to a match right now. Al accepts, but first we see footage of Goldberg dominating the SummerSlam "Elimination Chamber" match.

Jerry "the King" Lawler def. Al Snow. JR and Coach fight on commentary and call the action while their tag team partners this Sunday lock up. Al, wrestling in jeans, scores the first takedown and cover. While he might be a better technical wrestler, Lawler has a solid right hand and scores his own quick count with a fist. The two men then trade punches until "the King" gets a near fall with a DDT. Snow responds with an eye gouge and scoop slam. Following a back suplex, he tries to finish off Jerry with a suplex, but Lawler surprises him with a small package for the win. Coach can't stand it and starts to leave the announce table only to sucker punch JR from behind.

After a commercial break, JR is fine and says he needed some more motivation to fight Jonathan Coachman this Sunday. While he might not be able to wrestler, Ross promises a fight.

Inside the ring, an easel is set up for Triple H's retirement party on Goldberg's behalf. After the announcers preview Unforgiven, "Stone Cold" Steve Austin interrupts Evolution heading to the ring. He stops Randy Orton and Ric Flair from accompanying "the Game", unless Hunter doesn't have the guts to go out solo. Helmsley does and tells his stablemates to wait backstage for him.

After the final commercial break, Triple H heads to the ring in casual wear. He invites the fans to chant "Goldberg" louder than ever before because it will be the last time they do so. Tonight is a celebration and he invites everyone to live it up as balloons fall from the ceiling for the intense superstar's going away party. Hunter notes that he's been watching all of the videos for Bill tonight and couldn't help but realize that he's beaten everyone Goldberg has. Unlike the intense superstar, he's also beaten his opponent for this Sunday. After Helmsley calls himself a dynasty, his microphone goes out. Eventually, the champion is given a wired microphone. He didn't realize Bill was making microphones because they don't work either. Once back on track, "the Game" unveils a picture on the easel of Evolution leaving the intense superstar bloodied last week. He wants to give it to Goldberg as proof for his kids one day that he was in the ring with Triple H. He's also got a video package for the intense superstar, showing footage of Hunter destroying Bill. When he tries to play it again, Goldberg glares at him from the Titantron. The intense superstar invites him to take a look at the next World Champion before heading to the squared circle. There, he presses Helmsley into the air before dropping him into a powerslam for a big pop. JR says he's ready for Unforgiven.

SmackDown!

September 18, 2003
Raleigh, NC
Announcers: Michael Cole, Tazz

The show opens with a Vince McMahon statement. He is proud to announce that tonight we will see a one-hour "Iron Man" match for the WWE Title. His excitement is lowered when The Undertaker steps into the shot. He's not going to interfere in the main event because he has too much respect for the championship. However, he has no respect for Vince and "doesn't forget or forgive". After he threatens the WWE owner, the intro video plays and fireworks explode to kick off this season premiere episode.

Chris Benoit/Rey Mysterio def. Rhyno/Tajiri. As Tajiri heads to the ring, the announcers inform us that he'll challenge Rey for the Cruiserweight Title next week. Tonight, he receives a series of stiff chops from Benoit. When "the Crippler" attempts a corner charge though, the "Japanese Buzzsaw" moves and locks him in the Tarantula. Rhyno then illegally enters the ring for a spinebuster and corner shoulderblock, scoring a near fall. Benoit tries to answer with more chops, but a hard whip into the corner slows him temporarily. When the man-beast attempts to back suplex him, the "rabid wolverine" shifts his weight and falls onto Rhyno for a two-count. Afterwards, he back suplexes the man-beast before tagging in the masked man to catch Rhyno with a moonsault off the top rope. A DDT follows for a two-count before Tajiri makes the save. When Benoit rushes to his partner's defense, Jimmy Korderas cuts him off and forces him back to his corner. While he does so, the "Japanese Buzzsaw" tries to spray Mysterio with green mist. Unfortunately, the champion ducks and Tajiri hits his own partner. The babyfaces follow up with a combination 619 and German suplex to the "Japanese Buzzsaw" before Rey scores the victory courtesy of a 619 and Dropping the Dime onto Rhyno.

Shaniqua def. Nidia/Torrie Wilson (with Dawn Marie). After the announcers shill The Rock on the cover of *GQ* magazine, Torrie heads to the ring. Although The Basham Brothers accompany Shaniqua out onto the stage, she sends them backstage after they kiss her cheeks. Inside the ring, the babyfaces try to double-team the dominatrix, but Shaniqua drops them with a double clothesline. She follows up by slamming Torrie onto Nidia. Once she tosses Wilson out to the floor, Shaniqua Powerbombs Nidia for the win. Post-match, she kicks Dawn Marie and rams her into the ring post before flexing to celebrate.

Backstage, Stephanie McMahon draws on a picture of Sable and talks to someone on the phone about the upcoming "Iron Man" match. Vince McMahon, Sable, and Big Show interrupt, the WWE owner telling his daughter that he's surprised she didn't quit last week. She refuses to leave, but he promises to make her. He warns her that she played rough last week and he's going to get even rougher to the point where she'll beg him to let her quit.

A video package featuring Brock Lesnar and Kurt Angle wrestling at WrestleMania XIX and SummerSlam plays. They've each won one match and tonight they'll settle things.

Backstage, Chavo Guerrero Jr. tells Eddie Guerrero that Stephanie McMahon gave them a WWE Tag Title match. Eddie is proud of his nephew. He gets fired up when Chavo tells him that "Latino Heat" can become a double champion tonight and they should do it for their grandma.

The *WrestleMania XIX* video game replay is Eddie Guerrero Frog Splashing John Cena last week after Chavo Guerrero Jr.'s interference.

In a prerecorded promo, John Cena says he got cheated by the best, but he hasn't lost any steam. Next week, he promises to fulfill his patriotic duty as an "American thug".

MUST SEE! Los Guerreros def. The World's Greatest Tag Team (WWE Tag Title match). Chavo makes his in-ring return from injury. In the time he's been gone, Eddie has become a big star and the fans happily chant his name as he ties up with Benjamin. The challengers make quick tags to keep Shelton in their corner ahead of a double back elbow. Eventually, the champion drives "Latino Heat" back into the heel corner for Charlie to double-team him. Now it's the champions making quick tags, but a northern lights suplex allows Eddie to give his nephew the tag. Showing no ring rust, Chavo punches both heels and monkey flips Shelton. A dropkick to Haas follows before he chases Benjamin off with a head scissors. Following tandem slingshot splashes out to the floor, we take a commercial break with the challengers in control.

Afterwards, Eddie remains in control, chopping and elbowing Charlie. Chavo returns to drop a knee on Haas's back ahead of a dropkick to the chest. Luckily, Shelton breaks his cover. The champions briefly work the returning superstar over in their corner before "Latino Heat" tags in to try to back suplex the heel. Benjamin counters with a cross body block, but Chavo breaks his cover. When Shelton attempts to powerbomb him, Eddie rolls him up. The legal men then connect with simultaneous clotheslines, forcing them to both tag out. While Mike Chioda is distracted, Shelton superkicks Chavo's injured bicep. That turns the tide and the champions focus on Chavo's arm with slams, strikes, and hammerlocks. Despite the pain, he fights back with a flying forearm, but Benjamin prevents him from making the tag with a running forearm. While Chioda gets Shelton out of the ring, Chavo makes the tag but the referee doesn't see it. It doesn't matter as the challenger knocks Haas down and leaps over Benjamin for the hot tag. Eddie gets in several shots to both champions, but when he goes for his trio of suplexes to Shelton, Charlie stops the last one with a German suplex. Unfortunately, Benjamin recovers and attempts another superkick afterwards only to accidentally kick his own partner. "Latino Heat" capitalizes with a combination head scissors and headlock takedown. Afterwards, he attempts to head upstairs for a Frog Splash, but by the time he knocks Shelton out of the way to try to dive towards Haas, the champion recovers and moves. Fortunately, Eddie sees him rolling away and somersaults to his feet. That sends Charlie out to the floor to grab a chair. Benjamin joins him. While Haas distracts the referee, Shelton swings for the fences, but "Latino Heat" ducks. Chavo rushes to his uncle's aid, dropkicking the chair into Benjamin's knee. That takes him out of the match and lets Los Guerreros plant Charlie with a double-team hip toss neckbreaker. A Chavo suplex afterwards puts Haas back into position for a Frog Splash to crown new champions. Post-match, Los Guerreros celebrate in their lowrider.

Ahead of the main event, Tazz reads off his keys to victory for both men.

The Clearasil Smack of the Night is Brock Lesnar tossing Stephanie McMahon into the barricade.

At ringside, the announcers shill how big the upcoming WWE Title match is going to. They aren't the only ones excited as we see wrestlers in the back and at The APA's card table getting ready for the match. One of those wrestlers sitting at the card table is the future Mickie James making her first WWE appearance.

MUST SEE! Brock Lesnar def. Kurt Angle (WWE Title "Iron Man" match). As the wrestlers head to the ring, the announcers explain the rules for the match. It's basically a normal match where each man is looking to get as many falls as possible in sixty minutes. They also talk about the four other men who have competed in a sixty-minute WWE "Iron Man" match before Brock cheap shots Kurt and pounds him down to open the contest. In early control, the challenger stomps, chokes, and tosses around the Olympian. Angle responds with a series of clotheslines and a dropkick to the knee. A belly-to-belly suplex afterwards sends Lesnar retreating out to the floor. When he returns, the heel calls for a timeout. It's just to sucker the champion for another sneak attack. Once again, Kurt recovers quickly and chases off Brock. He threatens to use the ring steps before dropping them and breaking Brian Hebner's count. The fans aren't happy with his stalling as he refuses to return to the squared circle. He only briefly returns before retreating again when the Olympian teases a single leg takedown. This time, the challenger surprises Angle with a throat drop on the top rope before returning to club, stomp, and choke him. The champion answers with a belly-to-belly suplex and a clothesline back out to the floor, Lesnar grabbing his knee in agony. Kurt doesn't give him a chance to recover this time, leaving the squared circle to punch and ram the heel's head into the ring steps. Brock answers by ramming him back into the apron and ring post. Afterwards, Lesnar grabs a chair and smashes the Olympian's head for the disqualification. Angle 1. Lesnar 0.

More shots follow during the break between falls before the heel stomps and trash talks Angle. The announcers are confused why he would give up a fall. The answer is obvious when he hoists the champion up for an F5 and three-count. Angle 1. Lesnar 1.

Following another brief break, Brock traps Kurt in an anklelock. The Olympian has no choice but to tap out ahead of a commercial break. Lesnar 2. Angle 1.

During the break, Lesnar Angle Slams the champion. Somehow, Angle manages to kick out. Afterwards, he dodges a corner charge to punch the heel and rock him with a flying forearm. Kurt follows up with a trio of German suplexes, but the heel slows his momentum by flinging him out to the floor. There, he whips the Olympian into the railing. An F5 on the floor follows for Brock to get a count-out fall. Lesnar 3. Angle 1.

After a commercial break, Angle is back up and attempting a comeback only to see the challenger knock him out to the floor with a back elbow. Chokes and elbow drops back in the ring get Lesnar a near fall. When he misses a clothesline, the champion capitalizes with an Angle Slam to cut the lead. Lesnar 3. Angle 2.

In between falls, Cole reveals that UPN has granted *SmackDown!* additional time in the event of a tie for sudden death. Kurt tries to make that a possibility with a suplex for a two-count. The men exchange shots, but the Olympian cuts off his opponent's momentum with a German suplex. They then counter each other's finishers before Angle traps the heel in an Anklelock. Although the champion holds up from hitting Hebner when Brock kicks him off, his opponent doesn't do the same. That pays off for the challenger when there is no referee to count after Kurt's Angle Slam. Hebner also misses Lesnar giving the Olympian a low blow. He then heads to ringside and flings Mark Yeaton out of his way to grab the WWE Title. After bashing Angle's head, the heel wakes up the referee to score another fall. Lesnar 4. Angle 2.

After a commercial break, the champion pulls Brock out to the floor and whips him into the ring post. He follows up with a double ax-handle off the top rope for a two-count. He also gets a near fall with a top rope missile dropkick, but the challenger just kicks out. When he heads upstairs for a moonsault, Lesnar rolls out of the way and Kurt crashes hard onto the canvas. Despite that, he still gets a two-count with a roll-up, but the heel responds with a vicious clothesline. The momentum swings with that move and Brock nearly gets another fall with an overhead release belly-to-belly suplex. When he tries to lock on a bearhug, the Olympian counters with an Anklelock. He doesn't hold it for long before the challenger tosses him out to the floor. There, he repays Angle's earlier attack, tossing him into the ring steps for another near fall. Frustrated, he grabs the ring steps, but the champion baseball slide kicks them back into his head. That gets him a pair of close two-counts back in the squared circle. With just eighteen and a half minutes to go, Kurt scores a near fall ahead of a commercial break with a series of strikes. During the final break, Lesnar gets another fall with a top rope superplex. Lesnar 5. Angle 2.

Now up three falls, the heel tries to finish off the Olympian with an F5 into the ring post. Fortunately for Angle, he slips free and uses Brock's own move against him, driving his knee into the steel with an F5. Back in the squared circle, the champion cinches in a single leg crab. The challenger doesn't want to submit and crawls to the ropes, but Kurt pulls him back with an Anklelock. When he reaches the ropes again, Lesnar kicks free of the hold, but the damage is done. Smelling blood, the Olympian goes right back after the heel's leg only to run into an F5. Unfortunately, Brock is slow to make the cover for what would possibly give him an insurmountable lead. Angle capitalizes and just kicks out. He then surprises the challenger, rushing up to the top rope for a superplex and three-count. Lesnar 5. Angle 3.

A little over nine minutes left in the match, both men are down and work Hebner's standing ten-count to seven. Once up, the superstars trade right hands. The champion wins the exchange, hammering Lesnar down in a corner. A suplex fires up Kurt and he lowers his straps to attempt an Angle Slam. The heel slips free and responds with a DDT, but he can't hold the Olympian down for a three-count. Back up, Angle hammers him some more until Brock answers with a German suplex. A second puts both men down on the mat again. Tazz says the challenger doesn't need to make a cover. He doesn't, slowly pulling the champion up for a third German suplex. When he goes for a fourth, Kurt blocks and explodes around him for his own German suplex. A second follows, but Lesnar blocks a third. When he tries to deliver another German suplex, the Olympian rolls through and reapplies the Anklelock, finally scoring the tap-out. Lesnar 5. Angle 4.

Once the rest period ends, Angle goes right back to the Anklelock. This time, the heel escapes by flinging the champion into the ropes. Kurt is right back on him and applies a full body stretch. Cole wonders if it's a smart move to lock on a hold this late. Tazz thinks so, but it wastes time. By the time Brock escapes there's just two minutes left in the match and he rolls out to the floor. There, the Olympian applies another Anklelock, but he can't score the win on the floor. When he rolls the challenger back in the ring, Lesnar rolls back out to the floor. A head slam onto the ring steps stuns him enough for Angle to slow the heel and German suplex him back in the squared circle. Three more follow, but Brock holds onto the referee to low blow the champion afterwards. Instead of staying away from the downed Kurt and running out the time, the challenger gets too close to him and the Olympian traps Lesnar in an Anklelock. He refuses to give up, holding on for the final twenty seconds to score the victory and the championship. Lesnar 5. Angle 4.

Even without the title change, this is an incredible "Iron Man" match. Not only do the wrestlers showcase some great technical moves, but Brock breaks out a unique spot where he uses a chair to soften up Angle for the rest of the match. The nine falls are just two behind the record pace Triple H and The Rock set in the previous "Iron Man" match, but provide a good tempo for the contest and keep the fans engaged throughout. This is definitely a match to find for all wrestling fans.

PPV: Unforgiven
September 21, 2003
Hershey, PA
Announcers: Jim Ross, Jerry "the King" Lawler

The show opens with a video package featuring the top stars on the show and a creepy woman doing a voiceover talking about the days of "good and evil" going away. Instead, tonight is a battle of titans, Triple H promising that tonight will be Goldberg's last in the WWE. Afterwards, fireworks explode and the Unforgiven logo is set on fire to kick off the PPV.

MUST SEE! The Dudley Boyz def. La Resistance/Rob Conway ("Tables" World Tag Title match). Due to injury, Spike Dudley is out of this match. On the plus side, the World Titles are now on the line thanks to "Stone Cold" Steve Austin on *Heat*, but the Dudleys have to put all three members of the heel squad through tables to get the victory. D-Von is ready to go, punching and slamming Dupree's face to the canvas. When the champion forces him back into the heel corner, Rob tags in to wail on the challenger. Dudley answers with a slam and leg drop. He and Bubba Ray, from the apron, then work together to double clothesline Conway. Bubba tags in afterwards to slug the French sympathizer and tie him to the tree of woe. A vicious clothesline turns Rob inside out before Bubba Ray stacks all of the heels up in the challengers' corner for a big splash. The Dudleys follow with a double flapjack to Conway, but Rene swings the momentum for the heels, pounding Bubba down. Afterwards, the heels make quick tags and isolate Dudley in their corner for a series of fists and chokes. La Resistance also add in a double backward head slam while the fans chant "USA". When Rob applies a sleeper hold, Bubba Ray quickly escapes with a side suplex. Both men tag out afterwards for D-Von to clothesline Renee and Conway. A neckbreaker follows to Rob, but he recovers quickly only to miss a blind tag and walk into a double-team neckbreaker from the challengers. The Dudleys follow up with a wassup drop to Dupree's groin. It's finally time for tables and the fans go wild. When they set one up in the ring, the heels attack them from behind. Rene brings in a second table and props it up in a corner for his partners to whip D-Von through it. Interestingly, this is not an "Elimination" match. Despite going through the table, D-Von isn't eliminated from the match. However, if Bubba Ray goes through a table as well, The Dudley Boyz lose their shot at the titles. The three heels try to put Bubba through the other one, but he fights back until Conway slows him with a neckbreaker. Sylvan then trades shots with the babyface while his partners continue to work over D-Von at ringside. That proves costly as Bubba Ray surprises Grenier with a suplex through the set up table. He still has to put two men through tables while the heels only have to drive Bubba through one. They try to do that with a double back body drop, but D-Von pulls the table out of the way for the save. Bubba Ray takes advantage, Bubba Bombing Dupree before the Dudleys toss Rob over the top rope and through a table at ringside. There are two set up, but just like Spike, he clips the second table. While officials check on him, Sylvan tries to hit the challengers with the French flag. Instead, D-Von takes it away and bashes his skull. Rene comes to his rescue with a double clothesline. He then sets up a table, but tries to put D-Von through it by mistake. It doesn't matter as the challenger slips free and lifts Dupree up for a 3D through the table to win the championships for the eighth time.

Test (with Stacy Keibler) def. Scott Steiner. Following a music video package for the match, Stacy heads to the ring solo. After she stretches out between the ropes, Test comes out to do the same. She can't stand him. Neither can Scott. Keibler wants to go back to him and hugs him. If Steiner wins this match, she'll end up in his corner again. However, if the bodyguard wins, "Big Poppa Pump" will have to work for him too. Test tries to get the quick win attacking Scott from behind, but the babyface responds with a powerslam and stiff chops. A clothesline and elbow drop follows for a one-count before Steiner does a set of pushups. When the bodyguard retreats to the floor and hides behind Stacy, she slaps him. Despite that, Test seizes control and tosses "Big Poppa Pump" into the ring steps. A full nelson slam back in the squared circle nearly gets the bodyguard the win. He loses focus moments later, doing his own pushups after a corner clothesline. That lets Scott respond with some more hammering blows before Test traps him in a sleeper hold. Keibler cheers Steiner on, but the bodyguard remains in control until he leaps off the top rope into a belly-to-belly suplex. Catching a second wind, "Big Poppa Pump" clotheslines and chops Test before scoring a two-count with a belly-to-belly suplex. He tries to follow up, but the bodyguard hides behind Nick Patrick and pokes the babyface's eyes. Despite that, Scott recovers quickly for a double underhook powerbomb and two-count. When he tries to follow up, Test slows him with a low blow and nearly scores the win with a roll-up with his feet on the ropes. Fortunately, Keibler breaks the count. The bodyguard tries to make her pay, pulling her up onto the apron, but she drops down and throat drops him on the top rope into a reverse DDT for a close two-count. Back up, Test pumphandle slams his opponent, but Stacy hops onto the ropes and shows her backside to distract him for a Steiner roll-up and near fall. The bodyguard then chases after Keibler, forcing her into the ring where she runs into "Big Poppa Pump". Test capitalizes with a Big Boot, but Scott somehow kicks out. Frustrated, the bodyguard removes a turnbuckle pad right in front of the referee. While he attempts to tie it back on, Test gets a chair. Although Stacy takes it away, she misses him with her shot and nails Steiner. The bodyguard follows up with a Big Boot to score the win and Scott's services. Post-match, Test kisses a despondent Keibler.

A Trish Stratus VHS ad plays.

Randy Orton (with Ric Flair) def. Shawn Michaels. Following a video package for this rivalry, Shawn gives Orton a wrestling lesson and takes him down to the mat. In Randy's head, Michaels stays a step ahead of him with a series of headlock takedowns and struts to mock Ric. He then lays on the top rope, frustrating the "Legend Killer". The young heel responds with a side headlock, but the "Heartbreak Kid" quickly escapes and tosses him over the top rope. Unfortunately, Randy skins the cat and scores a two-count with a dropkick and clothesline. Fists and a scoop slam follow before Orton heads upstairs only to leap into an inverted atomic drop. Clotheslines follow, Shawn driving both men over the top rope only to show the young star how it's done by skinning the cat. He then interrupts the "Legend Killer's" conference with Flair by baseball slide kicking him. A flying cross body block off the top rope follows, JR talking about how bad Michaels's back is. Despite his injury, the "Heartbreak Kid" is back in the ring first to score a two-count with a bridging German suplex. A sunset flip also gets him a near fall before he runs into a corner boot. The two men then trade fists and chops until Earl Hebner intervenes. That lets Randy catch his breath and dodge a corner charge. After Shawn wraps his shoulder around the ring post and falls out to the floor, "The Nature Boy" rams him into the steel. Orton then heads to the floor to slam Michaels's shoulder into the ring post as well. Focusing on the injured arm, the "Legend Killer" drives it onto the top rope before slamming the "Heartbreak Kid" to the canvas by the arm. A hammerlock follows. Although Shawn fights free, one sledgehammer blow to the arm slows him for an armbar drop and two-count. Randy then stretches out the injured arm while Ric shouts instructions at ringside. After an extended stay in the stretch, Michaels rolls over to punch and cover Orton for a two-count. Moments later, he holds the ropes to dodge a dropkick before unloading with more chops and right hands. A flying forearm follows to put both men down. After laying on the mat for a few seconds, the "Heartbreak Kid" kips up. Catching a second wind, he hits both heels before tossing the "Legend Killer" out to the floor. Shawn follows him with a splash off the apron. Following shots at ringside, Michaels decks Ric again ahead of a flying double ax-handle to Randy for another near fall. Orton answers with a hard whip that sends the "Heartbreak Kid" upside down in a corner. Groggy, the "Legend Killer" tries to follow up with a second rope double ax-handle, but leaps into a boot to the jaw. Shawn doesn't waste time tuning up the band, but Randy catches his foot and plants him with an RKO. Unfortunately, he's slow to make the cover and Michaels just kicks out. Incensed, Flair yells for Orton to follow up. He tries to do so with a top rope flying cross body block, but the "Heartbreak Kid" dodges. After decking "The Nature Boy" one more time, Shawn drills the "Legend Killer" with a top rope flying elbow drop. That hurts his injured arm as well and he's also slow to make the cover, only getting a near fall. Reaching down deep, Michaels finds another gear and kips up to tune up the band. With the fans cheering him on, the "Heartbreak Kid" delivers Sweet Chin Music. That gets him a three-count, but while Hebner is making the count, Ric drapes Randy's foot on the bottom rope. That sees Earl restart the match and Shawn drop Flair with a second Sweet Chin Music. When he tries to back suplex Randy afterwards, the "Legend Killer" peppers Michaels with brass knuckles for the tainted victory.

Backstage, Chris Jericho tells La Resistance and Rob Conway that they look like a mess in the trainer's office. Y2J says this isn't their fault. He blames "Stone Cold" Steve Austin for making them put their titles on the line tonight. Jericho promises to stand up for the locker room against the "rattlesnake".

Lita/Trish Stratus def. Gail Kim/Molly Holly. Following over a year on the sidelines, Lita makes her return to the ring tonight only to see the heels attack her and Trish from behind. It doesn't take the babyfaces long to turn the tide and Lita to crush both heels in a corner, leaping off her partner's back. They follow up with a pair of baseball slide kicks. Once Chad Patton restores order, Lita tosses around Gail and suplexes her. The vixen then tags in to leap onto Kim and punch the rookie. Chops and clotheslines follow before Stratus scores a near fall with a Chick Kick after her Matrix dodge. Fortunately, Molly makes the save. She also helps out by pulling the ropes down for Trish to fall awkwardly out to the floor. While Patton forces Lita back to her corner, the heels double-team Stratus and drive her back into the apron. Holly then tags in to stretch the vixen's back. When Gail returns, she kicks Trish and locks her in a dragon sleeper. The vixen answers, pushing out of a corner for a modified backward head slam. Before she can tag out though, Molly runs around the ring to pull Lita off the apron and face-first into the canvas. That busts open the returning superstar's mouth and lets the heels continue to isolate Stratus, Holly nearly scoring the win with a backbreaker. Trish responds with a combination head scissors and headlock takedown to both heels, but a Kim clothesline prevents the tag again. Following a scoop slam, Gail tries to finish off the vixen with a second rope guillotine leg drop, but only hits canvas. Lita gets the hot tag afterwards to punch and head scissors the Women's Champion. A powerbomb follows to Kim. While she's down, Stratus tosses Molly off the top rope with a handstand head scissors. Lita follows up with a reverse twist of fate and Moonsault for the win.

Kane def. Shane McMahon ("Last Man Standing" match). Following a video package for this match, Kane makes his way to the squared circle first. Shane doesn't wait for him to get into the ring, rushing right behind him and hitting him with a chair repeatedly for Charles Robinson's standing ten-count. The only way to get the win here is by keeping your opponent down for ten seconds, but the "Big Red Machine" is up at four. McMahon changes tactics and hits the monster's knee with the chair to drop him to the mat. He then wraps the joint around the ring post until Kane kicks him back into the barricade. Shane refuses to stay down, chop blocking the "Big Red Machine" and ramming his face into the ring steps. He also slams the back of his head into the steel repeatedly. He tries to follow up with a flying dive off the barricade, but the monster catches and powerslams him for a five-count. JR says it wasn't a pretty slam, but it was effective. Regardless, it swings the momentum and Kane whips McMahon hard into the ring steps. He then picks them up and uses the steps as a weapon, running them into the babyface's skull. Somehow, Shane gets up at eight and the fight returns to the ring for a string of "Big Red Machine" boots. He follows up with a Chokeslam. McMahon won't stay down, pulling himself up with the help of Robinson's clothing. The monster tries to knock him back down with a big boot, but Shane moves and Kane rocks the referee. The "Big Red Machine" doesn't care. He tells McMahon that he's going to send him to his mom before setting up the ring steps base inside the squared circle. When he tries to Tombstone the babyface, Shane slips free and drives the monster face-first onto the steps. McMahon then repeatedly rams the steps back into Kane's head and shoulder in a corner. That gives him an idea and he props the steps up against the "Big Red Machine" for a top rope coast-to-coast flying dropkick. Unfortunately, there's no referee to count out the monster. When Shane recovers and crawls toward Kane, the "Big Red Machine" shoves the steps down onto his head. Robinson finally recovers to count both men down, but they both just make it to their feet. Afterwards, the monster tosses McMahon out to the floor again, stomping and punching him in the aisle. Shane answers with some short punches to the ribs and a big uppercut. The two men refuse to quit, crawling along the floor and punching each other. Kane gets the upper hand once again and scores a six-count with a whip into the entrance set. When Shane starts to stand, the "Big Red Machine" whips him into the set two more times. He gets a six-count again before hammering McMahon and tossing him out in front of the Spanish announce table. He then propels Shane into the upraised table. When he lands on the concrete floor, the monster heads up the stage and tosses the announce table down onto him. Unfortunately, he misses, and McMahon sneak attacks the "Big Red Machine" when he hops down to check his handiwork. Metal sign shots stun the monster ahead of Shane swinging the boom camera around to put Kane down for a nine-count. Since he can't knock him out, McMahon tries to choke out the "Big Red Machine" with a camera cable. He then dances, low blows, and DDTs the monster on the stage. That's still not enough for him to get the victory, so Shane smashes Kane with a monitor. The fans want McMahon to toss the "Big Red Machine" off the stage. Instead, he bashes the monster's head one more time before climbing on top of the set. Fifteen feet above Kane, Shane attempts a flying dive, but at the last second the "Big Red Machine" moves and McMahon crashes through the set. That finally gives the monster the victory before WWE officials rush out to help the babyface. JR bets he has a broken neck and the trainers treat him as such as they put him in a brace and stretcher him backstage in between replays of Shane's dive.

Backstage, Chris Jericho interrupts "Stone Cold" Steve Austin. The heel blames Austin for Shane McMahon's injuries since he turned Kane into a monster. He's also mad about La Resistance getting injured. Austin tells him to take his shot if he has a problem with the "rattlesnake". Y2J refuses to take a shot at him, but he promises to make "Stone Cold" crack. He'll start by winning the Intercontinental Title tonight.

Christian def. Chris Jericho and Rob Van Dam (Intercontinental Title match). The champion is out first for this match, watching as his opponents head to the squared circle. JR calls RVD the greatest superstar never to win a World Championship. That's lofty praise. The heels aren't impressed, double-teaming Rob until he flips over a double back body drop to dropkick both opponents. He then back body drops Christian out to the floor. Before he can follow up, Jericho forearms him only to be suplexed out of the ring. Van Dam then moonsaults off the second rope onto both heels. Back in the ring, he gets a near fall with a slingshot leg drop to the champion. Kicks in a corner follow ahead of a monkey flip and another two-count. Once he kicks Christian down again, Jericho surprises RVD with a flying attack. He then chops Rob until the popular superstar ducks a cross body block and answers with a moonsault and two-count. Van Dam also lands a springboard kick, but when he hits the ropes, Christian blocks rolling thunder and tosses RVD into the ring steps. The champion and Y2J take turns afterwards stomping Rob, but there's tension between the two. They set aside their differences for Christian to hold the babyface for Jericho's fists and a clothesline. Van Dam tries to flip over a Y2J corner charge but doesn't quite accomplish it. Instead, the heels reset the spot. This time, RVD dodges a Jericho charge to flatten the champion. Unfortunately, Y2J drops him with an enziguri kick. JR blames the last match for taking the air out of the crowd, but it might be the heels dominating that has the fans absolutely silent. Even Van Dam surprising the heels with a double DDT to counter a double flapjack doesn't make much of a difference to the crowd. Rob follows up with a flying somersault splash over the top rope onto the champion, but when he attempts to return to the ring, Jericho surprises him with a springboard dropkick. Nick Patrick tries to count out all three men when Y2J fights with RVD on the floor, but JR informs everyone that there are no count-outs. There also aren't disqualifications as Jericho chokes Rob with his wrist tape. When he applies a reverse chin lock, Lawler somberly reveals that Shane McMahon has been taken to a medical facility. Eventually, Van Dam escapes the rest hold and rolls up Y2J for a two-count. The heel answers with a clothesline and his one foot on the chest cover. When that doesn't score him the victory, Chris blocks a hurricanrana attempt and sits back into the Walls of Jericho. That finally wakes up the fans and they cheer for RVD to escape. He nearly reaches the ropes, but Jericho drags him back to the center of the ring. Before he can tap out, Christian breaks the hold and covers Rob for a two-count. That sets off Y2J and the friends end their partnership to trade shots at ringside. That culminates in Jericho whipping the champion into the ring steps. Back in the squared circle, Y2J scores a two-count with a top rope flying back elbow. When he attempts his running face slam, Christian dodges and answers with a poke to the eye and reverse DDT for a near fall with his feet on the ropes. He heads upstairs afterwards as Van Dam returns to the apron. When Jericho knocks the popular superstar back to the floor, he also shakes the ropes and crotches the champion. Y2J capitalizes with a superplex to put both men down for a Patrick nine-count. The announcers wonder if RVD would win the belt if the referee gets to ten, but we don't find out as Rob covers Christian for a near fall. He also gets a two-count with a springboard cross body block to Jericho. Y2J answers with a running face slam, but misses his Lionsault and hurts his knee. Van Dam doesn't miss a kick and twisting moonsault for a two-count. When Christian tries to make the save with a flying elbow drop, RVD moves and the champion hits his fellow heel. Jericho still manages to kick out of Rob's subsequent cover, but he can't get up before Van Dam drop toe holds Christian face-first into Y2J's crotch. With the heels stacked on top of each other, RVD goes upstairs and flies onto them with a Five-Star Frog Splash. It takes a lot out of Rob too and he's slow to get up. Instead of getting the three-count, he's only able to toss the champion out to the floor before setting Jericho into position for an electric chair drop off the second rope. Christian joins him, slipping under Van Dam to powerbomb him, Y2J flying to the canvas as well. The champion then covers both men for a pair of two-counts. He can't follow up as RVD kicks him out to the floor. Christian grabs his belt, but Rob sees him coming and rolls up the champion for a near fall. He heads upstairs afterwards, stopping only to kick a chair back into Jericho's face before attempting his Five-Star Frog Splash. At the last second, Christian hits Van Dam with the title belt to steal the victory.

Backstage, Marc Lloyd asks Triple H what he needs to do to defeat Goldberg tonight. Hunter tells him a fairytale about a hero beating monster after monster. Helmsley doesn't believe in fairytales or the hype. He only believes in himself and invites Bill to "play the Game".

Al Snow/Jonathan Coachman def. Jerry "the King" Lawler/Jim Ross. Following a video package for this match, the heels head to the ring for their opportunity to take over announcing duties on *Raw*. "The King" wonders who will announce this match before heading to the ring. JR says that's an executive problem because he's focused on keeping his job. He gets the final entrance and a nice pop as the Oklahoma Sooners' marching band music plays. Coach wants a piece of him, but Al starts the match for his team. Jerry takes advantage of the heels' confusion rolling up Snow and covering him for a quick two-count. The wrestlers then trade near falls, no one providing commentary. Instead, we hear JR and Coach yelling at each other while Lawler punches the crazed superstar for another two-count. Al answers in kind and threatens to slap Ross ahead of a two-count. After he only gets a near fall with a roll-up, Snow yells at Chad Patton. He still only gets a two-count with a clothesline before applying a sitting abdominal stretch. When "the King" powers out, the crazed superstar back body drops him. Coachman wants him to do it again. Instead, Jerry answers with a Piledriver, but Al drapes his foot on the rope to stop Patton's count. When Coach tags himself in, Snow can't believe it. He can only cheer on his partner as he punches and covers Lawler for another two-count. When he attempts a bronco buster though, "the King" moves and catches a second wind while Jonathan crotches himself. After he decks Al, Jerry goes to work hammering and slamming Coachman. The fans want tables, but get a second rope falling fist drop for a near fall. At the last second, Snow makes the save. That sends Lawler to his corner to tag JR. When Snow cuts him off, Ross gives him a low blow ahead of a clothesline out to the floor. He then clotheslines Coach from behind and kicks his ribs. While he mounts and punches the heel, Patton checks on the crazed superstar at ringside. That brings out Chris Jericho to dropkick the back of JR's head. After he pulls Coachman over onto Ross, the referee turns and spots the cover for the three-count. Post-match, Marc Lloyd asks Y2J why he did that. Jericho says there are multiple ways to get "Stone Cold" Steve Austin to crack and costing his friend his job is a good start. Inside the ring, JR can't believe that he's lost his job again.

MUST SEE! Goldberg def. Triple H (World Title versus Career match). Following a video package for the match, JR is back at the announce table apologizing to "the King" for costing them their jobs. Lawler doesn't blame him. Jim says Jerry is like a brother to him and they have one last job to call the World Title match. JR promises to give the fans something to remember. Lilian then explains that Triple H can lose the championship by any means, including count-out or disqualification, but if Goldberg loses, his career is over. Hunter then heads to the squared circle in his groin protecting biker shorts to spit water at the crowd. Goldberg follows with his customary entrance starting backstage and walking through sparks. The fans chant for the intense superstar as Earl Hebner goes over final instructions for the competitors. Bill is ready for a fight, press slamming and chasing off Helmsley. When Hebner counts to seven, Goldberg makes a mistake and interrupts his count. Lawler says that's not smart. The intense superstar wants to prove he's unquestionably the better man, punching and driving "the Game" back out to the floor. When he tries to pull him back in, the champion throat drops Bill onto the top rope. He then tosses the challenger out the other side of the ring only to see Goldberg return to hammer Triple H once again. When he sets up for a Spear, Hunter counters with a high knee to finally turn the tide. After catching his breath, Helmsley clotheslines the intense superstar out to the floor. He follows him and rams Bill's face into the ring post. Taking a rare risk, "the Game" scores a two-count with a middle rope flying elbow to the head. Shots follow in the squared circle and at ringside. Hunter tries to take the challenger's legs out from under him, wrapping his knee against the ring post. A chop block follows, but when he tries to apply a figure four leg lock, Goldberg kicks him back into a corner. The champion is tenacious and chop blocks his opponent once again before finally locking on the figure four. Triple H is close enough to the ropes to grab them for added leverage right beside Hebner. The intense superstar has to drag him to the center of the ring to block his extra leverage and turn over the hold. That forces Hunter to break it, but the damage has been done and he drops a knee on Bill's chest. When he attempts a second knee drop, the challenger catches his leg and fights back up to his feet to run through Helmsley. A tilt-a-whirl powerslam nearly wins him the championship afterwards. The fight then spills out to the floor where Goldberg drives him into the ring steps, busting open "the Game". Holding one of his arms awkwardly, the intense superstar refuses to quit and hip tosses the champion. When he picks him up for a powerslam, Triple H slips free and shoves Bill into Hebner, sending the referee out to the floor. Hunter capitalizes with a low blow, but when he sets up for a Pedigree, the challenger back body drops him out of the squared circle. There, he grabs a sledgehammer from under the ring to nail Goldberg. Despite that shot, the intense superstar surprises Helmsley with a Spear. After he kicks the weapon out to the floor, he Jackhammers "the Game" for the victory. The show ends with the new champion celebrating and JR saying goodbye to everyone.

The second *Raw* exclusive PPV, the WWE steps up their offering. It's much better than Bad Blood, but that's not a hard mark to top. The action tonight is good with some title changes and impactful moments. However, *Raw* still doesn't sport the in-ring action that *SmackDown!* does, and other than Randy Orton, doesn't have any young rising stars. It does start with an exciting "Tables" match and World Tag Title change. By this point, the Dudleys know exactly who they are and what they do in and out of the ring. The fans love them, and they are good for an opening pop. La Resistance are a team that's easy to hate and the pairing makes for a decent match, the tables covering up the rookies' skill level. Test and Steiner then pound each other through another tepid match. *Raw* doesn't have many other options, but Scott went from a main event contender to becoming Test's "property" in under a year. Randy and Shawn have a solid match that shows Orton has the potential to compete with the best. He's got great athleticism and good moves and Michaels helps him put it together here for a good match that features a tainted ending to help the "Heartbreak Kid" save face. The women's tag match follows and features Lita making a return, and bleeding. Other than the return, it's nothing above a typical *Raw* match, though the women do get almost seven-minutes here, a bit of an improvement thanks to the brand split. Kane and Shane then beat each other up for almost twenty minutes. It's not the most brutal match in WWE history, but it's good and features some impressive spots and one jaw-dropping fall from McMahon. Shane always entertains in his PPV matches and this is no different. If anything, the ending takes away a bit from Kane being a monster, but the big fall has the fans in shock and gives the event a tentpole moment. Unfortunately, it takes the steam out of the Intercontinental Title match. Everything the wrestlers do is good, there are no big mistakes, and all three men are over with their characters. Despite all that, the crowd is dead for most of this match. Part of it is the handicap like nature with the heels double-teaming RVD early on, but this match would have benefited from being earlier on the card. Christian continues to cheat to win and that's a good thing considering what happens in the main event. The WWE needs at least one heel champion to frustrate the fans and babyfaces. The tag match between commentary teams is long and feels even longer without commentary, but Snow and Lawler do most of the work. They don't do anything special here, but Jericho continues his war to get Austin fired by costing his friend his job in the end. The fans are firmly behind JR when he's in the ring, but the rest of the match doesn't really connect. It's hard to give it a bad rating because no one is expecting much, but it's not very good and gets a nice spot on the card over some other bigger matches. It also promises a heel commentary team tomorrow night. Finally, Goldberg winning the World Title should be a big moment and the fans cheer it as such, but the match is a little flat. Partly due to Triple H's injury and some due to a tired crowd, this one doesn't feel as big as it should. The WWE missed the opportunity to move the belt last month in front of a hot crowd, but the title change finally happens here. It's fifteen minutes long, but could probably be ten. Combined with Hunter's injury, the two men just don't gel in the ring. It's not bad, but it's not amazing. The fans want to see the title change, cheering for the new champion, but this doesn't feel like a huge coronation. Overall, Unforgiven is just that…not bad, but not great. It's a decent show, but even some of the big moments feel like they could be bigger. However, it is a big step up from Bad Blood and freshens up the World Title picture after a dominant Triple H run.

Monday Night Raw
September 22, 2003
Washington, D.C.
Announcers: Jonathan Coachman, Al Snow

Following the intro video and fireworks, Lilian Garcia introduces some injured soldiers in the crowd to a great pop. The announcers also get a special introduction, the fans booing the new team. They are at their heel best as they compliment each other and talk about seizing their opportunity last night.

Afterwards, Goldberg heads to the ring to a big pop. He tells the fans and Triple H to "believe the hype" as he holds up the World Title. "Stone Cold" Steve Austin then walks out, Coach saying he's stealing the champion's thunder. Steve says there are only a few things in the world that make him happy and that's beer, four-letter words, and the US armed forces. He's got another thing to add to that list—Bill beating Hunter for the championship. "Stone Cold" will drink to that, disgusting the announcers. The champion is happy to share a beer with him and the fans give the babyfaces another nice pop before Eric Bischoff steps through the curtain. The announcers love him and cheer as he heads to the ring as well. Eric congratulates the new champion and says he was just trying to motivate him when he made Randy Orton his partner two weeks ago. He claims that he knows what it takes to get Bill motivated since he created the intense superstar. That sets off Goldberg and he Spears Eric, the co-general manager's head hitting the ropes awkwardly, for a big pop and chant.

Rob Van Dam def. Christian (Intercontinental Title match) by disqualification. Following a wounded soldier saying hello to his friends and family in a sit down promo, RVD comes out to a nice cheer. When the champion follows, Rob flips over him and scores a two-count with a cross body block. He also gets a near fall with a standing moonsault, sending Christian out to the floor to grab his belt and threaten to leave. Van Dam stops him with a somersault splash over the top rope from the ring. He follows up with a leg drop off the ropes onto the apron. When he goes for the Five-Star Frog Splash though, the heel moves and finally gets in some offense with a series of kicks, punches, and a gutbuster for his own two-count. Slowing the pace, he then locks on an abdominal stretch and punches the challenger's ribs. Although RVD escapes and rolls him up for a near fall, the champion is right back on the attack with a string of fists until he runs into a heel kick. Rolling thunder follows for another close two-count. When he attempts to deliver a monkey flip, Christian shoves him back to the canvas, but Rob rolls to his feet and surprises the heel with a moonsault for another near fall. Following a pair of roll-ups that get Van Dam two-counts, Christian slides out to the floor and nails the challenger with the title belt for the disqualification. Post-match, the champion ignores Nick Patrick admonishing him and grabs a ladder to slam it into RVD's face. Still not done, he climbs up the ladder for his own Five-Star Frog Splash, Coach saying it looked a lot better than anything Van Dam has ever done.

Backstage, Chris Jericho interrupts trainers checking on Eric Bischoff. Y2J can't stand what Goldberg did to the co-GM, but he's even madder about "Stone Cold" Steve Austin laughing at him. Jericho wants to take up for the boss and asks for a World Title shot tonight. Eric is happy to give it to him.

The Stacker2 Burn of the Night is Shane McMahon leaping off the entrance set only to miss Kane and crash through the stage. The announcers say Shane is recuperating from an undisclosed location, but we'll hear from him later.

When Garrison Cade and Mark Jindrak head to the ring for their match, Evolution attack them from behind. In a foul mood, Triple H stomps the young superstars before marching down the aisle. The fans loudly chant for Goldberg. Hunter tells them that they don't bother him. Even though he lost one match, he's still the best wrestler in the world. In fact, Helmsley says the intense superstar didn't beat him, but rather "the Game" beat himself by taking Bill too lightly. He warns the new champion that "the Game has just started" and he will get his rematch.

After a commercial break and another wounded solider shouting out his friends and family, Theodore Long leads Mark Henry and Rodney Mack to the squared circle. Teddy says that he can't help but notice that there's never been a black president. He'd like to be the first and believes he'd look good on the "dollar-dollar bill". He then reinstates his "White Boy Challenge", asking for anyone to face Henry.

Mark Henry (with Theodore Long/Rodney Mack) def. Tommy Dreamer ("White Boy Challenge"). Dreamer answers and smashes the "World's Strongest Man" with a cane. Mark absorbs those shots and breaks the stick. Changing tactics, Tommy grabs a trashcan and smashes his opponent. When he drops Rodney too, Henry recovers and hoists up Dreamer for the World's Strongest Slam and the victory.

The announcers thank Sevendust for the use of "Enemy" last night for Unforgiven. Afterwards, we see Garrison Cade and Mark Jindrak trying to get to Evolution backstage. WWE officials and Maven hold them back. Triple H says they picked the wrong night to fight with Evolution and challenges the three babyfaces to a match.

Backstage, Chris Jericho and Christian watch Lita and Trish Stratus walk by in a bit of foreshadowing. "Stone Cold" Steve Austin interrupts the heels to ask Y2J if he's proud of himself costing Jim Ross his job last night. Jericho is. Austin promises to fix things and give the fans the match he should have given them originally. Next week, JR will wrestle Coach for the *Raw* announcing job. He then calls Christian "CLB". The Intercontinental Champion thinks it means "Christian Likes Blondes", but "Stone Cold" says it really means "Creepy Little Bastard". Since Christian likes using ladders so much, Austin signs him to a title defense next week against Rob Van Dam in a "Ladder" match.

Lita/Trish Stratus def. Gail Kim/Molly Holly. Following another wounded soldier promo, the heels head to the ring separately. The babyfaces also get separate entrances, the announcers shilling Trish's new DVD. She slams Gail to the canvas with a headlock takedown. A dropkick follows for a two-count while Coach says he's not afraid to put his and Snow's announcing jobs on the line next week. When Molly tags in, Stratus Matrix dodges a clothesline to head scissors the Women's Champion for a near fall. A Thesz press and fists follow before Lita tags in to kick and head scissors Holly. The champion answers with hammering blows, but misses a dropkick for the returning superstar to headbutt her gut and cover her. When she runs the ropes, Kim kicks her for Molly to score a two-count with a neckbreaker. A snap mare to the injured neck also gets Holly a near fall. Gail continues to focus on the neck when she tags in, elbowing it and choking the returning superstar on the ropes. A knee to the back and stretch has Charles Robinson asking Lita if she wants to quit, but instead she escapes with a leg sweep. She nearly tags out, but Kim kicks her from behind to slow the babyface. Molly returns afterwards for both heels to choke Lita. When the champion picks her up for a suplex, the babyface slips free and answers with a reverse DDT. Gail tags in before Lita can escape and knocks Trish off the apron. Unfortunately, Lita recovers afterwards to double clothesline the heels. She follows up with clotheslines and dropkicks to both heels. A tilt-a-whirl slam to Kim nearly gets her the win, but Holly makes the save. Stratus then rushes over to tackle the champion out of the ring while Lita scores the win with a twist of fate.

Backstage, Chris Jericho tells Eric Bischoff that he might not be able to fight "Stone Cold" Steve Austin and Goldberg physically, but he can outsmart them. He proposes that the co-GM serve as the outside the ring referee tonight for the World Title match and take advantage of any situation that arises. Eric thinks that's a great idea.

After a commercial break, Stacy Keibler apologizes to Scott Steiner. She says she never meant to hit him with a steel chair last night. Test interrupts. He wants Scott to carry his bags tonight. When Steiner yells at him, the bodyguard threatens to sue "Big Poppa Pump" if he doesn't fulfill his contract. After Test walks away though, Scott flings his bags away.

Following a teaser clip of Shane McMahon diving off the entrance set, the announcers talk to him via video from a medical facility. He's still in bed as nurses and doctors run tests on him. Shane says physically he's banged up, but mentally he feels great. He promises to take care of Kane whenever he's back, but the "Big Red Machine" doesn't wait, finding McMahon and hammering him in his hospital bed. After spraying blood on his face, the monster takes Shane for a ride, wheeling him into walls and equipment before tossing him down to the floor. When security arrives, Kane decks them to continue his assault. Once he's done, he mockingly tells McMahon to "get well soon".

Rosey/The Hurricane def. Rene Dupree/Rob Conway (with Sylvan Grenier). Despite being heels, the announcers aren't happy to see La Resistance waving their French flags in front of wounded soldiers. Al is glad they lost the belts last night. Tonight, a heavily bandaged Rob opens the match hitting The Hurricane. The superhero answers with a head scissors before taking the fight out to the floor, diving onto the heels. Sylvan makes the save with a shot from his flagpole. Also bandaged, Rene tags in to club and dropkick The Hurricane. He scores a two-count with a fist drop following his sidestepping dance before tagging back in Conway. He also gets a near fall before he slows the pace with a surfboard submission. It doesn't take the superhero long to fight free and plant Rob with an Eye of the Hurricane. Too injured to make the cover, he tags in Rosey to slam both heels and leg drop Conway for a near fall. At the last second, Rene makes the save. The super hero in training isn't bothered, double clotheslining his opponents ahead of a Hurricane flying cross body block to Dupree. Once he rolls out of the ring, the masked men score the win with a combination Samoan Drop and Neckbreaker to Rob. Post-match, The Dudley Boyz come out to shake hands with the winners and the wounded troops in the front row.

Footage of the WWE and Russell Simmons teaming up to get people to vote earlier today plays.

Randy Orton/Ric Flair/Triple H def. Garrison Cade/Mark Jindrak/Maven. After Evolution come out, the babyfaces race down the aisle together to chase off the heels. Once Earl Hebner restores order, Triple H wails on Jindrak. The babyface answers with his own shots before tagging in Maven. Hunter greets him with more fists. Flair then tags in to chop the babyface. Maven answers with fists, Snow rooting for him. He nearly gets the win with a backslide ahead of more fists. After he back body drops Ric, "The Nature Boy" slows the young superstar with a back elbow. Cade and Orton tag in afterwards, Garrison landing several strikes until the "Legend Killer" slows him with a backbreaker. Back in, Helmsley peppers the rookie with repeated fists. When Hebner admonishes "the Game", Flair chokes Cade behind the official's back. Randy tags in moments later to punch and choke Garrison. Trapping the rookie in their corner, Evolution make quick tags to punish Cade before Triple H locks him in a sleeper hold. Garrison escapes with a side suplex to put both men down on the mat. Although Hunter recovers first, Cade surprises him with a bulldog. When Orton tags in, the rookie back body drops him and tags Maven to fight all three heels. A six-man brawl erupts afterwards. Once everyone else powders out to the floor, Jindrak surprises "the Game" with a springboard back elbow. Earl spots Randy trying to use a chair at ringside and takes it away, missing Maven surprising Flair with a top rope flying cross body block. While the referee tries to restore order at ringside, Helmsley pulls the babyface up for a Pedigree. By the time Hebner returns to the squared circle, Ric drapes an arm on Maven for the win. Post-match, Orton RKOs Cade before Triple H tells the fans that they need him a lot more than he needs them.

Following another wounded soldier promo, Marc Lloyd talks to The Rock at the premiere of his new movie, *The Rundown*. The "People's Champ" wishes he was in the arena tonight, but he's thankful for all the fans, Vince McMahon, and the crew who have helped make him a star. Afterwards, the "Great One" insults Lloyd and calls him a "sick freak". When he walks away, Marc tells fans to "run down to the theaters". That sets off The Rock and he returns to talk smack and ask if the fans smell what he's cooking.

Goldberg def. Chris Jericho (World Title match). Eric Bischoff is out first to serve as the special "outside the ring referee". Goldberg is out last to toss Jericho around the ring and clothesline him. That sends the challenger out to the floor, the intense superstar following until Bischoff stops him. Y2J tries to sneak attack Bill, but hits Eric instead. That lets the champion run through him back in the squared circle until he speeds into a corner boot. The heel capitalizes with a series of strikes, but one hard whip into a corner turns the tide and Goldberg press slams Jericho crotch-first onto the top rope. He tries to Spear the challenger afterwards at ringside, but Y2J moves and the intense superstar hits the ring steps instead. That swings the momentum for a series of heel stomps and a top rope missile dropkick for a near fall. He focuses on the shoulder, clubbing it ahead of an armbar drop for another two-count. Afterwards, Jericho stretches Bill's arm until the champion fights free of his hold and kicks him. A clothesline slows the challenger, but Y2J has a few tricks up his sleeves and surprises the champion with a DDT. He tries to lock on the Walls of Jericho afterwards, but Goldberg powers out and press slams the heel for a two-count before Bischoff interrupts Charles Robinson's count. When the intense superstar grabs the co-GM, Jericho stuns Bill with a low blow ahead of a running face slam and Lionsault. That gets him a close two-count courtesy of Bischoff. "Stone Cold" Steve Austin has seen enough and runs out to deck Eric. Y2J can't stand it and yells at Austin until Goldberg Spears him. A Jackhammer follows for the champion's first successful title defense. Post-match, Bill celebrates with the troops at ringside.

SmackDown!
September 25, 2003
Philadelphia, PA
Announcers: Michael Cole, Tazz

Following the intro video and fireworks, the announcers talk about tonight's show with three title matches. Two of those will feature Eddie Guerrero as he defends both of his belts in one night.

Afterwards, Vince McMahon and Sable head to the ring to present Brock Lesnar with the WWE Title. Instead, Kurt Angle interrupts and stalks around the WWE owner. Vince thinks he's here to complain and challenge Lesnar to a rematch. The WWE owner says that's not going to happen tonight or any time soon because the Olympian is going to start at the bottom and work his way up. Kurt has heard enough and takes the microphone away. He says he's here to kick Brock's butt whether it's in the ring or backstage. He leaves that choice up to the new champion. Instead of Brock, John Cena responds. Everyone is confused why. When Cena insults Angle, the former champion decks him and chases off the rapping heel. He then heads backstage to look for Lesnar. Unfortunately, he can't find him. Even worse, John jumps the Olympian from behind before speeding out of the parking lot. Angle commandeers Mr. McMahon's limo and driver to chase after the rapping heel.

Los Guerreros def. Matt Hardy Version 1.0/Shannon Moore (WWE Tag Title match). The champions are out first, driving a lowrider with the company's name displayed on the front windshield. The challengers follow, Matt Facts revealing that Hardy has wrestled with strep throat and hates taking medicine. The champions start strong, making quick tags and staying a step ahead of Matt. A combination snap mare and dropkick lets Chavo nearly score the victory. When he runs the ropes though, Shannon pulls him out to the floor for Matt to surprise the champion with a baseball slide kick. The cheating gets the challengers a near fall, as does a Moore back suplex. Despite the heels driving the back of his head into their corner, Chavo surprises Shannon with a tornado DDT and tags in "Latino Heat". He fights both men until Matt stuns him with a kick to the gut followed by a Moore swinging neckbreaker and near fall. Moments later, Hardy drops Eddie and drags Shannon onto him for a two-count. Chavo recovers afterwards and surprises Moore with a top rope flying cross body block for a "Latino Heat" near fall. Shannon answers with a dropkick to the back of the head after Guerrero shoves Matt out to the floor for his own two-count. When he heads upstairs, Eddie dodges his second rope blockbuster neckbreaker. Chavo capitalizes with a back suplex followed by a "Latino Heat" Frog Splash for the win. Post-match, Hardy hits Eddie with a title belt followed by a side effect.

During the commercial break, Charlie Haas runs out to toss Chavo from the ring and lock Eddie in the Haas of Pain ahead of his US Title shot tonight.

Afterwards, A-Train storms down to the ring. After he tosses a pair of chairs into the squared circle, the hairy heel calls out the crowd and Chris Benoit. When no one offers to fight him, he drags Mark Yeaton into the ring and puts him in a Crossface. The "rabid wolverine" rushes out to show him how it's done, but A-Train shoves Benoit out to the floor and smashes his face with a chair.

Backstage, a trainer checks on Eddie Guerrero's ribs. "Latino Heat" doesn't want to listen to his recommendations. Eddie knows his body and will defend the US Title tonight.

After a commercial break, Vince McMahon gropes and kisses Sable. Their pointless display is interrupted by a member of the crew. Vince says he's late. The WWE owner wants to make sure the crew sets up the ring for Brock Lesnar's WWE Title ceremony again.

Further backstage, Josh Mathews says the odds have to be in Charlie Haas's favor tonight after Eddie Guerrero's injury earlier. Haas says the odds are always in his favor and he's going to pay "Latino Heat" back for taking The World's Greatest Tag Team's championships by taking Eddie's US Title.

MUST SEE! Tajiri def. Rey Mysterio (Cruiserweight Title match). Tajiri opens the match kicking and elbowing the champion. He follows up with a scoop slam and knee to the head for a quick two-count. Rey answers with a head scissors off the second rope, but when he goes for a victory roll, the challenger counters into his own pin for a near fall. The masked man scores his own two-count with a pop-up dropkick, but misses a corner charge and is trapped in the Tarantula. The "Japanese Buzzsaw" messes with the turnbuckle pad afterwards to distract Brian Hebner, but when he tries to spray Mysterio with his mist, the champion kicks his throat. He then knocks Tajiri out to the floor for a dive off the top rope ahead of a commercial break.

Afterwards, the challenger scores a near fall with a kick to the gut, countering a top rope dive. Once in control, Tajiri drops Rey sternum-first onto the top rope before punching and stretching out the masked man, targeting his ribs. A double boot to the gut gets the "Japanese Buzzsaw" another two-count, but Mysterio grabs the ropes to preserve the championship. He pays courtesy of more kicks and a body scissors for a challenger two-count. When he can't get the submission or pinfall from that hold, Tajiri picks up the champion for a gutbuster and another near fall. He then hooks his legs around Rey's ribs. With the fans cheering him on, the masked man elbows free only to be slowed with another kick. Mysterio will not give up, surprising the "Japanese Buzzsaw" with a bulldog out of a wheelbarrow suplex. He gets a two-count moments later with a moonsault off the ropes, but runs into a back suplex that nearly crowns a new champion. The challenger then drapes Rey on the top rope for a dropkick to the back of the head. A Michinoku driver afterwards scores Tajiri a close two-count. When he attempts a corner dive, the masked man moves. He dodges a kick to the head moments later, but Hebner doesn't. That puts the referee down while Mysterio counters a handspring back elbow and rocks the "Japanese Buzzsaw" with a 619. When he goes for the West Coast Pop, Tajiri moves and answers with a straight kick for a two-count from Mike Sparks when the replacement referee sprints down the aisle. Frustrated, the heel kicks the champion's gut and sets him up for a powerbomb. Rey counters with a hurricanrana, but Sparks doesn't see it because he's checking on Hebner. The challenger seizes the opportunity to spray red mist into Mysterio's eyes and steal the title with a Buzzsaw Kick.

After a commercial break, Cole teases an update on Zach Gowen's condition next week.

A SmackDown Your Vote video package plays.

Bradshaw/Jamie Noble (with Nidia) def. The Basham Brothers (with Shaniqua) by disqualification. Pre-match, Shaniqua whips the Bashams. Noble then comes out to say that Billy Gunn is injured, but Jamie is a smart man. He's also rich and he's putting his money to work for him, paying Bradshaw to serve as his partner tonight. He pays off initially, running through Doug and putting him down for the redneck. Unfortunately, when Noble runs the ropes, Danny holds them open to send Jamie crashing out to the floor. There, Shaniqua boots him before the Bashams give the redneck a double flapjack. Following a double kip up, Doug scores a two-count before the big Texan makes the save. Noble tries to tag out afterwards, but the heel cuts him off. Doug pays courtesy of a neckbreaker before both men tag out,

Bradshaw wailing on Danny. Following a suplex, he hip tosses Doug and runs through him. Doug tries to answer with a cross body block, but the big Texan catches him for a fallaway slam. When he sets up Danny for a Clothesline from Hell, Doug grabs Bradshaw's boot. Jamie rushes to his aid, baseball slide kicking Doug. Afterwards, Shaniqua delivers her own devastating clothesline, rocking Nidia. Inside the ring, the big Texan DDTs Danny, but Doug makes the save. The Bashams briefly double-team Bradshaw, but he drops Doug with a boot before rocking Danny with a Clothesline from Hell. Before he can score the three-count, the dominatrix rushes into the ring and stomps the big Texan for the disqualification. Post-match, the heels stomp and whip Bradshaw before heading backstage.

Following the announcers talking about *The Rundown*, a lengthy video package plays of last week's "Iron Man" match.

Eddie Guerrero def. Charlie Haas (US Title match). Big Show joins the announce table to provide guest commentary for this match. It's just a ruse though as the giant heads up the aisle after Eddie slowly makes his way to ringside, walking instead of driving his lowrider. Once Show passes him, he returns to toss the champion into the ring post. Cole doesn't understand why. Haas doesn't care, whipping "Latino Heat" into the squared circle for a back suplex and two-count. He follows up with elbows and a back body drop, but when he attempts a charge near the ropes, Guerrero low bridges him. He pumps himself up, yelling before pummeling and dropkicking the challenger. That hurts the champion too and he's slow to recover. When he does, he runs into a double leg slam and two-count. Charlie follows up with a backbreaker stretch over his knee. Although he escapes and head scissors Haas, the challenger recovers first to whip Eddie ribs-first into the ring post. That brings Chavo Guerrero Jr. down to check on his uncle. Charlie decks him before shoving "Latino Heat" into the ring. While Mike Sparks leads Chavo up the ramp, the challenger scores a near fall back in the ring. He then traps Guerrero in the Haas of Pain. It takes everything he's got, but the champion pops out of the hold and whips Haas out to the floor. That sets off Charlie and he grabs the US Title. Luckily, Mike Chioda spots him and takes the belt away. While he argues with the challenger, Eddie crawls to the belt and drapes it on the top rope. Haas tries to sneak attack him, but leaps into the belt face-first. Despite his injured ribs, "Latino Heat" heads upstairs and connects with a Frog Splash to retain the championship.

After a commercial break, the red carpet is rolled out again for Vince McMahon and Sable to introduce Brock Lesnar. This time, the new champion heads to the ring, the announcers arguing about how he won the belt last week. Vince calls him the face of *SmackDown!* and unstoppable before congratulating him on his win. Brock doesn't care that the fans are chanting that he tapped out because he's excited to have his belt back. He thanks Mr. McMahon for reminding him who he is. Lesnar agrees with the WWE owner that he's unrelenting and unstoppable. The Undertaker would beg to differ, riding his motorcycle to ringside. He stayed out of the WWE Title match last week because he respects the championship, but he doesn't respect Brock. He also hasn't forgotten that Lesnar hit him with a chair and he doesn't forgive. The biker tells the champion to enjoy his belt now, but his first title defense is against the "Deadman". Vince wants to know who he thinks he is signing title matches. He's not the one who signed the match. It was Stephanie McMahon who comes out to a nice pop. By her authority, she gives The Undertaker a WWE Title match at No Mercy. Mr. McMahon tells her to change her mind or she'll be in the first ever "Father/Daughter" match in history. Brock laughs that she doesn't make the rules, but Stephanie refuses to change her mind. Vince promises that she will quit, making their contest an "I Quit" match. Lesnar then sneak attacks the biker, but he can't keep him down and the "Deadman" responds with a Chokeslam to end the show standing tall, Stephanie applauding The Undertaker.

Monday Night Raw
September 29, 2003
Chicago, IL
Announcers: Jonathan Coachman, Al Snow, Chris Jericho (briefly)

Following the intro video and fireworks, Lilian Garcia introduces the announce team. The fans boo them before Chris Jericho and Eric Bischoff head to the ring for the Highlight Reel to even more boos. Eric has a special announcement tonight that gets even more boos. Due to "Stone Cold" Steve Austin attacking Bischoff last week, the "rattlesnake" has been suspended for a week. Y2J thinks he got off too easy. He blames "Stone Cold" for Jericho losing his World Title match last week. That was just payback for Y2J costing Jim Ross his job at Unforgiven. Ahead of his match tonight with Coach for the Raw announcing job, Jericho brings back JR. Before he says anything, Eric interrupts. Since Austin made the match for his friend, Bischoff offers to let Coachman pick the stipulation. Coach picks a "Country Whipping" match. Y2J interrupts and reminds everyone that it was just a month ago that Kane set Ross on fire and he's not one hundred percent recovered. Eric claims to be a compassionate man, but proves otherwise by signing the "Country Whipping" match and laughing. When JR finally gets to speak, he tells Bischoff that he's like Al and Coachman—he sucks! Jericho then gives Ross a low blow and locks him in the Walls of Jericho until "Stone Cold" runs out and chases the heels up the ramp. Eric has had enough of Steve and calls for security to escort him backstage. When they grab his right arm, he says it's his drinking arm. So is his left. Austin offers to leave calmly before turning on the guards and giving one a Stone Cold Stunner for a big pop.

After a commercial break, "Stone Cold" Steve Austin has been escorted out of the building.

The Dudley Boyz def. Scott Steiner/Test (with Stacy Keibler) (World Tag Title match). Test mocks Stacy by copying her entrance into the ring. He makes the fans madder when he refuses to let Keibler show him how it's done. Once the bell rings, Bubba Ray goes to work punching and elbowing the bodyguard until Test pokes his eyes. When the challenger tries to tag his partner, Scott steps back off the apron allowing Dudley to roll Test up for a near fall. The Dudleys tease a wassup drop, but Nick Patrick stops D-Von long enough for the bodyguard to give Bubba a low blow and shove the referee into the ropes to crotch D-Von. He follows up with a pumphandle slam to D-Von, but Steiner breaks his partner's cover. Frustrated, Test grabs a chair, but Stacy stops him from using it. After he shoves her down, Bubba Ray returns to give the bodyguard a Bubba Bomb. The champions follow up with a double-team neckbreaker to "Big Poppa Pump" ahead of a 3D to Test for the victory. Post-match, the bodyguard tries to slap Keibler, but Scott catches his arm and clotheslines Test. Steiner says the bodyguard got what he deserved and he'll never forgive him. However, he's not going to forgive Stacy for hitting him with a chair and costing him the World Tag Titles—even though he did the same—either. Suddenly, "Big Poppa Pump" belly-to-belly suplexes Keibler, shocking the announcers and bringing a smile to Test's face.

After a commercial break and WWE officials helping Stacy Keibler from the ring, Kane heads to the squared circle to call out Shane McMahon. The Hurricane interrupts to play footage of him and the "Big Red Machine" winning the World Tag Titles last year. The superhero says Kane went from a beloved hero to a monster. The "Big Red Machine" tells The Hurricane that he's everything that the monster hates and offers to take care of him tonight. The superhero doesn't want to fight. Kane does and looks around the arena for someone to attack. He spots a kid in a Hurricane mask and threatens him. Before he can get his hands on the fan, the superhero sprints down to attack the "Big Red Machine". It doesn't take the monster long to get the upper hand, but before he can Chokeslam The Hurricane, Rosey runs out for the save. Working together, the masked men drive Kane from the ring, but not off his feet.

Filmed earlier today, Maven interrupts Garrison Cade and Mark Jindrak playing *WrestleMania XIX*. La Resistance burst into the locker room to make fun of the babyfaces for being ignorant and wasting their time on videogames. The babyfaces know a lot about French history and point out that the heels are just like their country…always laying down. The six men then argue ahead of their match.

Garrison Cade/Mark Jindrak/Maven def. La Resistance/Rob Conway. Despite being heels, the announcers are against the Frenchmen here. Things break down quickly as all six competitors brawl until Chad Patton gets order for Dupree and Conway to pound Cade. They do most of the work as Sylvan watches from the apron. Eventually, he joins Rene in the ring, illegally tackling Garrison to stop him from tagging out. It's only a temporary reprieve as Maven gets the hot tag to fight all three heels. When Dupree and Rob whip him into the ropes, Jindrak blind tags himself into the match. He follows Rene out to the floor, brawling with him as Maven flies off the top rope to DDT Conway. La Resistance answer him with a Double Slam before Mark returns to surprise Dupree with a springboard flying clothesline. Cade joins his tag team partner in the ring, lifting up Rob for a Jindrak dropkick and the win.

Outside the arena, "Stone Cold" Steve Austin tells security guards that he just wants a beer back in the arena. Rob Van Dam interrupts to thank Austin for giving him an Intercontinental Title match tonight. Once he leaves, Jon Heidenreich introduces himself. He says he's trained his whole life to be a professional wrestler and bought tickets for him and Little Johnny to see the show. That gets "Stone Cold" thinking and he pulls the hopeful to the side to talk to him in private.

Via video, Triple H sits down and congratulates Goldberg on being the World Champion for one week. He wonders if paranoia has set in yet with everyone chasing the intense superstar. Hunter tells him that he's going to teach him a lesson. He's got one hundred thousand dollars of his own money for anyone who puts Bill on the shelf. Now, Helmsley says, "the Game got a lot more interesting".

Jim Ross def. Jonathan Coachman. ("Country Whipping" match). Pre-match, Al hypes up Coach, reminding him that both of their jobs on the line. Coachman looks ready, whipping the announce table before he heads to the squared circle. After JR enters with his leather strap, Chris Jericho joins Snow for commentary. He insults Ross and compliments Coach despite Jim repeatedly whipping him in and out of the ring. When he finally misses a shot, the Packers shirt wearing Coachman unloads with a series of lashes to JR's back. After several hard shots, Coach tries to pull off Ross's jersey. Instead, Jim slows him with a low blow. He then whips Coachman and Eric Bischoff when he tries to run out and interfere. A Stone Cold Stunner follows to Coach for JR to win his job back. Post-match, Al complains while Jerry "the King" Lawler runs out to celebrate with the winner. Y2J remains on commentary insulting Ross and "Stone Cold" Steve Austin. Speaking of, the "rattlesnake" makes his way through the crowd to raise JR's hand in victory. He welcomes back the new announce team, showing off his ticket to security to let him stay. Unlike normal fans, Austin has a beer bash in the ring with Jerry and JR.

Jim Ross and Jerry "the King" Lawler take over on commentary for the rest of the show. To keep the surprise, that is left off the Announcers section above. Their first act is to show footage of fans eagerly buying WrestleMania XX tickets.

Afterwards, Terri welcomes out Lita and hypes the returning superstar's new autobiography. Lita is happy to be back, but before she says anything else, Gail Kim and Molly Holly march out to take her book from Terri. The Women's Champion complains about Lita getting a book and Trish Stratus getting a DVD before Gail hits the returning superstar with her autobiography. When they try to double suplex her, Lita flips free. She's quickly joined by Stratus racing into the ring. Unfortunately, Victoria follows and trips the vixen from behind ahead of a Widow's Peak. Molly and Kim then double DDT Lita before the champion tears up the babyface's book and stuffs a page in her mouth.

Kane def. The Hurricane. The "Big Red Machine" tries to attack The Hurricane in the aisle, but the superhero dodges him to dropkick his knee and fly off the top rope out to the floor onto him. A shining wizard inside the ring gets The Hurricane just a one-count before the monster comes back to life with a powerslam. A Chokeslam follows for the three-count. Post-match, Kane Chokeslams his former partner a second time. JR believes the monster may get what's coming to him when Shane McMahon returns next week.

Backstage, Marc Lloyd asks Goldberg about the bounty Triple H put on him earlier. He wonders if Bill can trust his tag team partner tonight, Shawn Michaels. While the intense superstar warns the "Heartbreak Kid" not to cross him, Steven Richards sneak attacks Bill. It doesn't take Goldberg long to repel his attack and leave the heel laying.

Goldberg/Shawn Michaels def. Randy Orton/Ric Flair by disqualification. The announcers wonder if Goldberg can trust his partner here with a hundred thousand dollars on the line. The intense superstar takes matters into his own hands, shoving down Flair to start the match. When Orton tries to help his mentor, Bill overpowers both heels before tagging in Shawn to knock Ric from the squared circle. He attempts to finish off the match with a quick Sweet Chin Music to Randy, but the "Legend Killer" catches his foot and counters with a backbreaker. After he softens up Michaels, "The Nature Boy" returns to chop the babyface. The "Heartbreak Kid" responds with fists, but Ric slows him with an eye rake and drop toe hold. Back in, Orton stomps and dropkicks Shawn for a two-count. When Michaels tries to answer with a roll-up, Flair gets the blind tag to pummel the "Heartbreak Kid" again. He wastes time strutting afterwards before Shawn kips up and rocks him with a flying forearm. Both men then tag out for the World Champion to hammer the heels. Big back body drops follow to each man before Goldberg press slams Randy and Spears "The Nature Boy". That brings Rodney Mack out to the ring to hit Bill with a steel chair for the disqualification. The intense superstar answers with a Spear and Jackhammer while Mark Henry slams Michaels on the ring steps. The champion doesn't even notice until the "World's Strongest Man" drags a bloodied Shawn up the aisle and motions for money.

After a commercial break, Theodore Long tells Mark Henry that he's excited by what the "World's Strongest Man" just did. Mark says he showed everyone what he can do injuring Shawn Michaels. Next week, he promises to collect the hundred thousand dollars because he's challenging Goldberg to a match.

Further backstage, Christian heads to the squared circle and blows a kiss at Lita and Trish Stratus. When Tommy Dreamer wishes the "CLB" luck, Christian yells at him and promises to retain his Intercontinental Title. A heel, the champion even steals Dreamer's apple.

MUST SEE! Rob Van Dam def. Christian (Intercontinental Title "Ladder" match). After the men stare up at the Intercontinental Title, they trade shots in the center of the ring. Once RVD gets the upper hand, kicking Christian down, he heads to the floor for a ladder. He only manages to slide it into the ring before the champion attacks him and grabs a second ladder. Unfortunately, Rob baseball slide kicks it into his face ahead of a somersault splash over the top rope onto the ladder. That hurts Van Dam as much as Christian and the two men writhe on the floor until the champion pokes RVD's eyes. Afterwards, he places the ladder on the barricade and ring steps. It's Rob using it though, dropping Christian chest-first onto the ladder ahead of a twisting leg drop from the barricade. Back in the squared circle, the challenger props a ladder up in a corner. He tries to whip the heel into it, but Christian reverses the Irish whip. That turns the tide again and the champion wedges the ladder in a corner to slingshot Van Dam into the underside. Christian tries to grab his title afterwards, but RVD shoves the ladder over before press slamming the heel onto it. He immediately follows up with a standing moonsault for a nice pop, but that puts both men down again. The challenger is up first, ramming the ladder into Christian's ribs and knocking him out to the floor. That lets Rob head up the ladder, but the champion recovers to meet him at the top for a reverse DDT down to the canvas. He attempts to use a ladder in the corner, but Van Dam monkey flips him onto it ahead of rolling thunder against the steel. Exhausted, RVD sets up a ladder in another corner. Jerry says he's confused and needs to put it in the center of the ring. Instead, he heads up the ladder potentially for a Five-Star Frog Splash. We don't get to find out his plan because the heel yanks him down to the mat. Despite that, Rob recovers quickly and kicks a ladder into his face. When he tries to give Christian a Five-Star Frog Splash onto a ladder, the champion rolls out of the way and Van Dam crashes hard onto the steel. The heel follows up with a ladder shot to the face before heading up to grab his title. Before he can unlatch it, the challenger flies off the top rope and kicks the ladder out from under him, Christian's face falling onto the steel. Both men recover at the same time and head up opposite sides of the ladder to trade fists. That causes the ladder to topple over. Unfortunately for the champion, he falls onto the top rope while RVD lands on the other ladder. He quickly heads up to the top of it, the fans roaring as he sets up for a Five-Star Frog Splash. After he connects with his finisher, Van Dam puts the ladder on top of Christian and climbs up it to grab the belt and win this tremendous contest.

SmackDown!
October 2, 2003
Milwaukee, WI
Announcers: Michael Cole, Tazz, A-Train (briefly)

Eddie Guerrero (with Chavo Guerrero Jr.) def. Matt Hardy Version 1.0 (with Shannon Moore) (US Title match). Following the intro video and fireworks, Los Guerreros head to the ring in a lowrider. The heels follow to Matt Facts stating that Hardy has had four speeding tickets, but gotten out of twenty. Eddie is waiting to get revenge on him for his attack last week, stomping Matt down in a corner. When Jimmy Korderas gets in the way, "Latino Heat" shoves the referee aside. He then aggravates his injured ribs dropkicking the challenger. Guerrero doesn't care. He wants revenge and gets it with a back suplex and shoulderblock. When he tries to deliver his slingshot somersault from the apron, Shannon holds his foot for Hardy to take control with a suplex onto the top rope. He then focuses on the injured ribs with strikes and a hard whip into the corner for a two-count. A powerbomb nearly crowns a new champion, but Eddie just kicks out while the announcers talk about how hard it is to defend two titles. Matt tries to help him with that problem, scoring a near fall with a side effect. He then locks on a surfboard stretch, but the champion won't give up, powering into a swinging neckbreaker. Unfortunately, he misses a clothesline and runs into a back elbow for a two-count. A front slam also gets the challenger a near fall, as does an elbow drop. Changing tactics, he chokes "Latino Heat" before missing a second elbow drop. Guerrero capitalizes with a trio of suplexes, but when he heads upstairs, Hardy meets him for a superplex off the middle rope. That puts both men down for Korderas' standing seven-count. Matt is up first, kicking the champion and heading to the second rope. He wastes too much time posing and Eddie blocks his leg drop with a hurricanrana off the ropes for a two-count. When the challenger tries to answer with a side effect, "Latino Heat" rolls him up for a near fall. Hardy responds with a neckbreaker before going after Chavo. That distracts the referee for Moore to enter the ring to try to hit Guerrero with the title. Instead, the champion dropkicks the belt back into his face before tossing the title to Matt. The referee spots Hardy with it and takes it away, allowing Chavo to sneak in and blast the challenger with his own belt. A Frog Splash follows for the three-count.

An ad for Bradshaw's *Have More Money Now* book plays. Afterwards, we get a video package for WrestleMania XX ticket sales in New York City.

Backstage, Josh Mathews stops John Cena to ask him about his tag match main event and dropping "dope rhymes". That infuriates Cena and he makes fun of Mathews before telling everyone that he's tired of being in Kurt Angle's shadow. Tonight, he's going to put Angle in his shadow.

Further backstage, Los Guerreros celebrate Eddie's win until they walk past Big Show. "Latino Heat" wants to know if the giant tossed him into the ring post last week because of something personal or because he was in a bad mood. Show says he doesn't like Guerrero's kind, but he does like tacos and burritos. He tells the champions that there's nothing they can do about it before shoving them both down. After he leaves, Chavo tells his uncle that Big Show punked him out. Eddie promises to get revenge "Guerrero style".

The Basham Brothers (with Shaniqua) def. The APA. Pre-match, Shaniqua shoves around her men and orders them to get to work. They try, but the brawlers are ready and waiting to hammer them. While Bradshaw whips Doug into the ring steps, Faarooq manhandles Danny. Doug illegally enters to try to attack him and gets dropped to the mat. A double back suplex follows from The APA, but Danny breaks the big Texan's cover. Bradshaw remains in control, scoring another two-count with a back suplex. A fallaway slam follows soon afterwards before Doug whips the big Texan out to the floor. There, Shaniqua slaps and distracts Bradshaw for Danny to ram his head into the ring post. The Bashams then double-team and stomp the big Texan in their corner. Chokes and a chin lock follow until Bradshaw back suplexes Doug. Both men tag out afterwards for Faarooq to clothesline and powerslam the heels. A spinebuster to Danny nearly gets him the win, but Doug makes the save. Afterwards, Mike Chioda gets in the way and is knocked down for Shaniqua to big boot Bradshaw. The Bashams capitalize inside the ring with a Ball and Gag to Faarooq for the win. Post-match, the big Texan returns to the squared circle to club down the Bashams and give the dominatrix a Clothesline from Hell.

Chris Benoit def. Charlie Haas by disqualification. A-Train joins the announce table to provide guest commentary for this contest ahead of his No Mercy match with "the Crippler". As Haas comes out, Cole says Shelton Benjamin will be on the sidelines for a few weeks due to knee surgery, but should be back soon. While he's gone, Charlie trades submission holds with Benoit. The "rabid wolverine" gets the upper hand with a running shoulderblock before trapping the heel in a side headlock. He soon transitions into a surfboard, but Haas rams him back into a corner. Fists, kicks, and a corner choke follow. When Benoit tries to answer with a Crippler Crossface, Charlie shoves him out to the floor. There, the hairy heel distracts his No Mercy opponent for Haas to slam him into the announce table. A gutbuster follows before the heel takes the fight back to the squared circle. Moments later, a vicious clothesline gets Charlie a two-count before he applies an armbar stretch. While he attempts to make "the Crippler" submit, A-Train says a great big man can beat a great little man any day. Inside the ring, Haas scores another near fall with a dropkick. He then ties Benoit to the tree of woe for a pair of knees to the midsection. He continues to focus on the ribs with an abdominal stretch. It doesn't take the "rabid wolverine" long to fight free and respond with a German suplex. Charlie is right back up and nearly traps his opponent in the Haas of Pain, but Benoit grabs the ropes. Afterwards, he clotheslines and dropkicks the heel ahead of another German suplex and two-count. Sticking with what works, "the Crippler" German suplexes Charlie one more time before locking on a sharpshooter. Fortunately, the heel reaches the ropes for the break. Haas quickly responds with a belly-to-belly overhead suplex, dropping Benoit on his neck. Despite that, the "rabid wolverine" surprises Charlie with the Crippler Crossface out of nowhere. The hairy heel has seen enough and races into the ring to elbow drop Benoit for the disqualification. A-Train doesn't care, locking on his own Crossface until WWE officials pull him off "the Crippler".

An ad for Lita's new book plays.

Afterwards, Vince McMahon makes his way to the ring with Sable on his arm. The announcers debate whether he'll actually face his daughter at No Mercy. Vince says he's all about giving people second chances. Specifically, he wants Stephanie McMahon to rethink her decision to give The Undertaker a WWE Title match at No Mercy. He's giving her an opportunity tonight to cancel that match and quit as general manager. That brings out Stephanie to a nice pop. She tells her father no. She's not canceling the match or quitting her job. The WWE owner tells her she will quit at the PPV in their "I Quit" match. Not only will she quit that match, but she'll lose her job when she quits at No Mercy. Vince then accuses Stephanie of defying him and making him crush "Daddy's Little Girl". He can't believe she'd do that to him, but at No Mercy, he will "strike down the face of defiance". Sable tells Mr. McMahon not to think of Stephanie as his daughter, but as a "disrespectful little bitch". Stephanie tells her to head backstage and lay flat on her back because that's what she does best. Sable answers with a slap to the face. Stephanie immediately tackles and hits her until Vince pulls his daughter off the diva and slams her.

When he threatens to do so again to a crying Stephanie, The Undertaker runs out and decks him. He follows up with a big boot to Brock Lesnar when he rushes down the aisle. Cole says Vince broke Stephanie's heart.

After a commercial break, a Mexican deliveryman looks for Eddie Guerrero. He's got plenty of burritos for "Latino Heat". Unfortunately, he crosses paths with Big Show and the giant takes all the burritos. He leaves one for Eddie, handing it back to the deliveryman after he spits in it. Cole calls him a class act.

Tajiri def. Billy Kidman (Cruiserweight Title match). When the new champion gets in the ring, Mike Chioda checks his mouth for mist. He doesn't find anything. Afterwards, Billy attempts to end Tajiri's reign early with a roll-up. He follows up with a dive out to the floor onto the heel, but when he leaps back into the ring, the "Japanese Buzzsaw" catches him with a stiff kick. Afterwards, the champion works on Kidman's arm, stretching, striking, and driving it to the canvas. Kicks follow for a Tajiri two-count. Ignoring the referee's instructions, the "Japanese Buzzsaw" stretches the challenger's arm around the ropes before kicking him again and applying a hammerlock. Eventually, Billy comes back to life with a string of strikes and an enziguri for a two-count. When he attempts a springboard attack, the heel answers with a back kick. Fortunately, Kidman is in the ropes and Chioda refuses to count Tajiri's cover. The challenger responds with a bulldog and BK Bomb for a close two-count. Unfortunately, he then runs into a Tarantula. When the champion tries to finish him off with a Buzzsaw Kick, Billy ducks and answers with a dropkick for another near fall. The "Japanese Buzzsaw" is right back up to chop Kidman and low blow him when the referee dives out of the way to avoid the wrestlers running at him. A Buzzsaw Kick follows for the three-count. Post-match, Tajiri mockingly bows to his opponent.

Orlando Jordan def. Big Show by count-out. Show is struggling as he heads to the ring rubbing his stomach. When the bell rings, the giant drops Orlando with a kick, but clutches his own stomach. The rookie capitalizes with a string of corner shoulder blocks. Big Show answers with a hard chop and clothesline, but doubles over clutching his gut. He's had enough and tiptoes backstage clutching his backside while Mike Sparks counts him out. Tazz jokes that Mother Nature called. Cole wonders if it was the burritos, but whatever the case, Jordan gets his first win on the main shows.

Following a No Mercy ad featuring the WWE Title match, the announcers show the new issue of the *WWE Magazine* with Zach Gowen on the cover. He joins them via satellite to say that he's not feeling one hundred percent but is looking forward to getting back in the ring. He says it will be soon and he's not giving up on his wrestling dream. In fact, he'll be back in action next week.

Backstage, Big Show stinks up a bathroom. We hear plenty of pooping sound effects as Eddie Guerrero walks in to say that's what happens to people who cross "Latino Heat". He claims he gave Show some special sauce too, the kind that makes people sick. Things get even worse when Eddie reveals that he took all of the toilet paper. He offers to give the giant something to wipe with, kicking the door back into him. "Latino Heat" claims that Montezuma has nothing on him.

Brock Lesnar/John Cena def. Kurt Angle/The Undertaker. Pre-match, Cena raps that he's the reason people watch *SmackDown!* and root for the villain. He then calls out Kurt and says no one can stop him. They lock up while the fans remind Brock that he tapped out. The Olympian gets the better of John, whipping him to the canvas and working on his arm. The rapping heel answers with clubbing blows until he runs into a clothesline and two-count. The Undertaker tags in afterwards to work on Cena's arm, slamming him to the canvas by it. A shoulderblock and Old School follows before the biker nearly blindsides the WWE Champion. At the last second, Lesnar just slips off the apron and dodges the blow.

When Angle returns, he punches and back body drops John until Brock low bridges his rival running the ropes. Following a ram into the apron, the "Deadman" chases Lesnar off ahead of a commercial break.

Afterwards, Brock and Kurt trade shots, the champion getting the upper hand. The rapping heel also gets in some offense, stretching the Olympian and kneeing his gut for a two-count. Back in the ring, the champion stomps away at Angle. The fans are all over Lesnar's case as he press slams Kurt. When he picks up the Olympian again, Angle slips behind him for a German suplex. The Undertaker gets the hot tag afterwards, but Brian Hebner is distracted by Cena and misses it. While he gets the biker back out of the squared circle, John illegally enters the ring and scores a two-count with a back suplex. He wastes time taunting the "Deadman" and pays courtesy of a Kurt Anklelock. Fortunately, Brock makes the save. He also illegally switches places with his partner to cradle suplex the Olympian. This time, The Undertaker makes the save. The champion remains in control, powerslamming Angle, but when he turns to cheap shot the biker, Kurt small packages him. He follows up with an Angle Slam to finally make the legal hot tag. The "Deadman" proceeds to destroy both heels, clearing Lesnar from the ring with snake eyes and a clothesline. A big boot and chokeslam follow to the rapping heel, but Brock returns at the last moment to break the biker's cover. He follows up with a string of knees to the gut and a spinebuster to put everyone except the Olympian down. Kurt cheers for The Undertaker to crawl over and make the tag. When he does so, Angle clotheslines the heels and belly-to-belly suplexes Cena. The champion gets one too, chasing him from the ring. A trio of German suplexes follow to John before Kurt lowers his straps. While he does so, the rapping heel wraps his chain around his hand. The Olympian still traps him in an Anklelock, but Brock makes the save. The biker immediately rushes after his No Mercy opponent, distracting Hebner while Cena decks Angle with his loaded fist to steal the win.

Post-match, the "Deadman" and Lesnar continue their fight. Brock gets the upper hand whipping The Undertaker into the ring steps before teasing an F5 through the announce table. At the last second, the biker slips free and chokeslams the champion through the table to end the show standing tall for the second week in a row.

Monday Night Raw
October 6, 2003
Uncasville, CT
Announcers: Jim Ross, Jerry "the King" Lawler, Molly Holly (briefly)

Ahead of the intro video and fireworks, Triple H putting a bounty on Goldberg replays.

Kane def. Rosey. The super hero in training is looking to get revenge for his mentor after Kane destroyed him last week. He looks good early on, taking the "Big Red Machine" down and splashing him. Unfortunately, one big boot puts him down on the canvas. The monster follows up with chokes and clubbing blows ahead of a back suplex. Instead of going for the cover, he attacks Rosey on the apron, knocking his mask off. The babyface tries to fight back, but Kane cuts his momentum off with a sloppy spinebuster. Fortunately for Rosey, he dodges a top rope flying clothesline and answers with a DDT. A running leg drop follows, but the super hero in training makes a mistake and doesn't go for the cover. Instead, he waits for the "Big Red Machine" to stand up before running into a Chokeslam for the three-count. Post-match, The Hurricane runs out to help Rosey, but he also gets Chokeslammed. Shane McMahon then sneaks out from the crowd and nails the monster from behind before running away.

After a commercial break, Kane tears through the backstage area and ends up in the parking garage. After he looks for Shane McMahon in a control truck, he grabs a metal pipe and spots his nemesis by a limo. Shane tries to hide in it, but the "Big Red Machine" busts out the windows and crawls in. He can't catch McMahon before he slips out and tells him to have a nice ride, jamming a wooden post against the gas pedal to send the limo crashing hard into a truck. JR says we've "just witnessed a horrific accident". Jerry says it was no accident. After a commercial break, crew try to get Kane out of the wreckage. They're joined by firefighters attempting to use the jaws of life to free the monster. When "Stone Cold" Steve Austin approaches, emergency personnel tell him and the rest of the roster to stay back.

Lita def. Gail Kim. Molly Holly joins the announce table for this match, justifying her and Gail giving Lita a double DDT last week. She says if the babyface is ready to be back in the ring she's fair game. The fans certainly enjoy seeing her back, cheering Lita as she trades shots with Kim. A suplex gets the babyface a two-count and control. After dodging a dropkick, Lita surprises the heel with a unique roll-up. She tries to follow up with a corner bomb, but leaps into a pair of knees. Gail capitalizes with a knee to the neck and reverse chin lock. When that doesn't get her the submission, Kim clubs Lita's injured neck before trapping her in a dragon sleeper. Although the babyface escapes with a kick to the head, a dropkick puts her back down for a surfboard stretch. The announcers are more focused on Kane than the action in the ring until Lita surprises Gail with a leg sweep. She then catches a second wind, back body dropping and clotheslining the heel. A spinning slam follows for a near fall, but when she attempts a corner charge, Kim catches her with a boot to the jaw. She tries to follow up with a bulldog off the ropes, but the women collapse to the canvas instead in an ugly spot for a Lita two-count. Although Gail escapes a twist of fate afterwards, Lita is right back on the attack with a DDT for the victory.

Backstage, emergency personnel finally reach a bloodied Kane as police and Eric Bischoff arrive.

Filmed earlier today, Triple H sits in front of a briefcase filled with money. He offers to teach Goldberg a new lesson today. That's that anyone could come for the World Champion to buy anything they want with Hunter's money. He believes the man who takes out Bill could become the next member of Evolution before warning Goldberg that a "famous man" once said, "everyone's got a price".

After a commercial break, Shawn Michaels tells "Stone Cold" Steve Austin that he wants Mark Henry tonight. The co-general manager says that this isn't a good time and he can't give him that match. Shawn warns that he's going to take care of Henry anyway. Austin tells him to do whatever he wants.

At ringside, Scott Steiner leads Stacy Keibler out and says all he cares about are his "peaks and freaks". He refuses to take orders from Test, claiming that he only gives orders. Tonight, he wants Stacy to apologize on her knees. Eric Bischoff interrupts, excited to see the real "Big Poppa Pump". He offers to handpick Scott's opponent tonight to make sure the show has his seal of approval from now on.

Scott Steiner (with Stacy Keibler) def. Spike Dudley. Following a commercial break, Steiner press slams the runt out to the floor and whips him into the ring steps as emergency workers put a bloody Kane on a stretcher backstage. They load him into an ambulance before we return to the ring to see Scott belly-to-belly suplexing Spike. He follows up with a slam into the corner, but Dudley refuses to quit, surprising "Big Poppa Pump" with a battering ram headbutt to the gut. He attempts to score the win with a Dudley Dog, but Steiner slams him to the mat. Moments later, Scott scores a dominating victory with his Falling Face Slam. Post-match, he carries Spike up the ropes for a modified second rope Samoan drop. The Dudley Boyz have seen enough and run out to give Steiner a double-team neckbreaker. Stacy likes it, but before they can give "Big Poppa Pump" a 3D, Test rushes out and pulls him from the ring.

Backstage, Rob Conway and La Resistance discuss taking out Goldberg. They spot him in the distance and attempt to do so, but the World Champion fights them off and smashes them with their French flag.

After a commercial break, a crewmember explains to Eric Bischoff what he saw earlier with Kane and Shane McMahon. Eric says this is all on "Stone Cold" Steve Austin's head for pushing the monster.

Chris Jericho then leads Christian, Lance Storm, and Jonathan Coachman to the squared circle. There, he says he's sickened by "Stone Cold" Steve Austin. He blames what happened to Kane on the "rattlesnake" and is making a serious appeal to the WWE board of directors to have Austin fired. He's not alone and Coach takes the microphone to complain that "Stone Cold" took his job to help his friend, JR. Christian then complains about Austin calling him "CLB" and booking him in a brutal "Ladder" match. The former Intercontinental Champion yells that he hates "Stone Cold". Finally, Jericho says there's nothing worse than calling a wrestler "boring". He wants Storm to explain how it feels to be forced to head to the ring to "watered down techno music" doing the cabbage patch dance. Instead, Lance says Y2J is full of crap and for the first time in his career, Storm is having fun. He owes it all to the "rattlesnake" and thinks Austin is doing a great job. That sets off his fellow Canadians and they pound him down until "Stone Cold" heads to the squared circle. There, he can only watch as the heels stomp Lance and taunt him. Rob Van Dam can do something about it, running off to chase away the heels. The co-GM has his own appeal to the board of directors. He, and the fans, think that him being barred from touching WWE superstars sucks. While he still can't touch the heels, he can give them a match against RVD and Storm right now.

Lance Storm/Rob Van Dam def. Chris Jericho/Christian. Y2J complains that Christian is still injured from last week, but Austin doesn't care, grabbing a beer and heading backstage. After a commercial break, the heels are in control, hammering RVD in their corner. He doesn't stay on the defensive long, kicking Christian and tagging in Lance. The fresh man, he kicks both heels, scoring a two-count with a leg lariat to Christian. The CLB answers with a poke to the eye, but Storm traps him in a Single Leg Crab moments later. When Jericho makes the save, Rob follows. The babyfaces quickly toss their opponents out to the floor for tandem flying dives. That gets Lance a two-count before Christian doubles him over and tags in Y2J. Together, the heels chop Storm before Jericho unloads with a string of fists. Lance slows him with a jawbreaker and dropkick. When he heads upstairs, Christian distracts the babyface for Y2J to knock him out to the floor. There, he pulls back a piece of the barricade and drops Storm on the exposed steel. A flying back elbow follows for a near fall. Back in, Christian powerslams Lance for his own two-count before applying a reverse chin lock. Although Storm escapes and rolls up the former champion, Christian drops him with a clothesline to regain control. Y2J tags in afterwards, but can't lock Lance in the Walls of Jericho. Instead, Storm cradles him for a near fall. Jericho gets his own two-count following a dropkick and elbow drop before Christian tags back in. Lance meets him with a string of strikes and a rolling fireman's carry slam. Van Dam finally gets the hot tag afterwards to punch and dropkick Y2J. A springboard kick and hotshot follow before RVD slams the heel into position for a split legged moonsault. Fortunately for the heels, Christian breaks up Mike Chioda's count, the announcers not mentioning that he's suddenly on *Raw*. Although CLB rams Storm into the ring post, Rob surprises him with a drop toe hold into Jericho's crotch. He follows up with rolling thunder to both heels, but when he goes for the cover, Y2J extends his foot onto the bottom rope. Rob remains on the offensive, kicking Christian and delivering a Five-Star Frog Splash. Unfortunately, Jericho is the legal man and surprises the Intercontinental Champion with a Lionsault for a close two-count. He then locks on the Walls of Jericho, but Van Dam won't tap out. Instead, he crawls to his corner for the blind tag. Lance capitalizes with a top rope flying missile dropkick to steal the victory.

While workers try to tow the destroyed limo out from under a production truck, the announcers debate whether Kane deserved what happened to him earlier.

Backstage, Terri tries to interview Mark Henry about his match with Goldberg tonight. Theodore Long interrupts. He tells the interviewer that when she wants to talk to his men she needs to talk to Long first. Mark then tells everyone that not only is he going to collect the bounty on Goldberg tonight, but he's also going to claim the World Title. Theodore tells Terri to "believe that".

Randy Orton/Ric Flair def. Garrison Cade/Mark Jindrak. Orton and Cade lock up to start the match, JR calling them two of the best young superstars in the business. Jerry disagrees. He doesn't think Garrison is at Randy's level. He doesn't look it as the "Legend Killer" dropkicks and slugs him before getting distracted and cheap shotting Jindrak. That lets Cade recover and tag in his partner. Although Mark gets in a few shots, one stiff clothesline puts him down for Ric to tag in and stomp the babyface. Chops follow until Jindrak comes back to life with a back body drop and series of dropkicks to the heels. Even when he misses one, Mark surprises Flair with a small package for a two-count. Cade and Orton tag back in for the babyface to get in a few shots. When he attempts a roll-up, "The Nature Boy" cheap shots him to turn the tide. Randy capitalizes with a back suplex. Back in, Ric chops and stomps the rookie. The heels take turns punishing Garrison until he surprises the "Legend Killer" with a bulldog. That sends both men to their corners for tags. Jindrak is fired up and he punches and back body drops both heels. A springboard twisting double clothesline follows before Cade returns to pick up Flair for a Mark dropkick. While Chad Patton is trying to get Garrison out of the ring though, Randy surprises Jindrak with an RKO for "The Nature Boy" to steal the win while Orton drives Cade out to the floor.

Backstage, Ric Flair and Randy Orton celebrate their win until Maven and Trish Stratus pass them. Maven mockingly congratulates the heels on their "big win" and asks when they'll give Garrison Cade and Mark Jindrak a rematch. When Flair calls him a "boy", the babyface challenges Ric to a match next week. "The Nature Boy" is happy to accept, telling Maven he's had more championships than the babyface has had women. Lawler loves it.

Maven/Trish Stratus def. Steven Richards/Victoria. Maven isn't focused on this match after his exchange with Ric Flair and Richards takes advantage with an early assault. It doesn't take the babyface long to get focused and he responds with an inverted atomic drop and nice dropkick. That sends Steven to his corner to tag Victoria. Trish joins her for a stare down and exchange of slaps. The vixen gets the upper hand with a Thesz press and fists. A Matrix dodge and head scissors follow before she scores a two-count with a dropkick. Kicks and forearms follow, including one to the ropes when Richards tries to enter the ring, crotching the heel. When Stratus attempts to give the "black widow" a handstand head scissors from the top rope, Steven capitalizes on Jack Doan's back being turned to nail Trish from behind. Victoria takes advantage with a slingshot somersault leg drop for a near fall. Stiff kicks and shoulder blocks to the abdomen follow until the vixen surprises her opponent with a sunset flip and two-count. The "black widow" gets her own two-count with a knee to the gut. She then locks on a side bearhug, trying to crush Stratus's ribs. Trish quickly fights free and surprises her with another roll-up for a two-count. Afterwards, a spinebuster levels Victoria. When Richards tries to attack the vixen, Maven makes the save with a spinning heel kick. He then tags in to punch Steven for a two-count. A powerslam also gets him a near fall before Victoria makes the save. That brings Stratus back in to kick the "black widow" out of the ring. Behind her, Richards arm drags Maven off the top rope for a two-count. He then puts the babyface back on the top rope only to turn into a Chick Kick and Maven Blockbuster Neckbreaker for the three-count. Post-match, Victoria whips Trish into the ring steps.

Backstage, Theodore Long leads Mark Henry to the ring, pumping him up for his title shot.

Goldberg def. Mark Henry (with Theodore Long) (World Title match) by disqualification. Although Rodney Mack accompanies Henry to the ring also, Charles Robinson orders him to head backstage before Goldberg makes his entrance. He attempts to rush the challenger before the bell, but Mark is ready and waiting for him, hammering the intense superstar. The "World's Strongest Man" impresses, press slamming Bill. He can't keep the champion down and Goldberg responds with a series of fists, kicks, and clotheslines. Henry answers with a modified uranage for a near fall. When he attempts to follow up with a corner charge, the intense superstar meets him with a boot and clothesline to finally drop the challenger. Mark is right back up and rams Bill into a corner, crushing him to Long's delight. A leaping butt splash on the middle rope follows, Jerry calling it the "Take That". A shoulderbreaker afterwards nearly crowns a new champion before the "World's Strongest Man" applies an overhead hammerlock. The champion counters with an arm drag and armbar. When Henry reaches the ropes for the break, Goldberg hammers him until he runs into another uranage and two-count. Back up, the intense superstar punches the challenger ahead of a scoop slam for a big pop. Shoulder blocks follow before Bill sets up for a Spear. That brings Mack back out to hit the champion with a steel chair for the disqualification. Mark follows up with a corner splash before Shawn Michaels races out to give Rodney Sweet Chin Music. When he tries to do the same to Henry, the "World's Strongest Man" catches his foot and locks him in a bearhug. Michaels escapes with an eye rake, but his timing couldn't be worse as he turns into a Goldberg Spear. Not concerned at all about the "Heartbreak Kid", Bill Jackhammers Henry to end the show triumphant.

SmackDown!

October 9, 2003
Hartford, CT
Announcers: Michael Cole, Tazz, Rey Mysterio (briefly), Matt Hardy Version 1.0 (briefly)

The show opens with a video package featuring Vince McMahon and his daughter. Stephanie McMahon refuses to quit her job as general manager, but Vince promises she will at No Mercy. Shots of Stephanie as a little girl play as her father tells her that she's making him crush her for being defiant. When she later fights with Sable, Vince gets sickening pleasure slamming Stephanie. Afterwards, the intro video plays and fireworks explode before Linda McMahon heads to the squared circle. She says things have always been bizarre in her family, but with Shane McMahon attempting to kill Kane Monday night and her husband facing her daughter at No Mercy, Linda doesn't know what to think. Stephanie interrupts to talk to her mom and the fans. She knows how upsetting this all is for Linda, but Stephanie refuses to quit. Now it's Vince interrupting. He enters the squared circle and tells his daughter that he won't cancel their match even if she begs him. The WWE owner tells Stephanie that she's forcing him to "brutalize her". He'll do so with a clear conscience. Mr. McMahon believes Stephanie is forcing him to do this like Linda forced him to have a second kid. Linda acknowledges that Vince is twice as big and strong as their daughter, but doesn't think it's fair that Stephanie is putting her job on the line while the WWE owner isn't putting anything on the line. He says he doesn't have to, but he's not afraid of anything. After thinking it over, Vince offers to resign as WWE chairman if Stephanie wins. Sable then heads to the ring because this wrestling show hasn't had enough non-wrestlers opening the broadcast. Mr. McMahon says she looks fine and fawns over her before he introduces Linda to the diva. Sable calls his wife "Linda" condescendingly before saying that she's the great woman behind a great man and she'll be in his corner at No Mercy. Linda isn't surprised because she's heard that Sable offers her services freely to everyone. The heel immediately kicks her, setting off Stephanie. She tackles and punches Sable until Vince shoves her back. When she attempts another charge, the WWE owner clotheslines his daughter and says she made him do that before leaving with Sable. Of course, we also get a replay of this fifteen-minute segment after a commercial break.

Tajiri def. Ultimo Dragon. Rey Mysterio provides guest commentary here while he scouts Tajiri ahead of his Cruiserweight Title rematch at No Mercy. He respects both men in the ring, even if he doesn't like the current champion. The "Japanese Buzzsaw" tries to show him that he's in trouble in ten days, but Dragon blocks his handspring back elbow and knocks the heel out to the floor for an Asai moonsault. After that scores him a two-count, the masked man sets up for a victory roll, but Tajiri hotshots him on the top rope. He wastes time taunting Rey and pays courtesy of a tilt-a-whirl backbreaker and spinning heel kick for a two-count. Right back up, the champion responds with a Michinoku driver for his own near fall. He tries to follow up with a Tarantula, but Dragon slams him to the mat to escape ahead of a roll-up and two-count. When he flips over the "Japanese Buzzsaw" though, Tajiri surprises him with a straight kick to the jaw. A Buzzsaw Kick follows for the win. Post-match, the champion kicks Ultimo Dragon again. That brings Mysterio into the ring to trip the heel for a 619 and nice pop.

Backstage, Josh Mathews asks Stephanie McMahon how she's doing. She and Linda McMahon are fine. Linda's so good that Stephanie says she'll be in her daughter's corner at No Mercy.

The Undertaker def. Chuck Palumbo (with Johnny Stamboli/Nunzio). Pre-match, The Undertaker says Vince McMahon made this match to try to soften up the biker ahead of his No Mercy WWE Title shot.

He has his own equalizer, pulling out a large steel chain and wrapping it around the ring post before he gets to work. That includes working on Chuck's arm before delivering Old School. Stamboli hops onto the apron to distract him, but the "Deadman" knows all the tricks and dodges a corner charge that sees Palumbo hit the ring post and chain. Snake eyes and a big boot follow before The Undertaker sets up for a chokeslam. Once again Johnny hops onto the apron. This time, the biker decks him and big boots Nunzio before scoring the win with a chokeslam. Post-match, Brock Lesnar sneak attacks the "Deadman". When he leaves the ring to clear the announce table, The Undertaker recovers and chases off The FBI with shots from his chain wrapped right hand. Brock attempts a second sneak attack, but this time the biker is ready for him and punches the chair back into his face to drive off the champion.

Backstage, Paul London, in a dress shirt, interrupts Vince McMahon talking to Sable. He says he's a big fan and wants a try-out match tonight. Despite being annoyed, Vince agrees to give him an opportunity. It's a big opportunity as he gives Paul a WWE Title shot against Brock Lesnar in his first match. London isn't sure about the match, but the WWE owner is very convincing.

Backstage, a worker hides his burrito from Big Show. The giant is in a foul mood and slaps the man before shoving the burrito into his mouth, forcing him to eat it.

Earlier today, WWE officials and crew members are excited to see Zach Gowen entering the building.

Big Show def. Orlando Jordan. After giving the rookie a count-out victory last week, Big Show goes right to work pounding on Orlando. He manhandles Jordan until the giant runs into a drop toe hold driving him into the middle turnbuckle. That lets the rookie land a few strikes before Show grabs him by the throat for a definitive Chokeslam and the victory.

Backstage, Josh Mathews asks Eddie Guerrero if he's worried about Big Show getting revenge tonight or at No Mercy. "Latino Heat" jokes that he'll just give the giant another burrito if he tries to touch him. Eddie warns that he's got some cousins in the area and Show won't do anything to him tonight. However, he is nervous about putting his US Title on the line in ten days. Fortunately, Guerrero believes in himself. Big Show doesn't care, sneak attacking the champion and tossing him into the backdrop.

Instead of locking up to continue their rivalry, John Cena and Kurt Angle engage in a battle rap tonight ahead of their No Mercy match. Tazz moderates the competition inside the ring. He thinks Cena will have the upper hand here, but is impressed Kurt challenged the rapping heel to his own game. John says the Olympian has as much street cred as Cole. He then freestyles that Angle couldn't "rap a Christmas present". He also calls himself the "American nightmare" before giving Kurt a one-finger salute. The Olympian says he can't compete with Cena and his rap was good. Instead, Angle tells a story about how John just ran into the "king of kicking ass". Kurt promises to stick the rapping heel's chain up his butt if he tries to use it at No Mercy before warning that at the PPV, Cena will tap. The Olympian ends his story by telling John that he didn't come here to rap, but rather to fight. He then attacks the rapping heel in and out of the ring until Cena rocks him with a microphone shot to the head. Chokes and kicks follow, John telling Angle that he can't see him. Kurt proves him wrong, delivering a trio of German suplexes, but when he attempts to apply the Anklelock, Cena retreats backstage ahead of a No Mercy ad.

Shannon Moore def. Zach Gowen. Following a video package for Gowen, including Brock Lesnar injuring him, Matt Hardy leads Shannon to the ring with Matt Facts revealing that Hardy's not afraid to eat alone in public and likes portabella mushrooms. He then joins the announce table and complains about Zach getting a video package. When Moore taunts the babyface, Gowen surprises him with a missile dropkick. A leaping back elbow afterwards gets Zach a two-count while Matt tells the announcers that the babyface doesn't impress him. Shannon does with a northern lights suplex into the turnbuckles for a two-count. A suplex also scores Moore a near fall before he hammers the one-legged superstar in a corner. Following another two-count, slamming Gowen to the mat from the corner by his leg, the heel traps him in a reverse chin lock. It doesn't take Zach long to fight free and drop the MFer with a springboard kick. A reverse leg sweep follows for a near fall. Gowen gets under Hardy's skin when he screams ahead of a neckbreaker to Shannon. Zach knows what he's doing and baseball slide kicks Matt when approaches the apron. He doesn't see Moore coming though and the heel stacks him up for a near fall. Right back up, Gowen catches the MFer with a flying DDT off the second rope. When he heads back upstairs, Matt shoves him to the canvas behind Mike Sparks' back. Shannon capitalizes with a twisting neckbreaker for the win.

Backstage, The Undertaker chuckles as he leaves the general manager's office.

After a commercial break, the announcers run down the upcoming No Mercy card before replaying footage from the opening segment featuring the McMahons.

A-Train/The Basham Brothers def. Chris Benoit/The APA. The Bashams don't wait for the bell to ring, attacking The APA with chairs pre-match. Nick Patrick, now on *SmackDown!*, just watches as A-Train hurries out to join his partners. Faarooq gets the worse of the assault, officials checking on him at ringside while Doug scores a pair of two-counts on Bradshaw inside the squared circle. Danny gets in several shots in the heel corner ahead of his own two-count. The hairy heel then shows the Bashams how it's done, stomping the big Texan before scoring a near fall with a corner bomb. Back in, Doug slows the pace with a reverse chin lock. Bradshaw finally shows signs of life with elbows, but Basham slams him to the canvas by his hair while officials help Faarooq backstage. Inside the ring, the big Texan boots Doug and rocks Danny with a Clothesline from Hell. Benoit gets the hot tag afterwards to wrestle the heels and German suplex A-Train. When he locks him in a sharpshooter, Doug breaks it only to get trapped in his own sharpshooter. He quickly taps out, but he's not the legal man. The hairy heel is, and he scores the victory lifting "the Crippler" for a Train Wreck. Post-match, the Bashams give Bradshaw the Ball and Gag, paying him back for giving Shaniqua a Clothesline from Hell last week.

Brock Lesnar def. Paul London (WWE Title match). London is already in the ring as Lesnar's music plays. Tazz, as usual, says, "well, here comes the pain". Brock isn't happy about having to defend the title tonight, but he respects the young superstar for having the guts to face him. Paul is hesitant to get in the ring with him, but the champion offers to let him take a look at the belt that someday he might hold. Lesnar even offers to let him touch it, calling it a big honor. When the rookie reaches for the belt, Brock clotheslines him for the early advantage. Backbreakers and slams into the turnbuckles follow as Cole says this is an execution, not a try-out match. The champion enjoys it, powerbombing London ahead of an F5 for the win. Post-match, he tries to F5 the rookie against the ring post, but Spanky runs out for the save. He pays courtesy of a hard whip into the post, the back of the underdog's head hitting the steel. The Undertaker interrupts to tell Brock that he's not the only one with friends in high places. The biker says there've been some changes to their No Mercy WWE Title match. Now, it will be a "Biker Chain" match. The announcers don't know what that means, but don't think it's good for Lesnar.

Backstage, Josh Mathews waits outside the trainer's room to get word about Eddie Guerrero's condition. Chavo Guerrero Jr. exits the room and says his uncle is tough. While "Latino Heat" might not be able to do anything about Big Show's assault tonight, Chavo can and heads to the ring to call out the giant. Show is already dressed to go out on the town. He refuses to enter the squared circle to slap Guerrero. Chavo mocks him, drawing the giant into the ring by insulting his outfit and calling him chicken.

Big Show def. Chavo Guerrero Jr. by count-out. Once the giant is in the ring, Chavo rolls out to the floor. He refuses to return, staring at Show while Mike Sparks counts him out. The announcers don't think Eddie Guerrero will be proud of his nephew. Post-match, Chavo motions for someone to come out. It's "Latino Heat" on top of a sewage truck. Eddie tells Big Show that he warned him not to mess with the Guerreros. "Latino Heat" then introduces his cousin and tells the giant all about the truck he's on and how it sucks crap out of the ground. Apparently, it can hold thousands of pounds, mostly from what Show dropped last week. Since Big Show messed with him, Eddie promises to spray the crap on the giant. Show begs him to stop, but Chavo trips the giant for "Latino Heat" to spray him with sewage. Incensed, Big Show charges the US Champion only to be dropped with a concentrated blast. The fans love it and chant their appreciation as Eddie covers his No Mercy opponent in sewage. Once Los Guerreros leave, Show looks at his ruined clothing and holds up a shoe filled with excrement. He fights back tears as the show closes.

Monday Night Raw
October 13, 2003
Pittsburgh, PA
Announcers: Jim Ross, Jerry "the King" Lawler, Ric Flair (briefly)

The show opens with Ric Flair on crutches. He's joined by Randy Orton as he talks to Terri. "The Nature Boy" believes that despite him being injured last night, someone is going to collect on Triple H's bounty on Goldberg's head tonight. He excuses himself when he sees Shawn Michaels in the distance. Ric tells him that he's only given away the title of "best ever" to two people and Shawn is one of them. Flair can't believe that he'd let Mark Henry and Goldberg humble him. "The Nature Boy" wants him to act like the greatest ever again and to collect the hundred thousand dollars tonight. Michaels looks conflicted as he walks away ahead of the intro video and fireworks.

The announcers then reveal that Kane's condition has been upgraded and we'll hear from him in his hospital bed tonight. When they try to replay footage of Shane McMahon nearly killing the "Big Red Machine" last week, Chris Jericho interrupts from the squared circle. Christian stands behind the first ever Undisputed Champion as Y2J blames "Stone Cold" Steve Austin for all of this carnage. He also blames Austin for Shane injuring Test in Louisville, Kentucky, over the weekend. Footage plays of McMahon giving the bodyguard a coast-to-coast attack that breaks Test's foot. When Christian starts to badmouth Shane, he heads to the ring to take credit for his actions. If the heels don't like it, he tells them they can call a "wah-mbulance". Continuing to add to the heel numbers, Rene Dupree and Rob Conway head to the ring to complain about never getting a return match for the World Tag Titles. Instead of going through a long list of complaints, they join the other heels in attacking Shane until The Dudley Boyz run out to chase the foreigners from the squared circle. Bubba Ray is looking for a fight and challenges the heels to a match tonight. Despite having a four-on-three advantage, Y2J answers, "no".

In the parking lot, a car nearly runs over Goldberg, but he manages to leap on his car to escape injury.

Rob Van Dam def. Scott Steiner (with Stacy Keibler) (Intercontinental Title match) by disqualification. While Test recovers at home, he's ordered Stacy to remain in Scott's corner. "Big Poppa Pump" forces her to sit in a chair at ringside while he belly-to-belly suplexes and clubs RVD. A clothesline, elbow drop, and pushups follow until Rob answers a corner charge with a back elbow. He capitalizes with a scoop slam and split legged moonsault for a two-count, but can't keep Steiner down. Right back on the attack, he gives the champion a northern lights suplex before telling Keibler to give him her chair. She refuses, distracting "Big Poppa Pump" for Van Dam to repeatedly kick him, one from the top rope. Rolling thunder and a baseball slide kick follow before Scott drops RVD face-first on the apron. He tries to smash his skull afterwards against the ring post, but Rob dodges. When Van Dam tries to kick the chair back into Steiner's face, "Big Poppa Pump" beats him to the punch and bashes his skull for the disqualification. Post-match, Scott threatens to hit Stacy with the chair until "Stone Cold" Steve Austin marches down the aisle to ask what Steiner thinks he's doing. Austin dares "Big Poppa Pump" to hit him. Scott has never turned down a challenge and answers with a big right hand. Laying on the canvas, the "rattlesnake" smiles. Freed to fight back, "Stone Cold" punches, stomps, and chokes Steiner to Keibler's delight. Before he can finish off "Big Poppa Pump", Scott shoves Stacy into the co-general manager to escape. Once he's gone, Austin enjoys a few beers, even giving Keibler one. She doesn't like beer and shakes her head even after he opens it for her. When she grimaces after taking a hesitant sip, Steve gives her a Stone Cold Stunner. Somehow, that gets him a pop.

Maven def. Rico (with Miss Jackie). Ric Flair joins the announce table on crutches. He says he suffered his injury last night at a house show and is disappointed he can't wrestle tonight. Instead, Rico, sporting silver and blue face paint, steps in for "The Nature Boy" to pummel the babyface. Jackie also gets in on the act, choking Maven before the flamboyant superstar scores a two-count with a kick. When he attempts a second, the babyface ducks and answers with a string of clotheslines and a big back body drop. Following his own kick, Maven scores a near fall with a leaping DDT off the second rope. Post-match, Ric races down the aisle to smash the winner with his crutch and choke him. Jerry calls it a "miracle".

Backstage, Rosey, dressed as a mild-mannered photographer, spots Lance Storm wearing a Hurricane shirt. He'd love to take a picture of him. Before he can, The Hurricane leaps in to tell the Samoan about an emergency at a local orphanage. Rosey excuses himself to go change in the locker room, but his mentor says that superheroes don't change there. They change in phone booths. Unfortunately, when Rosey attempts to do so, he gets stuck.

Footage of Shane McMahon causing Kane to be a car wreck victim last week plays. Lawler says this has to stop, but Shane looks proud of his actions backstage. The Dudley Boyz interrupt to tell him that "Stone Cold" Steve Austin just signed them to an eight-man tag match against Chris Jericho, Christian, Rene Dupree, and Rob Conway tonight. Even better, they can pick their fourth partner. Even better than that, the Dudleys say that it will be a "Tables" match.

Further backstage, Goldberg tells a worker about the car that nearly ran him over. When he walks away, bricks fall off a shelf and nearly hit Bill.

After a commercial break, Goldberg heads to the ring and tells anyone who wants to collect on Triple H's bounty to come out and do it right now. That brings out Shawn Michaels. The World Champion says the rumors must be true that he can't be trusted. Shawn tells him that if someone offers him a hundred thousand dollars, he might take it or he might not. However, he'd collect it man-to-man. Instead, Michaels wants an explanation for why Bill Speared him last week. He's not even upset about the Spear, but the "Heartbreak Kid" noted that the intense superstar didn't care about the mistake. Shawn says he owes Goldberg now. Instead, it's Tommy Dreamer running out to hit the champion with a kendo stick. Michaels just watches until Bill Spears Dreamer. When the "Heartbreak Kid" grabs the stick, Ric Flair, joined by Randy Orton, hurries out to tell the "Heartbreak Kid" to finish off the intense superstar. Mark Henry and Theodore Long interrupt. They want the bounty themselves. Eric Bischoff has heard enough. He'd love to help Goldberg, but he hasn't forgotten that Bill Speared him. Because of that, he signs a handicap match pitting the World Champion and Shawn against Randy, Ric, and Mark.

Booker T/Shane McMahon/The Dudley Boyz def. Chris Jericho/Christian/Rene Dupree/Rob Conway ("Tables" match). The heels are out first. While they show unity heading to the ring together, the babyfaces make separate entrances. The heels, especially Christian, are shocked to see Booker make his return. The fans chant "USA" as the five-time champion locks up with Y2J. Although Jericho surprises him with a series of strikes, Booker T answers with kicks and chops in a corner. The fans already want tables. They'll have to wait as the babyface clotheslines Y2J and tags in Bubba Ray for his own round of strikes including a big elbow to the skull. Jericho quickly crawls to his corner and tags in Dupree. He fares no better, Bubba punching and slamming him. D-Von tags in to do the same ahead of a running bulldog. When he hits the ropes though, Y2J hits Dudley from behind. Conway then tags in to stomp and chop the dazed babyface. Christian gets in his own shots before Jericho returns with a top rope double ax-handle and back suplex. He lures Booker into the ring afterwards to distract Mike Chioda for Christian to join his partner stomping D-Von. Moments later, Rob returns for a string of fists before tagging Y2J again. He badmouths and leg drops Dudley on the middle rope ahead of a pair of stiff chops. Unfortunately, he misses a corner charge and D-Von nails him with a leaping shoulderblock. Both men tag out afterwards for Bubba Ray to back body drop Conway. When he starts fighting all of the heels, the other babyfaces jump into the brawl. While everyone else fights at ringside, Shane punches and spears Jericho. A leaping back elbow follows ahead of McMahon's shuffle and fists. A thumb to the eye slows him long enough for the other heels to make a wish and pull Shane's legs back, driving his groin into the ring post. Afterwards, Conway and Rene set up a table. The Dudleys chase them off from using it and check on McMahon ahead of a commercial break.

Afterwards, Christian is back in control, pummeling Shane before Y2J tags in to continue the assault. Unfortunately, he misses a running leg drop on the middle rope and crotches himself. Before McMahon can tag out, Christian sprints across the ring and hits the other babyfaces. That lets the heels retain control, Rob and Dupree taking turns wailing on Shane. When Rene does his French sidestep dance, the fans boo loudly. Even when McMahon starts to fight back, he can't string together enough moves to escape. Following a corner boot, Jericho surprises Shane with a flashback. Eventually, he answers a Y2J springboard attack with a kick and DDT. That finally lets him give Booker the hot tag. Fired up, he kicks everyone, dropping Jericho with a Scissors Kick. When Christian makes the save, the five-time champion stomps down his rival until the Canadian heel surprises him with a low blow. Bubba Ray comes to his partner's defense with a Bubba Bomb. Y2J answers with a top rope flying smash to the skull with a trashcan. D-Von is in next, dropping Jericho with the Saving Grace before Dupree plants him with a spinebuster. Booker T responds with his own spinebuster before putting the trashcan in Rene's lap for a McMahon coast-to-coast flying dropkick. When Booker teases a spinaroonie, Christian pulls him out to the floor. That leaves Conway to give Shane a neckbreaker. Unfortunately, the Dudleys are back up and give the French sympathizer a wassup drop. They grab a table afterwards and dodge Christian trying to dropkick it into their face. After they hit him with the table and set it up in the ring, Jericho smashes the Dudleys with the French flag. That brings Spike Dudley out to give Y2J a Dudley Dog. When he tries to do the same to Christian, the heel tosses him out to the floor. The Dudleys wait for Christian to turn and lift him up for a 3D, but Rob pulls the table out of the way. Unfortunately, Booker T puts Conway through it afterwards with a Book End to score the victory.

A video package of recent house shows plays to promote attendance. After a commercial break, Rosey is still stuck in the phone booth. People walk by, ignoring him.

Still in the ring, Booker T, Shane McMahon, and The Dudley Boyz continue celebrating their victory. Bubba even attempts a spinaroonie before Jonathan Coachman interrupts. He says it's time for his satellite interview with Kane and replays footage of Shane injuring the "Big Red Machine". McMahon takes the microphone away to say that the only thing "brutal" here is Coach's interviewing skills. He asks the other babyfaces to escort Coachman from the ring so he can handle the interview. They are all happy to do so before Shane asks for the satellite feed to be displayed on the Titantron. Bruised and bandaged, the monster looks unconscious. His doctor says that he might not be coherent. McMahon knows he can hear him and challenges Kane to a match at Survivor Series. The "Big Red Machine's" heart races as Shane teases that he locked the monster in the limo and heard him crying last week. That wakes up Kane and he assaults his doctor before Chokeslamming the nurse. Shane is impressed.

Ivory/Lita/Trish Stratus def. Gail Kim/Molly Holly/Victoria (with Steven Richards). Everyone gets separate entrances here before they open the match brawling. Ivory and Gail end up the legal women for the babyface to score a two-count with a bulldog. Lita then tags in to suplex Kim and jack her jaw. When she runs the ropes, Molly pulls the babyface's hair. The champion tags in afterwards to score a near fall with a dropkick to the face. Elbows and a reverse chin lock follow before Holly scores another two-count with a swinging neckbreaker. She then lures the babyfaces into the ring to distract Chad Patton for the heels to double-team Lita, Molly slamming her for a Victoria slingshot somersault splash. When that only scores her a two-count, Holly heads upstairs only to see Lita crotch her on the top rope and tag in Trish. She greets Holly with a handstand head scissors and neckbreaker. After dropkicking Gail out of the ring, she Matrix dodges Victoria ahead of a Chick Kick. Molly rushes to her partner's defense with a hair pull slam. Lita rewards her with a twist of fate, but Kim dropkicks her out of the ring. Ivory is back in and face slams Gail only to see the "black widow" plant her with a spinning side slam. When Trish attempts Stratusfaction, Steven shoves her into a Victoria back suplex and near fall. Incensed, he hops onto the apron only to see Lita pull him down. Richards responds by shoving her hard into the barricade. Inside the ring, Victoria picks up Stratus for a Widow's Peak, but she escapes with a roll-up for the victory. Post-match, Steven and the "black widow" attack Trish until Chris Jericho runs out and makes the save. After he tosses the heels from the ring, he brushes Stratus's face and smiles.

Following footage of "Stone Cold" Steve Austin attacking Scott Steiner and giving Stacy Keibler a Stone Cold Stunner, the "rattlesnake" stops Chris Jericho backstage. He wants to know if Y2J was trying to be a hero. Jericho says he was just showing Austin how to treat a lady and he's disgusted by him. When Y2J walks away, Jon Heidenreich stops the co-GM. He's got a highlight tape of his matches for "Stone Cold". After he gave Austin his ticket two weeks ago, Steve says watching that tape is the least he can do. Heidenreich does warn "Stone Cold" that Little Johnny made the tape, but promises it's good. Terri then asks the co-GM if he's found out who has been trying to attack Goldberg. He hasn't yet and plans to hit the bar instead. When he spots Rosey stuck in the phone booth, Austin forgets about the bar. He's ready to start drinking now. Rosey just needs to go to the bathroom.

Further backstage, Ric Flair tells Randy Orton that he needs to get serious to take out Goldberg and collect the hundred thousand dollar bounty. Mark Henry interrupts. He says the bounty is his, but the heels can watch up close. Randy is impressed with how Mark handles business and believes he's been behind the sneak attacks, but Theodore Long says that's not their style. Regardless, the heels are ready to finish off the World Champion tonight.

Goldberg/Shawn Michaels def. Mark Henry/Randy Orton/Ric Flair (with Theodore Long). Jerry questions if Goldberg can trust his partner as the World Champion comes out last. Despite his accusation, Shawn fights all three heels to open the match. He then trades chops with "The Nature Boy" before back body dropping both Evolution members. Following a Ric face-first flop, Flair dares Bill to enter the ring. He accepts the invitation and absorbs a series of fists and chops before also back body dropping "The Nature Boy". Both men tag out afterwards for Orton to punch and dropkick Michaels. Following several more strikes, Mark tags in and press slams the "Heartbreak Kid". He then whips Shawn upside down in a corner ahead of a pair of elbow drops. After slamming Michaels to the canvas, Henry tags Ric back in for more chops. Once again, the babyface answers in kind before the two men collide heads. Flair is closer to his corner, but the "Heartbreak Kid" lunges to give Goldberg the hot tag. He tackles the "World's Strongest Man" to the canvas before slamming both Ric and Randy. Impressing everyone, he also scoop slams Henry ahead of a Shawn top rope flying elbow drop. After Michaels somersaults over the top rope onto Evolution, Bill scores the win with a Spear and Jackhammer to Mark. Post-match, the "Heartbreak Kid" flattens Goldberg with Sweet Chin Music. Eric Bischoff is so excited to see the "real" Shawn back that he gives him a World Title match next week.

SmackDown!
October 16, 2003
Cincinnati, OH
Announcers: Michael Cole, Tazz

The show opens with Stephanie McMahon sitting on a couch telling fans that her father has banned her from the arena on what might be her last night as the general manager. She thinks it's petty, but that's Vince McMahon. Afterwards, the intro video plays and fireworks explode to kick off the go home episode of *SmackDown!* before No Mercy.

Afterwards, John Cena's music plays, but it's Kurt Angle coming out to the ring dressed as the rapping heel. He imitates John, cracking up the announcers as he dances and raps. When he gets the fans to yell "butt" after rhyming it with King Tut, Kurt explains how Cena's promos work. Angle's music then plays before a little person dressed like the Olympian heads to the squared circle. Kurt says it's "okay" and the man "can't see me". The little Olympian says, "John Cena, you're a wiener". After chasing the fake John from the ring, he leads the crowd in a "wiener" chant. That brings Angle, dressed as Cena, back into the squared circle. He tries to beat up the little man, "thuganomics style", but misses and taps out to an Anklelock. That brings the real Cena out in a foul mood. He gets in the real Olympian's face and tells him that what makes him really laugh is seeing Angle covered in his own blood at No Mercy. Unfortunately, the little Olympian low blows him ahead of a Kurt Angle Slam. Cole says the games are over this Sunday.

Chris Benoit def. Doug Basham (with Danny Basham). Shaniqua is still out after Bradshaw's clothesline. Doug could use her here as Benoit chops, suplexes, and teases an early Crippler Crossface. Even when Basham clubs his neck, "the Crippler" quickly recovers and fights both heels. A baseball kick drops Danny at ringside before Benoit tosses Doug out to the floor as well. Unfortunately, he misses a dive through the ropes, swinging the momentum when he hits his head on the floor. Afterwards, the Bashams take turns attacking Benoit legally and illegally, Doug leg dropping his neck twice before applying a neck vice. The "rabid wolverine" teases a comeback, but a hotshot and clothesline put him back down on the canvas. When Basham attempts to finish him off with a top rope guillotine leg drop, Benoit wisely moves. After catching his breath, he elbows and clotheslines Doug for a two-count. A German suplex puts the heel down, but when "the Crippler" motions for a diving headbutt, Danny slides a chair into the ring. Benoit spots it and dropkicks the weapon back into Doug's face before he can use it. While Jimmy Korderas deals with the weapon, Danny switches places with his brother. The "rabid wolverine" doesn't see it and misses a top rope diving headbutt for the illegal Basham to nearly steal the win. Afterwards, Benoit gives Danny a trio of German suplexes before locking Doug in the Crippler Crossface for the tap-out victory. Post-match, A-Train runs out to attack "the Crippler" ahead of their No Mercy match.

Filmed earlier today, Cole sits down with Stephanie McMahon. She talks about how ruthless her father is, taking away her opportunity to address the fans on what could be her last night on *SmackDown!*. Cole explains that she'll face Vince McMahon in an "I Quit" match this Sunday with their jobs on the line before asking if the McMahons are a normal family. It's all Stephanie has ever known. She doesn't know what she'll do if she loses. She also doesn't know what wrestling would be without Vince, saying that he might be the business itself. Fortunately, she knows her mother will always support her and be in her corner like she will be this Sunday. When Cole asks Stephanie if she's been given everything, she admits she probably has. However, she believes she's worked for everything she's got. Stephanie admits that there's some of her father in her, but she doesn't want to be feared like him. She never thought she'd come to blows with Vince. While they've had issues in the past, Stephanie never thought he'd put his hands on her. Crying, she says if they have their match this Sunday, he won't walk her down the aisle or be the grandfather to her kids if she has any. Despite all this, she says she loves Vince because he's her dad, but she hates him too. Cole calls it the toughest interview he's ever done. Back live, Tazz says he can't imagine Vince McMahon out of the industry. He'd find out in twenty years.

Backstage, Jamie Noble and Nidia argue about the upcoming father/daughter match. Jamie says *SmackDown!* may be better off without Vince McMahon around. Unfortunately, Tajiri overhears them and rats the rednecks out to the WWE owner. The "Japanese Buzzsaw" says he likes Vince. McMahon tells him to take out Noble tonight. He wants Tajiri to do something to Jamie that we've never seen before.

Jamie Noble and Tajiri (Cruiserweight Title match) wrestle to a no contest. The announcers wonder if Noble even knows why he's in this match. It doesn't seem to matter to him as he attacks the Cruiserweight Champion's arm to start the contest. A scoop slam and leg drop afterwards gets him a two-count. When he attempts a back suplex, Tajiri drives him into a corner for forearms and a kick to the side of the head. The "Japanese Buzzsaw" follows up with a dragon screw off the top rope. Focusing on the leg, he stomps the redneck's joint and grounds him with a knee breaker. Following a stretch, Jamie counters a second knee breaker with a roll-up and near fall. A neckbreaker then puts the champion down for Noble to catch his breath. Afterwards, he punches and clotheslines Tajiri. A powerslam follows for a near fall. When the "Japanese Buzzsaw" goes for a handspring back elbow, the redneck nails him instead. Unfortunately, his knee is still injured, and he can't lift up Tajiri for a Tiger Bomb. The champion tries to capitalize by using his title belt while Mike Sparks checks on Jamie, but Nidia grabs the championship. The "Japanese Buzzsaw" makes her pay for her actions, spraying black mist into her eyes. That stops the match as Sparks and Noble both check on the screeching diva.

After a commercial break, trainers and officials check on Nidia. She's still in pain as Jamie Noble storms back to the squared circle to warn Tajiri that if his girlfriend is permanently injured, there will be nowhere for the "Japanese Buzzsaw" to hide. He challenges Tajiri to come out and settle things like men, but when he doesn't, Jamie storms back up the aisle to find him. Unfortunately, he finds Brock Lesnar instead. The WWE Champion sends a message, tossing Noble into the guardrail before giving him an F5 at ringside. Afterwards, Vince McMahon and Sable walk down the aisle. Vince shakes Brock's hand and sends him backstage before stepping into the ring. He notes his daughter's award winning performance earlier. Especially when she lied that she loves her father. Only Vince understands the true meaning of love. He says it means hurting someone that he truly loves. This Sunday, he refuses to spare the rod. Mr. McMahon tells all those people that are hoping for some miracle at No Mercy with a Stephanie victory that he doesn't believe in miracles. Unlike the fans who play the lottery hoping for something better, Vince has worked hard for everything he's got. Ahead of their match this Sunday, he hopes God has mercy on Stephanie's soul because he won't. Sable rubs his shoulder and says she's happy to be in Vince's corner unlike his wife, Linda. Sable is proud to stand by her man and plans to take Mr. McMahon away at No Mercy, calling him a "genuine American icon". She seals things with a kiss.

Footage of *SmackDown!* superstars this week on a European tour plays.

Eddie Guerrero def. Rhyno. Eddie is out alone in a purple and yellow lowrider due to travel problems, according to Cole, for Chavo Guerrero Jr. Rhyno tries to make "Latino Heat" pay for being alone, shoulder blocking and hip tossing him. He then shows off his power advantage in a test of strength. Even when Guerrero tries to power up, the man-beast kicks him. The double champion responds in kind before stomping Rhyno's fingers. Fists follow until the man-beast drops him with a reverse powerbomb onto the top turnbuckle for a two-count. Afterwards, he wrenches Eddie's neck ahead of a spinebuster and another near fall. A press slam into a gutbuster also gets him a two-count before "Latino Heat" grabs the bottom rope. Frustrated, Rhyno grabs the US Title, but Nick Patrick takes it away. Guerrero capitalizes with a dropkick and head scissors. A trio of suplexes follow before Eddie heads upstairs only to Frog Splash onto a pair of knees. That puts both men down ahead of a commercial break.

Afterwards, the man-beast has "Latino Heat" trapped in a sharpshooter. Guerrero doesn't stay in it long, fighting free and back elbowing Rhyno into position for a slingshot somersault splash. When he heads upstairs, the man-beast meets him with a fist to the jaw and superplex off the second rope. That scores him a close two-count. Rhyno then heads upstairs only to see Eddie hurricanrana him to the canvas for his own near fall. When "Latino Heat" charges the man-beast, Rhyno flings him out to the floor. There, Guerrero unties his own boot and sticks the ring bell hammer into it. Tying the boot back on, Eddie returns to the ring to punch the man-beast. Rhyno answers with a clothesline before setting up for the Gore. At the last second, "Latino Heat" pulls the referee into the way. Fortunately, the man-beast holds up at the last second and only grazes Patrick. While he recovers, Guerrero tosses the man-beast his hammer. The referee spots it and takes it away for Eddie to blast Rhyno with the US Title for the win. Post-match, "Latino Heat" starts to back up his lowrider only to see Big Show smash out the back window with a lead pipe. After tossing Guerrero into his ride, Show smashes the lowrider with the pipe. Instead of using it on Eddie, he flings "Latino Heat" onto the windshield and broken glass. Guerrero's blood isn't enough to stop the giant from powerbombing his No Mercy opponent on the hood of the vehicle. Not done yet, he puts Eddie on top of the lowrider to Chokeslam him on the roof.

Rey Mysterio def. Johnny Stamboli. The FBI try to accompany Stamboli to the ring, but Brian Hebner sends them backstage for Rey to head scissors and kick "the Bull". Johnny responds with a backbreaker for a two-count. Afterwards, he traps the masked man in a reverse chin lock. Although he kicks free, Stamboli slams him into the tree of woe. When he attempts a charge, Mysterio moves and "the Bull" hits the ring post. A moonsault off the ropes follows for a two-count. Rey then dropkicks Johnny's knee for a springboard seated senton and two-count. Stamboli answers with a spinning side slam, but the masked man grabs the ropes for the break. When he pulls Mysterio in for a powerbomb, Rey punches free. A dropkick to the chest and one to the back put Johnny in position for a 619, but "the Bull" catches the masked man for a backbreaker. When he tries to press up Mysterio, Rey stuns him with a West Coast Pop for the three-count.

Backstage, Shannon Moore and other superstars look at Eddie Guerrero's lowrider being towed out of the arena. Matt Hardy Version 1.0 finds Moore and gives him a picture of Hardy for beating Zach Gowen last week. Jon Heidenreich interrupts with a videotape for Stephanie McMahon. Since she might be out of a job soon, Matt promises to get it where it belongs, tossing it in the trash when Jon walks away.

Afterwards, the announcers preview No Mercy before asking The Undertaker via video about the rules for the "Biker Chain" match. The "Deadman" says there are no rules other than a chain will be suspended above the ring for the wrestlers to grab and use it. By hook or crook, the biker plans to use the chain and win the WWE Title. When he hopes that Stephanie McMahon beats Vince McMahon this Sunday, Brock Lesnar ambushes The Undertaker and beats him with the chain. He continues his assault through a commercial break, dragging the biker to the ring and choking him with the chain. The "Deadman" tries to fight back, but the WWE Champion continues choking and hammering him before whipping The Undertaker into the ring steps. He nearly chokes out the biker around the ring post, but the "Deadman" fights free with a big boot. One clothesline inside the squared circle puts the biker back down for more chokes. When he picks up The Undertaker for an F5, the "Deadman" fights free and chokes Lesnar too. Just when he starts to build momentum, Brock slows him with a low blow. Despite that, the biker is the one standing tall to end the episode, chokeslamming the WWE Champion and chasing him from the ring ahead of their title match this Sunday.

PPV: No Mercy
October 19, 2003
Baltimore, MD
Announcers: Michael Cole, Tazz

The show opens with a video package for the Vince McMahon/Stephanie McMahon match. Afterwards, a shorter video for the WWE Title match plays before the logo spins around and fireworks explode.

Tajiri def. Rey Mysterio (Cruiserweight Title match). Pre-match, Brian Hebner checks Tajiri's mouth for any illegal mist. He doesn't find any. Instead, the wrestlers open the match trading shoves and kicks. Rey gets the upper hand with an arm drag and leg lock, but the heel is the champion for a reason and transitions into an armbar. He works on the shoulder with elbows until the masked man flips over only to turn into a chop and more elbows. When Mysterio starts to elbow in response, the "Japanese Buzzsaw" clubs his back. The challenger answers with a dropkick to the knee. Moments later, he counters a handspring back elbow with a dropkick to the back. Rey follows up with a flying dive over the top rope out to the floor. When he attempts another top rope maneuver back in the squared circle, Tajiri shoves him out to the floor to regain control. A whip into the ring post afterwards gets the champion a two-count before he returns to working on the arm, stretching it out with an armbar. Although the masked man escapes with an arm drag, he hurts himself doing so. A kick to the arm drops him afterwards for another two-count. Continuing to focus on the arm, the heel stretches and whips Mysterio around by the limb. The challenger answers with some kicks, but when he heads back upstairs, a "Japanese Buzzsaw" kick slows him. The champion follows up the ropes, but Rey shoves him down to the canvas for a flying DDT and two-count. With the fans chanting for the 619, the masked man scores a near fall with a springboard cross body block. The two men then trade roll-ups before Tajiri catapults Mysterio onto the apron. The challenger responds with a head scissors out to the floor. He quickly follows up with a running hurricanrana off the apron. Back in the squared circle, he goes for a flying senton, but the champion moves. Rey lands on his feet and surprises him with a kick to the gut, but his West Coast Pop attempt is answered with a powerbomb for an extremely close two-count. The masked man also gets a near fall landing on the top rope after a pop-up toss to moonsault the heel. Tajiri answers with a Tarantula, but misses a Buzzsaw Kick and receives a dropkick to the face instead. Mysterio follows up with a catapult onto the middle rope and 619. When he hits the West Coast Pop, two fans slide into the ring to distract everyone. The "Japanese Buzzsaw" capitalizes on Rey trying to figure out what they are doing to kick Mysterio and steal the victory.

Backstage, Josh Mathews asks Vince McMahon how he feels heading into his match with his daughter tonight. After insulting the interviewer for being nervous, Vince says that his fight with Stephanie is personal. He knows that a lot of people have personal issues with him, but if anyone on the roster interferes in his match tonight, he will fire them and make sure they never work again.

Chris Benoit def. A-Train. The hairy heel is obsessed with beating Benoit, driving him into a corner and trash talking him. Afterwards, a shoulderblock sends "the Crippler" out to the floor. The fans respond with a "shave your back" chant. When he returns to the ring, Benoit chops A-Train, but when he tries to apply the Crippler Crossface, the hairy heel shoves him back. A big back elbow follows, but the hairy heel misses an elbow drop to let the "rabid wolverine" land a string of punches. A-Train responds in kind until he misses a corner charge. Benoit capitalizes with more strikes and chops. That plays to the hairy heel's strengths and he responds with a scoop slam and body splash for a two-count while Cole announces that Stu Hart passed away over the week and offers the family the WWE's thoughts and prayers. Moments later, a bicycle kick scores A-Train a near fall. He proceeds to wail on "the Crippler" in a corner, overpowering his opponent ahead of a decapitator slingshot. Getting cocky, the hairy heel slaps Benoit ahead of a delayed butterfly suplex into a facebuster. Somehow, a bloodied Benoit just manages to kick out. When he starts to fight back, A-Train makes the mistake of arguing with Jimmy Korderas. The "rabid wolverine" capitalizes with another string of strikes, but one shot puts him right back down for a surfboard stretch. When he lets go, Benoit surprises him with a DDT to put both men down. The hairy heel is up first and German suplexes "the Crippler". He then shoots his opponent out to the floor to ram him into the barricade in front of some servicemen. Frustrated, A-Train grabs a chair and brings it back into the squared circle. There, he attempts to gorilla press slam Benoit, but drops him onto the chair headfirst. Despite that fall, the "rabid wolverine" comes back to life to trap the hairy heel in a Crippler Crossface. Although A-Train fights free of that hold, he can't escape a trio of German suplexes. With the fans cheering him on, Benoit heads upstairs only to be slammed to the mat. The hairy heel follows up with a clothesline before teasing going upstairs himself. He thinks better of it and returns to the canvas to deliver a Derailer, but "the Crippler" just manages to kick out. A-Train attempts to follow up with a corner kick, but hits the chair instead. Benoit capitalizes, trapping the hairy heel in a sharpshooter for the tap-out win.

Backstage, Jon Heidenreich chokes Shannon Moore. He tells Matt Hardy that Little Johnny told him that the heels threw away his wrestling tape. Matt assures him that there's been a mistake. He threw away a tape of Shannon's highlights because it wasn't very good. Heidenreich is confused and admits that he might have made a mistake. He tells Hardy that he's still number one with him and Little Johnny when Matt promises to get Jon's videotape to whoever is the general manager after tonight.

Ahead of the next match, Tony Chimel recognizes all of the troops in the crowd.

Zach Gowen def. Matt Hardy Version 1.0 (with Shannon Moore). Matt Facts tonight say that he cannot be grossed out and that he's survived five car wrecks. Inside the ring, he hammers and slams the t-shirt wearing babyface. Zach refuses to stay down, surprising him with a bulldog off the second rope for a one-count. When he attempts a springboard attack, Shannon trips him for Hardy to regain control. Cole wants to see a fair wrestling match, yelling at the heels. While Tazz tells him to calm down, Matt snake eyes and clotheslines Gowen. He then chokes him under the ropes before scoring a two-count. Hardy teases the babyface after a leg drop, pulling Zach's arm onto him for a two-count. After Matt gets his own two-count, he locks on a surfboard stretch. When that doesn't score him the win, Hardy slugs Gowen again ahead of a front slam in the corner. Unfortunately, he misses a top rope moonsault afterwards. That wakes up Zach and he drives the heel from the ring with a dropkick. The babyface follows him with a springboard somersault splash out to the floor. A flying cross body block back in the squared circle gets him a two-count. Matt immediately answers with a side effect for his own near fall. Hardy is still groggy and he runs into a back elbow before Gowen heads upstairs. The heel joins him only to get knocked down. Zach shows him how it's done, scoring his first and only singles WWE pinfall victory with a Moonsault.

Backstage, Linda McMahon begs her husband not to fight Stephanie McMahon tonight. Linda says she's turned her head for thirty-seven years on all his transgressions, but tonight she needs him to reconsider. Vince won't cancel the match, but he will make a concession. He offers to let Stephanie win their match by pinfall or submission while he can only win by submission. However, he's now making the match "no holds barred".

The Basham Brothers def. The APA. Shaniqua is still missing from the Bashams' entrance after Bradshaw gave her a Clothesline from Hell. He tries to injure Doug too, hammering him down in a corner. More fists follow before the big Texan runs through Basham. Faarooq then tags in for his own clubbing blows and a back elbow for a two-count. A powerslam follows before Danny tags in for his share of the punishment. The brawlers nearly score the win with a double spinebuster, but Basham just kicks out to receive a double shoulderblock as well. This time, Doug makes the save. Danny follows up with a jawbreaker and kick to Faarooq to turn the tide. Back in, Doug slams the brawler before leaping into a pair of knees. Bradshaw drags him out to the floor and whips the heel into the ring steps, barricade, and apron while Faarooq distracts Mike Sparks. The brawler tries to follow up with a Dominator, but Doug slips free. Danny joins his brother to double back suplex the brawler and illegally switch places for a two-count. Moments later, a double suplex gets Danny a near fall. After he knocks the big Texan off the apron, Bradshaw inadvertently distracts the referee for the Bashams to wail on Faarooq. Once he's down, Doug applies a reverse chin lock. It doesn't take the brawler long to start to elbow free, but Basham pulls his hair and tags in Danny for his own chin lock. When Faarooq elbows him, Danny slams the brawler. Unfortunately, he then runs into a spinebuster for both men to tag out. Bradshaw explodes into the ring, clotheslining, kicking, and shoulder blocking the heels. A vicious powerbomb follows to Doug, but somehow the heel kicks out. Danny then pokes the big Texan's eyes, but that doesn't slow him for long. After driving Doug from the ring, he gives Danny a fallaway slam. With Faarooq helping him, he follows up with a fallaway slam off the second rope to Doug, but Danny makes the save. Afterwards, Faarooq accidentally clubs the referee. While he's down, Bradshaw flattens Danny with a Clothesline from Hell. Unfortunately, Shaniqua makes her return and blasts the big Texan's skull with a steel pipe for Doug to score the win with a leaping leg drop.

Backstage, Josh Mathews congratulates Shaniqua and The Basham Brothers on their win. He's surprised to see the dominatrix back after Bradshaw's Clothesline from Hell. She knows the big Texan was surprised to see her too before noting her chest. She says it has permanently swelled. The Bashams like it, staring at her as she promises to "whip it good". This is Ruthless Aggression at its worst, trying to oversexualize everything.

Vince McMahon (with Sable) def. Stephanie McMahon (with Linda McMahon) ("'I Quit" match). Following a four-minute video package for the match, Stephanie and her mother head to the squared circle. If she wins, Vince will leave his job as chairman of the WWE, but if she loses, Stephanie will quit as the general manger. Sable is out next, getting her own entrance before Vince powerwalks down the aisle. Linda tries to talk some sense into him, but he's not listening. When Stephanie pulls her aside, Mr. McMahon clubs his daughter from behind. She responds by jumping on his back when he yells at his wife. One slam puts her back on the mat. Vince follows up with a shoulderblock, blaming his wife for this match. He then tosses Stephanie around by the hair and chokes her in a corner. To add insult to injury, he puts his daughter on the middle rope for Sable to slap. Linda chases after the diva, but Mr. McMahon intercepts his wife. Once she heads back to her side of the ring, Sable grinning as she goes, Vince returns to the squared circle to clothesline his daughter. He then turns her over into a single leg crab. She cries in agony, but will not submit. When he tires of that hold, Mr. McMahon locks on a surfboard as well. Stephanie escapes with an eye rake, bringing Sable onto the apron with a steel pipe. Fortunately, Linda grabs the heel and makes her drop her weapon. When Vince tries to separate the women, Stephanie scores a near fall with a low blow and roll-up. Repeated pipe shots follow for another close two-count, but Vince stretches his foot on the bottom rope to survive. Afterwards, Sable hops onto the apron to fight with Stephanie, but she spots her father's sneak attack and dodges. Once he runs into Sable, Stephanie scores another near fall with a bulldog. She tries to use the pipe again, but Vince catches her by the throat and whips his daughter to the canvas. Afterwards, Mr. McMahon hits his own daughter with the pipe before choking her out with it. Linda has seen enough and throws in a white towel to end the match on her daughter's behalf. Post-match, Vince pulls Linda off Stephanie and shoves his wife down to the canvas. Afterwards, trainers and WWE officials rush out to check on Stephanie, the former general manager asking her mom why she threw in the towel. Tazz wants to know who will be the next GM, but Cole is more concerned with what he just saw, calling out Mr. McMahon for the way he treated his daughter.

Kurt Angle def. John Cena. Following a video package for this match, notably half as long as the previous match's video package, Cena heads to the squared circle first. He raps that he's like a mad tiger and Kurt is Siegfried and Roy. A clash of styles, when the Olympian enters, he outwrestles the rapping heel. John answers with a kick to the gut and side headlock, the fans divided on who to cheer. Angle doesn't care who they cheer, hip tossing and arm dragging Cena ahead of an armbar. The rapping heel doesn't respect Kurt and the Olympian feels the same, flipping off John. He then stomps Cena down in a corner. The rapping heel responds with a clothesline for a two-count. He then unloads with fists in a corner, but control goes back and forth courtesy of an Angle back body drop. Kurt follows up with punches and a corner spear. When he attempts a second, John moves and the Olympian hits the ring post hard. Cena follows up with a clothesline and his own corner charge. He tells Angle he can't see him ahead of a neckbreaker and near fall. A big swinging sledgehammer blow afterwards busts open Kurt's mouth ahead of another two-count. The rapping heel slows the pace with a surfboard—a popular move tonight—until the Olympian fights free. That gets him driven to the canvas with a spinning slam ahead of a body vice. It doesn't take Angle long to fight free while the fans engage in dueling "Cena/Angle" chants. John gets the upper hand with a spinebuster, but when he heads upstairs, the Olympian tries to meet him with a run up belly-to-belly suplex. Although the rapping heel shoves him back to the canvas, Kurt recovers in time to dropkick his shin as Cena flies toward him. That swings the momentum and Angle unloads with clotheslines ahead of a leg sweep for a two-count. A drop toe hold into the Anklelock follows, but John grabs the ropes for the break. When he slides out to the floor, Kurt baseball slide kicks him into the announce table. He tries to take the fight back into the ring, but the rapping heel stuns him with a jawbreaker. The Olympian teases a German suplex off the apron, but Cena holds onto the ropes and answers with a DDT. Moments later, he catches Angle sliding back into the ring with a guillotine leg drop off the middle rope. That gets him a near fall before Kurt surprises him with a German suplex. John responds with a dropkick to the knee and throwback snap mare. Following another two-count, the rapping heel misses a corner charge. The Olympian capitalizes with a trio of German suplexes for a near fall. Once again, Cena clubs his opponent to regain control. He connects with a corner charge this time, clotheslining Angle before powerbombing him back into the buckles. Somehow, Kurt still manages to just kick out of his cover. John has had enough and picks the Olympian up for an FU. Somehow, he still only scores a near fall as Angle just kicks out. The rapping heel goes for a second FU, but Kurt slips free for an Angle Slam and his own close two-count. Frustrated, Cena crawls to his steel chain, but Jimmy Korderas takes it away before he can use it. The referee doesn't see John wrapping the Olympian's gold medals around his fist to deck Angle. Once again, Kurt just kicks out. He also scores a near fall with a roll-up before trapping the rapping heel in an Anklelock for the tap-out. Post-match, Angle shakes hands with some of the troops in the crowd.

MUST SEE! Big Show def. Eddie Guerrero (US Title match). Following footage of Eddie spraying Big Show with sewage, the giant marches to the squared circle in a foul mood. "Latino Heat" goes right after him, Cole talking about trainers pulling thirty pieces of glass from his body Thursday night. Despite a dropkick and several strikes, one big shot from Show flattens Guerrero. The challenger follows up with a massive chop and heavy forearm to the back. After he walks across the champion, Big Show continues his pounding assault. When he attempts a charge near the ropes, Eddie dodges and whips the champion out to the floor. He then flings a chair into the ring, distracting Nick Patrick as he gets rid of the weapon for "Latino Heat" to blast the giant with a trashcan lid. He follows up with a string of kicks to the knee back in the squared circle. That only makes Show mad and he takes the fight out to the floor to fling Guerrero into the ring post. A press slam back into the ring follows before the challenger drops his weight onto his opponent's lower back. Afterwards, he stretches out the champion, applying a modified surfboard stretch. Instead of looking for the submission, he kicks Eddie and stomps on his skull. Despite dominating the match legally, Big Show removes a turnbuckle pad to whip "Latino Heat" into the exposed steel. He promises to break Guerrero. When he puts the champion on the top rope though, Eddie slams his face onto the exposed steel. He follows up with a Frog Splash onto the standing giant for a two-count. Show's kick-out is so strong that he flings "Latino Heat" onto the referee. He then tries to leg drop Guerrero, but lands on Patrick. With no referee, the champion dons brass knuckles and lays out his opponent for a near fall. Eddie has another trick up his sleeve and grabs the US Title to blast the challenger. After nudging the referee to wake up, "Latino Heat" heads upstairs for a Frog Splash, but somehow, Big Show kicks out yet again. Guerrero can't believe it. He wastes time pleading with the referee before running into a spinebuster for a giant near fall. A Chokeslam follows, but this time the champion stretches his foot onto the bottom rope to break Patrick's count. He's still groggy and misses Eddie giving Show a low blow and DDT. That puts both men down for the referee's standing ten-count. On his knees, he gets to six before "Latino Heat" covers the challenger. This time he counts two before Big Show kicks out. He immediately responds with a Chokeslam to finally win the US Title. Post-match, Chavo Guerrero Jr. heads to the ring to yell at his uncle. Eddie is in no mood to hear him.

Backstage, Josh Mathews asks Big Show if he has anything he'd like to say. He says, "I told you so". Show claims that he took Eddie Guerrero's masculinity and gave him a beating only a giant could. The new champion warns that no one can take his belt from him.

Brock Lesnar def. The Undertaker (WWE Title "Biker Chain" match). Following a three-minute video package for the match, Tony Chimel makes note of the biker chain on a pole. He says the first man to reach it can use it. The challenger is out first, but it's Brock landing the first shots in a corner. The Undertaker responds in kind and starts working on the champion's arm. Lesnar has him well-scouted and drives the biker back into a corner for knees to the midsection. He attempts to follow up with a corner charge, but misses and hits the steel pole with the chain. The "Deadman" capitalizes with a string of shoulder blocks and shots to the injured arm. When he tries to head upstairs for Old School, Brock hammers him until the challenger drops him with a big boot. A leg drop afterwards gets The Undertaker a two-count before he heads back upstairs, this time delivering Old School to the shoulder. A quick roll-up follows for a near fall before he slugs the champion on the floor. After the biker gives him an elbow on the apron, Lesnar hits a second gear and responds with a string of strikes and a whip into the ring steps. Back in the squared circle, he continues his assault. Following a corner spear, a cradle suplex gets Brock a near fall. The "Deadman" answers with a kick, but when he races forward for a corner big boot, the champion dodges and The Undertaker straddles himself. The wrestlers exchange moves, the challenger dropping Lesnar's throat on the top rope before the heel knocks him off the apron into the barricade. They then trade shots, the biker getting the upper hand with a leaping clothesline and two-count. Although Brock answers with a knee to the gut, the "Deadman" drops him sternum-first onto the top rope before heading up for the chain. Before he can grab it, the lights go out. The champion takes advantage of the situation, grabbing his opponent's leg and stopping him ahead of a powerslam and near fall. With no disqualifications, Lesnar tosses the ring steps into the squared circle, but the challenger meets him with a series of shots. A drop toe hold onto the steps slows his assault, but The Undertaker won't stop. He unloads with more fists and a clothesline out to the floor. There, he gives the heel a piledriver onto the ring steps base. Somehow, Brock recovers in time to stop him from grabbing the chain. When he tries to give the biker an electric chair drop, the "Deadman" counters with a triangle choke. Unfortunately, a low blow puts the challenger down long enough for Lesnar to grab the ring steps and blast his opponent's skull for a pair of two-counts. He sets up for a second steps shot, but The Undertaker kicks them back into the champion's face. When the biker tries to use the steps, he misses the heel and flings them out to the floor. Brock wakes up afterwards, hammering the "Deadman" down in the corner before heading up for the chain. The challenger teases giving him a Last Ride from the corner, but Lesnar hops free before both men connect with simultaneous clotheslines. After they catch their breath, the two men trade fists in the center of the ring. The Undertaker wins the exchange and delivers snake eyes and a big boot. He tries to follow up with a chokeslam, but the champion slips free again and answers with a spinebuster. The biker won't stay down, responding with another triangle choke until the heel powerbombs his way free. When they get up, Brock clotheslines the "Deadman". This time, the challenger responds with Taking Care of Business, but Lesnar powers out and F5s The Undertaker. At the last second, the biker just manages to drape his boot on the bottom rope to keep his championship hopes alive. The champion then heads upstairs for the chain, but the "Deadman" meets him and chokeslams him to the canvas. Instead of going for the cover, he heads back up for the chain. This time, The FBI runs out to attack the challenger. Cole reminds us that there are no rules as The Undertaker takes care of all three heels, clearing them from the ring before Brock teases another F5. The biker is too fired up and slips free to give the champion the Last Ride. He then dives over the top rope onto Chuck Palumbo and Johnny Stamboli beside his motorcycle. While he does so, Nunzio tries to get the chain, but the "Deadman" spots him and knocks him off the pole out to the floor. Afterwards, he finally grabs the biker chain only to see Vince McMahon crawl out from under the ring and shove the challenger crotch-first onto the top rope. Lesnar then smashes The Undertaker with the chain to steal the victory while Vince sprints backstage.

No Mercy is a step down from Vengeance. While many of the same stars are involved, the show takes too long getting to the featured matches and spends far too much time on the McMahon family drama. The opening Cruiserweight Title match is fun, but we've seen Mysterio and Tajiri wrestle multiple times recently and this one doesn't stand out. It's good, but nothing spectacular. Benoit and A-Train then have a long twelve-minute match featuring the hairy heel clubbing his opponent. Like the opener, we've seen this match before and it's a lot better in smaller doses. Zach Gowen gets his only WWE PPV victory here over Matt in a short match that's just okay. The build to the match was slowed with Zach's injury and it loses a lot of the heat. The WWE tries to get some heat between The APA and Bashams, but other than being brothers and submissive to Shaniqua, the heels haven't shown any personality making them hard to boo or cheer. Faarooq is also struggling inside the ring at this point. The McMahons then have about fifteen minutes with video packages and entrances for Vince to dominate his daughter. Vince being a heel and fighting with his family is fine. It can even be entertaining, but too much of this show and the build up to it are on this storyline. It's not just that the McMahons have major storylines, they have massive amounts of television and PPV time building to what is usually a terrible match. Angle and Cena have the best match of the night and the crowd starts to get into the action. John is really starting to catch on with the crowd now. The US Title match doesn't connect, Show taking his time in the ring while Eddie tries to cheat in every way that he can. If anything, there are too many big moments in this match with both men kicking out of the other's finishers and illegal weapon shots. While that match is a disappointment due to the styles clash, the main event is another good match from Lesnar and The Undertaker. It's a little long at twenty-four minutes and the outside interference with both Vince and The FBI is a little much, but it's a good brawl and solid ending to the show. Overall, No Mercy is a step back for *SmackDown!*. For a show that has excelled with in-ring action, there's too much story and too many pairings featuring styles that don't mesh. It's not a terrible show, but there's little here to warrant your attention.

Monday Night Raw
October 20, 2003
Wilkes-Barre, PA
Announcers: Jim Ross, Jerry "the King" Lawler

The show opens with a still shot of Road Warrior Hawk who passed away yesterday, just forty-six years old. Afterwards, a video package of Triple H putting a bounty on Goldberg's head and Shawn Michaels kicking the intense superstar plays to set up tonight's World Title match ahead of the intro video and fireworks.

"Stone Cold" Steve Austin then heads to the ring. He's excited because someone left him a note earlier today to meet him in the squared circle at nine o'clock. Unfortunately, it's Test on crutches and Austin won't get a chance to fight. Instead, he watches as the bodyguard hobbles down with Stacy Keibler in tow. Test gets a big booing when he covers up Stacy's entrance in her short denim skirt. The bodyguard then blames his injury on Austin and wants an apology. The "rattlesnake" tells him that injuries happen in the ring and he's not apologizing. He's also not apologizing for giving Keibler a Stone Cold Stunner. He asks her in the future what she needs to do when he offers her a beer. Before she answers, Test interrupts and tells her that she only speaks when he lets her. "Stone Cold" wants him to go ahead and attack the co-general manager so he can respond. The bodyguard wonders if the "rattlesnake" would hit a crippled man. Steve would love that. He says he'd fight anyone and runs down a list of people he'd fight. Test has had enough and tries to pull Stacy backstage, but she shoves the bodyguard back into Austin who gives him a Stone Cold Stunner. From the Titantron, Eric Bischoff calls "Stone Cold" pathetic. He knows Steve is tired of not being able to do what he wants, almost as much as Eric is tired of having a co-GM. Bischoff has a proposal that the WWE board of directors has signed off on. At Survivor Series, the GMs will select teams to compete on their behalf. If Austin wins, he can go back to attacking superstars whenever he wants. However, if Eric's team wins, "Stone Cold" is fired. The "rattlesnake" isn't afraid of a little competition and accepts, even after finding out that Chris Jericho and Scott Steiner are Bischoff's first two team members. The possibility of getting his freedom back is cause for celebration for Austin and he calls for a beer. Keibler intercepts one, prompting JR to tell her that she's made a mistake. Instead, she entertains the crowd and "Stone Cold" by drinking several.

The Dudley Boyz def. Rene Dupree/Rob Conway (World Tag Title match). JR lets us know that both Spike Dudley and Sylvan Grenier are on the injured reserve after going down on house shows this week. D-Von tries to put the rest of the heel squad on the shelf alongside Grenier, taking an early advantage until Conway stuns him with a kick to the knee and neckbreaker. Once in control, the heels take turns slamming and pummeling Dudley. Rob even gets a pair of two-counts with a double suplex after Dupree lures Bubba Ray into the squared circle with his sidestep dance. When he can't score the three-count, Conway slows the pace with a reverse chin lock. Eventually, he stuns Rene with an enziguri kick before giving Bubba the hot tag to side slam Rob. Sporting a Hawk armband, he elbows and slams Conway into position for a wassup drop, but Dupree makes the save, straddling D-Von on the top rope. The heels follow up with a Double Slam to Bubba Ray, but D-Von recovers to make the save at the last second. Fights follow in and out of the ring before D-Von plants Rob with Saving Grace. The champions then point to the ceiling before hoisting up Conway for a Doomsday Device and the victory.

Following a commercial break, Eric Bischoff tells Chris Jericho and Scott Steiner that he wants to send a message ahead of Survivor Series tonight. The heels agree, but can't decide who is leading the team.

That's what Eric is worried about and tells his men to get on the same page before they face "Stone Cold" Steve Austin's squad at Survivor Series.

Further backstage, Terri stands with Randy Orton and Ric Flair. They are holding one hundred thousand dollars as Randy guarantees that the bounty will be collected tonight. Ric rants that Goldberg will be finished tonight before warning Maven to "strap on your jetpack" for their match later. Once the heels walk away, Booker T seizes the opportunity to tell Terri that he's going to make a statement tonight. Orton takes offense. He doesn't think anyone but Evolution will make a statement here. The five-time champion slaps him and challenges the "Legend Killer" to a fight next.

Booker T def. Randy Orton by count-out. Out of a commercial break, Booker chops and punches Randy. The heel is wearing dress pants as he catches the five-time champion with a hotshot and clothesline for a two-count. A backbreaker also gets him a near fall while the announcers question if Shawn Michaels will collect the bounty on Goldberg's head tonight. Orton slows the pace with a surfboard afterwards. It takes him some time, but Booker T eventually comes back to life with a string of strikes head of a Scissors Kick. Once the "Legend Killer" is down, the babyface entertains with a spinaroonie. That sends Randy out to the floor to claim that he doesn't need this for the count-out. Post-match, Booker grabs a microphone and volunteers to join "Stone Cold" Steve Austin's Survivor Series team.

The Goldberg/Shawn Michaels match doesn't officially start. After Shawn dances down to the aisle for his World Title shot, the cameras cut backstage for Goldberg's entrance. As soon as he leaves his locker room, Mark Henry attacks and slams him back into the steel door. Theodore Long tells him "it's all about the Benjamins".

After a commercial break, trainers check on Goldberg backstage. Shawn Michaels explains to "Stone Cold" Steve Austin what happened and wonders if he's going to get his title shot or not. Austin is more concerned with tossing Mark Henry out of the building.

Chris Jericho/Scott Steiner def. Lance Storm/Rob Van Dam. As Y2J heads to the ring, JR wonders what happened last week with him saving Trish Stratus. Ross isn't accustomed to Jericho doing good things. When the bell rings, Scott and RVD trade shots, Steiner with clubbing blows and Rob kicking the powerhouse heel. Eventually, "Big Poppa Pump" catches the popular superstar and slams him into a corner. Van Dam answers with a spinning heel kick and moonsault for a two-count. Lance then tags in for his own shots and a leg whip for a one-count. That sends Scott rolling out to the floor and the heels asking for a time-out. JR says there aren't any in the WWE, but Charles Robinson and the babyfaces certainly give the heels one. Y2J then tags in to receive his own share of the punishment. After dropping the Canadian heel face-first on the mat, Storm dances. Jericho responds with an eye rake and hip toss onto the apron. There, Lance fights both heels until Y2J knocks off into the barricade. Steiner follows up with a hard whip into the ring steps before threatening the fans. Back in the squared circle, Jericho scores a one-count with an arrogant cover. A back suplex and trio of elbow drops afterwards gets him a two-count. "Big Poppa Pump" soon returns to club Storm for his own two-count—for once not stopping after an elbow drop to do pushups—before hooking a reverse chin lock. Even when Lance gets free, a twisting suplex nearly scores Scott the victory before he tags Y2J. He imitates his partner and does a series of pushups. That almost costs him as Storm surprises him with a roll-up for a near fall. Moments later, he catches the heel with a springboard back elbow before tagging in RVD to fight both heels and northern lights suplex Jericho for a close two-count. A spinning heel kick puts Y2J down for a Five-Star Frog Splash, but before the popular superstar flies, Steiner hops onto the apron. Rob catches him with a leaping kick only to see Jericho nearly steal the win with a quick cover and his feet on the ropes. Back up, Van Dam slams Y2J in place for a split legged moonsault. Fortunately, "Big Poppa Pump" makes the save. Finally recovered, Lance slingshot splashes Scott from the ring, but is quickly tossed back into the steps. Inside the squared circle, RVD fights free of a Walls of Jericho and drops Y2J with a kick. When he runs the ropes though, Steiner hits him with a chair ahead of a Lionsault for the three-count. Post-match, "Big Poppa Pump" drops Storm with a Face-First Slam ahead of a second Lionsault. On the same page, the heels hug.

Backstage, Eric Bischoff interrupts trainers and Goldberg. The co-GM believes that Bill is faking his injury just to get out of his title match. The intense superstar grabs Eric and tells him that it's going to take a lot more than Mark Henry to cancel his match. Bischoff smiles while JR announces the match is still on.

From their desk, the announcers pass along news that both Hawk and Stu Hart passed away this week. A brief video package plays for Stu, narrated by Vince McMahon. He passes along the WWE's thoughts and prayers to the whole Hart family.

Backstage, Ric Flair tells Theodore Long on the phone that he's not paying him the bounty because Mark Henry didn't get the job done. However, Ric knows that someone is going to collect tonight.

Further backstage, Trish Stratus stops Chris Jericho. Y2J is in full heel mode as he tells her there's no reason to thank him for saving her last week. Trish stops him. She tells him that he doesn't need to be "Chris Jericho here". She knows he was trying to prove a point to "Stone Cold" Steve Austin last week and just wants him to know she appreciates him. Humbled, Jericho looks down as he says he respects her and was trying to help. Awkward, Stratus has a match to get to right now.

Even further backstage, Garrison Cade and Mark Jindrak enter Evolution's locker room. They tell Randy Orton that they are here for the bounty. He's glad they came to their senses and want to take out Goldberg. They've got another idea, attacking Randy and stealing the briefcase.

After a commercial break, Ric Flair tells Randy Orton to keep an eye on the money because he's got to take care of Maven. Randy doesn't know what to tell him, but he's smart enough not to admit that he lost a hundred thousand dollars.

Molly Holly/Victoria (with Steven Richards) def. Lita/Trish Stratus. Trish opens the match with a takedown and roll-up for a near fall on the Women's Champion. Chops and a head scissors soften up Molly afterwards for a dropkick and another two-count. When Richards hops onto the apron to distract Jack Doan though, Victoria hot shots the vixen on the top rope. A spinning side slam follows from the "black widow" for a near fall. Sadistic, she stretches Stratus before tagging back in Holly. Victoria isn't done attacking Trish, kicking her from the apron before the champion tries to score the victory with a Molly Go Round. At the last second, the vixen dodges and both women tag out. Fighting solo, Lita easily handles her opponents, dropping the "black widow" with a DDT. She then tags back in Stratus for a double hip toss. Following a Trish handstand head scissors to Holly, Lita tackles the champion. Doan watches that fight while Victoria lifts Stratus up on her shoulders. Steven capitalizes, slipping into the ring to slam Trish to the canvas for the three-count. Post-match, all three heels attack Lita. When Molly drapes the Women's Title on her face for a "black widow" slingshot somersault leg drop, Christian rushes out and makes the save, confusing JR.

Ric Flair def. Maven. The babyface is out first and doesn't wait for Ric to remove his robe, decking him before the bell. A back body drop follows before Maven clotheslines the veteran out to the floor.

There, Flair briefly slows him with an eye gouge, but the babyface quickly recovers and plants him with a spinebuster at ringside. Back in the squared circle, "The Nature Boy" quickly turns the tide with fists and chops. When he applies a chin lock, the announcers wonder what Randy Orton is going to do when Evolution finds out he lost a hundred thousand dollars. Ric has more pressing concerns right now as Maven nails him with fists and a flying forearm. Another back body drop and spinning heel kick have Flair seeing stars as the babyface heads upstairs for a flying cross body block and near fall. Once again, "The Nature Boy" goes to the eyes, but Maven rolls him up seconds later anyways. Ric has one more trick up his sleeve, grabbing the babyface's tights and rolling through for his own three-count.

Backstage, Randy Orton interrupts Ric Flair's celebration to tell him that Lance Cade and Mark Jindrak stole the money. Their car is still here, so Evolution rush to find them. Speaking of rushing, officers run past the heels to surround Kane who has just arrived to the building ahead of a Survivor Series ad.

After a commercial break, police officers follow Kane to ringside. He's still bloodied as he tells Shane McMahon to stay backstage and listen for once. The "Big Red Machine" says everything started with Linda McMahon when she tried to control the monster. Instead, Kane gave her a Tombstone. Even though she was screaming "no", he knew that she really meant "yes". The "Big Red Machine" adds that "inflicting pain turns (him) on". He promises there's no line he won't cross and suffering he won't inflict to destroy Shane. Survivor Series might be the end of their war, but McMahon's pain is only beginning.

In the parking lot, Lance Cade and Mark Jindrak rush to their car. Unfortunately, Triple H drops them with a two-by-four and recovers his briefcase without breaking a sweat.

After a commercial break, Randy Orton and Ric Flair wonder what they are going to do until Triple H enters the locker room. Ric immediately sells out the "Legend Killer". Hunter says since Goldberg is still wrestling tonight, they better have the money. He hands the briefcase back to Orton and tells him not to lose it again. Helmsley guarantees that someone will collect the bounty tonight and sits down to watch the main event.

Goldberg and Shawn Michaels (World Title match) wrestle to a no contest. Finally in the ring, Goldberg shoves around Shawn and grimaces to start the match. Michaels responds with a slap and forearms in a corner. He then kicks Bill down to size, but when he attempts a second rope flying attack, the champion catches the "Heartbreak Kid" and press slams him. A clothesline afterwards sends the challenger out to the floor. Goldberg brings him back in with a toss from the apron. Right back up, Shawn chops the intense superstar before being flipped up and over the top rope. Despite that, Michaels shoves Bill out to the floor and rams his lower back into the ring steps. With the fans cheering him on, the "Heartbreak Kid" chops the champion once more in a corner. Even when Goldberg starts to fight back, a flying forearm puts him down. The challenger then kips up and scores a near fall with a flying elbow drop. When he tunes up the band, the intense superstar blocks Sweet Chin Music with a clothesline. A powerslam and press into a front slam follow to soften up Shawn for a Spear. At the last second, he dodges and Bill runs over Earl Hebner. Sweet Chin Music follows to the champion to put everyone down. Charles Robinson sprints out to make a standing ten-count. He gets to eight before Batista returns and slams Michaels into the ring steps. He then gives Goldberg a spinebuster before chasing off Robinson for the no contest. Despite the fans chanting for Bill, "the Animal" gives him a Batista Bomb before Pillmanizing his ankle with a steel chair. Evolution then joins him on the stage, Triple H smiling as the heels reunite.

SmackDown!
October 23, 2003
Albany, NY
Announcers: Michael Cole, Tazz

The show opens with a video package featuring Stephanie and Vince McMahon. After her loss Sunday night, *SmackDown!* needs a new general manager. Following the intro video, instead of fireworks, Vince McMahon and Sable head to the squared circle. He's proud to say that he "kicked the snot out of" his daughter and that he's going to Hell when he dies. After bragging about sleeping with Sable following No Mercy, Vince turns his attention to Brock Lesnar and The Undertaker. Mr. McMahon was all too happy to teach the biker a lesson at the PPV, teaching him to "not cross the boss". Finally, Vince has thought long and hard about who should be the new general manager. While he tried to put him out of business and drives McMahon crazy, Vince is happy to introduce Paul Heyman. Tazz can't believe it and doesn't seem happy. The WWE owner is happy to shake Paul's hand as the new GM promises that things are going to change. Before he can make his first announcement, the "Deadman" marches out to chase the McMahon out through the crowd. When he gets in Heyman's face, the GM tells him that he's the only one who can get The Undertaker what he wants. That includes a match with Lesnar. Unfortunately, it's a handicap match with Big Show on Brock's side. However, if the biker wins, he'll be able to pick any kind of match he wants against anyone he wants. The "Deadman" knows he's not getting any favors and Paul being in his ring is like "someone taking a huge crap" in his yard. Regardless, The Undertaker promises to win his match tonight and get his revenge. He warns the new GM that he has no idea how sick and twisted the "Deadman" can be.

A-Train/John Cena and Chris Benoit/Kurt Angle wrestle to a no contest. Pre-match, Cena says she should thank Kurt for a great match Sunday, but instead he insults him and the fans. When the Olympian marches out, he starts the action with A-Train instead. Although he takes the hairy heel down with his superior mat skills, A-Train turns the tide with his size and power. John then tags in to drop Angle with a Michinoku driver for a two-count. Back in, the hairy heel kicks and butterfly suplexes Kurt for his own near fall. A backbreaker follows, but when he goes for a corner bomb, the Olympian moves and German suplexes him. Both men tag out afterwards for Benoit to fight the heels. That includes a German suplex to A-Train and back body drop to Cena. Afterwards, he locks the rapping heel in a sharpshooter, but the hairy heel makes the save. After "the Crippler" hammers him, Kurt tags back in to Angle Slam A-Train. He then traps John in an Anklelock, but the hairy heel makes the save with a big boot. The rapping heel has had enough and grabs his chain, but Brian Hebner spots him and stops him from using it. He doesn't see the hairy heel returning with a steel chair, but Benoit does. He takes away the weapon and tries to plaster A-Train with it only to see the hairy heel move and the "rabid wolverine" hit his own partner. That sets off the Olympian and he goes after his former rival. Benoit doesn't back down from a fight and locks Angle in the Crippler Crossface. When he taps out, the referee calls for the bell, presumably for the no decision.

The Subway Slam of the Week is Tajiri spraying Nidia's eyes with black mist. Apparently, it's extremely potent and the redneck still can't see. Recorded from his own webcam, Jamie Noble tells fans that money doesn't matter to him now. All he cares about is Nidia. Doctors are looking into surgical options to give her back her sight. If they don't, Tajiri better watch out because Noble is coming for him.

Backstage, Charlie Haas welcomes back Shelton Benjamin. He's a little worried that Paul Heyman is back too. He should be because the GM is lurking behind them. He remembers that The World's Greatest Tag Team never called to check on him after Brock Lesnar injured Heyman. He is a spiteful man and as one of his first acts, he's taking away their WWE Tag Title shot and giving it to The Basham Brothers. To prove he's a compassionate man, he doesn't fire the heels. Instead, he gives them a match next.

From their skybox, Sable makes Vince McMahon laugh saying hello to the "little people" in the crowd. Afterwards, the Stu Hart tribute video package plays.

Rikishi/Scotty 2 Hotty def. The World's Greatest Tag Team. The announcers are excited to see Scotty and Rikishi back together. Charlie isn't, trying to outwrestle Hotty. The fast-paced babyface isn't interested in mat wrestling. He picks up the pace fighting both heels. Following a back suplex to Haas, Scotty moonwalks. Unfortunately, he pays for it when Shelton trips him. Charlie follows up with his own back suplex for a near fall. Benjamin then tags in to slam the babyface for his own two-count before trapping him in a chin lock. When Scotty fights free, a knee doubles him over ahead of a double-team leapfrog splash. Haas follows up with stomps and a surfboard in a corner. Making quick tags, the heels wear down Hotty until he surprises Shelton with a back elbow and neckbreaker. Rikishi gets the hot tag afterwards to punch both heels and double clothesline them. Although he drops Charlie with a superkick, Benjamin responds with one of his own for a near fall. Scotty then drives Shelton's face into the canvas. When he motions for the Worm, Haas tosses him to the mat with a backward head slam. Fortunately, the big Samoan rushes to his partner's aid and stuns both heels. Another face slam follows to Shelton before Hotty finally drops the Worm. Rikishi then gives Charlie a Stinkface before dropping all his weight onto Benjamin's chest for the victory. Post-match, the babyfaces don hats and dance.

In the skybox, Vince McMahon and Sable dance until The Undertaker busts into their room. He grabs Vince and calls him a "real big man". If he was really a big man, the biker says he wouldn't have to pay Sable to sleep with him. The "Deadman" then warns McMahon that he better hope The Undertaker wins his match tonight or he'll come back to the skybox and finish him off here in Albany.

After a commercial break, Chavo Guerrero Jr. interrupts his uncle getting treatment on his cuts. Chavo tells him that he's not going to get any sympathy for losing the US Title Sunday night. He needs Eddie Guerrero at his best and focused for their family, fans, and each other. "Latino Heat" appreciates the pep talk and hard shove, focusing on the task at hand.

MUST SEE! The Basham Brothers (with Shaniqua) def. Los Guerreros (WWE Tag Title match). The challengers are out first, followed by Eddie driving the champions out in a black lowrider. Properly motivated, "Latino Heat" chops and kicks Doug before tagging in Chavo for a dropkick to the face and one-count. He follows up with a string of punches until Nick Patrick admonishes him. While the referee is distracted, Eddie chokes Basham. He then tags in to somersault splash Dough from the apron following a Chavo back suplex. A big uppercut and elbows follow from "Latino Heat". He also delivers his own back suplex. When Chavo returns, Basham surprises him with a right hand and tags in Danny for his own strikes. The champion quickly drops him with a back elbow before tagging his uncle. He tries to whip Danny into the ropes, but the challenger reverses the attempt for Shaniqua to trip and deck Eddie. That finally swings the momentum and the Bashams capitalize with a series of strikes and chokes in a corner. Doug nearly wins the titles with a suplex, but Guerrero just kicks out. He also kicks out following a leg drop, prompting Basham to trap him in a reverse chin lock. Back in, Danny punches and the heels double-team slam "Latino Heat". That brings Chavo into the ring to break his cover before the Bashams again double-team Eddie, Doug scoring a two-count with a back elbow drop from the second rope.

Taking matters into his own hands, "Latino Heat" drops both challengers with a combination head scissors and headlock takedown. Chavo then tags in to fight the heels and score a two-count with a swinging DDT to Doug. The Bashams respond with a double flapjack, but when they go for the Ball and Gag, Eddie pulls Danny out to the floor to clothesline him. Inside the squared circle, Chavo gets a two-count on Doug with a belly-to-belly suplex. Another near fall follows with a combination backbreaker and somersault splash from the champions. While "Latino Heat" gives Doug a trio of suplexes, Chavo slingshot dives out to the floor onto Danny. Unfortunately, he recovers and tosses the younger champion into the ring post while Eddie kicks Shaniqua off the apron. He doesn't see Danny switching places with his brother and taking Shaniqua's nightstick. Although Guerrero manages to roll to his feet after missing a Frog Splash moments later, Danny blasts him with a nightstick shot to steal the titles. Post-match, the new champions say it was only a matter of time before the dominatrix tells them it's time to celebrate. After La Resistance lost their titles on *Raw*, the Bashams get their run as one-dimensional heel champs here.

During the commercial break, Chavo Guerrero Jr. berates his uncle and leaves him on his own. Having lost two titles in less than a week, Chavo wants to know what it's going to take to get Eddie to focus.

Tajiri def. Zach Gowen. A non-title match, Zach surprises the champion with a quick takedown. When he embarrasses Tajiri by riding him, the heel responds with a stiff kick. Gowen tries to answer with a tornado DDT, but the "Japanese Buzzsaw" whips him to the canvas with a vicious spinebuster. Shots to the lower back follow before the champion slaps and suplexes Zach. Although he misses a knee drop, he holds the ropes to avoid a babyface dropkick. Gowen has plenty of fight left, rolling up Tajiri for a two-count ahead of a springboard leg lariat from the bottom rope. That also gets him a near fall before he heads upstairs. The heel meets him only to be thrown to the canvas. Unfortunately, Zach misses his Moonsault and is laid out with a big kick to the head for the three-count. Post-match, two Asian men enter the ring in black suits to raise the winner's hand. When Gowen gets up, they drive him back to the canvas with a Double Forward Leg Sweep Slam. This marks Zach's last WWE match.

After a commercial break, Brock Lesnar tells Big Show that he needs him to be on top of his game tonight because the WWE Champion doesn't want to defend his title against The Undertaker again. The US Champion tells Brock to worry about himself or else he might take away his championship too.

Footage of Brock Lesnar powerbombing and breaking Hardcore Holly's neck plays. In a prerecorded promo, Holly warns Lesnar that he's coming back to break his neck.

A tribute video package for Hawk plays.

The Undertaker def. Big Show/Brock Lesnar. Everyone comes out separately for this match, The Undertaker riding his motorcycle out last. Instead of getting his hands on Brock again, Big Show starts the match for the heels. He corners and headbutts the biker. When the heels double-team him in their corner, the "Deadman" fights free and grabs a chair to clear the squared circle. The announcers remind everyone that if he wins this match, he'll get to face anyone in any match he wants. They assume he will pick Lesnar. The champion tries to make sure that won't happen, returning to hammer and suplex The Undertaker for a two-count. The announcers speculate on what type of match the biker will pick, but it doesn't seem likely that he'll get it when Show returns to headbutt the "Deadman" for another near fall. The Undertaker refuses to stay down, fighting back and leveling the giant with a leaping clothesline for a two-count. Fortunately, Brock makes the save. He also receives a leaping clothesline before Big Show Chokeslams the biker. By the time the champion tags in to make the cover, the "Deadman" just recovers and kicks out. He then fights free of a Lesnar piledriver while Show climbs the ropes. Once he tosses Brock aside, The Undertaker chokeslams the giant off the top rope for the three-count. Unfortunately, Paul Heyman interrupts his celebration to admit he made a mistake. Now, this is a "Two out of Three Falls" match.

Following a commercial break, the biker is still on the attack, leveling the WWE Champion with a big boot and leg drop for a near fall. When he takes the fight out to the floor, Big Show clotheslines and headbutts the "Deadman". They only briefly return to the ring before the giant clotheslines The Undertaker back out to the floor. There, he misses a clothesline and is knocked over the barricade into the crowd. Lesnar joins him when the biker flings him over the barricade. He just manages to roll back in to beat Brian Hebner's count for the win. Once again, Heyman interrupts to say he made another mistake. He says this is actually a "No Count-out" match. Afterwards, Show blasts the biker with a steel chair for the disqualification. Once again, as expected, Paul admits that he made a mistake and this is a "No Disqualification" match. That comes back to cost the heels when the "Deadman" wraps a chain around his fist. Brock doesn't see it and tries to deliver an F5. Instead, The Undertaker slips free and knocks out both heels with the chain to score the three-count on the WWE Champion.

Post-match, Big Show pulls the "Deadman" off his bike and tosses him back into the squared circle. After Lesnar repeatedly stomps the biker, Show delivers several clubbing blows from his chain wrapped fist. A Chokeslam and leg drop follows. From his skybox, Vince McMahon watches intently. Not done yet, Brock takes the fight back out to the floor to F5 The Undertaker's knee against the ring post. McMahon tells the biker to stay right there because he's going to personally congratulate him.

After the final commercial break, Vince walks through the crowd and taunts the "Deadman". In the aisle, he wonders if what The Undertaker went through was worth it. Mr. McMahon promises that the biker will never be the WWE Champion again. He wants to know what kind of match the "Deadman" wants to have with Brock Lesnar. The Undertaker promises to get his revenge at Survivor Series in a "Buried Alive" match. Vince vows that Brock will bury the "Deadman" at Survivor Series, but he's wrong. The Undertaker takes the microphone away to tell McMahon that the biker won't face Lesnar at the PPV. Instead, he'll face Vince. The show ends with the WWE owner at a loss for words.

Monday Night Raw
October 27, 2003
Fayetteville, NC
Announcers: Jim Ross, Jerry "the King" Lawler

Once again, the show starts with a video package featuring Triple H putting a bounty on Goldberg's head. This week, the recap package also features Batista's return. Afterwards, the intro video plays and fireworks explode before the announcers note a steel cage hanging over the ring. They have no idea what it's here for tonight. Before they can speculate, Batista, Randy Orton, and Ric Flair head to the squared circle in business casual attire. When the fans chant for the World Champion, Ric tells them that he won't be here tonight because "the Animal" took him out. Batista then takes the microphone to tell Bill not to be mad. He should consider it an honor that Triple H wanted him eliminated and it was "the Animal's" privilege to do so. Randy says that since the champion is injured, the title should go back to the previous champion. That brings an angry Eric Bischoff down to the squared circle. He's just acting like he's upset though. He's really happy that Evolution took out Goldberg after the intense superstar Speared him. With a smile on his face, Eric pulls the World Title out of a bag. He says it's his honor to give away the belt as co-general manager. Before he can, "Stone Cold" Steve Austin steps through the curtain to a big pop. He heads to the squared circle to tell Bischoff that he left something in the bag, removing his hand and exposing a middle finger for his co-worker. Austin tells Eric that he can't strip Goldberg of the World Title because the intense superstar promises that he'll be back for revenge. To help him get it, "Stone Cold" books him in a match with Hunter at Survivor Series. Flair yells that the "rattlesnake" can't do that and Bill might not even be able to walk. In that case, Austin says it'll be a short night, but Goldberg will defend the World Title at Survivor Series. "Stone Cold" tries to walk away, but Batista follows him up the ramp. He warns the "rattlesnake" that he's "next". Before he can physically provoke the co-GM, Garrison Cade and Mark Jindrak sneak attack Ric and Randy, forcing "the Animal" to return to the squared circle to chase them off.

Backstage, Lita interrupts Trish Stratus on the phone. They are both in their bras as Trish confesses that Chris Jericho called her. Lita thinks it's weird that Christian saved her one week after Y2J saved Stratus. The extreme diva promises to find out what's going on.

Booker T def. Rico (with Miss Jackie). Jackie grabs Booker's foot as he enters the ring to distract him for Rico to attack the five-time champion before the bell. The flamboyant superstar capitalizes with several strikes and kicks before applying a chin lock. It doesn't take Booker T long to fight free and wail on Rico. A side kick afterwards scores him a near fall. When he sets up for the Scissors Kick, the heel dodges and the two men trade counters until Booker lands the decisive blow, finally hitting his Scissors Kick for the win. Before he can celebrate with a spinaroonie, Chris Jericho interrupts. He says the fans don't pay for his "breakdancing crap". They pay for impromptu Highlight Reels. Y2J kicks off the set-less version of his talk show to ask Booker T how stupid he can be joining "Stone Cold" Steve Austin's team at Survivor Series. Jericho introduces him to Bischoff's team, himself, Christian, and Scott Steiner. All three heels attack the five-time champion as the cage starts to lower. Before it can close around the ring, Rob Van Dam runs out with a chair to chase off the heels. Afterwards, RVD officially joins Austin's team.

After a commercial break, Chris Jericho and Eric Bischoff complain about Rob Van Dam interfering in their plan to send a message to "Stone Cold" Steve Austin. Y2J proposes that they send a different message. He wants Eric to give him an Intercontinental Title match with RVD tonight. Bischoff does.

Mark Henry (with Theodore Long) def. Lance Storm ("White Boy Challenge") by disqualification. Pre-match, Long complains that "Stone Cold" Steve Austin cost him and his client a hundred thousand dollars last week by tossing them out of the ring. Tonight, Mark is going to make "any 'Stone Cold' loving white boy" pay. Storm answers, rushing to the squared circle where Henry pounds on him. When he attempts a corner charge though, Lance wisely moves to punch and kick the "World's Strongest Man". Unfortunately, he misses a top rope missile dropkick and is flung out to the floor. Before Mark can follow up, Shawn Michaels slips into the ring out of nowhere to give Henry Sweet Chin Music for the disqualification. He doesn't care a bit about Storm, running around him to slap hands with the fans.

After a commercial break, The Hurricane flies onto the screen where Jon Heidenreich thanks him for teaming up with the hopeful for his try-out match. Unfortunately, Little Johnny isn't here tonight. Heidenreich says he got held up in traffic. Rosey, in his photographer disguise, enters just as the superhero asks Jon about his son. Heidenreich explains that Little Johnny isn't his son and whispers their relationship in the superhero's ear. Rosey gets a good shot of The Hurricane's stunned expression. When Jon walks away, the superhero says he's "off his rocker".

Further backstage, Lita asks Christian if he was trying to one-up Chris Jericho last week. The heel shows her a picture of the two of them in her book. Christian reminds her that they used to be good friends, but Lita says he's got the wrong idea and that was a long time ago.

Even further backstage, Jonathan Coachman reminds Shane McMahon that he's got a "No Disqualification" match later with a mystery opponent. Coach hopes it's not Kane. Shane does.

Jon Heidenreich/The Hurricane def. Rene Dupree/Rob Conway. Heidenreich is a big man, but he watches from the apron as The Hurricane teases giving a mask to a fan. Conway attacks him from behind before he can, but pays courtesy of a neckbreaker. When Rene tries to interfere, the superhero knocks him out to the floor for a flying dive over the top rope. Rob capitalizes with a spinning neckbreaker off the ropes when The Hurricane tries to return. After Dupree gets in his shots, Conway scores a two-count. Rene does too when he tags in and slams the superhero to the mat. The heels make quick tags and keep The Hurricane in their corner for more near falls and Dupree's patented dance. Although the superhero surprises him with a sunset flip and two-count, a clothesline puts The Hurricane back on the canvas. Eventually, he fights free of a neck vice and dodges a corner charge to tease chokeslamming Rene. Even though the heel fights free, the superhero surprises him with a leaping DDT. Jon gets the hot tag afterwards to toss Dupree out to the floor and nearly score the win with a bicycle kick to Conway. After dumping Rene back out of the ring, Heidenreich gets a three-count with a Uranage. Post-match, Dupree tries to hit Jon with the French flag, but the newcomer sees him coming and answers with a second Uranage.

The announcers hype Survivor Series and thank Limp Bizkit for the official theme song, "Build a Bridge". Afterwards, Shane McMahon heads to the ring to face his mystery opponent. Instead of Kane, he's surprised to see Test limping out on a crutch. He says he can't wrestle tonight, but is happy to introduce Shane's mystery opponent...himself.

Shane McMahon def. Test (with Stacy Keibler) ("No Disqualification" match). The bodyguard tries to open the match cheap shotting Shane with his crutch, but McMahon moves and drives him from the ring. There, Test motions for someone to come out from the back, but they don't show. Instead, Stacy slaps the bodyguard before Shane nails him on the floor. Test responds with a toss back into the ring ropes and whip into the steps. When Kane doesn't answer the bodyguard's pleas, Test takes the fight into the ring to full nelson slam McMahon. That hurts the bodyguard as much as his opponent. Sliding back out to the floor with a bloody lip, Test tosses trashcans, lids, and a steel chair into the squared circle. Instead of using them, he grabs his crutch. Keibler stops him from using it, but pays for getting involved when the bodyguard flings her to the canvas. Shane capitalizes with a string of trashcan lid shots before setting up Test for a coast-to-coast dropkick, putting a trashcan onto his lap. Fire explodes for the "Big Red Machine", but the monster is nowhere to be seen. The distraction does let the bodyguard hit McMahon with his crutch for a near fall. When he tries to slam Shane onto a trashcan, the babyface counters with a DDT onto the steel. Somehow, Test just manages to kick out. That proves to be a mistake as McMahon follows up with a chair shot and coast-to-coast dropkick, driving a trashcan into the bodyguard's face for the victory. Post-match, Shane pleads for Kane to come out, but the monster is nowhere to be found. McMahon decides to send him a message, hitting Test with a chair before placing his broken foot on the ring steps base for another savage shot. That finally brings out the "Big Red Machine", but he doesn't want to fight tonight. He'll wait until Survivor Series. Shane doesn't believe it's patience. He thinks it's fear that McMahon can be as "sick and dangerous" as the monster. Shane promises that one of them will end up in a hospital at Survivor Series and challenges Kane to an "Ambulance" match. The "Big Red Machine" happily accepts while trainers stretcher out Test.

Lita def. Gail Kim and Trish Stratus and Victoria (with Steven Richards) (#1 Contender's match). The heels immediately turn on Trish and drive her from the ring. Lita answers with a monkey flip to Kim and forward leg sweep to Victoria for a two-count. Back in, the vixen gets her own two-count with a Matrix dodge and spinebuster to Kim. The "black widow" makes the save and scores a near fall with a spinning side slam to Lita while Molly Holly watches from the top of the ramp. Stratus gets another two-count with a roll-up on Victoria before chopping her in a corner. Across the ring, Gail guillotine leg drops Lita. When Trish tries to finish off the "black widow" with Stratusfaction, Richards pulls the vixen over the top rope. Victoria throws her into the barricade before Lita sets the heel up for a twist of fate. Although Kim makes the save, she pays when the extreme superstar powerbombs her. Victoria breaks her cover and drops Lita with a Widow's Peak. At the last second, Gail breaks that cover with a boot to the face. That sets off the "black widow" and she tosses Kim out to the floor. When Steven grabs Lita, Victoria tries to sneak attack her, but hits her own man. The extreme diva capitalizes with a DDT for the victory.

Backstage, Janet puts makeup on Jonathan Coachman ahead of him reviewing "Stone Cold" Steve Austin's autobiography. Afterwards, the Hawk tribute video package plays.

After a commercial break, Jonathan Coachman takes offense to "Stone Cold" Steve Austin's book being titled *The Stone Cold Truth*. Coach is upset that Austin complains about being fired via FedEx from WCW. Coachman claims that Eric Bischoff called him multiple times and even drove out to Steve's house. The "rattlesnake" interrupts. He realizes that Coach has a problem with him. Coachman does. He's mad that he lost his announcing job thanks to "Stone Cold". Austin offers to let him take a shot right now. Maybe he'll get lucky and knock out the "rattlesnake". Coach turns the tables and tells Steve to take a shot, but he knows he won't. "Stone Cold" will wait until his team wins their Survivor Series match to do so. But once he wins, Austin wants Coachman to do the post-match interview because he really wants to see his face once he's free to stomp mudholes in whoever he wants.

Backstage, Garrison Cade and Mark Jindrak are excited to face Evolution tonight. They don't want to just hang with the heels. Tonight, they want to beat them. Shawn Michaels appreciates their intensity. He tells them that they can make friends or an impact in the WWE. When they leave to make an impact, Theodore Long wants to know what Shawn's problem is. Since he attacked Mark Henry earlier, Long offers to end things with a final match against the "World's Strongest Man" next week. Michaels happily accepts. Once Theodore leaves, Eric Bischoff enters the picture. He reminds everyone that "Stone Cold" Steve Austin had Henry kicked out of the building last week and has security escort the "Heartbreak Kid" out tonight for his earlier actions.

Garrison Cade/Mark Jindrak (with Maven) def. Randy Orton/Ric Flair (with Batista). Randy opens the match pounding down Jindrak. Mark answers with a big clothesline before Cade tags in to punch Orton. The "Legend Killer" seizes control with a clothesline from the corner and repeated boots. Ric then tags in to chop and elbow the rookie. Following a knee drop, Randy returns for more shots and a dropkick to score a near fall. Soon after, both men connect with simultaneous clotheslines and tag their partners. Jindrak has to fight both heels, back body dropping and dropkicking them until Garrison recovers. While Chad Patton forces him out of the ring, Orton cheap shots Mark into a Flair roll-up. Maven makes the save with a shot to Ric's head for Jindrak to steal the three-count with a handful of tights. Post-match, Batista joins his stablemates in destroying the babyfaces. That includes a Batista Bomb to Maven.

MUST SEE! Chris Jericho def. Rob Van Dam (Intercontinental Title match). Following a Survivor Series hype video, Y2J heads to the ring for a match that JR says is all about spite. Jericho proves that to be true, hitting and choking the champion to start the match. RVD answers with arm drags and a spinning heel kick for a two-count. An enziguri kick slows his attack and nearly crowns a new champion. The challenger follows up with a back suplex and elbow drops before mocking Rob's signature taunt. After he gets another near fall, Y2J briefly applies a surfboard stretch. When Van Dam escapes, the heel tries to spear him in a corner, but hits the post instead. The champion answers with kicks and a northern lights suplex for a two-count. He can't keep Jericho down as he comes back to life with a running face slam. Both men then miss their finishers for a challenger roll-up and two-count. Y2J follows up with a low blow lift up kick and the Walls of Jericho. Eric Bischoff rushes down the aisle to yell at Earl Hebner and distract him from RVD reaching the ropes. By the time Eric gets off the apron, Jericho pulls Rob back to the center of the ring and he taps out. Post-match, "Stone Cold" Steve Austin says he can't reverse the referee's decision, but he can sign Y2J's first title defense tonight against the former champion inside the steel cage. He also bars everyone, including GMs, from interfering. When Bischoff heads up the ramp, he trips and runs into Austin, the "rattlesnake" chasing him into a commercial break.

MUST SEE! Rob Van Dam def. Chris Jericho ("Steel Cage" Intercontinental Title match). Afterwards, the heel is in control with a backbreaker and stretch. RVD answers with a toss into the steel cage. More whips into the cage and kicks follow before Rob somersaults into the new champion against the steel. When Y2J stops him from climbing out, the challenger kicks him back into the cage. Right back up the cage, Jericho meets and slams Van Dam off the top rope. A running face slam follows, but he misses his Lionsault a second time. When he tries to dropkick RVD, the challenger makes the mistake of catapulting the heel into the corner. Unfortunately for Rob, Y2J lands on the top rope and nearly climbs out. Although the challenger pulls him down, Jericho hits a third running face slam. He nearly escapes again, Van Dam pulling him back into the ring at the last second. He follows up with a kick that sends the champion crashing to the canvas. While RVD climbs over the cage, the heel tries to escape through the door. Before he can, Rob kicks the door back into his face and drops down to regain the championship. Post-match, Christian and Scott Steiner hop out of the crowd to assault Van Dam. The Dudley Boyz follow them, pounding on the heels until Mark Henry hurries out to join them. Theodore Long chains the door shut for the heels to destroy what looks like their Survivor Series opponents. Booker T is the last man out, running out to climb the cage and fly off it onto the heels. Unfortunately, he's just one man and Henry recovers to give him the World's Strongest Slam. Bloodied, Y2J sits on top of the cage watching the carnage to end the show.

SmackDown!
October 30, 2003
Atlanta, GA
Announcers: Michael Cole, Tazz, Tajiri (briefly)

The show opens with a recap package featuring the debut of the new general manager, Paul Heyman, and The Undertaker winning a handicap match to earn a Survivor Series "Buried Alive" match with Vince McMahon. After that four-plus minute video package, the intro video plays.

Chris Benoit/Kurt Angle def. A-Train/John Cena. Instead of fireworks, Kurt heads to the ring to open the show with a rematch from last week. Once the babyfaces are out, Cena leads A-Train to the ring, rapping that the hairy heel is "like his Wookie" and he's Han Solo. Inside the squared circle, Benoit surprises the rapping heel with a backslide before unloading with chops and fists. The Olympian then tags in to deliver his own strikes and a suplex for a two-count. He also gets a near fall with a back elbow before John rakes his eyes and tags in A-Train. He absorbs Angle's punches, but can't absorb a German suplex. Cena sacrifices himself returning to the ring to be clotheslined to the floor. The hairy heel capitalizes with his own clothesline and corner bomb for a two-count. Once Kurt is down, the rapping heel tags back in for a sledgehammer blow and near fall. When the Olympian answers with an Anklelock, A-Train rushes in to make the save only to receive a series of fists to the jaw. Although John blindsides Angle, the babyface recovers to DDT him and send both men to their corners for tags. "The Crippler" unloads on the hairy heel with chops and a pair of flying forearms for a two-count. He also German suplexes A-Train before heading upstairs for a diving headbutt. At the last second, the hairy heel rolls out of the way and responds with a bicycle kick. Kurt returns afterwards to Angle Slam A-Train, but Cena surprises him with an FU. When the hairy heel tries to crush Benoit in a corner, the "rabid wolverine" moves and A-Train crushes his own partner. A trio of German suplexes and a top rope diving headbutt then scores Benoit the win. Post-match, the babyfaces shake hands and leave together. Inside the ring, John argues with the hairy heel. When A-Train shoves him, Cena gives him a low blow and FU for a nice pop.

Backstage, Vince McMahon is so mad that he can barely even speak. He grunts and slaps waters aside before getting in Paul Heyman's face. The WWE owner can't believe Paul put him in a "Buried Alive" match with The Undertaker. Heyman wants him to calm down, but McMahon flips over his desk and yells at the new GM. Vince promises that there won't be a Survivor Series match because he guarantees the "Deadman" will be carried out of the arena tonight. Paul tells him that can't happen because he gave the biker the night off. Even worse, he gave him off until Survivor Series due to the carnage he caused last week. McMahon loses his mind and promises that "terrorists will burn down" The Undertaker's house. He's also going to kidnap his children and have a biker gang "rape his wife". Vince wants Heyman to make it happen or he's going to choke the life out of him.

After we see Torrie Wilson checking out lingerie, Kurt Angle stops Chris Benoit backstage. The Olympian says they haven't always seen eye-to-eye, but when they are on the same page, they are unbeatable. That's why he wants Benoit on his Survivor Series team. "The Crippler" says they are just as likely to tear each other apart, but he's in. However, they are not friends. Angle doesn't want a friend; he wants to win.

Further backstage, Paul Heyman tells Vince McMahon that he has nothing for him. That makes the WWE owner upset and he promises to drag Paul to the ring to choke the life out of him. When he threatens to fire Heyman, the GM hopes he does. He doesn't want to work with a Vince that fights a one-legged wrestler and his daughter. Paul wants to work with the man who stared down the US government and drove Ted Turner's billion dollar empire into the ground. Heyman wonders what happened to his ruthless aggression and the Vince who refused to be buried. Paul wonders where the WWE owner who always had a masterplan is. Mr. McMahon is speechless, walking away determinedly.

Footage from this week's house shows plays.

Ultimo Dragon def. Rey Mysterio. Tajiri joins the announce table to provide guest commentary for this match. He's accompanied by his suited goons as he says he's here to scout his next opponent. He says Dragon is okay, but he's better. For Halloween, Rey has on an Incredible Hulk inspired costume as he trades holds with his fellow masked man. While Dragon gets the upper hand leveling Mysterio, Tajiri says he spewed black mist into Nidia's eyes by accident. The announcers continue talking about that situation while Ultimo kicks Rey for a two-count. Mysterio answers with a spinning head scissors and dropkick to the knee. He then leaps into Dragon's arms to drive him to the canvas with a bulldog for a two-count. A drop toe hold puts Ultimo into position for a 619, but he counters with a back body drop out to the apron. Although Rey drops him on the top rope, when he attempts to springboard off them, Dragon answers with a stiff kick to the ribs. Tajiri waits for his opportunity to strike, hopping onto the apron and kicking the back of Mysterio's head after he shoves Ultimo inadvertently into Brian Hebner. That scores Dragon the win. Post-match, the "Japanese Buzzsaw" bows to Ultimo, but the masked man walks away.

Backstage, Brock Lesnar yells at Big Show. The giant says he was at the top of his game last week, but Brock says if he wasn't so clumsy they would have beaten The Undertaker. Before the two heels come to blows, a worker interrupts to tell Lesnar that Paul Heyman wants to see him in the ring next.

After a commercial break, Paul Heyman leads Matt Morgan and Nathan Jones to the ring. He's proud to have the big superstars on *SmackDown!* and promises that they will help the new GM assert his greatness. With the monsters at his side, Paul calls out Brock Lesnar. The WWE Champion hasn't forgotten his history with Heyman and refuses to get into the squared circle for the GM's men to attack him. Heyman says he just wants to discuss business, but before Lesnar will do so, the champion calls out his big friend, Big Show. That gives Brock the confidence to enter the ring and tell Paul that he hates his guts. Despite that, Heyman tells Lesnar that Paul is the best at doing business. He thought he would get on the champion's good side by introducing him to three of his Survivor Series partners, Jones, Morgan, and Show. Brock likes the look of this massive team. Heyman has one other announcement, telling the giant and Big Show that he's signed them to a match tonight to shut up The APA who have been calling the GM all week questioning how good the US and WWE Champions really are.

Backstage, Dawn Marie gets Orlando Jordan and Paul London's opinion on her costume for the "Trick or Treat" contest next. They stop playing their video game briefly to lust after her, revealing that it's a good outfit.

Hardcore Holly threatens Brock Lesnar again in another teaser promo.

After a commercial break, Funaki wears a giant afro wig as he officiates the "Trick or Treat" costume contest. Torrie Wilson is out first dressed as the Easter Bunny. Dawn Marie follows in a Wonder

Woman costume. The women writhing around the ring has Funaki tongue-tied. He manages to find his voice to poll the audience and declare Torrie the winner of the first stage of the contest. The second stage sees the divas bending over a troth to bob for apples. Dawn wants to go first, but needs Funaki to help her remove her boots so she can step into the troth and sit in the chocolate. There, she removes her top to a nice pop. That drops Funaki's jaw and brings Tazz into the squared circle. The thug says he's seen the treat, but wants Wilson to show Funaki a trick. Tazz wants her to shove the interviewer into the chocolate, but Torrie tricks the thug and pushes him into the troth instead to end the contest.

An Ernest Miller teaser video plays.

Backstage, Brock Lesnar interrupts a downtrodden John Cena. The WWE Champion congratulates him prematurely on joining Brock's Survivor Series team. Lesnar says it's not official yet, but thinks it's going to happen. When he walks away, John stares at the camera conflicted.

After Tazz hugs and spreads chocolate on Cole, Chavo Guerrero Jr. yells at his uncle. He tells him that if he wants to lose the US Title that's his problem, but he dragged Chavo down losing the WWE Tag Titles. The incensed superstar tells Eddie Guerrero that he's sinking worse than when he was on drugs and he owes him, the fans, and their family an apology. Frustrated, "Latino Heat" heads to the ring while footage of The Basham Brothers winning the WWE Tag Titles last week plays. Instead of driving out in a lowrider, a morose Eddie steps into the squared circle and apologizes publicly. He can't believe Chavo would bring up his dark past, but "Latino Heat" promises to use that as motivation. Eddie refuses to lay down and die. He says the strength of a man is in how he fights when he's down. Guerrero vows that he will keep fighting until Los Guerreros are the WWE Tag Team Champions again. He'll also do it for the fans, drawing a big pop. When Shaniqua comes out with the title belts, Eddie calls her a "Mamacita wannabe". He warns her to stay back unless she's ready to face his "Latino Heat". Instead, she distracts him for The Basham Brothers to attempt to sneak attack him. Fortunately, Eddie knows all the dirty tricks and fights off the champions before back suplexing their dominatrix to the canvas. Not done yet, he heads upstairs for a Frog Splash. At the last second, Danny shoves him down to the floor. The Bashams then wail on him and whip "Latino Heat" into the ring steps. Finally, Chavo runs out to check on his uncle while the champions attend to Shaniqua.

After a commercial break, a trainer tries to get Eddie Guerrero to relax. He doesn't. He tells Paul Heyman that he wants a match with The Basham Brothers for the WWE Tag Titles. Heyman says he's the new GM and everyone starts with a clean slate. If "Latino Heat" wins a match against the Bashams next week he'll get a title shot. Eddie believes he and his nephew will take down the champions, but Paul didn't say anything about Chavo Guerrero Jr. He tells Eddie that he'll have to face the Bashams in a handicap match for a WWE Tag Title shot.

Further backstage, Josh Mathews asks Kurt Angle about facing Brock Lesnar's Survivor Series team, John Cena potentially rounding out the heel squad. Kurt calls them a big team, but he likes his squad. Not only does he have Chris Benoit on his side, but the Olympian just talked to Hardcore Holly on the phone and he's ready to return to get revenge on Lesnar for breaking his neck. Angle has two more members to announce and points down the hall. Unfortunately, it's just two members of the crew. Mathews isn't impressed. When Kurt realizes who he's looking at, he points another way to The APA.

After the announcers preview Survivor Series, a prerecorded interview with The Undertaker plays. He says that it was worth taking a beating last week to get his hands on Vince McMahon at the PPV. The "Deadman" believes that he won't win the WWE Title again until he takes out Vince. The biker adds that McMahon subconsciously planted the idea for the "Buried Alive" match in The Undertaker's brain. After Survivor Series, he promises the WWE owner won't be breathing anymore.

The APA def. Big Show/Brock Lesnar by disqualification. Bradshaw and Brock open the match trading heavy blows. Although the big Texan gets the upper hand, he gets too close to the heel corner and Show clubs him. The giant then tags in to chop and side slam Bradshaw for a two-count. When he attempts a corner charge, the big Texan moves and tags in Faarooq. He knocks Lesnar off the apron before slugging Big Show. One big boot puts him down. When Show tries to follow up with a Chokeslam, Bradshaw makes the save with a Clothesline from Hell. That gets Faarooq a two-count while the big Texan fights with Brock at ringside. There, Lesnar whips him into the ring steps before sliding into the squared circle to blast Faarooq with a chair for the disqualification. Post-match, the heels attack the brawler's ankle, Big Show Pillmanizing him like Batista did Goldberg on *Raw*. After Lesnar smashes Bradshaw's skull with the chair also, Chris Benoit and Kurt Angle run out for the save, German suplexing and Angle Slamming the heels before trapping them in the Crippler Crossface and Anklelock. Unfortunately, the heels have partners too and Matt Morgan and Nathan Jones run out to attack the babyfaces. Following big boots to them, Morgan gives Angle a sit-out powerbomb. Jones follows up with a gut wrench powerbomb to "the Crippler", the heels ending the show standing tall.

Monday Night Raw

November 3, 2003
Cleveland, OH
Announcers: Jim Ross, Jerry "the King" Lawler

Chris Jericho/Christian def. Booker T/Rob Van Dam. Following the intro video and fireworks, the babyfaces take turns heading to the squared circle for this Survivor Series preview match. The heels forego their normal entrances, ambushing their opponents. It doesn't pay off as the babyfaces quickly turn the tide and catapult Jericho out to the floor. RVD follows the heels with a dive over the top rope. Back inside the ring, Booker hammers on Christian, but misses a Scissors Kick. He doesn't miss a forearm to the jaw for a two-count. When Y2J gets the tag, the five-time champion slams him and tags in Rob for a reverse heel kick. More kicks follow for a near fall before Booker T returns to chop the heel. When he runs the ropes though, Christian hits the five-time champion. Moments later, he pulls Jericho out to the floor to avoid a spinning heel kick. Van Dam rushes over to make the heels pay, ramming their heads together. When Booker mounts Y2J moments later, Christian grabs the babyface and drops him throat-first onto the top rope. Jericho follows up with a second rope missile dropkick. Soon afterwards, Christian scores a two-count with his own dropkick. The heels then trap Booker T in their corner, Jericho back suplexing and Christian pounding the five-time champion. When he applies a reverse chin lock, Booker fights free and teases a Book End. Although Christian escapes, a side kick puts him down for the babyface to give RVD the hot tag. Y2J joins him, Rob scoring a two-count with a springboard cross body block. A step over kick and rolling thunder follow for a near fall. Van Dam spots Christian attempting a sneak attack afterwards and crotches him on the top rope. He then whips Jericho into his own partner's crotch for a two-count. A kick puts Y2J down afterwards, but when he heads upstairs for a Five-Star Frog Splash the popular superstar spots Christian again. This time he meets him with a flying cannonball smash. A split legged moonsault then gets him a two-count on Jericho before Christian makes the save. Moments later, Booker T impressed with a double Scissors Kick and spinaroonie. When Christian and Booker fight out at ringside, Van Dam stuns Y2J with a top rope flying kick. Unfortunately, Christian distracts Earl Hebner, preventing him from seeing RVD's cover. When Rob protests, Jericho recovers and plants the popular superstar with a flashback for the win, Christian holding down Van Dam's foot.

Backstage, "Stone Cold" Steve Austin is frustrated at his team's loss. As he storms away, Jonathan Coachman stops him. He's been thinking about Austin's offer to let him do the post-match interview at Survivor Series. With the way things are going, Coach accepts. "Stone Cold" warns him that if his team wins, he's going to kick Coachman's butt. However, if his team loses, he has nothing to lose and will kick his butt anyway. He then takes Coach's magazine, promising to do something he thought he never would.

After a commercial break, Terri asks Molly Holly about facing Lita for the Women's Title. The champion is tired of hearing about Lita and her comeback story. Holly tells the interviewer that she and Lita are going to have something in common—that they were both destroyed by the Women's Champion. Molly immediately slaps Terri and leads her out through the curtain, slamming the interviewer on the entrance stage. She then kicks her down the ramp, but when they get in the ring, Terri shows signs of life with a flurry of fists. It doesn't take Molly long to drop her again. Suddenly, Lita races out for the save, but when she follows Holly into the crowd, Gail Kim, wearing a hoodie over her head, hits the extreme diva with a wrench. The women then pull her back into the ring for a double DDT. JR says it was a setup.

Backstage, "Stone Cold" Steve Austin enters Shawn Michaels's locker room. He asks if Shawn knows what's happening. The "Heartbreak Kid" does and is ready for Mark Henry tonight. That's not what Austin is talking about. He's talking about the Survivor Series main event and that he has four guys. He needs one more, but Michaels isn't volunteering. After hemming and hawing, Steve asks Shawn to join him. It's an awkward moment and Michaels explains why, recapping their shared history dating back to even before their WrestleMania XIV match. "Stone Cold" doesn't need a history lesson. He "needs" the "Heartbreak Kid". Michaels tells him he has a "heck of a problem" on his hands, but Shawn is in.

After a commercial break, Lita tells a trainer that her neck is sore. Christian bursts in to check on her. He says he'll be right outside if she needs him, grinning as he leaves.

Batista (with Ric Flair) def. Maven. As Evolution head to the ring, we get a shot of Lebron James watching in the crowd. Maven then runs out only to be driven to the canvas with a spinebuster. A backbreaker follows before Batista whips him out to the floor and the ring steps. "The Animal" then pulls off the protective covering in front of Lebron and teases slamming Maven onto the barricade. Although the babyface slips free, a vicious clothesline puts him back down. Inside the ring, Maven comes back to life with a top rope missile dropkick. After he decks Flair, the babyface heads back upstairs only to see Batista counter his second rope bulldog with another clothesline. "The Animal" then scores the victory with a Batista Bomb.

After a commercial break, the announcers show video footage that has led to tonight's Mark Henry/Shawn Michaels match.

Backstage, Kane runs his hand along the side of an ambulance. He asks Shane McMahon if he's thought about how it will feel to be loaded into the ambulance at Survivor Series, a stylistic black and white shot from the perspective of the loser on the gurney looking up as EMTs work on them playing. The "Big Red Machine" says Shane will arrive at the hospital "DOA" after their "Ambulance" match.

Further backstage, Garrison Cade and Mark Jindrak are fired up after their victory last week over Ric Flair and Randy Orton. They want to keep the roll going tonight when they face The Dudley Boyz in a non-title match.

Garrison Cade/Mark Jindrak def. The Dudley Boyz. D-Von tries to stop the young superstars' momentum with a leaping back elbow to Jindrak. Cade gets one too when he tags into the match. Bubba Ray soon joins him to chop Garrison, but the rookie surprises him with a cross body block. Bleeding from his mouth, Cade is ready for a fight. Bubba gives him one until he runs into a corner boot and second rope flying shoulderblock for a near fall. When both men tag out, Garrison distracts D-Von for Mark to dropkick him. Right back in, Cade slows the pace with a reverse chin lock. It doesn't take D-Von long to fight free, but Garrison hammers both Dudleys ahead of a Jindrak dropkick and two-count. Cade attempts to follow up with a top rope flying elbow drop, but D-Von rolls out of the way and tags his half-brother. He proceeds to punch and clothesline both men. As soon as he drops Garrison, Scott Steiner interrupts from the top of the ramp, pressing Stacy Keibler high into the air. That distracts Bubba long enough for Cade to clothesline Dudley for the three-count. Post-match, Bubba Ray applauds the young stars while Garrison and Mark motion that they want the belts.

After a commercial break, "Stone Cold" Steve Austin heads to the ring for a Survivor Series contract signing. JR says Steve is having a hard time putting his fate in the hands of five other men considering he doesn't trust anyone. Austin says he has beer to drink and invites Eric Bischoff to come out and sign the contract. Eric teases that he made a change to it before introducing his fifth team member, a man who beat Shawn Michaels, Randy Orton. The "Legend Killer" steps onto the stage to arrogantly say that he's going to add a new legend to the list of careers he's ended with Austin at Survivor Series. The "rattlesnake" offers to go up and deal with him face-to-face, but Bischoff stops him and reminds his co-GM what's at stake at the PPV. Eric is happy to potentially be done with "Stone Cold" and signs their contract. Steve doesn't have any second thoughts and signs the contract too. Afterwards, Eric taunts him about having to depend on other people for the first time in his life. Austin is tired of Bischoff repeating himself, so he repeats himself too and flips off his co-GM. While "Stone Cold" doesn't like trusting people, he thinks the risk is worth the reward to be the "rattlesnake" that he used to be. The fans agree. Austin promises that after Survivor Series he's going to be the real "Stone Cold" again.

After a commercial break, Batista stops "Stone Cold" Steve Austin to tell him that the "rattlesnake" makes him sick. He thinks Austin is hiding behind the board of directors telling him not to touch anyone because he's a coward. "Stone Cold" can only seethe.

Lance Storm def. Rico (with Miss Jackie). Pre-match, Val Venis leads three women to ringside to watch the action. Afterwards, Lance dances out only to see Jackie trip him for a Rico kick and two-count. The flamboyant superstar follows up with stomps and elbows, "the big Valbowski" happily watching as Rico scores another near fall. Although Storm surprises him with a jawbreaker, Rico recovers quickly to apply a cobra clutch sleeper hold. He can't put the Canadian out and Lance fights free for a string of clotheslines and a drop toe hold into a Single Leg Crab for the tap-out. Post-match, Val brings the women into the ring to dance with the victor.

Backstage, Chris Jericho bumps into Trish Stratus. They're happy they bumped into each other. Trish is even happier that he asked for her number over the week and called her. She would have been happy to give it to him herself. Y2J is worried about her tag team match tonight with Jon Heidenreich. Jericho is concerned about Little Johnny, but Stratus says she's already seen it. That sets off Y2J, but before he can do anything, Heidenreich interrupts and leads the vixen to the ring. When they're gone, Jericho calls Jon a pervert.

Footage from *Raw* house shows this week plays to continue to hype up attending live events.

Jon Heidenreich/Trish Stratus def. Steven Richards/Victoria. The men start the match, Heidenreich absorbing Steven's shots to slam and toss him out of the ring. That sets off Richards, but he tags in Victoria rather than deal with the big rookie. She is willing to fight Jon, but can only lock up with Trish. Backstage, Chris Jericho watches as the vixen avoids the "black widow" with a Matrix dodge ahead of a head scissors. Chops follow until Stratus runs into a corner knee. Victoria tries to head upstairs, but Trish meets her with a handstand head scissors. When Heidenreich attempts to get involved, Charles Robinson holds him back allowing Steven to slip into the ring and back suplex the vixen. The "black widow" follows up with an over the shoulder backbreaker submission hold. When she doesn't get the win, she slams Stratus to the canvas for a two-count. While JR argues that Trish and Y2J wouldn't make a good couple, she comes back to life to pummel Victoria. The men tag in afterwards, Jon sidewalk slamming Richards. The "black widow" rushes to her man's aid, hopping onto Heidenreich's back, but Stratus peels her off and takes the fight out to the floor, wailing on Victoria again. That leaves Jon to pick up Steven in position for an over-the-shoulder backbreaker before slamming the heel to the mat for the three-count. Backstage, Jericho isn't happy to see the winners hug.

After a commercial break, Jonathan Coachman asks "Stone Cold" Steve Austin how it felt to get punked out by Batista. "Stone Cold" says there is something he can do about it and makes himself the special guest ring enforcer for the main event. He adds that if anyone wants to get involved in the match, he'll take it as physical provocation and deal with them. Afterwards, the announcers preview Survivor Series.

Backstage, Sgt. Slaughter rushes to give Kane an invitation from Shane McMahon. The "Big Red Machine" accepts, promising to meet Shane next week.

Shawn Michaels def. Mark Henry (with Theodore Long). "Stone Cold" Steve Austin is out first to keep order outside the ring. Long leads Henry to ringside, unleashing the "World's Strongest Man". Angry, Mark tosses around Shawn and weathers a pair of shots to his knees to slam the "Heartbreak Kid" to the canvas. Michaels will not give up and responds with a series of fists. When he nears the ropes, Theodore grabs his foot. Shawn knows all the tricks and dodges Henry's sneak attack before Austin ejects the manager from ringside. Alone, Mark catches the "Heartbreak Kid's" dive over the top rope and slams him into the apron. Back in the squared circle, he whips Shawn hard into the corner ahead of a clothesline and two-count. Unable to get the three-count, the "World's Strongest Man" locks on a bearhug. With the crowd cheering him on, Michaels fights free and repeatedly chops Henry. One big swipe puts the "Heartbreak Kid" back down for more clubbing blows. He tries to finish off Shawn with a corner charge, but the babyface moves and answers with ten fists to the head. That's not enough to drop Mark and the big man answers with more heavy blows. When he attempts a second rope corner bomb though, Michaels surprises him with a pair of knees and Sweet Chin Music for the victory.

Post-match, "Stone Cold" Steve Austin congratulates Shawn Michaels and thanks him for joining his Survivor Series team. Respectfully, the "rattlesnake" asks Shawn to leave the ring so he can take care of business. Eventually, Michaels does so for Austin to call out Batista. After a commercial break, "the Animal" joins him, the two men trading fists. "Stone Cold" gets the better of the exchange, driving Batista from the squared circle. When Mark Henry tries to sneak attack Austin, he gets a Stone Cold Stunner for his efforts. He does distract the "rattlesnake" long enough for Batista to sneak attack him and drive his head into the ring post. Goldberg responds to the fans' chant and returns with a chair. Limping down the aisle, he smashes Mark's head with a steel chair before Spearing "the Animal". He wants to repay Batista for his previous attack and Pillmanize him, but as the champion wraps the chair around "the Animal's" ankle, Ric Flair runs out for the save. That gets "The Nature Boy" a Spear too before the heels retreat backstage. Afterwards, "Stone Cold" offers Bill a beer, but the intense superstar doesn't accept it. He wants Austin to do something for him first. He wants a match with Batista next week. The co-GM is happy to make that match before the two superstars end the show drinking beer.

SmackDown!
November 6, 2003
Buffalo, NY
Announcers: Michael Cole, Tazz, Brock Lesnar (briefly)

John Cena def. Rey Mysterio. Following the intro video and fireworks, Rey pops out of the stage for a hot opener. Cena then raps to say the odds of him losing to the masked man is the same as Big Show eating one Cheerio at a buffet. He adds that they don't see eye-to-eye because Mysterio is too short. When the fans chant alongside John, Rey actually laughs. The two men continue taunting each other until the masked man picks up the pace with a drop toe hold and slide out to the floor. The rapping heel pursues, dropping Mysterio with a shoulderblock back in the squared circle. Although Rey counters a powerbomb with a hurricanrana, when he attempts a springboard attack, Cena decks him. The fans are behind him as he rams the masked man into the apron ahead of a two-count. A hard whip into the corner follows for another near fall, the announcers talking about how good Brock Lesnar's Survivor Series team will be with the rapping heel. John tries to finish off Mysterio with a corner charge, but at the last second, Rey moves. He takes too long heading upstairs though, and Cena capitalizes, pulling him back out for a delayed vertical suplex and two-count. The rapping heel then controls the pace with a reverse chin lock. When he escapes, the masked man kicks and bulldogs John for a two-count. A dropkick to the front of the knee and springboard cross body block follows. He gets a two-count moments later with a springboard senton splash, but one clothesline puts him back down. Afterwards, Cena drops Mysterio throat-first onto the top rope. Somehow, Rey quickly recovers to trip the rapping heel. When he hits the 619 though, John falls back into the referee, stunning Brian Hebner. Cena capitalizes, countering a West Coast Pop with a low blow followed by an FU for the win.

Post-match, Paul Heyman leads Brock Lesnar and his heel Survivor Series team to ringside to applaud John. Paul likes that Cena takes what he wants. Tonight, Heyman is going to give him something. It's not the WWE or US Titles because the general manager says people have to earn those. However, he is going to give him the final spot on Lesnar's Survivor Series team. The rapping heel has a problem with that. No one tells him what to do. Also, he doesn't think he'll fit in with "Team Sasquatch". That brings out A-Train to blindside him. Matt Morgan and Nathan Jones follow up with a double big boot. Not done, Big Show Chokeslams Cena before Brock blasts his skull with a steel chair.

After a commercial break, A-Train apologizes to Brock Lesnar's team and Paul Heyman, but he had a score to settle with John Cena. Paul likes people who take the initiative and offers the hairy heel a spot on the team. All of the big men are happy to shake hands. The announcers believe Team Angle is in trouble now.

Footage of Eddie Guerrero taking beatings, losing titles, and apologizing over recent weeks plays. Afterwards, Chavo Guerrero Jr. tells his uncle that he's got a big match tonight for Los Guerreros. However, he'll need to beat The Basham Brothers in a handicap match without Chavo at ringside to earn a WWE Tag Title shot for the former champions. Eddie didn't know he'd be out solo. Chavo says Paul Heyman just banned him. He wants his uncle to win the match tonight for him. While "Latino Heat" argues that they are a tag team, Chavo says he always had Eddie's back and he was on his side when he was going through his addiction issues. Chavo wants his uncle to make things right for him.

Big Show def. Bradshaw. Following footage of Faarooq getting injured last week, Cole tells fans that his status for Survivor Series is up in the air. He's not here tonight as Big Show marches out to try to eliminate Bradshaw too. The big Texan isn't afraid of a fight, storming the ring and wailing on the giant. When they end up outside the squared circle, Bradshaw shoves Show into the ring post. A top rope flying shoulderblock and elbow drop back in the ring gets him a two-count before Big Show comes back to life with a big boot and leg drop for his own near fall. After he headbutts and punches the big Texan, Big Show unloads with a vicious chop. Bradshaw refuses to stay down, punching and chop blocking the giant. A big clothesline afterwards topples Show out to the floor again. There, the big Texan pulls off a piece of the barricade covering and whips Big Show into the exposed steel. Despite that, the giant surprises him with a throat drop when he nears the apron. Moments later, Show interrupts a Clothesline from Hell with a Chokeslam for the win.

Backstage, Paul Heyman corners Torrie Wilson. He wants her to learn that he's in control, but she begs him to stop. Paul doesn't, telling her that she has three minutes to do what he wants and she better smile.

After a commercial break, Kurt Angle gets a phone call that says Faarooq is out of Survivor Series. Chris Benoit tells him that they just have to regroup before Torrie Wilson interrupts. She has a message for the babyfaces from Paul Heyman. Tonight, they'll face A-Train, Brock Lesnar, Matt Morgan, and Nathan Jones in a handicap match. Tazz says they are in trouble.

In a prerecorded interview, The Undertaker says that Survivor Series will mark thirteen years in the company for him. In all that time, Vince McMahon has shown him no respect because Vince doesn't respect anyone. The "Deadman" promises that McMahon will atone for the men he disrespected—men like "Stone Cold" Steve Austin and Bret Hart. The Undertaker promises to hold Vince accountable.

Another Ernest Miller vignette plays. In it, his assistant Lamont helps him with his jacket and says "the Cat" is the best looking and most entertaining man around.

Eddie Guerrero def. The Basham Brothers (with Shaniqua). After Eddie drives his lowrider to the ring, Shaniqua comes out in red to shove around her men and spank them. It motivates Doug to slam Guerrero to the canvas and tease a pumphandle slam. Eddie takes offense when Basham enjoys pulling him back to his groin. Despite "Latino Heat's" protests, Doug takes advantage of a Danny cheap shot to pumphandle slam Guerrero face-first moments later. Danny then tags in to score a two-count with a spinning side slam. Eddie has had enough and answers with a head scissors from the top rope. He then back body drops Doug out to the floor and follows him out with a slingshot splash. Unfortunately, Shaniqua comes to her men's aid, big booting "Latino Heat" down for a pair of Danny two-counts. The Bashams follow up with a double-team slingshot suplex for a Doug near fall. He then slows the pace with a reverse chin lock, the dominatrix yelling for him to finish off Guerrero. Danny also takes his turn applying a chin lock until Eddie escapes with a jawbreaker. One boot puts "Latino Heat" right back down. When Doug tags back in though, he misses a top rope guillotine leg drop to swing the momentum. Guerrero capitalizes with fists and a top rope hurricanrana. Following a pop-up dropkick, he fights both heels and nearly gets the win with a tilt-a-whirl backbreaker, but Danny breaks Nick Patrick's count. Outnumbered, Eddie drops the champions with a combination head scissors and headlock takedown. He follows up with a trio of suplexes to Doug, but when he heads upstairs, Shaniqua hops onto the apron to distract the referee and "Latino Heat". Behind their back, Danny switches places with his brother. Guerrero is ready for their tactics this week, taking Shaniqua's whip away from her to spank Danny and the referee. Before Patrick turns around, Eddie tosses the weapon to Danny. While he pleads innocence to the referee, "Latino Heat" rolls up Basham for the victory to earn a WWE Tag Title shot. Post-match, Chavo joins his uncle to celebrate their victory and leave the arena in the lowrider.

After a commercial break, Vince McMahon stoically heads to the ring. He asks the fans not to be afraid of him and to offer him their forgiveness. Vince then drops to a knee and asks for the lights to be lowered as he asks for his soul to be cleansed. He promises to follow the light to victory. However, McMahon isn't asking for forgiveness for his past sins. He doesn't care about those. He only cares about being forgiven for what he's about to do. The WWE owner claims that he's been chosen by a higher power to "slaughter the infidel" and bury The Undertaker alive.

A Hardcore Holly teaser plays.

Jamie Noble/Ultimo Dragon def. Nunzio/Tajiri. Noble goes right after Tajiri to get revenge for his girlfriend, but Nunzio cuts him off. The Italian heel pays for intervening as Jamie wails on him before tagging Dragon. The masked man targets Nunzio's legs with a series of kicks for an early two-count. The Italian heel answers with a trip and tag to Tajiri. The Cruiserweight Champion then trades kicks with Ultimo until the masked man chases him from the squared circle with a tilt-a-whirl backbreaker. A baseball slide kick follows, but when Dragon tries to follow the "Japanese Buzzsaw" out, Tajiri's goons give him pause. Nunzio capitalizes with a flying attack from behind. A Sicilian slice follows for a two-count, but Noble makes the save. The champion returns afterwards to rock Ultimo with a hard kick. One to the back of the head gets him a two-count. The "Japanese Buzzsaw" then mocks Jamie before tagging in the Italian heel for a snap mare. The heels make quick tags and continue taunting the redneck before Nunzio applies a triangle choke and uses the ropes for added leverage. When he attempts to finish off Dragon with a suplex off the top rope, the masked man answers with a face-first drop to the canvas. That sends both men crawling to their corners for tags. Noble finally gets his hands on Tajiri and unloads with fists and boots. He follows up with a swinging neckbreaker before the Italian heel surprises him with his Arrivederci armbar drop. Fortunately, Ultimo has caught his breath and drives Nunzio from the ring with a handspring back elbow. He follows the Italian heel out with an Asai moonsault while the "Japanese Buzzsaw" kicks Jamie. When he goes for his handspring back elbow, Noble ducks and rolls up the champion for the three-count. Post-match, Tajiri's men try to attack the redneck, but he escapes their assault.

Chris Benoit/Kurt Angle def. A-Train/Brock Lesnar/Matt Morgan/Nathan Jones by disqualification. Following a replay of the heels attacking John Cena earlier tonight, Brock kicks off the entrances for this match. By the time everyone makes their individual entrances, Lesnar joins the announce table. He says he can do anything he wants because he's the WWE Champion. As such, he watches as Jones runs over Kurt to open the match. He follows up with a slam, but when he presses up the Olympian, Angle slips free and attacks his knee. Benoit tags in afterwards, but he can't handle Nathan's size either. Things get worse when Morgan tags in to headbutt and toss around "the Crippler". When he picks up Benoit following a drop toe hold, Matt makes the mistake of ramming him into the babyface corner. That lets Kurt tag in to attack Morgan. His blows have little effect and Matt chases him from the ring before hammering the "rabid wolverine" again. A-Train joins in on the fun, pounding Benoit before trapping him in a bearhug. A butterfly suplex follows ahead of a commercial break.

Afterwards, the hairy heel tosses "the Crippler" out to the floor. Brock says it's time for him to go to work and stomps Benoit until the Olympian hurries over. When Angle returns to his corner though, the champion slams the "rabid wolverine" back into the ring post. He tags in moments later to suplex

Benoit and taunt Kurt. A delayed high angle cradle suplex gets him a pair of two-counts afterwards. "The Crippler" tries to fight back, but one knee stuns him for A-Train to tag back in for more fists and a big clothesline. When Morgan returns, he also applies a bearhug. The Olympian has seen enough and blindsides Matt to break the hold. When the hairy heel returns, he leaps into a knee to the face attempting a corner bomb. Benoit follows up with a German suplex to put both men on the mat and crawling to their corners. The fresh man, Angle knocks all of the heels off the apron except for Lesnar who he German suplexes twice. An Angle Slam follows to Morgan. When Jones misses a big boot, he straddles the top rope. A-Train then accidentally kicks Nathan out to the floor. Kurt capitalizes with a German suplex to the hairy heel. Brock tries to take advantage of the chaos and give the Olympian an F5, but the babyface slips free and plants him with an Angle Slam. While he traps the champion in an Anklelock, the "rabid wolverine" locks A-Train in a Crippler Crossface. That brings out Big Show to break both submissions for the disqualification before anyone can tap out. Post-match, Show Chokeslams Angle. When he tries to do the same to Benoit, "the Crippler" slips free and tries to lock on his finisher. Even though he doesn't succeed, Bradshaw sprints out to give the giant a Clothesline from Hell while he's tied up. Unfortunately, Jones big boots the big Texan ahead of a sit-out powerbomb from Morgan. John Cena sprints out afterwards to hit Matt and Nathan with a chair to a big pop. Unfortunately, Big Show punches the chair out of his hand ahead of a hairy heel Derailer. Lesnar then gets the chair and smashes Kurt, Benoit, and Cena with it to leave the babyfaces out cold and the heels standing tall to end the episode.

Monday Night Raw
November 10, 2003
Boston, MA
Announcers: Jim Ross, Jerry "the King" Lawler

Following the intro video and fireworks, Lita heads to the ring to kick off the final episode of *Raw* before Survivor Series. While she's happy to be back after suffering a serious injury, nothing will feel better than winning the Women's Title this Sunday. Triple H interrupts, leading Batista and Randy Orton to the squared circle. JR says Ric Flair is out for personal reasons. Inside the ring, Hunter gets a dollar bill and tells Lita to take a hike or start dancing for the cash. The extreme diva opts to leave. Once she's gone, Helmsley replays footage of "the Animal" attacking Goldberg. When the fans start chanting for the intense superstar, "the Game" calls him a man with more guts than brains. "Stone Cold" Steve Austin has heard enough and marches out to a big pop, Lawler telling fans this might be the last time we see him as the co-general manager. He tells the heels to take a hike too. Randy promises to end his career this Sunday, but the "rattlesnake" says Shawn Michaels may have something to say about that when he faces the "Legend Killer" later tonight. "Stone Cold" then tells Hunter if he's not prepared to wrestle, he needs to leave now. Helmsley and Batista wonder what the "rattlesnake" is going to do about it, "the Animal" calling him a coward. He's still the co-GM and he has security escort "the Game" from the building. Triple H says he'll leave, but only because he wants to. He shows security his lawyer's business card and promises to sue if they touch him. Wisely, they don't.

Backstage, Eric Bischoff and his Survivor Series team mocks "Stone Cold" Steve Austin. Eric says his co-GM is finally starting to understand what it means to be a general manager, but he's finding out a little too late. Bischoff promises to take away his job this Sunday. Booker T and the rest of Austin's team interrupt, getting in their Survivor Series opponents' faces to tell them that they are going to take care of business this Sunday.

Rob Van Dam def. Christian (Intercontinental Title match). The first of four Survivor Series preview matches tonight, Lawler says that none of the other team members can interfere in any of the contests. That lets RVD kick and monkey flip the challenger for an early two-count. Although Christian tosses him out to the apron, Rob back body drops the heel out to the floor. There, he drapes him on the barricade for a twisting leg drop. He tries to follow up with a slingshot attack from the apron, but the challenger rolls away and pokes his eyes. A DDT then scores Christian a pair of two-counts. When a neckbreaker only gets him a two-count, the heel resorts to choking Van Dam. Mike Chioda is all over his case, admonishing him when he turns his chin lock into a choke. Eventually, the champion punches his way free ahead of a spinning heel kick. While Jerry debates if Christian is creepy, RVD catches him with a split legged moonsault for a near fall. A springboard kick and rolling fireman's carry slam follows before Rob gets another two-count with a second rope moonsault. When Chioda gets in the way, Van Dam shoves him out of the way. The challenger capitalizes with a low blow. He tries to use a weapon, tossing Lilian Garcia aside to take her chair and the Intercontinental Title. Although the referee takes away the belt, he doesn't see the chair. RVD does, sweeping Christian's legs and stunning him with rolling thunder. A Five-Star Frog Splash afterwards gets Van Dam the win.

Shane McMahon enters a restaurant and asks for a table for two.

Back in the arena, Jonathan Coachman heads to the ring to boos. He tells Lilian Garcia that Eric Bischoff saw what happened to her in the last match. To keep her safe, Coach is taking over announcing duties.

Rene Dupree/Rob Conway def. Rosey/The Hurricane. The heels stop Lilian Garcia as she heads up the ramp, kissing her hands. She doesn't like it. The new version of La Resistance doesn't like that the superheroes cheated them last night on *Heat*. They're waiting for them to attack the babyfaces in the aisle. It doesn't take Rosey long to clothesline both heels down at the same time for a Hurricane top rope flying splash. Inside the ring Rosey slams Dupree before hip tossing his mentor onto the French heel. When the super hero in training goes for the cover after a falling headbutt, Conway makes the save. The heels then work on Rosey's knee, repeatedly stomping it. Rene gets so confident that he does his little dance to boos. When the big hero tries to respond with a powerslam, his knee gives out. It doesn't stop him from surprising Dupree with a Samoan drop. The Hurricane then tags in to fight both heels, stunning Rob with an inverted atomic drop and slam. When Rene makes the save, Rosey knocks him out to the floor. Conway sends the big hero out right behind him before escaping a chokeslam. He can't avoid a European uppercut, but Dupree stops The Hurricane from flying off the middle rope with a throat drop onto the top rope. Rob capitalizes with a swinging neckbreaker for the victory.

Backstage, Terri tells Lita that she doesn't have any gear tonight. She doesn't think she's going to be any help to Lita in their tag match. The extreme diva understands and will handle things. Eric Bischoff interrupts to remind Lita that he fired her before. Although "Stone Cold" Steve Austin brought her back, Eric believes the "rattlesnake" will be gone in six days. Bischoff smells Lita's hair and warns her that she better learn to "play ball".

After a commercial break, Chris Jericho reminds Christian, Mark Henry, and Scott Steiner why they all hate "Stone Cold" Steve Austin and need to beat him at Survivor Series. Randy Orton arrives late to the pep talk to tell everyone that if they have any trouble this Sunday, he will take care of it. To prove it, he tells the other heels to watch his match with Shawn Michaels later. When he leaves, Theodore Long calls him, "one cocky cracker". Scott adds, "believe that".

Further backstage, Val Venis leads two women into Lance Storm's locker room. He keeps one of the girls for himself as they stand outside Lance's shower. Storm's date is impressed with how big the Canadian is and is looking forward to their date tonight.

At a restaurant, Shane McMahon doesn't want to order until his guest arrives. JR wonders who it is.

Gail Kim/Molly Holly def. Lita/Terri. The heels go right after the denim dress wearing Terri to start the match. Lawler is concerned initially, but once he sees the she-devil's underwear, "the King" loses his mind. JR gets him to calm down speculating that Shane McMahon's dinner guest has to be Kane. While the announcers talk about that, Molly suplexes Terri and stretches her mouth. Eventually, the she-devil surprises the Women's Champion and whips her to the canvas before giving Lita the hot tag. She fights both heels, even dodging a Gail elbow drop that hits Holly. Using Molly as a springboard, she crushes Kim with a poetry in motion clothesline. Afterwards, Gail kicks Lita's face from the apron for Holly to steal the win with a roll-up and a handful of pants. Post-match, the women strip off Terri's dress and whip her into the barricade.

Shawn Michaels def. Randy Orton. An Unforgiven rematch, Orton comes out tonight without Ric Flair. Shawn follows, Lawler erroneously calling him the first Triple Crown winner in WWE history. He was the first Grand Slam winner. Randy doesn't care, looking to end the legend with an early dropkick. Michaels answers with chops and a back body drop. He tunes the band up for an early Sweet Chin Music, but the "Legend Killer" slides out to the floor and leads Shawn on a chase around the ring. Back in the squared circle, Michaels punches and rolls up the heel for a two-count. More chops follow until Randy uses the "Heartbreak Kid's" momentum against him and tosses him out to the floor. There, he rams Shawn's lower back into the apron. A series of fists gets him a two-count back in the squared circle, as does a back suplex. Orton then slows the pace with a reverse chin lock. JR is concerned with how much his announce partner talks about the "Legend Killer's" looks. Randy is more concerned with Michaels making a comeback with a string of strikes and a flying forearm. Orton only manages to slow his attack by running the "Heartbreak Kid" into Earl Hebner. While the referee is down, the "Legend Killer" stuns Shawn with a backbreaker. He takes Jonathan Coachman's chair afterwards and sets it up for a backbreaker inside the ring. Unfortunately, Michaels flips over and reverses the move, driving Randy through the chair. Sweet Chin Music follows for a groggy three-count to even both Shawn's series with Orton and Eric Bischoff and "Stone Cold" Steve Austin's Survivor Series teams facing off tonight.

At the restaurant, Kane, wearing a black polo shirt, arrives at the restaurant. He says he always keeps his word. Shane McMahon tells him that they have gone too far and Shane will stop at nothing to put the "Big Red Machine" in an ambulance this Sunday. The monster asks McMahon how his mother is doing. He adds that he tried to electrify Shane's crotch so he would never have any kids. Kane wonders if he succeeded. McMahon doesn't answer. The "Big Red Machine" doesn't care. He tells Shane that he only derives pleasure from injuring other people and there's no way to stop "pure evil". McMahon doesn't think he's a monster. He says deep down, Kane is a scared little boy, and at Survivor Series, Shane will put him out of his misery. The babyface then pays for dinner, leaving the monster seething.

The Dudley Boyz def. Mark Henry/Scott Steiner (with Stacy Keibler/Theodore Long) by disqualification. A non-title match, Steiner wastes no time suplexing and chopping D-Von. Dudley answers with a flying shoulderblock and dropkick. When Scott retreats out to the floor, Bubba Ray shoves him right back into the ring. Backstage, Garrison Cade and Mark Jindrak watch the action. They get to see Henry tag in to steamroll D-Von with a pair of shoulder blocks. Unfortunately, he misses an elbow drop allowing Bubba to tag into the match. He tries to match power with the "World's Strongest Man" and predictably loses. Henry then clubs Dudley down to the mat. When he lowers his head for a back body drop, Bubba Ray kicks Mark. D-Von joins his half-brother for a double-team attack, but Henry answers with a double clothesline. A twisting belly-to-belly suplex afterwards scores "Big Poppa Pump" a two-count. He also gets a near fall with an elbow drop before doing pushups and taunting Bubba. When he tries to hit him, Bubba Ray answers with his own fist for a D-Von roll-up and near fall. Scott is right back on the attack, but when he sets D-Von on the top rope, Dudley knocks Steiner back to the canvas. A diving headbutt follows before Bubba gets the hot tag to sidewalk slam "Big Poppa Pump" for a two-count. He also gets a near fall with a Bubba Bomb before the "World's Strongest Man" makes the save. That kicks off a four-man brawl, the Dudleys knocking Scott out to the floor. They tease giving Mark a 3D, but Steiner makes the save with a chair shot to Bubba Ray's back for the disqualification. After Henry gives D-Von the World's Strongest Slam, "Big Poppa Pump" wails on the World Tag Team Champions with the chair.

Backstage, Eric Bischoff loves it. He asks "Stone Cold" Steve Austin if he envisioned his career ending like this. Eric calls it ironic that it was Austin who helped put WCW out of business, but this Sunday Bischoff will put him out of the business. He also thinks it's ironic that the man who always said, "don't trust anybody", is going to have to trust his career to five men. Eric says it's been a blast working with Steve.

Backstage, Chris Jericho isn't happy that a woman finally brings him a warm water. He tells her that when Eric Bischoff is running the show next week, she'll be the first fired. Trish Stratus sees the exchange and wonders if Y2J is okay. He says he's stressed out about his upcoming Survivor Series match and isn't himself. She understands and tells him that he can vent to her anytime. Jericho finds the courage to ask her out on a date. She accepts. Wasting no time, Y2J says he'll find her after his match and they can go out tonight.

Both the *Raw* and *SmackDown!* announce teams preview the upcoming Survivor Series card.

Backstage, Booker T reads *WWE Unscripted* and calls Chris Jericho a "punk ass". Jon Heidenreich wants to get a book for him and Little Johnny. When he starts to leave, Heidenreich finds an envelope addressed to Booker. It has a note that says, "I still remember". Booker T doesn't have time for this. Neither does the WWE. Reportedly, this was supposed to be from Goldust, but he'll end up leaving the WWE officially before the storyline plays out.

Booker T def. Chris Jericho. Jonathan Coachman gives Jericho a huge introduction before Booker goes to work hip tossing and chopping the heel. When he attempts a side kick though, Y2J ducks and the five-time champion straddles the top rope. A missile dropkick sends Booker T out to the floor. When they return, Jericho gets a two-count with a top rope flying back elbow before applying a reverse chin lock. The babyface answers with more shots and a leaping forearm. A side kick afterwards gets him a two-count, the announcer speculating on the note Booker received. Jericho gives him a different kind of flashback for a near fall, but the five-time champion responds with a spinebuster. When Y2J attempts to apply his Walls of Jericho, Booker T powers free. He also avoids a Lionsault following a running face slam. Although Jericho fights free of a Book End, he walks into a roll-up out of the corner for the babyface to score the victory. Post-match, Y2J attacks the winner from behind and locks on the Walls of Jericho. Eric Bischoff's heel team follows behind, stomping Booker until "Stone Cold" Steve Austin's squad runs out for all ten men to brawl in a Survivor Series preview. The babyfaces get the upper hand and clear the ring before Coach declares Jericho the winner in his opinion. The babyfaces don't like that and chase Coachman into the ring where The Dudley Boyz draw a big pop with a 3D.

A video package for Kane and Shane McMahon's feud plays.

Goldberg def. Batista by disqualification. After the announcers shill the *WWE Unscripted* book, Lilian Garcia returns to announcing duties for this non-title match. Following Batista's entrance, Goldberg limps out with a cast on his right leg. "The Animal" has no sympathy, slugging him as he enters the ring. The champion responds with his own shots and a military press, still wearing the title belt. After he slings it aside, Batista slams Bill's injured ankle into the apron and ring post repeatedly. Stomps follow while the announcers wonder why the intense superstar isn't sitting at home tonight resting his injured leg. Blocking out the pain, Goldberg rolls out of the way of a corner charge to Spear "the Animal". Before he can finish off Batista with a Jackhammer, Triple H chop blocks the champion for the disqualification. He follows up with a Pedigree before grabbing a sledgehammer and chair. Trapping Bill's leg in the chair, Hunter looks to hit it with the sledgehammer, but the intense superstar escapes with a low blow. He then Spears Helmsley. When "the Animal" tries to help his leader, Goldberg sees him coming and hits Batista with the sledgehammer, chasing off the heels to end the show.

SmackDown!
November 13, 2003
East Rutherford, NJ
Announcers: Michael Cole, Tazz

Following the intro video and fireworks, the announcers preview the show. They inform us that we'll find out the fifth member of Team Angle's Survivor Series squad tonight when they team up with Chris Benoit.

Kurt Angle def. Nathan Jones by disqualification. Kurt is out first. When Matt Morgan tries to accompany Jones to the ring, Nick Patrick sends him backstage. Alone, Nathan drives the Olympian back to a corner. Angle answers with a roll-up for a two-count while the announcers speculate on potential members for Team Angle. Tazz thinks it could be John Cena. When Jones attempts a big boot, Kurt dodges and the big man straddles the top rope. The Olympian immediately knocks him out to the floor, but when he follows him out, Nathan slams Angle on top of the barricade. Back in the squared circle, Jones kicks Kurt until he runs into a corner back elbow and second rope missile dropkick for a two-count. When the Olympian attempts a cross body block, Nathan catches and slams him. He then slows the pace with a neck wrench. It doesn't take Angle long to fight free, but a knee to the gut slows him for another slam. An elbow drop follows for a two-count. Jones waits until Kurt stands to military press him, but the Olympian slips free and dropkicks his knee. Kicks and a clothesline follow before Angle delivers a trio of German suplexes. The fans roar to life as he lowers his straps, but Nathan slips free of an Angle Slam to big boot Kurt. When he tries to follow up, the Olympian counters and Angle Slams him. He then traps the big heel in an Anklelock. Before he can submit, Morgan returns to attack Angle for the disqualification. Suddenly, Hardcore Holly makes his return to *SmackDown!* to wail on both heels with a chair for the first "Holly" chant of his career. Hardcore wants Brock Lesnar to come out right now, but the WWE Champion is nowhere to be found.

After a commercial break, Hardcore Holly searches for Brock Lesnar. Paul Heyman, surrounded by security, offers to give Holly Lesnar, but not now. Paul says the returning superstar isn't even cleared to wrestle tonight. Heyman wants him to leave now. If he does, the general manager assures Hardcore that he'll get a piece of the WWE Champion at Survivor Series. Calming down, Holly promises to leave, but he wants Paul to tell Brock that this Sunday he is going to break the champion's neck like he did Hardcore's.

Further backstage, Sable tries to get Vince McMahon to calm down by looking at the *WWE Unscripted* book. Unfortunately, just when he starts to calm, he turns a page and sees The Undertaker. Vince then reveals that he had a dream about being buried alive and maggots eating his flesh. In the dream, he swallowed some of the maggots only to poop them out. That wasn't the end of the maggots and they crawled through his eyes and mouth again. When McMahon woke up, he had actually pooped himself.

After a commercial break, Jamie Noble heads to the ring to call out Tajiri. Although the "Japanese Buzzsaw" answers, it's his goons, Akio and Sakoda, doing most of the fighting. After they rock the redneck with a double enziguri kick, Tajiri orders them to pick him up for the Cruiserweight Champion to finish him off. Fortunately, Rey Mysterio rushes out to chase the heels from the ring.

Akio/Sakoda def. Jamie Noble/Rey Mysterio. After a commercial break, Noble stomps Akio, this match signed during the break by the GM. Akio answers with a dropkick before Sakoda tags in to stomp and chop the redneck. The announcers can't help but notice that Tajiri left ringside. Soon afterwards, Rey gets the hot tag to roll-up Sakoda and dropkick Akio. When he attempts to give Sakoda a victory roll, the heel hotshots him. Akio follows up with stomps and a triangle choke in the ropes. After working Jimmy Korderas' five-count, Akio applies a legal hold, a front face lock. Although Mysterio fights free, a dropkick puts him right back down. Sakoda then tags in to cheap shot Noble. He distracts the referee trying to get back into the ring, allowing the heels to double-team Rey. Trapping the masked man in their corner, the rookies make quick tags before Akio uses Mysterio's arms to choke him. When he runs up Rey though, the masked man answers his impressive flip with a spinning inverted DDT. Jamie gets the tag afterwards to hit both heels and stun Akio with a falling knee to the jaw. He gets a near fall with a powerslam before Sakoda makes the save. Noble answers him with a swinging neckbreaker only to rise up into a spinning heel kick. Mysterio then returns to stun Akio with a springboard flying senton splash. The 619 follows, but Korderas admonishes him before he can finish off the rookie with a West Coast Pop. That gives Sakoda time to pull Rey off the ropes out to the floor. Although Jamie plants Akio with a Tiger Bomb behind the referee's back, Tajiri returns to kick the redneck for his men to steal the victory.

Backstage, Chavo Guerrero Jr. tells Eddie Guerrero that they have a shot at the WWE Tag Titles tonight and "Latino Heat" can't screw it up. Eddie promises that he won't, reminding his nephew that he beat The Basham Brothers solo last week. Unfortunately, a detective enters to tell "Latino Heat" that his wife's sister was in a car wreck. Eddie grabs his stuff and starts to leave. Although Chavo doesn't like it, he understands that family comes first and promises to take care of their title shot. Surprisingly, Paul Heyman agrees that family comes first and postpones the WWE Tag Title match until this Sunday. The Basham Brothers don't like that, but they don't have any say. However, they do goad Chavo into a match tonight. To see if he's as tough as his uncle, the Bashams challenge him to a handicap match. When he accepts, Heyman tells him the match is next.

After the announcers shill *WWE Unscripted*, a vignette plays of The Undertaker walking in a graveyard. He's standing by a freshly dug grave to tell Vince McMahon that he's put himself in this situation. While the biker has taken out many great warriors, none of them ever threatened his wife and family. The "Deadman" promises that Vince is in for the most brutal evening of his life at Survivor Series, his punishment only ending when he's buried alive.

The Basham Brothers (with Shaniqua) def. Chavo Guerrero Jr. After Shaniqua whips her men, Chavo repeatedly takes Doug down to the canvas with arm drags, hip tosses, and a dropkick. Danny gets more of the same when he enters the ring illegally. That sends the Bashams out to the floor for Shaniqua to whip them. It doesn't help them focus as Guerrero continues to fight both men, diving off the apron onto Danny before trapping Doug in a Boston crab. When he lets go to attack Danny, Doug recovers and knocks him out to the floor. There, Danny rams him into the apron for a Doug two-count. Afterwards, the Bashams stomp Chavo in their corner, Cole saying that this is going to soften him up for the WWE Tag Title match Sunday. After Danny gets a two-count with a string of fists, Doug returns for a double flapjack and near fall. A chin lock follows while Shaniqua argues with the fans. It doesn't take Guerrero long to elbow free. When he attempts a corner charge though, Doug catches him with his own elbow. He can't follow up and Chavo counters his top rope dive with a boot to the jaw. After taking care of an illegally entering Danny again, Guerrero stuns Doug with an inverted atomic drop and back body drop. He heads upstairs, but dodges Doug's charge to flip over him and tornado DDT the legal Basham. Danny returns in time to break up the cover, but elbow drops his own brother. When Chavo dropkicks Doug out to the floor, Shaniqua hops onto the apron to distract Guerrero for her men to make a switch. Guerrero doesn't realize it, baseball slide kicking the dominatrix off the apron. Afterwards, he rolls a Basham back into the ring, but it's Danny and he small packages Chavo for the win. Post-match, Shaniqua big boots Guerrero ahead of a spinning side slam and double uranage from the Bashams. Still not done, Danny puts Chavo into Doug's arms on the second rope for a falling spinebuster.

Backstage, Josh Mathews is waiting outside Kurt Angle's locker room for word on who the fifth member of his team is. So far, the Olympian isn't answering.

After a commercial break, Chavo Guerrero Jr. complains to a trainer that he has a shooting pain down his back. Elsewhere, The Basham Brothers and Shaniqua laugh before shaking hands with the detective that told Eddie Guerrero his sister-in-law was in an accident. The WWE Tag Team Champions compliment his acting.

Bradshaw def. A-Train. For the next two Survivor Series preview matches, Paul Heyman has ordered that there will be no more outside interference. A-Train doesn't need the help, clubbing down the big Texan. Bradshaw soon answers with his own heavy blows including a big boot and elbow drop for a two-count. More brawl that wrestling match, the hairy heel responds with a clothesline and boot out on the floor. When he tries to use the stairs, the big Texan reverses his face slam. Back in the ring, Bradshaw connects with a leaping shoulderblock, but his suplex attempt is reversed. A-Train then scores a two-count with a decapitator slingshot. When he badmouths and slaps the big Texan, Bradshaw wakes up and unloads with a series of right hands. The hairy heel tries to slow his momentum with a sleeper hold, but the big Texan elbows free and reverses the hold. A-Train escapes with a side suplex to put both men down. When they get up, Bradshaw punches and dropkicks the hairy heel. A swinging neckbreaker and corner clotheslines have A-Train seeing stars until he surprises the big Texan with a back elbow. A corner bomb nearly gets him the win, but Bradshaw reaches the ropes. When he tries to respond with a Clothesline from Hell, the hairy heel ducks and answers with a Derailer. Somehow, the big Texan kicks out. A-Train attempts to follow up with a bicycle kick, but this time Bradshaw ducks and finally lands his Clothesline from Hell for the victory.

Backstage, Chris Benoit can't believe who Kurt Angle picked as the fifth member of their team. "The Crippler" says the mystery man isn't trustworthy and has tried to end their career. Kurt could say the same about Benoit. He thinks sometimes people need to make business decisions to win. John Cena interrupts to tell the "rabid wolverine" that he doesn't like him either. The only reason he's teaming with them is to get a piece of "Team Sasquatch". When John leaves, Benoit warns Angle that if the rapping heel does anything to mess with "the Crippler", Benoit will end him here tonight.

After a commercial break, Sable interrupts Vince McMahon and introduces him to a priest, Father Frank. She hopes he can alleviate Vince's fears. The WWE owner finds it funny that she brought him a priest. When Father Frank prays for him, McMahon repeatedly interrupts. He asks the priest to pray harder. That makes Vince laugh and he says Father Frank should be praying for The Undertaker. Mr. McMahon stands above the priest as he promises to bury the "Deadman" this Sunday.

A Survivor Series video package plays for the *Raw* PPV matches. Cole and Tazz then preview their show's matches.

A vignette featuring Ernest Miller in a limo with several women and Lamont praising "the Cat" plays.

Chris Benoit/John Cena def. Big Show/Brock Lesnar. Pre-match, Cena raps that he's the fifth member of Team Angle and there's no way he was going to join Brock's team. He then makes fun of the heel squad before the other competitors make individual entrances. Once the match starts, John and Lesnar trade strikes, the rapping heel eventually knocking down the champion. Benoit then tags in to elbow and snap suplex Brock for a two-count. He follows up with corner chops before Cena returns to continue his hammering assault. When he attempts a corner whip, the champion counters with an overhead belly-to-belly suplex. Show tags in afterwards to drop John with one big chop and a headbutt. He follows up with a Chokeslam, but "the Crippler" drags his partner out to the floor ahead of a commercial break.

During the break, Lesnar whips Benoit into the ring steps. Afterwards, Big Show slams the rapping heel before Brock tags back in for a German suplex. A fisherman's suplex moments later nearly gets him the victory, but Cena just kicks out. He then surprises the champion with a DDT and crawls to his corner for the hot tag. The "rabid wolverine" explodes into the ring with a running chop and big German suplex. With the fans cheering him on, Benoit connects with a top rope diving headbutt, but the giant breaks his cover. When he leaves, "the Crippler" kicks Show's back. Unfortunately, he turns into a hotshot and clothesline. Back in, Big Show slugs and chops Benoit. The fans insult the giant with a "Subway" chant, but that only makes him mad and he continues punishing the "rabid wolverine" ahead of a falling leg drop and two-count. Fortunately, John breaks his cover. Brock then tags in to squeeze Benoit's ribs and apply a rear naked choke. There's no quit in "the Crippler" and he surprises the champion with a back elbow followed by another German suplex. He nearly reaches his corner for the tag, but Lesnar holds him back long enough for Show to distract Brian Hebner. When the rapping heel finally gets the tag, the referee misses it and Brock capitalizes with a DDT to Benoit. The "rabid wolverine" responds with an enziguri. Hebner sees the tag this time and Cena explodes into the ring to punch the champion and knock down Big Show with a clothesline. Benoit follows up with a diving headbutt off the top rope, but Lesnar breaks John's cover. Chris answers by countering a clothesline to trap Brock in the Crippler Crossface. While the referee is distracted, Cena doubles over the giant with a low blow before knocking him out with his steel chain for the victory.

PPV: Survivor Series
November 16, 2003
Dallas, TX
Announcers: Jim Ross, Jerry "the King" Lawler, Michael Cole, Tazz

The PPV opens with a video package talking about what it takes to survive while footage from the major feuds plays. Afterwards, the show graphic featuring chains is displayed before fireworks explode to kick off the PPV.

Team Angle (Bradshaw/Chris Benoit/Hardcore Holly/John Cena/Kurt Angle) def. Team Lesnar (A-Train/Big Show/Brock Lesnar/Matt Morgan/Nathan Jones). Cena is out first to say the PPV is backwards because the main event is first tonight. He then runs down the heel squad, promising to put them in an ambulance and the grave. Everyone gets separate entrances to walk between the ambulance and a forklift before Holly attacks Brock before the bell. When he throws him into the ring steps, Brian Hebner tries to get the returning superstar to back off. Instead, Hardcore shoves the referee and gets disqualified before the bell rings. Inside the squared circle, A-Train crushes Bradshaw, but his corner bomb is countered with a boot to the chin. A Clothesline from Hell then evens the sides. The big Texan tries to get another elimination, bouncing into the ropes to give Big Show a Clothesline from Hell too, but Jones knees his back to stun him for a Chokeslam and three-count. The rapping heel tries to keep the rapid fire eliminations going, but he can't lift the giant for an FU. Instead, the heels hammer him in their corner until John clips Lesnar's knee. A pair of schoolboy roll-ups afterwards score Cena two-counts. One shot puts him back down before Morgan tags in to hammer and slam the rapping heel. Although he misses a leg drop, Matt quickly recovers to sidewalk slam John. Afterwards, Nathan tags in and whips Morgan into Cena in a corner. A scoop slam and choke follow from Jones before he tags back in the WWE Champion. He tries to finish off the rapping heel with a corner slam, but John slips free and gets a two-count with a throwback. Benoit then tags in to chop and suplex Brock. The champion responds with a hotshot and clothesline. Show returns afterwards to club and press slam "the Crippler". When he attempts to Chokeslam him, Benoit counters with a Crippler Crossface. Fortunately, Lesnar breaks the hold quickly. Back in control, Big Show applies an abdominal stretch. Being a heel, he uses Brock's hand for added leverage. Tiring of the submission hold, the giant leg drops a standing "rabid wolverine" for a near fall. Soon afterwards, Benoit ends up outside the ring where the heels wail on him. That kicks off a brawl at ringside. After Hebner restores order, Show headbutts "the Crippler". The heels make quick tags until Benoit dropkicks Morgan and tags in Kurt. He goes to town with a trio of German suplexes. When Nathan illegally enters the ring, the Olympian dropkicks his knee. Lesnar illegally enters the ring also. Although he hoists Angle up for an F5, Kurt slips free for a German suplex. Everyone starts fighting again, Matt accidentally big booting Jones. The Olympian capitalizes, Angle Slamming Morgan to even the sides. Afterwards, Nathan holds Kurt for a Big Show attack, but the Olympian dodges at the last second. With Jones stunned, Angle knocks the giant out of the ring and hooks Nathan in an Anklelock for the quick tap-out. Brock immediately grabs Kurt following the elimination for an F5 and the three-count. Down to two men on each team, Benoit attacks the WWE Champion's left arm. Lesnar answers with a back elbow, but when he tries to score another elimination with an F5, the "rabid wolverine" traps him in the Crippler Crossface. John stops Show from making the save, but Brock rolls over Benoit for a two-count. It doesn't take "the Crippler" long to reapply his submission hold for the tap-out. While the fans mock Lesnar for tapping out, Big Show attacks Benoit. The "rabid wolverine" answers with a top rope flying shoulderblock for a two-count. Benoit attempts to lock on his Crippler Crossface again, but the giant shoots him back into Team Angle's corner and Cena.

Hebner considers that a tag, but Show doesn't realize it. He Chokeslams "the Crippler" while John wraps his chain around his fist. While the referee checks on Benoit, Cena clocks Big Show ahead of a massive FU for the victory. Post-match, the survivors shake hands. Survivors: Chris Benoit/John Cena.

Backstage, Vince McMahon interrupts Shane McMahon preparing for his match. He feels a certain level of fate with the two McMahons facing a pair of brothers tonight. The only thing Shane feels is sorry for his father. When Vince walks away, "Stone Cold" Steve Austin stops and stares at him in the hall. Without saying a word, the two men laugh until Austin suddenly stops and leaves.

Molly Holly def. Lita (Women's Title match). The announcers note that Lita winning tonight would be a fairytale ending to her comeback, but she has never won at Survivor Series. She tries to get the quick victory tonight, tripping Molly at ringside and slamming her face onto the canvas for a two-count. A suplex follows, but when she attempts a corner head scissors, the champion tosses the extreme diva out to the floor. A hard whip back into the barricade follows for a Charles Robinson two-count. A swinging neckbreaker also gets Holly a near fall before she applies a reverse chin lock. After clubbing the challenger down, Molly locks on a dragon sleeper. Eventually, Lita kicks free, but the champion responds in kind. A handspring back elbow, kicks, and a choke follow until the extreme diva fights back and pulls herself up to the top rope for a flying cross body block and close two-count. After clotheslining Holly in a corner, the challenger mounts and punches her. A roll-up then scores Lita a two-count, but she runs into a sidewalk slam afterwards for a Molly near fall. When she mounts the extreme diva in a corner, the challenger answers with a powerbomb for another two-count. After the women catch their breath, they trade fists, Lita getting the upper hand and planting the champion with a leg sweep. She then heads upstairs for a Moonsault, but Holly moves. She capitalizes with a Molly Go Round, but somehow, the extreme diva just kicks out. Frustrated, Molly removes a middle turnbuckle pad, but the challenger rolls her up for a near fall. The champion answers, shoving Lita into the steel for the victory.

Kane def. Shane McMahon ("Ambulance" match). Following a video package for the match and an ambulance backing down the aisle, Shane cross body blocks Kane out to the floor. The rivals then brawl at ringside, the "Big Red Machine" attempting to use the ring steps only to see McMahon hit them with a steel chair. Following several shots, Shane drapes the monster on the Spanish announce table and smashes him with a television monitor. McMahon is willing to put his body on the line to get revenge on Kane for his attacks on him and his mother and heads upstairs for a flying elbow drop off the top rope. Once the wrestlers recover, Shane leads the "Big Red Machine" through the crowd and backstage. McMahon doubles around the monster and smashes him with a kendo stick repeatedly. He then backs a truck up, slamming Kane through a glass security booth. With radio in hand, Shane calls for a second ambulance. He pulls a stretcher from that emergency vehicle, but when he tries to put the "Big Red Machine" on it, the monster sits up and whips McMahon back and forth into walls and a trashcan. The fans boo as the camera feed goes out for the second time. Fortunately, a third camera is on hand to pick up Kane tossing around his nemesis, leading him back to ringside. There, he whips Shane hard into the ambulance, the back of McMahon's head cracking the front windshield. That's not enough to keep Shane down and he slams the "Big Red Machine" into the vehicle. He follows up with a pair of shots from the back door, scrambling the monster's brains. It's not enough to keep him down as Kane fights back and flings McMahon into the emergency vehicle. Although he closes one door, Shane kicks the second back into his head ahead of a tornado DDT on the floor. Not done yet, he smashes the "Big Red Machine" with a trashcan before putting a foam block between the monster's legs. The babyface crushes it moments later, flying off the top of the ambulance for a coast-to-coast dropkick. Winded himself, McMahon struggles to shove Kane into the ambulance. The "Big Red Machine" pulls him in as well. When they fight free, the monster picks up and slams Shane into the side of the vehicle. The fans try to wake up McMahon, cheering his name, but Kane Tombstones him on the floor to silence the crowd. Afterwards, he shoves Shane into the ambulance and closes the doors for the win. Post-match, the ambulance heads to a medical facility. JR tells us that the doctors were warned they'd have an admission tonight.

Backstage, Josh Mathews asks Brock Lesnar how he feels about his loss earlier. The WWE Champion says he didn't lose or tap-out. Brock blames the rest of his team before saying that he could beat anyone in the WWE. Goldberg interrupts to introduce himself and chuckle.

At ringside, Jonathan Coachman comes out in a neck brace to thank the fans for all their cards and well wishes after The Dudley Boyz gave him a 3D Monday night. Before he leaves the ring, he notices Dallas Mavericks owner Mark Cuban in the crowd. Coach hops out to shake his hand and interview him. He's here to see "Stone Cold" Steve Austin. When he starts to complain about referees, Eric Bischoff comes out to call out Cuban. He says that he rented the building tonight and can have Mark hauled out if he wants. The Mavericks owner doesn't take kindly to being threatened and shoves Eric down and out of the ring. Bischoff gets the last laugh as Randy Orton sprints out to give Cuban an RKO.

Backstage, Evolution is surrounded by women in their locker room. When they take off Triple H's shirt, Ric Flair interrupts. He says Hunter can't get "weak in the knees" before his World Title match tonight. Helmsley thinks he worries too much. Randy Orton interrupts to brag about what he just did. After eliminating Mark Cuban earlier, the "Legend Killer" promises to finish off "Stone Cold" Steve Austin too.

The Basham Brothers (with Shaniqua) def. Los Guerreros (WWE Tag Title match). The champions wear belts and handcuffs around their chests as they come out for Shaniqua to whip them ahead of this title match. Los Guerreros follow in a red and black lowrider. The former champions go right after the heels, dropkicking them from the squared circle. When Eddie goes after Shaniqua, Danny blindsides him. Inside the ring, Danny tries to continue his attack on Chavo, but the younger Guerrero quickly tags in his uncle to stomp down the champion. He follows up with a trio of suplexes for a near fall before Doug breaks Jimmy Korderas' count. Chavo returns afterwards with a low dropkick and slam before tagging "Latino Heat" for a slingshot somersault splash and two-count. Fighting both men, Eddie takes the champions down with a combination head scissors and headlock takedown. Unfortunately, they answer with a double hotshot. When he ends up outside the ring, Shaniqua clotheslines and slams "Latino Heat" for a Doug two-count. A double slingshot suplex moments later scores Danny another two-count before he slows the pace with a reverse chin lock. It doesn't take Guerrero long to elbow free. Following a head scissors, Chavo tags in to dropkick the Bashams and slam Doug for a near fall. The champions answer with a double flapjack, but when they try to slam Chavo off the second rope, Eddie makes the save with a hurricanrana to Doug. That scores the younger Guerrero a two-count with a somersault splash. Afterwards, Danny back body drops "Latino Heat" out to the floor, but Chavo fights both heels, dropkicking Danny before the challenger and Doug connect with simultaneous clotheslines. While they try to get up, Shaniqua distracts Korderas for Danny to switch places with his brother. Chavo doesn't care, dropkicking him out of the ring ahead of a clothesline to Shaniqua. Eddie follows up with a Frog Splash for a big pop. The fans get even louder when Chavo spanks the dominatrix over his knee. Unfortunately, Doug blindsides "Latino Heat". Although Chavo drops him with a swinging DDT, he accidentally kicks his uncle as he swings around. That lets Danny illegally switch places with his brother and steal the win with a handful of tights. Post-match, Eddie isn't happy about his nephew hitting him, but cooler heads prevail and Los Guerreros leave together.

Team Bischoff (Chris Jericho/Christian/Mark Henry/Randy Orton/Scott Steiner) (with Eric Bischoff/Stacy Keibler/Theodore Long) def. Team Austin (Booker T/Bubba Ray Dudley/D-Von Dudley/Rob Van Dam/Shawn Michaels) (with "Stone Cold" Steve Austin). "Stone Cold" Steve Austin has a lot on the line here. If he wins, he is no longer barred from attacking WWE superstars. However, if he loses, he loses his job. Ahead of the match, a video package plays for Austin and his run as co-general manager of *Raw*. JR calls this "the biggest match 'Stone Cold' never participated in". To show how unified his team is, Eric leads them all to the ring at one-time. The "rattlesnake" does the same, the babyfaces all entering to his theme song. Christian and D-Von open the contest trading arm wringers and hammerlocks. When the CLB slaps Dudley, D-Von goes to town with fists and a hair pull. A leaping clothesline follows for a two-count. RVD tags in afterwards to flip over and kick Christian for an early near fall. The heel responds with a few fists and limps to his corner to tag Jericho. Rob catches him with a kick too before scoring another two-count with a northern lights suplex. Y2J responds with an enziguri for his own near fall. Scott tags in afterwards to chop the popular superstar and flex. Van Dam answers with a springboard cross body block for another two-count. After he gets a near fall with a spinning kick, Steiner overhead belly-to-belly suplexes RVD. Instead of going for the cover, he does a few pushups and belly-to-belly suplexes Rob again. This time he gets a near fall. When Van Dam tries to answer with a top rope attack, "Big Poppa Pump" knocks him down onto the top rope ahead of a second rope twisting belly-to-belly suplex and another close two-count. Booker tags in moments later only to run into a clothesline and elbow drop. The five-time champion answers with a clothesline and Scissors Kick. Like Scott, he wastes time celebrating, this time with a spinaroonie. When he tries to score the elimination with a spinebuster, Booker T kicks off a ten-man brawl. Mike Chioda is distracted by everyone else fighting and misses Steiner giving the five-time champion a low blow. "Big Poppa Pump" then locks Booker in his Steiner Recliner, but Stacy hops onto the apron to distract him. When Scott lets Booker T go to grab Keibler, the Dudleys save her with a double-team neckbreaker. The five-time champion follows up with a Book End for the three-count and first elimination. Henry immediately evens back up the odds with a World's Strongest Slam to Booker for the three-count.

RVD is in afterwards, but his kicks have no effect. Neither does Bubba Ray's fists as the "World's Strongest Man" runs him over. Confident, he whips around Dudley until he makes the mistake of lowering his head too soon for a back body drop. Bubba answers with a kick, but when he tags in D-Von, Mark whips them into each other. He tries to finish off D-Von with a corner charge, but Dudley moves, and the World Tag Title holders capitalize with a 3D. Van Dam follows up with a Five-Star Frog Splash for the Dudleys and him to pile onto Henry for another elimination. Moments later, Rob surprises Jericho with a split legged moonsault for another near fall. At the last second, Y2J puts his foot on the ropes and tags in Orton for the first time. He proceeds to slug RVD and nearly take his head off with a clothesline. Following a two-count, Randy resumes his assault until he runs into a corner boot. A second rope springing kick and rolling thunder follow. When Van Dam heads upstairs for the Five-Star Frog Splash, Jericho shoves him down for an RKO and three-count. The sides evened again, D-Von slams the "Legend Killer" for a top rope diving headbutt and near fall. He wails on Y2J too until he runs into a corner boot and missile dropkick. Fortunately, Bubba Ray breaks the heel's cover. When D-Von knocks Jericho down, Chioda is distracted and misses his cover. Dudley gets his attention, but Y2J takes advantage of the break with a flashback for another elimination.

Rushing in to try to even the odds once again, Bubba gives Jericho a sidewalk slam before tagging in Shawn for the first time. Although he spots Christian attempting a sneak attack and drives him from the ring, Michaels turns into a Y2J clothesline. Following a double-team attack alongside Jericho, Orton tags in to pound on the "Heartbreak Kid". Unfortunately, he misses a dropkick. When both men tag out, Bubba Ray fights all three heels. He focuses on Christian, now the legal man, with a hotshot and big back body drop. When Randy breaks his cover, Dudley Samoan drops him. He continues fighting all three heels, Y2J accidentally running into Christian. When the babyface tries to capitalize with a Bubba Bomb, Jericho low blows him ahead of an Unprettier for the CLB to put Bischoff's squad up three men to one. Shawn won't lay down and quit, catching Christian with a flying forearm. When he runs the ropes, Y2J low bridges him for the heels to stomp the now solo superstar. Every time he tries to fight back, the heels capitalize on their superior numbers to take him down. That leads to Christian catapulting Michaels's head into the ring post, savagely busting him open. A suplex back into the ring scores the heel a two-count and sees him covered in blood as well. The "Heartbreak Kid" still won't stop, continuing to fight back, escaping an Unprettier. When Christian charges him seconds later, Sweet Chin Music out of nowhere scores Shawn a three-count. Y2J is back in afterwards to pound on Michaels's crimson mask and nearly earn the victory with a clothesline. Randy tags in afterwards to choke and kick the "Heartbreak Kid". Shawn answers with a sleeper hold, but a side suplex breaks it for Jericho to return and nearly get the three-count. When he attempts a springboard attack, Michaels kicks and DDTs him. Unfortunately, Orton breaks his cover. Once the "Heartbreak Kid" tosses him out to the floor, Jericho plants the bloodied superstar with a running face slam. Shawn still has the presence of mind to counter a Lionsault with a pair of knees. Both men struggle to get up to their feet, Michaels attempting to score the victory with Sweet Chin Music out of nowhere again. At the last second, Y2J ducks and attempts to lock on the Walls of Jericho. Before he can, the "Heartbreak Kid" rolls him up for the three-count. A sore loser, Jericho grabs a chair and plasters Shawn with it before yelling at Austin and heading backstage. That leaves the "Legend Killer" to crawl over Michaels for a close two-count. When he heads upstairs, Shawn dodges his flying cross body block, but the referee doesn't. After he pulls himself up, the "Heartbreak Kid" tunes up the band. Unfortunately, Bischoff makes the save with a kick to the ribs. That's all "Stone Cold" can take and he stomps a mudhole in Eric. He also gives Randy a Stone Cold Stunner before leading Bischoff up the aisle. That means there's no one watching as Batista hops out of the crowd to give Shawn a Batista Bomb. By the time Chioda rolls over, Orton covers Michaels for the three-count, ending the "rattlesnake's" run as co-general manager of *Raw*. Sole Survivor: Randy Orton.

Post-match, "Stone Cold" Steve Austin helps up Shawn Michaels. The "Heartbreak Kid" apologizes for letting him down, but Austin shakes his hand and helps Shawn backstage. While JR somberly says that the "rattlesnake's" career is over, "Stone Cold's" music plays and he returns to the squared circle. He can barely speak as he says he began his career here in Dallas, and at least he can say it ended here. After he tells the fans that he loves them, Jonathan Coachman returns to sing goodbye to the "rattlesnake". He's accompanied by four officers. They're here to escort Austin out, but Steve goes to town punching Coach and clearing the ring of the officers. One even gets a Stone Cold Stunner before only the "rattlesnake" and Coachman are left in the squared circle. "Stone Cold" proceeds to stomp him down ahead of a "final" Stunner. Afterwards, Austin leaves two cans of beer in the center of the ring to say goodbye.

Vince McMahon def. The Undertaker ("Buried Alive" match). Ahead of a video package for this match, the *SmackDown!* announcers say goodbye to "Stone Cold" Steve Austin. Tazz then offers his keys to victory. For The Undertaker, it's his experience and submission holds. For McMahon, the thug believes Vince must stay away from the grave and lean on his unmatched confidence. With the grave and equipment around the entrance, the "Deadman" can't ride his motorcycle out tonight. Instead, he walks out to watch as McMahon enters the ring, his hands clasped in prayer. He says another prayer in a corner before the biker decks him. That busts open the WWE owner before The Undertaker goes to work with a flurry of fists. Trying to one-up Shawn Michaels, Vince pours blood from his forehead. Only a minute into the match, he's wearing a crimson mask as the biker pulls him back crotch-first into the ring post. A second shot to the grapefruits follows before McMahon rolls out to the floor. There, the

"Deadman" introduces his bloodied face to the announce table. He dedicates his next shots to his wife before choking the WWE owner with a camera cable. The Undertaker follows up with a monitor shot to the skull. He warns everyone that we are just getting started, turning over the table and punching Vince some more. After he rolls McMahon into the squared circle, the biker heads to the dirt mount by the entrance to grab a steel shovel. Vince just manages to stand up only to be blasted with the shovel. Cole says that all that's left is for the "Deadman" to bury McMahon. That's not what The Undertaker wants, though. He drapes the WWE owner's foot on the ring steps base before driving the top onto them. Afterwards, he carries Vince up to the gravesite. Before he can shove McMahon into the already dug grave, the WWE owner slows the biker with a handful of dirt to the eyes. A low blow and shovel shot to the face then knocks the "Deadman" into the grave. He can't keep The Undertaker down. Grabbing the boss, the biker drags him into the grave and heads toward the loading truck. When he tries to open the door, a fireball hits his face. Kane is behind the attack and leads his brother to the grave, shoving him in and waking up Vince. After the "Big Red Machine" takes the biker's headband, McMahon operates the loader, dumping a mountain of dirt onto the "Deadman" for the victory.

Goldberg def. Triple H (with Ric Flair) (World Title match). Following a video package for the match, Triple H heads to the ring in his long shorts attire. JR informs fans that he's never won at Survivor Series. When Goldberg comes out, Ross says the longer the match goes, the worse for the already injured champion. He tries to get the win immediately with a Spear before the bell rings, but Flair distracts Earl Hebner and he doesn't see Bill with the match in hand. The intense superstar handles things personally, knocking Ric out to the floor before whipping Hunter into the announce table and ring steps. A slam on the barricade follows, Goldberg limping after Helmsley. When they get in the ring, the champion slams "the Game". He attempts to follow up with a press slam, but his injured ankle gives out and he drops the challenger. "The Nature Boy" is fired up and yells at the referee while Triple H tosses Bill back out to the floor. There, Hunter whips him into the ring steps while Flair distracts Hebner. A chair shot to the injured ankle follows before Ric whips the intense superstar's ankle against the ring post. Back in the squared circle, Helmsley focuses on the injured ankle, repeatedly stomping it. When Earl admonishes him, "The Nature Boy" chokes Goldberg. "The Game" also chokes the champion until Bill starts to fight back. One shot to the ankle drops the intense superstar for Ric to get in some cheap shots at ringside. The challenger then resumes his ankle attack before applying a single leg crab. For some reason, the referee doesn't break it even when Goldberg reaches under the ropes and grabs the apron. Moments later, the champion shows signs of life, fighting free of a stretch in the ropes to clothesline Triple H. When he attempts to powerslam Hunter, the challenger slips free and chop blocks him. Helmsley dedicates his next move to Flair and teases the Figure Four Leglock. Before he can cinch it in, Bill kicks "the Game" into Hebner. Triple H doesn't care, motioning for Ric to toss him brass knuckles. Even a shot with those can't keep the intense superstar down. When he only gets a groggy two-count, Hunter elbow drops the referee. Helmsley then grabs his sledgehammer, but Goldberg sees him coming and boots him with his injured foot. He also slams "The Nature Boy" off the top rope before clotheslining the heels. With everyone else down, the champion grabs the sledgehammer. Flair gets a shot to the ribs first. Bill follows up with shots to Batista and Randy Orton's midsections when they run out for the save. Even though "the Game" surprises him with a string of strikes, the intense superstar back body drops free of a Pedigree. He teases using the sledgehammer again, but tosses it aside to Spear and Jackhammer Triple H for the three-count. The announcers don't believe it. The show ends with Bill celebrating his victory to a loud "Goldberg" chant.

For the second major PPV featuring both brands in a row, no titles changed hands. In *SmackDown!*'s case, that makes some sense considering two of the champions were in the opening Survivor Series elimination match. While not groundbreaking, the match is very fast-paced and well-constructed. From

Holly not even getting into the match before being disqualified for going after Lesnar to Morgan and Jones being protected and eliminated quickly when they did get involved, the match was well laid out and let just about everyone shine. Cena continues his babyface turn, even shaking hands with Benoit, while the "rabid wolverine" proves that he is finally ready for a main event spot. Molly and Lita then have a fine match. *Raw* has started to give their women about five-to-seven minutes on PPVs and the competitors prove capable of entertaining for that long here. Unfortunately, there's no title change and nothing special that makes this contest feel any different than the shorter weekly matches. Still, it's an improvement for fans of women's wrestling and this match is actually competitive instead of just an excuse to have two women roll around while Jerry screams about puppies. Kane and Shane predictably pound on each other once again, but considering the brutality and blade jobs to follow, the match seems lost in the shuffle. This isn't as good as their Unforgiven match and doesn't feature a jaw-dropping Shane moment. *SmackDown!*'s only title match of the night features a bland team in the Bashams that still haven't caught on against a team that is clearly imploding in Los Guerreros. There's nothing bad about the match, but the Bashams don't bring anything to the table here. This could just as easily have been on the weekly shows. The longest match of the night, the *Raw* Survivor Series match goes almost thirty minutes. Not quite as well-paced as the opener, this match features more wrestlers ready for the big stage. Everyone plays their part well, even Mark Henry who squashes Booker T before calling it a night. Michaels is the star of the match, wearing a crimson mask and facing overwhelming odds before getting taken out by Batista's illegal interference. The best match of the night, this is a solid thirty minute investment on a show lacking in quality entertainment. Vince attempts to outdo Michaels in the next match. While he bleeds more, his comeback isn't as impressive as The Undertaker destroys him for the majority of this twelve-minute match. While McMahon does score the victory, it's only thanks to interference from Kane, setting up another chapter in the brothers' storybook rivalry. The "Deadman" dominating the match is the right call and the finish is even okay as it spins the story into new (familiar) directions. Finally, Goldberg overcomes the odds as well to defend the World Title. Maybe it's seeing both Vince and Shawn in the same spot, but Bill's win over Evolution doesn't seem special. After so many brawls earlier in the night, Goldberg winning is a nice moment, but there's nothing that stands out. Considering the night and his bandaged ankle, this could have been a good night for the intense superstar to squash Helmsley in just a few minutes. Maybe switching this match with the *Raw* Survivor Series would have worked better, then "Stone Cold" could have ended the show drinking one last time. Then again, maybe the WWE wanted the show to end on a big babyface victory. At this point it's obvious that Hunter and Goldberg won't tear down the house, but the WWE has no plans for the intense superstar other than running with Evolution as his contract winds down. There is the tease of a future meeting with Lesnar earlier in the show, but on *Raw* it's "the Game" and no one else in the title picture. A disappointing PPV, the pieces are all there, but they don't come together tonight. The Survivor Series elimination matches are the best parts of the evening. Also, take a minute and look at the crimson mask and pools of blood Vince leaves around the ring. It's not the most gruesome in wrestling history, but considering it's the owner of the company, it's quite impressive how much McMahon bleeds here.

Monday Night Raw

November 17, 2003
Beaumont, TX
Announcers: Jim Ross, Jerry "the King" Lawler, Randy Orton (briefly)

The show opens with Eric Bischoff spray painting over a picture of "Stone Cold" Steve Austin. A video package for the "rattlesnake" then plays after his team lost last night and the "rattlesnake" lost his general manager job. Live, Eric is standing in the ring with his Survivor Series team looking at the pair of beer cans "Stone Cold" left last night. Bischoff calls it the last legacy of Austin before stomping the cans. Tonight, the once again solo GM says it's a new beginning for those who supported him and the end for those who didn't. He's going to grant a favor to everyone on his team last night, but before anyone gets a chance to cash in one of those, the rest of Evolution head to the squared circle. Triple H believes he speaks for everyone in the arena when he congratulates Eric. However, he believes without Evolution, Bischoff wouldn't be the solo GM tonight. Eric sees where he's going and agrees to give Hunter a World Title match any time he wants. Helmsley appreciates that, but he cautions the GM that Goldberg is a dangerous animal who doesn't follow the rules. Instead of a singles match, "the Game" proposes to face Bill in a three-on-one handicap match. Bischoff loves it and signs the match for Evolution tonight.

Booker T def. Mark Henry (with Theodore Long). After Henry eliminated him last night, Booker comes out to a big pop looking for revenge. He starts fast, punching and chopping the big heel. A side kick doubles over Mark, but the five-time champion can't put him down before the "World's Strongest Man" clotheslines Booker T to the canvas. When Henry picks him up for a vertical suplex, the babyface slips free and locks on a sleeper hold. Although he drops to one knee, the "World's Strongest Man" has the presence of mind to fall back into a corner, crushing Booker. The five-time champion remains on the attack, but when he sets up Mark for a Scissors Kick, Long grabs his foot. That lets Henry club and toss around Booker T ahead of a neck wrench. The babyface eventually fights free, but one big shot puts him back down for an elbow drop and two-count before Mark returns to his submission hold. This time, Booker elbows out only to be crushed in a corner. When the big heel attempts a second charge, the five-time champion dodges and stuns him with a pair of kicks. A Scissors Kick finally puts the "World's Strongest Man" down for a hometown spinaroonie and top rope missile dropkick for a near fall. Mark answers with a powerslam, but Booker T also just kicks out. After countering another corner charge, the babyface rolls up Henry and steals the win with his feet on the ropes. Jerry calls him a criminal.

Garrison Cade/Mark Jindrak def. La Resistance (Rene Dupree/Rob Conway). The new iteration of La Resistance, Conway now wearing matching trunks, attacks the babyfaces as soon as they enter the ring. It doesn't take Cade and Jindrak long to chase them out to the floor. While the heels regroup, Garrison dedicates the match to the armed forces. Afterwards, Mark impresses with a springboard clothesline until Conway cheap shots him. That gives La Resistance control of the contest, clubbing Jindrak in their corner and making quick tags. He escapes by back suplexing Dupree. Back in, Cade back body drops Rene and tosses Rob out to the floor. He nearly scores the victory with a clothesline to Dupree afterwards, but Conway just makes the save. Once the babyfaces knock him back out to the floor, they score the win with a Garrison lift up and Mark dropkick to Rene.

After a commercial break, JR tries to interview Shawn Michaels via video. Eric Bischoff interrupts backstage to end the interview. Shawn doesn't take kindly to that. He says he might not have seen eye-to-eye with "Stone Cold" Steve Austin, but they both love this business. He blames Eric for taking away

Austin's job, but Bischoff corrects him. He didn't cost "Stone Cold" his job. Michaels did. The GM tells Shawn to go home and think about that because he doesn't have anything for him tonight. Security then escorts the "Heartbreak Kid" out of the arena.

Still shots from Kane and Shane McMahon's "Ambulance" match last night are shown. Due to the "Big Red Machine's" interference in Vince McMahon and The Undertaker's match last night, the monster will be on *SmackDown!* this week.

Backstage, Test thanks Scott Steiner for getting them a World Tag Title shot tonight. Scott says it's his favor that got them the match. As such, he wants a fresh start with the bodyguard. From now on, he's not Test's property. The bodyguard agrees to that, but he's keeping Stacy Keibler. After he smacks a drink out of her hand, Stacy says she'll do anything he says.

Rob Van Dam def. Ric Flair (Intercontinental Title match) by disqualification. Pre-match, Chad Patton tells RVD that Eric Bischoff has banned the Five-Star Frog Splash tonight. Randy Orton then joins the announce table to praise "The Nature Boy" and brag about giving Mark Cuban an RKO. Ric opens the match chopping and elbowing Rob, the announcers talking about the Intercontinental Title being one of the few titles that Flair hasn't held. Van Dam briefly takes the fight out to the floor, but a poke to the eyes slows him for more chops. When RVD tries to head upstairs to turn the tide, "The Nature Boy" shoves him out to the floor. There, he whips Rob into the ring steps while Orton threatens the "legendary" announce team because JR won't get off his back. When the fight returns to the ring, Van Dam surprises Ric with a spinning heel kick for a two-count. The heel answers with a chop block and Figure Four Leglock. It takes him a few seconds, but RVD manages to turn over the hold, forcing Flair to break it. "The Nature Boy" remains on the attack, chop blocking Rob again. Van Dam's legs are his strong point and he absorbs Ric's attacks to springboard cross body block him. When RVD connects with a top rope flying kick and rolling thunder, Randy heads to the squared circle. Van Dam meets him with a pair of kicks, but while the referee's back is turned, Flair low blows the champion. Incensed, "The Nature Boy" yells at Patton. RVD capitalizes with a spinning heel kick before heading upstairs. He doesn't care what Eric says and sets up for a Five-Star Frog Splash. Unfortunately, Orton recovers and sweeps his legs, crotching the champion ahead of an RKO and the disqualification. Post-match, the "Legend Killer" admires the Intercontinental Title and puts it around his waist before dropping it on Rob.

Backstage, Jonathan Coachman interrupts Rosey and The Hurricane making shadow puppets to tell them that their superhero act will "never fly". When he enters Eric Bischoff's office, the GM wants Coach to help him advertise next week's show featuring the return of "Raw Roulette". Coachman loves it.

After a commercial break, Chris Jericho is back with the Highlight Reel. He says it isn't his fault that "Stone Cold" Steve Austin was terrible at his job, but it is his fault that the "rattlesnake" is gone. He brags about hitting Shawn Michaels with a chair for Randy Orton to score the victory. He then introduces his guest, Lita. Y2J feels so bad that she lost last night and her dream didn't come true. Lita has had enough. She doesn't want to be insulted by Jericho. The Canadian heel tells her that she's got the wrong idea. He wants to make her feel better and he's got someone waiting to do just that. The extreme diva doesn't want to see Christian, but it's not him. It's Matt Hardy whose contract just expired on *SmackDown!*. Lita is happy to see him and gives her boyfriend a hug and kiss. Matt has something important to ask her, dropping to a knee. Before he can ask his question, Molly Holly steps onto the stage to ask what she has to do to get some respect. She complains that despite beating Lita last night, for some reason the show continues to revolve around the extreme diva. Jericho likes her passion and wants to take advantage of it. He wants Molly to team up with a partner of her choosing against Hardy and Lita. Holly picks Eric Bischoff.

After a commercial break, Eric Bischoff complains about Molly Holly picking him as her tag team partner. She was just following what Eric said about finishing off his enemies. Bischoff likes the sound of that, but he ups the stakes. If the heels win, Lita will be fired for good. If she wins, however, she'll get one more Women's Title shot.

The Dudley Boyz def. Scott Steiner/Test (with Stacy Keibler) (World Tag Title match). Stacy isn't happy as she's forced to accompany the heels to the ring. The fans already want tables before anyone locks up. Instead, Test hammers D-Von down in a corner. Dudley answers with a spinning back elbow for a two-count. Scott tags in afterwards to trade shots with D-Von. Bubba Ray enters the match moments later and scores a two-count with a sidewalk slam. When Keibler cheers, Test yells and forces her to sit in a chair at ringside. He then cheap shots Bubba ahead of a Steiner elbow drop and two-count. After "Big Poppa Pump" does some pushups, he lures D-Von into the ring to distract Jack Doan while the bodyguard chokes Bubba Ray. He then illegally enters the ring to hammer Dudley and hook a reverse chin lock. Stacy pounds the mat to cheer on Bubba and distract Test. It works as Bubba Ray comes back to life for a Bubba Bomb. Moments later, D-Von gets the tag to fight both challengers, scoring a pair of two-counts before Scott breaks his cover following a leaping shoulderblock. Bubba joins his half-brother afterwards to chase the heels out of the ring. When Test returns, Bubba Ray escapes his pumphandle slam to drop the bodyguard on the canvas for a wassup drop. Although Bubba tells his half-brother to get a table, Steiner returns and drops both champions. Frustrated, he gets a title belt, but the Dudleys see him coming and drop him with a double-team neckbreaker. Before they can score the win, the bodyguard returns to drop Bubba Ray and full nelson slam D-Von. He wants the title belt, but Keibler refuses to give it to him. While Test is distracted arguing, the Dudleys recover to 3D him for the win.

Backstage, Lita is so happy to see Matt Hardy again. She wonders what his question was, but he says he wants it to be special and in front of the fans like their first kiss. When he walks away, Lita turns to Trish Stratus. They hope Matt proposes.

Eric Bischoff/Molly Holly def. Lita/Matt Hardy Version 1.0. Lita's future is on the line here as the announcers inform everyone that this is an intergender match, meaning anyone can fight anyone. Eric doesn't look like he's here for a fight as he stands on the apron in his suit watching Molly drop the extreme diva on the canvas and stretch her. Lita responds with a reverse DDT to put both women down. Holly is closer to her corner and tags Bischoff. When he tries to grab the extreme diva, she slaps him. Lita attempts to tag Matt afterwards, but he drops off the apron for Eric to recover and slam Lita back to the canvas for the three-count. Post-match, the GM tells the extreme diva that she's fired before Hardy asks her how can she be so selfish. All she had to do was join Matt on *SmackDown!*, but she spent all her time training. Since her career means so much to her, Hardy is done with Lita.

Val Venis (with Lance Storm) def. Rico (with Miss Jackie). The babyfaces are out first and accompanied by two women. When Rico comes out, Lawler tells JR to get out of his bad mood and appreciate Jackie's beauty. Inside the ring, Val shoulder blocks, chops, and elbows Rico for the early advantage. He follows up with a suplex, but when he goes for a second, the flamboyant superstar flips free for a back stabber knee drop. Rico gets under the adult star's skin rubbing his chest before unloading with a step up kick. More kicks and a knee lift score the flamboyant superstar a two-count, as does an elbow drop. When Venis tries to fight back, Rico flattens him with a clothesline. He then locks on a cobra clutch while the announcers argue, JR not worried about Eric Bischoff firing him. "The King" says he's in "Stone Cold" shock. Eventually, "the big Valbowski" comes back to life with a string of strikes. When the heel tries to reapply his sleeper hold, Val escapes with a sit-out powerbomb for a near fall. Rico answers with a thumb to the eye and twisting neckbreaker for his own close two-count. He attempts to follow up with a corner charge, but runs into a boot and chokeslam for another near fall. Frustrated, the adult star hammers the flamboyant superstar before heading upstairs. When Jackie tries to stop him, Venis kicks her down to the floor. Rico tries to capitalize with a top rope attack, but is distracted by his valet backing into Lance's crotch, Jackie slipping out of her top. "The big Valbowski" capitalizes, shoving his opponent down for a Money Shot and the win. Post-match, the babyfaces grind with their girls.

Backstage, Lita is a mess as she drops her keys and bag. Christian stops her. He tells her that he used his favor to get the extreme diva her job back. She really appreciates it and leaves with Christian to talk about what a tough day it's been.

The "Stone Cold" Steve Austin video package plays again.

Mark Cuban shoving Eric Bischoff and Randy Orton giving the Dallas Mavericks owner an RKO last night replays. Afterwards, Randy tells Evolution that he just cashed in his favor for an Intercontinental Title match at Armageddon. He's looking to join the list of greats including the Honky Tonk Man. Triple H takes offense until Orton adds him to the list. Hunter then tells the rest of Evolution that they need to focus tonight on Goldberg. He's fine with his stablemates crippling and maiming Bill, but Helmsley wants the pin.

Further backstage, Chris Jericho stops to talk to Trish Stratus. She's distraught and wants him to explain why he set up her friend earlier. She's disgusted by him leading Lita into her match tonight and Matt Hardy dumping her. Trish doesn't want to get to know this Y2J. Jericho pleads innocence. He thought Matt was going to propose. When it comes to Stratus, Y2J says they have chemistry, and he would never disrespect her or her friends. Jericho can't stop thinking about her and doesn't want that to stop. The couple then slowly kisses to a nice pop from the crowd.

Batista/Randy Orton/Triple H (with Ric Flair) def. Goldberg. The heels are out together as a unified force. Goldberg follows, notably just stepping onto the stage rather than having the cameras follow him all the way from his locker room. His leg still bandaged, the World Champion shoulder blocks Randy to start the match. After knocking the other heels off the apron, he presses Orton overhead and tosses him out onto his partners at ringside. Back in the squared circle, the "Legend Killer" slows Bill with a thumb to the eye. Batista then tags in for the intense superstar to punch and clothesline. A powerslam follows for a two-count. Even though "the Animal" kicks out, Triple H illegally enters the ring to pummel Goldberg. He tags in moments later, but the champion suplexes him and sets up for a Spear. Before he can hit it, Ric trips Bill. A high knee from "the Game" follows before Batista returns for a corner clothesline. Randy also gets his shots in and dropkicks the intense superstar. When Hunter returns, Goldberg Spears him out of nowhere. Clotheslines follow to Orton and "the Animal", but when the champion sets up Helmsley for a Jackhammer, the "Legend Killer" hits him from behind. Bill absorbs his and Batista's shots to double clothesline the heels. Triple H answers with a facebuster ahead of an RKO. "The Animal" also delivers his finisher, Batista Bombing the intense superstar ahead of a Pedigree for the three-count. Post-match, Orton and Batista hold Goldberg for Hunter to grab a chair and warn the champion that he's cashing in his chips for a World Title match next week. He then wedges Bill's head into the chair, but Kane surprises everyone walking to the ring. Evolution wants nothing to do with him and flees the ring before the "Big Red Machine" Chokeslams the intense superstar to end the show.

SmackDown!
November 20, 2003
Houston, TX
Announcers: Michael Cole, Tazz

The show opens with Sable, sporting a barely there dress, helping Vince McMahon down the aisle. He's on crutches and heavily bandaged as he struggles to get into the squared circle. He asks for a little decency for once before recapping all of the damage he suffered at the hands of The Undertaker at Survivor Series. It led to him getting a transfusion, concussion, and shattered ankle. The fans love it. Despite all the punishment he received, Vince never gave up hope. He thanks Kane for serving as his "avenging angel" before noting that the WWE owner feels invincible and untouchable. When he starts to leave the ring, John Cena makes his entrance. He's upset that McMahon is stealing his catchphrases. Only Cena is "untouchable". He proceeds to get the Houston crowd on his side talking about Yao Ming. He then calls Vince stupid and says Sable is only with him for the money, implying that John is also sleeping with her. Cole is excited that McMahon got "punked out".

After a commercial break, Brock Lesnar blames his Survivor Series team for his loss Sunday night. He even blames them for making him tap-out to Chris Benoit. The WWE Champion believes he deserves respect and he's going to get it. Earlier tonight, he spoke to Paul Heyman and every member of the team is going to get a chance to redeem themselves. Lesnar expects Nathan Jones especially to take care of Benoit. Brock likes that Jones is so ugly that he is going to stand in his corner tonight. He then tells Big Show to get revenge on John Cena tonight for pinning him at Survivor Series. The giant is happy to get him because he wants a piece of the rapping superstar.

Rey Mysterio def. Akio. Rey kicks off the in-ring action, popping out of the stage for this fast-paced match. After trading strikes, Akio runs up the masked man in a corner only to run into a boot and twisting head scissors. The heel answers by whipping Mysterio out to the floor face-first. That gets him a two-count back in the squared circle. Afterwards, Akio stretches Rey's arms with a modified surfboard. When the masked man fights free, the heel flips him over with a vicious clothesline for another near fall. He then applies a neck wrench. Picking up the pace, a corner heel kick follows before Akio heads upstairs. Mysterio spots him and trips the heel, crotching him. Rey follows up with a springboard seated senton and low dropkick. A tornado DDT out of the corner afterwards gets the masked man a two-count. He teases a bulldog, but rolls up the heel for another near fall. Unfortunately, he misses a dropkick and Akio capitalizes with a spinning heel kick for a two-count. He heads upstairs afterwards for a corkscrew moonsault, but Mysterio rolls out of the way. A head scissors onto the middle rope then sets up Akio for a 619 and West Coast Pop on his head for the victory.

Backstage, Paul Heyman is on the phone. He stops talking to take credit for *SmackDown!* magazine, being read by a worker. He then passes Shaniqua whipping The Basham Brothers. They are bound and gagged as the dominatrix beats them and offers to give Paul a few shots. He passes before finding Shannon Moore. He doesn't blame Moore for Matt Hardy leaving *SmackDown!*. In fact, he blames Matt leaving on the change in administration between himself and Stephanie McMahon. Tonight, he promises to make Shannon an even bigger star than Hardy, signing him to a match with Matt Morgan.

Matt Morgan def. Shannon Moore. The announcers don't believe that this isn't punishment for Moore. He's giving up almost two feet and a hundred pounds, but he doesn't back down. He opens the match with a string of fists, but when he attempts a tilt-a-whirl head scissors, Matt drops the former MFer on the canvas. Fists, chokes, and slams follow before Shannon runs into a big boot. Toying with the smaller superstar, Morgan tosses him around and out of the ring. After he heaves Moore back into the squared circle, Matt teases taking the three-count. Instead, he picks up Shannon's head at the last second to give him a Sit-Out Powerbomb for the win.

A *SmackDown!* ad featuring Sable advises fans to "smack your tv".

A-Train def. Bradshaw. The hairy heel is out first and he doesn't wait for Bradshaw to get into the ring before clubbing him. When they finally get in the squared circle, the big Texan scores a two-count with a swinging neckbreaker. A-Train begs off and hides behind Nick Patrick to cheap shot Bradshaw. His tactic works as he scores a near fall with a big splash moments later. He also gets a two-count with a slam and elbow drop before hooking a reverse chin lock. Although he fights free, the big Texan runs into a back elbow. When the hairy heel attempts to follow up with a powerslam, Bradshaw slips free and DDTs him. That puts both men down for a Patrick six-count. Once up, the big Texan punches, kicks, and clotheslines A-Train. A back suplex puts the hairy heel down long enough for Bradshaw to head upstairs for a flying shoulderblock and near fall. He then clotheslines A-Train out to the floor where the hairy heel surprises him with a Derailer. Instead of taking the count-out victory, he breaks the referee's count and rolls the big Texan back into the ring for a pair of two-counts. Bradshaw responds with his own roll-ups, even putting his feet on the ropes at one point for a near fall. When he goes for the Clothesline for Hell though, A-Train beats the big Texan to the punch with a bicycle kick for the three-count.

Chris Benoit def. Nathan Jones (with Brock Lesnar). Brock is out first, the fans taunting him that he tapped out. Benoit follows, chasing the WWE Champion from the ring. Jones is out last, glaring at "the Crippler" as he marches out to boot him from the squared circle. After Benoit catches his breath, he dodges a rookie charge that sees Nathan fall out to the floor. Lesnar tells him to get back into the ring. He listens and powerslams the "rabid wolverine" for a two-count. He slows the pace afterwards with a chin lock. When that doesn't get him the win, Jones pounds Benoit in a corner ahead of a sidewalk slam and near fall. He returns to the chin lock while Brock riles up the crowd. When the rookie tries to finish off "the Crippler" with a slam, Benoit flips free. Moments later, he dodges a big boot that sees Nathan straddle the top rope. Although the rookie fights free of a sharpshooter, the "rabid wolverine" catches him with a trio of German suplexes. A top rope missile dropkick follows, but Chris misses a diving headbutt. When Jones tries to press slam him, Benoit counters with a Crippler Crossface. Lesnar tries to make the save, but "the Crippler" knocks him off the apron before returning to his submission hold for the tap-out victory. Post-match, Brock hits Benoit with the WWE Title. Before he can inflict any more damage, Hardcore Holly jumps out of the crowd and attacks the champion, whipping him into the guardrail and locking him in a full nelson until Paul Heyman leads police officers down to ringside to arrest the returning superstar. Paul calls Holly a disgrace before telling him that he's going to jail. Lesnar has a suggestion for the general manager and Heyman agrees. As of this moment, Hardcore is suspended indefinitely.

After a commercial break, Kane steps into the ring to deliver the eulogy for The Undertaker, the man he buried alive Sunday night. However, the "Big Red Machine" says the biker has been dead for a while—ever since he became weak like the people. Kane says his brother was a fraud and no monster. The "Big Red Machine" laughs about burying the imposter and tells him to rest in peace.

The Lugz Boot of the Week is Tajiri beating Jamie Noble on *Sunday Night Heat* thanks to Akio and Sakoda.

Tajiri def. Jamie Noble (Cruiserweight Title match). Mike Sparks stops Akio and Sakoda in the aisle and orders them to head backstage. That evens the playing field and Jamie capitalizes with strikes and a neckbreaker for an early two-count. When he attempts a corner head scissors, Tajiri tosses him crotch-first onto the top rope ahead of a kick to the back of the skull. At ringside, the champion whips Noble's arm into the steel post for a two-count. He follows up with a string of kicks and a hammerlock, targeting the injured arm. The challenger impresses, picking up the "Japanese Buzzsaw" for a Samoan drop to escape. He follows up with clotheslines from his good arm, but one kick puts Jamie back down. He does manager to avoid a handspring back elbow ahead of a la magistral roll-up for a near fall. When Tajiri tries to answer with a Tarantula, Noble shoves him out to the apron. There, the champion responds with a kick to the face, but when he climbs up the ropes, the challenger tosses him to the canvas. The two men then trade counters, the "Japanese Buzzsaw" escaping a Tiger Bomb with a slingshot into the corner. When Noble flies back, Tajiri kicks him for a near fall. He attempts to finish off the challenger with a Buzzsaw Kick, but Jamie dodges and scores his own close two-count with a Tiger Bomb before the champion drapes his foot on the bottom rope. That brings out Nidia with a walking cane. Her slowly walking down the aisle distracts Noble long enough for Tajiri to roll him up for the victory. Post-match, Jamie tells his girlfriend that he almost had the "Japanese Buzzsaw".

Backstage, Shelton Benjamin thanks Paul Heyman on behalf of The World's Greatest Tag Team. Shelton doesn't blame Paul for costing them the WWE Tag Titles. He blames Los Guerreros for injuring him and stealing his belt. Tonight, they plan on paying back the Guerreros. Charlie Haas adds, "what he said".

Los Guerreros def. The World's Greatest Tag Team. The babyfaces get a big pop as they come out in a yellow and blue lowrider this week. The heels go right after them, but Los Guerreros repel their attack until Haas surprises Chavo with a clothesline. Shelton then targets his leg before Charlie tags in to choke and kick the younger Guerrero. Haas follows up with a Boston crab. When Chavo reaches the ropes, Benjamin returns for a few quick shots. Back in, Charlie continues working on Guerrero's leg, locking on the Haas of Pain. That brings in Eddie for the break. Afterwards, Chavo catches an illegally entering Shelton with a spinning head scissors. "Latino Heat" gets the hot tag afterwards to fight both men and monkey flip Benjamin into Haas. Shelton answers with a powerslam, but Chavo returns to tornado DDT the heel. Charlie responds with a German suplex before Benjamin back body drops Eddie out to the floor. Haas tries to sneak attack Chavo, but he dodges his charge ahead of a second rope bulldog. While Chavo stomps Shelton, "Latino Heat" returns to Frog Splash Charlie for the win. Post-match, Benjamin knocks Eddie out to the floor before Haas chop blocks his nephew. A super kick follows to the younger Guerrero before Charlies slides Shelton a chair. While Haas holds off "Latino Heat", Benjamin applies a modified Haas of Pain, stretching Chavo's knee with the chair. Eventually, Eddie chases off the heels with another chair, but Chavo still yells at his uncle and asks where he was.

In a prerecorded vignette, Ernest Miller gets the key to the city of Boise, Idaho. In appreciation of this fake award, "the Cat" gives the executives a special "Cat" coin. They try to dance like him, but Ernest shows them how it's done. Cole is looking forward to Miller's debut next week, dancing around until Tazz tells him to sit down.

Afterwards, trainers are checking on Chavo Guerrero's knee. Despite being in agony, he sits up and says something isn't right with Eddie Guerrero. He notes his uncle has been letting him down and tells Eddie to leave him alone. When the trainer can't give him a shot for the returning pain, Chavo says he's going to have to start taking care of himself.

Further backstage, Vince McMahon tells Big Show to take out John Cena tonight. He doesn't want to see the rapping superstar ever again.

John Cena def. Big Show. Vince McMahon's pep talk works as the giant is fired up and waiting for Cena. The rapping superstar wisely leads Show on a chase around the ring before baseball slide kicking him. He follows up with a shoulderblock, but one clothesline turns the tide. Big Show adds a chop to the chest and scoop slam. Kicks and a headbutt follow before the giant clubs John's ribs. He also stretches Cena's face ahead of a leg drop onto the standing rapping superstar. Fortunately, John is close enough to the ropes for the break. That just gets him hammered and tossed around some more. Even though Show chops and stands on him, Cena won't stop fighting. He answers with his own strikes before dodging a boot that sees Big Show straddling the top rope. A throwback gets the rapping superstar a two-count and sends him out to the floor for a steel chair. When Brian Hebner takes it away, John gives the giant a low blow. Show recovers quickly to pound down Cena until Hebner gets in the way. The rapping superstar capitalizes with a shot from his steel chain wrapped fist, but he can't hold up Big Show for an FU. Both men collapse to the canvas, but the giant recovers first and teases slamming John through the announce table. Instead, he flings Cena back into the ring post. Instead of making the cover, Show grabs the ring steps and hurls them at the rapping superstar. Fortunately, John dodges. When Big Show returns to the ring, he accidentally kicks the referee out to the floor. The giant doesn't care, giving Cena a sidewalk slam. He attempts to use the ring steps again, but the rapping superstar dropkicks his knee, dropping Show face-first onto the steel. After catching his breath, John slams the steps into Big Show's face for Nick Patrick to run out and count to three for the rapping superstar victory. Cole wonders when his luck will run out.

Monday Night Raw
November 24, 2003
Salt Lake City, UT
Announcers: Jim Ross, Jerry "the King" Lawler

Following the intro video and fireworks, Eric Bischoff is in the ring with the Raw Roulette wheel and two showgirls. The general manager says he couldn't think of a better way to make life better for the dull fans of Utah than the return of Raw Roulette. On top of his giant wheel, he promises fans a World Title rematch tonight when Goldberg defends the championship against Triple H. Before Bischoff can spin the wheel, Shawn Michaels interrupts to a big pop. He tells Eric that he's repaying the favor for the GM interrupting his interview last week. After taking a week to look himself in the mirror, Shawn says he didn't cost "Stone Cold" Steve Austin his job at Survivor Series. The "Heartbreak Kid" did everything he could in his match and if it wasn't for Bischoff and Evolution, the "rattlesnake" would still be here. That brings out Batista. Shawn invites him to keep walking and join him in the ring. "The Animal" isn't worried about Michaels, telling him that he has "bigger chunks in his bowel movements". Batista then takes credit for ending Austin's career. The "Heartbreak Kid" has heard enough and tries to go after "the Animal", but Eric stops him. He's already done enough for Salt Lake City, so he's going to sign the duo to a match at Armageddon. The GM then notices that the wheel is sitting on "Bischoff's Choice". To give everyone a preview of the PPV match, he signs a tag match tonight pitting Batista and Ric Flair against Shawn and his WrestleMania XIX opponent, Chris Jericho.

Victoria def. Lita ("Steel Cage" match). As Lita heads to the ring, Eric Bischoff interrupts from the Titantron. He mocks the extreme diva for having a rough week, but is glad Christian used his favor to save her job because it'll be more fun to mess with her. That starts when he has Molly Holly spin the wheel to decide Lita's fate tonight. The Women's Champion is happy to spin, the wheel landing on a "Steel Cage" match, the first featuring two women in WWE history. Victoria doesn't seem to care, marching down the aisle, rubbing her hair, and stepping into the cage. Lita immediately shoots her into the steel twice. When she tries to DDT her, the "black widow" escapes and clotheslines the extreme diva. A catapult into the cage and spinning side slam follow for a two-count before Victoria tries to leave. Lita grabs and pounds her ahead of a head scissors takedown. After she topples the "black widow" with a drop toe hold, the extreme diva heads up the cage. Victoria follows her and flings Lita down to the canvas for a two-count. She then sets up for a Widow's Peak, but the extreme diva slips free and clotheslines her opponent. Unfortunately, she slips down the cage when she tries to escape, the "black widow" capitalizing with a spear into the steel. When she climbs up a corner, Lita powerbombs Victoria. A Moonsault follows to the standing "black widow". When the extreme diva tries to run out the door, Matt Hardy rushes down to slam it into his ex-girlfriend's face. That gives Victoria the victory. Before Matt can do any more damage, Christian runs out for the save.

Backstage, Eric Bischoff's showgirls are distracted by Randy Orton. He calls himself the next Intercontinental Champion before Eric notes that the wheel landed on a "Legend Killer" match. He's got a legend lined up for Randy tonight. When he leaves, Rosey and The Hurricane fly in to find out what kind of match they have tonight. The wheel lands on a "Capture the Midget" match. He introduces the superheroes to Fernando, a little man who runs out from behind the wheel and out of the office. The Hurricane doesn't believe this match is very politically correct and threatens not to compete. Bischoff tells him that's his choice, but the match could be a "loser gets fired" contest. That motivates the superhero and he runs after Fernando, leaving Rosey behind.

Randy Orton def. Sgt. Slaughter ("Legend Killer" match). As Slaughter heads to the ring, the announcers talk about him wrestling Randy's father and grandfather. The sergeant claims to have beaten both, but Lawler isn't so sure. He tries to get a win early here tonight with a Cobra Clutch, but Orton reaches the ropes for the break. The legend follows up with a gutbuster for a two-count before the "Legend Killer" turns the tide with a dropkick. When he locks on a sleeper hold, Slaughter reverses it back into the Cobra Clutch. Once again, Randy reaches the ropes. While Jack Doan tries to get the legend to make the break, Orton delivers a questionably low blow ahead of an RKO for the win. Post-match, the "Legend Killer" stomps Slaughter until Rob Van Dam runs out for the save, chasing Randy from the ring with a series of kicks.

A video package for the Goldberg/Triple H feud plays.

After a commercial break, Lance Storm and Val Venis are waiting on their dates. Val tells Storm that the girls are a little more conservative than they are used to so they'll have to take things slow. When the girls arrive, they are concerned that the wrestlers are wild. Lance assures them that they aren't, but Rosey and The Hurricane run past with a net on a pole trying to catch Fernando.

Further backstage, Jonathan Coachman compliments Ric Flair on having the fastest selling DVD in WWE history. "The Nature Boy" is already fired up, yelling about Randy Orton's victory, his and Batista's match with Shawn Michaels, and Triple H winning back the World Title tonight.

Even further backstage, Matt Hardy assures Eric Bischoff that their plan went off perfectly last week. He's not mad that Lita is back on the show. The GM offers to get him a new drink, using "Stone Cold" Steve Austin's autobiography as a coaster. He then taunts Austin and wishes him a happy Thanksgiving before Matt spins the wheel for his match. When it lands on "Strange Bedfellows", Hardy assures Eric that he's all man. Bischoff tells him the wheel doesn't mean that and it'll make for a great match next.

Footage of Goldberg and Triple H fighting on the PS2 *SmackDown!: Here Comes the Pain* videogame plays.

Bubba Ray Dudley/Garrison Cade def. Christian/Matt Hardy Version 1.0 ("Strange Bedfellows" match). The announcers are surprised to see the pairings here for this match, wondering how Christian and Hardy will be able to work together. After they exchange words, Bubba clubs Matt. He answers with a running clothesline and tags in Christian. Dudley welcomes him with a sidewalk slam for a two-count. Garrison then tags in to punch and trap the Canadian heel in a side headlock. While the fans chant for a table, Cade pounds on Christian in a neutral corner. A running bulldog gets him a two-count before Christian turns the tide with a backward head slam on the top rope. That scores him a near fall as well while JR talks about how disappointed he is that Hardy dumped Lita on live television. He should be more upset that we didn't get any Matt Facts as he entered the ring. Eventually, Garrison surprises the heel with a flying shoulderblock off the ropes before giving Bubba Ray the tag. He works over Christian, planting him with a Samoan drop, but misses a second rope senton splash. When the heel tries to tag Matt, Hardy drops off the apron and taunts Christian. Dudley capitalizes with a Bubba Bomb as Matt heads backstage. Before Bubba Ray can score the win, Cade tags himself in for a top rope flying elbow drop and the three-count. Post-match, Bubba is confused, but Garrison tries to calm him down by giving Dudley his World Tag Title. When Bubba Ray attempts to take it, Cade holds it tight, prompting Dudley to yank it away and threaten the rookie.

After a commercial break, Shawn Michaels tells Terri that the odds are stacked against him again tonight with Chris Jericho as a partner, but he's used to it. After expressing confidence in himself, Shawn tells Terri that there's a midget looking up her dress. It's Fernando and the interviewer joins The Hurricane and Rosey in chasing after him.

Goldberg def. Triple H (with Ric Flair) (World Title match) by disqualification. The challenger is out first for the only non-Raw Roulette match of the night. Goldberg gets his full entrance tonight, notably not wearing a cast on his leg for this big rematch. When the bell rings, the two men jaw with each other in the center of the ring. As soon as the champion turns to yell at Flair, Hunter hits him from behind. Triple H gets in several shots until Bill back body drops him and chases the challenger out to the floor. The intense superstar follows right behind, clotheslining Helmsley. When they return to the ring, "the Game" elbows Goldberg and shoots him back out to the floor for a whip into the ring steps. That hurts the champion's shoulder and gives Triple H a target. He goes to work hammering the shoulder ahead of a knee drop to the face. After Ric chokes Bill with his jacket, the challenger scores a two-count. The intense superstar refuses to quit, answering with fists and a press slam off the top rope when Hunter heads upstairs. A side slam puts Helmsley down afterwards and Goldberg sets up for a Spear, but "The Game" rolls out to the floor. While the fans boo, the champion follows for more right hands. When they return to the squared circle, Triple H counters a back body drop with a face buster. A high knee then gets him a near fall. Heading back upstairs, the challenger makes the mistake of leaping into a boot to the jaw. The champion follows up with a military press into a powerslam. "The Nature Boy" tries to intervene, but he gets decked. Randy Orton then runs out to attempt an RKO, but Bill shoves him and Spears the "Legend Killer". Once he's down, Helmsley takes advantage of Mike Chioda getting Orton out of the ring to give the intense superstar a low blow and Pedigree. Before he wins back the World Title, fire explodes and Kane marches down the aisle. "The Game" knocks him off the apron with a right hand, but turns into a Spear. The "Big Red Machine" then enters the ring and levels Goldberg with a big boot for the disqualification. Post-match, the monster hammers and Chokeslams the World Champion.

Backstage, Triple H yells at Eric Bischoff and tells him that if it wasn't for Evolution the GM wouldn't even have a job. Hunter wants his World Title back, but he's cut off by Kane standing behind him. The "Big Red Machine" wants a title match too. Eric has no choice but to give both of them a shot at the World Title in a triple threat match at Armageddon. Kane likes it, but Helmsley is less enthusiastic. When the monster leaves Bischoff's office, "the Game" seethes at the GM.

Out in the parking lot, The Hurricane continue chasing after Fernando.

Mark Henry (with Theodore Long) def. Booker T ("Salt Lake City Street Fight"). After Booker enters the ring, Eric Bischoff interrupts from the Titantron. Long is upset that Bischoff only has white showgirls. The GM promises to work on that before spinning the wheel to reveal that this match will be a "Salt Lake City Street Fight". Theodore warns the five-time champion to get ready for a beatdown. He sprints up the ramp to wait on the side of the stage to sneak attack Mark. Henry might have weapons, but Booker T sneak attacks him and takes away his stop sign. A shot from the sign doesn't knock the "World's Strongest Man" down. When they get in the ring, Mark takes away the stop sign and bends it with his bare hands. He then absorbs a shot from a two-by-four and choke to crush Booker in a corner. The five-time champion answers with a frying pan shot to the head. Once again, Henry absorbs his blows. After he slams Booker T, he bends the frying pan too before clotheslining the babyface out to the floor. There, Booker sprays him with a fire extinguisher before smashing him with it. A top rope missile dropkick follows. After he entertains the fans with a spinaroonie, the five-time champion drops the

"World's Strongest Man" with a Scissors Kick. Somehow, Mark manages to kick out. Back up, he whips Booker T into a trashcan in a corner. A second trashcan shot to the head follows for the three-count.

Following a *WWE Unscripted* ad, Eric Bischoff spins the wheel to reveal that Trish Stratus has a "Bra & Panties" match. She's not shocked. Chris Jericho offers to cash in his favor to get her out of it, but she looks at her chest and says she's got it under control. However, she wants Y2J to do the right thing tonight when he teams with Shawn Michaels. She wants him to be the man she knows he is and offers to be good to him if he's good to Shawn.

Back at the announce table, the announcers hype an upcoming "Stone Cold" Steve Austin special on UPN this Wednesday. In it, we'll hear from Austin's friends and family about his amazing career. Fernando then runs out and jumps into JR's lap. Lilian Garcia announces Ross as the winner of the "Capture the Midget" match. The Hurricane is disappointed.

Scott Steiner/Test (with Stacy Keibler) def. Rob Van Dam ("Singapore Cane" match). When RVD gets in the ring, Eric Bischoff tells him that he's already spun the wheel and Rob will compete in a handicap match. Randy Orton doesn't think that's enough for the Intercontinental Champion so Eric spins the wheel again to add Singapore canes to the mix. RVD goes right after the heels, knocking Scott off the apron before diving onto Test from the squared circle. Steiner answers with cane shots, but when he attempts a whip into the ring steps, Rob reverses it. The bodyguard slows the pace, taking his time entering the ring only to see Van Dam wail on him with his cane. He also hits and trips "Big Poppa Pump" until Test interrupts rolling thunder with a shot to the kidneys. When RVD goes after the bodyguard, he hides behind Stacy. Scott capitalizes with a shot to the back before the heels take turns battering Rob with the sticks. Van Dam will not quit, continuing to fight until Test accidentally hits Steiner with a cane. RVD follows up with a Five-Star Frog Splash, but before he can make the cover, the bodyguard returns to level him with a cane for the three-count. Post-match, Test forces Keibler to raise their hands in victory. As they leave, the bodyguard smacks Stacy's butt with a stick.

Backstage, Chris Jericho complains to Eric Bischoff about Trish Stratus being in a "Bra & Panties" match. He doesn't think that's quality entertainment. Eric thinks he's falling for her, but Y2J says he's just trying to make the show better. Bischoff tells him to worry about teaming with Shawn Michaels tonight and taking care of business for the GM. Jericho tells him that he'll do the right thing.

Trish Stratus def. Miss Jackie (with Rico) ("Bra & Panties" match). Jerry thinks Rico is competing in this match since he wears bras and panties. Instead, it's Jackie, Lawler happy to talk about her wardrobe malfunction last week. She's wearing more clothing tonight as she hammers Trish from behind. It's Stratus taking her opponent's top off first, but Jackie chokes the vixen with it. Afterwards, she ties Trish into the tree of woe to remove her top and even the match. The vixen responds with chops and attempts her handstand head scissors. Although the heel teases pulling down her pants, Stratus ends up tossing her to the canvas. When Rico hops into the ring, Trish pulls his pants off to reveal a shiny purple thong. He's not embarrassed. Jackie is moments later when Stratus dodges her boot and pulls off the heel's pants for the win. Post-match, Trish gives the fans a peek at her backside before Jackie heads out to the floor to strip off Lilian Garcia's shirt. She threatens Jackie before parading around happily, the fans cheering Lilian in her bra.

Backstage, Chris Jericho congratulates Trish Stratus. He asks if they are still on for tonight. She tells him that depends on him.

Chris Jericho/Shawn Michaels def. Batista/Ric Flair. After a commercial break, Lilian Garcia wears a WWE shirt as she introduces Evolution. Following their entrance together, Jericho and Shawn come out individually. Michaels and Ric open the match trading slaps. "The Nature Boy" can't intimidate the "Heartbreak Kid" so he doubles him over with a knee to the midsection followed by chops. Shawn responds in kind ahead of a back body drop. Y2J then tags in to score a two-count with a second rope missile dropkick. More chops see Flair fall face-first to the canvas. The smoke from the entrance fireworks fills the ring at this point while Jericho drives Ric face-first to the canvas again. When he misses a Lionsault, "The Nature Boy" tags in Batista to plaster Y2J with a spinebuster. Once the Canadian is down, Flair tags back in only to be slammed off the top rope. Michaels gets the hot tag afterwards to trade fists with Ric. When he whips him into the ropes, "The Nature Boy" busts his nose as he hits the ropes awkwardly. The show must go on and the "Heartbreak Kid" rocks Flair with a flying forearm moments later. Ric answers with a poke to the eyes, blinding Shawn. He still manages to fight off Batista before accidentally decking his tag team partner. Clearing his eyes, Michaels gives "The Nature Boy" Sweet Chin Music. Jericho pays his partner back with his own superkick, the "Heartbreak Kid" falling onto Flair for the three-count. Post-match, Y2J hurries up the ramp with a smile on his face. That leaves Shawn alone for "the Animal" to give him a Batista Bomb. He ends the show choking Michaels until he coughs up blood.

SmackDown!
November 27, 2003
Boise, ID
Announcers: Michael Cole, Tazz, Nidia (briefly)

The show opens with Paul Heyman in the center of the ring, *SmackDown!* superstars surrounding him on the apron. Paul says that twenty-men will compete in a battle royal for a WWE Title shot against Brock Lesnar tonight. That brings out Brock, the fans chanting that he tapped out. He tells them, "Happy Thanksgiving to you too" before noting that he's accomplished more than anyone else in the arena at just twenty-six. Lesnar says he's on his way to becoming the biggest WWE superstar of all-time and he's not afraid of Rey Mysterio's speed, Big Show's size, or John Cena who has never been champion. He then turns to Chris Benoit and tells him that he's not afraid of a man who will never be the champion. "The Crippler" reminds him that he tapped out. Lesnar promises to never tap out again. To prove how great he is, he promises to make the battle royal winner tap out tonight. Brock then whispers something to Heyman. The general manager tells him he has a great idea. Two men will have to earn their way into the battle royal tonight. First, John Cena will need to beat A-Train. Secondly, Benoit will need to beat an opponent of Paul's choosing and that match starts next.

Chris Benoit def. Matt Morgan. Benoit doesn't even let Morgan get into the ring, knocking him off the apron. He follows up with kicks and chops in and out of the ring ahead of a German suplex. When he goes for a second, Matt crushes him in a corner. Corner clotheslines and a leg drop on the middle rope follow before a suplex and leg drop score the big heel a two-count. Instead of going for the win after a sidewalk slam, Morgan works Nick Patrick's count to four on a choke. He then picks up "the Crippler" for a gutbuster, but misses a leg drop on the middle rope afterwards. Benoit tries to make him pay with a diving headbutt off the top rope all the way across the ring, but misses. Matt attempts to answer with a powerbomb, but the "rabid wolverine" counters into the Crippler Crossface for the tap-out.

Backstage, Jamie Noble runs his hands in front of Nidia's face. He thinks she might be faking for extra attention. When he screams, she tells him she's blind, not deaf. The redneck begs her not to accompany him to ringside tonight so he can get back in the Cruiserweight Title hunt. She compromises with him, offering to sit with the announcers during the next match.

Following a shot of the announcers as animated turkeys, Ernest Miller dances and tells someone to call his mama in a prerecorded vignette.

Akio (with Tajiri) def. Jamie Noble. Pre-match, Noble leads Nidia to the announce table to provide guest commentary. She hates Tajiri for blinding her, but says she has a good prognosis. Jamie doesn't as Akio attacks him from behind. When the redneck turns the tide, he wastes time chasing after Tajiri and is dropped by his opponent. Following an Akio jawbreaker, the competitors trade a series of roll-ups and two-counts. The exchange ends with both men delivering simultaneous clotheslines. Back up, Noble chops and clotheslines the heel, Nidia telling Cole to keep her updated on the action. Jamie nearly gets the win with a neckbreaker, but Akio just kicks out. He follows up with a triangle choke in the ropes. While he heads upstairs, the "Japanese Buzzsaw" stands in front of Nidia and mocks her. Noble counters Akio's attack with a superplex. With both men down, Nidia feels Tajiri's legs and gives him a low blow. Watching that distracts Jamie for Akio to roll him up for the three-count. Post-match, Noble helps his girlfriend backstage while Cole asks if she's a liability.

Backstage, Paul Heyman sits down beside Shannon Moore. The cruiserweight, his ribs taped up, asks Paul what he wants. Heyman sees a bright future for him. Even brighter than Matt Hardy's. To make him the kind of superstar who can appear on the cover of *SmackDown!* magazine, the GM signs Moore to a match tonight against Nathan Jones.

Rey Mysterio wishes everyone a "Happy Thanksgiving" and says that he's thankful for his job and fans.

Nathan Jones def. Shannon Moore. Like Chris Benoit, Moore attacks his opponent before the bell on the apron. Unfortunately, he doesn't knock down the big heel. Nathan responds with a toss off the top rope out to the floor. Inside the ring, Jones crushes Shannon with a corner clothesline. When he attempts a second, Moore counters with a pair of boots. He can't put Nathan down, though. Jones answers with a toss to the canvas followed by one out to the floor. Back in the ring, he teases pinning Shannon, but picks his head up twice before finally scoring the win with a gut wrench suplex.

Footage of the *SmackDown!* Thanksgiving dinner plays from earlier today. John Cena interrupts to rap about Torrie Wilson, Shaniqua, and the debuting Melina. Once he's said his own unique grace, everyone eats.

After a commercial break, Eddie Guerrero is surprised to see Chavo Guerrero Jr. here tonight. "Latino Heat" tells him to stay backstage and rest, but Chavo says he's feeling great. He promises to watch his uncle's back at ringside and wants to see him win the WWE Title tonight.

Eddie Guerrero (with Chavo Guerrero Jr.) def. Charlie Haas (with Shelton Benjamin). Los Guerreros are out second in a green lowrider. Tazz wants Eddie to get him an orange one. Inside the ring, "Latino Heat" wrestles in a WrestleMania XX t-shirt, stomping Charlie. He also plants him with a tilt-a-whirl backbreaker before Chavo gets involved with a few cheap shots. Haas quickly comes back to life with a back body drop and back suplex into a backbreaker. Shots to the lower back follow before Charlie scores a two-count with a back suplex. Afterwards, he slams Guerrero to the canvas and applies an armbar, the heel's knee in Eddie's ribs. It doesn't take "Latino Heat" long to fight free and slam Haas's face onto the top turnbuckle. A hurricanrana off the top rope follows before Guerrero clotheslines Charlie twice. A trio of suplexes put the heel down for Eddie to climb to the top rope. When Shelton gets on the apron, "Latino Heat" rolls over to knock him down. While Brian Hebner tries to keep Benjamin from getting into the ring, Eddie grabs his nephew's crutch and nails Haas for the roll-up and three-count. Post-match, Shelton attacks Chavo's injured knee until "Latino Heat" bends the crutch around Benjamin's back. Afterwards, Chavo yells at his uncle for leaving him alone for Shelton's attack.

The Xbox Smack of the Night is John Cena hitting Big Show with the ring steps.

John Cena def. A-Train. The *SmackDown!* magazine cover star, Cena gets a good pop when he comes out. Before he can rap, A-Train attacks John from behind. It doesn't take the rapping superstar long to recover and chase off his opponent. After he catches his breath, the hairy heel returns to the ring to club Cena while the fans chant for him to shave his back. A bicycle kick follows, the announcers reminding everyone that if John loses this match, he won't have a spot in the upcoming battle royal. A-Train tries to make that a reality, hammering the rapping superstar ahead of a powerslam and two-count. He then applies an abdominal stretch. Although Cena fights free, the damage is done and he can't slam the hairy heel, the big man falling on top of him for a near fall. Heading out to the floor, A-Train throat drops John on the top rope, but when he returns, the rapping superstar slows him with a low blow. A throwback, scoop slam, and five-knuckle shuffle falling fist drop then scores Cena a two-count. Although the hairy heel tries to fight back, John catches him with a spinning slam. He attempts to deliver an FU, but A-Train slips free and answers with a Derailer. Unfortunately, the rapping superstar is close enough to the ropes to break his cover. That sets off the hairy heel and he flings chairs into the ring. When he tries to use one, Cena surprises him with a kick to the gut ahead of the FU for the victory.

Following an Ernest Miller teaser, a *SmackDown!* ad featuring Big Show plays. After a commercial break, Hardcore Holly getting suspended last week plays. The angry superstar joins the announcers via satellite to say that he's appealing his suspension. When he returns, he is going to break Brock Lesnar's neck.

Inside the ring, Lamont carries a red cape and introduces "The Cat", Ernest Miller. He's here to dance to his "Somebody Call My Mama" music. Like James Brown, Lamont puts his cape on him when the show is over. "The Cat" isn't done. He needs help and invites Boise's own Torrie Wilson to come out and dance. She reluctantly tries to dance like him before doing her own hip swaying dance and enjoying a sucker. Ernest nearly has a seizure when she puts the sucker in his mouth. He's fired back up and dances like a madman until Lamont covers him with the cape again to end this fun, but goofy, segment. Afterwards, John Cena gives thanks to his fans and family, hoping his dad doesn't get drunk and arrested again.

Chris Benoit and John Cena win a twenty-man #1 Contender's battle royal.

Elimination Order	Wrestler	Eliminated By
1	Johnny Stamboli	Big Show
2	Ultimo Dragon	Big Show
3	Orlando Jordan	Big Show
4	Danny Basham	Big Show
5	Big Show	Everyone Left
6	Nathan Jones	Bradshaw
7	Bradshaw	Rikishi
8	Scotty 2 Hotty	A-Train
9	A-Train	Eddie Guerrero
10	Rhyno	Matt Morgan
11	Rikishi	Charlie Haas/Chris Benoit/Chuck Palumbo/John Cena/Matt Morgan
12	Chuck Palumbo	Chris Benoit/John Cena
13	Charlie Haas	Chris Benoit/John Cena
14	Matt Morgan	Chris Benoit/John Cena
15	Rey Mysterio	Chris Benoit/John Cena
16	Doug Basham	John Cena
17	Shelton Benjamin	Chris Benoit
18	Eddie Guerrero	Chris Benoit
19	Chris Benoit	Winner
20	John Cena	Winner

Big Show is out last for the battle royal. Cole picks him to win it. He looks like a good pick as he tosses Stamboli out almost immediately. He then headbutts Orlando Jordan while men punch and kick each other all around the squared circle. In the chaos, Ultimo Dragon surprises the giant with a string of kicks. He quickly recovers to toss him over the top rope. Jordan and Danny Basham, sporting a black mask, follow almost immediately. Big Show runs roughshod over the ring, clubbing Scotty 2 Hotty, Matt Morgan, and Rikishi. Eventually, everyone teams up on him, the remaining superstars clubbing him against the ropes. Despite everyone working together, Show shoves them aside. They stay on the attack, finally eliminating the giant thanks to fifteen men. As he leaves, he clotheslines Orlando in the aisle ahead of a commercial break.

Afterwards, we see that Bradshaw clotheslined Nathan Jones out only to be shoved out by Rikishi during the break. Eddie nearly eliminates Mysterio, but the masked man holds onto the ropes. The two men continue brawling while Morgan hammers Rhyno and Rikishi hoists Palumbo onto his shoulders. Rey gets a nice reaction when he head scissors Guerrero over the top rope, but "Latino Heat" holds on. So does Scotty when Chuck tosses him to the apron. He can't following an A-Train bicycle kick. Rhyno rewards him with a Gore ahead of an Eddie dropkick to eliminate the hairy heel. Seconds later, Morgan tosses out the man-beast. As the numbers start to thin out, the wrestlers begin pairing up. Curiously, The World's Greatest Tag Team don't work together to win the match. Instead, they split up, Shelton attempting to powerbomb Mysterio out of the ring. Instead, Rey hurricanranas him onto the middle rope for a 619. Cole wonders if the winner of this match will have anything left to take on Brock Lesnar tonight. It won't be Rikishi as several superstars team up to eliminate him. Benoit and Cena then send the men who helped them, Palumbo, Haas, and Morgan, out to the floor. Down to six men, Mysterio tries to surprise "the Crippler" and rapping superstar with a springboard cross body block, but they catch and toss him out to the floor as well. Moments later, Cena dumps Haas to get us to the final four. Benjamin is alone against three babyfaces now, the fans loudly chanting for the rapping superstar. He pairs up with Shelton while Guerrero hurricanranas Benoit. He tries to toss him over the top rope, but can't get the "rabid wolverine" out. Instead, he switches opponents and goes after Benjamin, but pays courtesy of a powerslam. Shelton then mounts Benoit in a corner while Cena stomps Eddie. Both men quickly recover, "the Crippler" snap suplexing Benjamin while Guerrero punches and chops John. "Latino Heat" follows up with a trio of suplexes, but the rapping superstar holds onto the ropes to avoid elimination until Shelton makes the save. He plasters Eddie to the canvas with a powerbomb, but Benoit rewards the heel with a trio of German suplexes. "Latino Heat" follows up with a Frog Splash, but stands up into an FU. The "rabid wolverine" catches Cena afterwards with a trio of German suplexes, but Benjamin almost gets the last laugh with a superkick. When he tosses Benoit over the top rope, "the Crippler" skins the cat and head scissors Shelton out. Eddie follows him courtesy of a Benoit back body drop. That leaves John and the "rabid wolverine" to trade shots. Benoit gets the upper hand with the Crippler Crossface, forcing the rapping superstar to tap-out. Unfortunately, a tap-out doesn't give him the victory. Instead, "the Crippler" inverted suplexes Cena onto the top rope. He tries to knock him out to the floor, but John ducks his shot and answers with an FU drop to the floor, both men's feet hitting at the same time.

Post-match, Brock Lesnar marches out while officials argue over who won the battle royal. After a commercial break, Paul Heyman asks Brian Hebner whose feet hit the ground first. He says Cena's, but Mike Sparks thinks it was Benoit. Both wrestlers want Lesnar. Paul believes a GM has to make tough decisions and the fans want to see a triple threat match. However, he makes the tough decision of signing the rapping superstar to face the "rabid wolverine" next week for a shot at the title. Afterwards, Brock blindsides Cena. When Benoit tries to help him, Big Show, Matt Morgan, A-Train, and Nathan Jones come out to attack the winners. The fans are not happy about losing a title match, and boo Brock as he gives his potential opponents a pair of F5s to end the show.

Monday Night Raw
December 1, 2003
Sacramento, CA
Announcers: Jim Ross, Jerry "the King" Lawler, Mick Foley (briefly)

The show opens with Eric Bischoff in front of a black screen. He's excited to announce tonight's main event, Shawn Michaels and Rob Van Dam against Batista, Kane, and Randy Orton in a handicap match. Afterwards, the intro video plays before Goldberg heads to the squared circle. He's tired of getting jumped from behind and challenges Kane and Triple H to fight him now. That sets off Eric and he storms out to tell Bill that he better not defy him again or he'll get fired. The general manager brags that this is no longer *Monday Night Raw*, but Bischoff's show. He threatens that no one can do anything about it. That's the cue for Mick Foley to come out in a suit to a big pop. He disagrees with Eric. Thanks to Linda McMahon deciding her husband is no longer making decisions that show he's in his right mind, she's hired Foley as a consultant to help the product. His first act is to give the World Champion what he wants. Specifically, he will join tonight's main event match alongside Shawn and RVD. For Mick's second act, he's starting a petition to bring back "Stone Cold" Steve Austin. First to sign is Lilian Garcia. Finally, Foley says after hours of research the only thing he's found wrong with *Raw* is Bischoff. To fix that, Mick hires himself as the new co-GM. He ends the segment telling Eric to "have a nice day".

After a commercial break, Eric Bischoff complains to Jonathan Coachman. Coach advises him not to call Linda McMahon, but Eric doesn't listen. He should have because Linda hangs up on Bischoff.

The Dudley Boyz def. Garrison Cade/Mark Jindrak (World Tag Title match). Bubba opens the match hammering and chopping Cade. Jindrak gets more of the same when he tags in, Dudley telling the challengers that they are going to teach them some respect. Although Mark surprises D-Von with a clothesline when he tags in, Dudley recovers quickly to powerslam Garrison. That kicks off a four-man brawl. While Bubba Ray and Jindrak fight at ringside, Cade rolls up D-Von and tries to steal the win with a handful of pants. That sets off D-Von and he slaps the rookie before claiming victory with his own handful of trunks. Post-match, Garrison says he was cheated and replays the finish before demanding a rematch.

Backstage, Al Snow and Jonathan Coachman debate whether Garrison Cade and Mark Jindrak deserve a rematch. When Mick Foley interrupts, Al rolls his eyes. Coach wonders if he's going to give Cade and Jindrak the shot. Foley will take it under advisement. Speaking of rematches, Mick is a glutton for punishment and he's giving Coachman a chance to lock up with Lawler again. Only this time, if Coach loses, he's fired.

Booker T def. Test (with Stacy Keibler). Stacy looks miserable as she comes out in a schoolgirl outfit. When Test stops her from making her customary entrance into the squared circle, Booker attacks him from behind. It doesn't take the bodyguard long to recover and knock down the five-time champion. After he mocks Booker T, Test applies a bearhug. Keibler pounds the mat to encourage the fans to cheer on the babyface. It works as Booker comes back to life with fists and a bicycle kick. The two men then trade counters until the bodyguard delivers a pumphandle slam near the ropes. When he puts his feet on the ropes, Stacy shoves them off to break his cover. Test yells at his valet until she slaps him. The five-time champion capitalizes with a Scissors Kick for the win. Post-match, Booker T celebrates with a spinaroonie. He stops his music for Keibler to perform two "leg-aroonies". While the fans enjoy seeing her underpants, Booker doesn't enjoy Mark Henry running out to clothesline him and deliver a World's Strongest Slam at Theodore Long's direction.

Backstage, Lita gives Trish Stratus a Chris Jericho action figure. After the two women have a laugh about it, Lita asks what's going on with the couple. Stratus says they have a connection she's never felt before. They spent last week talking and getting closer. She's got a Jericho jersey for him, but has even more special underwear that she's going to wear beneath it because tonight "might be the night".

After a commercial break, the announcers tell fans how they can sign the petition to bring back "Stone Cold" Steve Austin before playing footage of Batista choking and Batista Bombing Shawn Michaels last week. "The Animal" tells Terri that he's disappointed in himself. He's disappointed that he didn't finish off the "Heartbreak Kid". If he doesn't do it tonight, Batista promises to do so at Armageddon.

Afterwards, Scott Steiner leads Test and Stacy Keibler to the squared circle. "Big Poppa Pump" says the fans aren't going to see a "leg-aroonie" again because Stacey belongs to the heels and he and the bodyguard "share everything". That disgusts the announcers. Things get worse when the heels pull their pants down and tell Keibler to kiss their butts. Mick Foley has seen enough. He orders Stacy to join him on the ramp. He's got a way for her to get out of her contract with Test and that's by firing the bodyguard. Scott says that they're a tag team and he can't fire Test. Keibler has an idea that Foley likes, so he fires Steiner too.

Following a commercial break, Scott Steiner and Test complain to Eric Bischoff. While he can't get Linda McMahon on the phone, he promises to call Vince McMahon for them. When they storm off, a voice offscreen asks Eric if he's really going to call Vince. The co-GM isn't. He's going to handle things himself.

Lance Storm/Val Venis def. La Resistance. The babyfaces are accompanied once again by two women as Mick Foley joins the announce table. He thinks the fans want to love Rob Conway and Rene Dupree like they did The Rock. Dupree tries to give them something to cheer, immediately going after Val. Conway does the same, tagging in to whip the adult star hard into a corner ahead of a reverse chin lock. When he escapes, Venis slams Rob to the canvas. Rene tries to stop "the big Valbowski" from getting the tag, but Storm decks him first. He then tags in to clothesline both heels and dropkick Conway. An enziguri kick chases Dupree from the squared circle ahead of a rolling fireman's carry slam to Rob for a near fall. While he rolls up Conway into a Single Leg Crab, Foley teases a "Tag Team Turmoil" match at Armageddon. Although Rene breaks the submission hold, he's quickly driven from the ring for Val to lift Rob for a Hart Attack double-team clothesline and the three-count. Post-match, Mick grabs a microphone to tell the heels that the fans want to embrace him. They'll do it if La Resistance recites the national anthem with them. While Conway half-heartedly mumbles the words, Dupree doesn't at all. That forces Foley to tell him "au revoir" and fire another pair of heels.

Backstage, Chris Jericho asks Trish Stratus if she's ready for their match. She's a little distracted by how much she feels for Y2J, but heads to the ring for their mixed tag match anyway.

Chris Jericho/Trish Stratus def. Miss Jackie/Rico. When the heels come out, the announcers are distracted by Jackie's pants and cut out pockets on the backside. Rico gets under Jericho's skin when he shoves Trish down. The Canadian heel unloads with chops until the flamboyant heel pokes his eyes and clotheslines him. Following a two-count, Rico attempts a corner charge only to be hip tossed to the canvas. Y2J tries to quickly lock on the Walls of Jericho, but the flamboyant heel reaches the ropes. While he recovers on the apron, Jericho springboard dropkicks him out to the floor. Back in the squared circle, Rico surprises Y2J with a series of kicks, but one clothesline puts him down and scrambling to his corner for the tag. Jackie tries to kick Jericho, but he catches her foot and shoves her down to the canvas. Stratus tags in afterwards for a top rope flying cross body block. Forearms and chops follow for a near fall. When she attempts a suplex, Rico joins his partner for a double-team suplex and two-count. Once in control, Jackie kicks the vixen ahead of a neckbreaker and near fall. The heels take turns choking Trish, Y2J inadvertently distracting Charles Robinson trying to help his partner. He can only cheer her on when Jackie applies a dragon sleeper, but that's enough for Stratus to roll up the heel for a two-count. Jackie answers with a clothesline. A second misses by two feet, but the vixen sells it anyways. It doesn't matter as she comes back to life moments later with a spinebuster to send both women to their corners for tags. The aggressor, Jericho clotheslines Rico ahead of an enziguri kick and two-count. The flamboyant heel answers with a string of kicks, including one stepping up the Canadian in a corner. When he heads upstairs though, Y2J meets him with a fist to the gut. Although he hits his running face slam, Rico dodges a Lionsault. After having that move countered so many times, Jericho lands on his feet and tosses the flamboyant heel out of the ring. He also hits the ropes to crotch Jackie when she tries to sneak attack him. Trish follows up with a handstand head scissors ahead of Stratusfaction to Jackie for the win. Post-match, the winners can't keep their hands off each other as they leave.

Backstage, Eric Bischoff complains to someone offscreen. It's Kane, and he doesn't understand what Eric's problems have to do with him. Bischoff tells him that he's hearing word that Mick Foley may strip the "Big Red Machine" of his Armageddon World Title match. Eric assures him that he'll do everything to stop Mick, but the monster isn't happy with Foley.

Matt Hardy Version 1.0 def. Christian (with Lita). Hardy is out first, Matt Facts returning to say that he's more handsome than Christian. The Canadian has Lita on his side though, and she's enough motivation for him to punch and suplex Matt sternum-first onto the top rope. Afterwards, he knocks Hardy off the apron and into the barricade. A backward neck snap on the top rope scores Christian a two-count before Matt swings the momentum, whipping the Canadian into the ring post. A gut wrench suplex moments later gets Hardy a two-count. Focusing on the ribs, he kicks Christian twice and celebrates. Afterwards, he locks on an abdominal stretch and mocks Lita. The Canadian escapes with a back elbow before ramming Matt into a corner. Unfortunately, Hardy knocks him down quickly for a second rope guillotine leg drop and near fall. Afterwards, Matt applies a surfboard stretch, Lita cheering on her friend. When Hardy attempts to deliver a Twist of Fate, Christian fights free only to run into a side effect and close two-count. Frustrated, Matt clubs the Canadian. When he leaves the ring to stalk after Lita, Christian attempts to save her. That gets him hammered some more until Hardy misses a middle rope running leg drop and crotches himself. Christian capitalizes with an inverted atomic drop and clothesline. A gutbuster afterwards gets him a two-count. He follows up with a poke to the eye and reverse DDT for another near fall. Also frustrated, he yells at Matt to get up. While he sets Hardy up for an Unprettier, Molly Holly runs out to whip Lita into the ring steps. That distracts Christian long enough for Matt to roll him up for the three-count. Post-match, the Canadian checks on Lita. She assures him that she's okay.

Jerry "the King" Lawler def. Jonathan Coachman. JR tells fans to set their VCRs because he doesn't think Coach will be around much longer since if he loses this match he'll be fired. Jerry has no sympathy for him, punching Coachman before he even takes off his hat and sunglasses. A back suplex and falling fist drop off the second rope scores "the King" an easy victory. Post-match, Lawler reminds Coach that he sung goodbye to "Stone Cold" Steve Austin at Survivor Series. He wants the fans and JR to sing the same, making Coachman cry as he heads backstage.

Following a shot of fans signing the petition to bring back "Stone Cold" Steve Austin, the announcers remind the audience that they can sign up online before previewing Armageddon.

Backstage, Christian tells Chris Jericho that he's going to seal the deal with Lita tonight. Y2J says Trish Stratus has been falling for everything he's been doing for weeks. He promises that he's going to win their bet that he'll sleep with Stratus before Christian hooks up with Lita. Outside the room, Trish cries, overhearing him calling her stupid and mocking the vixen. While the WWE doesn't do romance well very often, this is a great story that takes cues from pop culture and spins it into the wrestling world.

Goldberg/Rob Van Dam/Shawn Michaels def. Batista/Kane/Randy Orton (with Ric Flair). As the heels head to the ring, JR wonders where Triple H is. The babyfaces follow, Goldberg coming out last to a big pop. Orton and RVD start the match slowly, trading tie-ups until Randy elbows Rob back into a corner. He follows up with fists until Van Dam surprises him with a springboard cross body block. A kick and standing moonsault scores the popular superstar a two-count before he boots the "Legend Killer" down and heads upstairs for a Five-Star Frog Splash. Before he can fly, Orton slides out to the floor to escape. RVD follows him, cross body blocking Randy from the top rope. Back in the squared circle, Rob slingshot leg drops the "Legend Killer", but Batista illegally enters the ring to clothesline him. Mike Chioda turns a blind eye to that, as well as Orton stomping and cheap shotting Van Dam when "the Animal" tags into the match. When Batista misses a corner charge, RVD kicks him and tags in Shawn for a flying forearm and kip up. After he knocks down the other heels, Michaels heads upstairs for a top rope flying elbow drop. He then tunes up the band, but Ric distracts him. Although "The Nature Boy" pays with a shot to the nose, Kane slips into the ring to Chokeslam the "Heartbreak Kid" ahead of a commercial break.

Afterwards, the "Big Red Machine" decks Shawn and teases a second Chokeslam. Although Michaels escapes, he runs into a big boot afterwards for a two-count. "The Animal" then slows the pace with a chin lock. It takes him a minute, but the "Heartbreak Kid" elbows free. When Batista picks him up for a hanging choke, Shawn pokes his eyes and low blows "the Animal". That puts both men down on the mat and crawling to their corners for tags. Goldberg explodes into the ring to back body drop Orton and clothesline Batista out to the floor. He follows up with a military press into a powerslam to the "Legend Killer" before daring Kane to get into the ring. The "Big Red Machine" answers the challenge, trading shots with the World Champion. Bill wins the exchange, hammering the monster down in a corner. When he attempts a corner charge though, Kane meets him with a boot. He wastes time fighting with the other babyfaces afterwards, enabling the intense superstar to recover and Spear the "Big Red Machine". When he picks him up for a Jackhammer, the other competitors join the brawl. Goldberg, Kane, Shawn, and Batista all disappear into the crowd brawling. That leaves RVD to give Orton rolling thunder, but Flair drags the referee out of the ring to break the count. After Ric decks Chioda, Van Dam punches "The Nature Boy". A spinning heel kick and Five-Star Frog Splash follow to Randy, but there's no referee to make the count. There is a co-GM as Mick Foley sprints out to make the three-count.

Post-match, Eric Bischoff power walks down to the ring to tell Mick that he ruined *Raw* on his first night. Eric says at least "Stone Cold" Steve Austin was competent and as soon as Foley signs all the release papers tonight, Paul Heyman is going to steal all *Raw*'s talent. Mick tells him that's not going to happen because Foley isn't actually going to fire anyone. He was just showing Bischoff what he's been doing for weeks. From now on, Mick is going to give the fans what they want. That includes Goldberg and Kane meeting next week for the World Title. First though, he gives the fans what they want by decking Eric and introducing him to Mr. Socko to end the show.

SmackDown!
December 4, 2003
San Jose, CA
Announcers: Michael Cole, Tazz

The show opens with footage from last week's number one contender's battle royal. After Paul Heyman signs a number one contender's match tonight between the two winners, Brock Lesnar attacking Chris Benoit and John Cena replays. Live, the WWE Champion heads to the squared circle. He tells the fans to enjoy chanting "you tapped out" now because he will never tap out again. Brock then tells everyone in the crowd that he could destroy them before talking about Cena and Benoit going out of the battle royal last week at the exact same time. He thinks they had it planned because they are scared to step into the squared circle with him. Lesnar warns that people are afraid to step into the ring with him because he injures people. If the fans don't believe him, the champion tells them to ask Kurt Angle and Hardcore Holly. Later tonight, he promises that he will make whoever wins the title shot tap out.

Rikishi/Scotty 2 Hotty def. The Basham Brothers (with Shaniqua). The champions wear masks to the ring, but take them off before Shaniqua whips them for this non-title match. Rikishi realizes how important this opportunity is, punching Danny before teasing a Samoan drop. Although the heel crawls out of that hold, the big Samoan drops his weight down onto him, sitting on Basham's head. The match briefly stops as everyone checks on Danny. When Doug tags in, the babyfaces team up on him with a drop toe hold and leg drop. Danny returns for Scotty to rock him with a flying forearm. He then low bridges the illegal Basham out to the floor. When Doug distracts Brian Hebner, Shaniqua pulls Hotty off the apron to the floor. The referee sees her handiwork and sends the dominatrix backstage. She doesn't get to see Doug score a near fall with a second rope elbow drop. Danny returns moments later to pound Scotty's ribs and apply an abdominal stretch. Eventually, Hotty hip tosses free and gives Rikishi the hot tag. He manhandles Danny before stunning Doug with a DDT. Once he kicks Danny out of the ring, the big Samoan crushes Doug in a corner. That brings Shaniqua back out to distract Hebner and Rikishi while the Bashams switch places. When the big Samoan tries to give Danny a Stinkface, the champion low blows him. Fortunately, Scotty comes to his partner's defense with a face slam and the Worm. Although Doug tosses Hotty out to the floor, Rikishi does the same to him before scoring the three-count on Danny with a Samoan drop. Post-match, the dominatrix yells at her men and calls them pathetic. She says they don't deserve her as their manager.

Following footage of Hardcore Holly attacking Brock Lesnar, Paul Heyman raises a fuss backstage. Dawn Marie, in black leather, tells him that everything is going to be okay and tries to seduce him. Paul tells her that he "doesn't do the help". However, she can take a message to inform Holly that his suspension remains intact due to his recent actions. He also wants Dawn to get him Shannon Moore.

After a commercial break, Paul Heyman is in the ring surrounded by Matt Morgan and Nathan Jones as he asks for the production team to play footage of the heels destroying Shannon Moore recently. He's impressed that Shannon keeps wanting more and invites the cruiserweight to get into the ring with him. Heyman says Moore deserves being in the squared circle. Paul likes that Shannon won't quit and is not holding him accountable for Matt Hardy leaving *SmackDown!*. Heyman promises to give him more opportunities. Moore is afraid that means a handicap match tonight, but Paul assures him that he's not facing the two big heels. Instead, he's facing Big Show. This segment ends Jones's run with the WWE as he'll quit on an Australian tour.

Big Show def. Shannon Moore. Shannon baseball slide kicks the US Champion before he can get in the ring, but his attack doesn't even slow the giant. Instead, Big Show slams him onto the top turnbuckle from the floor before shoving him down to ringside. When they finally get in the squared circle, Show chops and slams Moore out of a corner. After Jimmy Korderas admonishes him for stretching the young man's face, the giant delivers his standing leg drop slam. A Chokeslam follows for the victory.

After the announcers give the tale of the tape for the number one contender's match later tonight and a commercial break, Jamie Noble tells Nidia that she needs to stay backstage tonight. The last two weeks she's distracted him, and if he loses to Sakoda, he'll never get another Cruiserweight Title shot. She never wants to hurt him and reluctantly agrees to stay backstage waiting. On second thought, Jamie has an idea.

Jamie Noble (with Nidia) def. Sakoda (with Tajiri). Despite telling his girlfriend to stay backstage, Jamie ends up leading her to ringside. Cole says she was "temporarily blinded". Tazz covers for him before the wrestlers trade holds, Noble dropping Sakoda with a toe hold into the middle turnbuckle. The rookie answers with a leg sweep and clothesline. Stomps and a running slam into the corner follow, Nidia asking her boyfriend if he's okay. He can't answer because Sakoda stretches the redneck over his knee before covering him for a two-count. Jamie answers with a falling facebuster before whipping the heel out to the floor for a flying dive through the ropes. Tajiri teases interfering, but Mike Sparks sees him and stops the "Japanese Buzzsaw". While he's distracted, Noble flings Nidia into Sakoda, stunning him for the three-count. Post-match, Jamie tells her that Tajiri's men tossed her around before celebrating his victory. Cole can't believe it, calling Noble pathetic. Tazz has lost respect for him.

Backstage, Josh Mathews interviews John Cena. The rapping superstar says he's ready to beat Chris Benoit for a WWE Title shot. Benoit warns him that once the Crippler Crossface is on, Cena will tap.

Chris Benoit def. John Cena (#1 Contender's match). Pre-match, Cena says he doesn't want this match, but promises to kick Benoit's butt. "The Crippler" lets his actions do his talking, marching out to punch, kick, and suplex the rapping superstar for a two-count. The fans are behind John, chanting his name as Benoit unloads with chops. Cena answers with his ground and pound assault before scoring a two-count with a clothesline. A slam and five knuckle shuffle also gets him a near fall. When the "rabid wolverine" starts to fight back, the rapping superstar suplexes him for a two-count before slowing the pace with a surfboard stretch. Even when Benoit escapes, a spinebuster scores John a near fall. The two men then trade two-counts before Cena whips his opponent hard into the corner. A delayed vertical suplex follows for another near fall. When he misses a punch, "the Crippler" answers with a trio of German suplexes. He mocks the rapping superstar, motioning that John can't see him, but Benoit misses a top rope diving headbutt. Cena pumps up his shoes, but wastes time and the "rabid wolverine" answers with a string of chops. The rapping superstar blocks out his attack and surprises Benoit with an FU for the three-count despite "the Crippler's" feet being in the ropes. Post-match, Benoit tells Nick Patrick that his foot was on the ropes. Brian Hebner concurs, running out to talk to the official. Eventually, Patrick tells Justin Roberts that the match must continue after a commercial break.

Afterwards, the "rabid wolverine" dodges a clothesline and slams Cena's shoulder to the canvas. He follows up with a dropkick to the injured shoulder and northern lights suplex. Focusing on the arm, Benoit hammerlocks and suplexes the rapping superstar on his injured joint. Slams and elbow drops have John writhing and score "the Crippler" a near fall. Reaching down deep, Cena answers with a clothesline, but hurts himself doing so. Benoit is right back up, scoring another two-count before applying a standing armbar. The rapping superstar answers with a throwback for a near fall. When he tries to slam the "rabid wolverine", Benoit slips free and locks on a sharpshooter. With the fans cheering him on, John manages to reach the ropes for the break. The two men trade shots afterwards, Cena hitting a second FU out of nowhere. That brings Big Show running out, but the rapping superstar meets him with a fist to the jaw. When he turns around, Benoit traps John in the Crippler Crossface for the quick tap-out due to his injured shoulder.

Backstage, Eddie Guerrero tries to pump up his nephew. When "Latino Heat" says he'll accompany Chavo Guerrero Jr. to ringside, Chavo doesn't want his help. He blames his uncle for his injured knee and is tired of hearing all the "Eddie" chants. The younger Guerrero says tonight is about him and he wants "Latino Heat" to stay backstage. Eddie doesn't like it and says Chavo isn't being himself.

Chavo Guerrero Jr. (with Eddie Guerrero) def. Shelton Benjamin (with Charlie Haas). Despite his nephew's instructions, Eddie drives a fire emblazoned sports car down to ringside. He lets Chavo handle things himself, reading *SmackDown!* magazine in a lawn chair while sipping from a YJ Stinger hat. Unfortunately, "Latino Heat" distracts his nephew and Benjamin pounds him from behind before working on his knee. Following a knee breaker, Shelton applies a single leg stretch. Cole says Guerrero shouldn't even be in this match. Chavo proves him wrong, fighting back with an inverted atomic drop and dropkick for a near fall. Hopping around the ring, Guerrero plants Benjamin with a tornado DDT. When Haas hops onto the apron to distract the referee, Eddie capitalizes with a Frog Splash onto Shelton for Chavo to score the victory. Post-match, despite "Latino Heat" leading the fans in a "Chavo" chant, the younger Guerrero isn't happy with his uncle and tells him to go away for stealing his thunder.

Following footage of "The Cat" Ernest Miller, Tazz plays a sponsor's game, *Final Fantasy X-2*. Afterwards, a video package plays for Brock Lesnar.

Backstage, Chris Benoit tells Josh Mathews that Brock Lesnar's video package was missing him tapping out to the Crippler Crossface. Benoit promises that he will be the next WWE Champion.

After a commercial break, Johnny Stamboli shoves aside Spanky because he doesn't have any money. Everyone else gambles on who will win the WWE Title match, Nunzio giving Brock Lesnar the odds. A-Train puts ten grand on Chris Benoit.

Brock Lesnar def. Chris Benoit (WWE Title match). The champion is out first, charging Benoit when he steps into the ring for the early advantage. Despite the fans chanting that he tapped out, Brock looks strong here, standing on "the Crippler's" head and kicking him. When he misses a clothesline, Benoit answers with a trio of arm drags and a clothesline out to the floor. The "rabid wolverine" follows him to chop the heel and slam him into the announce table. A whip to the ring post sends Lesnar back into the squared circle where the challenger attempts to lock on the Crippler Crossface. Fortunately, the champion rolls back out to the floor. When Benoit chases him back into the ring, Brock surprises "the Crippler" with a hotshot. He follows up with a delayed cradle suplex for a two-count. The heel then whips Benoit back out to the floor to press slam him onto the announce table. Although he breaks Brian Hebner's count to make sure he lives up to his promise to make the "rabid wolverine" tap tonight, Lesnar scores a two-count moments later when he makes a cover. He then remembers his vow and locks on a reverse chin lock, wrapping his legs around the challenger. When Benoit escapes and busts open the champion's nose, Brock powerslams him for another near fall ahead of a commercial break.

Afterwards, "the Crippler" escapes a chin lock to chop the heel. Unfortunately, he misses a charge near the ropes and flies out to the floor. Lesnar follows him, whipping Benoit into the ring steps. Instead of breaking Hebner's count this time, he dares the "rabid wolverine" to get back into the squared circle. Instead, the challenger drags his opponent out and peppers him ahead of a whip into the steps. That sends the champion on the run, trying to get away from Benoit. "The Crippler" is all over him, stomping Brock until he surprises Benoit with a back elbow and release German suplex. That puts both men down for a Hebner standing nine-count. When they get up, the "rabid wolverine" unloads with a flurry of shots and dodges a corner charge. After the heel hits the corner post, the challenger delivers a trio of German suplexes. A running shoulderblock then puts Lesnar on the mat for a top rope diving headbutt and near fall. Frustrated, Benoit slams the canvas before ducking a clothesline and attempting to apply the Crippler Crossface. When he can't, "the Crippler" softens up the champion with a Fujiwara armbar. Brock tries to escape with a side slam, but Benoit swings free only to accidentally hit the referee. That means there's no one to give him the victory when the "rabid wolverine" traps the heel in a Crossface and he taps out. When Benoit goes to check on Hebner, Lesnar hoists the challenger up for an F5 and groggy near fall. The fans are all over the champion's case now, telling him that he tapped out as he slides out to get a chair and smash Benoit's knee. He then lifts "the Crippler" up, draping his knee over the back of the heel's neck and sitting on Benoit's back to try to score the submission. Instead, the "rabid wolverine" passes out for Lesnar to score the victory. Post-match, the champion puts an unconscious Benoit in the Crippler Crossface and uses his hand to make him tap-out. Cole says "the Crippler" never did so on his own.

Monday Night Raw
December 8, 2003
Anaheim, CA
Announcers: Jim Ross, Jerry "the King" Lawler

The show opens with still shots of the co-general managers before we see how Mick Foley got that job last week. Afterwards, the intro video plays ahead of Chris Jericho's fireworks replacing the show's normal display. He's joined by Christian, both heels carrying roses. Before they win the World Tag Titles, the Canadians want to address rumors that Lita and Trish Stratus are mad at them. Y2J says he's been calling Trish all week, but she hasn't responded. That brings out the divas and they are not happy. Stratus shows Jericho a Canadian dollar. Y2J gets it, but he says that was just a joke. They may have a stupid sense of humor, but the heels really care about the divas and wouldn't try to sleep with them just as a joke. He begs Trish to accept his apology because she knows the real Jericho. While she takes his flowers, she doesn't let him touch her, pulling her cheek away. When he begs her to accept his apology, she slaps him. The divas then wail on the heels with the flowers before The Dudley Boyz march out for the opener.

The Dudley Boyz def. Chris Jericho/Christian (World Tag Title match). Following a commercial break, D-Von powerslams Christian while Trish Stratus and Lita watch at ringside. After the Dudleys crush the heels in a corner, Christian turns the tide tripping Bubba Ray for Jericho to stomp him repeatedly. The announcers debate how the heels could have known that the divas knew about their bet in a brief discussion of how the fourth wall works in professional wrestling. Neither really knows, assuming someone else told them since apparently no one on the show can go back and watch a replay. Eventually, Y2J rocks Bubba with an enziguri, but before Charles Robinson can make a three-count, D-Von breaks the cover. Christian then switches places with his partner, punching and rubbing Bubba Ray's face across the canvas. The heels continue to make illegal switches, Jericho slapping his hands behind the ref's back before hammering Dudley in a corner. Bubba answers with a Samoan drop to put both men down. Trish likes it. When D-Von gets the hot tag, he wrestles both heels with back body drops, neckbreakers, and a sidewalk slam to Christian. Bubba Ray tags himself in moments later to clothesline Christian. He remains on the attack as D-Von takes Jericho out to the floor. While Bubba misses a second rope senton splash, Y2J tosses D-Von into the ring steps. He then gives Bubba Ray a Lionsault, but the champion just manages to kick out of Christian's cover. Bubba recovers quickly afterwards to give the heel a Bubba Bomb, but Jericho breaks Robinson's count by pulling him out to the floor. While the referee is down, the Dudleys hammer and slam their opponents to the canvas for Lita and Stratus to join them for stereo wassup drops. A 3D follows to Christian for the three-count.

Following an Armageddon ad, Ric Flair tells Batista and Randy Orton that he knows Triple H better than anyone. Flair promises that Hunter is here tonight, but won't go anywhere near the ring for Goldberg's match against Kane. Ric believes that Helmsley will let them tear each other apart before picking up the pieces this Sunday. Randy chimes in that "the Game" won't be the only Evolution champion at Armageddon because he's going to beat Rob Van Dam too. "The Animal" says that's only if he leaves enough of RVD to make it to the PPV after their match tonight. He also promises victory this Sunday.

Further backstage, Chris Jericho and Christian complain about what just happened to them to Eric Bischoff. They want him to make things right, but Eric wants to know first if they really made a bet about sleeping with Lita and Trish Stratus. Christian confirms that they did before Bischoff signs the heels to a match with the divas at Armageddon. While Christian loves it, Y2J looks hesitant.

Batista (with Ric Flair) def. Rob Van Dam. Although Batista starts strong, RVD answers with a string of kicks and a top rope flying cross body block for a two-count. When "the Animal" retreats to the floor, he trips Rob to briefly slow him. Van Dam quickly answers with a baseball kick and leg drop off the second rope for another near fall. One big clothesline puts him back down. Batista then softens up the Intercontinental Champion, whipping him around the ring and driving him out to the floor. Following a double ax-handle off the apron, "the Animal" shoves RVD back into the squared circle for a vertical suplex and two-count. He then slows the pace with a reverse chin lock. Even when Rob fights free, a spinebuster puts him down for a two-count. Afterwards, Batista ties Van Dam up in the tree of woe only to run into a knee on a corner charge. Refusing to give up, the champion stuns his opponent with a cannonball kick off the second rope. A step over kick and rolling thunder follow for a near fall. More kicks, including a springboard kick off the second rope put "the Animal" down, but when he sets up for the Five-Star Frog Splash, Ric pulls him down. Although he gets dropped, RVD accidentally rolls into Chad Patton when he flips over Batista. Things get worse when he tries to counter a Batista Bomb with a sunset flip, but falls on his head. Afterwards, Flair interrupts a Van Dam split legged moonsault with a fist to the jaw for "the Animal" to score the win with a Batista Bomb.

Garrison Cade/Mark Jindrak def. Lance Storm/Val Venis. Pre-match, Cade sets the record straight that they are not whiners. He says they are "winners", and they wanted a rematch with The Dudley Boyz after the champions cheated them last week. This Sunday, they promise to win the World Tag Titles. The babyfaces then come out, accompanied by two women. The young stars aren't impressed, attacking Storm and Val from behind before taking turns pounding on Lance. They also join up for a series of boots and a double suplex. That gets Garrison a two-count before the adult star breaks his cover. After fighting out of a chin lock, Storm surprises Cade with a second rope missile dropkick. Venis then gets the hot tag to fight both heels and toss Garrison out in front of the girls. He can only watch as "the big Valbowski" scores a two-count with a uranage. When he delivers a sit-out powerbomb, Cade returns for the save. He then brawls with Lance, driving him into the barricade outside the ring while Val punches Jindrak. When Garrison returns, the adult star decks him only to see Mark roll Venis up and steal the win with a handful of trunks.

Backstage, Kane recalls that a German shepherd used to bark at him until he killed it and dragged the carcass into the woods. He liked to watch the maggots eat the dog. Goldberg reminds him of the dog and the people are maggots. This Sunday, he promises to put the World Champion out of his misery.

After a commercial break, Mick Foley heads to the ring with a clipboard. He says he's here on *Raw* to make things right. If Ric Flair or Evolution interfere in the Intercontinental Title match this Sunday, that wouldn't be right. That's why Mick is naming a special referee for the match…himself. He then talks about reinstating "Stone Cold" Steve Austin. Although his petition has already collected half a million signatures, he needs more. Before he can pass around the clipboard, La Resistance interrupt. They say that Foley didn't treat them right last week. After warning him that the French are better fighters than Americans, they want the co-GM to salute the French flag. Mick has nothing against French fries or even French's mustard, but he refuses to salute the flag. When the heels corner him, The Rock returns to a massive pop. After he says he's finally come back to Anaheim, the "People's Champ" tells everyone that he came here tonight to surprise his friend, Foley. However, he's confused. He knows Mick, Lilian Garcia—stopping to ask her if she still likes strudel—and even the cross-dressing cameraman Marty, but he doesn't know the heels. When he asks them who they are, he predictably tells them that it doesn't matter who they are. He then threatens to slap off their lips before Rene Dupree demands respect. He promises that the heels will win the World Tag Titles this Sunday. The "Great One" tells them that they won't win because they are French and they suck. The fans agree. Afterwards, the "Brahma Bull" makes fun of the French army before Mick says they don't want a piece of the "Sock 'n' Rock Connection". When The Rock takes offense to the order of their names, La Resistance attack and drive him out of the ring. They then stomp Foley in a corner until the "People's Champ" returns to give Rob Conway a Rock Bottom. Dupree sneak attacks the "Great One" afterwards, but doesn't see the "Brahma Bull" kipping up behind him when he does his sidestep dance. That gets him a spinebuster and People's Elbow. Conway returns afterwards for another spinebuster and Mick People's Elbow to the groin. Foley tries to end the segment by telling them to run "if you smell"…but The Rock cuts him off. He says he loves Mick, but he'd better never steal his catchphrases. The "People's Champ" then shows him how it's done to a big pop. Afterwards, the "Great One" signs the petition to bring back Austin.

Following a replay of the previous segment, Jonathan Coachman admits The Rock's return was a big surprise. Eric Bischoff isn't impressed. He had the "People's Champ" removed during the break. To make sure his villainous plans come to fruition from here on out, he changes the Goldberg/Kane contest later tonight to a "Lumberjack" match.

Mark Henry/Scott Steiner/Test (with Theodore Long) def. Booker T/Rosey/The Hurricane. The announcers wonder where Stacy Keibler is as the heels come out. JR hopes she was able to get out of her contract with Test after last week. Lawler thinks she was bad luck for the heels, but the bodyguard isn't doing too well without her here as Rosey clotheslines and body splashes him for a two-count. The Hurricane then tags in for a second rope guillotine leg drop and his own near fall. Following a superhero uppercut, Test comes back to life with a tilt-a-whirl slam. Scott follows up with a clothesline and elbow drop for a two-count. After he does a series of pushups, he gives The Hurricane a spinning belly-to-belly suplex and threatens to do the same to the super hero in training. Instead, the bodyguard returns to stomp and mock the superhero. The Hurricane counters a back body drop with a boot to the face afterwards before tagging in Booker to kick all of the heels and entertain with a spinaroonie. When he tries to finish off Test with a Scissors Kick, Henry illegally enters the ring and runs through him. He then press slams The Hurricane out of the ring before impressing with a spinebuster to Rosey ahead of a commercial break.

Afterwards, Test stomps the five-time champion and mocks him with jumping jacks. Mark tags in legally moments later to elbow drop his Armageddon opponent. When he tags out, Booker T surprises the bodyguard with a roll-up and two-count. Right back up, Test hammers him down again before Henry returns to punch and squeeze the babyface's shoulder. When Booker fights free, the "World's Strongest Man" flattens him with a clothesline. Fortunately, The Hurricane breaks his cover. Afterwards, Scott tags in to northern lights suplex the five-time champion. The fans are all over Steiner's case, booing him as he clubs Booker T and tags back in Test. He keeps the babyface trapped with a bearhug, but eventually Booker fights free and surprises him with a spinebuster. The superhero tags in moments later to catch the bodyguard with a top rope flying cross body block. He then knocks the other heels off the apron before slipping free of a pumphandle slam for the Eye of the Hurricane and a near fall. Unfortunately, he misses a shining wizard afterwards for Test to plant him with a full nelson slam. Rosey answers with a Spinning Side Slam only to see "Big Poppa Pump" overhead belly-to-belly suplex him. Booker T responds with a Book End to Scott before kicking Mark's jaw and driving him out to the floor. He returns after Booker clotheslines himself and the bodyguard out to the floor. Although The Hurricane surprises him with a neckbreaker off the ropes, Henry kicks out of his cover and traps the superhero in a bearhug for the win. Post-match, Booker T makes the save but gets trapped in a bearhug himself.

After a commercial break, Eric Bischoff names Evolution and Mark Henry the lumberjacks for tonight's main event. He says they can do anything they want to Goldberg or Kane if they leave the ring.

We then see footage of Goldberg and Kane facing off virtually in *SmackDown!: Here Comes the Pain*. Afterwards, the announcers preview Armageddon.

Molly Holly/Victoria def. Lita/Trish Stratus. Joined in progress after a commercial break, Trish chops Molly in a corner while Chris Jericho and Christian watch from the entrance stage. They see the vixen score a two-count with a dropkick. When she nears the ropes though, Victoria pulls her hair and slaps Stratus for a Holly two-count. The "black widow" tags in afterwards for a slingshot somersault leg drop and near fall. When Victoria only gets a two-count with a spinning side slam, Y2J wants Trish to show him what she's got. Instead, the heels trap her in their corner for a backbreaker and Molly face stretch. When the champion attempts a handspring back elbow, the vixen catches her only to see Holly slip free and powerbomb her to the canvas. Fortunately, Lita breaks her cover with a dropkick. She gets the tag soon afterwards to kick and trip the heels. Following a sit-out spinning slam to the "black widow", the extreme diva head scissors Molly. That brings Matt Hardy out to distract Lita. The heels capitalize with a double-team side slam to the extreme diva for the victory.

Ads for *WWE Unscripted* and Armageddon play.

Goldberg def. Kane ("Lumberjack" match) by disqualification. Goldberg is out last, getting his full entrance from his locker room this week while the announcers question where Triple H is. Although the intense superstar tackles Kane, the "Big Red Machine" quickly recovers to toss him out to the floor for the four lumberjacks to assault him. That scores the monster a two-count. He follows up with clubbing blows until the champion side suplexes him. Unfortunately, Bill is tossed back out to the floor for another heel assault moments later. Once again, that scores Kane a two-count. The "Big Red Machine" and Ric Flair then take turns choking the intense superstar before the monster scores another near fall with a corner clothesline. An unorthodox sidewalk slam follows where Kane picks up Goldberg from the back. That also gets him a two-count before he applies a sleeper hold. JR thinks it's a choke, but Charles Robinson doesn't check. He doesn't need to because the champion fights his way free ahead of a fireman's carry takeover. A kick sends the "Big Red Machine" out to the floor, but the lumberjacks don't touch him. Instead, Bill leaves to deck the four lumberjacks. Back in the squared circle, a powerslam puts the monster down for a Spear, but Randy Orton hops into the ring to attack the intense superstar from behind. Batista joins him, Robinson calling for the bell. Rob Van Dam tries to even up the odds, but the heels swarm him. They do the same to Booker T when he runs out. Finally, Shawn Michaels gets a big pop when he sprints out to give Flair Sweet Chin Music. He tunes up the band afterwards and stuns Kane with Sweet Chin Music before Goldberg Spears Kane ahead of Armageddon.

SmackDown!
December 11, 2003
San Diego, CA
Announcers: Michael Cole, Tazz

The show opens with a close-up of Paul Heyman's face. He tells Chris Benoit that he will never get another shot at the WWE Title so long as Heyman is the general manager ahead of the intro video and fireworks. Afterwards, Justin Roberts introduces Heyman to boos. Paul says he's just following the company tradition by building the company on the back of a dominant champion. That champion is Brock Lesnar, and Benoit came a little too close to beating the champion and ruining the GM's plans. Brock then comes out to boos. He doesn't ask for the fans' respect; he demands it. Lesnar adds that "the Crippler" doesn't deserve another title shot because he tapped out. The fans mock Brock for being the one who tapped out, but the champion shows footage of him making Benoit tap after the "rabid wolverine" was unconscious. Lesnar adds that no one is in his league. He calls Paul a smart man for wanting to build the company around him. When the fans start to taunt him, Brock says he can make anyone in the crowd tap out or deport them from here in Mexico. Heyman corrects him that they are in San Diego, but Lesnar doesn't care. He continues insulting the town until Rey Mysterio comes out. The hometown star enters the squared circle to tell the champion that he's not insulting his people while the masked man is around. Rey issues a challenge to Brock for a match tonight. When the champion says he doesn't have the power to make matches, Mysterio accuses him of lacking testicles. That sets off Lesnar and he agrees to give Rey a non-title match. If Mysterio wins, he'll get a title shot next week. Brock then shoves the masked man down, but Rey refuses to be intimidated. He promises that after tonight the fans will chant "619".

Rhyno def. Bradshaw. After Rhyno Gored him on *Velocity*, Bradshaw marches out for a piece of the man-beast. He gets it, punching and chasing off Rhyno by teasing an early Clothesline from Hell. The big Texan follows him out to slam the man-beast into the ring steps and barricade. Back in the squared circle, Bradshaw knocks Rhyno down with a shoulderblock, but misses an elbow drop. The man-beast doesn't miss his DDT for a two-count. Afterwards, the two men trade shots, the big Texan getting the upper hand with another shoulderblock and neckbreaker. A second neckbreaker gets him a near fall. Although Rhyno counters his corner charge with a back elbow, Bradshaw recovers quickly to give the man-beast a fallaway slam off the second rope. That scores him a near fall moments later. The big Texan follows up with a big boot and corner clothesline. Going back upstairs, Bradshaw superplexes the man-beast from the second rope. When they hit the mat though, Rhyno hooks his legs for the win.

Backstage, Paul Heyman tells A-Train that he dealt with Nathan Jones and he doesn't want to deal with the hairy heel tonight. "Dealt with" is code for him quitting on an Australian tour. Paul's having an issue with A-Train betting on Chris Benoit last week. Since he upset Brock Lesnar, Heyman signs him to a match against a man who might have a spot on Team Lesnar, the man stealing the show of late…Shannon Moore. Matt Morgan tells the hairy heel that they have a lot of money riding on his match and he better not blow it.

After a commercial break, The FBI take bets on the A-Train/Shannon Moore match. The Basham Brothers want to know the odds on their match next week with Rikishi and Scotty 2 Hotty. With the odds favoring them, the WWE Tag Team Champions put money on themselves. Matt Morgan then finds out the odds on Moore/A-Train. When he's told it's ten-to-one for the hairy heel, Morgan puts his cash on A-Train.

Shannon Moore def. A-Train. Tazz mocks Nathan Jones for getting homesick as A-Train crushes Moore in a corner. He follows up with a swing into the barricade. Back in the ring, Shannon surprises the hairy heel with a springboard cross body block off the second rope to the back. It doesn't take A-Train long to answer with a back body drop out to the floor. Back in the squared circle, he lifts up the cruiserweight for a powerbomb, but Moore sunset flips him for the three-count. Post-match, Matt Morgan hits Shannon from behind and tosses him back into the ring. Big Show joins the heels, applauding Morgan crushing Moore in a corner. When A-Train tries the same, Matt stuns him with a big boot. A giant clothesline and Chokeslam follow.

Backstage, the camera focuses on Ernest Miller's feet as he dances and Lamont praises his skills. After a commercial break, Lamont introduces "the Cat" to the excited crowd, including Rey Mysterio's family, Dominik sitting front row. Miller dances out solo, but he wants a diva to join him and invites Sable to the ring. She says she only dances for Vince McMahon and yells at "the Cat". Ernest doesn't mind getting yelled at, but he tells her that she's going to dance for the people. He then grabs and leads her in a dance before he kisses the diva. She can't believe it and storms backstage while Miller strips down to his boxer shorts.

Backstage, Eddie Guerrero asks Chavo Guerrero Jr. if he's going to ride with him tonight. Chavo says he'll ride with him if his uncle doesn't steal the spotlight again. "Latino Heat" has no idea what he's talking about. Eddie isn't worried about spotlights. He wants to know if Chavo's knee is good. The younger Guerrero says it's so good that he might not even tag in his uncle. "Latino Heat" can't promise he won't steal the spotlight, but he will steal the victory. Chavo says he'll have to steal it from him, making his uncle smile.

Los Guerreros def. The World's Greatest Tag Team. The babyfaces are out first in a green lowrider. The announcers are glad to see them back on the same page. So are the fans. After Eddie and Charlie trade shots, Shelton tags in to challenge Guerrero to a test of strength. "Latino Heat" escapes with a head scissors before tagging in Chavo to stomp Benjamin in a corner. When Haas tries to help his partner and distracts the referee, Eddie chokes Shelton. Benjamin answers with an armbar drop when "Latino Heat" tags in. He then heads out to the floor to open the hood of the lowrider. Eddie follows him out and gets tossed into the steel post ahead of a commercial break.

Afterwards, Charlie hammerlocks "Latino Heat's" arm. The heels focus on the arm, trapping Guerrero in their corner. Although Eddie manages to toss Haas down, the heel stops him from tagging out and knocks Chavo off the apron. It doesn't matter as Chavo tags himself in moments later to back body drop Charlie and head scissors Shelton. A twisting senton splash off the second rope follows to Haas for a near fall. When the heel tries to answer with a press slam, Chavo slips free and rolls him up for another two-count before applying an armbar. Eddie can barely stay conscious on the apron as he watches his nephew. Unfortunately, The World's Greatest Tag Team is at full strength and Benjamin surprises Chavo with a shot to his injured knee. Charlie follows with a knee lock before Shelton tags in to leap onto the injured joint and apply his own submission stretch. Eventually, "Latino Heat" pulls the tag rope out of the corner, forcing Jimmy Korderas to fix it while Eddie cheap shots Benjamin to save his nephew. Moments later, Chavo dropkicks Shelton out of the ring, but when he crawls to his corner for the tag, the heel pulls his uncle out to the floor. Despite that, "Latino Heat" gets the tag moments later to fight both heels and arm drag Benjamin across the squared circle. He then dodges a Haas charge that sees the heels run into each other. They do the same moments later when Eddie dropkicks Shelton into Charlie. With Chavo down and out at ringside, "Latino Heat" back suplexes Benjamin into position for a Frog Splash, but Haas meets Guerrero on the top rope for a superplex. After the men in the ring catch their breath, Charlie hotshots Eddie for a heel double-team leapfrog splash. Thankfully, Chavo returns for the save. After low bridging Haas out to the floor, the younger Guerrero follows him out with a slingshot plancha. That leaves "Latino Heat" alone to give Benjamin a trio of suplexes. Before the third, Haas tries to sneak attack Guerrero, but Eddie back body drops him. Chavo then tags himself in to Frog Splash Shelton for a near fall. "Latino Heat" wants the tag, but Chavo doesn't want to leave the ring. Instead, Charlie dropkicks him into his uncle, the referee counting it as a tag. While The World's Greatest Tag Team lays out Chavo with a combination Inverted Atomic Drop and Superkick, the older Guerrero grabs something from his lowrider. Inside the ring, Korderas tells the heels that Eddie is the legal man. While they argue, "Latino Heat" smashes Benjamin with an air filter for the victory.

A Tribute to the Troops video package plays. The WWE also invites fans to donate twenty-five dollars to send care packages to the troops.

Afterwards, Big Show comes out dressed in hip hop clothing like John Cena. Since he's already proven that he's physically superior to Cena, he challenges him to his own game this week, a battle rap. It doesn't take long for the rapping superstar to answer to a big pop. This week, John is sporting an old school WWF logo with the "F" removed. Show taunts him, rapping about "punking out" Cena. He draws a big reaction when he calls John the "white girl" and the giant is "Kobe Bryant". It's a pretty solid insult, but the rapping superstar says he didn't hear him over all his neck fat. He then mocks him for being overweight and having stinky breath. Hilarious, Big Show checks it. Cena wins the battle rap, implying that he slept with the giant's mom and calling him "Fat Albert". He then tosses Show the microphone, but when he looks up, John kicks his crotch.

Following footage of Brock Lesnar's match with Chris Benoit last week, Josh Mathews interviews "the Crippler". Benoit admits that he didn't win that match and now it's not a matter of when he gets another shot at the WWE Title, it's "if". The "rabid wolverine" refuses to let Paul Heyman or anyone else take away his dreams of being the champion.

Ahead of the main event, we see the tale of the tape for the competitors.

Brock Lesnar def. Rey Mysterio. Rey's wife, daughter, and son, Dominik, watch this match from the front row. At least two of them do. His daughter is asleep. When Brock comes out, the fans instantly start chanting that he tapped out. The champion ignores them to laugh at the masked man's size. When they lock up, Lesnar shoves Mysterio down effortlessly. He then slings Rey around by the leg until the masked man answers with fist to the jaw and dropkick to the front of the knee. A drop toe hold onto the middle turnbuckle has the champion seeing red and he chases his opponent all around ringside. Cole says it will tire out Lesnar. It definitely gets the crowd popping for Mysterio and telling the heel that he tapped out. Brock has had enough and grabs the ring steps, but it's Rey baseball slide kicking them back into his face. Despite that blow, the champion recovers to slam the masked man's back into the ring post. Back in the squared circle, he chokes Mysterio before missing a clothesline near the ropes. When he topples out to the floor, Rey sunset flips him into the barricade. A head scissors into the ring post and springboard splash off the ropes follow ahead of a commercial break.

Afterwards, Brock catches the masked man for a backbreaker. When Brian Hebner gets in the way, the champion shoves him aside and low blows Mysterio. Elbows and clotheslines follow before Lesnar squeezes Rey with a crisscross submission. Tiring of that, he lets the masked man up to toss him out to the floor. When he taunts him, Mysterio kicks the middle rope into his groin ahead of a 619. He Drops the Dime afterwards for a near fall to almost win a title shot next week. A head scissors follows before Rey lands on the top rope when Lesnar tosses him for a roll-up and another near fall. When he tries to hit the West Coast Pop though, Brock answers with a powerbomb. Instead of going for the cover, he hoists Mysterio's leg over his head and hooks the new Brock Lock, named by the announcers. He holds on for a few seconds, but the masked man has no choice but to submit. Post-match, a man in a Rey Mysterio mask tries to hop into the ring to help Rey, but security holds him back. The man surprises everyone when he pulls his mask off to reveal it's actually Hardcore Holly. With security stunned, he finally gets his hands on the WWE Champion, hammering him out of the ring, the show ending with Brock running backstage and Holly smiling.

PPV: Armageddon
December 14, 2003
Orlando, FL
Announcers: Jim Ross, Jerry "the King" Lawler

The show opens with Howard Finkel introducing Lilian Garcia to sing the national anthem. A video package then plays featuring Goldberg, Kane, and Triple H, promising that the great day of Armageddon has come. Afterwards, a wrecking ball graphic destroys the logo before fireworks explode and fire rages on the entrance stage to kick off the PPV.

Booker T def. Mark Henry (with Theodore Long). As Mark heads to the ring, we see footage of him fighting with the babyface over recent weeks. After staring down the big heel, Booker unloads with a series of strikes. It only takes one shot to slow the five-time champion. Henry follows up with a scoop slam and clothesline out to the floor. Outside the ring, the "World's Strongest Man" whips Booker T into the ring steps before shoving him back into the squared circle. The babyface refuses to let Mark back in, baseball slide kicking him before diving over the top rope onto him. When Henry does get in the ring, a top rope missile dropkick scores Booker a two-count. He motions for a Scissors Kick, but Long hops onto the apron to distract him. When the five-time champion goes after him, the "World's Strongest Man" capitalizes with a backbreaker for a near fall. He then slows the pace with a side bow and arrow, stretching Booker T's lower back. When that doesn't score him the victory, Mark chokes and leg drops the babyface on the middle rope for a two-count. Afterwards, he hooks a reverse chin lock. Although Booker fights free, he runs into a bearhug afterwards. It takes him some time, but he fights free again only to run into a clothesline. When Henry tries to follow up with a leg drop, the five-time champion rolls out of the way at the last second. That lets him turn the tide with a string of kicks. A running forearm and shot to the gut follow to double over the "World's Strongest Man" for a Scissors Kick and near fall. Mark immediately answers with a spinebuster for his own close two-count. After catching his breath, he crushes Booker T in a corner. A clothesline and leg drop get him another near fall and frustrate the big heel. That's not good for the babyface because Henry picks him up and powerbombs him to the canvas. Running out of steam, the "World's Strongest Man" misses a corner charge for Booker to steal the win with a second Scissors Kick.

Backstage, Eric Bischoff says that's not how he wanted to start Armageddon. He's counting on Chris Jericho and Christian winning the "battle of the sexes" match with Lita and Trish Stratus. Jericho wants to talk about that, but Christian cuts him off to exclaim how excited he is for the match after the divas cost the Canadians the World Tag Titles Monday night. Y2J again tries to interrupt, but Eric hears Mick Foley's music playing and watches his co-general manager head to the ring.

Inside the squared circle, Mick Foley gets a cheap pop saying the name of the town. He's excited to be here for his first PPV as the co-general manager. He's also excited to announce that the "Stone Cold" Steve Austin petition has one million signatures. That shows how much people want to see the "rattlesnake" and Foley believes it's cause for celebration. Stacy Keibler then comes out in a cheerleader outfit to kick and cartwheel inside the ring. Lawler loves seeing her underwear, while the fans are entertained by Mick flipping over as he attempts his own cartwheel. Unfortunately, Randy Orton and Ric Flair interrupt the festivities. Randy hopes that Foley didn't hurt his hand because he'll need it to count to three later tonight for Orton's Intercontinental Title shot. He is also fired up about the "Stone Cold" petition, telling the co-GM that he retired Austin. Since Randy is in such a combative spirit, Foley takes off his shirt to reveal his referee's attire underneath and orders the Intercontinental Title match to start right now.

MUST SEE! Randy Orton (with Ric Flair) def. Rob Van Dam (Intercontinental Title match). RVD is always ready for a fight and heads down the aisle to sweep Randy's leg and chase him out to the floor. Lawler doesn't think this is fair since Ric didn't get time to give Orton his "official pep talk". He has to wing it tonight, trading holds with Rob. When neither gets the advantage, they try to hit each other, but dodge and square off again. This time, the "Legend Killer" clubs Van Dam only to see the champion kick him. A second shot to the gut puts the challenger down for RVD to head upstairs and score a Mick Foley two-count with a cross body block. Moments later, Randy ends up on the apron where Rob kicks him out to the floor. Van Dam follows up with a cannonball over the top rope. Back in the squared circle, a slingshot leg drop scores the champion a near fall. When he heads back upstairs though, Orton shoves the popular superstar all the way out face-first into the barricade. The "Legend Killer" follows for a dropkick on the floor and two-count. Afterwards, he stomps and punches RVD for another near fall. Surprisingly, the challenger follows the referee's instructions, choking Rob on the ropes for a four-count. When he chokes him a second time, Randy ignores the referee's count forcing Foley to take things into his own hands and pull the heel back. He also threatens Flair when he gets too close to the ropes and complains. Orton remains in control until Rob surprises him with a cross body block and two-count. Right back up, the "Legend Killer" unloads with a stiff clothesline. A European uppercut and face rams into the top turnbuckle follow for another near fall. He then slows the pace with a reverse chin lock. It doesn't take Van Dam long to fight free only to run into another hard clothesline. The challenger is so impressed with himself that he poses before laying on the popular superstar for a two-count. Randy also gets a near fall with a low dropkick before returning to the chin lock. The champion escapes and briefly picks up the pace with a roll-up and split legged moonsault, but Orton cuts off his momentum by picking him up into position for a powerbomb before dropping RVD with a neckbreaker. He returns to his chin lock until Rob punches free. A dropkick from Van Dam puts both men down. Mick just watches as they struggle to regain their footing. It's the champion on the offensive first, mounting and punching the "Legend Killer" ahead of a corner monkey flip. Building momentum, he clotheslines and northern lights suplexes the challenger for a near fall. When Randy rolls out to the floor, RVD follows him for a sternum-first suplex onto the barricade and twisting leg drop off the apron. Rob makes the mistake of rolling Orton back into the ring first and the "Legend Killer" capitalizes by grabbing Van Dam's head for a DDT off the ropes and a pair of near falls. The challenger can't believe that's not enough to score the victory and yells at the special guest referee. That comes back to cost him as the champion recovers in time to avoid his knee drop. A roll-up afterwards scores the popular superstar a two-count before he kicks Randy down for a dropkick to the face and rolling thunder. When Ric tells his man to get up, Orton kicks Rob out to the floor. The "Legend Killer" follows up with a roll-up, but only scores a two-count. RVD immediately answers with a step over heel kick before heading upstairs. "The Nature Boy" tries to stop the champion with a foreign object, but Foley knocks Flair off the apron before he can interfere. On his own, the challenger dropkicks Van Dam in the corner, crotching the popular superstar. When he falls to the canvas, Orton delivers an RKO out of nowhere to win the championship. JR wonders if this is a sign of things to come tonight for Evolution.

Chris Jericho/Christian def. Lita/Trish Stratus. Following a lengthy video package for the match, Y2J heads to the ring first. JR is disgusted by this match, but thinks it's ironic that Jericho's first Survivor Series contest was an intergender match with Chyna in 1999, though he doesn't name her. Chris looks conflicted here tonight as the divas step into the squared circle. Y2J tries to talk to Trish and tell her that he doesn't want this. When he touches her chin, she slaps him. Instead of fighting back, he tries to hold her back. She won't stop and leaps into his arms attempting a cross body block. He tells her to calm down and spanks her. That sets off the vixen and she kicks and dropkicks the heel back into his corner where Christian tags himself into the ring. He is not conflicted, shoving Stratus hard back into her corner. He then dares Lita to hit him when she tags in. Instead, she headbutts him and leads him around the ring to stomp and wail on the Canadian heel. When he attempts to answer with a corner charge, she moves and responds with a monkey flip and head scissors. Jericho has no qualms hitting the extreme diva and knocks her down as she runs the ropes. Christian follows up with a scoop slam before Y2J tags in for his own slam. He then stands on Lita's hair and pulls her up by the arms, Charles Robinson yelling for him to stop. Instead, he pulls the extreme diva up for a powerbomb, but she surprises him with a hurricanrana for a near fall. Christian returns afterwards to pull off Lita's shirt. While he and Jericho taunt her, the extreme diva recovers to give Christian a low blow. Trish gets the hot tag afterwards to forearm the heel ahead of a Chick Kick. She tries to follow up with Stratusfaction, but Christian flips her over only to miss a charge and fall out to the floor. Y2J teases attacking the vixen from the top rope, but Lita trips him. Stratus tries to follow up with her handstand head scissors, but Jericho shoves her down to the canvas. That scores Christian a two-count, but he picks up Trish's head at the last second to inflict more punishment. Unfortunately, he then runs into Jericho, knocking him off the apron and into the Spanish announce table. Although Christian levels the vixen with a clothesline, Lita surprises him with a flying hurricanrana off the top rope. Before she can follow up, Y2J pulls the extreme diva out to the floor and whips her back hard into the barricade. He then slides into the ring to help Stratus up. They share a look before Christian rolls up Trish for the win. Once again, Jericho looks conflicted as his partner celebrates.

Shawn Michaels def. Batista (with Ric Flair). Following a video package for the match, Shawn peppers "the Animal" with fists. The fans are firmly behind Michaels as he hits and moves. One shot from the big heel puts the "Heartbreak Kid" down. He refuses to stay there, kicking and chopping Batista. When Shawn slides out to the floor to taunt "the Animal", he stops and decks Ric. That upsets Batista and he gives chase until Flair calms him down. Back in the squared circle, he corners Michaels and hammers him. After choking the "Heartbreak Kid", the big heel scores a two-count with a vicious clothesline. He shows off his power with a vertical suplex for another near fall. "The Nature Boy" wants his man to hurt Shawn. He tries, whipping Michaels hard into a corner before raking his elbow across the "Heartbreak Kid's" face. Shawn answers with chops and a boot to the face before knocking "the Animal" down to the canvas when Batista puts him on the top rope. A moonsault follows for a two-count. Afterwards, Michaels rocks "the Animal" with a flying forearm. After working Earl Hebner's count to six, the "Heartbreak Kid" kips up only to see Batista clothesline him. He then takes the fight out to the floor where he whips Shawn into the ring steps for a two-count. A backbreaker also gets him a near fall. Following a second backbreaker, "the Animal" stretches his opponent over his knee. When Michaels starts to fight back, Batista shoves him to the canvas for another two-count. Back up, the "Heartbreak Kid" unloads with a series of chops and another flying forearm. This time he immediately kips up to inverted atomic drop "the Animal". When Batista catches him by the throat and tries to lift Shawn up, the babyface answers with a DDT. He then heads upstairs for a flying elbow drop and big pop. Feeling it, Michaels tunes up the band. Unfortunately, "the Animal" blocks Sweet Chin Music with a spinebuster. A second spinebuster follows before Batista flexes and sets up for his finisher. When he picks up the "Heartbreak Kid" though, Shawn flips back to the canvas and nails him with Sweet Chin Music for the victory. Post-match, Batista is so stunned that he thinks he won until Flair tells him otherwise.

The Matt Hardy Version 1.0/Maven match never officially starts. Batista and Ric Flair are still in the ring as a confused Maven comes out. Hardy follows, Matt Facts revealing that his fingernails grow extremely fast. With the ring already occupied, Matt attacks Maven in the aisle and shoves him into the squared circle for a Batista Bomb. Both Hardy and Flair love it as "the Animal" delivers a second Batista Bomb before finally leaving the ring. Wisely, Matt gives him a wide berth. Jack Doan tells Lilian Garcia that Maven is no longer able to compete and cancels the match. Hardy doesn't like that. He shoves the referee aside to splash Maven and count to three himself. Afterwards, he declares himself the winner.

Backstage, Batista throws a fit and yells that he's better than Shawn Michaels. Ric Flair agrees. He tries to calm "the Animal" by telling him that he has greatness in him and even the best slip on occasion. Ric believes it's more important how he responds. Tonight, Flair promises that the duo will leave with gold.

Rosey/The Hurricane def. La Resistance (Rene Dupree/Rob Conway) ("Tag Team Turmoil" World Tag Title match). "Tag Team Turmoil" will see a number of tag teams face each other in a series of head-to-head matches, the last team standing winning the belts. The superheroes try to make it them, attacking the heels until The Hurricane clips the ropes on a dive out of the ring and crashes to the floor. Conway capitalizes with a running neckbreaker before Dupree tags in to powerslam the superhero for a two-count. When he lowers his head for a back body drop, The Hurricane counters with a falling face slam. Both men tag out afterwards for Rosey to back body drop the heels and Samoan drop Rene. A Spinning Side Slam follows to Rob, but Dupree makes the save. That gets him slammed over the top rope. Rosey then tosses Conway to the canvas before tagging in The Hurricane to fly off his partner's shoulders, the super hero in training sitting on the middle rope, for a body splash and three-count.

Garrison Cade/Mark Jindrak def. Rosey/The Hurricane ("Tag Team Turmoil" World Tag Title match). The young superstars immediately hop out of the crowd to attack the superheroes from behind. After Cade knocks Rosey to the floor, Jindrak rolls up The Hurricane for the three-count.

Garrison Cade/Mark Jindrak def. Lance Storm/Val Venis ("Tag Team Turmoil" World Tag Title match). The babyfaces are ready and waiting to immediately walk out with their dates for this third "Tag Team Turmoil" match. Val and Mark open the fall trading shots. When the adult star gets the upper hand, both men tag out for Lance to work on Cade's arm. The two men then trade holds, the fans chanting "boring". The babyfaces' dates aren't bored, applauding Storm's efforts as he flips off the top rope. When he attempts a springboard attack though, Jindrak jacks his jaw for a Garrison two-count. Mark then tags in to apply a surfboard stretch. It doesn't take long for Lance to fight free, but Jindrak remains on the offensive with a clubbing blow to the back. When he attempts a corner splash though, Storm moves and tags in Venis to fight both heels. That includes slams and neckbreakers before Cade breaks up a cover on Mark. Soon after, Lance recovers to clothesline himself and Garrison out to the floor. That leaves "the big Valbowski" to give Jindrak a sit-out powerbomb for a near fall. Mark tries to roll out to the apron to regroup, but Val won't let him go and sets up for a suplex. Before he can bring the young star back into the squared circle, Cade clips the adult star's leg for Jindrak to land on him for the three-count, Garrison holding down Val's foot.

The Dudley Boyz def. Garrison Cade/Mark Jindrak ("Tag Team Turmoil" World Tag Title match). The champions get a bad draw as they don't enter as the final team. Cade is waiting to punch Bubba Ray, but when he attempts a corner leapfrog, Dudley moves and ties him to the tree of woe. Following a pair of hammering blows, D-Von tags in for a double shoulderblock and two-count. Garrison answers with a right hand before Jindrak tags in only to catch a spinning back elbow and near fall. Mark responds with a big clothesline and his own two-count. After he cheap shots D-Von from the apron, Cade tags in to choke the champion and slow him with a chin lock. Moments later, he heads upstairs for a nice looking flying elbow drop, but ultimately misses. That lets Bubba tag back in to squash both challengers in a corner. While he fights with Garrison at ringside, D-Von deals with Jindrak in the ring. They trade roll-ups and two-counts while Cade whips Bubba Ray into the ring steps. By the time Mark misses a dropkick, Bubba recovers to join his half-brother for a 3D and the elimination.

The Dudley Boyz def. Scott Steiner/Test ("Tag Team Turmoil" World Tag Title match). Before the heels head to the ring, Garrison Cade hits the Dudleys from behind. Once the sore loser leaves, Scott and Test run out to whip D-Von into the ring steps and hammer Bubba Ray. Although Bubba tries to fight back, a Steiner northern lights suplex slows his comeback. The bodyguard follows up with a trio of whips into the ring post, focusing on the champion's shoulder. An elbow drop back in the ring scores "Big Poppa Pump" a near fall and sees him celebrating with pushups. After the heels take turns choking Dudley, Scott traps him in an armbar. When he won't submit, Test tags in to stomp, choke, and punch the champion ahead of his own armbar. Although Bubba Ray fights free, the bodyguard remains in control and puts Dudley on the top rope. Bubba reaches down deep and shoves Test to the canvas before landing his rarely successful second rope senton splash. D-Von then gets the hot tag to fight both challengers and nearly finish off Test with a swinging neckbreaker. When the heels get back up, Steiner northern lights suplexes D-Von ahead of a bodyguard sidewalk slam and near fall. JR says that would have crowned new champions because these are the last two teams. Test attempts to win the belts again with a Big Boot, but D-Von dodges and the bodyguard hits his own partner. Test isn't concerned about "Big Poppa Pump" and attempts to finish off Dudley with a pumphandle slam, but the champion slips free only to turn into a full nelson slam. Despite putting his feet on the ropes, the bodyguard still can't score the three-count. Frustrated, he slides a title belt into the ring to distract Mike Chioda. While the referee gets rid of it, Test blasts D-Von with a chair. Before he can score the win, Bubba Ray pulls the bodyguard out to the floor. Test answers with a clothesline, but makes the mistake of shoving Bubba into the ring. That comes back to haunt him moments later when he surprises the bodyguard with a Bubba Bomb for D-Von to score the three-count and retain the titles. Unfortunately, Eric Bischoff marches out to tell the champions that they haven't went through all of the teams. He then introduces Batista and Ric Flair.

MUST SEE! Batista/Ric Flair def. The Dudley Boyz ("Tag Team Turmoil" World Tag Title match). JR is upset that Eric Bischoff just added a seventh team to "Tag Team Turmoil". He says the Dudleys don't stand a chance. He's right as the challengers march out to pummel Bubba Ray and D-Von. While Ric traps Bubba in a Figure Four Leglock by the ropes, "the Animal" finishes off D-von with a Batista Bomb to crown new champions. Jerry notes that Evolution has both the World Tag and Intercontinental Titles.

The Tribute to the Troops video package from *SmackDown!* replays.

Molly Holly def. Ivory (Women's Title match). Just added, Molly marches out to defend her title. Ivory follows, dropkicking and rolling up the champion for a two-count. The fans do not care. Regardless, the challenger scores another near fall with a top rope flying cross body block before catapulting Holly out to the floor. Ivory follows with a dive off the apron. When she tries to return to the ring, Molly surprises her with a low dropkick to the ankles for a two-count. A northern lights suplex also gets the champion a near fall before she applies an overhead hammerlock. When the challenger fights free, Holly tosses her down onto the bottom rope for another two-count. Following a suplex and near fall, Molly stretches Ivory's jaw, drawing a warning from Chad Patton. A handspring back elbow also gets the champion a near fall before she clubs and stomps her opponent. She then removes the top turnbuckle pad, but when she tries to ram Ivory's face into it, the challenger reverses the attempt. That still only gets Ivory a two-count before Holly reverses her roll-up for the victory.

MUST SEE! Triple H def. Goldberg and Kane (World Title match). Following a video package for the match, Kane is out first. Triple H follows, back to his customary trunks as he spits water and poses on the apron by himself. The announcers are surprised that no one from Evolution joined him. Goldberg is out last, the fans loudly chanting his name as the camera follows his entrance from his locker room to the squared circle. There, Hunter taunts him before the heels team up to wear down the champion. Although Bill manages to surprise Helmsley with a clothesline, the "Big Red Machine" immediately drops the intense superstar. He can't keep him down as Goldberg recovers to clothesline and slam the heels. After knocking "the Game" out to the floor, the champion tries to follow him only to see the monster sit up. That brings Bill back over to fight with Kane, the two men trading shots. The announcers say the "Big Red Machine" is one of the few men in the world who can trade shots with the intense superstar, and he proves it, scoring a two-count with a clothesline. When Goldberg answers with a slam, Triple H returns only to be knocked down again. After the champion slams the monster off the top rope, he powerslams Hunter. He tries to finish off Kane with a Spear, but the "Big Red Machine" answers with a big boot to finally put Bill down. Once again, the challengers team up to punch, stomp, and choke the intense superstar. Together, they double suplex Goldberg. Helmsley tells the monster to finish him off with a powerslam, but when Kane does so, "the Game" tries to steal the pin. While Triple H begs off, the champion recovers. The "Big Red Machine" tries to clothesline him, but Bill ducks and the monster knocks Hunter out to the floor. That sees him grab a chair to block a Chokeslam and blast Kane's skull. The intense superstar takes advantage of the heels turning on each other to kick "the Game" and powerslam him. He then wraps the chair around Triple H's leg to Pillmanize him. Fortunately, the "Big Red Machine" makes the save and tosses Goldberg out to the floor. The monster follows him, whipping the champion into the ring steps. He then clears the Spanish announce table and sets up for a Chokeslam. Instead, Bill fights free and teases a Jackhammer until Hunter drives the chair into the intense superstar's ribs. Kane finally delivers his Chokeslam onto the table, but it doesn't break. Helmsley makes it do so, elbow dropping Goldberg from the barricade. When he celebrates with the chair, the "Big Red Machine" asks "the Game" what he's doing. He begs off and walks away, leaving the monster to grab the champion. Before he can do anything, Triple H tosses Kane into the steps and sets up for a Pedigree. The "Big Red Machine" escapes with a back body drop. That's the final straw for the heels and the monster takes their fight back into the ring for a big boot, corner clothesline, and sidewalk slam. He then heads upstairs and connects with a flying clothesline. He teases a Chokeslam, but Hunter slows him with a poke to the eye and DDT. When Kane sits up, Helmsley delivers a neckbreaker. He can't keep the "Big Red Machine" down and he fights "the Game" out to the floor to Chokeslam him on the ramp. When he carries Triple H back into the ring, Bill Spears the monster for a near fall before Hunter breaks his cover. All three men then stagger up to their feet and trade haymakers. When the heels try to work together again, the intense superstar drops them with a double clothesline. He then Spears Kane again. Afterwards, he Spears Helmsley as Randy Orton and Ric Flair run down to ringside. Goldberg fights them off and gives Helmsley a short Spear, but the "Big Red Machine" breaks his cover. He and the champion then grab each other's throats until "the Game" low blows Bill. The monster follows up with a Chokeslam, but before he can make the cover, Batista drags Kane out to the floor for Triple H to steal the three-count and the World Title, his eighth WWF/WWE championship. The show ends with Evolution celebrating their third title win of the night.

Armageddon is almost exclusively about Evolution with the heels competing in four of the seven matches and winning three championships. The WWE tries to start the night off with a feel good victory as Booker T beats Mark Henry, but ten-minutes is too long for the "World's Strongest Man". Orton and RVD go nearly twenty in a solid Intercontinental Title match. It stretches in places, but it's a fun contest and it's time for Randy to take a step forward. Van Dam certainly doesn't need the Intercontinental Title to get a reaction at this point. The intergender tag match continues the Jericho/Trish story. It's one of the best slow builds of the year and Y2J continues to tell a good story with his facial reactions, conflicted on hurting a girl that he wasn't supposed to like, but clearly does. Shawn Michaels helps carry Batista through one of his early PPV matches. With the "Heartbreak Kid" on the other side, "the Animal" is put over strong even in defeat. Shawn is really settling into his role with the company and is able to make young stars look good while keeping himself elevated as one of the most exciting in-ring competitors of all-time. The "Tag Team Turmoil" match follows and gives Batista redemption as he wins his first championship alongside Ric Flair. This is Ric's first tag title victory in the WWE and adds to his impressive list of accolades. The match itself is good with seven teams going through a series of matches in twenty minutes that showcases Garrison Cade and Mark Jindrak as well as The Dudley Boyz before Evolution take their second championships of the night. The Women's Title match is hard to watch, not for the competitors, but because the fans do not care. Ivory hasn't gotten a reaction since her time in The Right to Censor and that doesn't change here as she hasn't been featured on television in a long time. It's just a match and the fans know it, sitting quietly or chanting for puppies while the women have what turns out to be an average in-ring confrontation with absolutely no emotion. This is barely *Heat* worthy and only fills time and lets fans go to the bathroom or snack stand ahead of the main event. JR describes the World Title match as "bowling shoe ugly" and he's not wrong. Kane and Goldberg don't tell many stories in the ring. In fact, they tell the same one—a monster destroying his competition. While Triple H can sell, he can also gobble up opponents and hammer them too. That's what he wants to do here, but it doesn't work as everyone is just clubbing each other for twenty minutes. Shawn Michaels would have been a good addition here to sell for everyone. Instead, it's three men hitting each other before Evolution interferes and Helmsley wins back the World Title at Armageddon for the second straight year. After Hunter dominated *Raw* for the last year and a half, there's no sign of that ending now that Evolution has all of the belts. Curiously, the WWE hasn't changed belts on the major PPVs lately, but this brand exclusive show features three title changes. The company is probably trying to boost PPV buys for traditionally weaker shows. If so, that's the only reason to watch this PPV unless you are invested in the Jericho/Stratus storyline. Featuring a large number of heel victories and matches that are bad to just okay, there's not a lot of great in-ring action to enjoy. *Raw* has some solid pieces in place, but the show is too heel heavy at the top and with Goldberg losing the World Title, there's no one waiting to step in and give the show a shot of excitement. Armageddon is a weak ending to 2003's PPVs and is a bit of a worrying sign for 2004 with heels dominating both shows.

Monday Night Raw
December 15, 2003
Tampa, FL
Announcers: Jim Ross, Jerry "the King" Lawler

The show opens with Evolution standing on the stage holding up their newly won title belts. Triple H says that he promised Evolution was going to change the game and they delivered last night, winning all the gold. From now on, he says *Raw* is going to follow the "Golden Rule". Since they have all the gold, they make the rules. Afterwards, the intro video plays and fireworks explode.

Chris Jericho/Christian and Lita/Trish Stratus wrestle to a no contest. A rematch from last night, Lilian Garcia calls this "Eric Bischoff's Battle of the Sexes II". Trish opens the rematch yelling at Jericho. He doesn't even want to face her, tagging Christian and turning his back on the apron. When the CLB turns to argue with Lita, she slaps him and Stratus rolls Christian up for a two-count. The heel shoots up and shoves her down. When Lita tags in, the heel corners her, but she climbs onto his back and scratches his eyes. Fortunately, Y2J saves his partner by pulling Lita off by her hair. After he tags in to slam the extreme diva, Christian returns and puts Lita on the top rope. Unfortunately, she elbows free and knocks the CLB down for a moonsault, but doesn't rotate completely and rams her surgically repaired neck into the heel. Luckily, she avoids serious injury and tags in Trish to surprise Christian with a top rope flying cross body block and two-count. Lita joins her partner for both women to wail on the CLB until he responds with a double clothesline. Instead of taking the win, he pulls the vixen up at the last second to break Charles Robinson's count. He then delivers the Unprettier, but Jericho pulls his partner off Stratus and yells at the referee. When Christian gets in Y2J's face, Jericho shoves him down and the referee waves off this match.

Afterwards, Eric rushes out to yell at Y2J. He wants to know what Jericho is thinking stopping his match. Y2J tells him to shut up. He didn't want the match and he hopes Bischoff is satisfied. Jericho calls him stupid and storms off. The co-general manager doesn't appreciate being yelled at. He tells Y2J that if he's so angry he can take his frustrations out on another man who is angry tonight…Kane. Once Jericho steps through the curtain, Eric invites Mick Foley to come to the ring to hear his big idea.

After a commercial break, Mick comes out to hear Bischoff's idea that will "reshape the face of *Raw*". Foley has his own idea to make *Raw* better—the return of "Stone Cold" Steve Austin. He says that with all the signatures he's gotten for the "rattlesnake's" return, Mick has called for a special meeting in two weeks to decide "Stone Cold's" fate. Eric congratulates Foley on his hard work and says the fans love him, but not as a co-GM. They love him as a hardcore legend. Bischoff reminds Mick that the fans loved seeing him back in the ring last week with The Rock before playing a career retrospective video for the hardcore legend. Eric believes the fans would rather see Foley in the ring. He admits he's been playing around with the idea and would love to wrestle Bischoff. However, it will be on his own terms and when he wants to do so. Eric has had enough of sharing power with co-GMs. He challenges Mick to step into the ring tonight with Randy Orton. If Foley wins, Bischoff will quit as *Raw* general manager. However, if Mick loses, he has to quit. Foley doesn't take that deal. It's not the hardcore legend's first day in the WWE. He knows that as soon as he starts beating Orton, Evolution will interfere. Mick wants a few concessions. First, he wants Earl Hebner as the referee. Second, he wants Evolution banned from ringside. And finally, he wants Eric himself banned from interfering. Bischoff hesitates, but accepts his proposal. The fans love it, but Foley has one last stipulation. Since he's never held the Intercontinental Title, he puts that on the line tonight too.

Booker T/Maven def. Mark Henry/Matt Hardy Version 1.0 (with Theodore Long). Hardy is out last, his Matt Fact revealing that he always uses toilet seat covers. Sort of a rematch from last night, Maven looks for revenge on Matt after he threw him to the wolves at Armageddon. That includes Maven delivering fists and a dropkick until he misses a corner charge. Henry capitalizes with a clothesline from the apron. When he tags in, he tosses around and pounds on the babyface. Back in, Hardy scores a one-count with a side effect before Booker breaks the cover. Matt is right back on the attack, locking on a surfboard submission. It takes him a while, but Maven powers free only to run into a clothesline and two-count. Fists, elbows, and kicks afterwards score the heel another two-count. When he sets up for a powerbomb, the babyface slips free and plants Hardy with a leg sweep. The five-time champion tags in afterwards to hit both heels and drop Matt with a spinebuster. After he entertains with a spinaroonie, Booker T low bridges Mark attempting a sneak attack. Maven follows him out to the floor with a flying cross body block off the top rope before Booker scores the win with a Scissors Kick to Hardy.

Backstage, Jonathan Coachman stands outside Goldberg's locker room. He's at his heel best, promising to get a word with the "former champion". When Bill slams the door in his face, Coach arrogantly says that no one does that to him and enters the locker room. There, Goldberg destroys him and tosses the crying heel back out into the hallway.

Afterwards, La Resistance head to the ring for their scheduled match. Before their opponents come out, Rene Dupree and Rob Conway mock The Rock. They talk big because he's not here tonight. Since they don't like the "People's Champ" or Mick Foley, they put their support behind Randy Orton in his match with the hardcore legend. Instead of their opponents coming out, it's Goldberg in a foul mood. He decimates both heels, Spearing them before giving Rob Conway a Jackhammer. Afterwards, Bill tosses aside the French flag and waves the American flag. That's the last straw for Eric Bischoff. Since Bill attacked his "top announcer", Eric is "deactivating" him for thirty days.

Following a commercial break, Mick Foley talks to Shawn Michaels. The "Heartbreak Kid" says he came back for just one more match, but the WWE is like the mob and always draws you back in. He tells Mick that punching Triple H for the first time in his return match was worth it. That's all Foley needed to hear and he asks Shawn to hand him his flannel shirt.

Rob Van Dam/Shawn Michaels def. Batista/Ric Flair/Triple H. Due to Goldberg being deactivated, this is now a handicap match. While the babyfaces come out separately, Evolution is unified as they step into the ring. Shawn wants another shot at Batista, but the big heel hammers him down. Michaels soon picks up the pace to punch all three heels and frustrate "the Animal". The "Heartbreak Kid" takes advantage of his anger, drop toe holding him. Unfortunately, Batista quickly recovers and rams Shawn back into the heel corner. Triple H then tags in, Michaels meeting his former friend with a series of fists. When he knocks down the World Champion, the "Heartbreak Kid" struts and mocks Flair. RVD tags in afterwards to work on Hunter's arm with strikes and an armbar. Helmsley responds with a thumb to the eye before Ric tags in only to run into a spinning kick. Back in, Shawn trades chops with "The Nature Boy". Although Michaels wins the exchange and back body drops Ric, the legend responds with a poke to the eye. Moments later, "the Game" surprises Shawn with a shot to the face when the "Heartbreak Kid" tries to run Flair into the ropes. Triple H tags in afterwards for a high knee and two-count. Batista then returns to clothesline and rake his elbow across Michaels's face. While Hunter distracts Mike Chioda, "The Nature Boy" joins his tag team partner in punishing the "Heartbreak Kid". Ric tries to follow up with a top rope attack, but that almost never works. It doesn't here either, Shawn slamming him to the canvas before the two men trade chops again. Afterwards, both men tag out for Rob to dropkick "the Animal". He also surprises Hunter with a mule kick before kicking Batista back into a corner. Unfortunately, he crushes Chioda behind him. Things get worse when Van Dam accidentally spears the official. That means there's no referee to see RVD give Batista rolling thunder and a Five-Star Frog Splash. With the official down, Helmsley Pedigrees Rob, but Chioda is too dazed to count "the Animal" covering Van Dam at first. By the time he does, RVD just kicks out. That sees Flair trap the popular superstar in a Figure Four Leglock afterwards as the show takes an abrupt commercial break.

Afterwards, "the Game" works on Rob's leg, dropping a knee on it and applying a leg lock. Ric tags back in to punch and shoulderblock Van Dam. Although RVD answers with a sleeper hold, Flair side suplexes free and tags in Batista. A pair of clotheslines score him a two-count before Triple H returns. Rob greets him with a kick to the face, but "The Nature Boy" gets the tag first to prevent Van Dam from leaving the ring. Reaching down deep, the popular superstar kicks Ric too before giving Shawn the hot tag. He unloads with a string of fists and a flying forearm to Hunter. Clotheslines and forearms follow to the other two heels before Michaels kips up and slams Helmsley for a top rope flying elbow drop. He then tunes up the band, but "the Animal" grabs him from behind for a Batista Bomb. That brings RVD back into the fight, knocking Batista out to the floor. When Flair joins his partner, Rob flies off the top rope onto the World Tag Team Champions to put everyone down in and out of the ring. "The Game" is the first to recover, just barely beating Chioda's standing ten-count. When he pulls Michaels in for a Pedigree, the "Heartbreak Kid" back body drops free and finally hits Sweet Chin Music for the victory.

Rico (with Miss Jackie) def. Jon Heidenreich. After Jackie distracted him last night on *Heat*, costing the rookie a win, Heidenreich marches out for this rematch. He looks good early on as he hammers Rico and traps him in a bearhug, but the flamboyant superstar escapes by kissing the side of Jon's face. He then kicks, stomps, and rakes the big man's eyes. A step up kick in a corner gets him a near fall where he sits on Heidenreich's crotch. Unable to get the pinfall, he applies a chin lock. It doesn't take the rookie long to fight free, but he quickly runs into a sleeper hold, some vocal fans chanting that this is boring. Heidenreich escapes the sleeper moments later to sidewalk slam Rico. He follows up with a shoulderblock and big back body drop for a near fall. The flamboyant heel tries to answer with a neckbreaker, but Heidenreich spins around and continues to club Rico. Although he connects with one corner clothesline, he misses Rico on the second. He nearly hits Charles Robinson, but the referee just manages to dodge out of the way. While he's out of position, Jackie throat drops Heidenreich on the top rope for her man to score the win with a Neckbreaker.

Backstage, Chris Jericho knocks on Trish Stratus's door. She's got ice on her neck as he asks if she's okay. She says she's not physically, but at least she knows the real Jericho now. She'll be much better if he never talks to her again.

Kane def. Chris Jericho by disqualification. Jericho is out first, the announcers debating if he sincerely cares about Trish Stratus. JR doesn't believe Y2J. Jericho has more pressing concerns as Kane storms into the ring in a bad mood. Although Jericho surprises him with a dropkick, it doesn't take the "Big Red Machine" long to slow the Canadian with an onslaught of clubbing blows. Y2J has been in the ring with big men before and uses the monster's size against him, drop toe holding him onto the middle rope for a leg drop. A top rope missile dropkick follows for a one-count. He follows up with a running face slam and Lionsault, but Kane sits up and lifts Jericho by the throat. Before he can Chokeslam him, Y2J climbs down his back and rolls him up to attempt the Walls of Jericho. Unfortunately, he can't turn over the "Big Red Machine". Instead, the monster slugs Jericho again and press slams him out to the floor.

There, Kane introduces him to the barricade. Although Y2J grabs a chair, the "Big Red Machine" throws him back into the ring. Jericho doesn't stay there, sliding back out to grab the chair and smash the monster's skull for the disqualification. Post-match, Y2J tries to deliver a second shot, but Kane surprises him with a big boot. He then ties the Canadian to the tree of woe to choke him with a camera cable. The "Big Red Machine" finally ends his assault, Chokeslamming Jericho. Afterwards, Christian hurries out to help Y2J up before shoving him back down as payback for earlier tonight.

Footage of *Raw* superstars visiting a local air force base plays.

Backstage, Eric Bischoff wants to talk strategy with Randy Orton. The GM tells Randy that he's in great shape and he needs to tire out Mick Foley. Most importantly, Bischoff wants Orton to tune out the locker room rumors. The "Legend Killer" wants to know what people are saying. Eric doesn't want to tell him that several people think he doesn't have what it takes to succeed. That fires up Orton and he promises to show everyone that he is the "greatest talent" in the business.

Further backstage, WWE superstars wish Mick Foley luck. The Dudley Boyz want to talk to him about getting their World Tag Titles back, but he's got other things to worry about. That doesn't stop him from telling Shawn Michaels that he has a World Title match in two weeks as he passes the "Heartbreak Kid".

The Mick Foley/Randy Orton match never officially starts. With just five minutes left in the show, Foley walks out sporting his familiar red and black flannel and a Mankind shirt. He slaps his face to pump himself up. The fans join him, chanting his name. He circles the ring and teases a run from the ramp before heading backstage without a word. Orton is confused. After a second, he grabs his belt and follows Mick backstage. There, Foley grabs his stuff and walks out of the arena. Eric Bischoff briefly stops him to tell Mick that if he walks out, he's walking out on his job. That gives Randy time to catch up and ask the hardcore legend what's going on. He mocks Foley for having a tear in his eye. Orton tells him that legends don't' walk out or cry. He just thinks of Mick as a coward and spits in his face. Foley doesn't say a word, dropping his bag to walk out of the arena as the show ends.

SmackDown!

December 18, 2003
Jacksonville, FL
Announcers: Michael Cole, Tazz, John Cena (briefly)

The show opens with footage from last week's Brock Lesnar/Rey Mysterio match and Hardcore Holly attacking the WWE Champion post-match. Afterwards, the intro video plays and fireworks explode.

John Cena then heads to the ring to a big pop to rap about Christmas and getting crappy presents like "yellow snow". This year he wants to seduce Mrs. Claus. He then joins the announce table for the next match and to talk about his match next week against Big Show.

Big Show def. Orlando Jordan. Show is distracted by Cena at ringside and Orlando capitalizes with a series of fists and a top rope flying cross body block for a two-count. One clothesline slows the rookie and the giant unloads with chops and his standing leg drop. While he punishes Jordan, the rapping superstar teaches Cole a lesson on how to talk like he's from the streets. When Big Show attempts to Chokeslam Orlando, the rookie slips free and kicks him. His boot has no effect as the giant grabs him by the throat again to score the win with a Chokeslam. Post-match, Cena and Show stare each other down.

A security guard stops Hardcore Holly backstage. The announcers are shocked to hear that Holly is Paul Heyman's invited guest tonight.

After a commercial break, A-Train paces the ring. Brock Lesnar, Matt Morgan, and Paul Heyman follow him out. Lesnar wants to ask the hairy heel something face-to-face. Specifically, he wants to know how A-Train's match went with Shannon Moore last week since he missed it getting ready for his match with Rey Mysterio. Instead of letting the hairy heel answer, Brock turns to Morgan. Matt informs the WWE Champion that not only did A-Train lose to Moore, but he lost a lot of their money. Lesnar can't believe it. He wants to know why the hairy heel lost. A-Train has been looking forward to this opportunity to say something to Brock face-to-face. While he talks tough, he backs down and apologizes. Not only for losing to Shannon, but for betting against Lesnar two weeks ago. The hairy heel just wants to make things right. Heyman has a way for him to do so. Since the WWE board of directors has lifted Hardcore Holly's suspension and Paul is being forced to put him in the ring tonight, the general manager is signing him to an "All or Nothing" match. If Holly wins, he will get a WWE Title match with Brock. However, if he loses, Heyman is free to fire him. Since he can't make it a handicap match due to the board of directors, Paul signs A-Train to team up with Morgan against Hardcore and Moore. Lesnar doesn't look confident in his team.

A teaser for next week's Tribute for the Troops episode plays.

The Basham Brothers (with Shaniqua) def. Los Guerreros and Rikishi/Scotty 2 Hotty and The World's Greatest Tag Team (WWE Tag Title match). Los Guerreros are out first, stopping their lowrider at the entrance stage as Cole promotes Eddie on the cover of *Lowrider* magazine. The champions come out last, the announcers revealing that this is a one fall to a finish match and the Bashams don't even have to be involved in the decision to lose their belts. Rikishi starts strong suplexing both Guerreros at the same time. After Scotty helps him stack the former champions up in a corner, the big Samoan squashes them and teases a Stinkface. Fortunately, they bail out to the floor while Haas enters only to see Rikishi slam him and tag in Hotty for a trio of elbow drops and a near fall before Doug breaks the cover. Afterwards, Scotty and Shelton trade fists. Benjamin eventually gets the upper hand to T-bone suplex the babyface. Unfortunately, he gets too close to the ropes and Doug tags himself in. Eddie does the same, fighting both Bashams with a combination head scissors and headlock takedown. When Chavo joins him, Los Guerreros knock the champions down in a corner before tagging in Rikishi. The World's Greatest Tag Team briefly stop the big Samoan before deciding that they don't care and step aside for a double Stinkface ahead of a commercial break.

Afterwards, Danny shoulder blocks Scotty in a corner. Hotty answers with a running face slam. The fans go bananas as he hops around and delivers the Worm for a two-count before Charlie breaks the cover. After a brief fight on the floor, Danny covers Hotty for a two-count. When he makes another cover, The World's Greatest Tag Team makes the save and Shelton tags himself in to trap Scotty in a reverse chin lock. Even when the babyface fights free, a knee to the gut drops him for Haas to tag in and stomp Hotty. Back in, Danny stomps and elbows Scotty for another near fall. When Doug returns, he slows the pace with a sleeper hold. Hotty escapes with a jawbreaker, but the champion is closer to his corner and tags Danny. When Scotty nears the ropes though, Chavo tags himself in for a top rope flying cross body block and his own close two-count. "Latino Heat" returns afterwards to triple suplex Hotty, but Rikishi answers with a superkick. The World's Greatest Tag Team attack afterwards, knocking the big Samoan out to the floor before stunning Danny for a double-team leapfrog splash. Chavo responds and gives Benjamin a spinning head scissors, but Doug surprises him with a leaping leg lariat. Charlie then German suplexes Basham before Scotty recovers and rocks him with an enziguri kick. When he attempts to charge Danny, the champion answers with a back elbow and heads upstairs. Chavo follows him up for a superplex, but Doug frog splashes Chavo when he hits the canvas to steal the win despite not being the legal man. Cole admits that it was hard for Nick Patrick to keep track of everything with eight men.

Backstage, Paul Heyman wants Dawn Marie to envision Brock Lesnar defending the WWE Title tonight. While Lesnar may not appreciate it, Paul is all about opportunity. That's why he has put every *SmackDown!* superstar's name on a ping pong ball inside a tumbler. Everyone except Chris Benoit, that is. Tonight, Brock will draw out the name of the man he will face.

After a commercial break, Lamont is in the ring to introduce Ernest Miller. "The Cat" dances out in a black jumpsuit before Sable interrupts. She wants to know what he was thinking trying to kiss her last week. Miller says he did kiss her and was just trying to heat her up. She warns "the Cat" to never try it again before trying to slap him. Ernest sees her slap coming and grabs her hand before attempting another kiss. That brings Vince McMahon out. When Lamont holds the ropes open for him, Vince pulls up the middle rope and tosses him aside. The WWE owner wants to know who "the Cat" thinks he is. Miller says he's the "greatest of all-time", but Mr. McMahon corrects him. He says he's the greatest. To prove it, he tells the production crew to play Ernest's music. Everyone starts dancing, Sable distracting "the Cat" for a Vince low blow. McMahon says somebody better call Miller's mama before heading backstage with Sable.

Rey Mysterio def. Jamie Noble (with Nidia). The announcers debate what's going on with the rednecks as Jamie and Rey trade holds and takedowns. They both have the same idea and go for dropkicks at the same time, the crowd applauding them as they reset. Afterwards, Noble unloads on the masked man in a corner before countering a head scissors with a slam to the canvas. An inverted suplex onto the top rope scores the redneck a two-count before he sits back into a camel clutch. When Mysterio escapes, he shoves Jamie out to the floor. That only briefly slows him as he returns to catch a springboard attack and slam Rey into a corner. Fortunately, the masked man dodges his corner charge and answers with a top rope moonsault onto the standing redneck for a near fall. He follows up with a spinning head scissors before running into a powerslam and Noble two-count. Jamie tries to deliver a Tiger Bomb, but Mysterio fights free and kicks off a series of roll-ups and near falls. Afterwards, Rey trips the redneck into position for a 619, but Noble sees him coming and dodges. After the masked man falls out to the floor, Jamie shoves him back in before doing the same to Nidia. Once again, he takes advantage of her blindness to dropkick her into the referee and Mysterio. He attempts to score the win with a Tiger Bomb afterwards, but Rey counters with a hurricanrana for the three-count. Post-match, Jamie tells Nidia that Mysterio was the one who attacked her while a vocal fan keeps telling her that he's lying.

Backstage, Hardcore Holly tells security to back away from him while he ties his boots. Josh Mathews wonders why he would agree to Paul Heyman's stipulations tonight. Holly answers that he had no choice if he wanted to get his hands on Brock Lesnar. After he deals with A-Train and Matt Morgan tonight, he promises to break Lesnar's neck and take the WWE Title.

Footage of Brock Lesnar in *SmackDown!: Here Comes the Pain* plays.

Chris Benoit def. Chuck Palumbo. When The FBI come out with Chuck and distract Benoit for a Palumbo sneak attack, Mike Sparks orders the heels to head backstage. They've already helped their man and he pounds "the Crippler" for an early two-count. A clothesline also gets him a near fall while the announcers talk about what an honor it will be to participate in the Tribute to the Troops. Eventually, Benoit fights free of a vice lock only to be driven hard into a corner. A Chuck choke and back suplex scores him another two-count. After he argues with the referee, he returns to his neck hold. Once again, the "rabid wolverine" fights free and wrenches Palumbo down to the mat by the arm. Although Chuck remains on the attack, his shoulder looks weakened. That comes back to haunt him when he misses a corner charge and hits the steel shoulder-first. Benoit capitalizes, locking him in a Crippler Crossface. Fortunately for the heel, he's close enough to the ropes for the break. "The Crippler" continues to build momentum, dropkicking Palumbo's leg ahead of a trio of German suplexes. He follows up with a top rope diving headbutt for a near fall. When he tries to finish off his opponent, Chuck surprises him with a whip into the top turnbuckle for another close two-count. Afterwards, Palumbo attempts to take Benoit's head off with a clothesline, but the "rabid wolverine" ducks and locks on the Crippler Crossface in the center of the ring for the tap-out. Post-match, The FBI return to attack Benoit. Although he initially holds his own, a Chuck Superkick flattens "the Crippler".

Backstage, trainers check on Nidia. She wants to know where Jamie Noble is until Rey Mysterio enters the room. She's terrified of him as he tries to explain to her what Noble did earlier. Nidia refuses to believe him.

As Rhyno heads to the ring, the announcers promote a WWE special magazine, *The 50 Greatest WWE Superstars of All-Time*. The man-beast then calls out Bradshaw, telling him that they have each got a win in their series and they can settle things tonight. He wants the big Texan to come out, but he's not here. When Rhyno tells Nick Patrick to declare him the winner by forfeit, Faarooq answers.

Faarooq def. Rhyno by disqualification. The brawler is always ready for a fight, and he's happy to take up for his friend and tag team partner. Early on, he hammers Rhyno. When the man-beast starts to turn the tide, Faarooq plants him with a spinebuster for a near fall. On the defensive, Rhyno blatantly low blows the brawler for the disqualification. Afterwards, he Gores Faarooq and celebrates.

Backstage, Paul Heyman tells Dawn Marie that Brock Lesnar will have to accept that his title match is in the best interest of *SmackDown!*. He runs down some of the names that could face Lesnar tonight including John Cena and Big Show ahead of a *SmackDown!* ad.

After a commercial break, Paul Heyman stands with security behind him and the ping pong ball hopper in front of him. He introduces Brock Lesnar, the general manager looking terrified as the WWE Champion heads out to find out who he'll face tonight. When Lesnar reaches in and grabs the ball, he wants to draw again. Paul doesn't understand why, but Brock says he just drew Shannon Moore, the hottest guy on the show. He laughs while Cole says this is very convenient.

Brock Lesnar def. Shannon Moore (WWE Title match). His ribs bandaged, Shannon limps out. Not only does he get this title shot, but he'll also team with Hardcore Holly in the main event. Before the bell rings, Brock shoves the challenger down to the canvas. Moore answers by stomping his foot and kicking Lesnar's leg. He then dodges a clothesline and slips free of a slam for more kicks. A pair of dropkicks to the head nearly crowns a new champion before Brock finally flattens Shannon with a clothesline. A second clothesline follows before Lesnar cinches in the Brock Lock for the tap-out victory. Post-match, the champion says that was a close one, but he's the greatest in WWE history. Brock says he's the only champion who would defend his title against anyone. He tries to prove it by pulling out more balls from the hopper. They all read "Shannon Moore". Lesnar tells him that his and Holly's luck just ran out.

Hardcore Holly/Shannon Moore def. A-Train/Matt Morgan. Brock Lesnar watches from ringside as security leads Holly down the aisle. The announcers can't believe the WWE Champion's evil plan while security surrounds him. They keep Hardcore back from Lesnar while the heels run down to wail on Moore. That makes Shannon the legal man for A-Train and Morgan to take turns punishing him. That includes a Matt headbutt and choke before the hairy heel knees Shannon's already injured ribs. He follows up with a series of backbreakers and a whip into Morgan's boot. When Matt returns, he locks on a bearhug and swings around the cruiserweight, but Shannon won't submit. He holds on as A-Train cheap shots Holly before he gives Moore a Derailer. Fortunately, Hardcore breaks his cover. Moments later, Shannon counters a corner bomb with a boot to the jaw. Holly gets the hot tag afterwards to punch Morgan and dropkick A-Train. Fighting two men, Hardcore stuns them with boots in a corner ahead of a top rope flying clothesline to Matt for a two-count. He then punches the hairy heel and kicks his groin. Unfortunately, Morgan capitalizes and whips Holly neck-first into the top rope. While Matt distracts the referee, Brock smashes Hardcore with a chair to the back. Back in the ring, Morgan scores a near fall with a Sit-out Powerbomb. Lesnar can't believe it. Matt tries to squeeze the life out of him with a bearhug, but Holly fights free and dodges an A-Train bicycle kick that levels Morgan. Hardcore then clotheslines the hairy heel out of the ring to score the three-count with an Alabama Slam to Matt. Post-match, Brock throws a fit while Holly celebrates and the announcers promote Tribute to the Troops one last time.

Monday Night Raw

December 22, 2003
Hosts: Jonathan Coachman, Jerry "the King" Lawler

Following the intro video, Coach, his arm in a sling, and "the King" host this highlight show for 2023. Coachman is happy that Eric Bischoff made him the co-host tonight, but Lawler warns the heel that if he gets out of line, Jerry will take care of him.

Footage from Chris Jericho and Shawn Michaels's WrestleMania XIX match plays.

After a commercial break, Lawler reads *WWE Unscripted* and says it would make a great Christmas gift. When he sees a picture of Triple H, "the King" looks forward to his match with Shawn Michaels next week.

The Trish Stratus/Victoria "Chicago Street Fight" replays.

Highlights from the *Raw* tenth anniversary show early in the year play. Afterwards, Coach brags about *Raw* being the longest-running weekly show on television. Jerry would rather talk about Stacy Keibler's long legs, welcoming her out to sit between the hosts. She shills Bod Man body spray and squirts some on Coachman to help him with the ladies. Stacy says he needs it.

Christian and Rob Van Dam's Intercontinental Title "Ladder" match replays.

Goldberg's debut replays. Afterwards, footage from his Backlash match with The Rock plays.

Chris Jericho and Trish Stratus kissing plays.

Eric Bischoff signing "Stone Cold" Steve Austin to a contract to keep Eric's job plays. Afterwards, their No Way Out match replays.

Footage of "Mean" Gene Okerlund from *Confidential* talking about how proud the WWE is about the upcoming Tribute to the Troops show plays.

Kane unmasking replays. Afterwards, he goes on a path of destruction before we see a replay of his "Ambulance" match with Shane McMahon at Survivor Series.

The Rock and The Hurricane verbally jousting backstage replays. Coach says the only two men more entertaining are himself and the "People's Champ".

A video package for the wrestlers that passed away this year plays. That includes Stu Hart, Crash Holly, Miss Elizabeth, Hawk, Mr. Perfect, and "Classy" Freddie Blassie.

Ric Flair cutting an impassioned promo on Triple H plays before we see their World Title match replay and Coach shill "The Nature Boy's" DVD.

Footage of Eric Bischoff kissing Mae Young and receiving a bronco buster from the octogenarian plays.

Footage from the Team Austin versus Team Bischoff Survivor Series match replays, including "Stone Cold" Steve Austin's farewell to the WWE.

Randy Orton chasing off Mick Foley last week on *Raw* replays.

The show ends with Coach praising Eric Bischoff who is once again the sole general manager of *Raw*. Jerry says it will be a nightmare before wishing everyone happy holidays.

SmackDown!
December 25, 2003
Baghdad, Iraq
Announcers: Michael Cole, Tazz

The show opens with Tony Chimel introducing Spc. Marilynn Anderson to sing the national anthem in front of the troops gathered for this special episode. Taped in Iraq, the ring is surrounded by service men and women and tanks. While this will get lumped into the Tribute to the Troops series, it's called "Christmas from Baghdad" tonight.

Following the national anthem, Vince McMahon proudly walks to the ring to say thank you to the troops from all the "freedom loving people" of the world. He thanks the armed forces for letting them perform tonight and for protecting America. Just when he starts to wrap up, Santa Claus heads to the squared circle. While he climbs in, McMahon makes fun of his bulbous belly. When Vince asks if he's getting a present, Santa shakes his head. He's got presents for the troops, but McMahon wants him to save one for the WWE owner. Santa then hops out into the crowd to throw out shirts. When he starts to leave, Vince calls him back into the squared circle. Mr. McMahon is mad that Santa didn't bring him a gift and knocks him down. While the WWE owner warns everyone that he will kick anyone's butt who doesn't show him the proper respect, Old Saint Nick removes his hat and beard. It's "Stone Cold" Steve Austin and he gives Vince a Stone Cold Stunner to a big pop. Afterwards, the "rattlesnake" enjoys a beer bash, still wearing the Santa pants. Once he takes those off, Austin stops his music to talk to the fans. He tells them that his throat is hoarse so he's not going to sing any Christmas carols. Instead, he plans to go backstage and drink some beer for the troops. Before he does so, he thanks them for all they do.

Footage of troops warning WWE superstars about the potential dangers of this show play. The troops tell the superstars that if anything happens, they need to duck. Faarooq says it's good he's from Atlanta, because he's used to ducking.

Troops watching the ring being set up plays.

The APA def. The World's Greatest Tag Team. Bradshaw gets a big pop as he comes out in a flak jacket and hardhat. The announcers credit him for helping put this show together. He watches from the apron as Faarooq locks up with Benjamin. Shelton gets an early advantage with a cheap shot in a corner, but the brawler answers with a second rope flying shoulderblock for a two-count. The big Texan then tags in to hammer Benjamin until he rakes Bradshaw's eyes. Haas tags in afterwards for the Big Texan to manhandle. That includes a shoulderblock to the back and powerslam for a pair of near falls. As Faarooq returns, he hoists Charlie up for a Dominator, but the heel slips free and shoves him into Shelton for a cheap shot. When Benjamin tags in, he punches and stomps the brawler for his own near fall. A double suplex follows from the heels before Haas slams Faarooq to the mat. When he attempts to follow up with a charge, the brawler back body drops him and gives Bradshaw the hot tag. He kicks and shoulder blocks both heels before scoring a two-count with a DDT to Charlie. When Shelton breaks his cover, Faarooq joins his partner for a double shoulderblock, knocking Benjamin out to the floor. The big Texan follows up with a second rope fallaway slam to Haas, but Shelton comes to his partner's aid with a Superkick. Unfortunately, he then runs into a Faarooq powerslam. Once Charlie shoves the brawler out of the ring, Bradshaw surprises Haas with a Clothesline from Hell for the three-count.

Backstage, "Stone Cold" Steve Austin gives Chris Benoit a pep talk. "The Crippler" has something for Eddie Guerrero tonight and shakes the "rattlesnake's" hand.

A serviceman talks about his newborn and missing his wife. Afterwards, troops wish their families a Merry Christmas. The announcers do the same to all the fans back home.

Backstage, Torrie Wilson zips up her Santa's little helper costume and sucks on a candy cane.

Rikishi def. Rhyno. While Rhyno punches the big Samoan, the WWE runs credits for the small crew who helped set up this show. The man-beast tries to sunset flip Rikishi, but the big man holds his ground and attempts to answer with a falling butt splash. Although Rhyno moves out of the way and lands a few more blows, the big Samoan drops him with a superkick. He tries to finish him off with a Rump Shaker, but the man-beast counters with a pair of knees. When he rushes forward with a Gore afterwards, Rikishi moves and scores the victory with a Samoan drop. Rhyno makes the mistake of crawling into a corner post-match and pays courtesy of a Stinkface. The troops love it. They also love seeing the big Samoan dancing with two service women.

Footage of WWE superstars and Vince McMahon meeting with the troops plays.

After a commercial break, footage of superstars flying in helicopters to visit another camp plays.

Back at ringside, John Cena comes out to say that one of his dreams came true appearing here tonight, but he's got a huge challenge with Big Show. However, Cena knows that Show beating him is like "trying to get the French to fight". The American troops love it. He thanks them for fighting for him and all the people of America.

Backstage, Eddie Guerrero tells "Stone Cold" Steve Austin that he wasn't allowed to bring over a lowrider. Austin informs him that Chris Benoit is planning on lying, cheating, and stealing from him tonight in the ring. That's "Latino Heat's" shtick and he takes offense.

After we see troops send well wishes to their families, WWE superstars partying with the armed forces plays.

Eddie Guerrero def. Chris Benoit. Instead of driving a lowrider, Eddie walks down the ramp to a big pop. As Benoit comes out, we see a sniper perched above the entrance with a gun pointed toward him. Inside the ring, "the Crippler" knocks his former friend down with a shoulderblock. "Latino Heat" answers with a headlock takedown and tilt-a-whirl backbreaker for a pair of near falls. He then returns to his headlock until Benoit shoots him into the ropes for a monkey flip. When the "rabid wolverine" unloads with chops, Guerrero crawls to the corner and hugs Jimmy Korderas' waist. Afterwards, a Blackhawk chopper circles over head while Eddie puts on a flak jacket. When the referee makes him take it off, "Latino Heat" tosses it into Benoit's face for the advantage. He follows up with chops, but when he attempts a back suplex, "the Crippler" flips free and back suplexes both men out to the floor ahead of a commercial break.

Afterwards, Benoit has Guerrero trapped in a surfboard stretch until Eddie runs him into a corner. He follows up with a spot that doesn't quite work, attempting to turn a hurricanrana into a sunset flip to toss the "rabid wolverine" off the top rope. It actuality, Benoit just falls back to the mat for "Latino Heat" to cover him for a two-count. Guerrero follows up with a pair of suplexes, but when he goes for the third, Chris traps him briefly in a Crippler Crossface. Fortunately, Eddie rolls to the ropes for the break. Afterwards, "the Crippler" slugs "Latino Heat" and rams his face into the top turnbuckle. Chops follow from both men, Benoit slowing Guerrero with a pop up slam. He follows up with a pair of German suplexes, but like his former friend, Eddie counters the third and teases a second tilt-a-whirl backbreaker. This time, Benoit flips the hold over for a shoulderbreaker. When he heads upstairs though, "Latino Heat" just dodges his diving headbutt. Guerrero goes upstairs afterwards, but misses his own high risk move, Frog Splashing the canvas. Once they get up, the two men trade counters culminating in an Eddie roll-up and three-count with his feet on the ropes. Post-match, the "rabid wolverine" wants "Latino Heat" to get back in the ring. Guerrero only does so wearing a flak jacket and helmet. He denies using the ropes for the win before leading the crowd in a "USA" chant. Afterwards, the wrestlers shake hands and hug.

Footage of Vince McMahon hitting Santa Claus from behind and getting a Stone Cold Stunner earlier tonight replays. Afterwards, more troops wish their families and the fans a Merry Christmas.

A video package of wrestlers meeting the troops and talking about how honored they are to be here plays. Afterwards, even more troops wish their friends and families a Merry Christmas.

After a commercial break, WWE superstars firing guns at a shooting range plays.

Back at ringside, Tony Chimel introduces the divas for a "Santa's Little Helper" contest with the troops as the judges. Torrie Wilson is out first in a red Santa's outfit, tossing candy canes to the fans. Dawn Marie follows in her own skimpy red outfit. Sable is the last one to be introduced, but she goes first in the dance contest, slowly removing her silver garland and belt as she shakes her backside for the fans. Dawn Marie then dances and strips off her top to reveal a patriotic bikini. Torrie gets the final dance, but she just strips off her outfit to reveal a red and white thong. Predictably, Wilson wins. The losers take offense and attack her, but Torrie quickly recovers and strips off Sable's top, sending the heels backstage while Wilson parades around the ring and hugs the troops.

Footage of armed forces escorting WWE superstars to a hospital to meet injured service men and women plays. We also see the director of armed forces, Art Myers, saying that this has been the best tour he's ever seen and hopes the WWE does it again in 2004. Afterwards, troops say hello to their friends and family again.

John Cena def. Big Show. Cena sprints right down to the ring for a fight, but Show greets him with an early Chokeslam. That sends the rapping superstar out to the floor to try to gather his thoughts. When the giant tries to pull him back in, John surprises him with a throat drop on the top rope. He recovers quickly to clothesline and chop Cena. Big Show follows up with headbutts and a chin lock. He soon transitions into an abdominal stretch. When the rapping superstar rakes his eyes to get free, Show headbutts him again. Afterwards, he tries to big boot John, but Cena dodges and the giant nails Brian Hebner. Big Show follows up with a sidewalk slam before grabbing the rapping superstar's chain. Fortunately, John ducks his punch and answers with a low blow kick. A shot from the chain follows before Cena wakes up the referee for a near fall. Back up, Show grabs the rapping superstar's throat for a second Chokeslam, but John slips free and impresses with an FU for the victory. Post-match, "Stone Cold" Steve Austin comes out to copy Cena's "you can't see me" taunt before giving the rapping superstar a Stone Cold Stunner. Big Show gets a pair of Stunners too. Austin then invites the divas, superstars, and Vince McMahon all out to thank the troops. Show gets one last Stunner ahead of a second beer bash.

Monday Night Raw
December 29, 2003
San Antonio, TX
Announcers: Jim Ross, Jerry "the King" Lawler

The show opens with a recap package of Mick Foley walking out two weeks ago ahead of the intro video and fireworks. Afterwards, Randy Orton walks out to Mick's music. He again calls Foley a coward, but adds that he's a "smart coward". Since Mick knew he didn't have a chance to beat the "Legend Killer", Randy says he was smart to leave the arena rather than fight Orton. Tonight, the "Legend Killer" wants Lilian Garcia to get into the ring and announce him as the winner of the match. JR can't believe it. When she does, Randy tells her to call him the new "hardcore legend" too. That brings out Booker T to challenge Orton to a match. Out of nowhere, Mark Henry attacks the five-time champion from behind. Once he's pounded him down, Randy accepts Booker's challenge.

Backstage, Eric Bischoff yells at Mark Henry and Theodore Long. He can't believe they would try to injure Booker T and potentially ruin his first night as the sole general manager again. On top of that, he's got the board of directors meeting to address the "Stone Cold" Steve Austin petition. Long wants to cash in the favor Bischoff owes the heels, but he tells them to take the night off and cool off. Theodore warns the GM that he will pay them back soon.

Rob Van Dam def. Scott Steiner. When RVD does his pointing taunt, Scott kicks him and slams the popular superstar to start the contest. Rob answers with a pair of spinning heel kicks and a standing moonsault for a two-count. A second rope karate kick stuns Steiner long enough for Van Dam to hop onto the top rope, but "Big Poppa Pump" recovers and hits the ropes to crotch him. A belly-to-belly suplex off the second rope follows for a near fall. Scott follows up with a questionably low blow kick, but Chad Patton lets the match continue without questioning the shot. That gives Steiner control and he capitalizes with a whip into the ring steps before taking the action back into the squared circle for chops and a twisting belly-to-belly suplex. When that only gets him a two-count, "Big Poppa Pump" chokes RVD and yells at the referee. He then ties Rob up in the tree of woe and pulls his head back from outside the ring. More chokes follow before Scott scores a two-count with an elbow drop. As usual, he mocks his opponent with pushups. That gives Van Dam time to recover and answer a corner charge with a boot to the jaw. Rolling thunder and a split legged moonsault follow for a near fall. Right back up, Steiner tosses RVD over with a modified northern lights suplex. He then puts the popular superstar back on the top rope, but this time Rob fights free of his belly-to-belly suplex and shoves "Big Poppa Pump" down for a flying kick. Afterwards, Van Dam scores the win with a Five-Star Frog Splash.

Ahead of his upcoming World Title match tonight, Shawn Michaels winning the WWF Title at the 1997 Survivor Series plays in a replay segment called the "Heart Break Klassic".

Backstage, Chris Jericho and Christian argue. Christian believes Y2J owes him an apology for turning his back on him "for a girl". Jericho argues otherwise, but Christian storms off.

Back in Stamford, Connecticut, Jonathan Coachman is posted outside the board of directors' meeting room. He'll be waiting for word from the "Stone Cold" Steve Austin reinstatement hearing. Linda McMahon will represent "Stone Cold" to the board, but it will be Vince McMahon arguing to keep the "rattlesnake" away. While Vince might have influence, since the WWE is a publicly traded company, he has to go through the motions of this hearing. However, he notes that the board almost always sees his way. Coach is sure the board will make a "fair decision". JR believes Vince is going to try to get revenge tonight for Austin giving him a Stone Cold Stunner on *SmackDown!*. We then see a video package featuring WWE superstars visiting armed forces bases and performing at "Christmas from Baghdad".

The Dudley Boyz talking about their new song on the *WWE Originals* CD coming out next month plays. We then see a prerecorded promo from them earlier today. D-Von says the Dudleys looked up to Mick Foley, but now Bubba Ray is afraid that he's turning into a coward.

Eddie Kramer/Russell Simpson def. The Dudley Boys by disqualification. Everyone is shocked to see Ric Flair come out in khaki pants to serve as the guest referee. He watches as D-Von scoop slams Kramer, but misses an elbow drop. Simpson then tags in for the Dudleys to give him a double flapjack. Bubba Ray follows up with a series of kicks and fists, drawing the referee's ire. When Bubba continues punching Russell, Ric calls for the bell and disqualifies the Dudleys. Post-match, Bubba Ray decks Flair. That brings out Batista to give Bubba a spinebuster before dropping D-Von too with a Batista Bomb.

Another "Heart Break Klassic" shows Shawn Michaels beating Triple H at last year's SummerSlam.

After the announcers shill the *50 Greatest WWE Superstars* magazine, Eric Bischoff talks to the *Raw* referees. He tells them that Ric Flair did the right thing and exerted his authority in the last match. Eric wants his referees to do their job and exert their authority in the ring too.

Back in Stamford, Vince McMahon tells Jonathan Coachman that he made his points about "Stone Cold" Steve Austin. While he appreciates all Austin did for the WWE, there's no place for his antics in this new publicly traded company. Vince says it's his job to give the fans what's best for them and that's to keep "Stone Cold" out of the WWE.

Backstage, Terri interviews Lita, Stacy Keibler, and Trish Stratus about their upcoming "Happy Holidays" match. They are all dressed up like Santa's little helpers. When Terri asks if they got anything special, "Stone Cold" Steve Austin nearly runs over the women backing up his truck. He's here to await word from the WWE board of directors.

Randy Orton def. Booker T (Intercontinental Title match). Lawler credits Booker for not walking out on this match like Mick Foley. Instead, he traps the champion in a side headlock. When Randy shoves him off, the challenger levels him with a leaping shoulderblock. Orton answers with kicks and forearm uppercuts in a corner. Booker T is fine with a fight, responding with chops and a side kick for a two-count until the "Legend Killer" slows him with a hotshot. A dropkick afterwards gets Randy a two-count before he starts to choke the babyface. When he attempts a hip toss, Booker backslides him for a near fall. One clothesline puts the challenger back down for a two-count. Afterwards, the champion hooks a reverse chin lock. It doesn't take Booker T long to fight free and kick Orton down to the mat. The two men then trade fists, the babyface scoring a two-count with a leaping clothesline. A bicycle kick afterwards puts the "Legend Killer" down for Booker to entertain with a spinaroonie. Both men then counter each other's finishers before the challenger drives Randy to the canvas with a spinebuster. When he tries to follow up with a Scissors Kick, Kane marches down the aisle to distract everyone but Orton. The "Legend Killer" quickly capitalizes with an RKO for the victory. Post-match, he bails out of the ring for the "Big Red Machine" to sidewalk slam and Chokeslam Booker T.

Another "Heart Break Klassic" sees Shawn Michaels beat Triple H for the World Title in the first ever "Elimination Chamber" match last year at Survivor Series.

Back in Stamford, Jonathan Coachman asks Linda how she did arguing for "Stone Cold" Steve Austin to the WWE board of directors. She thinks it went well because she put the WWE fans first unlike Eric Bischoff. Coach wonders if she's letting her dislike of Bischoff dictate her actions. Linda disagrees. She believes "Stone Cold" balances out Eric.

Back in the arena, Chris Jericho gives Trish Stratus a Christmas gift. She doesn't appreciate it, asking him if he thinks that will make her forget that he had a bet to sleep with her. Trish is really disgusted that she was only worth seventy-five cents to him and he broke her heart. Fighting back tears, she says she really cared about him. Y2J tells her he made a mistake, but she disagrees. Stratus says she was the one who made the mistake.

After a commercial break, "Stone Cold" Steve Austin's phone rings. Unfortunately, it's not from the board of directors.

Lita/Stacy Keibler/Trish Stratus def. Miss Jackie/Molly Holly/Victoria. Everyone is dressed up in red and white Santa's little helpers outfits for this "Happy Holidays" match. Victoria is the early aggressor, shoving Stacy until she tries to answer with a spinning heel kick. Although the "black widow" ducks, Keibler chases her off to tag in Molly. Stacy greets her with kicks and a choke with her boot in a corner. Lita then tags in for a quick cover and two-count. When she runs the ropes, Jackie kicks the extreme diva to swing the momentum. The Women's Champion capitalizes with some clubbing blows until Lita rolls her up. That brings Jackie in to break up the cover. For some reason, Victoria takes offense and pulls her partner out to the floor and whips her into the barricade. She then gets back in the heel corner and cheers on Holly as she stretches Lita. Eventually, the extreme diva surprises the champion with a head scissors. Trish tags in moments later to punch Molly and give her a handstand head scissors. Stratusfaction follows for the three-count. Post-match, the "black widow" checks on Holly before decking her with the Women's Title to a nice pop.

Backstage, "Stone Cold" Steve Austin's phone rings again. He's told that he's back as the co-general manager of *Raw*. That's not what he wants to hear. He didn't want to be the GM again. If that's all the board of directors has for him, the "rattlesnake" tells them to "take your job and shove it". He then speeds out of the arena in his truck.

Shawn Michaels and Triple H (with Ric Flair) (World Title match) wrestle to a draw. Very familiar with each other, the competitors open the match trading amateur holds while waiting for the other to make a mistake. While Shawn gets the early upper hand with a headlock, Triple H slows him with a back elbow. He then attempts to whip the challenger out to the floor, but Michaels skins the cat. The "Heartbreak Kid" surprises Hunter when he turns around with a head scissors out of the ring. When he celebrates with a Flair strut, "The Nature Boy" hops onto the apron only to be knocked down to the floor. Shawn follows both heels out with a springboard cross body block off the ropes. Back in the squared circle, Helmsley tries to slow the pace with an arm ringer, but the challenger reverses the hold. An arm drag and armbar follow until "the Game" reaches the ropes for the break. Michaels takes advantage of Earl Hebner being out of position to kick the ropes and crotch the champion. He then returns to the arm until Triple H unloads with fists in a corner. The two men soon trade fists and chops, the "Heartbreak Kid" getting the advantage and whipping Hunter out to the floor for another chop. When they return to the ring, Shawn briefly locks on a sleeper hold. Helmsley tries to escape with a side suplex, but the challenger flips over and rolls him up for a two-count. He almost gets the win moments later with a backslide before chopping "the Game" once again. When he attempts a corner charge though, the champion back body drops him out to the floor ahead of a commercial break.

Afterwards, Triple H throat drops Michaels on the top rope before going to work stomping the "Heartbreak Kid". Chokes and fists follow, but Shawn won't stay down. Just as he starts to build momentum with his own punches, Hunter surprises him with a backbreaker for a near fall. More fists soften up the challenger ahead of a pair of elbow drops to the lower back. He scores a two-count with more punches before Michaels starts to fight back. Helmsley answers by tossing him out to the floor for a whip into the ring steps. Although the "Heartbreak Kid" surprises him with a sunset flip for a near fall, a clothesline scores "the Game" a pair of two-counts afterwards. The champion then applies an abdominal stretch, pulling Shawn's hair for added leverage, punishment, and insult. Predictably, Flair grabs his man's hand for additional punishment. Eventually, Hebner catches the heels cheating and kicks Ric's hand. That lets the challenger hip toss free. He then catches a second wind with kicks and chops until he runs into a high knee. Despite scoring a two-count, that blows hurts the champion too. Michaels capitalizes with a knee breaker before trapping Triple H in a figure four leg lock. After Hunter has been in the hold for over a minute, Flair rakes the "Heartbreak Kid's" eyes behind the referee's back for the break. Shawn tries to answer with a top rope attack, but Helmsley counters with a kick to the gut. When he sets up for the Pedigree, the challenger back body drops free to put both men down for Earl's eight-count. Back up, the two men trade fists and chops. When they collide moments later, Michaels inadvertently bounces off the ropes and falls headfirst into "the Game's" groin. Once again, they work Hebner's count to eight before the "Heartbreak Kid" unloads with fists. The champion responds in kind, but Shawn gets the upper hand with a pair of inverted atomic drops. A flying forearm and kip up follows, the fans roaring to life. They get louder following a top rope flying elbow drop. Afterwards, the challenger tunes up the band, but "The Nature Boy" interferes. After Michaels drops him, Triple H attempts a sneak attack. Unfortunately for Hebner, the "Heartbreak Kid" moves and Hunter hits the official. Shawn remains in control, dropping Helmsley with a DDT, but he doesn't have any fight left. While he catches his breath, Flair tosses "the Game" the World Title. He uses it to blast the challenger. By the time Earl recovers, Michaels just kicks out. Moments later, the champion kicks the "Heartbreak Kid" back into the referee, knocking Hebner out to the floor. Eric Bischoff runs out to check on him while Triple H removes a turnbuckle pad. He tries to ram Shawn into it, but the challenger reverses the attempt to knock out Hunter. Unfortunately, there's no referee to count his cover. Eric takes matters into his own hands and slides into the ring for a close two-count. He does the same following a string of fists, Helmsley bleeding. When "the Game" counters a back body drop with a facebuster, Bischoff also gives him a two-count. The champion tries to follow up with a second rope flying attack, but leaps into a boot. Moments later, Michaels surprises him with Sweet Chin Music for the three-count. The fans go absolutely bananas as the "Heartbreak Kid's" music plays and the announcers say that "lightning has struck again". Unfortunately, Eric announces Triple H as the World Champion. He says that since both men's shoulders were down, the title stays with the champion. Footage proves that both men's shoulders were down on the canvas, making this the right call. When Bischoff starts to taunt Shawn, the "Heartbreak Kid" answers with a fist to the jaw and Sweet Chin Music to Ric. That's all Eric can take and he fires Michaels. JR says you can't fire a man in his hometown. That brings out "Stone Cold" Steve Austin to a big pop. He takes the microphone away to say that he's back on his own terms and Shawn is rehired. Not only does he hire him back, but he says he deserves a rematch. Austin adds that from now on there is a new sheriff in town and he drops Bischoff with a Stone Cold Stunner to end a big show and year of WWE action.

Top Tag Team of the Year

The World's Greatest Tag Team. Tag team wrestling took a backseat in the Ruthless Aggression era. After a renaissance in the Attitude Era, tag team wrestling began focusing more on singles wrestlers pairing up than established teams. The WWE tried to change that in 2003 with the introduction of La Resistance, The Basham Brothers, and The World's Greatest Tag Team. While all three would hold title belts during the year, it was Charlie Haas and Shelton Benjamin who would prove to be not only the top rookie team, but top tag team of the year. As Kurt Angle's henchmen, and originally named Team Angle, Haas and Benjamin got the opportunity to wrestle with some of the top talent in the WWE including Chris Benoit, Eddie Guerrero, and Brock Lesnar. Not only did they wrestle them, but they looked right at home with them in the ring. Angle and Paul Heyman would do most of the talking for them, but that just made the rookies look more focused and like a big deal. They'd win the belts twice, successfully defend them six times, and win more matches than any other tag team in the WWE for the year. While Kane and Rob Van Dam had more successful title defenses, they didn't make it through the whole year together and won fewer matches. The Dudley Boyz also won the World Tag Titles twice, but they didn't win as many matches and weren't involved in featured storylines like The World's Greatest Tag Team, giving the *SmackDown!* rookies just enough of an edge to claim this award.

Top Wrestler of the Year

10. Kane. 2003 was a return to stardom for Kane. After several years of languishing, Kane went through quite the character arc in 2003. He was part of a popular tag team alongside Rob Van Dam, winning the World Tag Titles. He lost his mask and showed his face for the first time…admittedly ruining a bit of the menace to the character. He went on a monster rampage, destroying anyone in his path including Linda McMahon before feuding with her son for most of the second half of 2003. Together, Kane and Shane McMahon beat each other to a pulp, a war that saw them try to electrocute testicles, toss people into burning dumpsters, and dive off the entrance set. In the end, it was Kane standing tall as he won an "Ambulance" match before turning his attention to the World Title. Finally a monster heel again, the "Big Red Machine" was a demented demon hellbent on destroying anyone that found happiness. He even buried his own brother alive as Kane showed there was no depths to which he wouldn't sink.

9. John Cena. After a good, but not great debut year, Cena really picked up momentum in 2003. Embracing his "doctor of thuganomics" character, he rapped and insulted babyface after babyface throughout the year. His act got so popular that Brock Lesnar offered him a spot on his heel Survivor Series squad. After feuding with Eddie Guerrero, Chris Benoit, and Kurt Angle for a year, the rapping superstar refuted Lesnar and joined them on the babyface side of the roster. He still cheated and insulted his opponents in raps, but now he was focused on the heels. That's what the fans wanted, and they cheered his antics. He was different than every other babyface and earned a special place on the card, ending the year feuding with the US Champion, Big Show. Finally given the spotlight, Cena broke through in 2003, his talent promising a bright future ahead.

8. Chris Jericho. Although he didn't hold the World Title in 2003 like he did the two previous years, 2003 was hardly a step back for Y2J. He remained the number two heel on *Raw*, feuded with top superstars like Rob Van Dam and Goldberg, and was consistently given solid amounts of television time whether in-ring or as the host of the Highlight Reel. He won the Intercontinental Title once and spent a good portion of the year teaming up with Christian to infuriate the babyfaces of *Raw*. By the end of the year, Jericho began to show a change of heart. What started as a bet to sleep with Trish Stratus blossomed into a real romance. Y2J's acting helped change him from a cocky heel to a believable babyface over time. Instead of changing overnight, Jericho slowly transitioned to a guy worthy of Stratus's love and connected with the audience in a way he hadn't before. Showing more character than ever before, 2003 proved that Y2J didn't need to win championships or be in the main event picture to be one of the most entertaining men on the roster.

7. Rob Van Dam. While he didn't get a World Title push, RVD did tease going for the championship. In a year with Shawn Michaels and Goldberg dominating on top of the babyface ranks, Van Dam did everything he could to make the undercard matter. He won the Tag Titles with Kane and the Intercontinental Title twice. He feuded with almost every heel on the roster, including his former partner Kane, and helped elevate Randy Orton at the end of the year. He was consistently one of the most popular wrestlers on *Raw* and always entertained inside the ring. His only knocks are that he didn't win a singles PPV match during the year and that he never had a run with the World Title. By 2003, the WWE knew what they had in RVD. He was one of their most popular superstars that would never disappoint in the ring. Clearly the company wasn't comfortable with his personality as the champion. He had charisma, it just wasn't what the company had ever featured before and it would take time for the WWE to finally wrap their heads around what they had. Regardless, 2003 proved to be another fantastic year for the popular superstar, even if it looked like there was a ceiling to his career.

6. Eddie Guerrero. From the day Eddie arrived in the WWF it was obvious that he had talent. His wrestling skills were nearly as good as anyone's and he could fly better than just about everyone. What set him apart from the other Radicalz and WCW castoffs is that Eddie could entertain with his facial expressions and words. Adopting the nickname "Latino Heat", Guerrero proved to be one of the breakout stars from WCW. The only thing holding him back was his size and personal demons. After clearing up those demons, Eddie began wrestling with some of the best in the world including Brock Lesnar, Chris Benoit, Kurt Angle, and Edge. His style meshed with everyone and proved it didn't matter how big someone was if they were talented. In 2003, "Latino Heat" lied, cheated, and stole his way to three championship wins, holding the US and WWE Tag Titles at the same time. He was a fixture on PPVs and always had engaging stories. His ability to steal a win each week entertained fans so much that the WWE had no choice but to make him a babyface, Guerrero stealing the hearts of fans in 2003.

5. **Chris Benoit.** One of the best technical wrestlers, this ranking is solely based on what Benoit did in 2003. For 2003, Benoit was hugely successful despite not winning a single championship belt. While he had fought for secondary titles since his arrival in 2000, Benoit stopped pursuing secondary belts in 2003. It was the first year he didn't win a championship with the company. Instead, he focused on climbing the ranks into the WWE Title picture. That included wars with John Cena, Rhyno, Eddie Guerrero, Kurt Angle, and of course, Brock Lesnar. By the end of the year, it was obvious that Benoit was being positioned as a top star with the general manager targeting him specifically to block any championship opportunities. Intense in the ring and able to get anyone over, Benoit finally had the proper storytelling around him to make him a star. With all that in place, Benoit climbed up the ladder of success in 2003 and set himself up for what promised to be the biggest of his career in 2004.

4. **Goldberg.** Possibly WCW's biggest homegrown talent, Goldberg made a tremendous impact when he debuted after WrestleMania XIX and Speared The Rock. As the "People's Champ" left the WWE to head to Hollywood, he put Bill over strong and created a number one babyface for *Raw*. Goldberg would defeat The Rock at Backlash before targeting Triple H and the World Title. It would take him a while to get it, but there was no question that the intense superstar was Helmsley's number one challenge throughout the year. With the fans chanting his name as he made his unique entrance from his locker room through sparks and smoke, Goldberg was all about intensity. He'd parlay that into a large number of wins, big matches, and of course, a World Title victory. Even in defeat, heels tried to get the advantage over him so much that he led the entire federation in disqualification victories with five because very few men could conceivably beat Goldberg in a fair match. While Bill has later said that he did not love this run, it's a bit odd considering how successful it was.

3. **Kurt Angle.** A wrestling machine, Kurt held the WWE Title on two occasions throughout the year despite battling injuries. He was both the top babyface and heel on *SmackDown!* at different times, and any time he was healthy he was at the top of the card. He helped make The World's Greatest Tag Team stars. He put over Brock Lesnar in a fantastic WrestleMania XIX match only to come back and help turn the new champion heel. Near the top of the card in promo skills and wrestling ability, there's nothing Kurt can't do except block injuries. Only injuries drop him down on this countdown. Had he been able to wrestle more often and not need so much time off, it's debatable if he or Lesnar would be the face of *SmackDown!*. When healthy, there's no one who can touch Angle and he proved that in 2003 with two great runs while dealing with a broken neck.

2. **Triple H.** Helmsley dominated *Raw* in 2003 and almost takes his third Top Wrestler of the Year award. All that holds him back is that his run on top of *Raw* isn't especially loved. Whether he was fighting Shawn Michaels, Rob Van Dam, Kevin Nash, or Goldberg, Hunter was too dominant. He gobbled up Booker T in a terrible storyline with racist undertones heading into WrestleMania XIX only to beat him at the PPV. With Evolution at his side, he continued gobbling up opposition. A strong heel champion is one thing, but an unbeatable heel champion is another.

Even when Goldberg beat him for the belt, Hunter was the only credible challenger to his reign, once again seeing him and Evolution dominating screen time. There's no question that "the Game" is a great wrestler with all the tools needed to be a top star. He's a trusted superstar in the ring and money on the microphone. 2003 was an absolutely dominant year for him as he main evented six PPVs (in the brand split era) and defended a major championship successfully more than anyone in the year. He certainly has some argument for being the top star, but his lack of great stories hold him back this go around.

1. **Brock Lesnar.** Lesnar did it all in 2003. He won the Royal Rumble, main evented and won the WWE Title at WrestleMania XIX, and dominated *SmackDown!*. He worked well as a babyface, a little better as a heel, and always as an unstoppable monster in the ring. His year is most remembered for his wars with Kurt Angle, but he had matches with Chris Benoit, Big Show, John Cena, and The Undertaker among others. He fought free of Paul Heyman's control only to join up with Vince McMahon as the dominant heel presence on Thursday nights. He won the WWE Title twice during the year, was in four PPV main event matches plus the aforementioned Royal Rumble, and won far more matches than he lost. Most of his matches felt like a big deal, none bigger than his "Iron Man" and WrestleMania XIX matches with Angle. A big man who was able to wrestle with anyone, Brock stood out inside the squared circle. There may be a few better technical wrestlers around, but none have the look to go along with their ability like Brock Lesnar. As the WWE's biggest new face, Lesnar looked to be the lead man for the promotion for years to come. He left 2003 wearing the WWE Title with a very bright future ahead after two of the greatest years in WWE history. Thanks to a full schedule of matches, great storytelling with top stars like McMahon and Angle, and his incredible in-ring ability, Lesnar just beats out Triple H on *Raw* as the biggest star of 2003. Sadly, it would be a long time before WWE fans got to see another full year out of him.

Ruthless Aggression was alive and well in 2003. Young superstars like Randy Orton, John Cena, and Batista were starting to find their footing in the WWE while Triple H and Goldberg were representing the superstars of the Monday Night War. Angle, Benoit, Guerrero, and Lesnar were providing match of the year candidates regularly on *SmackDown!* while "Stone Cold" Steve Austin returned for one final match with The Rock at WrestleMania XIX before becoming an onscreen foil to Eric Bischoff. 2003 was also a year of transition for the WWE as the company lost three of their biggest stars of all-time, Austin, The Rock, and Hulk Hogan, from the active roster. None of the three would ever again be a full-time competitor for the company. The WWE tried to offset those losses with an increased focus on in-ring competition, risqué storylines, and divas prancing around in various states of undress. The brand split was starting to show signs of success as each program looked and felt different. Separate PPVs also allowed more superstars a chance to shine. While 2003 might not be remembered as the greatest year of all-time and is certainly a bit of a letdown after the Attitude Era and 2002, it's still a good showing for the WWE. The roster was starting to show signs of weakness with some talent pushed ahead of their ability, but for the most part, weekly shows remained entertaining and **MUST SEE!** affairs. While the days of Austin showing up and creating watercooler moments were over, the in-ring action was better, many storylines entertained, and the WWE featured enough talent to survive until the next crop of icons was ready to take over. The company wouldn't have to wait long.

Printed in Great Britain
by Amazon